W9-BDS-779

EX LIBRIS

Louise Walters

9422 McKenzie Rd., Affton, Mo.
13310 West Watson (27)
Vi 3-5074

THE NEW COVENANT

COMMONLY CALLED

THE

NEW TESTAMENT

OF OUR LORD AND SAVIOR

JESUS CHRIST

REVISED STANDARD VERSION

TRANSLATED FROM THE GREEK
BEING THE VERSION SET FORTH A. D. 1611
REVISED A. D. 1881 AND A. D. 1901

COMPARED WITH THE MOST ANCIENT AUTHORITIES AND REVISED
A. D. 1946

THOMAS NELSON & SONS
NEW YORK

COPYRIGHT, 1901,
BY THOMAS NELSON & SONS

COPYRIGHT RENEWED, 1929,
BY THE INTERNATIONAL COUNCIL OF RELIGIOUS EDUCATION

COPYRIGHT, 1946,
BY THE INTERNATIONAL COUNCIL OF RELIGIOUS EDUCATION

TO INSURE PURITY OF TEXT

Norwood Press
J. S. Cushing Co. — Berwick & Smith Co.
Norwood, Mass., U.S.A.

PREFACE

THE Revised Standard Version of the New Testament is an authorized revision of the American Standard Version, published in 1901, which was a revision of the King James Version, published in 1611.

The King James Version was itself a revision rather than a new translation. The first English version of the New Testament made by translation from the Greek was that of William Tyndale, 1525; and this became the foundation for successive versions, notably those of Coverdale, 1535; the Great Bible, 1539; Geneva, 1560; and the Bishop's Bible, 1568. In 1582 a translation of the New Testament, made from the Latin Vulgate by Roman Catholic scholars, was published at Rheims. The translators of the King James Version took into account all of these preceding versions; and comparison shows that it owes something to each of them. It kept felicitous turns of phrase and apt expressions, from whatever source, which had stood the test of public usage.

As a result of the discovery of manuscripts of the New Testament more ancient than those used by the translators in 1611, together with a marked development in Biblical studies, a demand for revision of the King James Bible arose in the middle of the nineteenth century. In 1870 the Convocation of Canterbury authorized a revision, and organized a committee of British scholars to undertake it. With this committee was associated by correspondence a committee of American scholars organized a year later. In 1881 the English Revised Version of the New Testament was published, with an appendix containing recommendations of the American Committee which had not been approved by the British Committee. In 1901, at the expiration of an agreed period, the American Standard Version was published, embodying these recommendations and printing in an appendix the British readings which they replaced.

The American Standard Version was copyrighted to protect the text from unauthorized changes; and in 1928 Thomas Nelson and Sons, its publishers, transferred the copyright to the International Council of Religious Education, in which the educational boards of forty of the major Protestant denominations of the United States and Canada are associated. This body appointed a committee of scholars to have charge of the text, and authorized it to undertake further revision if deemed necessary. The charter of the Committee contains the provision that "all changes in the text shall be agreed upon by a two-thirds vote of the total membership of the Committee" — a more conservative rule than that which had governed revision hitherto, which required only a two-thirds vote of members present.

In 1937 a comprehensive revision of the American Standard Version of the Bible was authorized by vote of the Council. Conversations with British scholars looked toward correspondence with a similar committee to be organized in Great Britain; but this proved to be impracticable during the years of war.

The Committee has worked in two Sections, one dealing with the Old Testament and one with the New Testament. As with former revisions, the work upon the New Testament has been completed first; and the revision of the Old Testament will take about four years more. All changes in the translation of the New Testament have been submitted to the entire Committee, and in a few cases a majority vote in the Section has been reversed by failure to receive the support of two-thirds of the members of the Committee.

This preface does not undertake to set forth the lines along which the revision has proceeded. That is done in a small book entitled *An Introduction to the Revised Standard Version of the New Testament*, written by the members of the New Testament Section, and designed to help the general public to understand the main principles which have guided this comprehensive revision of the King James and American Standard Versions.

Let it be said here simply that all of the reasons which led to the demand for revision of the King James Version one hundred years ago are still valid, and are even more cogent now than then. And we cannot be content with the Versions of 1881 and 1901 for two main reasons. One is that these are mechanically exact, literal, word-for-word translations, which follow the order of the Greek words, so far as this is possible, rather than the order which is natural to English; they are more accurate than the King James Version, but have lost some of its beauty and power as English literature. The second reason is that the discovery of a few more ancient manuscripts of the New Testament and of a great body of Greek papyri dealing with the everyday affairs of life in the early centuries of the Christian era, has furnished scholars with new resources, both for seeking to recover the original text of the Greek New Testament and for understanding its language.

In the Bible we have not merely an historical document and a classic of English literature, but the Word of God. The Bible carries its full message, not to those who regard it simply as a heritage of the past or praise its literary style, but to those who read it that they may discern and understand God's Word to men. And men need the Word of God in our time and hereafter as never before. That Word must not be disguised in phrases that are no longer clear, or hidden under words that have changed or lost their meaning. It must stand forth in language that is direct and plain and meaningful to people today. It is our hope and our earnest prayer that this Revised Standard Version of the New Testament may be used by God to speak to men in these momentous times, and to help them to understand and believe and obey His Word.

THE NAMES AND ORDER

OF THE

BOOKS OF THE NEW TESTAMENT.

1. { first Book written 50 A.D.

THE GOSPEL ACCORDING TO
MATTHEW

1 The book of the genealogy of Jesus Christ, the son of David, the son of Abraham.

2 Abraham was the father of Isaac, and Isaac the father of Jacob, and Jacob the father of Judah and his brothers, ³ and Judah the father of Per'ez and Ze'rah by Ta'mar, and Per'ez the father of Hez'ron, and Hez'ron the father of Ram,ᵃ ⁴ and Ramᵃ the father of Am-min'a-dab, and Am-min'a-dab the father of Nah'shon, and Nah'shon the father of Sal'mon, ⁵ and Sal'mon the father of Bo'az by Ra'hab, and Bo'az the father of O'bed by Ruth, and O'bed the father of Jesse, ⁶ and Jesse the father of David the king.

And David was the father of Solomon by the wife of U-ri'ah, ⁷ and Solomon the father of Re-ho-bo'am, and Re-ho-bo'am the father of A-bi'jah, and A-bi'jah the father of Asa,ᵇ ⁸ and Asaᵇ the father of Je-hosh'a-phat, and Je-hosh'a-phat the father of Jo'ram, and Jo'ram the father of Uz-zi'ah, ⁹ and Uz-zi'ah the father of Jo'tham, and Jo'tham the father of A'haz, and A'haz the father of Hez-e-ki'ah, ¹⁰ and Hez-e-ki'ah the father of Ma-nas'seh, and Ma-nas'seh the father of Amon,ᶜ and Amonᶜ the father of Jo-si'ah, ¹¹ and Jo-si'ah the father of Jech-o-ni'ah and his brothers, at the time of the deportation to Babylon.

12 And after the deportation to Babylon: Jech-o-ni'ah was the father of She-al'ti-el,ᵈ and She-al'ti-elᵈ the father of Ze-rub'ba-bel, ¹³ and Ze-rub'ba-bel the father of A-bi'ud, and A-bi'ud the father of E-li'a-kim, and E-li'a-kim the father of A'zor, ¹⁴ and A'zor the father of Za'dok, and Za'dok the father of A'chim, and A'chim the father of

ᵃ Greek *Aram.*   ᵇ Greek *Asaph.*   ᶜ Some authorities read *Amos.*   ᵈ Greek *Salathiel.*
1. 1-17: Lk. 3. 23-38.   **1. 3-6:** Ruth 4. 18-22; 1 Chr. 2. 1-15.   **1. 11:** 2 Kings 24. 14; Jer. 27. 20.

E-li'ud, [15] and E-li'ud the father of E-le-a'zar, and E-le-a'zar the father of Matthan, and Matthan the father of Jacob, [16] and Jacob the father of Joseph the husband of Mary, of whom Jesus was born, who is called Christ.

17 So all the generations from Abraham to David were fourteen generations, and from David to the deportation to Babylon fourteen generations, and from the deportation to Babylon to the Christ fourteen generations.

18 Now the birth of Jesus Christ[e] took place in this way. When his mother Mary had been betrothed to Joseph, before they came together she was found to be with child of the Holy Spirit; [19] and her husband Joseph, being a just man and unwilling to put her to shame, resolved to divorce her quietly. [20] But as he considered this, behold, an angel of the Lord appeared to him in a dream, saying, "Joseph, son of David, do not fear to take Mary your wife, for that which is conceived in her is of the Holy Spirit; [21] she will bear a son, and you shall call his name Jesus, for he will save his people from their sins." [22] All this took place to fulfill what the Lord had spoken by the prophet:

[23] "Behold, a virgin shall conceive and bear a son,
and his name shall be called Em-man'u-el"

(which means, God with us). [24] When Joseph woke from sleep, he did as the angel of the Lord commanded him; he took his wife, [25] but knew her not until she had borne a son; and he called his name Jesus.

2 Now when Jesus was born in Bethlehem of Judea in the days of Herod the king, behold, wise men from the East came to Jerusalem, saying, [2] "Where is he who has been born king of the Jews? For we have seen his star in the East, and have come to worship him." [3] When Herod

[e] Some ancient authorities read *of the Christ*.

1. 18: Lk. 1. 26–38.   **1. 21:** Lk. 2. 21; Jn. 1. 29; Acts 13. 23.   **1. 23:** Is. 7. 14.
2. 1: Lk. 2. 4–7; 1. 5.   **2. 2:** Jer. 23. 5; Zech. 9. 9; Mk. 15. 2; Jn. 1. 49; Num. 24. 17.

the king heard this, he was troubled, and all Jerusalem with him; [4] and assembling all the chief priests and scribes of the people, he inquired of them where the Christ was to be born. [5] They told him, "In Bethlehem of Judea; for so it is written by the prophet:

> [6] 'And thou Bethlehem, in the land of Judah,
> art by no means least among the rulers of Judah;
> for from thee shall come a ruler
> who will govern my people Israel.'"

7 Then Herod summoned the wise men secretly and ascertained from them what time the star appeared; [8] and he sent them to Bethlehem, saying, "Go and search diligently for the child, and when you have found him bring me word, that I too may come and worship him." [9] When they had heard the king they went their way; and lo, the star which they had seen in the East went before them, till it came to rest over the place where the child was. [10] When they saw the star, they rejoiced exceedingly with great joy; [11] and going into the house they saw the child with Mary his mother, and they fell down and worshiped him. Then, opening their treasures, they offered him gifts, gold and frankincense and myrrh. [12] And being warned in a dream not to return to Herod, they departed to their own country by another way.

13 Now when they had departed, behold, an angel of the Lord appeared to Joseph in a dream and said, "Rise, take the child and his mother, and flee to Egypt, and remain there till I tell you; for Herod is about to search for the child, to destroy him." [14] And he rose and took the child and his mother by night, and departed to Egypt, [15] and remained there until the death of Herod. This was to fulfill what the Lord had spoken by the prophet, "Out of Egypt have I called my son."

2. 5: Jn. 7. 42.   2. 6: Mic. 5. 2; Jn. 21. 16.   2. 11: Mt. 1. 18; 12. 46.   2. 12: Mt. 2. 22; Acts 10. 22; Heb. 11. 7.   2. 15: Hos. 11. 1; Ex. 4. 22.

16 Then Herod, when he saw that he had been tricked by the wise men, was in a furious rage, and he sent and killed all the male children in Bethlehem and in all that region who were two years old or under, according to the time which he had ascertained from the wise men. ¹⁷ Then was fulfilled what was spoken by the prophet Jeremiah:

> ¹⁸ "A voice was heard in Ra'mah,
> wailing and loud lamentation,
> Rachel weeping for her children;
> she refused to be consoled,
> because they were no more."

19 But when Herod died, behold, an angel of the Lord appeared in a dream to Joseph in Egypt, saying, ²⁰ "Rise, take the child and his mother, and go to the land of Israel, for those who sought the child's life are dead." ²¹ And he rose and took the child and his mother, and went to the land of Israel. ²² But when he heard that Ar-che-la'us reigned over Judea in place of his father Herod, he was afraid to go there, and being warned in a dream he withdrew to the district of Galilee. ²³ And he went and dwelt in a city called Nazareth, that what was spoken by the prophets might be fulfilled, "He shall be called a Nazarene."

3 In those days came John the Baptist, preaching in the wilderness of Judea, ² "Repent, for the kingdom of heaven is at hand." ³ For this is he who was spoken of by the prophet Isaiah when he said,

> "The voice of one crying in the wilderness:
> Prepare the way of the Lord,
> make his paths straight."

⁴ Now John wore a garment of camel's hair, and a leather girdle around his waist; and his food was locusts and wild

2. 18: Jer. 31. 15.   2. 19: Mt. 1. 20; 2. 13.   2. 23: Lk. 1. 26; Is. 11. 1; Mk. 1. 24.
3. 1–12: Mk. 1. 3–8; Lk. 3. 2–17; Jn. 1. 6–8, 19–28.   3. 2: Mt. 4. 17; Dan. 2. 44; 4. 17;
Mt. 10. 7.   3. 3: Is. 40. 3.   3. 4: 2 Kings 1. 8; Zech. 13. 4; Lev. 11. 22.

honey. [5] Then went out to him Jerusalem and all Judea and all the region about the Jordan, [6] and they were baptized by him in the river Jordan, confessing their sins.

7 But when he saw many of the Pharisees and Sad'du-cees coming for baptism, he said to them, "You brood of vipers! Who warned you to flee from the wrath to come? [8] Bear fruit that befits repentance, [9] and do not presume to say to yourselves, 'We have Abraham as our father'; for I tell you, God is able from these stones to raise up children to Abraham. [10] Even now the ax is laid to the root of the trees; every tree therefore that does not bear good fruit is cut down and thrown into the fire.

11 "I baptize you with water for repentance, but he who is coming after me is mightier than I, whose sandals I am not worthy to carry; he will baptize you with the Holy Spirit and with fire. [12] His winnowing fork is in his hand, and he will clear his threshing floor and gather his wheat into the granary, but the chaff he will burn with unquenchable fire."

13 Then Jesus came from Galilee to the Jordan to John, to be baptized by him. [14] John would have prevented him, saying, "I need to be baptized by you, and do you come to me?" [15] But Jesus answered him, "Let it be so now; for thus it is fitting for us to fulfill all righteousness." Then he consented. [16] And when Jesus was baptized, he went up immediately from the water, and behold, the heavens were opened[f] and he saw the Spirit of God descending like a dove and alighting on him; [17] and lo, a voice from heaven, saying, "This is my beloved Son,[g] with whom I am well pleased."

4 Then Jesus was led up by the Spirit into the wilderness to be tempted by the devil. [2] And he fasted forty days

[f] Some ancient authorities add *to him.*   [g] Or *my Son, my* (or *the*) *Beloved.*

3. 7: Mt. 12. 34; 23. 33; 1 Thess. 1. 10.   3. 9: Jn. 8. 33; Rom. 4. 16.   3. 10: Mt. 7. 19.
3. 12: Mt. 13. 30.   3. 13–17: Mk. 1. 9–11; Lk. 3. 21–22; Jn. 1. 31–34.
3. 17: Mt. 12. 18; 17. 5; Mk. 9. 7; Lk. 9. 35; Ps. 2. 7; Is. 42. 1.
4. 1–11: Mk. 1. 12–13; Lk. 4. 1–13; Heb. 2. 18; 4. 15.   4. 2: Ex. 34. 28; 1 Kings 19. 8.

and forty nights, and afterward he was hungry. [3] And the tempter came and said to him, "If you are the Son of God, command these stones to become loaves of bread." [4] But he answered, "It is written,

'Man shall not live by bread alone,
   but by every word that proceeds from the mouth of
      God.'"

[5] Then the devil took him to the holy city, and set him on the pinnacle of the temple, [6] and said to him, "If you are the Son of God, throw yourself down; for it is written,

'He will give his angels charge of you,'
and

'On their hands they will bear you up,
   lest you strike your foot against a stone.'"

[7] Jesus said to him, "Again it is written, 'You shall not tempt the Lord your God.'" [8] Again, the devil took him to a very high mountain, and showed him all the kingdoms of the world and the glory of them; [9] and he said to him, "All these I will give you, if you will fall down and worship me." [10] Then Jesus said to him, "Begone, Satan! for it is written,

'You shall worship the Lord your God,
   and him only shall you serve.'"

[11] Then the devil left him, and behold, angels came and ministered to him.

12 Now when he heard that John had been arrested, he withdrew into Galilee; [13] and leaving Nazareth he went and dwelt in Ca-per'na-um by the sea, in the territory of Zeb'u-lun and Naph'ta-li, [14] that what was spoken by the prophet Isaiah might be fulfilled:

[15] "The land of Zeb'u-lun and the land of Naph'ta-li,
   toward the sea, across the Jordan,

4. 4: Deut. 8. 3.   **4. 5:** Mt. 27. 53; Neh. 11. 1; Dan. 9. 24; Rev. 21. 10.   **4. 6:** Ps. 91. 11–12.   **4. 7:** Deut. 6. 16.   **4. 10:** Deut. 6. 13; Mk. 8. 33.   **4. 11:** Mt. 26. 53; Lk. 22. 43.   **4. 12:** Mk. 1. 14; Lk. 4. 14; Mt. 14. 3; Jn. 1. 43.   **4. 13:** Jn. 2. 12; Mk. 1. 21; Lk. 4. 23.   **4. 15:** Is. 9. 1–2.

Galilee of the Gentiles —
[16] the people who sat in darkness
have seen a great light,
and for those who sat in the region and shadow of
death
light has dawned."

[17] From that time Jesus began to preach, saying, "Repent, for the kingdom of heaven is at hand."

18 As he walked by the sea of Galilee, he saw two brothers, Simon who is called Peter and Andrew his brother, casting a net into the sea; for they were fishermen. [19] And he said to them, "Follow me, and I will make you fishers of men." [20] Immediately they left their nets and followed him. [21] And going on from there he saw two other brothers, James the son of Zeb'e-dee and John his brother, in the boat with Zeb'e-dee their father, mending their nets, and he called them. [22] Immediately they left the boat and their father, and followed him.

23 And he went about all Galilee, teaching in their synagogues and preaching the gospel of the kingdom and healing every disease and every infirmity among the people. [24] So his fame spread throughout all Syria, and they brought him all the sick, those afflicted with various diseases and pains, demoniacs, epileptics, and paralytics, and he healed them. [25] And great crowds followed him from Galilee and the De-cap'o-lis and Jerusalem and Judea and from beyond the Jordan.

5 Seeing the crowds, he went up on the mountain, and when he sat down his disciples came to him. [2] And he opened his mouth and taught them, saying:

3 "Blessed are the poor in spirit, for theirs is the kingdom of heaven.

4. 17: Mk. 1. 15; Mt. 3. 2; 10. 7.   4. 18–22: Mk. 1. 16–20; Lk. 5. 1–11; Jn. 1. 35–42.
4. 23–25: Mk. 1. 39; Lk. 4. 15, 44; Mt. 9. 35; Mk. 3. 7–8; Lk. 6. 17.
5. 1–12: Lk. 6. 17, 20–23; Mk. 3. 13; Jn. 6. 3.   5. 3: Mk. 10. 14; Lk. 22. 29.

4 "Blessed are those who mourn, for they shall be comforted.

5 "Blessed are the meek, for they shall inherit the earth.

6 "Blessed are those who hunger and thirst for righteousness, for they shall be satisfied.

7 "Blessed are the merciful, for they shall obtain mercy.

8 "Blessed are the pure in heart, for they shall see God.

9 "Blessed are the peacemakers, for they shall be called sons of God.

10 "Blessed are those who are persecuted for righteousness' sake, for theirs is the kingdom of heaven.

11 "Blessed are you when men revile you and persecute you and utter all kinds of evil against you falsely on my account. [12] Rejoice and be glad, for your reward is great in heaven, for so men persecuted the prophets who were before you.

13 "You are the salt of the earth; but if salt has lost its taste, how can its saltness be restored? It is no longer good for anything except to be thrown out and trodden under foot by men.

14 "You are the light of the world. A city set on a hill cannot be hid. [15] Nor do men light a lamp and put it under a bushel, but on a stand, and it gives light to all in the house. [16] Let your light so shine before men, that they may see your good works and give glory to your Father who is in heaven.

17 "Think not that I have come to abolish the law and the prophets; I have come not to abolish them but to fulfill them. [18] For truly, I say to you, till heaven and earth pass away, not an iota, not a dot, will pass from the law until all is accomplished. [19] Whoever then relaxes one of the least of these commandments and teaches men so, shall be called least in

5. 4: Is. 61. 2; Jn. 16. 20; Rev. 7. 17.   **5. 5:** Ps. 37. 11.   **5. 6:** Is. 55. 1–2; Jn. 4. 14; 6. 48–51.   **5. 8:** Ps. 24. 4; Heb. 12. 14; 1 Jn. 3. 2; Rev. 22. 4.   **5. 10:** 1 Pet. 3. 14; 4. 14.   **5. 12:** 2 Chr. 36. 16; Mt. 23. 37; Acts 7. 52; 1 Thess. 2. 15; Jas. 5. 10.   **5. 13:** Mk. 9. 49–50; Lk. 14. 34–35.   **5. 14:** Eph. 5. 8; Phil. 2. 15; Jn. 8. 12.   **5. 15–16:** Lk. 11. 33; Mk. 4. 21; 1 Pet. 2. 12.   **5. 18:** Lk. 16. 17; Mk. 13. 31.   **5. 19:** Jas. 2. 10.

the kingdom of heaven; but he who does them and teaches them shall be called great in the kingdom of heaven. [20] For I tell you, unless your righteousness exceeds that of the scribes and Pharisees, you will never enter the kingdom of heaven.

21 "You have heard that it was said to the men of old, 'You shall not kill; and whoever kills shall be liable to judgment.' [22] But I say to you that every one who is angry with his brother[h] shall be liable to judgment; whoever insults[i] his brother shall be liable to the council, and whoever says, 'You fool!' shall be liable to the hell[j] of fire. [23] So if you are offering your gift at the altar, and there remember that your brother has something against you, [24] leave your gift there before the altar and go; first be reconciled to your brother, and then come and offer your gift. [25] Make friends quickly with your accuser, while you are going with him to court, lest your accuser hand you over to the judge, and the judge to the guard, and you be put in prison; [26] truly, I say to you, you will never get out till you have paid the last penny.

27 "You have heard that it was said, 'You shall not commit adultery.' [28] But I say to you that every one who looks at a woman lustfully has already committed adultery with her in his heart. [29] If your right eye causes you to sin, pluck it out and throw it away; it is better that you lose one of your members than that your whole body be thrown into hell.[j] [30] And if your right hand causes you to sin, cut it off and throw it away; it is better that you lose one of your members than that your whole body go into hell.[j]

31 "It was also said, 'Whoever divorces his wife, let him give her a certificate of divorce.' [32] But I say to you that every one who divorces his wife, except on the ground of

---

[h] Many ancient authorities insert *without cause*.   [i] Greek *says Raca to* (an obscure term of abuse).   [j] Greek *Gehenna*.

5. 21: Ex. 20. 13; Deut. 5. 17; 16. 18.   **5. 25–26:** Lk. 12. 57–59.   **5. 27:** Ex. 20. 14; Deut. 5. 18.   **5. 29–30:** Mk. 9. 43–48; Mt. 18. 8–9.   **5. 31–32:** Lk. 16. 18; Mk. 10. 11–12; Mt. 19. 9; 1 Cor. 7. 10–11; Deut. 24. 1–4.

unchastity, makes her an adulteress; and whoever marries a divorced woman commits adultery.

33 "Again you have heard that it was said to the men of old, 'You shall not swear falsely, but shall perform to the Lord what you have sworn.' [34] But I say to you, Do not swear at all, either by heaven, for it is the throne of God, [35] or by the earth, for it is his footstool, or by Jerusalem, for it is the city of the great King. [36] And do not swear by your head, for you cannot make one hair white or black. [37] Let what you say be simply 'Yes' or 'No'; anything more than this comes from evil.[k]

38 "You have heard that it was said, 'An eye for an eye and a tooth for a tooth.' [39] But I say to you, Do not resist one who is evil. But if any one strikes you on the right cheek, turn to him the other also; [40] and if any one would sue you and take your coat, let him have your cloak as well; [41] and if any one forces you to go one mile, go with him two miles. [42] Give to him who begs from you, and do not refuse him who would borrow from you.

43 "You have heard that it was said, 'You shall love your neighbor and hate your enemy.' [44] But I say to you, Love your enemies and pray for those who persecute you, [45] so that you may be sons of your Father who is in heaven; for he makes his sun rise on the evil and on the good, and sends rain on the just and on the unjust. [46] For if you love those who love you, what reward have you? Do not even the tax collectors do the same? [47] And if you salute only your brethren, what more are you doing than others? Do not even the Gentiles do the same? [48] You, therefore, must be perfect, as your heavenly Father is perfect.

[k] Or *the evil one.*

5. 33–37: Mt. 23. 16–22; Jas. 5. 12; Lev. 19. 12; Num. 30. 2; Deut. 23. 21. **5. 35:** Is. 66. 1; Acts 7. 49; Ps. 48. 2. **5. 38:** Ex. 21. 24; Lev. 24. 20; Deut. 19. 21. **5. 39–42:** Lk. 6. 29–30; 1 Cor. 6. 7; Rom. 12. 17; 1 Pet. 2. 19; 3. 9; Prov. 24. 29. **5. 43–48:** Lk. 6. 27–28, 32–36; Lev. 19. 18; Prov. 25. 21–22. **5. 48:** Lev. 19. 2.

6 "Beware of practicing your piety before men in order to be seen by them; for then you will have no reward from your Father who is in heaven.

2 "Thus, when you give alms, sound no trumpet before you, as the hypocrites do in the synagogues and in the streets, that they may be praised by men. Truly, I say to you, they have their reward. ³ But when you give alms, do not let your left hand know what your right hand is doing, ⁴ so that your alms may be in secret; and your Father who sees in secret will reward you.

5 "And when you pray, you must not be like the hypocrites; for they love to stand and pray in the synagogues and at the street corners, that they may be seen by men. Truly, I say to you, they have their reward. ⁶ But when you pray, go into your room and shut the door and pray to your Father who is in secret; and your Father who sees in secret will reward you.

7 "And in praying do not heap up empty phrases as the Gentiles do; for they think that they will be heard for their many words. ⁸ Do not be like them, for your Father knows what you need before you ask him. ⁹ Pray then like this:

'Our Father who art in heaven,
    Hallowed be thy name.
¹⁰ Thy kingdom come,
    Thy will be done,
        On earth as it is in heaven.
¹¹ Give us this day our daily bread;*
¹² And forgive us our debts,
    As we also have forgiven our debtors;

Or our bread for the morrow.

6. 1: Mt. 23. 5.   **6. 4:** Col. 3. 23–24.   **6. 5:** Mk. 11. 25; Lk. 18. 10–14.
6. 7: 1 Kings 18. 25–29.   **6. 8:** Mt. 6. 32; Lk. 12. 30.   **6. 9–13:** Lk. 11. 2–4.

11

¹³ And lead us not into temptation,
But deliver us from evil.' ^m

¹⁴ For if you forgive men their trespasses, your heavenly Father also will forgive you; ¹⁵ but if you do not forgive men their trespasses, neither will your Father forgive your trespasses.

16 "And when you fast, do not look dismal, like the hypocrites, for they disfigure their faces that their fasting may be seen by men. Truly, I say to you, they have their reward. ¹⁷ But when you fast, anoint your head and wash your face, ¹⁸ that your fasting may not be seen by men but by your Father who is in secret; and your Father who sees in secret will reward you.

19 "Do not lay up for yourselves treasures on earth, where moth and rustⁿ consume and where thieves break in and steal, ²⁰ but lay up for yourselves treasures in heaven, where neither moth nor rustⁿ consumes and where thieves do not break in and steal; ²¹ for where your treasure is, there will your heart be also.

22 "The eye is the lamp of the body. So, if your eye is sound, your whole body will be full of light; ²³ but if your eye is not sound, your whole body will be full of darkness. If then the light in you is darkness, how great is the darkness!

24 "No one can serve two masters; for either he will hate the one and love the other, or he will be devoted to the one and despise the other. You cannot serve God and mammon.

25 "Therefore I tell you, do not be anxious about your life, what you shall eat or what you shall drink, nor about your body, what you shall put on. Is not life more than food, and

^m Or *the evil one.* Many authorities, some ancient, add, in some form, *For thine is the kingdom and the power and the glory, forever. Amen.*   ⁿ Or *worm.*

6. 13: 2 Thess. 3. 3; Jn. 17. 15; Jas. 1. 13.   **6. 14–15:** Mt. 18. 35; Mk. 11. 25; Eph. 4. 32; Col. 3. 13.   **6. 16:** Is. 58. 5.   **6. 18:** Mt. 6. 4, 6.   **6. 19–21:** Lk. 12. 33–34; Mk. 10. 21; 1 Tim. 6. 17–19; Jas. 5. 1–3.   **6. 22–23:** Lk. 11. 34–36; Mt. 20. 15; Mk. 7. 22. **6. 24:** Lk. 16. 13.   **6. 25–33:** Lk. 12. 22–31; 10. 41; 12. 11; Phil. 4. 6; 1 Pet. 5. 7.

the body more than clothing? [26] Look at the birds of the air: they neither sow nor reap nor gather into barns, and yet your heavenly Father feeds them. Are you not of more value than they? [27] And which of you by being anxious can add one cubit to his span of life?[o] [28] And why be anxious about clothing? Consider the lilies of the field, how they grow; they neither toil nor spin; [29] yet I tell you, even Solomon in all his glory was not arrayed like one of these. [30] But if God so clothes the grass of the field, which today is alive and tomorrow is thrown into the oven, will he not much more clothe you, O men of little faith? [31] Therefore do not be anxious, saying, 'What shall we eat?' or 'What shall we drink?' or 'What shall we wear?' [32] For the Gentiles seek all these things; and your heavenly Father knows that you need them all. [33] But seek first his kingdom and his righteousness, and all these things shall be yours as well.

34 "Therefore do not be anxious about tomorrow, for tomorrow will be anxious for itself. Let the day's own trouble be sufficient for the day.

7 "Judge not, that you be not judged. [2] For with the judgment you pronounce you will be judged, and the measure you give will be the measure you get. [3] Why do you see the speck that is in your brother's eye, but do not notice the log that is in your own eye? [4] Or how can you say to your brother, 'Let me take the speck out of your eye,' when there is the log in your own eye? [5] You hypocrite, first take the log out of your own eye, and then you will see clearly to take the speck out of your brother's eye.

6 "Do not give dogs what is holy; and do not throw your pearls before swine, lest they trample them underfoot and turn to attack you.

[o] Or *to his stature.*

6. 26: Mt. 10. 29.   **6. 27:** Ps. 39. 5.   **6. 29:** 1 Kings 10. 4–7.   **6. 30:** Mt. 8. 26;
14. 31; 16. 8.   **6. 33:** Mt. 19. 28; Mk. 10. 29–30; Lk. 18. 29–30.
7. 1–2: Lk. 6. 37–38; Mk. 4. 24; Rom. 2. 1; 14. 10.   **7. 3–5:** Lk. 6. 41–42.

7 "Ask, and it will be given you; seek, and you will find; knock, and it will be opened to you.[8] For every one who asks receives, and he who seeks finds, and to him who knocks it will be opened. [9] Or what man of you, if his son asks him for a loaf, will give him a stone? [10] Or if he asks for a fish, will give him a serpent? [11] If you then, who are evil, know how to give good gifts to your children, how much more will your Father who is in heaven give good things to those who ask him? [12] So whatever you wish that men would do to you, do so to them; for this is the law and the prophets.

13 "Enter by the narrow gate; for the gate is wide and the way is easy,[p] that leads to destruction, and those who enter by it are many. [14] For the gate is narrow and the way is hard, that leads to life, and those who find it are few.

15 "Beware of false prophets, who come to you in sheep's clothing but inwardly are ravenous wolves. [16] You will know them by their fruits. Are grapes gathered from thorns, or figs from thistles? [17] So, every sound tree bears good fruit, but the bad tree bears evil fruit. [18] A sound tree cannot bear evil fruit, nor can a bad tree bear good fruit. [19] Every tree that does not bear good fruit is cut down and thrown into the fire. [20] Thus you will know them by their fruits.

21 "Not every one who says to me, 'Lord, Lord,' shall enter the kingdom of heaven, but he who does the will of my Father who is in heaven. [22] On that day many will say to me, 'Lord, Lord, did we not prophesy in your name, and cast out demons in your name, and do many mighty works in your name?' [23] And then will I declare to them, 'I never knew you; depart from me, you evil-doers.'

24 "Every one then who hears these words of mine and

---

[p] Some ancient authorities read *for the way is wide and easy.*

7. 7–11: Lk. 11. 9–13; Mk. 11. 24; Jn. 15. 7; 16. 23–24; Jas. 4. 3; 1 Jn. 3. 22; 5. 14. **7. 12:** Lk. 6. 31. **7. 13–14:** Lk. 13. 23–24; Jer. 21. 8; Deut. 30. 19; Jn. 14. 6; 10. 7. **7. 15:** Mt. 24. 11, 24; Ezek. 22. 27; 1 Jn. 4. 1; Jn. 10. 12. **7. 16–20:** Lk. 6. 43–44; Mt. 12. 33–35; Mt. 3. 10; Jas. 3. 12; Lk. 13. 7. **7. 21:** Lk. 6. 46. **7. 22–23:** Lk. 13. 26–27; Mt. 25. 12; Ps. 6. 8. **7. 24–27:** Lk. 6. 47–49; Jas. 1. 22–25.

does them will be like a wise man who built his house upon the rock; [25] and the rain fell, and the floods came, and the winds blew and beat upon that house, but it did not fall, because it had been founded on the rock. [26] And every one who hears these words of mine and does not do them will be like a foolish man who built his house upon the sand; [27] and the rain fell, and the floods came, and the winds blew and beat against that house, and it fell; and great was the fall of it."

28 And when Jesus finished these sayings, the crowds were astonished at his teaching, [29] for he taught them as one who had authority, and not as their scribes.

8 When he came down from the mountain, great crowds followed him; [2] and behold, a leper came to him and knelt before him, saying, "Lord, if you will, you can make me clean." [3] And he stretched out his hand and touched him, saying, "I will; be clean." And immediately his leprosy was cleansed. [4] And Jesus said to him, "See that you say nothing to any one; but go, show yourself to the priest, and offer the gift that Moses commanded, for a proof to the people."[q]

5 As he entered Ca-per'na-um, a centurion came forward to him, beseeching him [6] and saying, "Lord, my servant is lying paralyzed at home, in terrible distress." [7] And he said to him, "I will come and heal him." [8] But the centurion answered him, "Lord, I am not worthy to have you come under my roof; but only say the word, and my servant will be healed. [9] For I am a man under authority, with soldiers under me; and I say to one, 'Go,' and he goes, and to another, 'Come,' and he comes, and to my slave, 'Do this,' and he does it." [10] When Jesus heard him, he marveled, and said to those who followed him, "Truly, I say to you, not even[r] in Israel

[q] Greek *to them*.   [r] Some ancient authorities read *with no one*.

7. 28–29: Mk. 1. 22; Lk. 4. 32; Mt. 11. 1; 13. 53; 19. 1; 26. 1.
8. 2–4: Mk. 1. 40–44; Lk. 5. 12–14.   8. 2: Mt. 9. 18; 15. 25; 18. 26; 20. 20; Jn. 9. 38.
8. 4: Mk. 3. 12; 5. 43; 7. 36; 8. 30; 9. 9; Lev. 14. 2.   8. 5–13: Lk. 7. 1–10;
Jn. 4. 46–53.

have I found such faith. [11] I tell you, many will come from east and west and sit at table with Abraham, Isaac, and Jacob in the kingdom of heaven, [12] while the sons of the kingdom will be thrown into the outer darkness; there men will weep and gnash their teeth." [13] And to the centurion Jesus said, "Go; be it done for you as you have believed." And the servant was healed at that very moment.

14 And when Jesus entered Peter's house, he saw his mother-in-law lying sick with a fever; [15] he touched her hand, and the fever left her, and she rose and served him. [16] That evening they brought to him many who were possessed with demons; and he cast out the spirits with a word, and healed all who were sick. [17] This was to fulfill what was spoken by the prophet Isaiah, "He took our infirmities and bore our diseases."

18 Now when Jesus saw great crowds around him, he gave orders to go over to the other side. [19] And a scribe came up and said to him, "Master, I will follow you wherever you go." [20] And Jesus said to him, "Foxes have holes, and birds of the air have nests; but the Son of man has nowhere to lay his head." [21] Another of the disciples said to him, "Lord, let me first go and bury my father." [22] But Jesus said to him, "Follow me, and leave the dead to bury their own dead."

23 And when he got into the boat, his disciples followed him. [24] And behold, there arose a great storm on the sea, so that the boat was being swamped by the waves; but he was asleep. [25] And they went and woke him, saying, "Save, Lord; we are perishing." [26] And he said to them, "Why are you afraid, O men of little faith?" Then he rose and rebuked the winds and the sea; and there was a great calm. [27] And

8. 11–12: Lk. 13. 28–29; Is. 49. 12; 59. 19; Mal. 1. 11; Ps. 107. 3.   8. 12: Mt. 13. 42, 50; 22. 13; 24. 51; 25. 30; Lk. 13. 28.   8. 14–16: Mk. 1. 29–34; Lk. 4. 38–41; Mt. 4. 23–24.   8. 17: Is. 53. 4.   8. 18–22: Lk. 9. 57–60; Mk. 4. 35; Lk. 8. 22.   8. 22: Mt. 9. 9; Jn. 1. 43; 21. 19.   8. 23–27: Mk. 4. 36–41; Lk. 8. 22–25.   8. 26: Mt. 6. 30; 14. 31; 16. 8.

the men marveled, saying, "What sort of man is this, that even winds and sea obey him?"

28 And when he came to the other side, to the country of the Gad-a-renes',[s] two demoniacs met him, coming out of the tombs, so fierce that no one could pass that way. [29] And behold, they cried out, "What have you to do with us, O Son of God? Have you come here to torment us before the time?" [30] Now a herd of many swine was feeding at some distance from them. [31] And the demons begged him, "If you cast us out, send us away into the herd of swine." [32] And he said to them, "Go." So they came out and went into the swine; and behold, the whole herd rushed down the steep bank into the sea, and perished in the waters. [33] The swineherds fled, and going into the city they told everything, and what had happened to the demoniacs. [34] And behold, all the city came out to meet Jesus; and when they saw him, they begged him to leave their neighborhood.

9 And getting into a boat he crossed over and came to his own city. [2] And behold, they brought to him a paralytic, lying on his bed; and when Jesus saw their faith he said to the paralytic, "Take heart, my son; your sins are forgiven." [3] And behold, some of the scribes said to themselves, "This man is blaspheming." [4] But Jesus, knowing[t] their thoughts, said, "Why do you think evil in your hearts? [5] For which is easier, to say, 'Your sins are forgiven,' or to say, 'Rise and walk'? [6] But that you may know that the Son of man has authority on earth to forgive sins" — he then said to the paralytic — "Rise, take up your bed and go home." [7] And he rose and went home. [8] When the crowds saw it, they were

---

[s] Many ancient authorities read *Gergesenes;* some, *Gerasenes.*
[t] Many ancient authorities read *seeing.*

8. 28–34: Mk. 5. 1–17; Lk. 8. 26–37.   **8. 29:** Judg. 11. 12; 2 Sam. 16. 10; Mk. 1. 24;
Jn. 2. 4.
9. 1–8: Mk. 2. 1–12; Lk. 5. 17–26.   **9. 2:** Mt. 9. 22; Mk. 6. 50; 10. 49; Jn. 16. 33;
Acts 23. 11; Lk. 7. 48.

afraid, and they glorified God, who had given such authority to men.

9 As Jesus passed on from there, he saw a man called Matthew sitting at the tax office; and he said to him, "Follow me." And he rose and followed him.

10 And as he sat at table[u] in the house, behold, many tax collectors and sinners came and sat down with Jesus and his disciples. 11 And when the Pharisees saw this, they said to his disciples, "Why does your master eat with tax collectors and sinners?" 12 But when he heard it, he said, "Those who are well have no need of a physician, but those who are sick. 13 Go and learn what this means, 'I desire mercy, and not sacrifice.' For I came not to call the righteous, but sinners."

14 Then the disciples of John came to him, saying, "Why do we and the Pharisees fast,[v] but your disciples do not fast?" 15 And Jesus said to them, "Can the wedding guests mourn as long as the bridegroom is with them? The days will come, when the bridegroom is taken away from them, and then they will fast. 16 And no one puts a piece of unshrunk cloth on an old garment, for the patch tears away from the garment, and a worse tear is made. 17 Neither is new wine put into old wineskins; if it is, the skins burst, and the wine is spilled, and the skins are destroyed; but new wine is put into fresh wineskins, and so both are preserved."

18 While he was thus speaking to them, behold, a ruler came in and knelt before him, saying, "My daughter has just died; but come and lay your hand on her, and she will live." 19 And Jesus rose and followed him, with his disciples. 20 And behold, a woman who had suffered from a hemorrhage for twelve years came up behind him and touched the fringe

---

[u] Greek *reclined*.   [v] Many ancient authorities add *much* or *often*.

9. 9–13: Mk. 2. 13–17; Lk. 5. 27–32; 15. 1–2; 7. 34.   **9. 13:** Hos. 6. 6; Mt. 12. 7; 1 Tim. 1. 15.   **9. 14–17:** Mk. 2. 18–22; Lk. 5. 33–39; 18. 12.   **9. 18–26:** Mk. 5. 21–43; Lk. 8. 40–56.   **9. 18:** Mt. 8. 2; 15. 25; 18. 26; 20. 20; Jn. 9. 38.   **9. 20:** Num. 15. 38; Deut. 22. 12; Mt. 14. 36; Mk. 3. 10.

of his garment; [21] for she said to herself, "If I only touch his garment, I shall be made well." [22] Jesus turned, and seeing her he said, "Take heart, my daughter; your faith has made you well." And instantly the woman was made well. [23] And when Jesus came to the ruler's house, and saw the flute players, and the crowd making a tumult, [24] he said, "Depart; for the girl is not dead but sleeping." And they laughed at him. [25] But when the crowd had been put outside, he went in and took her by the hand, and the girl arose. [26] And the report of this went through all that district.

27 And as Jesus passed on from there, two blind men followed him, crying aloud, "Have mercy on us, Son of David." [28] When he entered the house, the blind men came to him; and Jesus said to them, "Do you believe that I am able to do this?" They said to him, "Yes, Lord." [29] Then he touched their eyes, saying, "According to your faith be it done to you." [30] And their eyes were opened. And Jesus sternly charged them, "See that no one knows it." [31] But they went away and spread his fame through all that district.

32 As they were going away, behold, a dumb demoniac was brought to him. [33] And when the demon had been cast out, the dumb man spoke; and the crowds marveled, saying, "Never was anything like this seen in Israel." [34] But the Pharisees said, "He casts out demons by the prince of demons."

35 And Jesus went about all the cities and villages, teaching in their synagogues and preaching the gospel of the kingdom, and healing every disease and every infirmity. [36] When he saw the crowds, he had compassion for them, because they were harassed and helpless, like sheep without a shepherd. [37] Then he said to his disciples, "The harvest is plentiful, but

9. 22: Mk. 10. 52; Lk. 7. 50; 17. 19; Mt. 15. 28; 9. 29.   **9. 27–31:** Mt. 20. 29–34.
9. 32–34: Lk. 11. 14–15; Mt. 12. 22–24; Mk. 3. 22; Jn. 7. 20.   **9. 35:** Mt. 4. 23;
Mk. 6. 6.   **9. 36:** Mk. 6. 34; Mt. 14. 14; 15. 32; Num. 27. 17; Zech. 10. 2.
9. 37–38: Lk. 10. 2; Jn. 4. 35.

the laborers are few; [38] pray therefore the Lord of the harvest to send out laborers into his harvest."

10 And he called to him his twelve disciples and gave them authority over unclean spirits, to cast them out, and to heal every disease and every infirmity. [2] The names of the twelve apostles are these: first, Simon, who is called Peter, and Andrew his brother; James the son of Zeb'e-dee, and John his brother; [3] Philip and Bartholomew; Thomas and Matthew the tax collector; James the son of Alphaeus, and Thaddaeus;[w] [4] Simon the Cananaean, and Judas Iscariot, who betrayed him.

5 These twelve Jesus sent out, charging them, "Go nowhere among the Gentiles, and enter no town of the Samaritans, [6] but go rather to the lost sheep of the house of Israel. [7] And preach as you go, saying, 'The kingdom of heaven is at hand.' [8] Heal the sick, raise the dead, cleanse lepers, cast out demons. You received without pay, give without pay. [9] Take no gold, nor silver, nor copper in your purses,[x] [10] no bag for your journey, nor two tunics, nor sandals, nor a staff; for the laborer deserves his food. [11] And whatever town or village you enter, find out who is worthy in it, and stay with him until you depart. [12] As you enter the house, salute it. [13] And if the house is worthy, let your peace come upon it; but if it is not worthy, let your peace return to you. [14] And if any one will not receive you or listen to your words, shake off the dust from your feet as you leave that house or town. [15] Truly, I say to you, it shall be more tolerable on the day of judgment for the land of Sodom and Go-mor'rah than for that town.

16 "Lo, I send you out as sheep in the midst of wolves; so

[w] Some ancient authorities read *Lebbaeus* or *Lebbaeus called Thaddaeus.*   [x] Greek *girdles.*
10. 1–4: Mk. 6. 7; 3. 16–19; Lk. 9. 1; 6. 14–16; Acts 1. 13.   **10. 5:** Lk. 9. 52; Jn. 4. 9; Acts 8. 5, 25.   **10. 6:** Mt. 15. 24; 10. 23.   **10. 7–8:** Lk. 9. 2; 10. 9–11; Mt. 4. 17. **10. 9–14:** Mk. 6. 8–11; Lk. 9. 3–5, 10. 4–12; 22. 35–36.   **10. 10:** 1 Cor. 9. 14; 1 Tim. 5. 18.   **10. 14:** Acts 13. 51.   **10. 15:** Mt. 11. 24; Lk. 10. 12; Jude 7; 2 Pet. 2. 6.   **10. 16:** Lk. 10. 3; Gen. 3. 1; Rom. 16. 19.

be wise as serpents and innocent as doves. [17] Beware of men; for they will deliver you up to councils, and flog you in their synagogues, [18] and you will be dragged before governors and kings for my sake, to bear testimony before them and the Gentiles. [19] When they deliver you up, do not be anxious how you are to speak or what you are to say; for what you are to say will be given to you in that hour; [20] for it is not you who speak, but the Spirit of your Father speaking through you. [21] Brother will deliver up brother to death, and the father his child, and children will rise against parents and have them put to death; [22] and you will be hated by all for my name's sake. But he who endures to the end will be saved. [23] When they persecute you in one town, flee to the next; for truly, I say to you, you will not have gone through all the towns of Israel, before the Son of man comes.

24 "A disciple is not above his teacher, nor a servant[y] above his master; [25] it is enough for the disciple to be like his teacher, and the servant[y] like his master. If they have called the master of the house Be-el'ze-bub,[z] how much more will they malign those of his household.

26 "So have no fear of them; for nothing is covered that will not be revealed, or hidden that will not be known. [27] What I tell you in the dark, utter in the light; and what you hear whispered, proclaim upon the housetops. [28] And do not fear those who kill the body but cannot kill the soul; rather fear him who can destroy both soul and body in hell.[a] [29] Are not two sparrows sold for a penny? And not one of them will fall to the ground without your Father's will. [30] But even the hairs of your head are all numbered. [31] Fear not, therefore;

[y] Or *slave*.   [z] Greek *Beelzebul*.   [a] Greek *Gehenna*.

10. 17–22: Mk. 13. 9–13; Lk. 12. 11–12; 21. 12–19; Jn. 16. 2.   **10. 18:** Acts 25. 24–26.
10. 20: Jn. 16. 7–11.   **10. 21:** Mt. 10. 35–36; Lk. 12. 52–53.   **10. 22:** Jn. 15, 18;
Mt. 24. 9.   **10. 23:** Mt. 16. 27; 1 Thess. 4. 17.   **10. 24:** Lk. 6. 40; Jn. 13. 16;
15. 20.   **10. 25:** Mt. 9. 34; 12. 24; Mk. 3. 22; Lk. 11. 15; 2 Kings 1. 2.   **10. 26–33:**
Lk. 12. 2–9.   **10. 26:** Mk. 4. 22; Lk. 8. 17; Eph. 5. 13.   **10. 28:** Heb. 10. 31.
10. 31: Mt. 12. 12.

you are of more value than many sparrows. [32] So every one who acknowledges me before men, I also will acknowledge before my Father who is in heaven; [33] but whoever denies me before men, I also will deny before my Father who is in heaven.

34 "Do not think that I have come to bring peace on earth; I have not come to bring peace, but a sword. [35] For I have come to set a man against his father, and a daughter against her mother, and a daughter-in-law against her mother-in-law; [36] and a man's foes will be those of his own household. [37] He who loves father or mother more than me is not worthy of me; and he who loves son or daughter more than me is not worthy of me; [38] and he who does not take his cross and follow me is not worthy of me. [39] He who finds his life will lose it, and he who loses his life for my sake will find it.

40 "He who receives you receives me, and he who receives me receives him who sent me. [41] He who receives a prophet because he is a prophet shall receive a prophet's reward, and he who receives a righteous man because he is a righteous man shall receive a righteous man's reward. [42] And whoever gives to one of these little ones even a cup of cold water because he is a disciple, truly, I say to you, he shall not lose his reward."

11 And when Jesus had finished instructing his twelve disciples, he went on from there to teach and preach in their cities.

2 Now when John heard in prison about the deeds of the Christ, he sent word by his disciples [3] and said to him, "Are you he who is to come, or shall we look for another?" [4] And

10. 32: Mk. 8. 38; Lk. 9. 26; Rev. 3. 5; 2 Tim. 2. 12.   **10. 34–36:** Lk. 12. 51–53; Mt. 10. 21; Mk. 13. 12; Mic. 7. 6.   **10. 37–39:** Lk. 14. 25–27; 17. 33, 9. 23–24; Mt. 16. 24–25; Mk. 8. 34–35; Jn. 12. 25.   **10. 40:** Lk. 10. 16; Jn. 13. 20; Gal. 4. 14; Mk. 9. 37; Mt. 18. 5; Lk. 9. 48.   **10. 42:** Mk. 9. 41; Mt. 25. 40.   **11. 1:** Mt. 7. 28; 13. 53; 19. 1; 26. 1.   **11. 2–19:** Lk. 7. 18–35.   **11. 3:** Mk. 1. 7–8; Hab. 2. 3; Jn. 11. 27.

Jesus answered them, "Go and tell John what you hear and see: ⁵ the blind receive their sight and the lame walk, lepers are cleansed and the deaf hear, and the dead are raised up, and the poor have good news preached to them. ⁶ And blessed is he who takes no offense at me."

7 As they went away, Jesus began to speak to the crowds concerning John: "What did you go out into the wilderness to behold? A reed shaken by the wind? ⁸ Why then did you go out? To see a man *ᵇ* clothed in soft raiment? Behold, those who wear soft raiment are in kings' houses. ⁹ Why then did you go out? To see a prophet? *ᶜ* Yes, I tell you, and more than a prophet. ¹⁰ This is he of whom it is written,

'Behold, I send my messenger before thy face,
who shall prepare thy way before thee.'

¹¹ Truly, I say to you, among those born of women there has risen no one greater than John the Baptist; yet he who is least in the kingdom of heaven is greater than he. ¹² From the days of John the Baptist until now the kingdom of heaven has suffered violence, *ᵈ* and men of violence take it by force. ¹³ For all the prophets and the law prophesied until John; ¹⁴ and if you are willing to accept it, he is Elijah who is to come. ¹⁵ He who has ears to hear, *ᵉ* let him hear.

16 "But to what shall I compare this generation? It is like children sitting in the market places and calling to their playmates,

¹⁷ 'We piped to you, and you did not dance;
we wailed, and you did not mourn.'

¹⁸ For John came neither eating nor drinking, and they say, 'He has a demon'; ¹⁹ the Son of man came eating and drink-

---

ᵇ Or *What then did you go out to see? A man.* *ᶜ* Many ancient authorities read *What then did you go out to see? A prophet?* *ᵈ* Or *has been coming violently.* *ᵉ* Some ancient authorities omit *to hear.*

11. 5: Is. 35. 5–6, 61. 1; Lk. 4. 18–19. **11. 9:** Mt. 14. 5; 21. 26; Lk. 1. 76. **11. 10:** Mal. 3. 1; Mk. 1. 2. **11. 12–13:** Lk. 16. 16. **11. 14:** Mal. 4. 5; Mt. 17. 10–13; Jn. 1. 21; Lk. 1. 17. **11. 15:** Mt. 13. 9, 43; Mk. 4. 23; Rev. 13. 9; 2. 7. **11. 16–19:** Lk. 7. 31–35.

ing, and they say, 'Behold, a glutton and a drunkard, a friend of tax collectors and sinners!' Yet wisdom is justified by her deeds."[f]

20 Then he began to upbraid the cities where most of his mighty works had been done, because they did not repent. [21] "Woe to you, Cho-ra'zin! woe to you, Beth-sa'i-da! for if the mighty works done in you had been done in Tyre and Sidon, they would have repented long ago in sackcloth and ashes. [22] But I tell you, it shall be more tolerable on the day of judgment for Tyre and Sidon than for you. [23] And you, Ca-per'na-um, will you be exalted to heaven? You shall be brought down to Hades. For if the mighty works done in you had been done in Sodom, it would have remained until this day. [24] But I tell you that it shall be more tolerable on the day of judgment for the land of Sodom than for you."

25 At that time Jesus declared, "I thank thee, Father, Lord of heaven and earth, that thou hast hidden these things from the wise and understanding and revealed them to babes; [26] yea, Father, for such was thy gracious will.[g] [27] All things have been delivered to me by my Father; and no one knows the Son except the Father, and no one knows the Father except the Son and any one to whom the Son chooses to reveal him. [28] Come to me, all who labor and are heavy-laden, and I will give you rest. [29] Take my yoke upon you, and learn from me; for I am gentle and lowly in heart, and you will find rest for your souls. [30] For my yoke is easy, and my burden is light."

12 At that time Jesus went through the grainfields on the sabbath; his disciples were hungry, and they began to pluck ears of grain and to eat. [2] But when the Phar-

---

[f] Many ancient authorities read *children* (Luke 7.35).   [g] Or *so it was well-pleasing before thee.*

11. 20–24: Lk. 10. 13–15.   **11. 24:** Mt. 10. 15; Lk. 10. 12.   **11. 25–27:** Lk. 10. 21–22.
11. 25: 1 Cor. 1. 26–29.   **11. 27:** Jn. 3. 35; 5. 20; 13. 3; 7. 29; 10. 15; 17. 25; Mt. 28. 18.
11. 29: Jn. 13. 15; Phil. 2. 5; 1 Pet. 2. 21; Jer. 6. 16.
12. 1–8: Mk. 2. 23–28; Lk. 6. 1–5.   **12. 1:** Deut. 23. 25.

isees saw it, they said to him, "Look, your disciples are doing what is not lawful to do on the sabbath." [3] He said to them, "Have you not read what David did, when he was hungry, and those who were with him: [4] how he entered the house of God and ate the bread of the Presence, which it was not lawful for him to eat nor for those who were with him, but only for the priests? [5] Or have you not read in the law how on the sabbath the priests in the temple profane the sabbath, and are guiltless? [6] I tell you, something greater than the temple is here. [7] And if you had known what this means, 'I desire mercy, and not sacrifice,' you would not have condemned the guiltless. [8] For the Son of man is lord of the sabbath."

9 And he went on from there, and entered their synagogue. [10] And behold, there was a man with a withered hand. And they asked him, "Is it lawful to heal on the sabbath?" so that they might accuse him. [11] He said to them, "What man of you, if he has one sheep and it falls into a pit on the sabbath, will not lay hold of it and lift it out? [12] Of how much more value is a man than a sheep! So it is lawful to do good on the sabbath." [13] Then he said to the man, "Stretch out your hand." And the man stretched it out, and it was restored, whole like the other. [14] But the Pharisees went out and took counsel against him, how to destroy him.

15 Jesus, aware of this, withdrew from there. And many followed him, and he healed them all, [16] and ordered them not to make him known.[17] This was to fulfill what was spoken by the prophet Isaiah:

[18] "Behold, my servant whom I have chosen,
  my beloved with whom my soul is well pleased.

12. 3: 1 Sam. 21. 1–6; Lev. 24. 9.   **12. 5:** Num. 28. 9–10.   **12. 6:** Mt. 12. 41–42; Lk. 11. 31–32.   **12. 7:** Hos. 6. 6; Mt. 9. 13.   **12. 8:** Jn. 5. 1–18; 7. 19–24; 9. 1–41. **12. 9–14:** Mk. 3. 1–6; Lk. 6. 6–11.   **12. 11:** Lk. 14. 5.   **12. 12:** Mt. 10. 31.   **12. 14:** Mk. 14. 1; Jn. 7. 30; 8. 59; 10. 39; 11. 53.   **12. 15–16:** Mk. 3. 7–12; Lk. 6. 17–19. **12. 18–21:** Is. 42. 1–4.

> I will put my Spirit upon him,
>> and he shall proclaim justice to the Gentiles.
> [19] He will not wrangle or cry aloud,
>> nor will any one hear his voice in the streets;
> [20] he will not break a bruised reed
>> or quench a smoldering wick,
>> till he brings justice to victory;
> [21] and in his name will the Gentiles hope."

22 Then a blind and dumb demoniac was brought to him, and he healed him, so that the dumb man spoke and saw. [23] And all the people were amazed, and said, "Can this be the Son of David?" [24] But when the Pharisees heard it they said, "It is only by Be-el′ze-bub,[h] the prince of demons, that this man casts out demons." [25] Knowing their thoughts, he said to them, "Every kingdom divided against itself is laid waste, and no city or house divided against itself will stand; [26] and if Satan casts out Satan, he is divided against himself; how then will his kingdom stand? [27] And if I cast out demons by Be-el′ze-bub,[h] by whom do your sons cast them out? Therefore they shall be your judges. [28] But if it is by the Spirit of God that I cast out demons, then the kingdom of God has come upon you. [29] Or how can one enter a strong man's house and plunder his goods, unless he first binds the strong man? Then indeed he may plunder his house. [30] He who is not with me is against me, and he who does not gather with me scatters. [31] Therefore I tell you, every sin and blasphemy will be forgiven men, but the blasphemy against the Spirit will not be forgiven. [32] And whoever says a word against the Son of man will be forgiven; but whoever speaks against the Holy Spirit will not be forgiven, either in this age or in the age to come.

[h] Greek *Beelzebul.*

12. 22–29: Mk. 3. 22–27; Lk. 11. 14–22.　12. 22: Mt. 9. 32–33.　12. 24: Mt. 9. 34; 10. 25; Jn. 7. 20; 8. 52; 10. 20.　12. 30: Lk. 11. 23; Mk. 9. 40.　12. 31–32: Mk. 3. 28–30; Lk. 12. 10.

33 "Either make the tree good, and its fruit good; or make the tree bad, and its fruit bad; for the tree is known by its fruit. ³⁴ You brood of vipers! how can you speak good, when you are evil? For out of the abundance of the heart the mouth speaks. ³⁵ The good man out of his good treasure brings forth good, and the evil man out of his evil treasure brings forth evil. ³⁶ I tell you, on the day of judgment men will render account for every careless word they utter; ³⁷ for by your words you will be justified, and by your words you will be condemned."

38 Then some of the scribes and Pharisees said to him, "Teacher, we wish to see a sign from you." ³⁹ But he answered them, "An evil and adulterous generation seeks a sign; but no sign shall be given to it except the sign of the prophet Jonah. ⁴⁰ For as Jonah was three days and three nights in the belly of the whale, so will the Son of man be three days and three nights in the heart of the earth. ⁴¹ The men of Nin'e-veh will arise at the judgment with this generation and condemn it; for they repented at the preaching of Jonah, and behold, something greater than Jonah is here. ⁴² The queen of the South will arise at the judgment with this generation and condemn it; for she came from the ends of the earth to hear the wisdom of Solomon; and behold, something greater than Solomon is here.

43 "When the unclean spirit has gone out of a man, he passes through waterless places seeking rest, but he finds none. ⁴⁴ Then he says, 'I will return to my house from which I came.' And when he comes he finds it empty, swept, and put in order. ⁴⁵ Then he goes and brings with him seven other spirits more evil than himself, and they enter and dwell there;

12. 33–35: Lk. 6. 43–45; Mt. 7. 16–20; Jas. 3. 11–12; Mt. 15. 18.   **12. 38–42:** Lk. 11. 16, 29–32; Mk. 8. 11–12; Mt. 16. 1–4; Jn. 2. 18; 6. 30; 1 Cor. 1. 22.   **12. 40:** Jon. 1. 17. **12. 41:** Jon. 3. 5.   **12. 42:** 1 Kings 10. 1; 2 Chr. 9. 1.   **12. 43–45:** Lk. 11. 24–26; 2 Pet. 2. 20.

and the last state of that man becomes worse than the first. So shall it be also with this evil generation."

46 While he was still speaking to the people, behold, his mother and his brothers stood outside, asking to speak to him.[i] [48] But he replied to the man who told him, "Who is my mother, and who are my brothers?" [49] And stretching out his hand toward his disciples, he said, "Here are my mother and my brothers! [50] For whoever does the will of my Father in heaven is my brother, and sister, and mother."

13 That same day Jesus went out of the house and sat beside the sea. [2] And great crowds gathered about him, so that he got into a boat and sat there; and the whole crowd stood on the beach. [3] And he told them many things in parables, saying: "A sower went out to sow. [4] And as he sowed, some seeds fell along the path, and the birds came and devoured them. [5] Other seeds fell on rocky ground, where they had not much soil, and immediately they sprang up, since they had no depth of soil, [6] but when the sun rose they were scorched; and since they had no root they withered away. [7] Other seeds fell upon thorns, and the thorns grew up and choked them. [8] Other seeds fell on good soil and brought forth grain, some a hundredfold, some sixty, some thirty. [9] He who has ears,[j] let him hear."

10 Then the disciples came and said to him, "Why do you speak to them in parables?" [11] And he answered them, "To you it has been given to know the secrets of the kingdom of heaven, but to them it has not been given. [12] For to him who has will more be given, and he will have abundance; but from him who has not, even what he has will be taken away.

---

[i] Some ancient authorities insert verse 47: *Some one told him, "Your mother and your brothers are standing outside, asking to speak to you."*
[j] Some ancient authorities add here and in verse 43 *to hear.*

12. 46–50: Mk. 3. 31–35; Lk. 8. 19–21.   **12. 46:** Jn. 2. 1–12; 19. 25–27; 7. 1–10; Mk. 6. 3; 1 Cor. 9. 5.   **12. 50:** Jn. 15. 14.
13. 1–9: Mk. 4. 1–9; Lk. 8. 4–8; 5. 1–3.   **13. 10–13:** Mk. 4. 10–12; Lk. 8. 9–10.
13. 12: Mk. 4. 25; Lk. 8. 18; Mt. 25. 29; Lk. 19. 26.

[13] This is why I speak to them in parables, because seeing they do not see, and hearing they do not hear, nor do they understand. [14] With them indeed is fulfilled the prophecy of Isaiah which says:

'You shall indeed hear but never understand,
    and you shall indeed see but never perceive.
[15] For this people's heart has grown dull,
    and their ears are heavy of hearing,
    and their eyes they have closed,
lest they should perceive with their eyes,
    and hear with their ears,
    and understand with their heart,
    and turn for me to heal them.'

[16] But blessed are your eyes, for they see, and your ears, for they hear. [17] Truly, I say to you, many prophets and righteous men longed to see what you see, and did not see it, and to hear what you hear, and did not hear it.

18 "Hear then the parable of the sower. [19] When any one hears the word of the kingdom and does not understand it, the evil one comes and snatches away what is sown in his heart; this is what was sown along the path. [20] As for what was sown on rocky ground, this is he who hears the word and immediately receives it with joy; [21] yet he has no root in himself, but endures for a while, and when tribulation or persecution arises on account of the word, immediately he falls away.[k] [22] As for what was sown among thorns, this is he who hears the word, but the cares of the world and the delight in riches choke the word, and it proves unfruitful. [23] As for what was sown on good soil, this is he who hears the word and understands it; he indeed bears fruit, and yields, in one case a hundredfold, in another sixty, and in another thirty."

[k] Or *stumbles.*

13. 14–15: Is. 6. 9–10; Mk. 8. 18; Jn. 12. 39–41; Acts 28. 26–27.   **13. 16–17:** Lk. 10. 23–24; Jn. 8. 56; Heb. 11. 13; 1 Pet. 1. 10–12.   **13. 18–23:** Mk. 4. 13–20; Lk. 8. 11–15. **13. 22:** Mt. 19. 23; 1 Tim. 6. 9–10, 17.

24 Another parable he put before them, saying, "The kingdom of heaven may be compared to a man who sowed good seed in his field; [25] but while men were sleeping, his enemy came and sowed weeds among the wheat, and went away. [26] So when the plants came up and bore grain, then the weeds appeared also. [27] And the servants[l] of the householder came and said to him, 'Sir, did you not sow good seed in your field? How then has it weeds?' [28] He said to them, 'An enemy has done this.' The servants[l] said to him, 'Then do you want us to go and gather them?' [29] But he said, 'No; lest in gathering the weeds you root up the wheat along with them. [30] Let both grow together until the harvest; and at harvest time I will tell the reapers, Gather the weeds first and bind them in bundles to be burned, but gather the wheat into my barn.'"

31 Another parable he put before them, saying, "The kingdom of heaven is like a grain of mustard seed which a man took and sowed in his field; [32] it is the smallest of all seeds, but when it has grown it is the greatest of shrubs and becomes a tree, so that the birds of the air come and make nests in its branches."

33 He told them another parable. "The kingdom of heaven is like leaven which a woman took and hid in three measures of meal, till it was all leavened."

34 All this Jesus said to the crowds in parables; indeed he said nothing to them without a parable. [35] This was to fulfill what was spoken by the prophet:[m]

"I will open my mouth in parables,
I will utter what has been hidden since the
    foundation of the world."

36 Then he left the crowds and went into the house. And

[l] Or *slaves.*   [m] Some ancient authorities read *the prophet Isaiah.*
13. 24–30: Mk. 4. 26–29.   **13. 31–32:** Mk. 4. 30–32; Lk. 13. 18–19; Mt. 17. 20.
13. 33: Lk. 13. 20–21; Gal. 5. 9; Gen. 18. 6.   **13. 34:** Mk. 4. 33–34; Jn. 10. 6; 16. 25.
13. 35: Ps. 78. 2.

his disciples came to him, saying, "Explain to us the parable of the weeds of the field." [37] He answered, "He who sows the good seed is the Son of man; [38] the field is the world, and the good seed means the sons of the kingdom; the weeds are the sons of the evil one, [39] and the enemy who sowed them is the devil; the harvest is the close of the age, and the reapers are angels. [40] Just as the weeds are gathered and burned with fire, so will it be at the close of the age. [41] The Son of man will send his angels, and they will gather out of his kingdom all causes of sin and all evil-doers, [42] and throw them into the furnace of fire; there men will weep and gnash their teeth. [43] Then the righteous will shine like the sun in the kingdom of their Father. He who has ears, let him hear.

44 "The kingdom of heaven is like treasure hidden in a field, which a man found and covered up; then in his joy he goes and sells all that he has and buys that field.

45 "Again, the kingdom of heaven is like a merchant in search of fine pearls, [46] who, on finding one pearl of great value, went and sold all that he had and bought it.

47 "Again, the kingdom of heaven is like a net which was thrown into the sea and gathered fish of every kind; [48] when it was full, men drew it ashore and sat down and sorted the good into vessels but threw away the bad. [49] So it will be at the close of the age. The angels will come out and separate the evil from the righteous, [50] and throw them into the furnace of fire; there men will weep and gnash their teeth.

51 "Have you understood all this?" They said to him, "Yes." [52] And he said to them, "Therefore every scribe who has been trained for the kingdom of heaven is like a householder who brings out of his treasure what is new and what is old."

13. 38: Jn. 8. 44; 1 Jn. 3. 10.　　**13. 41:** Mt. 24. 31.　　**13. 42:** Mt. 13. 50; 8. 12; 22. 13; 24. 51; 25. 30; Lk. 13. 28.　　**13. 47–50:** Mt. 13. 40–42.

53 And when Jesus had finished these parables, he went away from there, [54] and coming to his own country he taught them in their synagogue, so that they were astonished, and said, "Where did this man get this wisdom and these mighty works? [55] Is not this the carpenter's son? Is not his mother called Mary? And are not his brothers James and Joseph and Simon and Judas? [56] And are not all his sisters with us? Where then did this man get all this?" [57] And they took offense at him. But Jesus said to them, "A prophet is not without honor except in his own country and in his own house." [58] And he did not do many mighty works there, because of their unbelief.

14 At that time Herod the tetrarch heard about the fame of Jesus; [2] and he said to his servants, "This is John the Baptist, he has been raised from the dead; that is why these powers are at work in him." [3] For Herod had seized John and bound him and put him in prison, for the sake of He-ro'di-as, his brother Philip's wife;[n] because John said to him, [4] "It is not lawful for you to have her." [5] And though he wanted to put him to death, he feared the people, because they held him to be a prophet. [6] But when Herod's birthday came, the daughter of He-ro'di-as danced before the company, and pleased Herod, [7] so that he promised with an oath to give her whatever she might ask. [8] Prompted by her mother, she said, "Give me the head of John the Baptist here on a platter." [9] And the king was sorry; but because of his oaths and his guests he commanded it to be given; [10] he sent and had John beheaded in the prison, [11] and his head was brought on a platter and given to the girl, and she brought it to her mother. [12] And his disciples came and took the body and buried it; and they went and told Jesus.

n A few ancient authorities read *his brother's wife.*
13. 53: Mt. 7. 28; 11. 1; 19. 1; 26. 1.   13. 54–58: Mk. 6. 1–6; Lk. 4. 16–30.
14. 1–2: Mk. 6. 14–16; Lk. 9. 7–9; Mk. 8. 28.   14. 3–4: Mk. 6. 17–18; Lk. 3. 19–20;
Lev. 18. 16; 20. 21.   14. 5–12: Mk. 6. 19–29.

13 Now when Jesus heard this, he withdrew from there in a boat to a lonely place apart. But when the crowds heard it, they followed him on foot from the towns. [14] As he went ashore he saw a great throng; and he had compassion on them, and healed their sick. [15] When it was evening, the disciples came to him and said, "This is a lonely place, and the day is now over; send the crowds away to go into the villages and buy food for themselves." [16] Jesus said, "They need not go away; you give them something to eat." [17] They said to him, "We have only five loaves here and two fish." [18] And he said, "Bring them here to me." [19] Then he ordered the crowds to sit down on the grass; and taking the five loaves and the two fish he looked up to heaven, and blessed, and broke and gave the loaves to the disciples, and the disciples gave them to the crowds. [20] And they all ate and were satisfied. And they took up twelve baskets full of the broken pieces left over. [21] And those who ate were about five thousand men, besides women and children.

22 Then he made the disciples get into the boat and go before him to the other side, while he dismissed the crowds. [23] And after he had dismissed the crowds, he went up into the hills by himself to pray. When evening came, he was there alone, [24] but the boat by this time was out on the sea,[o] beaten by the waves; for the wind was against them. [25] And in the fourth watch of the night he came to them, walking on the sea. [26] But when the disciples saw him walking on the sea, they were terrified, saying, "It is a ghost!" And they cried out for fear. [27] But immediately he spoke to them, saying, "Take heart, it is I; have no fear."

28 And Peter answered him, "Lord, if it is you, bid me come to you on the water." [29] He said, "Come." So Peter

[o] Some ancient authorities read *was many furlongs distant from the land.*

14. 13–21: Mk. 6. 32–44; Lk. 9. 10–17; Jn. 6. 1–13; Mt. 15. 32–38.   **14. 19:** Mk. 14. 22; Lk. 24. 30.   **14. 22–23:** Mk. 6. 45–46; Jn. 6. 15–17.   **14. 24–33:** Mk. 6. 47–52; Jn. 6. 16–21.   **14. 26:** Lk. 24. 37.   **14. 29:** Jn. 21. 7.

got out of the boat and walked on the water and came to Jesus; [30] but when he saw the wind,[p] he was afraid, and beginning to sink he cried out, "Lord, save me." [31] Jesus immediately reached out his hand and caught him, saying to him, "O man of little faith, why did you doubt?" [32] And when they got into the boat, the wind ceased. [33] And those in the boat worshiped him, saying, "Truly you are the Son of God."

34 And when they had crossed over, they landed at Gen-nes'a-ret. [35] And when the men of that place recognized him, they sent round to all that region and brought to him all that were sick, [36] and besought him that they might only touch the fringe of his garment; and as many as touched it were made well.

15 Then Pharisees and scribes came to Jesus from Jerusalem and said, [2] "Why do your disciples transgress the tradition of the elders? For they do not wash their hands when they eat." [3] He answered them, "And why do you transgress the commandment of God for the sake of your tradition? [4] For God commanded, 'Honor your father and your mother,' and, 'He who speaks evil of father or mother, let him surely die.' [5] But you say, 'If any one tells his father or his mother, What you would have gained from me is given to God,[q] he need not honor his father.' [6] So, for the sake of your tradition, you have made void the law[r] of God. [7] You hypocrites! Well did Isaiah prophesy of you, when he said:

[8] 'This people honors me with their lips,
    but their heart is far from me;
[9] in vain do they worship me,
    teaching as doctrines the precepts of men.'"

[p] Many ancient authorities read *strong wind.*
[q] Or *an offering.*   [r] Many ancient authorities read *word.*

14. 31: Mt. 6. 30; 8. 26; 16. 8.   **14. 33:** Mt. 28. 9, 17.   **14. 34–36:** Mk. 6. 53–56; Jn. 6. 22–26.   **14. 36:** Mk. 3. 10; Num. 15. 38; Mt. 9. 20.   **15. 1–20:** Mk. 7. 1–23.   **15. 4:** Ex. 20. 12; Deut. 5. 16; Ex. 21. 17; Lev. 20. 9.   **15. 8–9:** Is. 29. 13.

10 And he called the people to him and said to them, "Hear and understand: [11] not what goes into the mouth defiles a man, but what comes out of the mouth, this defiles a man." [12] Then the disciples came and said to him, "Do you know that the Pharisees were offended when they heard this saying?" [13] He answered, "Every plant which my heavenly Father has not planted will be rooted up. [14] Let them alone; they are blind guides. And if a blind man leads a blind man, both will fall into a pit." [15] But Peter said to him, "Explain the parable to us." [16] And he said, "Are you also still without understanding? [17] Do you not see that whatever goes into the mouth passes into the stomach, and so passes on?[s] [18] But what comes out of the mouth proceeds from the heart, and this defiles a man. [19] For out of the heart come evil thoughts, murder, adultery, fornication, theft, false witness, slander. [20] These are what defile a man; but to eat with unwashed hands does not defile a man."

21 And Jesus went away from there and withdrew to the district of Tyre and Sidon. [22] And behold, a Canaanite woman from that region came out and cried, "Have mercy on me, O Lord, Son of David; my daughter is severely possessed by a demon." [23] But he did not answer her a word. And his disciples came and begged him, saying, "Send her away, for she is crying after us." [24] He answered, "I was sent only to the lost sheep of the house of Israel." [25] But she came and knelt before him, saying, "Lord, help me." [26] And he answered, "It is not fair to take the children's bread and throw it to the dogs." [27] She said, "Yes, Lord, yet even the dogs eat the crumbs that fall from their masters' table." [28] Then Jesus answered her, "O woman, great is your faith! Be it

[s] Or *is evacuated.*

15. 11: Acts 10. 14–15; 1 Tim. 4. 3.   **15. 13:** Is. 60. 21; Jn. 15. 2.   **15. 14:** Lk. 6. 39; Mt. 23. 16, 24; Rom. 2. 19.   **15. 19:** Gal. 5. 19–21; 1 Cor. 6. 9–10; Rom. 14. 14. **15. 21–28:** Mk. 7. 24–30.   **15. 24:** Mt. 10. 6, 23.   **15. 25:** Mt. 8. 2; 18. 26; 20. 20; Jn. 9. 38.   **15. 28:** Mt. 9. 22, 28; Mk. 10. 52; Lk. 7. 50; 17. 19.

done for you as you desire." And her daughter was healed instantly.

29 And Jesus went on from there and passed along the sea of Galilee. And he went up into the hills, and sat down there. [30] And great crowds came to him, bringing with them the lame, the maimed, the blind, the dumb, and many others, and they put them at his feet, and he healed them, [31] so that the throng wondered, when they saw the dumb speaking, the maimed whole, the lame walking, and the blind seeing; and they glorified the God of Israel.

32 Then Jesus called his disciples to him and said, "I have compassion on the crowd, because they have been with me now three days, and have nothing to eat; and I am unwilling to send them away hungry, lest they faint on the way." [33] And the disciples said to him, "Where are we to get bread enough in the desert to feed so great a crowd?" [34] And Jesus said to them, "How many loaves have you?" They said, "Seven, and a few small fish." [35] And commanding the crowd to sit down on the ground, [36] he took the seven loaves and the fish, and having given thanks he broke them and gave them to the disciples, and the disciples gave them to the crowds. [37] And they all ate and were satisfied; and they took up seven baskets full of the broken pieces left over. [38] Those who ate were four thousand men, besides women and children. [39] And sending away the crowds, he got into the boat and went to the region of Mag'a-dan.

16 And the Pharisees and Sad'du-cees came, and to test him they asked him to show them a sign from heaven. [2] He answered them,[f] "When it is evening, you say, 'It will be fair weather; for the sky is red.' [3] And in the morning, 'It will be stormy today, for the sky is red and threatening.'

[f] Many ancient authorities omit the following words to the end of verse 3.
15. 29–31: Mk. 7. 31–37.   **15. 32–39:** Mk. 8. 1–10; Mt. 14. 13–21.   **15. 32:** Mt. 9. 36.
16. 1–4: Mk. 8. 11–12; Lk. 11. 16, 29; 12. 54–56; Mt. 12. 38–39; Jn. 2. 18; 6. 30.

You know how to interpret the face of the heaven, but you cannot interpret the signs of the times. ⁴ An evil and adulterous generation seeks for a sign, but no sign shall be given to it except the sign of Jonah." So he left them and departed.

5 When the disciples reached the other side, they had forgotten to bring any bread. ⁶ Jesus said to them, "Take heed and beware of the leaven of the Pharisees and Sad'du-cees." ⁷ And they discussed it among themselves, saying, "We brought no bread." ⁸ But Jesus, aware of this, said, "O men of little faith, why do you discuss among yourselves the fact that you have no bread? ⁹ Do you not yet perceive? Do you not remember the five loaves of the five thousand, and how many baskets you gathered? ¹⁰ Nor the seven loaves of the four thousand, and how many baskets you gathered? ¹¹ How is it that you fail to perceive that I did not speak about bread? Beware of the leaven of the Pharisees and Sad'du-cees." ¹² Then they understood that he did not tell them to beware of the leaven of bread, but of the teaching of the Pharisees and Sad'du-cees.

13 Now when Jesus came into the district of Caes-a-re'a Philippi, he asked his disciples, "Who do men say that the Son of man is?" ¹⁴ And they said, "Some say John the Baptist, others say Elijah, and others Jeremiah or one of the prophets." ¹⁵ He said to them, "But who do you say that I am?" ¹⁶ Simon Peter replied, "You are the Christ, the Son of the living God." ¹⁷ And Jesus answered him, "Blessed are you, Simon Bar-Jona! For flesh and blood has not revealed this to you, but my Father who is in heaven. ¹⁸ And I tell you, you are Peter,ᵘ and on this rockᵛ I will build my church,

ᵘ Greek *Petros.*   ᵛ Greek *petra.*

16. 4: Jon. 3. 4–5. **16. 5–12:** Mk. 8. 13–21. **16. 6:** Lk. 12. 1. **16. 8:** Mt. 6. 30; 8. 26; 14. 31. **16. 9:** Mt. 14. 17–21. **16. 10:** Mt. 15. 34–38. **16. 13–16:** Mk. 8. 27–30; Lk. 9. 18–21. **16. 14:** Mt. 14. 2; Mk. 6. 15; Lk. 9. 7–8; Jn. 1. 21. **16. 16:** Mt. 1. 16; Jn. 11. 27; 1. 49. **16. 17:** 1 Cor. 15. 50; Gal. 1. 16; Eph. 6. 12; Heb. 2. 14. **16. 18:** Jn. 1. 40–42; 21. 15–17; 1 Cor. 15. 5.

37

and the powers of death[w] shall not prevail against it. [19] I will give you the keys of the kingdom of heaven, and whatever you bind on earth shall be bound in heaven, and whatever you loose on earth shall be loosed in heaven." [20] Then he strictly charged the disciples to tell no one that he was the Christ.

21 From that time Jesus began to show his disciples that he must go to Jerusalem and suffer many things from the elders and chief priests and scribes, and be killed, and on the third day be raised. [22] And Peter took him and began to rebuke him, saying, "God forbid, Lord! This shall never happen to you." [23] But he turned and said to Peter, "Get behind me, Satan! You are a hindrance[x] to me; for you are not on the side of God, but of men."

24 Then Jesus told his disciples, "If any man would come after me, let him deny himself and take up his cross and follow me. [25] For whoever would save his life will lose it, and whoever loses his life for my sake will find it. [26] For what will it profit a man, if he gains the whole world and forfeits his life? Or what shall a man give in return for his life? [27] For the Son of man is to come with his angels in the glory of his Father, and then he will repay every man for what he has done. [28] Truly, I say to you, there are some standing here who will not taste death before they see the Son of man coming in his kingdom."

17 And after six days Jesus took with him Peter and James and John his brother, and led them up a high mountain apart. [2] And he was transfigured before them, and his face shone like the sun, and his garments became white

---

[w] Greek *the gates of Hades.*   [x] Greek *stumbling-block.*

16. 19: Is. 22. 22; Rev. 1. 18; Mt. 18. 18; Jn. 20. 23.   **16. 20:** Mt. 8. 4; Mk. 3. 12; 5. 43; 7. 36; 9. 9.   **16. 21–28:** Mk. 8. 31–9. 1; Lk. 9. 22–27.   **16. 21:** Mt. 17. 22–23; 20. 17–19; Lk. 17. 25; Mt. 17. 12; 26. 2.   **16. 23:** Mt. 4. 10.   **16. 24–26:** Mt. 10. 38–39; Lk. 14. 27; 17. 33; Jn. 12. 25.   **16. 27:** Mt. 10. 33; Lk. 12. 9; 1 Jn. 2. 28; Rom. 2. 6; Rev. 22. 12.   **16. 28:** Mt. 10. 23; 1 Cor. 16. 22; 1 Thess. 4. 15–18; Rev. 1. 7; Jas. 5. 7. **17. 1–9:** Mk. 9. 2–10; Lk. 9. 28–36; 2 Pet. 1. 17–18.   **17. 1:** Mt. 26. 37; Mk. 5. 37; 13. 3.

as light. ³ And behold, there appeared to them Moses and Elijah, talking with him. ⁴ And Peter said to Jesus, "Lord, it is well that we are here; if you wish, I will make three booths here, one for you and one for Moses and one for Elijah." ⁵ He was still speaking, when lo, a bright cloud over-shadowed them, and a voice from the cloud said, "This is my beloved Son,ʸ with whom I am well pleased; listen to him." ⁶ When the disciples heard this, they fell on their faces, and were filled with awe. ⁷ But Jesus came and touched them, saying, "Rise, and have no fear." ⁸ And when they lifted up their eyes, they saw no one but Jesus only.

9 And as they were coming down the mountain, Jesus commanded them, "Tell no one the vision, until the Son of man is raised from the dead." ¹⁰ And the disciples asked him, "Then why do the scribes say that first Elijah must come?" ¹¹ He replied, "Elijah does come, and he is to restore all things; ¹² but I tell you that Elijah has already come, and they did not know him, but did to him whatever they pleased. So also the Son of man will suffer at their hands." ¹³ Then the disciples understood that he was speaking to them of John the Baptist.

14 And when they came to the crowd, a man came up to him and kneeling before him said, ¹⁵ "Lord, have mercy on my son, for he is an epileptic and he suffers terribly; for often he falls into the fire, and often into the water. ¹⁶ And I brought him to your disciples, and they could not heal him." ¹⁷ And Jesus answered, "O faithless and perverse generation, how long am I to be with you? How long am I to bear with you? Bring him here to me." ¹⁸ And Jesus rebuked him, and the demon came out of him, and the boy was cured instantly.

ʸ Or *my Son, my* (or *the*) *Beloved.*

17. 5: Mt. 3. 17; Is. 42. 1; Ps. 2. 7; Jn. 12. 28.   **17. 9:** Mt. 8. 4; 16. 20; Mk. 3. 12; 5. 43; 7. 36.   **17. 10–13:** Mk. 9. 11–13; Mt. 11. 14; Mal. 4. 5.   **17. 12:** Mt. 16. 21; 17. 22; 20. 17; 26. 2; Lk. 17. 25.   **17. 14–18:** Mk. 9. 14–27; Lk. 9. 37–43.

[19] Then the disciples came to Jesus privately and said, "Why could we not cast it out?" [20] He said to them, "Because of your little faith. For truly, I say to you, if you have faith as a grain of mustard seed, you will say to this mountain, 'Move hence to yonder place,' and it will move; and nothing will be impossible to you."[z]

22 As they were gathering[a] in Galilee, Jesus said to them, "The Son of man is to be delivered into the hands of men, [23] and they will kill him, and he will be raised on the third day." And they were greatly distressed.

24 When they came to Ca-per'na-um, the collectors of the half-shekel tax went up to Peter and said, "Does not your teacher pay the tax?" [25] He said, "Yes." And when he came home, Jesus spoke to him first, saying, "What do you think, Simon? From whom do kings of the earth take toll or tribute? From their sons or from others?" [26] And when he said, "From others," Jesus said to him, "Then the sons are free. [27] However, not to give offense to them, go to the sea and cast a hook, and take the first fish that comes up, and when you open its mouth you will find a shekel; take that and give it to them for me and for yourself."

18 At that time the disciples came to Jesus, saying, "Who is the greatest in the kingdom of heaven?" [2] And calling to him a child, he put him in the midst of them, [3] and said, "Truly, I say to you, unless you turn and become like children, you will never enter the kingdom of heaven. [4] Whoever humbles himself like this child, he is the greatest in the kingdom of heaven.

5 "Whoever receives one such child in my name receives

---

[z] Some ancient authorities insert verse 21, "*But this kind never comes out except by prayer and fasting.*" [a] Some ancient authorities read *abode*.

17. 19, 21: Mk. 9. 28–29.   **17. 20:** Lk. 17. 6; Mt. 21. 21; Mk. 11. 22–23; 1 Cor. 13. 2; Mk. 9. 23.   **17. 22–23:** Mk. 9. 30–32; Lk. 9. 43–45; Mt. 16. 21; 20. 17–19; 26. 2. **17. 24:** Ex. 30. 13; 38. 26.   **17. 25:** Rom. 13. 7; Mt. 22. 17–21.   **17. 27:** Mt. 5. 29; 18. 6–9; Jn. 6. 61; 1 Cor. 8. 13.   **18. 1–5:** Mk. 9. 33–37; Lk. 9. 46–48.   **18. 3:** Mk. 10. 15; Lk. 18. 17; 1 Pet. 2. 2.   **18. 5:** Mt. 10. 40; Lk. 10. 16; Jn. 13. 20.

me; [6] but whoever causes one of these little ones who believe in me to sin,[b] it would be better for him to have a great millstone fastened round his neck and to be drowned in the depth of the sea.

7 "Woe to the world for temptations to sin![c] For it is necessary that temptations come, but woe to the man by whom the temptation comes! [8] And if your hand or your foot causes you to sin, cut it off and throw it from you; it is better for you to enter life maimed or lame than with two hands or two feet to be thrown into the eternal fire. [9] And if your eye causes you to sin, pluck it out and throw it from you; it is better for you to enter life with one eye than with two eyes to be thrown into the hell[d] of fire.

10 "See that you do not despise one of these little ones; for I tell you that in heaven their angels always behold the face of my Father who is in heaven.[e] [12] What do you think? If a man has a hundred sheep, and one of them has gone astray, does he not leave the ninety-nine on the hills and go in search of the one that went astray? [13] And if he finds it, truly, I say to you, he rejoices over it more than over the ninety-nine that never went astray. [14] So it is not the will of my[f] Father who is in heaven that one of these little ones should perish.

15 "If your brother sins against you, go and tell him his fault, between you and him alone. If he listens to you, you have gained your brother. [16] But if he does not listen, take one or two others along with you, that every word may be confirmed by the evidence of two or three witnesses. [17] If he refuses to listen to them, tell it to the church; and if he refuses to listen even to the church, let him be to you as a

[b] Greek *causes . . . to stumble.*   [c] Greek *stumbling-blocks.*   [d] Greek *Gehenna.*   [e] Some ancient authorities add verse 11, *For the Son of man came to save that which was lost.*
[f] Some ancient authorities read *your.*
18. 6–9: Mk. 9. 42–48; Lk. 17. 1–2.   **18. 8–9:** Mt. 5. 29–30; 17. 27.   **18. 10:** Acts 12. 11.   **18. 11:** Lk. 19. 10.   **18. 12–14:** Lk. 15. 3–7.   **18. 15–17:** Lk. 17. 3; 1 Cor. 6. 1–6; Gal. 6. 1; Jas. 5. 19–20; Lev. 19. 17; Deut. 19. 15.

Gentile and a tax collector. [18] Truly, I say to you, whatever you bind on earth will be bound in heaven, and whatever you loose on earth will be loosed in heaven. [19] Again I say to you, if two of you agree on earth about anything they ask, it will be done for them by my Father in heaven. [20] For where two or three are gathered in my name, there am I in the midst of them."

21 Then Peter came up and said to him, "Lord, how often shall my brother sin against me, and I forgive him? As many as seven times?" [22] Jesus said to him, "I do not say to you seven times, but seventy times seven.[g]

23 "Therefore the kingdom of heaven may be compared to a king who wished to settle accounts with his servants. [24] When he began the reckoning, one was brought to him who owed him ten thousand talents;[h] [25] and as he could not pay, his lord ordered him to be sold, with his wife and children and all that he had, and payment to be made. [26] So the servant fell on his knees, imploring him, 'Lord, have patience with me, and I will pay you everything.' [27] And out of pity for him the lord of that servant released him and forgave him the debt. [28] But that same servant, as he went out, came upon one of his fellow servants who owed him a hundred denarii;[i] and seizing him by the throat he said, 'Pay what you owe.' [29] So his fellow servant fell down and besought him, 'Have patience with me, and I will pay you.' [30] He refused and went and put him in prison till he should pay the debt. [31] When his fellow servants saw what had taken place, they were greatly distressed, and they went and reported to their lord all that had taken place. [32] Then his lord summoned him and said to him, 'You wicked servant! I for-

---

[g] Or *seventy-seven times.*   [h] This talent was probably worth about a thousand dollars.
[i] The denarius was worth about twenty cents.

18. 18: Mt. 16. 19; Jn. 20. 23.   **18. 19–20:** Mt. 7. 7; 21. 22; Jas. 1. 5–7; 1 Jn. 5. 14; Jn. 14. 13.   **18. 21–22:** Lk. 17. 4; Gen. 4. 24.   **18. 23:** Mt. 25. 19.   **18. 25:** Lk. 7. 42. **18. 26:** Mt. 8. 2.

gave you all that debt because you besought me; [33] and should not you have had mercy on your fellow servant, as I had mercy on you?' [34] And in anger his lord delivered him to the jailers,[j] till he should pay all his debt. [35] So also my heavenly Father will do to every one of you, if you do not forgive your brother from your heart."

19 Now when Jesus had finished these sayings, he went away from Galilee and entered the region of Judea beyond the Jordan; [2] and large crowds followed him, and he healed them there.

3 And Pharisees came up to him and tested him by asking, "Is it lawful to divorce one's wife for any cause?" [4] He answered, "Have you not read that he who made them from the beginning made them male and female, [5] and said, 'For this reason a man shall leave his father and mother and be joined to his wife, and the two shall become one'?[k] [6] So they are no longer two but one.[k] What therefore God has joined together, let not man put asunder." [7] They said to him, "Why then did Moses command one to give a certificate of divorce, and to put her away?" [8] He said to them, "For your hardness of heart Moses allowed you to divorce your wives, but from the beginning it was not so. [9] And I say to you: whoever divorces his wife, except for unchastity,[l] and marries another, commits adultery."[m]

10 The disciples said to him, "If such is the case of a man with his wife, it is not expedient to marry." [11] But he said to them, "Not all men can receive this precept, but only those to whom it is given. [12] For there are eunuchs who have been so from birth, and there are eunuchs who have been

---

[j] Greek *torturers.*   [k] Greek *one flesh.*
[l] Some ancient authorities, after *unchastity*, read *makes her commit adultery.*
[m] Some ancient authorities insert *and he who marries a divorced woman commits adultery.*

18. 35: Mt. 6. 14.   **19. 1:** Mt. 7. 28; 11. 1; 13. 53; 26. 1.   **19. 1–9:** Mk. 10. 1–12.
19. 5: Gen. 1. 27; 2. 24; Eph. 5. 31; 1 Cor. 6. 16.   **19. 7:** Deut. 24. 1–4.   **19. 9:** Mt. 5. 32; Lk. 16. 18; 1 Cor. 7. 10–13.   **19. 11:** 1 Cor. 7. 7–9.

made eunuchs by men, and there are eunuchs who have made themselves eunuchs for the sake of the kingdom of heaven. He who is able to receive this, let him receive it."

13 Then children were brought to him that he might lay his hands on them and pray. The disciples rebuked the people; [14] but Jesus said, "Let the children come to me, and do not hinder them; for to such belongs the kingdom of heaven." [15] And he laid his hands on them and went away.

16 And behold, one came up to him, saying, "Teacher, what good deed must I do, to have eternal life?" [17] And he said to him, "Why do you ask me about what is good? One there is who is good. If you would enter life, keep the commandments." [18] He said to him, "Which?" And Jesus said, "You shall not kill, You shall not commit adultery, You shall not steal, You shall not bear false witness, [19] Honor your father and your mother, and, You shall love your neighbor as yourself." [20] The young man said to him, "All these I have observed; what do I still lack?" [21] Jesus said to him, "If you would be perfect, go, sell what you possess and give it to the poor, and you will have treasure in heaven; and come, follow me." [22] When the young man heard this he went away sorrowful; for he had great possessions.

23 And Jesus said to his disciples, "Truly, I say to you, it will be hard for a rich man to enter the kingdom of heaven. [24] Again I tell you, it is easier for a camel to go through the eye of a needle than for a rich man to enter the kingdom of God." [25] When the disciples heard this, they were greatly astonished, saying, "Who then can be saved?" [26] But Jesus looked at them and said to them, "With men this is impossible, but with God all things are possible." [27] Then Peter

19. 13–15: Mk. 10. 13–16; Lk. 18. 15–17; Mt. 18. 2–3; 1 Cor. 14. 20.   **19. 16–22:** Mk. 10. 17–22; Lk. 18. 18–23.   **19. 16:** Lk. 10. 25; Lev. 18. 5.   **19. 18:** Ex. 20. 12–16; Deut. 5. 16–20; Rom. 13. 9; Jas. 2. 11.   **19. 19:** Lev. 19. 18; Mt. 22. 39.   **19. 21:** Lk. 12. 33; Acts 2. 45; 4. 34; Mt. 6. 20.   **19. 23–26:** Mk. 10. 23–27; Lk. 18. 24–27. **19. 26:** Gen. 18. 14; Job 42. 2.   **19. 27–30:** Mk. 10. 28–31; Lk. 18. 28–30; Mt. 4. 18–22.

said in reply, "Lo, we have left everything and followed you. What then shall we have?" [28] Jesus said to them, "Truly, I say to you, in the new world, when the Son of man shall sit on his glorious throne, you who have followed me will also sit on twelve thrones, judging the twelve tribes of Israel. [29] And every one who has left houses or brothers or sisters or father or mother or children or lands, for my name's sake, will receive a hundredfold,[n] and inherit eternal life. [30] But many that are first will be last, and the last first.

20 "For the kingdom of heaven is like a householder who went out early in the morning to hire laborers for his vineyard. [2] After agreeing with the laborers for a denarius[o] a day, he sent them into his vineyard. [3] And going out about the third hour he saw others standing idle in the market place; [4] and to them he said, 'You go into the vineyard too, and whatever is right I will give you.' So they went. [5] Going out again about the sixth hour and the ninth hour, he did the same. [6] And about the eleventh hour he went out and found others standing; and he said to them, 'Why do you stand here idle all day?' [7] They said to him, 'Because no one has hired us.' He said to them, 'You go into the vineyard too.' [8] And when evening came, the owner of the vineyard said to his steward, 'Call the laborers and pay them their wages, beginning with the last, up to the first.' [9] And when those hired about the eleventh hour came, each of them received a denarius. [10] Now when the first came, they thought they would receive more; but each of them also received a denarius. [11] And on receiving it they grumbled at the householder, [12] saying, 'These last worked only one hour, and you have made them equal to us who have borne the burden of the day and the scorching heat.' [13] But he replied to one of

[n] Some ancient authorities read *manifold.*   [o] See note on 18. 28.
19. 28: Lk. 22. 30; Mt. 20. 21; Rev. 3. 21.   **19. 30:** Mt. 20. 16; Lk. 13. 30.
20. 1: Mt. 21. 28, 33.   **20. 8:** Lev. 19. 13; Deut. 24. 15.   **20. 13:** Mt. 22. 12; 26. 50.

them, 'Friend, I am doing you no wrong; did you not agree with me for a denarius? [14] Take what belongs to you, and go; I choose to give to this last as I give to you. [15] Am I not allowed to do what I choose with what belongs to me? Or do you begrudge my generosity[p] ?' [16] So the last will be first, and the first last."

17 And as Jesus was going up to Jerusalem, he took the twelve disciples aside, and on the way he said to them, [18] "Behold, we are going up to Jerusalem; and the Son of man will be delivered to the chief priests and scribes, and they will condemn him to death, [19] and deliver him to the Gentiles to be mocked and scourged and crucified, and he will be raised on the third day."

20 Then the mother of the sons of Zeb'e-dee came up to him, with her sons, and kneeling before him she asked him for something. [21] And he said to her, "What do you want?" She said to him, "Command that these two sons of mine may sit, one at your right hand and one at your left, in your kingdom." [22] But Jesus answered, "You do not know what you are asking. Are you able to drink the cup that I am to drink?" They said to him, "We are able." [23] He said to them, "You will drink my cup, but to sit at my right hand and at my left is not mine to grant, but it is for those for whom it has been prepared by my Father." [24] And when the ten heard it, they were indignant at the two brothers. [25] But Jesus called them to him and said, "You know that the rulers of the Gentiles lord it over them, and their great men exercise authority over them. [26] Not so shall it be among you; but whoever would be great among you must be your servant, [27] and whoever would be first among you must be

---

[p] Or *is your eye evil because I am good?*

20. 15: Mt. 6. 23; Mk. 7. 22; Deut. 15. 9.   **20. 16:** Lk. 13. 30; Mt. 19. 30; Mk. 10. 31.   **20. 17–19:** Mk. 10. 32–34; Lk. 18. 31–34; Mt. 16. 21; 17. 12, 22–23; 26. 2. **20. 20–24:** Mk. 10. 35–41.   **20. 20:** Mt. 8. 2; 9. 18; 15. 25; 18. 26; Jn. 9. 38.   **20. 21:** Mt. 19. 28.   **20. 22:** Mt. 26. 39; Jn. 18. 11.   **20. 23:** Acts 12. 2; Rev. 1. 9; Mt. 13. 11. **20. 25–28:** Mk. 10. 42–45; Lk. 22. 25–27.   **20. 26:** Mt. 23. 11; Mk. 9. 35; Lk. 9. 48.

your slave; [28] even as the Son of man came not to be served but to serve, and to give his life as a ransom for many."

29 And as they went out of Jericho, a great crowd followed him. [30] And behold, two blind men sitting by the roadside, when they heard that Jesus was passing by, cried out,[q] "Have mercy on us, Son of David!" [31] The crowd rebuked them, telling them to hold their peace; but they cried out the more, "Lord, have mercy on us, Son of David!" [32] And Jesus stopped and called them, saying, "What do you want me to do for you?" [33] They said to him, "Lord, let our eyes be opened." [34] And Jesus in pity touched their eyes, and immediately they received their sight and followed him.

21 And when they drew near to Jerusalem and came to Beth′pha-ge, to the Mount of Olives, then Jesus sent two disciples, [2] saying to them, "Go into the village opposite you, and immediately you will find an ass tied, and a colt with her; untie them and bring them to me. [3] If any one says anything to you, you shall say, 'The Lord has need of them,' and he will send them immediately." [4] This took place to fulfill what was spoken by the prophet, saying,

[5] "Tell the daughter of Zion,

    Behold, your king is coming to you,

    humble, and mounted on an ass,

    and on a colt, the foal of an ass."

[6] The disciples went and did as Jesus had directed them; [7] they brought the ass and the colt, and put their clothes on them, and he sat thereon. [8] Most of the crowd spread their clothes on the road, and others cut branches from the trees and spread them on the road. [9] And the crowds that went before him and that followed him shouted, "Hosanna to the

---

[q] Many ancient authorities insert *Lord*.

20. 28: Mt. 26. 28; 1 Tim. 2. 5–6; Jn. 13. 15–16; Tit. 2. 14; 1 Pet. 1. 18.   **20. 29–34:**
Mk. 10. 46–52; Lk. 18. 35–43; Mt. 9. 27–31.
21. 1–9: Mk. 11. 1–10; Lk. 19. 29–38; Jn. 12. 12–18.   **21. 5:** Is. 62. 11; Zech. 9. 9.
21. 8: 2 Kings 9. 13.   **21. 9:** Ps. 118. 26; Lk. 2. 14; Mt. 21. 15; 23. 39.

Son of David! Blessed be he who comes in the name of the Lord! Hosanna in the highest!" [10] And when he entered Jerusalem, all the city was stirred, saying, "Who is this?" [11] And the crowds said, "This is the prophet Jesus from Nazareth of Galilee."

12 And Jesus entered the temple of God[r] and drove out all who sold and bought in the temple, and he overturned the tables of the money-changers and the seats of those who sold pigeons. [13] He said to them, "It is written, 'My house shall be called a house of prayer'; but you make it a den of robbers."

14 And the blind and the lame came to him in the temple, and he healed them. [15] But when the chief priests and the scribes saw the wonderful things that he did, and the children crying out in the temple, "Hosanna to the Son of David!" they were indignant; [16] and they said to him, "Do you hear what these are saying?" And Jesus said to them, "Yes; have you never read,

'Out of the mouth of babes and sucklings
thou hast brought perfect praise'?"

[17] And leaving them, he went out of the city to Bethany and lodged there.

18 In the morning, as he was returning to the city, he was hungry. [19] And seeing a fig tree by the wayside he went to it, and found on it nothing but leaves. And he said to it, "May no fruit ever come from you again!" And the fig tree withered at once. [20] When the disciples saw it they marveled, saying, "How did the fig tree wither at once?" [21] And Jesus answered them, "Truly, I say to you, if you have faith and never doubt, you will not only do what has been done to the fig tree,

---

[r] Some ancient authorities omit *of God.*

21. 11: Jn. 6. 14; 7. 40; Acts 3. 22; Mk. 6. 15; Lk. 13. 33.   **21. 12-13:** Mk. 11. 15-17; Lk. 19. 45-46; Jn. 2. 13-17; Ex. 30. 13; Lev. 1. 14.   **21. 13:** Is. 56. 7; Jer. 7. 11. **21. 15:** Lk. 19. 39; Mt. 21. 9.   **21. 16:** Ps. 8. 2.   **21. 17-19:** Mk. 11. 11-14; Lk. 13. 6-9.   **21. 20-22:** Mk. 11. 20-24.   **21. 21:** Mt. 17. 20; Lk. 17. 6; 1 Cor. 13. 2; Jas. 1. 6.

but even if you say to this mountain, 'Be taken up and cast into the sea,' it will be done. [22] And whatever you ask in prayer, you will receive, if you have faith."

23 And when he entered the temple, the chief priests and the elders of the people came up to him as he was teaching, and said, "By what authority are you doing these things, and who gave you this authority?" [24] Jesus answered them, "I also will ask you a question; and if you tell me the answer, then I also will tell you by what authority I do these things. [25] The baptism of John, whence was it? From heaven or from men?" And they argued with one another, "If we say, 'From heaven,' he will say to us, 'Why then did you not believe him?' [26] But if we say, 'From men,' we are afraid of the multitude; for all hold that John was a prophet." [27] So they answered Jesus, "We do not know." And he said to them, "Neither will I tell you by what authority I do these things.

28 "What do you think? A man had two sons; and he went to the first and said, 'Son, go and work in the vineyard today.' [29] And he answered, 'I will not'; but afterward he repented and went. [30] And he went to the second and said the same; and he answered, 'I go, sir,' but did not go. [31] Which of the two did the will of his father?" They said, "The first." Jesus said to them, "Truly, I say to you, the tax collectors and the harlots go into the kingdom of God before you. [32] For John came to you in the way of righteousness, and you did not believe him, but the tax collectors and the harlots believed him; and even when you saw it, you did not afterward repent and believe him.

33 "Hear another parable. There was a householder who planted a vineyard, and set a hedge around it, and dug a

---

21. 22: Jn. 14. 13–14, 16. 23.   **21. 23–27:** Mk. 11. 27–33; Lk. 20. 1–8; Jn. 2. 18–22.
21. 26: Mt. 11. 9; 14. 5; Lk. 1. 76.   **21. 28:** Mt. 20. 1; 21. 33.   **21. 32:** Lk. 7. 29–30.
21. 33–46: Mk. 12. 1–12; Lk. 20. 9–19; Is. 5. 1–7.

wine press in it, and built a tower, and let it out to tenants, and went into another country. [34] When the season of fruit drew near, he sent his servants to the tenants, to get his fruit; [35] and the tenants took his servants and beat one, killed another, and stoned another. [36] Again he sent other servants, more than the first; and they did the same to them. [37] Afterward he sent his son to them, saying, 'They will respect my son.' [38] But when the tenants saw the son, they said to themselves, 'This is the heir; come, let us kill him and have his inheritance.' [39] And they took him and cast him out of the vineyard, and killed him. [40] When therefore the owner of the vineyard comes, what will he do to those tenants?" [41] They said to him, "He will put those wretches to a miserable death, and let out the vineyard to other tenants who will give him the fruits in their seasons."

42 Jesus said to them, "Have you never read in the scriptures:

' The very stone which the builders rejected
     has become the head of the corner;
     this was the Lord's doing,
     and it is marvelous in our eyes'?

[43] Therefore I tell you, the kingdom of God will be taken away from you and given to a nation producing the fruits of it."[s]

45 When the chief priests and the Pharisees heard his parables, they perceived that he was speaking about them. [46] But when they tried to arrest him, they feared the multitudes, because they held him to be a prophet.

22   And again Jesus spoke to them in parables, saying, [2] "The kingdom of heaven may be compared to a king who gave a marriage feast for his son, [3] and sent his

---

[s] Some ancient authorities add verse 44, "*And he who falls on this stone will be broken to pieces; but when it falls on anyone, it will crush him.*"

21. 34: Mt. 22. 3.   **21. 41:** Mt. 8. 11; Acts 13. 46; 18. 6; 28. 28.   **21. 42:** Ps. 118. 22–23; Acts 4. 11; 1 Pet. 2. 7.   **22. 1–10:** Lk. 14. 16–24.   **22. 3:** Mt. 21. 34.

servants to call those who were invited to the marriage feast; but they would not come. ⁴ Again he sent other servants, saying, 'Tell those who are invited, Behold, I have made ready my dinner, my oxen and my fat calves are killed, and everything is ready; come to the marriage feast.' ⁵ But they made light of it and went off, one to his farm, another to his business, ⁶ while the rest seized his servants, treated them shamefully, and killed them. ⁷ The king was angry, and he sent his troops and destroyed those murderers and burned their city. ⁸ Then he said to his servants, 'The wedding is ready, but those invited were not worthy. ⁹ Go therefore to the thoroughfares, and invite to the marriage feast as many as you find.' ¹⁰ And those servants went out into the streets and gathered all whom they found, both bad and good; so the wedding hall was filled with guests.

11 "But when the king came in to look at the guests, he saw there a man who had no wedding garment; ¹² and he said to him, 'Friend, how did you get in here without a wedding garment?' And he was speechless. ¹³ Then the king said to the attendants, 'Bind him hand and foot, and cast him into the outer darkness; there men will weep and gnash their teeth.' ¹⁴ For many are called, but few are chosen."

15 Then the Pharisees went and took counsel how to entangle him in his talk. ¹⁶ And they sent their disciples to him, along with the He-ro'di-ans, saying, "Master, we know that you are true, and teach the way of God truthfully, and care for no man; for you do not regard the position of men. ¹⁷ Tell us, then, what you think. Is it lawful to pay taxes to Caesar, or not?" ¹⁸ But Jesus, aware of their malice, said, "Why put me to the test, you hypocrites? ¹⁹ Show me the money for the tax." And they brought him a coin.ᵗ ²⁰ And

ᵗ Greek *a denarius.*
22. 10: Mt. 13. 47.   **22. 12:** Mt. 20. 13; 26. 50.   **22. 13:** Mt. 8. 12; 13. 42, 50; 24. 51; 25. 30; Lk. 13. 28.   **22. 15–22:** Mk. 12. 13–17; Lk. 20. 20–26.   **22. 15:** Mk. 3. 6; 8. 15.

Jesus said to them, "Whose likeness and inscription is this?" [21] They said, "Caesar's." Then he said to them, "Render therefore to Caesar the things that are Caesar's, and to God the things that are God's." [22] When they heard it, they marveled; and they left him and went away.

23 The same day Sad'du-cees came to him, who say that there is no resurrection; and they asked him a question, [24] saying, "Teacher, Moses said, 'If a man dies, having no children, his brother must marry the widow, and raise up children for his brother.' [25] Now there were seven brothers among us; the first married, and died, and having no children left his wife to his brother. [26] So too the second and third, down to the seventh. [27] After them all, the woman died. [28] In the resurrection, therefore, to which of the seven will she be wife? For they all had her."

29 But Jesus answered them, "You are wrong, because you know neither the scriptures nor the power of God. [30] For in the resurrection they neither marry nor are given in marriage, but are like angels[u] in heaven.[31] And as for the resurrection of the dead, have you not read what was said to you by God, [32] 'I am the God of Abraham, and the God of Isaac, and the God of Jacob'? He is not God of the dead, but of the living." [33] And when the crowd heard it, they were astonished at his teaching.

34 But when the Pharisees heard that he had silenced the Sad'du-cees, they came together. [35] And one of them, a lawyer, asked him a question, to test him. [36] "Teacher, which is the great commandment in the law?" [37] And he said to him, "You shall love the Lord your God with all your heart, and with all your soul, and with all your mind. [38] This is

[u] Many ancient authorities add *of God.*

22. 21: Rom. 13. 7.   **22. 23–33:** Mk. 12. 18–27; Lk. 20. 27–38.   **22. 23:** Acts 4. 1–2; 23. 6–10.   **22. 24:** Deut. 25. 5.   **22. 32:** Ex. 3. 6.   **22. 33:** Mt. 7. 28.   **22. 34–40:** Mk. 12. 28–34; Lk. 20. 39–40; 10. 25–28.   **22. 35:** Lk. 7. 30; 11. 45; 14. 3.   **22. 37:** Deut. 6. 5.

the great and first commandment. [39] And a second is like it, You shall love your neighbor as yourself. [40] On these two commandments depend all the law and the prophets."

[41] Now while the Pharisees were gathered together, Jesus asked them a question, [42] saying, "What do you think of the Christ? Whose son is he?" They said to him, "The son of David." [43] He said to them, "How is it then that David, inspired by the Spirit,[v] calls him Lord, saying,

[44] 'The Lord said to my Lord,

Sit at my right hand,

till I put thy enemies under thy feet'?

[45] If David thus calls him Lord, how is he his son?" [46] And no one was able to answer him a word, nor from that day did any one dare to ask him any more questions.

23 Then said Jesus to the crowds and to his disciples, [2] "The scribes and the Pharisees sit on Moses' seat; [3] so practice and observe whatever they tell you, but not what they do; for they preach, but do not practice. [4] They bind heavy burdens, hard to bear,[w] and lay them on men's shoulders; but they themselves will not move them with their finger. [5] They do all their deeds to be seen by men; for they make their phylacteries broad and their fringes long, [6] and they love the place of honor at feasts and the best seats in the synagogues, [7] and salutations in the market places, and being called rabbi by men. [8] But you are not to be called rabbi, for you have one teacher, and you are all brethren. [9] And call no man your father on earth, for you have one Father, who is in heaven. [10] Neither be called masters, for you have one master, the Christ. [11] He who is greatest

[v] Or *in the Spirit.*   [w] Some ancient authorities omit *hard to bear.*

22. 39: Lev. 19. 18; Mt. 19. 19; Gal. 5. 14; Rom. 13. 9; Jas. 2. 8.   **22. 41–46:** Mk. 12. 35–37; Lk. 20. 41–44.   **22. 44:** Ps. 110. 1; Acts 2. 34–35; Heb. 1. 13; 10. 13. **22. 46:** Mk. 12. 34; Lk. 20. 40.   **23. 4:** Lk. 11. 46; Acts 15. 10.   **23. 5:** Mt. 6. 1; 5, 16; Ex. 13. 9; Deut. 6. 8; Mt. 9. 20.   **23. 6–7:** Mk. 12. 38–39; Lk. 20. 46; 14. 7–11; 11. 43. **23. 8:** Jas. 3. 1.   **23. 11:** Mt. 20. 26; Mk. 9. 35; 10. 43; Lk. 9. 48; 22. 26.

among you shall be your servant; [12] whoever exalts himself shall be humbled, and whoever humbles himself shall be exalted.

13 "But woe to you, scribes and Pharisees, hypocrites! because you shut the kingdom of heaven against men; for you neither enter yourselves, nor allow those who would enter to go in.[x] [15] Woe to you, scribes and Pharisees, hypocrites! for you traverse sea and land to make a single proselyte, and when he becomes a proselyte, you make him twice as much a child of hell[y] as yourselves.

16 "Woe to you, blind guides, who say, 'If any one swears by the temple, it is nothing; but if any one swears by the gold of the temple, he is bound by his oath.' [17] You blind fools! For which is greater, the gold or the temple that has made the gold sacred? [18] And you say, 'If any one swears by the altar, it is nothing; but if any one swears by the gift that is on the altar, he is bound by his oath.' [19] You blind men! For which is greater, the gift or the altar that makes the gift sacred? [20] So he who swears by the altar, swears by it and by everything on it; [21] and he who swears by the temple, swears by it and by him who dwells in it; [22] and he who swears by heaven, swears by the throne of God and by him who sits upon it.

23 "Woe to you, scribes and Pharisees, hypocrites! for you tithe mint and dill and cummin, and have neglected the weightier matters of the law, justice and mercy and faith; these you ought to have done, without neglecting the others. [24] You blind guides, straining out a gnat and swallowing a camel!

25 "Woe to you, scribes and Pharisees, hypocrites! for

---

[x] Some authorities add here (or after verse 12) verse 14, *Woe to you, scribes and Pharisees, hypocrites! for you devour widows' houses, and for a pretence you make long prayers; therefore you will receive the greater condemnation.*   [y] Greek *Gehenna.*

23. 12: Lk. 14. 11; 18. 14; Mt. 18. 4; 1 Pet. 5. 6.   **23. 13:** Lk. 11. 52.   **23. 15:** Acts 2. 10; 6. 5; 13. 43.   **23. 16–22:** Mt. 5. 33–37; 15. 14.   **23. 17:** Ex. 30. 29.   **23. 21:** 1 Kings 8. 13; Ps. 26. 8.   **23. 23–24:** Lk. 11. 42; Lev. 27. 30; Mic. 6. 8.   **23. 25–26:** Lk. 11. 39–41; Mk. 7. 4.

you cleanse the outside of the cup and of the plate, but inside they are full of extortion and rapacity. [26] You blind Pharisee! first cleanse the inside of the cup and of the plate, that the outside also may be clean.

27 " Woe to you, scribes and Pharisees, hypocrites! for you are like whitewashed tombs, which outwardly appear beautiful, but within they are full of dead men's bones and all uncleanness. [28] So you also outwardly appear righteous to men, but within you are full of hypocrisy and iniquity.

29 "Woe to you, scribes and Pharisees, hypocrites! for you build the tombs of the prophets and adorn the monuments of the righteous, [30] saying, 'If we had lived in the days of our fathers, we would not have taken part with them in shedding the blood of the prophets.' [31] Thus you witness against yourselves, that you are sons of those who murdered the prophets. [32] Fill up, then, the measure of your fathers. [33] You serpents, you brood of vipers, how are you to escape being sentenced to hell?[y] [34] Therefore I send you prophets and wise men and scribes, some of whom you will kill and crucify, and some you will scourge in your synagogues and persecute from town to town, [35] that upon you may come all the righteous blood shed on earth, from the blood of innocent Abel to the blood of Zech-a-ri′ah the son of Bar-a-chi′ah, whom you murdered between the sanctuary and the altar. [36] Truly, I say to you, all this will come upon this generation.

37 "O Jerusalem, Jerusalem, killing the prophets and stoning those who are sent to you! How often would I have gathered your children together as a hen gathers her brood under her wings, and you would not! [38] Behold, your house is forsaken and desolate.[z] [39] For I tell you, you will not see me

[y] Greek *Gehenna*.   [z] Some ancient authorities omit *and desolate*.

23. 27–28: Lk. 11. 44; Acts 23. 3; Ps. 5. 9.   **23. 29–32:** Lk. 11. 47–48; Acts 7. 51–53.
23. 33: Mt. 3. 7; Lk. 3. 7.   **23. 34–36:** Lk. 11. 49–51; 2 Chr. 36. 15–16.   **23. 34:**
Mt. 10. 17, 23.   **23. 35:** Gen. 4. 8; Heb. 11. 4; Zech. 1. 1; 2 Chr. 24. 21.   **23. 36:**
Mt. 10. 23; 16. 28; 24. 34.   **23. 37–39:** Lk. 13. 34–35.   **23. 38:** 1 Kings 9. 7; Jer. 22. 5.
23. 39: Mt. 21. 9; Ps. 118. 26.

again, until you say, 'Blessed be he who comes in the name of the Lord.'"

24 Jesus left the temple and was going away, when his disciples came to point out to him the buildings of the temple. [2] But he answered them, "You see all these, do you not? Truly, I say to you, there will not be left here one stone upon another, that will not be thrown down."

3 As he sat on the Mount of Olives, the disciples came to him privately, saying, "Tell us, when will this be, and what will be the sign of your coming and of the close of the age?" [4] And Jesus answered them, "Take heed that no one leads you astray. [5] For many will come in my name, saying, 'I am the Christ,' and they will lead many astray. [6] And you will hear of wars and rumors of wars; see that you are not alarmed; for this must take place, but the end is not yet. [7] For nation will rise against nation, and kingdom against kingdom, and there will be famines and earthquakes in various places: [8] all this is but the beginning of the sufferings.

9 "Then they will deliver you up to tribulation, and put you to death; and you will be hated by all nations for my name's sake. [10] And then many will fall away,[a] and betray one another, and hate one another. [11] And many false prophets will arise and lead many astray. [12] And because wickedness is multiplied, most men's love will grow cold. [13] But he who endures to the end will be saved. [14] And this gospel of the kingdom will be preached throughout the whole world, as a testimony to all nations; and then the end will come.

15 "So when you see the desolating sacrilege spoken of by the prophet Daniel, standing in the holy place (let the reader

[a] Or *stumble*.

24. 1–35: Mk. 13. 1–31; Lk. 21. 1–33.   24. 2: Mt. 26. 61; 27. 39–40; Lk. 19. 44; Jn. 2. 19.   24. 3: Lk. 17. 20; Mt. 13. 39, 40, 49; 28. 20; 16. 27.   24. 5: Mt. 24. 11, 23–24; 1 Jn. 2. 18.   24. 6–7: Rev. 6. 3–8, 12–17; Is. 19. 2.   24. 9: Mt. 10. 17–18, 22; Jn. 15. 18; 16. 2.   24. 13: Mt. 10. 22; Rev. 2. 7.   24. 14: Mt. 28. 19; Rom. 10. 18. 24. 15: Dan. 9. 27; 11. 31; 12. 11.

understand), [16] then let those who are in Judea flee to the mountains; [17] let him who is on the housetop not go down to take what is in his house; [18] and let him who is in the field not turn back to take his mantle. [19] And alas for those who are with child and for those who give suck in those days! [20] Pray that your flight may not be in winter or on a sabbath. [21] For then there will be great tribulation, such as has not been from the beginning of the world until now, no, and never will be. [22] And if those days had not been shortened, no human being would be saved; but for the sake of the elect those days will be shortened. [23] Then if any one says to you, 'Lo, here is the Christ!' or 'There he is!' do not believe it. [24] For false Christs and false prophets will arise and show great signs and wonders, so as to lead astray, if possible, even the elect. [25] Lo, I have told you beforehand. [26] So, if they say to you, 'Lo, he is in the wilderness,' do not go out; if they say, 'Lo, he is in the inner rooms,' do not believe it. [27] For as the lightning comes from the east and shines as far as the west, so will be the coming of the Son of man. [28] Wherever the body is, there the eagles[b] will be gathered together.

29 "Immediately after the tribulation of those days the sun will be darkened, and the moon will not give its light, and the stars will fall from heaven, and the powers of the heavens will be shaken; [30] then will appear the sign of the Son of man in heaven, and then all the tribes of the earth will mourn, and they will see the Son of man coming on the clouds of heaven with power and great glory; [31] and he will send out his angels with a loud trumpet call, and they will gather his elect from the four winds, from one end of heaven to the other.

[b] Or *vultures.*

24. 17–18: Lk. 17. 31.   **24. 19:** Lk. 23. 29.   **24. 21:** Dan. 12. 1; Joel 2. 2. **24. 26–27:** Lk. 17. 22–24; Rev. 1. 7.   **24. 28:** Lk. 17. 37; Job 39. 30.   **24. 29:** Rev. 8. 12; Is. 13. 10; Ezek. 32. 7; Joel 2. 10–11; Zeph. 1. 15.   **24. 30:** Mt. 16. 27; Dan. 7. 13.   **24. 31:** 1 Cor. 15. 52; 1 Thess. 4. 16; Is. 27. 13; Zech. 9. 14.

32 "From the fig tree learn its lesson: as soon as its branch becomes tender and puts forth its leaves, you know that summer is near. [33] So also, when you see all these things, you know that he is near, at the very gates. [34] Truly, I say to you, this generation will not pass away till all these things take place. [35] Heaven and earth will pass away, but my words will not pass away.

36 "But of that day and hour no one knows, not even the angels of heaven, nor the Son, but the Father only. [37] As were the days of Noah, so will be the coming of the Son of man. [38] For as in those days before the flood they were eating and drinking, marrying and giving in marriage, until the day when Noah entered the ark, [39] and they did not know until the flood came and swept them all away, so will be the coming of the Son of man. [40] Then two men will be in the field; one is taken and one is left. [41] Two women will be grinding at the mill; one is taken and one is left. [42] Watch therefore, for you do not know on what day your Lord is coming. [43] But know this, that if the householder had known in what part of the night the thief was coming, he would have watched and would not have let his house be broken into. [44] Therefore you also must be ready; for the Son of man is coming at an hour you do not expect.

45 "Who then is the faithful and wise servant, whom his master has set over his household, to give them their food at the proper time? [46] Blessed is that servant whom his master when he comes will find so doing. [47] Truly, I say to you, he will set him over all his possessions. [48] But if that wicked servant says to himself, 'My master is delayed,' [49] and begins to beat his fellow servants, and eats and drinks with the drunken, [50] the master of that servant will come on a

24. 34: Mt. 16. 28.   24. 35: Mt. 5. 18; Lk. 16. 17.   24. 36: Acts 1. 6–7.
24. 37–39: Lk. 17. 26–27; Gen. 6. 5–8; 7. 6–24.   24. 40–41: Lk. 17. 34–35.   24. 42: Mk. 13. 35; Lk. 12. 40; Mt. 25. 13.   24. 43–51: Lk. 12. 39–46.   24. 43: 1 Thess. 5. 2; Rev. 3. 3; 16. 15; 2 Pet. 3. 10.   24. 45: Mt. 25. 21, 23.   24. 49: Lk. 21. 34.

day when he does not expect him and at an hour he does not know, [51] and will punish[c] him and put him with the hypocrites; there men will weep and gnash their teeth.

25 "Then the kingdom of heaven shall be compared to ten maidens who took their lamps and went to meet the bridegroom.[d] [2] Five of them were foolish, and five were wise. [3] For when the foolish took their lamps, they took no oil with them; [4] but the wise took flasks of oil with their lamps. [5] As the bridegroom was delayed, they all slumbered and slept. [6] But at midnight there was a cry, 'Behold, the bridegroom! Come out to meet him.' [7] Then all those maidens rose and trimmed their lamps. [8] And the foolish said to the wise, 'Give us some of your oil, for our lamps are going out.' [9] But the wise replied, 'Perhaps there will not be enough for us and for you; go rather to the dealers and buy for yourselves.' [10] And while they went to buy, the bridegroom came, and those who were ready went in with him to the marriage feast; and the door was shut. [11] Afterward the other maidens came also, saying, 'Lord, Lord, open to us.' [12] But he replied, 'Truly, I say to you, I do not know you.' [13] Watch therefore, for you know neither the day nor the hour.

[14] "For it will be as when a man going on a journey called his servants and entrusted to them his property; [15] to one he gave five talents,[e] to another two, to another one, to each according to his ability. Then he went away. [16] He who had received the five talents went at once and traded with them; and he made five talents more. [17] So too, he who had the two talents made two talents more. [18] But he who had received the one talent, went and dug in the ground and hid his master's money. [19] Now after a long time the master

---

[c] Or *cut him in pieces.*   [d] Some ancient authorities add *and the bride.*
[e] See note on 18. 24.

24. 51: Mt. 8. 12; 13. 42, 50; 22. 13; 25. 30; Lk. 13. 28.
25. 1: Lk. 12. 35–38; Mk. 13. 34.   **25. 2:** Mt. 7. 24–27.   **25. 10:** Rev. 19. 9.
25. 11–12: Lk. 13. 25; Mt. 7. 21–23.   **25. 13:** Mt. 24. 42; Mk. 13. 35; Lk. 12. 40.
25. 14–30: Lk. 19. 12–28.   **25. 19:** Mt. 18. 23.

of those servants came and settled accounts with them. [20] And he who had received the five talents came forward, bringing five talents more, saying, 'Master, you delivered to me five talents; here I have made five talents more.' [21] His master said to him, 'Well done, good and faithful servant; you have been faithful over a little, I will set you over much; enter into the joy of your master.' [22] And he also who had the two talents came forward, saying, 'Master, you delivered to me two talents; here I have made two talents more.' [23] His master said to him, 'Well done, good and faithful servant; you have been faithful over a little, I will set you over much; enter into the joy of your master.' [24] He also who had received the one talent came forward, saying, 'Master, I knew you to be a hard man, reaping where you did not sow, and gathering where you did not winnow; [25] so I was afraid, and I went and hid your talent in the ground. Here you have what is yours.' [26] But his master answered him, 'You wicked and slothful servant! You knew that I reap where I have not sowed, and gather where I have not winnowed? [27] Then you ought to have invested my money with the bankers, and at my coming I should have received what was my own with interest. [28] So take the talent from him, and give it to him who has the ten talents. [29] For to every one who has will more be given, and he will have abundance; but from him who has not, even what he has will be taken away. [30] And cast the worthless servant into the outer darkness; there men will weep and gnash their teeth.'

31 "When the Son of man comes in his glory, and all the angels with him, then he will sit on his glorious throne. [32] Before him will be gathered all the nations, and he will separate them one from another as a shepherd separates the sheep

25. 21: Lk. 16. 10; Mt. 24. 45.   **25. 29:** Mt. 13. 12; Mk. 4. 25; Lk. 8. 18.
25. 30: Mt. 8. 12; 13. 42, 50; 22. 13; Lk. 13. 28.   **25. 31:** Mt. 16. 27; 19. 28.
25. 32: Ezek. 34. 17.

from the goats,[33] and he will place the sheep at his right hand, but the goats at the left. [34] Then the King will say to those at his right hand, 'Come, O blessed of my Father, inherit the kingdom prepared for you from the foundation of the world; [35] for I was hungry and you gave me food, I was thirsty and you gave me drink, I was a stranger and you welcomed me, [36] I was naked and you clothed me, I was sick and you visited me, I was in prison and you came to me.' [37] Then the righteous will answer him, 'Lord, when did we see thee hungry and feed thee, or thirsty and give thee drink? [38] And when did we see thee a stranger and welcome thee, or naked and clothe thee? [39] And when did we see thee sick or in prison and visit thee?' [40] And the King will answer them, 'Truly, I say to you, as you did it to one of the least of these my brethren, you did it to me.' [41] Then he will say to those at his left hand, 'Depart from me, you cursed, into the eternal fire prepared for the devil and his angels; [42] for I was hungry and you gave me no food, I was thirsty and you gave me no drink, [43] I was a stranger and you did not welcome me, naked and you did not clothe me, sick and in prison and you did not visit me.' [44] Then they also will answer, 'Lord, when did we see thee hungry or thirsty or a stranger or naked or sick or in prison, and did not minister to thee?' [45] Then he will answer them, 'Truly, I say to you, as you did it not to one of the least of these, you did it not to me.' [46] And they will go away into eternal punishment, but the righteous into eternal life."

26 When Jesus had finished all these sayings, he said to his disciples, [2] "You know that after two days the Passover is coming, and the Son of man will be delivered up to be crucified."

25. 34: Lk. 12. 32; Mt. 5. 3; Rev. 13. 8; 17. 8.   **25. 35–36:** Is. 58. 7; Jas. 1. 27; 2. 15–16; Heb. 13. 2; 2 Tim. 1. 16.   **25. 40:** Mt. 10. 42; Mk. 9. 41; Heb. 6. 10; Prov. 19. 17.   **25. 41:** Mk. 9. 48; Lk. 16. 23; Rev. 20. 10.   **25. 46:** Dan. 12. 2; Jn. 5. 29. **26. 1:** Mt. 7. 28; 11. 1; 13. 53; 19. 1.   **26. 2–5:** Mk. 14. 1–2; Lk. 22. 1–2; Jn. 11. 47–53.

3 Then the chief priests and the elders of the people gathered in the palace of the high priest, who was called Ca'iaphas, ⁴ and took counsel together in order to arrest Jesus by stealth and kill him. ⁵ But they said, "Not during the feast, lest there be a tumult among the people."

6 Now when Jesus was at Bethany in the house of Simon the leper, ⁷ a woman came up to him with an alabaster jar of very expensive ointment, and she poured it on his head, as he sat at table. ⁸ But when the disciples saw it, they were indignant, saying, "Why this waste? ⁹ For this ointment might have been sold for a large sum, and given to the poor." ¹⁰ But Jesus, aware of this, said to them, "Why do you trouble the woman? For she has done a beautiful thing to me. ¹¹ For you always have the poor with you, but you will not always have me. ¹² In pouring this ointment on my body she has done it to prepare me for burial. ¹³ Truly, I say to you, wherever this gospel is preached in the whole world, what this woman has done will be told in memory of her."

14 Then one of the twelve, who was called Judas Iscariot, went to the chief priests ¹⁵ and said, "What will you give me if I deliver him to you?" And they paid him thirty pieces of silver. ¹⁶ And from that moment he sought an opportunity to betray him.

17 Now on the first day of Unleavened Bread the disciples came to Jesus, saying, "Where will you have us prepare for you to eat the passover?" ¹⁸ He said, "Go into the city to such a one, and say to him, 'The Teacher says, My time is at hand; I will keep the passover at your house with my disciples.'" ¹⁹ And the disciples did as Jesus had directed them, and they prepared the passover.

26. 6–13: Mk. 14. 3–9; Jn. 12. 1–8; Lk. 7. 36–38.   **26. 11:** Deut. 15. 11.   **26. 12:** Jn. 19. 40.   **26. 14–16:** Mk. 14. 10–11; Lk. 22. 3–6.   **26. 15:** Ex. 21. 32; Zech. 11. 12.   **26. 17–19:** Mk. 14. 12–16; Lk. 22. 7–13.   **26. 18:** Mt. 26. 45; Jn. 7. 6; 12. 23; 13. 1; 17. 1.   **26. 19:** Mt. 21. 6; Deut. 16. 5–8.

20 When it was evening, he sat at table with the twelve disciples;*ᶠ* ²¹ and as they were eating, he said, "Truly, I say to you, one of you will betray me." ²² And they were very sorrowful, and began to say to him one after another, "Is it I, Lord?" ²³ He answered, "He who has dipped his hand in the dish with me, will betray me. ²⁴ The Son of man goes as it is written of him, but woe to that man by whom the Son of man is betrayed! It would have been better for that man if he had not been born." ²⁵ Judas, who betrayed him, said, "Is it I, Master?"*ᵍ* He said to him, "You have said so."

26 Now as they were eating, Jesus took bread, and blessed, and broke it, and gave it to the disciples and said, "Take, eat; this is my body." ²⁷ And he took a cup, and when he had given thanks he gave it to them, saying, "Drink of it, all of you; ²⁸ for this is my blood of the*ʰ* covenant, which is poured out for many for the forgiveness of sins. ²⁹ I tell you I shall not drink again of this fruit of the vine until that day when I drink it new with you in my Father's kingdom."

30 And when they had sung a hymn, they went out to the Mount of Olives. ³¹ Then Jesus said to them, "You will all fall away because of me this night; for it is written, 'I will strike the shepherd, and the sheep of the flock will be scattered.' ³² But after I am raised up, I will go before you to Galilee." ³³ Peter declared to him, "Though they all fall away because of you, I will never fall away." ³⁴ Jesus said to him, "Truly, I say to you, this very night, before the cock crows, you will deny me three times." ³⁵ Peter said to him, "Even if I must die with you, I will not deny you." And so said all the disciples.

ᶠ Many authorities omit *disciples.*   *ᵍ* Or *Rabbi.*   *ʰ* Many ancient authorities insert *new.*
26. 20–24: Mk. 14. 17–21; Lk. 22. 14, 21–23; Jn. 13. 21–30.   **26. 24:** Ps. 41. 9; Lk. 24. 25; 1 Cor. 15. 3; Acts 17. 2–3; Mt. 18. 7.   **26. 26–29:** Mk. 14. 22–25; Lk. 22. 17–19; 1 Cor. 10. 16; 11. 23–26; Mt. 14. 19; 15. 36.   **26. 28:** Heb. 9. 20; Mt. 20. 28; Mk. 1. 4; Ex. 24. 6–8.   **26. 30–35:** Mk. 14. 26–31; Lk. 22. 33–34, 39; Jn. 14. 31; 18. 1; 13. 36–38.   **26. 31:** Zech. 13. 7; Jn. 16. 32.   **26. 32:** Mt. 28. 7, 10, 16.

36 Then Jesus went with them to a place called Geth-sem'a-ne, and he said to his disciples, "Sit here, while I go yonder and pray." ³⁷ And taking with him Peter and the two sons of Zeb'e-dee, he began to be sorrowful and troubled. ³⁸ Then he said to them, "My soul is very sorrowful, even to death; remain here, and watch*ⁱ* with me." ³⁹ And going a little farther he fell on his face and prayed, "My Father, if it be possible, let this cup pass from me; nevertheless, not as I will, but as thou wilt." ⁴⁰ And he came to the disciples and found them sleeping; and he said to Peter, "So, could you not watch*ⁱ* with me one hour? ⁴¹ Watch*ⁱ* and pray that you may not enter into temptation; the spirit indeed is willing, but the flesh is weak." ⁴² Again, for the second time, he went away and prayed, "My Father, if this cannot pass unless I drink it, thy will be done." ⁴³ And again he came and found them sleeping, for their eyes were heavy. ⁴⁴ So, leaving them again, he went away and prayed for the third time, saying the same words. ⁴⁵ Then he came to the disciples and said to them, "Are you still sleeping and taking your rest? Behold, the hour is at hand, and the Son of man is betrayed into the hands of sinners. ⁴⁶ Rise, let us be going; see, my betrayer is at hand."

47 While he was still speaking, Judas came, one of the twelve, and with him a great crowd with swords and clubs, from the chief priests and the elders of the people. ⁴⁸ Now the betrayer had given them a sign, saying, "The one I shall kiss is the man; seize him." ⁴⁹ And he came up to Jesus at once and said, "Hail, Master!"*ʲ* And he kissed him. ⁵⁰ Jesus said to him, "Friend, why are you here?"*ᵏ* Then they came up and laid hands on Jesus and seized him. ⁵¹ And behold, one

---

ⁱ Or *keep awake.*   *ʲ* Or *Rabbi.*   *ᵏ* Or *do that for which you have come.*

26. 36–46: Mk. 14. 32–42; Lk. 22. 40–46.   **26. 38:** Jn. 12. 27; Heb. 5. 7–8.   **26. 39:** Jn. 18. 11; Mt. 20. 22.   **26. 41:** Mt. 6. 13; Lk. 11. 4.   **26. 42:** Jn. 4. 34; 5. 30; 6. 38.   **26. 45:** Mt. 26. 18; Jn. 12. 23; 13. 1; 17. 1.   **26. 47–56:** Mk. 14. 43–50; Lk. 22. 47–53; Jn. 18. 2–11.   **26. 50:** Mt. 20. 13; 22. 12.

of those who were with Jesus stretched out his hand and
drew his sword, and struck the slave of the high priest, and
cut off his ear. ⁵² Then Jesus said to him, "Put your sword
back into its place; for all who take the sword will perish
by the sword. ⁵³ Do you think that I cannot appeal to my
Father, and he will at once send me more than twelve legions
of angels? ⁵⁴ But how then should the scriptures be fulfilled,
that it must be so?" ⁵⁵ At that hour Jesus said to the crowds,
"Have you come out as against a robber with swords and
clubs to capture me? Day after day I sat in the temple
teaching, and you did not seize me. ⁵⁶ But all this has taken
place, that the scriptures of the prophets might be fulfilled."
Then all the disciples forsook him and fled.

57 Then those who had seized Jesus led him to Ca′ia-phas
the high priest, where the scribes and the elders had gathered.
⁵⁸ But Peter followed him at a distance, as far as the courtyard of the high priest, and going inside he sat with the
guards to see the end. ⁵⁹ Now the chief priests and the whole
council sought false witness against Jesus, that they might
put him to death, ⁶⁰ but they found none, though many witnesses came forward. At last two came forward ⁶¹ and said,
"This fellow said, 'I am able to destroy the temple of God,
and to build it in three days.'" ⁶² And the high priest stood up
and said, "Have you no answer to make? What is it that
these men testify against you?" ⁶³ But Jesus was silent. And
the high priest said to him, "I adjure you by the living God,
tell us if you are the Christ, the Son of God?" ⁶⁴ Jesus said to
him, "You have said so. But I tell you, hereafter you will
see the Son of man seated at the right hand of Power, and
coming on the clouds of heaven." ⁶⁵ Then the high priest tore
his robes, and said, "He has uttered blasphemy. Why do we

26. 52: Gen. 9. 6; Rev. 13. 10.   26. 55: Lk. 19. 47; Jn. 18. 19–21.   26. 57–75:
Mk. 14. 53–72; Lk. 22. 54–71; Jn. 18. 12–27.   26. 61: Mt. 24. 2; 27. 40; Acts 6. 14;
Jn. 2. 19.   26. 63: Mt. 27. 11; Jn. 18. 33.   26. 64: Mt. 16. 28; Dan. 7. 13; Ps. 110. 1.
26. 65: Num. 14. 6; Acts 14. 14; Lev. 24. 16.

still need witnesses? You have now heard his blasphemy. [66] What is your judgment?" They answered, "He deserves death." [67] Then they spat in his face, and struck him; and some slapped him, [68] saying, "Prophesy to us, you Christ! Who was it that struck you?"

69 Now Peter was sitting outside in the courtyard. And a maid came up to him, and said, "You also were with Jesus the Galilean." [70] But he denied it before them all, saying, "I do not know what you mean." [71] And when he went out to the porch, another maid saw him, and she said to the bystanders, "This fellow was with Jesus of Nazareth." [72] And again he denied it with an oath, "I do not know the man." [73] After a little while the bystanders came up and said to Peter, "Certainly you are also one of them, for your accent betrays you." [74] Then he began to invoke a curse on himself and to swear, "I do not know the man." And immediately the cock crowed. [75] And Peter remembered the saying of Jesus, "Before the cock crows, you will deny me three times." And he went out and wept bitterly.

27 When morning came, all the chief priests and the elders of the people took counsel against Jesus to put him to death; [2] and they bound him and led him away and delivered him to Pilate the governor.

3 When Judas, his betrayer, saw that he was condemned, he repented and brought back the thirty pieces of silver to the chief priests and the elders, [4] saying, "I have sinned in betraying innocent blood." They said, "What is that to us? See to it yourself." [5] And throwing down the pieces of silver in the temple, he departed; and he went and hanged himself. [6] But the chief priests, taking the pieces of silver, said, "It is not lawful to put them into the treasury, since they are

26. 75: Mt. 26. 34.   **27. 1–2**: Mk. 15. 1; Lk. 23. 1; Jn. 18. 28.   **27. 3–10**: Acts 1. 16–20.
27. 3: Mt. 26. 15; Ex. 21. 32.   **27. 6**: Deut. 23. 18.

blood money." [7] So they took counsel, and bought with them the potter's field, to bury strangers in. [8] Therefore that field has been called the Field of Blood to this day. [9] Then was fulfilled what had been spoken by the prophet Jeremiah, saying, "And they took the thirty pieces of silver, the price of him on whom a price had been set by some of the sons of Israel, [10] and they gave them for the potter's field, as the Lord directed me."

11 Now Jesus stood before the governor; and the governor asked him, "Are you the King of the Jews?" Jesus said to him, "You have said so." [12] But when he was accused by the chief priests and elders, he made no answer. [13] Then Pilate said to him, "Do you not hear how many things they testify against you?" [14] But he gave him no answer, not even to a single charge; so that the governor wondered greatly.

15 Now at the feast the governor was accustomed to release for the crowd any one prisoner whom they wanted. [16] And they had then a notorious prisoner, called Bar-ab′bas.[*l*] [17] So when they had gathered, Pilate said to them, "Whom do you want me to release for you, Bar-ab′bas[*l*] or Jesus who is called Christ?" [18] For he knew that it was out of envy that they had delivered him up. [19] Besides, while he was sitting on the judgment seat, his wife sent word to him, "Have nothing to do with that righteous man, for I have suffered much over him today in a dream." [20] Now the chief priests and the elders persuaded the people to ask for Bar-ab′bas and destroy Jesus. [21] The governor again said to them, "Which of the two do you want me to release for you?" And they said, "Bar-ab′bas." [22] Pilate said to them, "Then what shall I do with Jesus who is called Christ?" [23] They all said, "Let him be crucified." And he said, "Why, what evil

[*l*] Some ancient authorities read *Jesus Barabbas.*
27. 9: Zech. 11. 12–13; Jer. 32. 6–15; 18. 2–3.   **27. 11–26:** Mk. 15. 2–15; Lk. 23. 3, 18–25; Jn. 18. 29–19. 16.   **27. 14:** Lk. 23. 9; Mt. 26. 62; Mk. 14. 60; 1 Tim. 6. 13.
27. 19: Lk. 23. 4.   **27. 21:** Acts 3. 13–14.

has he done?" But they shouted all the more, "Let him be crucified."

24 So when Pilate saw that he was gaining nothing, but rather that a riot was beginning, he took water and washed his hands before the crowd, saying, "I am innocent of this man's blood;*m* see to it yourselves." [25] And all the people answered, "His blood be on us and on our children!" [26] Then he released for them Bar-ab'bas, and having scourged Jesus, delivered him to be crucified.

27 Then the soldiers of the governor took Jesus into the praetorium, and they gathered the whole battalion before him. [28] And they stripped him and put a scarlet robe upon him, [29] and plaiting a crown of thorns they put it on his head, and put a reed in his right hand. And kneeling before him they mocked him, saying, "Hail, King of the Jews!" [30] And they spat upon him, and took the reed and struck him on the head. [31] And when they had mocked him, they stripped him of the robe, and put his own clothes on him, and led him away to crucify him.

32 As they were marching out, they came upon a man of Cy-re'ne, Simon by name; this man they compelled to carry his cross. [33] And when they came to a place called Gol'go-tha, which means the place of a skull, [34] they offered him wine to drink, mingled with gall; but when he tasted it, he would not drink it. [35] And when they had crucified him, they divided his garments among them by casting lots; [36] then they sat down and kept watch over him there. [37] And over his head they put the charge against him, which read, "This is Jesus the King of the Jews." [38] Then two robbers were crucified with him, one on the right and one on the left.

---

m Some authorities read *this righteous blood* or *this righteous man's blood.*

27. 24: Deut. 21. 6–9; Ps. 26. 6.   **27. 25:** Acts 5. 28; Josh. 2. 19.   **27. 27–31:** Mk. 15. 16–20; Lk. 23. 11; Jn. 19. 2–3.   **27. 32:** Mk. 15. 21; Lk. 23. 26; Jn. 19. 17; Heb. 13. 12.   **27. 33–44:** Mk. 15. 22–32; Lk. 23. 33–39; Jn. 19. 17–24.   **27. 35:** Ps. 22. 18.

[39] And those who passed by derided him, wagging their heads [40] and saying, "You who would destroy the temple and build it in three days, save yourself! If you are the Son of God, come down from the cross." [41] So also the chief priests, with the scribes and elders, mocked him, saying, [42] "He saved others; he cannot save himself. He is the King of Israel; let him come down now from the cross, and we will believe in him. [43] He trusts in God; let God deliver him now, if he desires him; for he said, 'I am the Son of God.'" [44] And the robbers who were crucified with him also reviled him in the same way.

45 Now from the sixth hour there was darkness over all the land[n] until the ninth hour. [46] And about the ninth hour Jesus cried with a loud voice, "Eli, Eli, la'ma sa-bach-tha'ni?" that is, "My God, my God, why hast thou forsaken me?" [47] And some of the bystanders hearing it said, "This man is calling Elijah." [48] And one of them at once ran and took a sponge, filled it with vinegar, and put it on a reed, and gave it to him to drink. [49] But the others said, "Wait, let us see whether Elijah will come to save him."[o] [50] And Jesus cried again with a loud voice and yielded up his spirit.

51 And behold, the curtain of the temple was torn in two, from top to bottom; and the earth shook, and the rocks were split; [52] the tombs also were opened, and many bodies of the saints who had fallen asleep were raised, [53] and coming out of the tombs after his resurrection they went into the holy city and appeared to many. [54] When the centurion and those who were with him, keeping watch over Jesus, saw the earthquake and what took place, they were filled with awe, and said, "Truly this was a son of God!"

[n] Or *earth*.
[o] Many ancient authorities insert *And another took a spear and pierced his side, and out came water and blood.*
27. 39: Ps. 22. 7–8; 109. 25.   27. 40: Mt. 26. 61; Acts 6. 14; Jn. 2. 19.   27. 45–56: Mk. 15. 33–41; Lk. 23. 44–54; Jn. 19. 28–30.   27. 46: Ps. 22. 1.   27. 48: Ps. 69. 21. 27. 51: Heb. 9. 8; 10. 19; Ex. 26. 31–35; Mt. 28. 2.   27. 54: Mt. 3. 17; 17. 5.

55 There were also many women there, looking on from afar, who had followed Jesus from Galilee, ministering to him; [56] among whom were Mary Mag'da-lene, and Mary the mother of James and Joseph, and the mother of the sons of Zeb'e-dee.

57 When it was evening, there came a rich man from Ar-i-ma-the'a, named Joseph, who also was a disciple of Jesus. [58] He went to Pilate and asked for the body of Jesus. Then Pilate ordered it to be given to him. [59] And Joseph took the body, and wrapped it in a clean linen shroud, [60] and laid it in his own new tomb, which he had hewn in the rock; and he rolled a great stone to the entrance of the tomb, and departed. [61] And Mary Mag'da-lene and the other Mary were there, sitting opposite the tomb.

62 Next day, that is, after the day of Preparation, the chief priests and the Pharisees gathered before Pilate [63] and said, "Sir, we remember how that impostor said, while he was still alive, 'After three days I will rise again.' [64] Therefore order the tomb to be made secure until the third day, lest his disciples go and steal him away, and tell the people, 'He has risen from the dead,' and the last fraud will be worse than the first." [65] Pilate said to them, "You have a guard[p] of soldiers; go, make it as secure as you can."[q] [66] So they went and made the tomb secure by sealing the stone and setting a guard.

28 Now after the sabbath, toward the dawn of the first day of the week, Mary Mag'da-lene and the other Mary went to see the tomb. [2] And behold, there was a great earthquake; for an angel of the Lord descended from heaven and came and rolled back the stone, and sat upon it.

[p] Or *Take a guard.*   [q] Greek *know.*

27. 56: Lk. 24. 10.   27. 57–61: Mk. 15. 42–47; Lk. 23. 50–56; Jn. 19. 38–42; Acts 13. 29.
27. 63: Mt. 16. 21; 17. 23; 20. 19.   27. 66: Mt. 27. 60; 28. 11–15.
28. 1–8: Mk. 16. 1–8; Lk. 24. 1–9; Jn. 20. 1–2.   28. 1: Lk. 8. 2; Mt. 27. 56.
28. 2: Mt. 27. 51, 60.

³ His appearance was like lightning, and his raiment white as snow. ⁴ And for fear of him the guards trembled and became like dead men. ⁵ But the angel said to the women, "Do not be afraid; for I know that you seek Jesus who was crucified. ⁶ He is not here; for he has risen, as he said. Come, see the place where he' lay. ⁷ Then go quickly and tell his disciples that he has risen from the dead, and behold, he is going before you to Galilee; there you will see him. Lo, I have told you." ⁸ So they departed quickly from the tomb with fear and great joy, and ran to tell his disciples. ⁹ And behold, Jesus met them and said, "Hail!" And they came up and took hold of his feet and worshiped him. ¹⁰ Then Jesus said to them, "Do not be afraid; go and tell my brethren to go to Galilee, and there they will see me."

11 While they were going, behold, some of the guard went into the city and told the chief priests all that had taken place. ¹² And when they had assembled with the elders and taken counsel, they gave a sum of money to the soldiers ¹³ and said, "Tell people, 'His disciples came by night and stole him away while we were asleep.' ¹⁴ And if this comes to the governor's ears, we will satisfy him and keep you out of trouble." ¹⁵ So they took the money and did as they were directed; and this story has been spread among the Jews to this day.

16 Now the eleven disciples went to Galilee, to the mountain to which Jesus had directed them. ¹⁷ And when they saw him they worshiped him; but some doubted. ¹⁸ And Jesus came and said to them, "All authority in heaven and on earth has been given to me. ¹⁹ Go therefore and make disciples of all nations, baptizing them in the name of the Father

---

ʳ Some ancient authorities read *the Lord.*

28. 4: Mt. 27. 62–66.   **28. 7:** Mt. 26. 32; 28. 16; Jn. 21. 1–23.   **28. 9:** Jn. 20. 14–18.   **28. 11:** Mt. 27. 62–66.   **28. 16–17:** 1 Cor. 15. 5; Jn. 21. 1–23.   **28. 18:** Mt. 11. 27; Lk. 10. 22; Phil. 2. 9; Eph. 1. 20–22.   **28. 19:** Lk. 24. 47; Acts 1. 8.

and of the Son and of the Holy Spirit, [20] teaching them to observe all that I have commanded you; and lo, I am with you always, to the close of the age."

THE GOSPEL ACCORDING TO

MARK

1 The beginning of the gospel of Jesus Christ, the Son of God.[a]

2 As it is written in Isaiah the prophet,[b]

"Behold, I send my messenger before thy face,
who shall prepare thy way;
[3] the voice of one crying in the wilderness:
Prepare the way of the Lord,
make his paths straight —"

[4] John the baptizer appeared in the wilderness, preaching a baptism of repentance for the forgiveness of sins. [5] And there went out to him all the country of Judea, and all the people of Jerusalem; and they were baptized by him in the river Jordan, confessing their sins. [6] Now John was clothed with camel's hair, and had a leather girdle around his waist, and ate locusts and wild honey. [7] And he preached, saying, "After me comes he who is mightier than I, the thong of whose sandals I am not worthy to stoop down and untie. [8] I have baptized you with water; but he will baptize you with the Holy Spirit."

9 In those days Jesus came from Nazareth of Galilee and was baptized by John in the Jordan. [10] And when he came up out of the water, immediately he saw the heavens opened

[a] Some ancient authorities omit *the Son of God.*   [b] Some ancient authorities read *in the prophets.*

28. 20: Mt. 13. 39, 49; 24. 3; 18. 20; Acts 18. 10.
1. 2–8: Mt. 3. 1–12; Lk. 3. 2–16; Jn. 1. 6, 15, 19–28.   **1. 2:** Mal. 3. 1; Mt. 11. 10;
Lk. 7. 27.   **1. 3:** Is. 40. 3.   **1. 4:** Acts 13. 24.   **1. 9–11:** Mt. 3. 13–17; Lk. 3. 21–22;
Jn. 1. 29–34.

and the Spirit descending upon him like a dove; [11] and a voice came from heaven, "Thou art my beloved Son;[c] with thee I am well pleased."

12 The Spirit immediately drove him out into the wilderness. [13] And he was in the wilderness forty days, tempted by Satan; and he was with the wild beasts; and the angels ministered to him.

14 Now after John was arrested, Jesus came into Galilee, preaching the gospel of God, [15] and saying, "The time is fulfilled, and the kingdom of God is at hand; repent, and believe in the gospel."

16 And passing along by the sea of Galilee, he saw Simon and Andrew the brother of Simon casting a net in the sea; for they were fishermen. [17] And Jesus said to them, "Follow me and I will make you become fishers of men." [18] And immediately they left their nets and followed him. [19] And going on a little farther, he saw James the son of Zeb'e-dee and John his brother, who were in their boat mending the nets. [20] And immediately he called them; and they left their father Zeb'e-dee in the boat with the hired servants, and followed him.

21 And they went into Ca-per'na-um; and immediately on the sabbath he entered the synagogue and taught. [22] And they were astonished at his teaching, for he taught them as one who had authority, and not as the scribes. [23] And immediately there was in their synagogue a man with an unclean spirit; [24] and he cried out, "What have you to do with us, Jesus of Nazareth? Have you come to destroy us? I know who you are, the Holy One of God." [25] But Jesus rebuked him, saying, "Be silent, and come out of him!" [26] And the unclean spirit, convulsing him and crying with

[c] Or *my Son, my* (or *the*) *Beloved.*

1. 11: Ps. 2. 7; Is. 42. 1.   1. 12-13: Mt. 4. 1-11; Lk. 4. 1-13.   1. 14-15: Mt. 4. 12-17; Lk. 4. 14-15.   1. 16-20: Mt. 4. 18-22; Lk. 5. 1-11; Jn. 1. 40-42.   1. 21-22: Mt. 7. 28-29; Lk. 4. 31-32.   1. 23-28: Lk. 4. 33-37.   1. 24: Jn. 6. 69.

a loud voice, came out of him. [27] And they were all amazed, so that they questioned among themselves, saying, "What is this? A new teaching! With authority he commands even the unclean spirits, and they obey him." [28] And at once his fame spread everywhere throughout all the surrounding region of Galilee.

29 And immediately he[d] left the synagogue, and entered the house of Simon and Andrew, with James and John. [30] Now Simon's mother-in-law lay sick with a fever, and immediately they told him of her. [31] And he came and took her by the hand and lifted her up, and the fever left her; and she served them.

32 That evening, at sundown, they brought to him all who were sick or possessed with demons. [33] And the whole city was gathered together about the door. [34] And he healed many who were sick with various diseases, and cast out many demons; and he would not permit the demons to speak, because they knew him.

35 And in the morning, a great while before day, he rose and went out to a lonely place, and there he prayed. [36] And Simon and those who were with him followed him, [37] and they found him and said to him, "Every one is searching for you." [38] And he said to them, "Let us go on to the next towns, that I may preach there also; for that is why I came out." [39] And he went throughout all Galilee, preaching in their synagogues and casting out demons.

40 And a leper came to him beseeching him, and kneeling said to him, "If you will, you can make me clean." [41] And being moved with pity, he stretched out his hand and touched him, and said to him, "I will; be clean." [42] And

---

[d] Many ancient authorities read *they*.

1. 29–31: Mt. 8. 14–15; Lk. 4. 38–39.   **1. 32–34**: Mt. 8. 16–17; Lk. 4. 40–41.
1. 35–38: Lk. 4. 42–43.   **1. 39**: Mt. 4. 23–25; Lk. 4. 44.   **1. 40–45**: Mt. 8. 2–4;
Lk. 5. 12–16.

immediately the leprosy left him, and he was made clean.
[43] And he sternly charged him, and sent him away at once,
[44] and said to him, "See that you say nothing to any one;
but go, show yourself to the priest, and offer for your
cleansing what Moses commanded, for a proof to the
people."[e] [45] But he went out and began to talk freely about
it, and to spread the news, so that Jesus[f] could no longer
openly enter a town, but was out in the country; and people
came to him from every quarter.

2 And when he returned to Ca-per'na-um after some
days, it was reported that he was at home. [2] And many
were gathered together, so that there was no longer room
for them, not even about the door; and he was preaching
the word to them. [3] And they came, bringing to him a
paralytic carried by four men. [4] And when they could not
get near him because of the crowd, they removed the roof
above him; and when they had made an opening, they let
down the pallet on which the paralytic lay. [5] And when
Jesus saw their faith, he said to the paralytic, "My son,
your sins are forgiven." [6] Now some of the scribes were
sitting there, questioning in their hearts, [7] "Why does this
man speak thus? It is blasphemy! Who can forgive sins
but God alone?" [8] And immediately Jesus, perceiving in
his spirit that they thus questioned within themselves, said
to them, "Why do you question thus in your hearts?
[9] Which is easier, to say to the paralytic, 'Your sins are forgiven'; or to say, 'Rise, take up your pallet and walk'?
[10] But that you may know that the Son of man has authority
on earth to forgive sins" — he said to the paralytic — [11] "I
say to you, rise, take up your pallet and go home." [12] And
he rose, and immediately took up the pallet and went out

[e] Greek *to them.*   [f] Greek *he.*
1. 44: Lev. 13. 49; 14. 2–32.
2. 3–12: Mt. 9. 2–8; Lk. 5. 18–26.   **2. 12:** Mt. 9. 33.

before them all; so that they were all amazed and glorified God, saying, "We never saw anything like this!"

13 He went out again beside the sea; and all the crowd gathered about him, and he taught them. [14] And as he passed on, he saw Levi the son of Alphaeus sitting at the tax office, and he said to him, "Follow me." And he rose and followed him.

15 And as he sat at table in his house, many tax collectors and sinners were sitting with Jesus and his disciples; for there were many who followed him. [16] And the scribes of[g] the Pharisees, when they saw that he was eating with sinners and tax collectors, said to his disciples, "Why does he eat and drink[h] with tax collectors and sinners?" [17] And when Jesus heard it, he said to them, "Those who are well have no need of a physician, but those who are sick; I came not to call the righteous, but sinners."

18 Now John's disciples and the Pharisees were fasting; and people came and said to him, "Why do John's disciples and the disciples of the Pharisees fast, but your disciples do not fast?" [19] And Jesus said to them, "Can the wedding guests fast while the bridegroom is with them? As long as they have the bridegroom with them, they cannot fast. [20] The days will come, when the bridegroom is taken away from them, and then they will fast on that day. [21] No one sews a piece of unshrunk cloth on an old garment; if he does, the patch tears away from it, the new from the old, and a worse tear is made. [22] And no one puts new wine into old wineskins; if he does, the wine will burst the skins, and the wine is lost, and so are the skins."[i]

23 One sabbath he was going through the grainfields; and

[g] Some ancient authorities read *and*.   [h] Some ancient authorities omit *and drink*.
[i] Some ancient authorities add *but new wine is for fresh skins*.
2. 14–17: Mt. 9. 9–13; Lk. 5. 27–32.   **2. 16:** Acts 23. 9.   **2. 18–22:** Mt. 9. 14–17;
Lk. 5. 33–38.   **2. 20:** Lk. 17. 22.   **2. 23–28:** Mt. 12. 1–8; Lk. 6. 1–5.   **2. 23:**
Deut. 23. 25.

as they made their way his disciples began to pluck ears of grain. ²⁴ And the Pharisees said to him, "Look, why are they doing what is not lawful on the sabbath?" ²⁵ And he said to them, "Have you never read what David did, when he was in need and was hungry, he and those who were with him: ²⁶ how he entered the house of God, when A-bi'-a-thar was high priest, and ate the bread of the Presence, which it is not lawful for any but the priests to eat, and also gave it to those who were with him?" ²⁷ And he said to them, "The sabbath was made for man, not man for the sabbath; ²⁸ so the Son of man is lord even of the sabbath."

3 Again he entered the synagogue, and a man was there who had a withered hand. ² And they watched him, to see whether he would heal him on the sabbath, so that they might accuse him. ³ And he said to the man who had the withered hand, "Come here." ⁴ And he said to them, "Is it lawful on the sabbath to do good or to do harm, to save life or to kill?" But they were silent. ⁵ And he looked around at them with anger, grieved at their hardness of heart, and said to the man, "Stretch out your hand." He stretched it out, and his hand was restored. ⁶ The Pharisees went out, and immediately held counsel with the He-ro'-di-ans against him, how to destroy him.

7 Jesus withdrew with his disciples to the sea, and a great multitude from Galilee followed; also from Judea ⁸ and Jerusalem and Id-u-me'a and from beyond the Jordan and from about Tyre and Sidon a great multitude, hearing all that he did, came to him. ⁹ And he told his disciples to have a boat ready for him because of the crowd, lest they should crush him; ¹⁰ for he had healed many, so that all who had diseases pressed upon him to touch him. ¹¹ And

2. 26: 1 Sam. 21. 1–6; 2 Sam. 8. 17.   **2. 27:** Ex. 23. 12; Deut. 5. 14.
3. 1–6: Mt. 12. 9–14; Lk. 6. 6–11.   **3. 2:** Lk. 11. 54.   **3. 6:** Mk. 12. 13.   **3. 7–12:** Mt. 4. 24–25; 12. 15–16; Lk. 6. 17–19.   **3. 8:** Mt. 11. 21.   **3. 10:** Mk. 5. 29, 34; 6. 56.

whenever the unclean spirits beheld him, they fell down before him and cried out, "You are the Son of God." [12] And he strictly ordered them not to make him known.

13 And he went up into the hills, and called to him those whom he desired; and they came to him. [14] And he appointed twelve,[j] to be with him, and to be sent out to preach [15] and have authority to cast out demons: [16] Simon whom he surnamed Peter; [17] James the son of Zeb'e-dee and John the brother of James, whom he surnamed Bo-a-ner'ges, that is, sons of thunder; [18] Andrew, and Philip, and Bartholomew, and Matthew, and Thomas, and James the son of Alphaeus, and Thaddaeus, and Simon the Cananaean, [19] and Judas Iscariot, who betrayed him.

Then he went home; [20] and the crowd came together again, so that they could not even eat. [21] And when his friends heard it, they went out to seize him, for they said, "He is beside himself." [22] And the scribes who came down from Jerusalem said, "He is possessed by Be-el'ze-bub,[k] and by the prince of demons he casts out the demons." [23] And he called them to him, and said to them in parables, "How can Satan cast out Satan? [24] If a kingdom is divided against itself, that kingdom cannot stand. [25] And if a house is divided against itself, that house will not be able to stand. [26] And if Satan has risen up against himself and is divided, he cannot stand, but is coming to an end. [27] But no one can enter a strong man's house and plunder his goods, unless he first binds the strong man; then indeed he may plunder his house.

28 "Truly, I say to you, all sins will be forgiven the sons of men, and whatever blasphemies they utter; [29] but who-

---

[j] Some ancient authorities add *whom also he named apostles.*   [k] Greek *Beelzebul.*

3. **12**: Mk. 1. 45.   3. **13**: Mt. 5. 1; Lk. 6. 12.   3. **14–15**: Mt. 10. 1.   3. **16–19**: Mt. 10. 2–4; Lk. 6. 14–16; Acts 1. 13.   3. **19**: Mk. 2. 1; 7. 17.   3. **20**: Mk. 6. 31. 3. **21**: Mk. 3. 31–35; Jn. 10. 20.   3. **22–27**: Mt. 12. 24–29; Lk. 11. 15–22.   3. **22**: Mt. 9. 34; 10. 25.   3. **27**: Is. 49. 24–25.   3. **28–30**: Mt. 12. 31–32; Lk. 12. 10.

ever blasphemes against the Holy Spirit never has forgiveness, but is guilty of an eternal sin" — [30] for they had said, "He has an unclean spirit."

31 And his mother and his brothers came; and standing outside they sent to him and called him. [32] And a crowd was sitting about him; and they said to him, "Your mother and your brothers[*l*] are outside, asking for you." [33] And he answered, "Who are my mother and my brothers?" [34] And looking around on those who sat about him, he said, "Here are my mother and my brothers! [35] Whoever does the will of God is my brother, and sister, and mother."

4 Again he began to teach beside the sea. And a very large crowd gathered about him, so that he got into a boat and sat in it on the sea; and the whole crowd was beside the sea on the land. [2] And he taught them many things in parables, and in his teaching he said to them: [3] "Listen! A sower went out to sow. [4] And as he sowed, some seed fell along the path, and the birds came and devoured it. [5] Other seed fell on rocky ground, where it had not much soil, and immediately it sprang up, since it had no depth of soil; [6] and when the sun rose it was scorched, and since it had no root it withered away. [7] Other seed fell among thorns and the thorns grew up and choked it, and it yielded no grain. [8] And other seeds fell into good soil and brought forth grain, growing up and increasing and yielding thirtyfold and sixtyfold and a hundredfold." [9] And he said, "He who has ears to hear, let him hear."

10 And when he was alone, those who were about him with the twelve asked him concerning the parables. [11] And he said to them, "To you has been given the secret of the

---

[*l*] Some early authorities add *and your sisters.*

3. 31–35: Mt. 12. 46–50; Lk. 8. 19–21.
4. 1–9: Mt. 13. 1–9; Lk. 8. 4–8.   **4. 10–12:** Mt. 13. 10–15; Lk. 8. 9–10.
4. 11: 1 Cor. 5. 12–13; Col. 4. 5; 1 Thess. 4. 12; 1 Tim. 3. 7.

kingdom of God, but for those outside everything is in parables; [12] so that they may indeed see but not perceive, and may indeed hear but not understand; lest they should turn again, and be forgiven." [13] And he said to them, "Do you not understand this parable? How then will you understand all the parables? [14] The sower sows the word. [15] And these are the ones along the path, where the word is sown; when they hear, Satan immediately comes and takes away the word which is sown in them. [16] And these in like manner are the ones sown upon rocky ground, who, when they hear the word, immediately receive it with joy; [17] and they have no root in themselves, but endure for a while; then, when tribulation or persecution arises on account of the word, immediately they fall away."[m] [18] And others are the ones sown among thorns; they are those who hear the word, [19] but the cares of the world, and the delight in riches, and the desire for other things, enter in and choke the word, and it proves unfruitful. [20] But those that were sown upon the good soil are the ones who hear the word and accept it and bear fruit, thirtyfold and sixtyfold and a hundredfold."

21 And he said to them, "Is a lamp brought in to be put under a bushel, or under a bed, and not on a stand? [22] For there is nothing hid, except to be made manifest; nor is anything secret, except to come to light. [23] If any man has ears to hear, let him hear." [24] And he said to them, "Take heed what you hear; the measure you give will be the measure you get, and still more will be given you. [25] For to him who has will more be given; and from him who has not, even what he has will be taken away."

[m] Or *stumble*.

4. 12: Is. 6. 9–10.   **4. 13–20:** Mt. 13. 18–23; Lk. 8. 11–15.   **4. 21:** Mt. 5. 15; Lk. 8. 16; 11. 33.   **4. 22:** Mt. 10. 26; Lk. 8. 17; 12. 2.   **4. 23:** Mt. 11. 15; Mk. 4. 9. **4. 24:** Mt. 7. 2; Lk. 6. 38.   **4. 25:** Mt. 13. 12; 25. 29; Lk. 8. 18; 19. 26.

26 And he said, "The kingdom of God is as if a man should scatter seed upon the ground, [27] and should sleep and rise night and day, and the seed should sprout and grow, he knows not how. [28] The earth produces of itself, first the blade, then the ear, then the full grain in the ear. [29] But when the grain is ripe, at once he puts in the sickle, because the harvest has come."

30 And he said, "With what can we compare the kingdom of God, or what parable shall we use for it? [31] It is like a grain of mustard seed, which, when sown upon the ground, is the smallest of all the seeds on earth; [32] yet when it is sown it grows up and becomes the greatest of all shrubs, and puts forth large branches, so that the birds of the air can make nests in its shade."

33 With many such parables he spoke the word to them, as they were able to hear it; [34] he did not speak to them without a parable, but privately to his own disciples he explained everything.

35 On that day, when evening had come, he said to them, "Let us go across to the other side." [36] And leaving the crowd, they took him with them, just as he was, in the boat. And other boats were with him. [37] And a great storm of wind arose, and the waves beat into the boat, so that the boat was already filling. [38] But he was in the stern, asleep on the cushion; and they woke him and said to him, "Master, do you not care if we perish?" [39] And he awoke and rebuked the wind, and said to the sea, "Peace! Be still!" And the wind ceased, and there was a great calm. [40] He said to them, "Why are you afraid? Have you no faith?" [41] And they were filled with awe, and said to one another, "Who then is this, that even wind and sea obey him?"

4. 26–29: Mt. 13. 24–30.   **4. 30–32:** Mt. 13. 31–32; Lk. 13. 18–19.   **4. 34:** Mt. 13. 34; Jn. 16. 25.   **4. 35–41:** Mt. 8. 18, 23–27; Lk. 8. 22–25.

5 They came to the other side of the sea, to the country of the Ger'a-senes.[n] [2] And when he had come out of the boat, there met him out of the tombs a man with an unclean spirit, [3] who lived among the tombs; and no one could bind him any more, even with a chain; [4] for he had often been bound with fetters and chains, but the chains he wrenched apart, and the fetters he broke in pieces; and no one had the strength to subdue him. [5] Night and day among the tombs and on the mountains he was always crying out, and bruising himself with stones. [6] And when he saw Jesus from afar, he ran and worshiped him; [7] and crying out with a loud voice, he said, "What have you to do with me, Jesus, Son of the Most High God? I adjure you by God, do not torment me." [8] For he had said to him, "Come out of the man, you unclean spirit!" [9] And Jesus[o] asked him, "What is your name?" He replied, "My name is Legion; for we are many." [10] And he begged him eagerly not to send them out of the country. [11] Now a great herd of swine was feeding there on the hillside; [12] and they begged him, "Send us to the swine, let us enter into them." [13] So he gave them leave. And the unclean spirits came out, and entered into the swine; and the herd, numbering about two thousand, rushed down the steep bank into the sea, and were drowned in the sea.

14 The swineherds fled, and told it in the city and in the country. And people came to see what it was that had happened. [15] And they came to Jesus, and saw the demoniac sitting there, clothed and in his right mind, the man who had had the legion; and they were afraid. [16] And those who saw it told what had happened to the demoniac and to the swine. [17] And they began to beg Jesus[p] to depart from

---

[n] Some ancient authorities read *Gergesenes*, some *Gadarenes*.
[o] Greek *he.*   [p] Greek *him.*
5. 1–20: Mt. 8. 28–34; Lk. 8. 26–39.   **5. 7:** Acts 16. 17; Heb. 7. 1; Mk. 1. 24.

their neighborhood. [18] And as he was getting into the boat, the man who had been possessed with demons begged him that he might be with him. [19] But he refused, and said to him, "Go home to your friends, and tell them how much the Lord has done for you, and how he has had mercy on you." [20] And he went away and began to proclaim in the De-cap'o-lis how much Jesus had done for him; and all men marveled.

21 And when Jesus had crossed again in the boat to the other side, a great crowd gathered about him; and he was beside the sea. [22] Then came one of the rulers of the synagogue, Ja'i-rus by name; and seeing him, he fell at his feet, [23] and besought him, saying, "My little daughter is at the point of death. Come and lay your hands on her, so that she may be made well, and live." [24] And he went with him.

And a great crowd followed him and thronged about him. [25] And there was a woman who had had a flow of blood for twelve years, [26] and who had suffered much under many physicians, and had spent all that she had, and was no better but rather grew worse. [27] She had heard the reports about Jesus, and came up behind him in the crowd and touched his garment. [28] For she said, "If I touch even his garments, I shall be made well." [29] And immediately the hemorrhage ceased; and she felt in her body that she was healed of her disease. [30] And Jesus, perceiving in himself that power had gone forth from him, immediately turned about in the crowd, and said, "Who touched my garments?" [31] And his disciples said to him, "You see the crowd pressing around you, and yet you say, 'Who touched me?'" [32] And he looked around to see who had done it. [33] But the woman, knowing what had been done to her, came in fear and

5. 20: Mk. 7. 31.　　**5. 21–43:** Mt. 9. 18–26; Lk. 8. 40–56.　　**5. 22:** Lk. 13. 14;
Acts 13. 15; 18. 8, 17.　　**5. 23:** Mk. 6. 5; 7. 32; 8. 23; Acts 9. 17; 28. 8.　　**5. 30:**
Lk. 5. 17.

trembling and fell down before him, and told him the whole truth. ³⁴ And he said to her, "Daughter, your faith has made you well; go in peace, and be healed of your disease."

35 While he was still speaking, there came from the ruler's house some who said, "Your daughter is dead. Why trouble the Teacher any further?" ³⁶ But ignoring*q* what they said, Jesus said to the ruler of the synagogue, "Do not fear, only believe." ³⁷ And he allowed no one to follow him except Peter and James and John the brother of James. ³⁸ When they came to the house of the ruler of the synagogue, he saw a tumult, and people weeping and wailing loudly. ³⁹ And when he had entered, he said to them, "Why do you make a tumult and weep? The child is not dead but sleeping." ⁴⁰ And they laughed at him. But he put them all outside, and took the child's father and mother and those who were with him, and went in where the child was. ⁴¹ Taking her by the hand he said to her, "Tal′i-tha cu′mi"; which means, "Little girl, I say to you, arise." ⁴² And immediately the girl got up and walked; for she was twelve years old. And immediately they were overcome with amazement. ⁴³ And he strictly charged them that no one should know this, and told them to give her something to eat.

6 He went away from there and came to his own country; and his disciples followed him. ² And on the sabbath he began to teach in the synagogue; and many who heard him were astonished, saying, "Where did this man get all this? What is the wisdom given to him? What mighty works are wrought by his hands! ³ Is not this the carpenter, the son of Mary and brother of James and Joses and Judas

q Or *overhearing*. Many ancient authorities read *hearing*.

5. 34: Lk. 7. 50; Mk. 10. 52.   5. 37: Mk. 9. 2; 13. 3.   5. 41: Lk. 7. 14; Acts 9. 40.
5. 43: Mk. 1. 43–44; 7. 36.
6. 1–6: Mt. 13. 53–58; Lk. 4. 16–30.   6. 2: Mk. 1. 21; Mt. 7. 28.   6. 3: Mt. 11. 6.

and Simon, and are not his sisters here with us?" And they took offense[7] at him. [4] And Jesus said to them, "A prophet is not without honor, except in his own country, and among his own kin, and in his own house." [5] And he could do no mighty work there, except that he laid his hands upon a few sick people and healed them. [6] And he marveled because of their unbelief.

And he went about among the villages teaching.

[7] And he called to him the twelve, and began to send them out two by two, and gave them authority over the unclean spirits. [8] He charged them to take nothing for their journey except a staff; no bread, no bag, no money in their purses;[8] [9] but to wear sandals and not put on two tunics. [10] And he said to them, "Where you enter a house, stay there until you leave the place. [11] And if any place will not receive you and they refuse to hear you, when you leave, shake off the dust that is on your feet for a testimony against them." [12] So they went out and preached that men should repent. [13] And they cast out many demons, and anointed with oil many that were sick and healed them.

[14] King Herod heard of it; for Jesus' name had become known. Some[t] said, "John the baptizer has been raised from the dead; that is why these powers are at work in him." [15] But others said, "It is Elijah." And others said, "It is a prophet, like one of the prophets of old." [16] But when Herod heard of it he said, "John, whom I beheaded, has been raised." [17] For Herod had sent and seized John, and bound him in prison for the sake of He-ro'di-as, his brother Philip's wife; because he had married her. [18] For John had said to Herod, "It is not lawful for you to have your brother's

---

[7] Or *stumbled*.   [8] Greek *girdles*.   [t] Some ancient authorities read *he*.

6. 5: Mk. 5. 23; 7. 32; 8. 23.   **6. 6:** Mt. 9. 35.   **6. 7–11:** Mt. 10. 1, 5, 7–11; Lk. 9. 1–5.   **6. 7:** Lk. 10. 1.   **6. 11:** Mt. 10. 14.   **6. 12–13:** Mt. 11. 1; Lk. 9. 6. **6. 13:** Jas. 5. 14.   **6. 14–16:** Mt. 14. 1–2; Lk. 9. 7–9; 9. 19; Mt. 21. 11.   **6. 17–18:** Mt. 14. 3–4; Lk. 3. 19–20.

wife." [19] And He-ro'di-as had a grudge against him, and wanted to kill him. But she could not, [20] for Herod feared John, knowing that he was a righteous and holy man, and kept him safe. When he heard him, he was much perplexed; and yet he heard him gladly. [21] But an opportunity came when Herod on his birthday gave a banquet for his courtiers and officers and the leading men of Galilee. [22] For when He-ro'di-as' daughter came in and danced, she pleased Herod and his guests; and the king said to the girl, "Ask me for whatever you wish, and I will grant it." [23] And he vowed to her, "Whatever you ask me, I will give you, even half of my kingdom." [24] And she went out, and said to her mother, "What shall I ask?" And she said, "The head of John the baptizer." [25] And she came in immediately with haste to the king, and asked, saying, "I want you to give me at once the head of John the Baptist on a platter." [26] And the king was exceedingly sorry; but because of his oaths and his guests he did not want to break his word to her. [27] And immediately the king sent a soldier of the guard and gave orders to bring his head. He went and beheaded him in the prison, [28] and brought his head on a platter, and gave it to the girl; and the girl gave it to her mother. [29] When the disciples heard of it, they came and took his body, and laid it in a tomb.

30 The apostles returned to Jesus, and told him all that they had done and taught. [31] And he said to them, "Come away by yourselves to a lonely place, and rest a while." For many were coming and going, and they had no leisure even to eat. [32] And they went away in the boat to a lonely place by themselves. [33] Now many saw them going, and knew them, and they ran there on foot from all the towns, and got there ahead of them. [34] As he landed he saw a great throng,

6. 19–29: Mt. 14. 5–12.   **6. 20:** Mt. 21. 26.   **6. 23:** Esth. 5. 3, 6.   **6. 30–31:** Lk. 9. 10; Mk. 3. 20.   **6. 32–44:** Mt. 14. 13–21; Lk. 9. 11–17; Jn. 6. 5–13; Mk. 8. 1–10; Mt. 15. 32–39.   **6. 34:** Mt. 9. 36.

and he had compassion on them, because they were like sheep without a shepherd; and he began to teach them many things. [35] And when it grew late, his disciples came to him and said, "This is a lonely place, and the hour is now late; [36] send them away, to go into the country and villages round about and buy themselves something to eat." [37] But he answered them, "You give them something to eat." And they said to him, "Shall we go and buy two hundred denarii[u] worth of bread, and give it to them to eat?" [38] And he said to them, "How many loaves have you? Go and see." And when they had found out, they said, "Five, and two fish." [39] Then he commanded them all to sit down by companies upon the green grass. [40] So they sat down in groups, by hundreds and by fifties. [41] And taking the five loaves and the two fish he looked up to heaven, and blessed, and broke the loaves, and gave them to the disciples to set before the people; and he divided the two fish among them all. [42] And they all ate, and were satisfied. [43] And they took up twelve baskets full of broken pieces and of the fish. [44] And those who ate the loaves were five thousand men.

45 Immediately he made his disciples get into the boat and go before him to the other side, to Beth-sa'i-da, while he dismissed the crowd. [46] And after he had taken leave of them, he went into the hills to pray. [47] And when evening came, the boat was out on the sea, and he was alone on the land. [48] And he saw that they were distressed in rowing, for the wind was against them. And about the fourth watch of the night he came to them, walking on the sea. He meant to pass by them, [49] but when they saw him walking on the sea they thought it was a ghost, and cried out; [50] for they all saw him, and were terrified. But immediately he spoke

[u] See note on Matthew 18. 28.

6. 37: 2 Kings 4. 42–44.   6. 41: Mk. 14. 22; Lk. 24. 30–31.   6. 45–52: Mt. 14. 22–33; Jn. 6. 15–21.   6. 48: Mk. 13. 35.   6. 50: Mt. 9. 2.

to them and said, "Take heart, it is I; have no fear." [51] And he got into the boat with them and the wind ceased. And they were utterly astounded, [52] for they did not understand about the loaves, but their hearts were hardened.

53 And when they had crossed over, they came to land at Gen-nes′a-ret, and moored to the shore. [54] And when they got out of the boat, immediately the people recognized him, [55] and ran about the whole neighborhood and began to bring sick people on their pallets to any place where they heard he was. [56] And wherever he came, in villages, cities, or country, they laid the sick in the market places, and besought him that they might touch even the fringe of his garment; and as many as touched it were made well.

7 Now when the Pharisees gathered together to him, with some of the scribes, who had come from Jerusalem, [2] they saw that some of his disciples ate with hands defiled, that is, unwashed. [3] (For the Pharisees, and all the Jews, do not eat unless they wash their hands, observing the tradition of the elders; [4] and when they come from the market place, they do not eat unless they purify[w] themselves; and there are many other traditions which they observe, the washing of cups and pots and vessels of bronze.[x]) [5] And the Pharisees and the scribes asked him, "Why do your disciples not live[y] according to the tradition of the elders, but eat with hands defiled?" [6] And he said to them, "Well did Isaiah prophesy of you hypocrites, as it is written,

' This people honors me with their lips,
     but their heart is far from me;
    [7] in vain do they worship me,
     teaching as doctrines the precepts of men.'

---

[w] Some ancient authorities read *baptize.*   [x] Some ancient authorities add *and beds.*
[y] Greek *walk.*

6. 52: Mk. 8. 17.   **6. 53–56:** Mt. 14. 34–36.   **6. 56:** Mk. 3. 10; Mt. 9. 20.
7. 1–15: Mt. 15. 1–11; Lk. 11. 38.   **7. 4:** Mt. 23. 25; Lk. 11. 39.   **7. 5:** Gal. 1. 14.
7. 6–7: Is. 29. 13.

[8] You leave the commandment of God, and hold fast the tradition of men."

9 And he said to them, "You have a fine way of rejecting the commandment of God, in order to keep your tradition! [10] For Moses said, 'Honor your father and your mother'; and, 'He who speaks evil of father or mother, let him surely die'; [11] but you say, 'If a man tells his father or his mother, What you would have gained from me is Corban' (that is, given to God)[z] — [12] then you no longer permit him to do anything for his father or mother, [13] thus making void the word of God through your tradition which you hand on. And many such things you do."

14 And he called the people to him again, and said to them, "Hear me, all of you, and understand: [15] there is nothing outside a man which by going into him can defile him; but the things which come out of a man are what defile him."[a] [17] And when he had entered the house, and left the people, his disciples asked him about the parable. [18] And he said to them, "Then are you also without understanding? Do you not see that whatever goes into a man from outside cannot defile him, [19] since it enters, not his heart but his stomach, and so passes on[b]?" (Thus he declared all foods clean.) [20] And he said, "What comes out of a man is what defiles a man. [21] For from within, out of the heart of man, come evil thoughts, fornication, theft, murder, adultery, [22] coveting, wickedness, deceit, licentiousness, an evil eye, slander, pride, foolishness. [23] All these evil things come from within, and they defile a man."

24 And from there he arose and went away to the region of Tyre and Sidon.[c] And he entered a house, and would not

---

[z] Or *an offering.*   [a] Many ancient authorities add verse 16, "*If any man has ears to hear, let him hear.*"   [b] Or *is evacuated.*   [c] Some ancient authorities omit *and Sidon.*

7. 10: Ex. 20. 12; Deut. 5. 16; Ex. 21. 17; Lev. 20. 9.   **7. 17–23:** Mt. 15. 15–20; Mk. 4. 10.   **7. 18–19:** 1 Cor. 10. 25–27; Rom. 14. 14; Tit. 1. 15; Acts 10. 15.   **7. 20–23:** Rom. 1. 28–31; Gal. 5. 19–21.   **7. 22:** Mt. 6. 23; 20. 15.   **7. 24–30:** Mt. 15. 21–28.

have any one know it; yet he could not be hid. [25] But immediately a woman, whose little daughter was possessed by an unclean spirit, heard of him, and came and fell down at his feet. [26] Now the woman was a Greek, a Sy-ro-phoe-ni'cian by race. And she begged him to cast the demon out of her daughter. [27] And he said to her, "Let the children first be fed, for it is not right to take the children's bread and throw it to the dogs." [28] But she answered him, "Yes, Lord; yet even the dogs under the table eat the children's crumbs." [29] And he said to her, "For this saying you may go your way; the demon has left your daughter." [30] And she went home, and found the child lying in bed, and the demon gone.

31 Soon after this he returned from the region of Tyre, and went through Sidon to the sea of Galilee, through the region of the De-cap'o-lis. [32] And they brought to him a man who was deaf and had an impediment in his speech; and they besought him to lay his hand upon him. [33] And taking him aside from the multitude privately, he put his fingers into his ears, and he spat and touched his tongue; [34] and looking up to heaven, he sighed, and said to him, "Eph'pha-tha," that is, "Be opened." [35] And his ears were opened, his tongue was released, and he spoke plainly. [36] And he charged them to tell no one; but the more he charged them, the more zealously they proclaimed it. [37] And they were astonished beyond measure, saying, "He has done all things well; he even makes the deaf hear and the dumb speak."

8 In those days, when again a great crowd had gathered, and they had nothing to eat, he called his disciples to him, and said to them, [2] "I have compassion on the crowd, because they have been with me now three days, and have nothing to eat; [3] and if I send them away hungry to their homes, they will faint on the way; and some of them have

7. 31–37: Mt. 15. 29–31.   7. 32: Mk. 5. 23.   7. 33: Mk. 8. 23.   7. 36: Mk. 1. 44; 5. 43.
8. 1–10: Mt. 15. 32–39; Mk. 6. 32–44; Mt. 14. 13–21; Lk. 9. 11–17; Jn. 6. 5–13.

come a long way." [4] And his disciples answered him, "How can one feed these men with bread here in the desert?" [5] And he asked them, "How many loaves have you?" They said, "Seven." [6] And he commanded the crowd to sit down on the ground; and he took the seven loaves, and having given thanks he broke them and gave them to his disciples to set before the people; and they set them before the crowd. [7] And they had a few small fish; and having blessed them, he commanded that these also should be set before them. [8] And they ate, and were satisfied; and they took up the broken pieces left over, seven baskets full. [9] And there were about four thousand people. [10] And he sent them away; and immediately he got into the boat with his disciples, and went to the district of Dal-ma-nu'tha.[d]

11 The Pharisees came and began to argue with him, seeking from him a sign from heaven, to test him. [12] And he sighed deeply in his spirit, and said, "Why does this generation seek for a sign? Truly, I say to you, no sign shall be given to this generation." [13] And he left them, and getting into the boat again he departed to the other side.

14 Now they had forgotten to bring bread; and they had only one loaf with them in the boat. [15] And he cautioned them, saying, "Take heed, beware of the leaven of the Pharisees and the leaven of Herod."[e] [16] And they discussed it with one another, saying, "We have no bread." [17] And being aware of it, Jesus said to them, "Why do you discuss the fact that you have no bread? Do you not yet perceive or understand? Are your hearts hardened? [18] Having eyes do you not see, and having ears do you not hear? And do you not remember? [19] When I broke the five loaves for the five

[d] Some ancient authorities read *Magadan* or *Magdala.*
[e] Some ancient authorities read *the Herodians.*

8. 11–12: Mt. 16. 1–4; 12. 38–39; Lk. 11. 29. **8. 13–21:** Mt. 16. 4–12. **8. 15:** Lk. 12. 1; Mk. 6. 14; 12. 13.   **8. 17:** Mk. 6. 52; Jer. 5. 21; Is. 6. 9–10; Mt. 13. 10–15.   **8. 19:** Mk. 6. 41–44.

thousand, how many baskets full of broken pieces did you take up?" They said to him, "Twelve." [20] "And the seven for the four thousand, how many baskets full of broken pieces did you take up?" And they said to him, "Seven." [21] And he said to them, "Do you not yet understand?"

22 And they came to Beth-sa'i-da. And some people brought to him a blind man, and begged him to touch him. [23] And he took the blind man by the hand, and led him out of the village; and when he had spit on his eyes and laid his hands upon him, he asked him, "Do you see anything?" [24] And he looked up and said, "I see men; but they look like trees, walking." [25] Then again he laid his hands upon his eyes; and he looked intently and was restored, and saw everything clearly. [26] And he sent him away to his home, saying, "Do not even enter the village."

27 And Jesus went on with his disciples, to the villages of Caes-a-re'a Philippi; and on the way he asked his disciples, "Who do men say that I am?" [28] And they told him, "John the Baptist"; and others, "Elijah"; and others, "One of the prophets." [29] And he asked them, "But who do you say that I am?" Peter answered him, "You are the Christ." [30] And he charged them to tell no one about him.

31 And he began to teach them that the Son of man must suffer many things, and be rejected by the elders and the chief priests and the scribes, and be killed, and after three days rise again. [32] And he said this plainly. And Peter took him, and began to rebuke him. [33] But turning and seeing his disciples, he rebuked Peter, and said, "Get behind me, Satan! For you are not on the side of God, but of men."

34 And he called to him the multitude with his disciples, and said to them, "If any man would come after me, let

8. 20: Mk. 8. 1–10.   8. 22–26: Mk. 10. 46–52; Jn. 9. 1–7.   8. 22: Mk. 6. 45; Lk. 9. 10.
8. 23: Mk. 7. 33; 5. 23.   8. 27–30: Mt. 16. 13–20; Lk. 9. 18–21; Jn. 6. 66–69.
8. 28: Mk. 6. 14.   8. 30: Mk. 9. 9; 1. 34.   8. 31–9. 1: Mt. 16. 21–28; Lk. 9. 22–27.
8. 33: Mt. 4. 10.   8. 34: Mt. 10. 38; Lk. 14. 27.

him deny himself and take up his cross and follow me. [35] For whoever would save his life will lose it; and whoever loses his life for my sake and the gospel's will save it. [36] For what does it profit a man, to gain the whole world and forfeit his life? [37] For what can a man give in return for his life? [38] For whoever is ashamed of me and of my words in this adulterous and sinful generation, of him will the Son of man also be ashamed, when he comes in the glory of his 9 Father with the holy angels." [1] And he said to them, "Truly, I say to you, there are some standing here who will not taste death before they see the kingdom of God come with power."

2 And after six days Jesus took with him Peter and James and John, and led them up a high mountain apart by themselves; and he was transfigured before them, [3] and his garments became glistening, intensely white, as no fuller on earth could bleach them. [4] And there appeared to them Elijah with Moses; and they were talking to Jesus. [5] And Peter said to Jesus, "Master,[f] it is well that we are here: let us make three booths, one for you and one for Moses and one for Elijah." [6] For he did not know what to say, for they were exceedingly afraid. [7] And a cloud overshadowed them, and a voice came out of the cloud, "This is my beloved Son;[g] listen to him." [8] And suddenly looking around they no longer saw any one with them but Jesus only.

9 And as they were coming down the mountain, he charged them to tell no one what they had seen, until the Son of man should have risen from the dead. [10] So they kept the matter to themselves, questioning what the rising from the dead meant. [11] And they asked him, "Why do the

[f] Or *Rabbi.*   [g] Or *my Son, my* (or *the*) *Beloved.*

8. 35: Mt. 10. 39; Lk. 17. 33; Jn. 12. 25.   **8. 38:** Mt. 10. 33; Lk. 12. 9.
9. 1: Mk. 13. 30; Mt. 10. 23; Lk. 22. 18.   **9. 2–8:** Mt. 17. 1–8; Lk. 9. 28–36.   **9. 2:** Mk. 5. 37; 13. 3.   **9. 3:** Mt. 28. 3.   **9. 7:** 2 Pet. 1. 17–18; Mt. 3. 17; Jn. 12. 28–29.
9. 9–13: Mt. 17. 9–13; Lk. 9. 36.   **9. 9:** Mk. 8. 30; 5. 43; 7. 36.   **9. 11:** Mt. 11. 14.

scribes say that first Elijah must come?" [12] And he said to them, "Elijah does come first to restore all things; and how is it written of the Son of man, that he should suffer many things and be treated with contempt? [13] But I tell you that Elijah has come, and they did to him whatever they pleased, as it is written of him."

14 And when they came to the disciples, they saw a great crowd about them, and scribes arguing with them. [15] And immediately all the crowd, when they saw him, were greatly amazed, and ran up to him and greeted him. [16] And he asked them, "What are you discussing with them?" [17] And one of the crowd answered him, "Teacher, I brought my son to you, for he has a dumb spirit; [18] and wherever it seizes him, it dashes him down; and he foams and grinds his teeth and becomes rigid; and I asked your disciples to cast it out, and they were not able." [19] And he answered them, "O faithless generation, how long am I to be with you? How long am I to bear with you? Bring him to me." [20] And they brought the boy to him; and when the spirit saw him, immediately it convulsed the boy, and he fell on the ground and rolled about, foaming at the mouth. [21] And Jesus[h] asked his father, "How long has he had this?" And he said, "From childhood. [22] And it has often cast him into the fire and into the water, to destroy him; but if you can do anything, have pity on us and help us." [23] And Jesus said to him, "If you can! All things are possible to him who believes." [24] Immediately the father of the child cried out[i] and said, "I believe; help my unbelief!" [25] And when Jesus saw that a crowd came running together, he rebuked the unclean spirit, saying to it, "You dumb and deaf spirit, I command you, come out of him, and never enter him

[h] Greek *he*.   [i] Many ancient authorities add *with tears*.
9. 12: Mk. 8. 31; 9. 31; 10. 33.   **9. 14–27:** Mt. 17. 14–18; Lk. 9. 37–43.   **9. 23:** Mt. 17. 20; Lk. 17. 6; Mk. 11. 22–24.

again." ²⁶ And after crying out and convulsing him terribly, it came out, and the boy was like a corpse; so that most of them said, "He is dead." ²⁷ But Jesus took him by the hand and lifted him up, and he arose. ²⁸ And when he had gone home, his disciples asked him privately, "Why could we not cast it out?" ²⁹ And he said to them, "This kind cannot be driven out by anything but prayer."ʲ

30 They went on from there and passed through Galilee. And he would not have any one know it; ³¹ for he was teaching his disciples, saying to them, "The Son of man will be delivered into the hands of men, and they will kill him; and when he is killed, after three days he will rise." ³² But they did not understand the saying, and they were afraid to ask him.

33 And they came to Ca-per′na-um; and when he was in the house he asked them, "What were you discussing on the way?" ³⁴ But they were silent; for on the way they had discussed with one another who was the greatest. ³⁵ And he sat down and called the twelve; and he said to them, "If any one would be first, he must be last of all and servant of all." ³⁶ And he took a child, and put him in the midst of them; and taking him in his arms, he said to them, ³⁷ "Whoever receives one such child in my name, receives me; and whoever receives me, receives not me but him who sent me."

38 John said to him, "Teacher, we saw a man casting out demons in your name;ᵏ and we forbade him, because he was not following us." ³⁹ But Jesus said, "Do not forbid him; for no one who does a mighty work in my name will be able soon after to speak evil of me. ⁴⁰ For he that is not

ʲ Many ancient authorities add *and fasting.*
ᵏ Some ancient authorities add *who does not follow us.*

9. 30–32: Mt. 17. 22–23; Lk. 9. 43–45.   **9. 31:** Mk. 8. 31; 10. 33.   **9. 32:** Jn. 12. 16.
9. 33–37: Mt. 18. 1–5; Lk. 9. 46–48.   **9. 34:** Lk. 22. 24.   **9. 35:** Mk. 10. 43–44;
Mt. 20. 26–27; 23. 11; Lk. 22. 26.   **9. 36:** Mk. 10. 16.   **9. 37:** Mt. 10. 40; Lk. 10. 16;
Jn. 12. 44; 13. 20.   **9. 38–40:** Lk. 9. 49–50; 11–23; Mt. 12. 30; Num. 11. 27–29

against us is for us. [41] For truly, I say to you, whoever gives you a cup of water to drink because you bear the name of Christ, will by no means lose his reward.

42 "Whoever causes one of these little ones who believe in me to sin,[l] it would be better for him if a great millstone were hung round his neck and he were thrown into the sea. [43] And if your hand causes you to sin,[l] cut it off; it is better for you to enter life maimed than with two hands to go to hell,[m] to the unquenchable fire.[n] [45] And if your foot causes you to sin,[l] cut it off; it is better for you to enter life lame than with two feet to be thrown into hell.[m, n] [47] And if your eye causes you to sin,[l] pluck it out; it is better for you to enter the kingdom of God with one eye than with two eyes to be thrown into hell,[m] [48] where their worm does not die, and the fire is not quenched. [49] For every one will be salted with fire.[o] [50] Salt is good; but if the salt has lost its saltness, how will you season it? Have salt in yourselves, and be at peace with one another."

10 And he left there and went to the region of Judea and beyond the Jordan, and crowds gathered to him again; and again, as his custom was, he taught them.

2 And Pharisees came up and in order to test him asked, "Is it lawful for a man to divorce his wife?" [3] He answered them, "What did Moses command you?" [4] They said, "Moses permitted a man to write a certificate of divorce, and to put her away." [5] But Jesus said to them, "For your hardness of heart he wrote you this commandment. [6] But from the beginning of creation, 'God made them male and female.' [7] 'For this reason a man shall leave his father and

---

[l] Or *stumble.*   [m] Greek *Gehenna.*   [n] Verses 44 and 46 (which are identical with verse 48) are omitted by the best ancient authorities.   [o] Many ancient authorities add *and every sacrifice will be salted with salt.*

9. 41: Mt. 10. 42.   **9. 42–48:** Mt. 18. 6–9; 5. 29–30; Lk. 17. 1–2.   **9. 48:** Is. 66. 24.
9. 49–50: Mt. 5. 13; Lk. 14. 34–35.   **9. 50:** Col. 4. 6; 1 Thess. 5. 13.
10. 1–12: Mt. 19. 1–9.   **10. 1:** Lk. 9. 51; Jn. 10. 40; 11. 7.   **10. 4:** Deut. 24. 1–4.
10. 6: Gen. 1. 27; 5. 2.   **10. 7–8:** Gen. 2. 24.

mother and be joined to his wife,[p] 8 and the two shall become one.'[q] So they are no longer two but one.[q] 9 What therefore God has joined together, let not man put asunder."

10 And in the house the disciples asked him again about this matter. 11 And he said to them, "Whoever divorces his wife and marries another, commits adultery against her; 12 and if she divorces her husband and marries another, she commits adultery."

13 And they were bringing children to him, that he might touch them; and the disciples rebuked them. 14 But when Jesus saw it he was indignant, and said to them, "Let the children come to me, do not hinder them; for to such belongs the kingdom of God. 15 Truly, I say to you, whoever does not receive the kingdom of God like a child shall not enter it." 16 And he took them in his arms and blessed them, laying his hands upon them.

17 And as he was setting out on his journey, a man ran up and knelt before him, and asked him, "Good teacher, what must I do to inherit eternal life?" 18 And Jesus said to him, "Why do you call me good? No one is good but God alone. 19 You know the commandments: 'Do not kill, Do not commit adultery, Do not steal, Do not bear false witness, Do not defraud, Honor your father and mother.'" 20 And he said to him, "Teacher, all these I have observed from my youth." 21 And Jesus looking upon him loved him, and said to him, "You lack one thing; go, sell all that you have, and give it to the poor, and you will have treasure in heaven; and come, follow me." 22 At that saying his countenance fell, and he went away sorrowful; for he had great possessions.

---

[p] Some ancient authorities omit *and be joined to his wife.*   [q] Greek *one flesh.*

10. 11: Mt. 5. 32; Lk. 16. 18; 1 Cor. 7. 10–11; Rom. 7. 2–3.   **10. 13–16:** Mt. 19. 13–15; 18. 3; Lk. 18. 15–17.   **10. 16:** Mk. 9. 36.   **10. 17–31:** Mt. 19. 16–30; Lk. 18. 18–30. **10. 17:** Lk. 10. 25; Mk. 1. 40.   **10. 19:** Ex. 20. 12–16; Deut. 5. 16–20.   **10. 21:** Mt. 6. 20; Lk. 12. 33; Acts 2. 45; 4. 34–35.

23 And Jesus looked around and said to his disciples, "How hard it will be for those who have riches to enter the kingdom of God!" ²⁴ And the disciples were amazed at his words. But Jesus said to them again, "Children, how hard it is^r to enter the kingdom of God! ²⁵ It is easier for a camel to go through the eye of a needle than for a rich man to enter the kingdom of God." ²⁶ And they were exceedingly astonished, and said to him,^s "Then who can be saved?" ²⁷ Jesus looked at them and said, "With men it is impossible, but not with God; for all things are possible with God." ²⁸ Peter began to say to him, "Lo, we have left everything, and followed you." ²⁹ Jesus said, "Truly, I say to you, there is no one who has left house or brothers or sisters or mother or father or children or lands, for my sake and for the gospel, ³⁰ who will not receive a hundredfold now in this time, houses and brothers and sisters and mothers and children and lands, with persecutions, and in the age to come eternal life. ³¹ But many that are first will be last, and the last first."

32 And they were on the road, going up to Jerusalem, and Jesus was walking ahead of them; and they were amazed, and those who followed were afraid. And he took the twelve again, and began to tell them what was to happen to him, ³³ saying, "Behold, we are going up to Jerusalem; and the Son of man will be delivered to the chief priests and the scribes, and they will condemn him to death, and deliver him to the Gentiles; ³⁴ and they will mock him, and spit upon him, and scourge him, and kill him; and after three days he will rise."

35 And James and John, the sons of Zeb'e-dee, came for-

---

^r Some ancient authorities add *for those who trust in riches.*
^s Many ancient authorities read *to one another.*

10. 28: Mk. 1. 16–20.   **10. 30:** Mt. 6. 33.   **10. 31:** Mt. 20. 16; Lk. 13. 30.
10. 32–34: Mt. 20. 17–19; Lk. 18. 31–34.   **10. 33:** Mk. 8. 31; 9. 12; 9. 33.   **10. 34:** Mk. 14. 65; 15. 19, 26–32.   **10. 35–45:** Mt. 20. 20–28.

ward to him, and said to him, "Teacher, we want you to do for us whatever we ask of you." [36] And he said to them, "What do you want me to do for you?" [37] And they said to him, "Grant us to sit, one at your right hand and one at your left, in your glory." [38] But Jesus said to them, "You do not know what you are asking. Are you able to drink the cup that I drink, or to be baptized with the baptism with which I am baptized?" [39] And they said to him, "We are able." And Jesus said to them, "The cup that I drink you will drink; and with the baptism with which I am baptized, you will be baptized; [40] but to sit at my right hand or at my left is not mine to grant; but it is for those for whom it has been prepared." [41] And when the ten heard it, they began to be indignant at James and John. [42] And Jesus called them to him and said to them, "You know that those who are supposed to rule over the Gentiles lord it over them, and their great men exercise authority over them. [43] But it shall not be so among you; but whoever would be great among you must be your servant, [44] and whoever would be first among you must be slave of all. [45] For the Son of man also came not to be served but to serve, and to give his life as a ransom for many."

46 And they came to Jericho; and as he was leaving Jericho with his disciples and a great multitude, Bar-ti-mae′us, a blind beggar, the son of Ti-mae′us, was sitting by the roadside. [47] And when he heard that it was Jesus of Naza-reth, he began to cry out and say, "Jesus, Son of David, have mercy on me!" [48] And many rebuked him, telling him to be silent; but he cried out all the more, "Son of David, have mercy on me!" [49] And Jesus stopped and said, "Call him." And they called the blind man, saying to him,

10. 37: Mt. 19. 28; Lk. 22. 30.   **10. 38**: Lk. 12. 50; Jn. 18. 11.   **10. 39**: Acts 12. 2; Rev. 1. 9.   **10. 42–45**: Lk. 22. 25–27.   **10. 43**: Mk. 9. 35.   **10. 45**: 1 Tim. 2. 5–6. **10. 46–52**: Mt. 20. 29–34; Lk. 18. 35–43; Mk. 8. 22–26.   **10. 47**: Mt. 9. 27.

"Take heart; rise, he is calling you." [50] And throwing off his mantle he sprang up and came to Jesus. [51] And Jesus said to him, "What do you want me to do for you?" And the blind man said to him, "Master,[t] let me receive my sight." [52] And Jesus said to him, "Go your way; your faith has made you well." And immediately he received his sight and followed him on the way.

11 And when they drew near to Jerusalem, to Beth'-pha-ge and Bethany, at the Mount of Olives, he sent two of his disciples, [2] and said to them, "Go into the village opposite you, and immediately as you enter it you will find a colt tied, on which no one has ever sat; untie it and bring it. [3] If any one says to you, 'Why are you doing this?' say, 'The Lord has need of it and will send it back here immediately.'" [4] And they went away, and found a colt tied at the door out in the open street; and they untied it. [5] And those who stood there said to them, "What are you doing, untying the colt?" [6] And they told them what Jesus had said; and they let them go. [7] And they brought the colt to Jesus, and threw their clothes on it; and he sat upon it. [8] And many spread their clothes on the road, and others spread leafy branches which they had cut from the fields. [9] And those who went before and those who followed cried out, "Hosanna! Blessed be he who comes in the name of the Lord! [10] Blessed be the kingdom of our father David that is coming! Hosanna in the highest!"

11 And he entered Jerusalem, and went into the temple; and when he had looked round at everything, as it was already late, he went out to Bethany with the twelve.

12 On the following day, when they came from Bethany,

[t] Or *Rabbi.*

10. 52: Mt. 9. 22; Mk. 5. 34; Lk. 7. 50; 8. 48; 17. 19.
11. 1–10: Mt. 21. 1–9; Lk. 19. 29–38.   11. 4: Mk. 14. 16.   11. 7–10: Jn. 12. 12–15.
11. 9: Ps. 118. 26; Mt. 21. 15; 23. 39.   11. 11: Mt. 21. 10–11, 17.   11. 12–14:
Mt. 21. 18–19; Lk. 13. 6–9.

he was hungry. [13] And seeing in the distance a fig tree in leaf, he went to see if he could find anything on it. When he came to it, he found nothing but leaves, for it was not the season for figs. [14] And he said to it, "May no one ever eat fruit from you again." And his disciples heard it.

15 And they came to Jerusalem. And he entered the temple and began to drive out those who sold and those who bought in the temple, and he overturned the tables of the money-changers and the seats of those who sold pigeons; [16] and he would not allow any one to carry anything through the temple. [17] And he taught, and said to them, "Is it not written, 'My house shall be called a house of prayer for all the nations'? But you have made it a den of robbers." [18] And the chief priests and the scribes heard it and sought a way to destroy him; for they feared him, because all the multitude was astonished at his teaching. [19] And when evening came they[u] went out of the city.

20 As they passed by in the morning, they saw the fig tree withered away to its roots. [21] And Peter remembered and said to him, "Master,[v] look! The fig tree which you cursed has withered." [22] And Jesus answered them, "Have faith in God. [23] Truly, I say to you, whoever says to this mountain, Be taken up and cast into the sea, and does not doubt in his heart, but believes that what he says will come to pass, it will be done for him. [24] Therefore I tell you, whatever you ask in prayer, believe that you receive it, and you will. [25] And whenever you stand praying, forgive, if you have anything against any one; so that your Father also who is in heaven may forgive you your trespasses."[w]

[u] Some ancient authorities read *he.*
[v] Or *Rabbi.*
[w] Many ancient authorities add verse 26, "*But if you do not forgive, neither will your Father who is in heaven forgive your trespasses.*"

11. 15–18: Mt. 21. 12–16; Lk. 19. 45–48; Jn. 2. 13–16.   **11. 17:** Is. 56. 7; Jer. 7.11.
11. 19: Lk. 21. 37.   **11. 20–25:** Mt. 21. 20–22; Mt. 17. 20; Lk. 17. 6.   **11. 24:** Jn. 14. 13–14; 16. 23; Mt. 7. 7–11.   **11. 25:** Mt. 6. 14–15; 18. 35.

27 And they came again to Jerusalem. And as he was walking in the temple, the chief priests and the scribes and the elders came to him, [28] and they said to him, "By what authority are you doing these things, or who gave you this authority to do them?" [29] Jesus said to them, "I will ask you a question; answer me, and I will tell you by what authority I do these things. [30] Was the baptism of John from heaven or from men? Answer me." [31] And they argued with one another, "If we say, 'From heaven,' he will say, 'Why then did you not believe him?' [32] But shall we say, 'From men'?" — they were afraid of the people, for all held that John was a real prophet. [33] So they answered Jesus, "We do not know." And Jesus said to them, "Neither will I tell you by what authority I do these things."

12 And he began to speak to them in parables. "A man planted a vineyard, and set a hedge around it, and dug a pit for the wine press, and built a tower, and let it out to tenants, and went into another country. [2] When the time came, he sent a servant to the tenants, to get from them some of the fruit of the vineyard. [3] And they took him and beat him, and sent him away empty-handed. [4] Again he sent to them another servant, and they wounded him in the head, and treated him shamefully. [5] And he sent another, and him they killed; and so with many others, some they beat and some they killed. [6] He had still one other, a beloved son; finally he sent him to them, saying, 'They will respect my son.' [7] But those tenants said to one another, 'This is the heir; come, let us kill him, and the inheritance will be ours.' [8] And they took him and killed him, and cast him out of the vineyard. [9] What will the owner of the vineyard do? He will come and destroy the tenants, and

11. 27–33: Mt. 21. 23–27; Lk. 20. 1–8; Jn. 2. 18.
12. 1–12: Mt. 21. 33–46; Lk. 20. 9–19; Is. 5. 1–7.

give the vineyard to others. ¹⁰ Have you not read this scripture:

> 'The very stone which the builders rejected
> has become the head of the corner;
> ¹¹ this was the Lord's doing,
> and it is marvelous in our eyes'?"

12 And they tried to arrest him, but feared the multitude, for they perceived that he had told the parable against them; so they left him and went away.

13 And they sent to him some of the Pharisees and some of the He-ro′di-ans, to entrap him in his talk. ¹⁴ And they came and said to him, "Teacher, we know that you are true, and care for no man; for you do not regard the position of men, but truly teach the way of God. Is it lawful to pay taxes to Caesar, or not? ¹⁵ Should we pay them, or should we not?" But knowing their hypocrisy, he said to them, "Why put me to the test? Bring me a coin,ˣ and let me look at it." ¹⁶ And they brought one. And he said to them, "Whose likeness and inscription is this?" They said to him, "Caesar's." ¹⁷ Jesus said to them, "Render to Caesar the things that are Caesar's, and to God the things that are God's." And they were amazed at him.

18 And Sad′du-cees came to him, who say that there is no resurrection; and they asked him a question, saying, ¹⁹ "Teacher, Moses wrote for us that if a man's brother dies and leaves a wife, but leaves no child, the manʸ must take the wife, and raise up children for his brother. ²⁰ There were seven brothers; the first took a wife, and when he died left no children; ²¹ and the second took her, and died, leaving no children; and the third likewise; ²² and the seven left

---

ˣ Greek *a denarius*.   ʸ Greek *his brother*.

12. 10–11: Ps. 118. 22–23; Acts 4. 11; 1 Pet. 2. 7.   **12. 12:** Mk. 11. 18.   **12. 13–17:** Mt. 22. 15–22; Lk. 20. 20–26.   **12. 13:** Mk. 3. 6; Lk. 11. 54.   **12. 17:** Rom. 13. 7.   **12. 18–27:** Mt. 22. 23–33; Lk. 20. 27–38.   **12. 19:** Deut. 25. 5.

no children. Last of all the woman also died. [23] In the resurrection whose wife will she be? For the seven had her as wife."

24 Jesus said to them, "Is not this why you are wrong, that you know neither the scriptures nor the power of God? [25] For when they rise from the dead, they neither marry nor are given in marriage, but are like angels in heaven. [26] And as for the dead being raised, have you not read in the book of Moses, in the passage about the bush, how God said to him, 'I am the God of Abraham, and the God of Isaac, and the God of Jacob'? [27] He is not God of the dead, but of the living; you are quite wrong."

28 And one of the scribes came up and heard them disputing with one another, and seeing that he answered them well, asked him, "Which commandment is the first of all?" [29] Jesus answered, "The first is, 'Hear, O Israel: The Lord our God, the Lord is one; [30] and you shall love the Lord your God with all your heart, and with all your soul, and with all your mind, and with all your strength.' [31] The second is this, 'You shall love your neighbor as yourself.' There is no other commandment greater than these." [32] And the scribe said to him, "You are right, Teacher; you have truly said that he is one, and there is no other but he; [33] and to love him with all the heart, and with all the understanding, and with all the strength, and to love one's neighbor as oneself, is much more than all whole burnt offerings and sacrifices." [34] And when Jesus saw that he answered wisely, he said to him, "You are not far from the kingdom of God." And after that no one dared to ask him any question.

35 And as Jesus taught in the temple, he said, "How can

12. 26: Ex. 3. 6.   **12. 28–34:** Mt. 22. 34–40; Lk. 20. 39–40; 10. 25–28.   **12. 29:** Deut. 6. 4.   **12. 31:** Lev. 19. 18; Rom. 13. 9; Gal. 5. 14; Jas. 2. 8.   **12. 33:** 1 Sam. 15. 22; Hos. 6. 6; Mic. 6. 6–8; Mt. 9. 13.

the scribes say that the Christ is the son of David? [36] David
himself, inspired by[z] the Holy Spirit, declared,

> 'The Lord said to my Lord,
> Sit at my right hand,
> till I put thy enemies under thy feet.'

[37] David himself calls him Lord; so how is he his son?"
And the great throng heard him gladly.

38 And in his teaching he said, "Beware of the scribes,
who like to go about in long robes, and to have salutations
in the market places [39] and the best seats in the synagogues
and the places of honor at feasts, [40] who devour widows'
houses and for a pretense make long prayers. They will
receive the greater condemnation."

41 And he sat down opposite the treasury, and watched
the multitude putting money into the treasury. Many rich
people put in large sums. [42] And a poor widow came, and
put in two copper coins, which make a penny. [43] And he
called his disciples to him, and said to them, "Truly, I say
to you, this poor widow has put in more than all those who
are contributing to the treasury. [44] For they all contributed
out of their abundance; but she out of her poverty has put
in everything she had, her whole living."

13 And as he came out of the temple, one of his disciples said to him, "Look, Teacher, what wonderful
stones and what wonderful buildings!" [2] And Jesus said to
him, "Do you see these great buildings? There will not
be left here one stone upon another, that will not be thrown
down."

3 And as he sat on the Mount of Olives opposite the
temple, Peter and James and John and Andrew asked him

---

[z] Or *himself, in.*

12. 35–37: Mt. 22. 41–46; Lk. 20. 41–44.   **12. 36:** Ps. 110. 1; Acts 2. 34–35; Heb. 1. 13.
12. 38–40: Mt. 23. 5–7; Lk. 20. 46–47; Lk. 11. 43.   **12. 41–44:** Lk. 21. 1–4; Jn. 8. 20.
13. 1–37: Mt. 24; Lk. 21. 5–36.   **13. 2:** Lk. 19. 43–44; Mk. 14. 58; 15. 29; Jn. 2. 19;
Acts 6. 14.   **13. 3:** Mk. 5. 37; 9. 2.

privately,[4] "Tell us, when will this be, and what will be the sign when these things are all to be accomplished?" [5] And Jesus began to say to them, "Take heed that no one leads you astray. [6] Many will come in my name, saying, 'I am he!' and they will lead many astray. [7] And when you hear of wars and rumors of wars, do not be alarmed; this must take place, but the end is not yet. [8] For nation will rise against nation, and kingdom against kingdom; there will be earthquakes in various places, there will be famines; this is but the beginning of the sufferings.

9 "But take heed to yourselves; for they will deliver you up to councils; and you will be beaten in synagogues; and you will stand before governors and kings for my sake, to bear testimony before them. [10] And the gospel must first be preached to all nations. [11] And when they bring you to trial and deliver you up, do not be anxious beforehand what you are to say; but say whatever is given you in that hour, for it is not you who speak, but the Holy Spirit. [12] And brother will deliver up brother to death, and the father his child, and children will rise against parents and have them put to death; [13] and you will be hated by all for my name's sake. But he who endures to the end will be saved.

14 "But when you see the desolating sacrilege set up where it ought not to be (let the reader understand), then let those who are in Judea flee to the mountains; [15] let him who is on the housetop not go down, nor enter his house, to take anything away; [16] and let him who is in the field not turn back to take his mantle. [17] And alas for those who are with child and for those who give suck in those days! [18] Pray that it may not happen in winter. [19] For in those days there

13. 4: Lk. 17. 20.   13. 6: Jn. 8. 24; 1 Jn. 2. 18.   13. 9–13: Mt. 10. 17–22.   13. 11: Jn. 14. 26; 16. 7–11; Lk. 12. 11–12.   13. 13: Jn. 15. 21.   13. 14: Dan. 9. 27; 11. 31; 12. 11.   13. 17: Lk. 23. 29.

will be such tribulation as has not been from the beginning of the creation which God created until now, and never will be. [20] And if the Lord had not shortened the days, no human being would be saved; but for the sake of the elect, whom he chose, he shortened the days. [21] And then if any one says to you, 'Look, here is the Christ!' or 'Look, there he is!' do not believe it. [22] False Christs and false prophets will arise and show signs and wonders, to lead astray, if possible, the elect. [23] But take heed; I have told you all things beforehand.

24 "But in those days, after that tribulation, the sun will be darkened, and the moon will not give its light, [25] and the stars will be falling from heaven, and the powers in the heavens will be shaken. [26] And then they will see the Son of man coming in clouds with great power and glory. [27] And then he will send out the angels, and gather his elect from the four winds, from the ends of the earth to the ends of heaven.

28 "From the fig tree learn its lesson: as soon as its branch becomes tender and puts forth its leaves, you know that summer is near. [29] So also, when you see these things taking place, you know that he is near, at the very gates. [30] Truly, I say to you, this generation will not pass away before all these things take place. [31] Heaven and earth will pass away, but my words will not pass away.

32 "But of that day or that hour no one knows, not even the angels in heaven, nor the Son, but only the Father. [33] Take heed, watch and pray;[a] for you do not know when the time will come. [34] It is like a man going on a journey, when he leaves home and puts his servants in charge, each

---

a Some ancient authorities omit *and pray.*

13. 22: Mt. 7. 15; Jn. 4. 48.   **13. 26:** Mk. 8. 38; Mt. 10. 23; Dan. 7. 13.   **13. 30:** Mk. 9. 1. **13. 31:** Mt. 5. 18; Lk. 16. 17.   **13. 32:** Acts 1. 7.   **13. 33:** Eph. 6. 18; Col. 4. 2.   **13. 34:** Mt. 25. 14.

with his work, and commands the doorkeeper to be on the watch. [35] Watch therefore — for you do not know when the master of the house will come, in the evening, or at midnight, or at cockcrow, or in the morning — [36] lest he come suddenly and find you asleep. [37] And what I say to you I say to all: Watch."

14 It was now two days before the Passover and the feast of Unleavened Bread. And the chief priests and the scribes were seeking how to arrest him by stealth, and kill him; [2] for they said, "Not during the feast, lest there be a tumult of the people."

3 And while he was at Bethany in the house of Simon the leper, as he sat at table, a woman came with an alabaster jar of ointment of pure nard, very costly, and she broke the jar and poured it over his head. [4] But there were some who said to themselves indignantly, "Why was the ointment thus wasted? [5] For this ointment might have been sold for more than three hundred denarii,[b] and given to the poor." And they reproached her. [6] But Jesus said, "Let her alone; why do you trouble her? She has done a beautiful thing to me. [7] For you always have the poor with you, and whenever you will, you can do good to them; but you will not always have me. [8] She has done what she could; she has anointed my body beforehand for burying. [9] And truly, I say to you, wherever the gospel is preached in the whole world, what she has done will be told in memory of her."

10 Then Judas Iscariot, who was one of the twelve, went to the chief priests in order to betray him to them. [11] And when they heard it they were glad, and promised to give him money. And he sought an opportunity to betray him.

[b] See note on Matthew 18. 28.

13. 35: Lk. 12. 35–40.
14. 1–2: Mt. 26. 1–5; Lk. 22. 1–2; Jn. 11. 47–53.   **14. 3–9:** Mt. 26. 6–13; Lk. 7. 36–38;
Jn. 12. 1–8.   **14. 7:** Deut. 15. 11.   **14. 8:** Jn. 19. 40.   **14. 10–11:** Mt. 26. 14–16;
Lk. 22. 3–6.

12 And on the first day of Unleavened Bread, when they sacrificed the passover lamb, his disciples said to him, "Where will you have us go and prepare for you to eat the passover?" [13] And he sent two of his disciples, and said to them, "Go into the city, and a man carrying a jar of water will meet you; follow him, [14] and wherever he enters, say to the householder, 'The Teacher says, Where is my guest room, where I am to eat the passover with my disciples?' [15] And he will show you a large upper room furnished and ready; there prepare for us." [16] And the disciples set out and went to the city, and found it as he had told them; and they prepared the passover.

17 And when it was evening he came with the twelve. [18] And as they were at table eating, Jesus said, "Truly, I say to you, one of you will betray me, one who is eating with me." [19] They began to be sorrowful, and to say to him one after another, "Is it I?" [20] He said to them, "It is one of the twelve, one who is dipping bread in the same dish with me. [21] For the Son of man goes, as it is written of him, but woe to that man by whom the Son of man is betrayed! It would have been better for that man if he had not been born."

22 And as they were eating, he took bread, and blessed, and broke it, and gave it to them, and said, "Take; this is my body." [23] And he took a cup, and when he had given thanks he gave it to them, and they all drank of it. [24] And he said to them, "This is my blood of the[c] covenant, which is poured out for many. [25] Truly, I say to you, I shall not drink again of the fruit of the vine until that day when I drink it new in the kingdom of God."

26 And when they had sung a hymn, they went out to

---

[c] Some ancient authorities insert *new*.

14. 12–16: Mt. 26. 17–19; Lk. 22. 7–13.   **14. 17–21:** Mt. 26. 20–25; Lk. 22. 14, 21–23; Jn. 13. 21–30; Ps. 41. 9.   **14. 22–25:** Mt. 26. 26–29; Lk. 22. 17–19; 1 Cor. 11. 23–26. **14. 22:** Mk. 6. 41; 8. 6; Lk. 24. 30.   **14. 23:** 1 Cor. 10. 16.   **14. 24:** Ex. 24. 8; Heb. 9. 20.   **14. 26–31:** Mt. 26. 30–35; Lk. 22. 39, 33–34.

the Mount of Olives. [27] And Jesus said to them, "You will all fall away; for it is written, 'I will strike the shepherd, and the sheep will be scattered.' [28] But after I am raised up, I will go before you to Galilee." [29] Peter said to him, "Even though they all fall away, I will not." [30] And Jesus said to him, "Truly, I say to you, this very night, before the cock crows twice, you will deny me three times." [31] But he said vehemently, "If I must die with you, I will not deny you." And they all said the same.

32 And they went to a place which was called Geth-sem'a-ne; and he said to his disciples, "Sit here, while I pray." [33] And he took with him Peter and James and John, and began to be greatly distressed and troubled. [34] And he said to them, "My soul is very sorrowful, even to death; remain here, and watch." [d] [35] And going a little farther, he fell on the ground and prayed that, if it were possible, the hour might pass from him. [36] And he said, "Abba, Father, all things are possible to thee; remove this cup from me; yet not what I will, but what thou wilt." [37] And he came and found them sleeping, and he said to Peter, "Simon, are you asleep? Could you not watch[d] one hour? [38] Watch[d] and pray that you may not enter into temptation; the spirit indeed is willing, but the flesh is weak." [39] And again he went away, and prayed, saying the same words. [40] And again he came and found them sleeping, for their eyes were very heavy; and they did not know what to answer him. [41] And he came the third time, and said to them, "Are you still sleeping and taking your rest? It is enough; the hour has come; the Son of man is betrayed into the hands of sinners. [42] Rise, let us be going; see, my betrayer is at hand."

[d] Or *keep awake.*

14. 27: Zech. 13. 7; Jn. 16. 32.   **14. 28**: Mk. 16. 7.   **14. 30**: Mk. 14. 66–72; Jn. 13. 36–38; 18. 17–18, 25–27.   **14. 32–42**: Mt. 26. 36–46; Lk. 22. 40–46; Heb. 5. 7–8. **14. 34**: Jn. 12. 27.   **14. 36**: Rom. 8. 15; Gal. 4. 6; Mk. 10. 38; Jn. 18. 11.   **14. 38**: Mt. 6. 13; Lk. 11. 4.

43 And immediately, while he was still speaking, Judas came, one of the twelve, and with him a crowd with swords and clubs, from the chief priests and the scribes and the elders. ⁴⁴ Now the betrayer had given them a sign, saying, "The one I shall kiss is the man; seize him and lead him away safely." ⁴⁵ And when he came, he went up to him at once, and said, "Master!*ᵉ*" And he kissed him. ⁴⁶ And they laid hands on him and seized him. ⁴⁷ But one of those who stood by drew his sword, and struck the slave of the high priest and cut off his ear. ⁴⁸ And Jesus said to them, "Have you come out as against a robber, with swords and clubs to capture me? ⁴⁹ Day after day I was with you in the temple teaching, and you did not seize me. But let the scriptures be fulfilled." ⁵⁰ And they all forsook him, and fled.

51 And a young man followed him, with nothing but a linen cloth about his body; and they seized him, ⁵² but he left the linen cloth and ran away naked.

53 And they led Jesus to the high priest; and all the chief priests and the elders and the scribes were assembled. ⁵⁴ And Peter had followed him at a distance, right into the courtyard of the high priest; and he was sitting with the guards, and warming himself at the fire. ⁵⁵ Now the chief priests and the whole council sought testimony against Jesus, to put him to death; but they found none. ⁵⁶ For many bore false witness against him, and their witness did not agree. ⁵⁷ And some stood up and bore false witness against him, saying, ⁵⁸ "We heard him say, 'I will destroy this temple that is made with hands, and in three days I will build another, not made with hands.'" ⁵⁹ Yet not even so did their testimony agree. ⁶⁰ And the high priest stood up in the midst,

ᵉ Or *Rabbi.*

14. 43–50: Mt. 26. 47–56; Lk. 22. 47–53; Jn. 18. 2–11. **14. 49:** Lk. 19. 47; Jn. 18. 19–21. **14. 53–65:** Mt. 26. 57–68; Lk. 22. 54–55, 63–71; Jn. 18. 12–24. **14. 58:** Mk. 13. 2; 15. 29; Acts 6. 14; Jn. 2. 19.

and asked Jesus, "Have you no answer to make? What is it that these men testify against you?" [61] But he was silent and made no answer. Again the high priest asked him, "Are you the Christ, the Son of the Blessed?" [62] And Jesus said, "I am; and you will see the Son of man sitting at the right hand of Power, and coming with the clouds of heaven." [63] And the high priest tore his mantle, and said, "Why do we still need witnesses? [64] You have heard his blasphemy. What is your decision?" And they all condemned him as deserving death. [65] And some began to spit on him, and to cover his face, and to strike him, saying to him, "Prophesy!" And the guards received him with blows.

66 And as Peter was below in the courtyard, one of the maids of the high priest came; [67] and seeing Peter warming himself, she looked at him, and said, "You also were with the Nazarene, Jesus." [68] But he denied it, saying, "I neither know nor understand what you mean." And he went out into the gateway.*f* [69] And the maid saw him, and began again to say to the bystanders, "This man is one of them." [70] But again he denied it. And after a little while again the bystanders said to Peter, "Certainly you are one of them; for you are a Galilean." [71] But he began to invoke a curse on himself and to swear, "I do not know this man of whom you speak." [72] And immediately the cock crowed a second time. And Peter remembered how Jesus had said to him, "Before the cock crows twice, you will deny me three times." And he broke down and wept.

15 And as soon as it was morning the chief priests, with the elders and scribes, and the whole council held a consultation; and they bound Jesus and led him away

---

f Or *fore-court*. Some ancient authorities add *and the cock crowed*.

14. 62: Dan. 7. 13; Mk. 9. 1; 13. 26.   **14. 63:** Acts 14. 14; Num. 14. 6.   **14. 64:** Lev. 24. 16.   **14. 66–72:** Mt. 26. 69–75; Lk. 22. 56–62; Jn. 18. 16–18, 25–27; Mk. 14. 30. **15. 1:** Mt. 27. 1–2; Lk. 23. 1; Jn. 18. 28.

and delivered him to Pilate. [2] And Pilate asked him, "Are you the King of the Jews?" And he answered him, "You have said so." [3] And the chief priests accused him of many things. [4] And Pilate again asked him, "Have you no answer to make? See how many charges they bring against you." [5] But Jesus made no further answer, so that Pilate wondered.

6 Now at the feast he used to release for them any one prisoner whom they asked. [7] And among the rebels in prison, who had committed murder in the insurrection, there was a man called Bar-ab'bas. [8] And the crowd came up and began to ask Pilate to do as he was wont to do for them. [9] And he answered them, "Do you want me to release for you the King of the Jews?" [10] For he perceived that it was out of envy that the chief priests had delivered him up. [11] But the chief priests stirred up the crowd to have him release for them Bar-ab'bas instead. [12] And Pilate again said to them, "Then what shall I do with the man whom you call the King of the Jews?" [13] And they cried out again, "Crucify him." [14] And Pilate said to them, "Why, what evil has he done?" But they shouted all the more, "Crucify him." [15] So Pilate, wishing to satisfy the crowd, released for them Bar-ab'bas; and having scourged Jesus, he delivered him to be crucified.

16 And the soldiers led him away inside the palace (that is, the praetorium); and they called together the whole battalion. [17] And they clothed him in a purple cloak, and plaiting a crown of thorns they put it on him. [18] And they began to salute him, "Hail, King of the Jews!" [19] And they struck his head with a reed, and spat upon him, and they knelt down in homage to him. [20] And when they had mocked him, they stripped him of the purple cloak, and put his own clothes on him. And they led him out to crucify him.

15. 2–15: Mt. 27. 11–26; Lk. 23. 2–3, 18–25; Jn. 18. 29–19. 16.   **15. 11:** Acts 3. 14.
15. 16–20: Mt. 27. 27–31; Lk. 23. 11; Jn. 19. 2–3.

21 And they compelled a passer-by, Simon of Cy-re′ne, who was coming in from the country, the father of Alexander and Rufus, to carry his cross. ²² And they brought him to the place called Gol′go-tha (which means the place of a skull). ²³ And they offered him wine mingled with myrrh; but he did not take it. ²⁴ And they crucified him, and divided his garments among them, casting lots for them, to decide what each should take. ²⁵ And it was the third hour, when they crucified him. ²⁶ And the inscription of the charge against him read, "The King of the Jews." ²⁷ And with him they crucified two robbers, one on his right and one on his left.*ᵍ* ²⁹ And those who passed by derided him, wagging their heads, and saying, "Aha! You who would destroy the temple and build it in three days, ³⁰ save yourself, and come down from the cross!" ³¹ So also the chief priests mocked him to one another with the scribes, saying, "He saved others; he cannot save himself. ³² Let the Christ, the King of Israel, come down now from the cross, that we may see and believe." Those who were crucified with him also reviled him.

33 And when the sixth hour had come, there was darkness over the whole land*ʰ* until the ninth hour. ³⁴ And at the ninth hour Jesus cried with a loud voice, "E′lo-i, E′lo-i, la′ma sa-bach-tha′ni?" which means, "My God, my God, why hast thou forsaken me?" ³⁵ And some of the bystanders hearing it said, "Behold, he is calling Elijah." ³⁶ And one ran and, filling a sponge full of vinegar, put it on a reed and gave it to him to drink, saying, "Wait, let us see whether Elijah will come to take him down." ³⁷ And Jesus uttered a loud cry, and breathed his last. ³⁸ And the curtain

ᵍ Many ancient authorities insert verse 28, *And the scripture was fulfilled which says, " He was reckoned among the transgressors."* *ʰ* Or *earth.*

15. 21: Mt. 27. 32; Lk. 23. 26; Rom. 16. 13. **15. 22–32:** Mt. 27. 33–44; Lk. 23. 33–39; Jn. 19. 17–24. **15. 24:** Ps. 22. 18. **15. 29:** Mk. 13. 2; 14. 58; Jn. 2. 19. **15. 31:** Ps. 22. 7–8. **15. 33–41:** Mt. 27. 45–56; Lk. 23. 44–49; Jn. 19. 28–30. **15. 34:** Ps. 22. 1. **15. 36:** Ps. 69. 21. **15. 38:** Heb. 10. 19–20.

of the temple was torn in two, from top to bottom. [39]And when the centurion, who stood facing him, saw that he thus[i] breathed his last, he said, "Truly this man was a son of God."

40 There were also women looking on from afar, among whom were Mary Mag'da-lene, and Mary the mother of James the younger and of Joses, and Sa-lo'me, [41] who, when he was in Galilee, followed him, and ministered to him; and also many other women who came up with him to Jerusalem.

42 And when evening had come, since it was the day of Preparation, that is, the day before the sabbath, [43] Joseph of Ar-i-ma-the'a, a respected member of the council, who was also himself looking for the kingdom of God, took courage and went to Pilate, and asked for the body of Jesus. [44] And Pilate wondered if he were already dead; and summoning the centurion, he asked him whether he was already dead.[j] [45] And when he learned from the centurion that he was dead, he granted the body to Joseph. [46] And he bought a linen shroud, and taking him down, wrapped him in the linen shroud, and laid him in a tomb which had been hewn out of the rock; and he rolled a stone against the door of the tomb. [47] Mary Mag'da-lene and Mary the mother of Joses saw where he was laid.

16 And when the sabbath was past, Mary Mag'da-lene, and Mary the mother of James, and Sa-lo'me, bought spices, so that they might go and anoint him. [2] And very early on the first day of the week they went to the tomb when the sun had risen. [3] And they were saying to one another, "Who will roll away the stone for us from the door

---

[i] Many ancient authorities insert *cried out and. he had been some time dead.*   [j] Some ancient authorities read *whether*

15. 39: Mk. 1. 11; 9. 7.   **15. 40:** Jn. 19. 25.   **15. 41:** Lk. 8. 1–3.   **15. 42–47:** Mt. 27. 57–61; Lk. 23. 50–56; Jn. 19. 38–42; Acts 13. 29.   **15. 42:** Deut. 21. 22–23.
16. 1–8: Mt. 28. 1–8; Lk. 24. 1–10; Jn. 20. 1–2.   **16. 1:** Lk. 23. 56; Jn. 19. 39.

of the tomb?" [4] And looking up, they saw that the stone was rolled back; for it was very large. [5] And entering the tomb, they saw a young man sitting on the right side, dressed in a white robe; and they were amazed. [6] And he said to them, "Do not be amazed; you seek Jesus of Nazareth, who was crucified. He has risen, he is not here; see the place where they laid him. [7] But go, tell his disciples and Peter that he is going before you to Galilee; there you will see him, as he told you." [8] And they went out and fled from the tomb; for trembling and astonishment had come upon them; and they said nothing to any one, for they were afraid.[k]

[k] Some texts and versions add as 16. 9–20 the following passage:

[9] *Now when he rose early on the first day of the week, he appeared first to Mary Magdalene, from whom he had cast out seven demons.* [10] *She went and told those who had been with him, as they mourned and wept.* [11] *But when they heard that he was alive and had been seen by her, they would not believe it.*

[12] *After this he appeared in another form to two of them, as they were walking into the country.* [13] *And they went back and told the rest, but they did not believe them.*

[14] *Afterward he appeared to the eleven themselves as they sat at table; and he upbraided them for their unbelief and hardness of heart, because they had not believed those who saw him after he had risen.* [15] *And he said to them, "Go into all the world and preach the gospel to the whole creation.* [16] *He who believes and is baptized will be saved; but he who does not believe will be condemned.* [17] *And these signs will accompany those who believe: in my name they will cast out demons; they will speak in new tongues;* [18] *they will pick up serpents, and if they drink any deadly thing, it will not hurt them; they will lay their hands on the sick, and they will recover."*

[19] *So then the Lord Jesus, after he had spoken to them, was taken up into heaven, and sat down at the right hand of God.* [20] *And they went forth and preached everywhere, while the Lord worked with them and confirmed the message by the signs that attended it. Amen.*

Other ancient authorities add after verse 8 the following: *But they reported briefly to Peter and those with him all that they had been told. And after this, Jesu himself sent out by means of them, from east to west, the sacred and imperishable proclamation of eternal salvation.*

16. 7: Mk. 14. 28; Jn. 21. 1–23; Mt. 28. 17.

THE GOSPEL ACCORDING TO

LUKE

1 Inasmuch as many have undertaken to compile a narrative of the things which have been accomplished among us, [2] just as they were delivered to us by those who from the beginning were eyewitnesses and ministers of the word, [3] it seemed good to me also, having followed all things closely[a] for some time past, to write an orderly account for you, most excellent The-oph'i-lus, [4] that you may know the truth concerning the things of which you have been informed.

5 In the days of Herod, king of Judea, there was a priest named Zech-a-ri'ah,[b] of the division of A-bi'jah; and he had a wife of the daughters of Aaron, and her name was Elizabeth. [6] And they were both righteous before God, walking in all the commandments and ordinances of the Lord blameless. [7] But they had no child, because Elizabeth was barren, and both were advanced in years.

8 Now while he was serving as priest before God when his division was on duty, [9] according to the custom of the priesthood, it fell to him by lot to enter the temple of the Lord and burn incense. [10] And the whole multitude of the people were praying outside at the hour of incense. [11] And there appeared to him an angel of the Lord standing on the right side of the altar of incense. [12] And Zech-a-ri'ah was troubled when he saw him, and fear fell upon him. [13] But the angel said to him, "Do not be afraid, Zech-a-ri'ah, for your prayer is heard, and your wife Elizabeth will bear you a son, and you shall call his name John.

[a] Or *accurately*.   [b] Greek *Zacharias*.

1. 2: 1 Jn. 1. 1; Acts 1. 21; Heb. 2. 3.   1. 3: Acts 1. 1.   1. 4: Jn. 20. 31.
1. 5: Mt. 2. 1; 1 Chr. 24. 10; 2 Chr. 31. 2.   1. 9: Ex. 30. 7.   1. 11: Lk. 2. 9;
Acts 5. 19.   1. 13: Lk. 1. 30, 60.

¹⁴ And you will have joy and gladness,
and many will rejoice at his birth;
¹⁵ for he will be great before the Lord,
and he shall drink no wine nor strong drink,
and he will be filled with the Holy Spirit,
even from his mother's womb.
¹⁶ And he will turn many of the sons of Israel to the
Lord their God,
¹⁷ and he will go before him in the spirit and power
of Elijah,
to turn the hearts of the fathers to the children,
and the disobedient to the wisdom of the just,
to make ready for the Lord a people prepared."

¹⁸ And Zech-a-ri'ah said to the angel, "How shall I know this? For I am an old man, and my wife is advanced in years." ¹⁹ And the angel answered him, "I am Gabriel, who stand in the presence of God; and I was sent to speak to you, and to bring you this good news. ²⁰ And behold, you will be silent and unable to speak until the day that these things come to pass, because you did not believe my words, which will be fulfilled in their time." ²¹ And the people were waiting for Zech-a-ri'ah, and they wondered at his delay in the temple. ²² And when he came out, he could not speak to them, and they perceived that he had seen a vision in the temple; and he made signs to them and remained dumb. ²³ And when his time of service was ended, he went to his home.

24 After these days his wife Elizabeth conceived, and for five months she hid herself, saying, ²⁵ "Thus the Lord has done to me in the days when he looked on me, to take away my reproach among men."

26 In the sixth month the angel Gabriel was sent from God to a city of Galilee named Nazareth, ²⁷ to a virgin

1. 15: Num. 6. 3; Lk. 7. 33.   **1. 17:** Mt. 11. 14; 17. 13; Mal. 4. 5.   **1. 18:** Lk. 1. 34.
1. 19: Dan. 8. 16; 9. 21; Mt. 18. 10.   **1. 25:** Gen. 30. 23; Is. 4. 1.

betrothed to a man whose name was Joseph, of the house of David; and the virgin's name was Mary. [28] And he came to her and said, "Hail, O favored one, the Lord is with you!"[c] [29] But she was greatly troubled at the saying, and considered in her mind what sort of greeting this might be. [30] And the angel said to her, "Do not be afraid, Mary, for you have found favor with God. [31] And behold, you will conceive in your womb and bear a son, and you shall call his name Jesus.

> [32] He will be great, and will be called the Son of the
> Most High;
> and the Lord God will give to him the throne of
> his father David,
> [33] and he will reign over the house of Jacob forever;
> and of his kingdom there will be no end."

[34] And Mary said to the angel, "How can this be, since I have no husband?"[35] And the angel said to her,

> "The Holy Spirit will come upon you,
> and the power of the Most High will overshadow you;
> therefore the child to be born[d] will be called holy,
> the Son of God.

[36] And behold, your kinswoman Elizabeth in her old age has also conceived a son; and this is the sixth month with her who was called barren. [37] For with God nothing will be impossible." [38] And Mary said, "Behold I am the handmaid of the Lord; let it be to me according to your word." And the angel departed from her.

39 In those days Mary arose and went with haste into the hill country, to a city of Judah, [40] and she entered the house of Zech-a-ri′ah and greeted Elizabeth. [41] And when Elizabeth heard the greeting of Mary, the babe leaped in her womb; and Elizabeth was filled with the Holy Spirit

[c] Some ancient authorities add "*Blessed are you among women!*"
[d] Some ancient authorities add *of you.*

1. 30: Lk. 1. 13.   **1. 31:** Lk. 2. 21; Mt. 1. 21.   **1. 33:** Mt. 28. 18; Dan. 2. 44.
1. 34: Lk. 1. 18.   **1. 35:** Mt. 1. 20.   **1. 37:** Gen. 18. 14.

[42] and she exclaimed with a loud cry, "Blessed are you among women, and blessed is the fruit of your womb! [43] And why is this granted me, that the mother of my Lord should come to me? [44] For behold, when the voice of your greeting came to my ears, the babe in my womb leaped for joy. [45] And blessed is she who believed that there would be[e] a fulfillment of what was spoken to her from the Lord." [46] And Mary said,

> "My soul magnifies the Lord,
>
> [47] and my spirit rejoices in God my Savior,
>
> [48] for he has regarded the low estate of his handmaiden.
>
> For behold, henceforth all generations will call me blessed;
>
> [49] for he who is mighty has done great things for me, and holy is his name.
>
> [50] And his mercy is on those who fear him from generation to generation.
>
> [51] He has shown strength with his arm, he has scattered the proud in the imagination of their hearts,
>
> [52] he has put down the mighty from their thrones, and exalted those of low degree;
>
> [53] he has filled the hungry with good things, and the rich he has sent empty away.
>
> [54] He has helped his servant Israel, in remembrance of his mercy,
>
> [55] as he spoke to our fathers, to Abraham and to his posterity forever."

[56] And Mary remained with her about three months, and returned to her home.

57 Now the time came for Elizabeth to be delivered, and she gave birth to a son. [58] And her neighbors and kinsfolk

---

[e] Or *believed, for there will be.*

1. 42: Lk. 11. 27–28.   **1. 46–55:** 1 Sam. 2. 1–10.   **1. 47:** 1 Tim. 2. 3; Tit. 2. 10; Jude 25.
1. 55: Mic. 7. 20; Gen. 17. 7; 18. 18; 22. 17.

heard that the Lord had shown great mercy to her, and they rejoiced with her. [59] And on the eighth day they came to circumcise the child; and they would have named him Zech-a-ri′ah after his father, [60] but his mother said, "Not so; he shall be called John." [61] And they said to her, "None of your kindred is called by this name." [62] And they made signs to his father, inquiring what he would have him called. [63] And he asked for a writing tablet, and wrote, "His name is John." And they all marveled. [64] And immediately his mouth was opened and his tongue loosed, and he spoke, blessing God. [65] And fear came on all their neighbors. And all these things were talked about through all the hill country of Judea; [66] and all who heard them laid them up in their hearts, saying, "What then will this child be?" For the hand of the Lord was with him.

67 And his father Zech-a-ri′ah was filled with the Holy Spirit, and prophesied, saying,

[68] "Blessed be the Lord God of Israel,
　　for he has visited and redeemed his people,
[69] and has raised up a horn of salvation for us
　　in the house of his servant David,
[70] as he spoke by the mouth of his holy prophets from of old,
[71] that we should be saved from our enemies,
　　and from the hand of all who hate us;
[72] to perform the mercy promised to our fathers,
　　and to remember his holy covenant,
[73] the oath which he swore to our father Abraham,
　　　[74] to grant us
　　that we, being delivered from the hand of our enemies,
　　might serve him without fear,
[75] in holiness and righteousness before him all the days
　　　of our life.

1. 59: Lev. 12. 3; Gen. 17. 12.　　1. 63: Lk. 1. 13.

⁷⁶ And thou, child, shalt be called the prophet of the
    Most High;

    for thou shalt go before the Lord to prepare his ways,
⁷⁷ to give knowledge of salvation to his people
    in the forgiveness of their sins,
⁷⁸ through the tender mercy of our God,
    when the day shall dawn upon^f us from on high
⁷⁹ to give light to those who sit in darkness and in
    the shadow of death,

    to guide our feet into the way of peace."

⁸⁰ And the child grew and became strong in spirit, and he was in the wilderness till the day of his manifestation to Israel.

2 In those days a decree went out from Caesar Augustus that all the world should be enrolled. ² This was the first enrollment, when Qui-rin'i-us was governor of Syria. ³ And all went to be enrolled, each to his own city. ⁴ And Joseph also went up from Galilee, from the city of Nazareth, to Judea, to the city of David, which is called Bethlehem, because he was of the house and lineage of David, ⁵ to be enrolled with Mary, his betrothed, who was with child. ⁶ And while they were there, the time came for her to be delivered. ⁷ And she gave birth to her first-born son and wrapped him in swaddling cloths, and laid him in a manger, because there was no place for them in the inn.

8 And in that region there were shepherds out in the field, keeping watch over their flock by night. ⁹ And an angel of the Lord appeared to them, and the glory of the Lord shone around them, and they were filled with fear. ¹⁰ And the angel said to them, "Be not afraid; for behold, I

---

^f Or *whereby the dayspring will visit.* Many ancient authorities read *since the dayspring has visited.*

1. 76: Lk. 7. 26; Mal. 4. 5.   **1. 77:** Mk. 1. 4.   **1. 78:** Mal. 4. 2; Eph. 5. 14.
1. 79: Is. 9. 2; Mt. 4. 16.   **1. 80:** Lk. 2. 40; 2. 52.
2. 1: Lk. 3. 1.   **2. 4:** Lk. 1. 27.   **2. 9:** Lk. 1. 11; Acts 5. 19.

bring you good news of a great joy which will come to all the people; [11] for to you is born this day in the city of David a Savior, who is Christ the Lord. [12] And this will be a sign for you: you will find a babe wrapped in swaddling cloths and lying in a manger." [13] And suddenly there was with the angel a multitude of the heavenly host praising God and saying,

[14] "Glory to God in the highest,
    and on earth peace among men with whom he is pleased!"*g*

15 When the angels went away from them into heaven, the shepherds said to one another, "Let us go over to Bethlehem and see this thing that has happened, which the Lord has made known to us." [16] And they went with haste, and found Mary and Joseph, and the babe lying in a manger. [17] And when they saw it they made known the saying which had been told them concerning this child; [18] and all who heard it wondered at what the shepherds told them. [19] But Mary kept all these things, pondering them in her heart. [20] And the shepherds returned, glorifying and praising God for all they had heard and seen, as it had been told them.

21 And at the end of eight days, when he was circumcised, he was called Jesus, the name given by the angel before he was conceived in the womb.

22 And when the time came for their purification according to the law of Moses, they brought him up to Jerusalem to present him to the Lord [23] (as it is written in the law of the Lord, "Every male that opens the womb shall be called holy to the Lord") [24] and to offer a sacrifice according to

---

g Some ancient authorities read "*peace, goodwill among men.*"

2. 11: Jn. 4. 42; Acts 5. 31; Mt. 16. 16; Acts 2. 36.   **2. 12:** 1 Sam. 2. 34; 2 Kings 19. 29; Is. 7. 14.   **2. 14:** Lk. 19. 38; 3. 22.   **2. 19:** Lk. 2. 51.   **2. 21:** Lk. 1. 59, 31; Mt. 1. 25.   **2. 22–24:** Lev. 12. 2–8.   **2. 23:** Ex. 13. 2, 12.

what is said in the law of the Lord, "a pair of turtledoves, or two young pigeons." [25] Now there was a man in Jerusalem, whose name was Simeon, and this man was righteous and devout, looking for the consolation of Israel, and the Holy Spirit was upon him. [26] And it had been revealed to him by the Holy Spirit that he should not see death before he had seen the Lord's Christ. [27] And inspired by the Spirit[h] he came into the temple; and when the parents brought in the child Jesus, to do for him according to the custom of the law, [28] he took him up in his arms and blessed God and said,

> [29] "Lord, now lettest thou thy servant depart in peace,
>   according to thy word;
> [30] for mine eyes have seen thy salvation
> [31] which thou hast prepared in the presence of all
>   peoples,
> [32] a light for revelation to the Gentiles,
>   and for glory to thy people Israel."

33 And his father and his mother marveled at what was said about him; [34] and Simeon blessed them and said to Mary his mother,

> "Behold, this child is set for the fall and rising of
>   many in Israel,
> and for a sign that is spoken against
> [35] (and a sword will pierce through your own soul also),
>   that thoughts out of many hearts may be revealed."

36 And there was a prophetess, Anna, the daughter of Phan'u-el, of the tribe of Asher; she was of a great age, having lived with her husband seven years from her virginity, [37] and as a widow till she was eighty-four. She did not depart from the temple, worshiping with fasting and

[h] Or *in the Spirit*.

2. 25: Lk. 2. 38; 23. 51.   **2. 30:** Is. 52. 10; Lk. 3. 6.   **2. 32:** Is. 42. 6; 49. 6; Acts 13. 47; 26. 23.   **2. 36:** Acts 21. 9; Josh. 19. 24; 1 Tim. 5. 9.

prayer night and day. [38] And coming up at that very hour she gave thanks to God, and spoke of him to all who were looking for the redemption of Jerusalem.

39 And when they had performed everything according to the law of the Lord, they returned into Galilee, to their own city, Nazareth. [40] And the child grew and became strong, filled with wisdom; and the favor of God was upon him.

41 Now his parents went to Jerusalem every year at the feast of the Passover. [42] And when he was twelve years old, they went up according to custom; [43] and when the feast was ended, as they were returning, the boy Jesus stayed behind in Jerusalem. His parents did not know it, [44] but supposing him to be in the company they went a day's journey, and they sought him among their kinsfolk and acquaintances; [45] and when they did not find him, they returned to Jerusalem, seeking him. [46] After three days they found him in the temple, sitting among the teachers, listening to them and asking them questions; [47] and all who heard him were amazed at his understanding and his answers. [48] And when they saw him they were astonished; and his mother said to him, "Son, why have you treated us so? Behold, your father and I have been looking for you anxiously." [49] And he said to them, "How is it that you sought me? Did you not know that I must be in my Father's house?" [50] And they did not understand the saying which he spoke to them. [51] And he went down with them and came to Nazareth, and was obedient to them; and his mother kept all these things in her heart.

52 And Jesus increased in wisdom and in stature,[i] and in favor with God and man.

[i] Or *years*.

2. 40: Judg. 13. 24; 1 Sam. 2. 26.   **2. 41:** Deut. 16. 1–8; Ex. 23. 15.   **2. 48:** Mk. 3. 31–35.
2. 51: Lk. 2. 19.   **2. 52:** Lk. 1. 80; 2. 40.

3 In the fifteenth year of the reign of Ti-be′ri-us Caesar, Pontius Pilate being governor of Judea, and Herod being tetrarch of Galilee, and his brother Philip tetrarch of the region of It-u-rae′a and Trach-o-ni′tis, and Ly-sa′ni-as tetrarch of Ab-i-le′ne, ² in the high-priesthood of Annas and Ca′ia-phas, the word of God came to John the son of Zech-a-ri′ah in the wilderness; ³ and he went into all the region about the Jordan, preaching a baptism of repentance for the forgiveness of sin. ⁴ As it is written in the book of the words of Isaiah the prophet,

> "The voice of one crying in the wilderness:
> Prepare the way of the Lord,
> make his paths straight.
> ⁵ Every valley shall be filled,
> and every mountain and hill shall be brought low,
> and the crooked shall be made straight,
> and the rough ways shall be made smooth;
> ⁶ and all flesh shall see the salvation of God."

7 He said therefore to the multitudes that came out to be baptized by him, "You brood of vipers! Who warned you to flee from the wrath to come? ⁸ Bear fruits that befit repentance, and do not begin to say to yourselves, 'We have Abraham as our father'; for I tell you, God is able from these stones to raise up children to Abraham. ⁹ Even now the ax is laid to the root of the trees; every tree therefore that does not bear good fruit is cut down and thrown into the fire."

10 And the multitudes asked him, "What then shall we do?" ¹¹ And he answered them, "He who has two coats, let him share with him who has none; and he who has food, let him do likewise." ¹² Tax collectors also came to be bap-

3. 1: Lk. 23. 1; 9. 7; 13. 31; 23. 7.   3. 2: Jn. 18. 13; Acts 4. 6; Mt. 26. 3; Jn. 11. 49.
3. 3–9: Mt. 3. 1–10; Mk. 1. 1–5; Jn. 1. 6, 23.   3. 4–6: Is. 40. 3–5.   3. 6: Lk. 2. 30.
3. 7: Mt. 12. 34; 23. 33.   3. 8: Jn. 8. 33, 39.   3. 9: Mt. 7. 19; Heb. 6. 7–8.   3. 11: Lk. 6. 29.

tized, and said to him, "Teacher, what shall we do?" [13] And he said to them, "Collect no more than is appointed you." [14] Soldiers also asked him, "And we, what shall we do?" And he said to them, "Rob no one by violence or by false accusation, and be content with your wages."

15 As the people were in expectation, and all men questioned in their hearts concerning John, whether perhaps he were the Christ, [16] John answered them all, "I baptize you with water; but he who is mightier than I is coming, the thong of whose sandals I am not worthy to untie; he will baptize you with the Holy Spirit and with fire. [17] His winnowing fork is in his hand, to clear his threshing floor, and to gather the wheat into his granary, but the chaff he will burn with unquenchable fire."

18 So, with many other exhortations, he preached good news to the people. [19] But Herod the tetrarch, who had been reproved by him for He-ro'di-as, his brother's wife, and for all the evil things that Herod had done, [20] added this to them all, that he shut up John in prison.

21 Now when all the people were baptized, and when Jesus also had been baptized and was praying, the heaven was opened, [22] and the Holy Spirit descended upon him in bodily form, as a dove, and a voice came from heaven, "Thou art my beloved Son;[j] with thee I am well pleased."[k]

23 Jesus, when he began his ministry, was about thirty years of age, being the son (as was supposed) of Joseph, the son of He'li, [24] the son of Matthat, the son of Levi, the son of Mel'chi, the son of Jan'na-i, the son of Joseph, [25] the son of Mat-ta-thi'as, the son of Amos, the son of Na'hum,

---

[j] Or *my Son, my* (or *the*) *Beloved.*   [k] Some ancient authorities read *today have I begotten thee.*

3. 15: Acts 13. 25; Jn. 1. 19–22.   **3. 16–18:** Mt. 3. 11–12; Mk. 1. 7–8; Jn. 1. 26–27, 33; Acts 1. 5; 11. 16; 19. 4.   **3. 19–20:** Mt. 14. 3–4; Mk. 6. 17–18.   **3. 21–22:** Mt. 3. 13–17; Mk. 1. 9–11; Jn. 1. 29–34.   **3. 21:** Lk. 5. 16; 6. 12; 9. 18; 9. 28; 11. 1; Mk. 1. 35.   **3. 22:** Ps. 2. 7; Is. 42. 1; Lk. 9. 35; Acts 10. 38; 2 Pet. 1. 17.   **3. 23–38:** Mt. 1. 1–17; Gen. 5. 3–32; 11. 10–26; Ruth 4. 18–22; 1 Chr. 1. 1–4, 24–28; 2. 1–15. **3. 23:** Jn. 8. 57; Lk. 1. 27.

the son of Es'li, the son of Nag'ga-i, [26] the son of Ma'ath, the son of Mat-ta-thi'as, the son of Sem'e-in, the son of Jo'sech, the son of Joda, [27] the son of Jo-an'an, the son of Rhesa, the son of Ze-rub'ba-bel, the son of She-al'ti-el,[l] the son of Ne'ri, [28] the son of Mel'chi, the son of Addi, the son of Cosam, the son of El-ma'dam, the son of Er, [29] the son of Jesus, the son of E-li-e'zer, the son of Jorim, the son of Matthat, the son of Levi, [30] the son of Symeon, the son of Judas, the son of Joseph, the son of Jonam, the son of E-li'a-kim, [31] the son of Me'le-a, the son of Men'na, the son of Mat'ta-tha, the son of Nathan, the son of David, [32] the son of Jesse, the son of O'bed, the son of Bo'az, the son of Sal'mon,[m] the son of Nah'shon, [33] the son of Am-min'a-dab,[n] the son of Ar'ni,[o] the son of Hez'ron, the son of Pe'rez, the son of Judah, [34] the son of Jacob, the son of Isaac, the son of Abraham, the son of Te'rah, the son of Na'hor, [35] the son of Se'rug, the son of Re'u, the son of Pe'leg, the son of Eber, the son of She'lah, [36] the son of Ca-i'nan, the son of Ar-pha'xad, the son of Shem, the son of Noah, the son of Lamech, [37] the son of Methuselah, the son of Enoch, the son of Ja'red, the son of Ma-ha'la-le-el, the son of Ca-i'nan, [38] the son of Enos, the son of Seth, the son of Adam, the son of God.

4 And Jesus, full of the Holy Spirit, returned from the Jordan, and was led by the Spirit [2] for forty days in the wilderness, tempted by the devil. And he ate nothing in those days; and when they were ended, he was hungry. The devil said to him, "If you are the Son of God, command this stone to become bread." [4] And Jesus answered him, "It is written, 'Man shall not live by bread alone.'"

---

[l] Greek *Salathiel*.   [m] Some ancient authorities read *Sala*.
[n] Many ancient authorities insert *son of Admin* or *son of Aram*.
[o] Some ancient authorities read *Aram*.

4. 1–13: Mt. 4. 1–11; Mk. 1. 12–13.   **4. 2:** Deut. 9. 9; 1 Kings 19. 8.   **4. 4:** Deut. 8. 3.

⁵ And the devil took him up, and showed him all the kingdoms of the world in a moment of time, ⁶ and said to him, "To you I will give all this authority and their glory; for it has been delivered to me, and I give it to whom I will. ⁷ If you, then, will worship me, it shall all be yours." ⁸ And Jesus answered him, "It is written,

> 'You shall worship the Lord your God,
> and him only shall you serve.'"

⁹ And he took him to Jerusalem, and set him on the pinnacle of the temple, and said to him, "If you are the Son of God, throw yourself down from here; ¹⁰ for it is written,

> 'He will give his angels charge of you, to guard you,

¹¹ and

> 'On their hands they will bear you up,
> lest you strike your foot against a stone.'"

¹² And Jesus answered him, "It is said, 'You shall not tempt the Lord your God.'" ¹³ And when the devil had ended every temptation, he departed from him until an opportune time.

14 And Jesus returned in the power of the Spirit into Galilee, and a report concerning him went out through all the surrounding country. ¹⁵ And he taught in their synagogues, being glorified by all.

16 And he came to Nazareth, where he had been brought up; and he went to the synagogue, as his custom was, on the sabbath day. And he stood up to read; ¹⁷ and there was given to him the book of the prophet Isaiah. He opened the book, and found the place where it was written,

> ¹⁸ "The Spirit of the Lord is upon me,
>
> because he has anointed me to preach good news to the poor.

4. 6: 1 Jn. 5. 19.   **4. 8:** Deut. 6. 13.   **4. 10–11:** Ps. 91. 11–12.   **4. 12:** Deut. 6. 16.
4. 13: Lk. 22. 28.   **4. 14:** Mt. 4. 12; Mk. 1. 14; Mt. 9. 26; Lk. 4. 37.
4. 15: Mt. 4. 23; 9. 35; 11. 1.   **4. 16–30:** Mt. 13. 53–58; Mk. 6. 1–6; Acts 13. 14–16.
4. 18–19: Is. 61. 1–2.

He has sent me to proclaim release to the captives
and recovering of sight to the blind,
to set at liberty those who are oppressed,
[19] to proclaim the acceptable year of the Lord."

[20] And he closed the book, and gave it back to the attendant, and sat down; and the eyes of all in the synagogue were fixed on him. [21] And he began to say to them, "Today this scripture has been fulfilled in your hearing." [22] And all spoke well of him, and wondered at the gracious words which proceeded out of his mouth; and they said, "Is not this Joseph's son?" [23] And he said to them, "Doubtless you will quote to me this proverb, 'Physician, heal yourself; what we have heard you did at Ca-per'na-um, do here also in your own country.'" [24] And he said, "Truly, I say to you, no prophet is acceptable in his own country. [25] But in truth, I tell you, there were many widows in Israel in the days of Elijah, when the heaven was shut up three years and six months, when there came a great famine over all the land; [26] and Elijah was sent to none of them but only to Zar'e-phath, in the land of Sidon, to a woman who was a widow. [27] And there were many lepers in Israel in the time of the prophet Elisha; and none of them was cleansed, but only Na'a-man the Syrian." [28] When they heard this, all in the synagogue were filled with wrath. [29] And they rose up and put him out of the city, and led him to the brow of the hill on which their city was built, that they might throw him down headlong. [30] But passing through the midst of them he went away.

31 And he went down to Ca-per'na-um, a city of Galilee. And he was teaching them on the sabbath; [32] and they were astonished at his teaching, for his word was with authority.

4. 22: Jn. 6. 42; 7. 15.   **4. 23:** Mk. 1. 21, 2. 1; Jn. 4. 46.   **4. 24:** Jn. 4. 44.
4. 25: 1 Kings 17. 1, 8–16; 18. 1; Jas. 5. 17–18.   **4. 27:** 2 Kings 5. 1–14.   **4. 29:** Acts
7. 58; Num. 15. 35.   **4. 30:** Jn. 8. 59; 10. 39.   **4. 31–37:** Mk. 1. 21–28.
4. 32: Mt. 7. 28; 13. 54; 22. 33; Mk. 11. 18; Jn. 7. 46.

[33] And in the synagogue there was a man who had the spirit of an unclean demon; and he cried out with a loud voice, [34] "Ah!*p* What have you to do with us, Jesus of Nazareth? Have you come to destroy us? I know who you are, the Holy One of God." [35] But Jesus rebuked him, saying, "Be silent, and come out of him!" And when the demon had thrown him down in the midst, he came out of him, having done him no harm. [36] And they were all amazed and said to one another, "What is this word? For with authority and power he commands the unclean spirits, and they come out." [37] And reports of him went out into every place in the surrounding region.

38 And he arose and left the synagogue, and entered Simon's house. Now Simon's mother-in-law was ill with a high fever, and they besought him for her. [39] And he stood over her and rebuked the fever, and it left her; and immediately she rose and served them.

40 Now when the sun was setting, all those who had any that were sick with various diseases brought them to him; and he laid his hands on every one of them and healed them. [41] And demons also came out of many, crying, "You are the Son of God!" But he rebuked them, and would not allow them to speak, because they knew that he was the Christ.

42 And when it was day he departed and went into a lonely place. And the people sought him and came to him, and would have kept him from leaving them; [43] but he said to them, "I must preach the good news of the kingdom of God to the other cities also; for I was sent for this purpose." [44] And he was preaching in the synagogues of Judea.*q*

p Or *Let us alone.*
q Some ancient authorities read *Galilee.*

4. 37: Lk. 4. 14; 5. 15; Mt. 9. 26.   **4. 38–41**: Mt. 8. 14–17; Mk. 1. 29–34.
4. 42–43: Mk. 1. 35–38.   **4. 44**: Mt. 4. 23; Mk. 1. 39; Mt. 9. 35.

5 While the people pressed upon him to hear the word of God, he was standing by the lake of Gen-nes'a-ret. ² And he saw two boats by the lake; but the fishermen had gone out of them and were washing their nets. ³ Getting into one of the boats, which was Simon's, he asked him to put out a little from the land. And he sat down and taught the people from the boat. ⁴ And when he had ceased speaking, he said to Simon, "Put out into the deep and let down your nets for a catch." ⁵ And Simon answered, "Master, we toiled all night and took nothing! But at your word I will let down the nets." ⁶ And when they had done this, they enclosed a great shoal of fish; and as their nets were breaking, ⁷ they beckoned to their partners in the other boat to come and help them. And they came and filled both the boats, so that they began to sink. ⁸ But when Simon Peter saw it, he fell down at Jesus' knees, saying, "Depart from me, for I am a sinful man, O Lord." ⁹ For he was astonished, and all that were with him, at the catch of fish which they had taken; ¹⁰ and so also were James and John, sons of Zeb'e-dee, who were partners with Simon. And Jesus said to Simon, "Do not be afraid; henceforth you will be catching men." ¹¹ And when they had brought their boats to land, they left everything and followed him.

12 While he was in one of the cities, there came a man full of leprosy; and when he saw Jesus, he fell on his face and besought him, "Lord, if you will, you can make me clean." ¹³ And he stretched out his hand, and touched him, saying, "I will; be clean." And immediately the leprosy left him. ¹⁴ And he charged him to tell no one; but "go and show yourself to the priest, and make an offering for your cleansing, as Moses commanded, for a proof to the people."ʳ

ʳ Greek *to them.*

5. 1–11: Mt. 4. 18–22; Mk. 1. 16–20; Jn. 1. 40–42; 21. 1–19.　　　**5. 3:** Mt. 13. 1–2;
Mk. 4. 1.　　**5. 5:** Lk. 8. 24, 45; 9. 33, 49; 17. 13.　　**5. 12–16:** Mt. 8. 1–4; Mk. 1. 40–45;
Lk. 17. 11–19.　　**5. 14:** Lev. 13. 49; 14. 2–32.

[15] But so much the more the report went abroad concerning him; and great multitudes gathered to hear and to be healed of their infirmities. [16] But he withdrew to the wilderness and prayed.

17 On one of those days, as he was teaching, there were Pharisees and teachers of the law sitting by, who had come from every town of Galilee and Judea and from Jerusalem; and the power of the Lord was with him to heal.[s] [18] And behold, men were bringing on a bed a man who was paralyzed, and they sought to bring him in and lay him before Jesus;[t] [19] but finding no way to bring him in, because of the crowd, they went up on the roof and let him down with his bed through the tiles into the midst before Jesus. [20] And when he saw their faith he said, "Man, your sins are forgiven you." [21] And the scribes and the Pharisees began to question, saying, "Who is this that speaks blasphemies? Who can forgive sins but God only?" [22] When Jesus perceived their questionings, he answered them, "Why do you question in your hearts? [23] Which is easier, to say, 'Your sins are forgiven you,' or to say, 'Rise and walk'? [24] But that you may know that the Son of man has authority on earth to forgive sins" — he said to the man who was paralyzed — "I say to you, rise, take up your bed and go home." [25] And immediately he rose before them, and took up that on which he lay, and went home, glorifying God. [26] And amazement seized them all, and they glorified God and were filled with awe, saying, "We have seen strange things today."

27 After this he went out, and saw a tax collector, named Levi, sitting at the tax office; and he said to him, "Follow me." [28] And he left everything, and rose and followed him.

29 And Levi made him a great feast in his house; and

[s] Some ancient authorities read *was present to heal them.*   [t] Greek *him.*
5. 15: Lk. 4. 14, 37; Mt. 9. 26.   **5. 16:** Lk. 3. 21; 6. 12; 9. 18, 28; 11. 1.
5. 17–26: Mt. 9. 1–8; Mk. 2. 1–12; Jn. 5. 1–9.   **5. 17:** Mt. 15. 1; Mk. 5. 30;
Lk. 6. 19.   **5. 20:** Lk. 7. 48–49.   **5. 27–32:** Mt. 9. 9–13; Mk. 2. 13–17.

there was a large company of tax collectors and others sitting at table[u] with them. [30] And the Pharisees and their scribes murmured against his disciples, saying, "Why do you eat and drink with tax collectors and sinners?" [31] And Jesus answered them, "Those who are well have no need of a physician, but those who are sick; [32] I have not come to call the righteous, but sinners to repentance."

[33] And they said to him, "The disciples of John fast often and offer prayers, and so do the disciples of the Pharisees, but yours eat and drink." [34] And Jesus said to them, "Can you make wedding guests fast while the bridegroom is with them? [35] The days will come, when the bridegroom is taken away from them, and then they will fast in those days." [36] He told them a parable also: "No one tears a piece from a new garment and puts it upon an old garment; if he does, he will tear the new, and the piece from the new will not match the old. [37] And no one puts new wine into old wineskins; if he does, the new wine will burst the skins and it will be spilled, and the skins will be destroyed. [38] But new wine must be put into fresh wineskins. [39] And no one after drinking old wine desires new; for he says, 'The old is good.' "[v]

6 On a sabbath,[w] while he was going through the grainfields, his disciples plucked and ate some ears of grain, rubbing them in their hands. [2] But some of the Pharisees said, "Why are you doing what is not lawful to do on the sabbath?" [3] And Jesus answered, "Have you not read what David did when he was hungry, he and those who were with him: [4] how he entered the house of God, and took and

---

[u] Greek *reclining.*   [v] Many ancient authorities read *better.*
[w] Many ancient authorities read *On the second first sabbath* (on the second sabbath after the first).

5. 30: Lk. 15. 1–2.   **5. 32:** 1 Tim. 1. 15.   **5. 33–38:** Mt. 9. 14–17; Mk. 2. 18–22.
5. 33: Lk. 7. 18; 11. 1; Jn. 3. 25–26.   **5. 35:** Lk. 9. 22; 17. 22.
6. 1–5: Mt. 12. 1–8; Mk. 2. 23–28.   **6. 1:** Deut. 23. 25.   **6. 2:** Ex. 20. 10; 23. 12;
Deut. 5. 14.   **6. 3:** 1 Sam. 21. 1–6.   **6. 4:** Lev. 24. 9.

ate the bread of the Presence, which it is not lawful for any but the priests to eat, and also gave it to those with him?" [5] And he said to them, "The Son of man is lord of the sabbath."

6 On another sabbath, when he entered the synagogue and taught, a man was there whose right hand was withered. [7] And the scribes and the Pharisees watched him, to see whether he would heal on the sabbath, so that they might find an accusation against him. [8] But he knew their thoughts, and he said to the man who had the withered hand, "Come and stand here." And he rose and stood there. [9] And Jesus said to them, "I ask you, is it lawful on the sabbath to do good or to do harm, to save life or to destroy it?" [10] And he looked around on them all, and said to him, "Stretch out your hand." And he did so, and his hand was restored. [11] But they were filled with fury and discussed with one another what they might do to Jesus.

12 In these days he went out into the hills to pray; and all night he continued in prayer to God. [13] And when it was day, he called his disciples, and chose from them twelve, whom he named apostles; [14] Simon, whom he named Peter, and Andrew his brother, and James and John, and Philip, and Bartholomew, [15] and Matthew, and Thomas, and James the son of Alphaeus, and Simon who was called the Zealot, [16] and Judas the son[x] of James, and Judas Iscariot, who became a traitor.

17 And he came down with them and stood on a level place, with a great crowd of his disciples and a great multitude of people from all Judea and Jerusalem and the seacoast of Tyre and Sidon, who came to hear him and to be healed of their diseases; [18] and those who were troubled

---

[x] Or *brother*.

6. **6–11:** Mt. 12. 9–14; Mk. 3. 1–6.   6. **12–16:** Mk. 3. 13–19; Mt. 10. 2–4; Acts 1. 13.
6. **12:** Lk. 3. 21; 5. 16; 9. 18, 28; 11. 1.   6. **17–19:** Mt. 5. 1–2; 4. 24–25; Mk. 3. 7–12.

with unclean spirits were cured. ¹⁹ And all the crowd sought to touch him, for power came forth from him and healed them all.

20 And he lifted up his eyes on his disciples, and said:

"Blessed are you poor, for yours is the kingdom of God.

21 "Blessed are you that hunger now, for you shall be satisfied.

"Blessed are you that weep now, for you shall laugh.

22 "Blessed are you when men hate you, and when they exclude you and revile you, and cast out your name as evil, on account of the Son of man! ²³ Rejoice in that day, and leap for joy, for behold, your reward is great in heaven; for so their fathers did to the prophets.

24 "But woe to you that are rich, for you have received your consolation.

25 "Woe to you that are full now, for you shall hunger.

"Woe to you that laugh now, for you shall mourn and weep.

26 "Woe to you, when all men speak well of you, for so their fathers did to the false prophets.

27 "But I say to you that hear, Love your enemies, do good to those who hate you, ²⁸ bless those who curse you, pray for those who abuse you. ²⁹ To him who strikes you on the cheek, offer the other also; and from him who takes away your cloak do not withhold your coat as well. ³⁰ Give to every one who begs from you; and of him who takes away your goods, do not ask them again. ³¹ And as you wish that men would do to you, do so to them.

32 "If you love those who love you, what credit is that to you? For even sinners love those who love them. ³³ And if you do good to those who do good to you, what credit is

6. 19: Mk. 3. 10; Mt. 9. 21; 14. 36; Lk. 5. 17.   6. 20–23: Mt. 5. 3–12.
6. 22: 1 Pet. 4. 14; Jn. 9. 22; 16. 2.   6. 24–26: Lk. 10. 13–15; 11. 38–52; 17. 1; 21. 23;
22. 22.   6. 24: Lk. 16. 25; Jas. 5. 1–5; Mt. 6. 2.   6. 27–30: Mt. 5. 39–44;
Rom. 12. 17; 1 Cor. 6. 7.   6. 31: Mt. 7. 12.   6. 32–36: Mt. 5. 44–48.

that to you? For even sinners do the same. [34] And if you lend
to those from whom you hope to receive, what credit is that
to you? Even sinners lend to sinners, to receive as much
again. [35] But love your enemies, and do good, and lend,
expecting nothing in return;[y] and your reward will be great,
and you will be sons of the Most High; for he is kind to the
ungrateful and the selfish. [36] Be merciful, even as your Father
is merciful.

37 "Judge not, and you will not be judged; condemn
not, and you will not be condemned; forgive, and you will
be forgiven; [38] give, and it will be given to you; good measure,
pressed down, shaken together, running over, will be put
into your lap. For the measure you give will be the measure
you get back."

39 He also told them a parable: "Can a blind man lead
a blind man? Will they not both fall into a pit? [40] A disciple
is not above his teacher, but every one when he is fully taught
will be like his teacher. [41] Why do you see the speck that
is in your brother's eye, but do not notice the log that is
in your own eye? [42] Or how can you say to your brother,
'Brother, let me take out the speck that is in your eye,'
when you yourself do not see the log that is in your own
eye? You hypocrite, first take the log out of your own eye,
and then you will see clearly to take out the speck that is
in your brother's eye.

43 "For no good tree bears bad fruit, nor again does a
bad tree bear good fruit; [44] for each tree is known by its
own fruit. For figs are not gathered from thorns, nor are
grapes picked from a bramble bush. [45] The good man out
of the good treasure of his heart produces good, and the

[y] Some ancient authorities read *despairing of no man*.

6. 35: Mt. 5. 9.   6. 37–38: Mt. 7. 1–2; Rom. 2. 1.   6. 38: Mk. 4. 24; Acts 20. 35.
6. 39: Mt. 15. 14.   6. 40: Mt. 10. 24–25; Jn. 13. 16; 15. 20.   6. 41–42: Mt. 7. 3–5.
6. 43–45: Mt. 7. 18–19; 12. 33–35; Jas. 3. 11–12.   6. 45: Mk. 7. 20.

evil man out of his evil treasure produces evil; for out of the abundance of the heart his mouth speaks.

46 "Why do you call me Lord and not do what I tell you? [47] Every one who comes to me and hears my words and does them, I will show you what he is like: [48] he is like a man building a house, who dug deep, and laid the foundation upon rock; and when a flood arose, the stream broke against that house, and could not shake it, because it had been well built.[z] [49] But he who hears and does not do them is like a man who built a house on the ground without a foundation; against which the stream broke, and immediately it fell, and the ruin of that house was great."

7 After he had ended all his sayings in the hearing of the people he entered Ca-per'na-um. [2] Now a centurion had a slave who was dear[a] to him, who was sick and at the point of death. [3] When he heard of Jesus, he sent to him elders of the Jews, asking him to come and heal his slave. [4] And when they came to Jesus, they besought him earnestly, saying, "He is worthy to have you do this for him, [5] for he loves our nation, and he built us our synagogue." [6] And Jesus went with them. When he was not far from the house, the centurion sent friends to him, saying to him, "Lord, do not trouble yourself, for I am not worthy to have you come under my roof; [7] therefore I did not presume to come to you. But say the word, and let my servant be healed. [8] For I am a man set under authority, with soldiers under me: and I say to one, 'Go,' and he goes; and to another, 'Come,' and he comes; and to my slave, 'Do this,' and he does it." [9] When Jesus heard this he marveled at him, and turned and said to the multitude that followed him, "I tell you, not even in

[z] Some ancient authorities read *founded upon the rock.*
[a] Or *valuable.*

6. 46: Mt. 7. 21. **6. 47–49:** Mt. 7. 24–27; Jas. 1. 22–25.
7. 1–10: Mt. 8. 5–10, 13; Jn. 4. 46–53. **7. 5:** Acts 10. 2.

Israel have I found such faith." [10] And when those who had been sent returned to the house, they found the slave well.

11 Soon afterward[b] he went to a city called Na'in, and his disciples and a great crowd went with him. [12] As he drew near to the gate of the city, behold, a man who had died was being carried out, the only son of his mother, and she was a widow; and a large crowd from the city was with her. [13] And when the Lord saw her, he had compassion on her and said to her, "Do not weep." [14] And he came and touched the bier, and the bearers stood still. And he said, "Young man, I say to you, arise." [15] And the dead man sat up, and began to speak. And he gave him to his mother. [16] Fear seized them all; and they glorified God, saying, "A great prophet has arisen among us!" and "God has visited his people!" [17] And this report concerning him spread through the whole of Judea and all the surrounding country.

18 The disciples of John told him of all these things. [19] And John, calling to him two of his disciples, sent them to the Lord, saying, "Are you he who is to come, or shall we look for another?" [20] And when the men had come to him, they said, "John the Baptist has sent us to you, saying, 'Are you he who is to come, or shall we look for another?'" [21] In that hour he cured many of diseases and plagues and evil spirits, and on many that were blind he bestowed sight. [22] And he answered them, "Go and tell John what you have seen and heard: the blind receive their sight, the lame walk, lepers are cleansed, and the deaf hear, the dead are raised up, the poor have good news preached to them. [23] And blessed is he who takes no offence at me!"

24 When the messengers of John had gone, he began to

[b] Many ancient authorities read *Next day.*

7. 11–17: Mk. 5. 21–24, 35–43; Jn. 11. 1–44; 1 Kings 17. 17–24; 2 Kings 4. 32–37. 7. 13: Lk. 7. 19; 10. 1; 11. 39; 12. 42; 13. 15; 17. 5–6; 18. 6; 19. 8; 22. 61; 24. 3. 7. 16: Lk. 7. 39; 24. 19; Mt. 21. 11; Jn. 6. 14. 7. 18–35: Mt. 11. 2–19. 7. 21: Mt. 4. 23; Mk. 3. 10. 7. 22: Is. 29. 18–19; 35. 5–6; 61. 1; Lk. 4. 18–19.

speak to the crowds concerning John: "What did you go out into the wilderness to behold? A reed shaken by the wind? [25] What then did you go out to see? A man clothed in soft raiment? Behold, those who are gorgeously appareled and live in luxury are in kings' courts. [26] What then did you go out to see? A prophet? Yes, I tell you, and more than a prophet. [27] This is he of whom it is written,

'Behold, I send my messenger before thy face,
who shall prepare thy way before thee.'

[28] I tell you, among those born of women none is greater than John; yet he who is least in the kingdom of God is greater than he." [29] (When they heard this all the people and the tax collectors justified God, having been baptized with the baptism of John; [30] but the Pharisees and the lawyers rejected the purpose of God for themselves, not having been baptized by him.)

31 "To what then shall I compare the men of this generation, and what are they like? [32] They are like children sitting in the market place and calling to one another,

'We piped to you, and you did not dance;
we wailed, and you did not weep.'

[33] For John the Baptist has come eating no bread and drinking no wine; and you say, 'He has a demon.' [34] The Son of man has come eating and drinking; and you say, 'Behold, a glutton and a drunkard, a friend of tax collectors and sinners!' [35] Yet wisdom is justified by all her children."

36 One of the Pharisees asked him to eat with him, and he went into the Pharisee's house, and sat at table. [37] And behold, a woman of the city, who was a sinner, when she learned that he was sitting at table in the Pharisee's house, brought an alabaster flask of ointment, [38] and standing be-

7. 27: Mal. 3. 1; Mk. 1. 2.   **7. 29–30:** Mt. 21. 32; Lk. 3. 12.   **7. 33:** Lk. 1. 15.
7. 34: Lk. 5. 29; 15. 1–2; 7. 36–50.   **7. 36–50:** Mt. 26. 6–13; Mk. 14. 3–9; Jn. 12. 1–8.
7. 36: Lk. 11. 37; 14. 1.

hind him at his feet, weeping, she began to wet his feet with her tears, and wiped them with the hair of her head, and kissed his feet, and anointed them with the ointment. [39] Now when the Pharisee who had invited him saw it, he said to himself, "If this man were a prophet, he would have known who and what sort of woman this is who is touching him, for she is a sinner." [40] And Jesus answering said to him, "Simon, I have something to say to you." And he answered, "What is it, Teacher?" [41] "A certain creditor had two debtors; one owed five hundred denarii, and the other fifty. [42] When they could not pay, he forgave them both. Now which of them will love him more?" [43] Simon answered, "The one, I suppose, to whom he forgave more." And he said to him, "You have judged rightly." [44] Then turning toward the woman he said to Simon, "Do you see this woman? I entered your house, you gave me no water for my feet, but she has wet my feet with her tears and wiped them with her hair. [45] You gave me no kiss, but from the time I came in she has not ceased to kiss my feet. [46] You did not anoint my head with oil, but she has anointed my feet with ointment. [47] Therefore I tell you, her sins, which are many, are forgiven, for she loved much; but he who is forgiven little, loves little." [48] And he said to her, "Your sins are forgiven." [49] Then those who were at table with him began to say among themselves, "Who is this, who even forgives sins?" [50] And he said to the woman, "Your faith has saved you; go in peace."

8 Soon afterward he went on through cities and villages, preaching and bringing the good news of the kingdom of God. And the twelve were with him, [2] and also some women who had been healed of evil spirits and infirmities:

7. 39: Lk. 7. 16; 24. 19; Mt. 21. 11; Jn. 6. 14.   **7. 42**: Mt. 18. 25.   **7. 43**: Lk. 10. 28.
7. 48: Mt. 9. 2; Mk. 2. 5; Lk. 5. 20.   **7. 50**: Mt. 9. 22; Mk. 5. 34; Lk. 8. 48.
8. 1-3: Lk. 4. 15; Mk. 15. 40–41; Mt. 27. 55–56; Lk. 23. 49.

Mary, called Mag'da-lene, from whom seven demons had gone out, [3] and Jo-an'na, the wife of Chu'za, Herod's steward, and Susanna, and many others, who provided for them[c] out of their means.

4 And when a great crowd came together and people from town after town came to him, he said in a parable: [5] "A sower went out to sow his seed; and as he sowed, some fell along the path, and was trodden under foot, and the birds of the air devoured it. [6] And some fell on the rock; and as it grew up, it withered away, because it had no moisture. [7] And some fell among thorns; and the thorns grew with it and choked it. [8] And some fell into good soil and grew, and yielded a hundredfold." As he said this, he called out, "He who has ears to hear, let him hear."

9 And when his disciples asked him what this parable meant, [10] he said, "To you it has been given to know the secrets of the kingdom of God; but for others they are in parables, so that seeing they may not see, and hearing they may not understand. [11] Now the parable is this: The seed is the word of God. [12] The ones along the path are those who have heard; then the devil comes and takes away the word from their hearts, that they may not believe and be saved. [13] And the ones on the rock are those who, when they hear the word, receive it with joy; but these have no root, they believe for a while and in time of temptation fall away. [14] And as for what fell among the thorns, they are those who hear, but as they go on their way they are choked by the cares and riches and pleasures of life, and their fruit does not mature. [15] And as for that in the good soil, they are those who, hearing the word, hold it fast in an honest and good heart, and bring forth fruit with patience.

[c] Some ancient authorities read *him.*

8. 4–8: Mt. 13. 1–9; Mk. 4. 1–9.   **8. 8:** Mt. 11. 15.   **8. 9–10:** Mt. 13. 10–13; Mk. 4. 10–12; Is. 6. 9–10; Jer. 5. 21; Ezek. 12. 2.   **8. 11–15:** Mt. 13. 18–23; Mk. 4. 13–20. **8. 11:** 1 Thess. 2. 13; 1 Pet. 1. 23.

16 "No one after lighting a lamp covers it with a vessel, or puts it under a bed, but puts it on a stand, that those who enter may see the light. ¹⁷ For nothing is hid that shall not be made manifest, nor anything secret that shall not be known and come to light. ¹⁸ Take heed then how you hear; for to him who has will more be given, and from him who has not, even what he thinks that he has will be taken away."

19 Then his mother and his brothers came to him, but they could not reach him for the crowd. ²⁰ And he was told, "Your mother and your brothers are standing outside, desiring to see you." ²¹ But he said to them, "My mother and my brothers are those who hear the word of God and do it."

22 One day he got into a boat with his disciples, and he said to them, "Let us go across to the other side of the lake." So they set out, ²³ and as they sailed he fell asleep. And a storm of wind came down on the lake, and they were filling with water, and were in danger. ²⁴ And they went and woke him, saying, "Master, Master, we are perishing!" And he awoke and rebuked the wind and the raging waves; and they ceased, and there was a calm. ²⁵ He said to them, "Where is your faith?" And they were afraid, and they wondered, saying to one another, "Who then is this, that he commands even wind and water, and they obey him?"

26 Then they arrived at the country of the Ger′a-senes,^d which is opposite Galilee. ²⁷ And as he stepped out on land, there met him a man from the city who had demons; for a long time he had worn no clothes, and he lived not in a house but in the tombs. ²⁸ When he saw Jesus, he cried out and fell down before him, and said with a loud voice, "What have you to do with me, Jesus, Son of the Most High God?

---

^d Some ancient authorities read *Gadarenes*, some *Gergesenes*.

8. 16: Mk. 4. 21; Mt. 5. 15; Lk. 11. 33.   **8. 17:** Mk. 4. 22–23; Mt. 10. 26–27; Lk. 12. 2–3; Eph. 5. 13.   **8. 18:** Mk. 4. 24–25; Mt. 13. 12; 25. 29; Lk. 19. 26.   **8. 19–21:** Mt. 12. 46–50; Mk. 3. 31–35.   **8. 21:** Lk. 11. 28; Jn. 15. 14.   **8. 22–25:** Mt. 8. 23–27; Mk. 4. 35–41; 6. 47–52; Jn. 6. 16–21.   **8. 24:** Lk. 5. 5; 8. 45; 9. 33, 49; 17. 13.   **8. 26–39:** Mt. 8. 28–34; Mk. 5. 1–20.   **8. 28:** Mk. 1. 24; Jn. 2. 4.

I beseech you, do not torment me." ²⁹ For he had commanded the unclean spirit to come out of the man. (For many a time it had seized him; he was kept under guard, and bound with chains and fetters, but he broke the bonds and was driven by the demon into the desert.) ³⁰ Jesus then asked him, "What is your name?" And he said, "Legion"; for many demons had entered him. ³¹ And they begged him not to command them to depart into the abyss. ³² Now a large herd of swine was feeding there on the hillside; and they begged him to let them enter these. And he allowed them. ³³ Then the demons came out of the man and entered the swine, and the herd rushed down the steep bank into the lake and were drowned.

34 When the herdsmen saw what had happened, they fled, and told it in the city and in the country. ³⁵ Then people went out to see what had happened, and they came to Jesus, and found the man from whom the demons had gone, sitting at the feet of Jesus, clothed and in his right mind; and they were afraid. ³⁶ And those who had seen it told them how he who had been possessed with demons was healed. ³⁷ Then all the people of the surrounding country of the Ger′a-senes*ᵉ* asked him to depart from them; for they were seized with great fear; so he got into the boat and returned. ³⁸ The man from whom the demons had gone begged that he might be with him; but he sent him away, saying, ³⁹ "Return to your home, and declare how much God has done for you." And he went away, proclaiming throughout the whole city how much Jesus had done for him.

40 Now when Jesus returned, the crowd welcomed him, for they were all waiting for him. ⁴¹ And there came a man named Ja′i-rus, who was a ruler of the synagogue; and fall-

---

*ᵉ Some ancient authorities read *Gadarenes*, some *Gergesenes*.*

8. 40–56: Mt. 9. 18–26; Mk. 5. 21–43.

ing at Jesus' feet he besought him to come to his house, [42] for he had an only daughter, about twelve years of age, and she was dying.

As he went, the people pressed round him. [43] And a woman who had suffered from a flow of blood for twelve years[f] and could not be healed by any one, [44] came up behind him, and touched the fringe of his garment; and immediately her flow of blood ceased. [45] And Jesus said, "Who was it that touched me?" When all denied it, Peter and those who were with him[g] said, "Master, the multitudes surround you and press upon you!" [46] But Jesus said, "Some one touched me; for I perceive that power has gone forth from me." [47] And when the woman saw that she was not hidden, she came trembling, and falling down before him declared in the presence of all the people why she had touched him, and how she had been immediately healed. [48] And he said to her, "Daughter, your faith has made you well; go in peace."

49 While he was still speaking, a man from the ruler's house came and said, "Your daughter is dead; do not trouble the Teacher any more." [50] But Jesus on hearing this answered him, "Do not fear; only believe, and she shall be well." [51] And when he came to the house, he permitted no one to enter with him, except Peter and John and James, and the father and mother of the maiden. [52] And all were weeping and bewailing her; but he said, "Do not weep; for she is not dead but sleeping." [53] And they laughed at him, knowing that she was dead. [54] But taking her by the hand he called, saying, "Child, arise." [55] And her spirit returned, and she got up at once; and he directed that something should be given her to eat. [56] And her parents were amazed; but he charged them to tell no one what had happened.

[f] Some ancient authorities add *and had spent all her living upon physicians.*   [g] Some ancient authorities omit *and those who were with him.*
8. 45: Lk. 8. 24.   **8. 46:** Lk. 5. 17; 6. 19.   **8. 48:** Mt. 9. 22; Lk. 7. 50; 17. 19; 18. 42.
8. 56: Mt. 8. 4; Mk. 3. 12; 7. 36; Lk. 9. 21.

9 And he called the twelve together and gave them power and authority over all demons and to cure diseases, [2] and he sent them out to preach the kingdom of God and to heal. [3] And he said to them, "Take nothing for your journey, no staff, nor bag, nor bread, nor money; and do not have two tunics. [4] And whatever house you enter, stay there, and from there depart. [5] And wherever they do not receive you, when you leave that city shake off the dust from your feet as a testimony against them." [6] And they departed and went through the villages, preaching the gospel and healing everywhere.

7 Now Herod the tetrarch heard of all that was done, and he was perplexed, because it was said by some that John had been raised from the dead, [8] by some that Elijah had appeared, and by others that one of the old prophets had risen. [9] Herod said, "John I beheaded; but who is this about whom I hear such things?" And he sought to see him.

10 On their return the apostles told him what they had done. And he took them and withdrew apart to a city called Beth-sa'i-da. [11] When the crowds learned it, they followed him; and he welcomed them and spoke to them of the kingdom of God, and cured those who had need of healing. [12] Now the day began to wear away; and the twelve came and said to him, "Send the crowd away, to go into the villages and country round about, to lodge and get provisions; for we are here in a lonely place." [13] But he said to them, "You give them something to eat." They said, "We have no more than five loaves and two fish — unless we are to go and buy food for all these people." [14] For there were about five thousand men. And he said to his disciples, "Make them sit down in companies, about fifty each." [15] And they did so,

9. 1–6: Mt. 10. 1, 5, 7–11, 14; Mk. 6. 7–12; Lk. 10. 4–11.   **9. 5:** Acts 13. 51.   **9. 7–9:** Mt. 14. 1–2; Mk. 6. 14–16; Lk. 9. 19.   **9. 9:** Lk. 23. 8.   **9. 10:** Mk. 6. 30–31; Lk. 10. 17; Jn. 1. 44.   **9. 11–17:** Mt. 14. 13–21; Mk. 6. 32–44; Jn. 6. 1–14; Mk. 8. 4–10.   **9. 13:** 2 Kings 4. 42–44.

and made them all sit down. [16] And taking the five loaves and the two fish he looked up to heaven, and blessed and broke them, and gave them to the disciples to set before the crowd. [17] And all ate and were satisfied. And they took up what was left over, twelve baskets of broken pieces.

18 Now it happened that as he was praying alone the disciples were with him; and he asked them, "Who do the people say that I am?" [19] And they answered, "John the Baptist; but others say, Elijah; and others, that one of the old prophets has risen." [20] And he said to them, "But who do you say that I am?" And Peter answered, "The Christ of God." [21] But he charged and commanded them to tell this to no one, [22] saying, "The Son of man must suffer many things, and be rejected by the elders and chief priests and scribes, and be killed, and on the third day be raised."

23 And he said to all, "If any man would come after me, let him deny himself and take up his cross daily and follow me. [24] For whoever would save his life will lose it; but whoever loses his life for my sake, he will save it. [25] For what does it profit a man if he gains the whole world and loses or forfeits himself? [26] For whoever is ashamed of me and of my words, of him will the Son of man be ashamed when he comes in his glory and the glory of the Father and of the holy angels. [27] But I tell you truly, there are some standing here who will not taste of death before they see the kingdom of God."

28 Now about eight days after these sayings he took with him Peter and John and James, and went up on the mountain to pray. [29] And as he was praying, the appearance of

9. 16: Lk. 22. 19; 24. 30–31; Acts 2. 42; 20. 11; 27. 35.   **9. 18–21:** Mt. 16. 13–20; Mk. 8. 27–30; Jn. 1. 49; 11. 27; 6. 66–69.   **9. 18:** Lk. 3. 21; 5. 16; 6. 12; 9. 28; 11. 1. **9. 19:** Lk. 9. 9; Mk. 9. 11–13.   **9. 22:** Mt. 16. 21; Mk. 8. 31; Lk. 9. 43–45; 18. 31–34; 17. 25.   **9. 23–27:** Mt. 16. 24–28; Mk. 8. 34–9. 1.   **9. 24–25:** Mt. 10. 38–39; Lk. 14. 27; 17. 33; Jn. 12. 25.   **9. 26:** Mt. 10. 33; Lk. 12. 9; 1 Jn. 2. 28. **9. 27:** Lk. 22. 18; Mt. 10. 23; 1 Thess. 4. 15–18; Jn. 21. 22.   **9. 28–36:** Mt. 17. 1–8; Mk. 9. 2–8; 2 Pet. 1. 17–18.   **9. 28:** Lk. 8. 51; 3. 21; 5. 16; 6. 12; 9. 18; 11. 1.

his countenance was altered, and his raiment became dazzling white. [30] And behold, two men talked with him, Moses and Elijah, [31] who appeared in glory and spoke of his departure, which he was to accomplish at Jerusalem. [32] Now Peter and those who were with him were heavy with sleep but kept awake, and they saw his glory and the two men who stood with him. [33] And as the men were parting from him, Peter said to Jesus, "Master, it is well that we are here; let us make three booths, one for you and one for Moses and one for Elijah" — not knowing what he said. [34] As he said this, a cloud came and overshadowed them; and they were afraid as they entered the cloud. [35] And a voice came out of the cloud, saying, "This is my Son, my Chosen;[h] listen to him!" [36] And when the voice had spoken, Jesus was found alone. And they kept silence and told no one in those days anything of what they had seen.

37 On the next day, when they had come down from the mountain, a great crowd met him. [38] And behold, a man from the crowd cried, "Master, I beg you to look upon my son, for he is my only child; [39] and behold, a spirit seizes him, and he suddenly cries out; it convulses him till he foams, and shatters him, and will hardly leave him. [40] And I begged your disciples to cast it out, but they could not." [41] Jesus answered, "O faithless and perverse generation, how long am I to be with you and bear with you? Bring your son here." [42] While he was coming, the demon tore him and convulsed him. But Jesus rebuked the unclean spirit, and healed the boy, and gave him back to his father. [43] And all were astonished at the majesty of God.

But while they were all marveling at everything he did,

[h] Many ancient authorities read *my Beloved*.

9. 30: Acts 1. 9–11.   **9. 32:** Jn. 1. 14.   **9. 33:** Lk. 5. 5; 8. 24, 45; 9. 49; 17. 13.
9. 35: Lk. 3. 22; Jn. 12. 28–30.   **9. 36:** Mt. 17. 9; Mk. 9. 9–10. **9. 37–43:** Mt. 17. 14–18;
Mk. 9. 14–27.   **9. 43–45:** Mt. 17. 22–23; Mk. 9. 30–32; Lk. 9. 22; 18. 31–34; 17. 25.

he said to his disciples, [44] "Let these words sink into your ears; for the Son of man is to be delivered into the hands of men." [45] But they did not understand this saying, and it was concealed from them, that they should not perceive it; and they were afraid to ask him about this saying.

46 And an argument arose among them as to which of them was the greatest. [47] But when Jesus perceived the thought of their hearts, he took a child and put him by his side, [48] and said to them, "Whoever receives this child in my name receives me, and whoever receives me receives him who sent me; for he who is least among you all is the one who is great."

49 John answered, "Master, we saw a man casting out demons in your name, and we forbade him, because he does not follow with us." [50] But Jesus said to him, "Do not forbid him; for he that is not against you is for you."

51 When the days drew near for him to be received up, he set his face to go to Jerusalem. And he sent messengers ahead of him, [52] who went and entered a village of the Samaritans, to make ready for him; [53] but the people would not receive him, because his face was set toward Jerusalem. [54] And when his disciples James and John saw it, they said, "Lord, do you want us to bid fire come down from heaven and consume them?"[i] [55] But he turned and rebuked them.[j] [56] And they went on to another village.

57 As they were going along the road, a man said to him, "I will follow you wherever you go." [58] And Jesus said to him, "Foxes have holes, and birds of the air have nests; but the Son of man has nowhere to lay his head." [59] To another

[i] Some ancient authorities add *as Elijah did.*   [j] Some ancient authorities add *and he said,* "*You do not know what manner of spirit you are of; for the Son of man came not to destroy men's lives but to save them.*"

9. 46–48: Mt. 18. 1–5; Mk. 9. 33–37.   **9. 48:** Lk. 10. 16; Mt. 10. 40.   **9. 49–50:** Mk. 9. 38–40; Lk. 11. 23.   **9. 49:** Lk. 5. 5; 8. 24, 45; 9. 33; 17. 13.   **9. 51–56:** Mk. 10. 1; Lk. 17. 11; Jn. 4. 40–42.   **9. 52:** Mt. 10. 5; Jn. 4. 4.   **9. 54:** Mk. 3. 17; 2 Kings 1. 9–16. **9. 57–60:** Mt. 8. 19–22.

he said, "Follow me." But he said, "Lord, let me first go and bury my father." ⁶⁰ But he said to him, "Leave the dead to bury their own dead; but as for you, go and proclaim the kingdom of God." ⁶¹ Another said, "I will follow you, Lord; but let me first say farewell to those at my home." ⁶² Jesus said to him, "No one who puts his hand to the plow and looks back is fit for the kingdom of God."

10 After this the Lord appointed seventy*ᵏ* others, and sent them on ahead of him, two by two, into every town and place where he himself was about to come. ² And he said to them, "The harvest is plentiful, but the laborers are few; pray therefore the Lord of the harvest to send out laborers into his harvest. ³ Go your way; behold, I send you out as lambs in the midst of wolves. ⁴ Carry no purse, no bag, no sandals; and salute no one on the road. ⁵ Whatever house you enter, first say, 'Peace be to this house!' ⁶ And if a son of peace is there, your peace shall rest upon him; but if not, it shall return to you. ⁷ And remain in the same house, eating and drinking what they provide, for the laborer deserves his wages; do not go from house to house. ⁸ Whenever you enter a town and they receive you, eat what is set before you; ⁹ heal the sick in it and say to them, 'The kingdom of God has come near to you.' ¹⁰ But whenever you enter a town and they do not receive you, go into its streets and say, ¹¹ 'Even the dust of your town that clings to our feet, we wipe off against you; nevertheless know this, that the kingdom of God has come near.' ¹² I tell you, it shall be more tolerable on that day for Sodom than for that town.

13 "Woe to you, Cho-ra′zin! woe to you, Beth-sa′i-da! For if the mighty works done in you had been done in Tyre

ᵏ Many ancient authorities read *seventy-two.*
9. 61: 1 Kings 19. 20; Phil. 3. 13.
10. 1: Lk. 9. 1–2, 51–52; 7. 13.   **10. 2:** Mt. 9. 37–38; Jn. 4. 35.   **10. 3–12:**
Mt. 10. 7–16; Mk. 6. 8–11; Lk. 9. 2–5; 22. 35–36.   **10. 5:** 1 Sam. 25. 6.   **10. 7:**
1 Cor. 10. 27; 9. 14; 1 Tim. 5. 18; Deut. 24. 15.   **10. 11:** Acts 13. 51.   **10. 12:**
Mt. 11. 24; Gen. 19. 24–28; Jude 7.   **10. 13–15:** Mt. 11. 21–23; Lk. 6. 24–26.
150

and Sidon, they would have repented long ago, sitting in sackcloth and ashes. [14] But it shall be more tolerable in the judgment for Tyre and Sidon than for you. [15] And you, Ca-per′na-um, will you be exalted to heaven? You shall be brought down to Hades.

16 "He who hears you hears me, and he who rejects you rejects me, and he who rejects me rejects him who sent me."

17 The seventy[l] returned with joy, saying, "Lord, even the demons are subject to us in your name!" [18] And he said to them, "I saw Satan fall like lightning from heaven. [19] Behold, I have given you authority to tread upon serpents and scorpions, and over all the power of the enemy; and nothing shall hurt you. [20] Nevertheless do not rejoice in this, that the spirits are subject to you; but rejoice that your names are written in heaven."

21 In that same hour he rejoiced in the Holy Spirit and said, "I thank thee, Father, Lord of heaven and earth, that thou hast hidden these things from the wise and understanding and revealed them to babes; yea, Father, for such was thy gracious will.[m] [22] All things have been delivered to me by my Father; and no one knows who the Son is except the Father, or who the Father is except the Son and any one to whom the Son chooses to reveal him."

23 Then turning to the disciples he said privately, "Blessed are the eyes which see what you see! [24] For I tell you that many prophets and kings desired to see what you see, and did not see it, and to hear what you hear, and did not hear it."

25 And behold, a lawyer stood up to put him to the test, saying, "Teacher, what shall I do to inherit eternal life?"

---

[l] Many ancient authorities read *seventy-two*.   [m] Or *so it was well-pleasing before thee.*

10. 16: Mt. 10. 40; 18. 5; Mk. 9. 37; Lk. 9. 48; Jn. 13. 20; 12. 48.   **10. 18:** Rev. 12. 9; Jn. 12. 31.   **10. 20:** Ex. 32. 32; Ps. 69. 28; Dan. 12. 1; Phil. 4. 3; Heb. 12. 23; Rev. 3. 5; 13. 8; 21. 27.   **10. 21–22:** Mt. 11. 25–27.   **10. 21:** 1 Cor. 1. 26–29.   **10. 22:** Mt. 28. 18; Jn. 3. 35; 13. 3; 10. 15; 17. 25.   **10. 23–24:** Mt. 13. 16–17; Jn. 8. 56; Heb. 11. 13; 1 Pet. 1. 10–12.   **10. 25–28:** Mt. 22. 34–39; Mk. 12. 28–31.   **10. 25:** Mk. 10. 17; Mt. 19. 16; Lk. 18. 18.

²⁶ He said to him, "What is written in the law? How do you read?" ²⁷ And he answered, "You shall love the Lord your God with all your heart, and with all your soul, and with all your strength, and with all your mind; and your neighbor as yourself." ²⁸ And he said to him, "You have answered right; do this, and you will live."

29 But he, desiring to justify himself, said to Jesus, "And who is my neighbor?" ³⁰ Jesus replied, "A man was going down from Jerusalem to Jericho, and he fell among robbers, who stripped him and beat him, and departed, leaving him half-dead. ³¹ Now by chance a priest was going down that road; and when he saw him he passed by on the other side. ³² So likewise a Levite, when he came to the place and saw him, passed by on the other side. ³³ But a Samaritan, as he journeyed, came to where he was; and when he saw him, he had compassion, ³⁴ and went to him and bound up his wounds, pouring on oil and wine; then he set him on his own beast and brought him to an inn, and took care of him. ³⁵ And the next day he took out two denarii[n] and gave them to the innkeeper, saying, 'Take care of him; and whatever more you spend, I will repay you when I come back.' ³⁶ Which of these three, do you think, proved neighbor to the man who fell among the robbers?" ³⁷ He said, "The one who showed mercy on him." And Jesus said to him, "Go and do likewise."

38 Now as they went on their way, he entered a village; and a woman named Martha received him into her house. ³⁹ And she had a sister called Mary, who sat at the Lord's feet and listened to his teaching. ⁴⁰ But Martha was distracted with much serving; and she went to him and said,

---

[n] See note on Matt. 18. 28.

10. 27: Deut. 6. 5; Lev. 19. 18; Rom. 13. 9; Gal. 5. 14; Jas. 2. 8.   **10. 28:** Lk. 20. 39;
Lev. 18. 5.   **10. 33:** Lk. 9. 51–56; 17. 11–19; Jn. 4. 4–42.   **10. 38–42:** Jn. 12. 1–3;
11. 1–45.

"Lord, do you not care that my sister has left me to serve alone? Tell her then to help me." [41] But the Lord answered her, "Martha, Martha, you are anxious and troubled about many things; [42] one thing is needful[o]. Mary has chosen the good portion, which shall not be taken away from her."

11 He was praying in a certain place, and when he ceased, one of his disciples said to him, "Lord, teach us to pray, as John taught his disciples." [2] And he said to them, "When you pray, say:

"Father, hallowed be thy name. Thy kingdom come. [3] Give us each day our daily bread;[p] [4] and forgive us our sins, for we ourselves forgive every one who is indebted to us; and lead us not into temptation."

5 And he said to them, "Which of you who has a friend will go to him at midnight and say to him, 'Friend, lend me three loaves; [6] for a friend of mine has arrived on a journey, and I have nothing to set before him'; [7] and he will answer from within, 'Do not bother me; the door is now shut, and my children are with me in bed; I cannot get up and give you anything'? [8] I tell you, though he will not get up and give him anything because he is his friend, yet because of his importunity he will rise and give him whatever he needs. [9] And I tell you, Ask, and it will be given you; seek, and you will find; knock, and it will be opened to you. [10] For every one who asks receives, and he who seeks finds, and to him who knocks it will be opened. [11] What father among you, if his son asks for[q] a fish, will instead of a fish give him a serpent; [12] or if he asks for an egg, will give him a scorpion? [13] If you then, who are evil, know how to give good

[o] Many ancient authorities read *few things are needful, or only one*.
[p] Or *our bread for the morrow*.
[q] Some ancient authorities insert *a loaf, will give him a stone; or if he asks for*.

10. 41: Lk. 7. 13.
11. 1: Mk. 1. 35; Lk. 3. 21; 5. 16; 6. 12; 9. 18, 28; 5. 33; 7. 18.   **11. 2–4:** Mt. 6. 9–13.
11. 4: Mk. 11. 25; Mt. 18. 35.   **11. 5–8:** Lk. 18. 1–8.   **11. 9–13:** Mt. 7. 7–11.
11. 9: Mt. 18. 19; 21. 22; Mk. 11. 24; Jas. 1. 5–8; 1 Jn. 5. 14–15; Jn. 15. 7; 16. 23–24.

gifts to your children, how much more will the heavenly Father give the Holy Spirit to those who ask him?"

[14] Now he was casting out a demon that was dumb; when the demon had gone out, the dumb man spoke, and the people marveled. [15] But some of them said, "He casts out demons by Be-el'ze-bub,[r] the prince of demons"; [16] while others, to try him, sought from him a sign from heaven. [17] But he, knowing their thoughts, said to them, "Every kingdom divided against itself is laid waste, and house falls upon house. [18] And if Satan also is divided against himself, how will his kingdom stand? For you say that I cast out demons by Be-el'ze-bub. [19] And if I cast out demons by Be-el'ze-bub, by whom do your sons cast them out? Therefore they shall be your judges. [20] But if it is by the finger of God that I cast out demons, then the kingdom of God has come upon you. [21] When a strong man, fully armed, guards his own palace, his goods are in peace; [22] but when one stronger than he assails him and overcomes him, he takes away his armor in which he trusted, and divides his spoil. [23] He who is not with me is against me; and he who does not gather with me scatters.

24 "When the unclean spirit has gone out of a man, he passes through waterless places seeking rest; and finding none he says, 'I will return to my house from which I came.' [25] And when he comes he finds it swept and put in order. [26] Then he goes and brings seven other spirits more evil than himself, and they enter and dwell there; and the last state of that man becomes worse than the first."

27 As he said this, a woman in the crowd raised her voice and said to him, "Blessed is the womb that bore

[r] Greek *Beelzebul*.

11. 14–23: Mt. 12. 22–30; 10. 25; Mk. 3. 23–27.   11. 14–15: Mt. 9. 32–34.   11. 16: Mt. 12. 38; 16. 1; Mk. 8. 11; Jn. 2. 18; 6. 30.   11. 23: Lk. 9. 50.   11. 24–26: Mt. 12. 43–45. 11. 27: Lk. 1. 42; 23. 29.

you, and the breasts that you sucked!" [28] But he said,
"Blessed rather are those who hear the word of God and
keep it!"

29 When the crowds were increasing, he began to say,
"This generation is an evil generation; it seeks a sign, but
no sign shall be given to it except the sign of Jonah. [30] For as
Jonah became a sign to the men of Nin'e-veh, so will the Son
of man be to this generation. [31] The queen of the South will
arise at the judgment with the men of this generation and
condemn them; for she came from the ends of the earth to
hear the wisdom of Solomon, and behold, something greater
than Solomon is here. [32] The men of Nin'e-veh will arise at
the judgment with this generation and condemn it; for they
repented at the preaching of Jonah, and behold, something
greater than Jonah is here.

33 "No one after lighting a lamp puts it in a cellar or under
a bushel, but on a stand, that those who enter may see the
light. [34] Your eye is the lamp of your body; when your eye is
sound, your whole body is full of light; but when it is not
sound, your body is full of darkness. [35] Therefore be careful
lest the light in you be darkness. [36] If then your whole body is
full of light, having no part dark, it will be wholly bright,
as when a lamp with its rays gives you light."

37 While he was speaking, a Pharisee asked him to dine
with him; so he went in and sat at table. [38] The Pharisee
was astonished to see that he did not first wash before dinner.
[39] And the Lord said to him, "Now you Pharisees cleanse the
outside of the cup and of the dish, but inside you are full
of extortion and wickedness. [40] You fools! Did not he who
made the outside make the inside also? [41] But give for alms

11. 28: Lk. 8. 21; Jn. 15. 14.   **11. 29–32:** Mt. 12. 39–42.   **11. 29:** Mt. 16. 4;
Mk. 8. 12; Lk. 11. 16; Jon. 3. 4–5.   **11. 31:** 1 Kings 10. 1–10; 2 Chr. 9. 1–12.
11. 32: Mt. 12. 6.   **11. 33:** Mt. 5. 15; Mk. 4. 21; Lk. 8. 16.   **11. 34–35:** Mt. 6. 22–23.
11. 37: Lk. 7. 36; 14. 1.   **11. 38:** Mk. 7. 1–5.   **11. 39–41:** Mt. 23. 25–26.
11. 39: Lk. 7. 13.   **11. 41:** Tit. 1. 15; Mk. 7. 19.

those things which are within; and behold, everything is clean for you.

42 "But woe to you Pharisees! For you tithe mint and rue and every herb, and neglect justice and the love of God; these you ought to have done without neglecting the others. [43] Woe to you Pharisees! For you love the best seats in synagogues and salutations in the market places. [44] Woe to you! For you are like graves which are not seen, and men walk over them without knowing it."

45 One of the lawyers answered him, "Teacher, in saying this you reproach us also." [46] And he said, "Woe to you lawyers also! For you load men with burdens hard to bear, and you yourselves do not touch the burdens with one of your fingers. [47] Woe to you! For you build the tombs of the prophets whom your fathers killed. [48] So you are witnesses and consent to the deeds of your fathers; for they killed them, and you build their tombs. [49] Therefore also the Wisdom of God said, 'I will send them prophets and apostles, some of whom they will kill and persecute,' [50] that the blood of all the prophets, shed from the foundation of the world, may be required of this generation, [51] from the blood of Abel to the blood of Zech-a-ri'ah, who perished between the altar and the sanctuary. Yes, I tell you, it shall be required of this generation. [52] Woe to you lawyers! For you have taken away the key of knowledge; you did not enter yourselves, and you hindered those who were entering."

53 As he went away from there, the scribes and the Pharisees began to press him hard, and to provoke him to speak of many things, [54] lying in wait for him, to catch at something he might say.

11. 42: Mt. 23. 23–24; Lev. 27. 30; Mic. 6. 8.   **11. 43**: Mt. 23. 6–7; Mk. 12. 38–39; Lk. 20. 46.   **11. 44**: Mt. 23. 27.   **11. 46**: Mt. 23. 4.   **11. 47–48**: Mt. 23. 29–32; Acts 7. 51–53.   **11. 49–51**: Mt. 23. 34–36.   **11. 49**: 1 Cor. 1. 24; Col. 2. 3. **11. 51**: Gen. 4. 8; 2 Chr. 24. 20–21; Zech. 1. 1.   **11. 52**: Mt. 23. 13.   **11. 53–54**: Mk. 12. 13.

12 In the meantime, when so many thousands of the multitude had gathered together that they trod upon one another, he began to say to his disciples first, "Beware of the leaven of the Pharisees, which is hypocrisy. ² Nothing is covered up that will not be revealed, or hidden that will not be known. ³ Whatever you have said in the dark shall be heard in the light, and what you have whispered in private rooms shall be proclaimed upon the housetops.

4 "I tell you, my friends, do not fear those who kill the body, and after that have no more that they can do. ⁵ But I will warn you whom to fear: fear him who, after he has killed, has power to cast into hell;ˢ yes, I tell you, fear him! ⁶ Are not five sparrows sold for two pennies? And not one of them is forgotten before God. ⁷ Why, even the hairs of your head are all numbered. Fear not; you are of more value than many sparrows.

8 "And I tell you, every one who acknowledges me before men, the Son of man also will acknowledge before the angels of God; ⁹ but he who denies me before men will be denied before the angels of God. ¹⁰ And every one who speaks a word against the Son of man will be forgiven; but he who blasphemes against the Holy Spirit will not be forgiven. ¹¹ And when they bring you before the synagogues and the rulers and the authorities, do not be anxious how or what you are to answer or what you are to say; ¹² for the Holy Spirit will teach you in that very hour what you ought to say."

13 One of the multitude said to him, "Teacher, bid my brother divide the inheritance with me." ¹⁴ But he said to

ˢ Greek *Gehenna*.

12. 1: Mt. 16. 6; Mk. 8. 15. Eph. 5. 13.   **12. 4:** Jn. 15. 14–15. **12. 7:** Lk. 21. 18; Acts 27. 34; Mt. 12. 12. **12. 10:** Mt. 12. 31–32; Mk. 3. 28–29. Lk. 21. 14–15.   **12. 2–3:** Mt. 10. 26–27; Mk. 4. 22; Lk. 8. 17; **12. 4–9:** Mt. 10. 28–33.   **12. 5:** Heb. 10. 31. **12. 9:** Mk. 8. 38; Lk. 9. 26; 2 Tim. 2. 12. **12. 11–12:** Mt. 10. 19–20; Mk. 13. 11;

him, "Man, who made me a judge or divider over you?" [15] And he said to them, "Take heed, and beware of all covetousness; for a man's life does not consist in the abundance of his possessions." [16] And he told them a parable, saying, "The land of a rich man brought forth plentifully; [17] and he thought to himself, 'What shall I do, for I have nowhere to store my crops?' [18] And he said, 'I will do this: I will pull down my barns, and build larger ones; and there I will store all my grain and my goods. [19] And I will say to my soul, Soul, you have ample goods laid up for many years; take your ease, eat, drink, be merry.' [20] But God said to him, 'Fool! This night your soul is required of you; and the things you have prepared, whose will they be?' [21] So is he who lays up treasure for himself, and is not rich toward God."

22 And he said to his disciples, "Therefore I tell you, do not be anxious about your life, what you shall eat, nor about your body, what you shall put on. [23] For life is more than food, and the body more than clothing. [24] Consider the ravens: they neither sow nor reap, they have neither storehouse nor barn, and yet God feeds them. Of how much more value are you than the birds! [25] And which of you by being anxious can add a cubit to his span of life?[t] [26] If then you are not able to do as small a thing as that, why are you anxious about the rest? [27] Consider the lilies, how they grow; they neither toil nor spin;[u] yet I tell you, even Solomon in all his glory was not arrayed like one of these. [28] But if God so clothes the grass which is alive in the field today and tomorrow is thrown into the oven, how much more will he clothe you, O men of little faith? [29] And do not seek what you are to eat and what you are to drink, nor be of anxious

[t] Or *to his stature.*
[u] A few ancient authorities read *Consider the lilies; they neither spin nor weave.*

12. 15: 1 Tim. 6. 6–10.   **12. 20:** Jer. 17. 11; Job 27. 8; Ps. 39. 6; Lk. 12. 33–34.
12. 22–31: Mt. 6. 25–33.   **12. 24:** Lk. 12. 6–7.   **12. 27:** 1 Kings 10. 1–10.

mind. [30] For all the nations of the world seek these things; and your Father knows that you need them. [31] Instead, seek his[v] kingdom, and these things shall be yours as well.

[32] "Fear not, little flock, for it is your Father's good pleasure to give you the kingdom. [33] Sell your possessions, and give alms; provide yourselves with purses that do not grow old, with a treasure in the heavens that does not fail, where no thief approaches and no moth destroys. [34] For where your treasure is, there will your heart be also.

[35] "Let your loins be girded and your lamps burning, [36] and be like men who are waiting for their master to come home from the marriage feast, so that they may open to him at once when he comes and knocks. [37] Blessed are those servants whom the master finds awake when he comes; truly, I say to you, he will gird himself and have them sit at table and come and serve them. [38] If he comes in the second watch, or in the third, and finds them so, blessed are those servants! [39] But know this, that if the householder had known at what hour the thief was coming, he would have been awake and[w] would not have left his house to be broken into. [40] You also must be ready; for the Son of man is coming at an hour you do not expect."

[41] Peter said, "Lord, are you telling this parable for us or for all?" [42] And the Lord said, "Who then is the faithful and wise steward, whom his master will set over his household, to give them their portion of food at the proper time? [43] Blessed is that servant whom his master finds so doing when he comes. [44] Truly I tell you, he will set him over all his possessions. [45] But if that servant says in his heart, 'My

[v] Some ancient authoities read *God's*.
[w] Some ancient authorities omit *would have been awake and*.

12. 30: Mt. 6. 8.   12. 32: Jn. 21. 15–17.   12. 33–34: Mt. 6. 19–21; Lk. 18. 22.
12. 35: Eph. 6. 14; Mt. 25. 1–13; Mk. 13. 33–37.   12. 37: Jn. 13. 3–5; Mt. 24. 42;
Lk. 21. 36.   12. 39–40: Mt. 24. 43–44; 1 Thess. 5. 2; Rev. 3. 3; 16. 15; 2 Pet. 3. 10.
12. 42–46: Mt. 24. 45–51.   12. 42: Lk. 7. 13.

master is delayed in coming,' and begins to beat the men-servants and the maidservants, and to eat and drink and get drunk, [46] the master of that servant will come on a day when he does not expect him and at an hour he does not know, and will punish[x] him, and put him with the unfaithful. [47] And that servant who knew his master's will, but did not make ready or act according to his will, shall receive a severe beating. [48] But he who did not know, and did what deserved a beating, shall receive a light beating. Every one to whom much is given, of him will much be required; and of him to whom men commit much they will demand the more.

49 "I came to cast fire upon the earth; and would that it were already kindled! [50] I have a baptism to be baptized with; and how I am constrained until it is accomplished! [51] Do you think that I have come to give peace on earth? No, I tell you, but rather division; [52] for henceforth in one house there will be five divided, three against two and two against three; [53] they will be divided, father against son and son against father, mother against daughter and daughter against her mother, mother-in-law against her daughter-in-law and daughter-in-law against her mother-in-law."

54 He also said to the multitudes, "When you see a cloud rising in the west, you say at once, 'A shower is coming'; and so it happens. [55] And when you see the south wind blow-ing, you say, 'There will be scorching heat'; and it happens. [56] You hypocrites! You know how to interpret the appearance of earth and sky; but why do you not know how to interpret the present time?

57 "And why do you not judge for yourselves what is right? [58] As you go with your accuser before the magistrate,

[x] Or *cut him in pieces.*

12. 47–48: Deut. 25. 2–3; Num. 15. 29–30; Lk. 8. 18; 19. 26.   **12. 49:** Lk. 22. 15.
12. 50: Mk. 10. 38–39; Jn. 12. 27.   **12. 51–53:** Mt. 10. 34–36; Lk. 21. 16; Mic. 7. 6.
12. 54–56: Mt. 16. 2–3.   **12. 57–59:** Mt. 5. 25–26.

make an effort to settle with him on the way, lest he drag you to the judge, and the judge hand you over to the officer, and the officer put you in prison. [59] I tell you, you will never get out till you have paid the very last copper!"

13 There were some present at that very time who told him of the Galileans whose blood Pilate had mingled with their sacrifices. [2] And he answered them, "Do you think that these Galileans were worse sinners than all the other Galileans, because they suffered thus? [3] I tell you, No; but unless you repent you will all likewise perish. [4] Or those eighteen upon whom the tower in Si-lo'am fell and killed them, do you think that they were worse offenders than all the others who dwelt in Jerusalem? [5] I tell you, No; but unless you repent you will all likewise perish."

6 And he told this parable: "A man had a fig tree planted in his vineyard; and he came seeking fruit on it and found none. [7] And he said to the vinedresser, 'Lo, these three years I have come seeking fruit on this fig tree, and I find none. Cut it down; why should it use up the ground?' [8] And he answered him, 'Let it alone, sir, this year also, till I dig about it and put on manure. [9] And if it bears fruit next year, well and good; but if not, you can cut it down.'"

10 Now he was teaching in one of the synagogues on the sabbath. [11] And there was a woman who had had a spirit of infirmity for eighteen years; she was bent over and could not fully straighten herself. [12] And when Jesus saw her, he called her and said to her, "Woman, you are freed from your infirmity." [13] And he laid his hands upon her, and immediately she was made straight, and she praised God. [14] But the ruler of the synagogue, indignant because Jesus had healed on the sabbath, said to the people, "There are six days on which

13. 2: Jn. 9. 1–3; 7. 19; Lk. 3. 9.   **13. 6–9**: Mt. 21. 18–20; Mk. 11. 12–14, 20–21.   **13. 7**: Mt. 3. 10; **13. 14**: Ex. 20. 9–10; Lk. 6. 6–11; 14. 1–6; Jn. 5. 1–18.

work ought to be done; come on those days and be healed, and not on the sabbath day." [15] Then the Lord answered him, "You hypocrites! Does not each of you on the sabbath untie his ox or his ass from the manger, and lead it away to water it? [16] And ought not this woman, a daughter of Abraham whom Satan bound for eighteen years, be loosed from this bond on the sabbath day?" [17] As he said this, all his adversaries were put to shame; and all the people rejoiced at all the glorious things that were done by him.

18 He said therefore, "What is the kingdom of God like? And to what shall I compare it? [19] It is like a grain of mustard seed which a man took and sowed in his garden; and it grew and became a tree, and the birds of the air made nests in its branches."

20 And again he said, "To what shall I compare the kingdom of God? [21] It is like leaven which a woman took and hid in three measures of meal, till it was all leavened."

22 He went on his way through towns and villages, teaching, and journeying toward Jerusalem. [23] And some one said to him, "Lord, will those who are saved be few?" And he said to them, [24] "Strive to enter by the narrow door; for many, I tell you, will seek to enter and will not be able. [25] When once the householder has risen up and shut the door, you will begin to stand outside and to knock at the door, saying, 'Lord, open to us.' He will answer you, 'I do not know where you come from.' [26] Then you will begin to say, 'We ate and drank in your presence, and you taught in our streets.' [27] But he will say, 'I tell you, I do not know where you come from; depart from me, all you workers of iniquity!' [28] There you will weep and gnash your teeth, when you see Abraham and Isaac and Jacob and all the prophets in the

13. 15: Lk. 7. 13; 14. 5; Mt. 12. 11.   **13. 16:** Lk. 19. 9.   **13. 18–19:** Mt. 13. 31–32; Mk. 4. 30–32.   **13. 20–21:** Mt. 13. 33.   **13. 22:** Lk. 9. 51; 17. 11; 18. 31; 19. 11. **13. 23–24:** Mt. 7. 13–14; Jn. 10. 7.   **13. 25:** Mt. 25. 10–12.   **13. 26–27:** Mt. 7. 21–23, 25. 41; Lk. 6. 46.   **13. 28–29:** Mt. 8. 11–12.

kingdom of God and you yourselves thrust out. [29] And men
will come from east and west, and from north and south, and
sit at table in the kingdom of God. [30] And behold, some are
last who will be first, and some are first who will be last."

31 At that very hour some Pharisees came, and said to him,
"Get away from here, for Herod wants to kill you." [32] And
he said to them, "Go and tell that fox, 'Behold, I cast out
demons and perform cures today and tomorrow, and the
third day I finish my course. [33] Nevertheless I must go on my
way today and tomorrow and the day following; for it cannot be that a prophet should perish away from Jerusalem.'
[34] O Jerusalem, Jerusalem, killing the prophets and stoning
those who are sent to you! How often would I have gathered
your children together as a hen gathers her brood under her
wings, and you would not! [35] Behold, your house is forsaken!
And I tell you, you will not see me until you say, 'Blessed be
he who comes in the name of the Lord!'"

14 One sabbath when he went to dine at the house of a
ruler who belonged to the Pharisees, they were watching him. [2] And behold, there was a man before him who had
dropsy. [3] And Jesus spoke to the lawyers and Pharisees,
saying, "Is it lawful to heal on the sabbath, or not?" [4] But
they were silent. Then he took him and healed him, and let
him go. [5] And he said to them, "Which of you, having an
ass[y] or an ox that has fallen into a well, will not immediately
pull him out on a sabbath day?" [6] And they could not reply
to this.

7 Now he told a parable to those who were invited, when
he marked how they chose the places of honor, saying to
them, [8] "When you are invited by any one to a marriage

[y] Many ancient authorities read *a son*.

13. 30: Mt. 19. 30; Mk. 10. 31.   **13. 32:** Heb. 2. 10; 7. 28.   **13. 34–35:** Mt. 23. 37–39;
Lk. 19. 41.   **13. 35:** Jer. 22. 5; Ps. 118. 26; Lk. 19. 38.
14. 1: Lk. 7. 36; 11. 37; Mk. 3. 2.   **14. 3:** Mt. 12. 10; Mk. 3. 4; Lk. 6. 9.   **14. 5:**
Mt. 12. 11; Lk. 13. 15.   **14. 8:** Prov. 25. 6–7; Lk. 11. 43; 20. 46.

feast, do not sit down in a place of honor, lest a more eminent man than you be invited by him; [9] and he who invited you both will come and say to you, 'Give place to this man,' and then you will begin with shame to take the lowest place. [10] But when you are invited, go and sit in the lowest place, so that when your host comes he may say to you, 'Friend, go up higher'; then you will be honored in the presence of all who sit at table with you. [11] For every one who exalts himself will be humbled, and he who humbles himself will be exalted."

12 He said also to the man who had invited him, "When you give a dinner or a banquet, do not invite your friends or your brothers or your kinsmen or rich neighbors, lest they also invite you in return, and you be repaid. [13] But when you give a feast, invite the poor, the maimed, the lame, the blind, [14] and you will be blessed, because they cannot repay you. You will be repaid at the resurrection of the just."

15 When one of those who sat at table with him heard this, he said to him, "Blessed is he who shall eat bread in the kingdom of God!" [16] But he said to him, "A man once gave a great banquet, and invited many; [17] and at the time for the banquet he sent his servant to say to those who had been invited, 'Come; for all is now ready.' [18] But they all alike began to make excuses. The first said to him, 'I have bought a field, and I must go out and see it; I pray you, have me excused.' [19] And another said, 'I have bought five yoke of oxen, and I go to examine them; I pray you, have me excused.' [20] And another said, 'I have married a wife, and therefore I cannot come.' [21] So the servant came and reported this to his master. Then the householder in anger said to his servant, 'Go out quickly to the streets and lanes of the city, and bring in the poor and maimed and blind and

14. 11: Mt. 23. 12; Lk. 18. 14; Mt. 18. 4; 1 Pet. 5. 6.   **14. 12:** Jas. 2. 2–4.   **14. 13:** Lk. 14. 21.   **14. 15:** Rev. 19. 9.   **14. 16–24:** Mt. 22. 1–10.   **14. 20:** Deut. 24. 5; 1 Cor. 7. 33.   **14. 21:** Lk. 14. 13.

lame.' ²² And the servant said, 'Sir, what you commanded has been done, and still there is room.' ²³ And the master said to the servant, 'Go out to the highways and hedges, and compel people to come in, that my house may be filled. ²⁴ For I tell you, none of those men who were invited shall taste my banquet.'"

25 Now great multitudes accompanied him; and he turned and said to them, ²⁶ "If any one comes to me and does not hate his own father and mother and wife and children and brothers and sisters, yes, and even his own life, he cannot be my disciple. ²⁷ Whoever does not bear his own cross and come after me, cannot be my disciple. ²⁸ For which of you, desiring to build a tower, does not first sit down and count the cost, whether he has enough to complete it? ²⁹ Otherwise, when he has laid a foundation, and is not able to finish, all who see it begin to mock him, ³⁰ saying, 'This man began to build, and was not able to finish.' ³¹ Or what king, going to encounter another king in war, will not sit down first and take counsel whether he is able with ten thousand to meet him who comes against him with twenty thousand? ³² And if not, while the other is yet a great way off, he sends an embassy and asks terms of peace. ³³ So therefore, whoever of you does not renounce all that he has cannot be my disciple.

34 "Salt is good; but if salt has lost its taste, how shall its saltness be restored? ³⁵ It is fit neither for the land nor for the dunghill; men throw it away. He who has ears to hear, let him hear."

15 Now the tax collectors and sinners were all drawing near to hear him. ² And the Pharisees and the scribes murmured, saying, "This man receives sinners and eats with them."

14. 26–27: Mt. 10. 37–38.
14. 33: Lk. 18. 29–30; Phil. 3. 7.
15. 1–2: Lk. 5. 29–30; 19. 7.
14. 27: Mt. 16. 24; Mk. 8. 34; Lk. 9. 23.
14. 34–35: Mt. 5. 13; Mk. 9. 49–50; Mt. 11. 15.

3 So he told them this parable: ⁴ "What man of you, having a hundred sheep, if he has lost one of them, does not leave the ninety-nine in the wilderness, and go after the one which is lost, until he finds it? ⁵ And when he has found it, he lays it on his shoulders, rejoicing. ⁶ And when he comes home, he calls together his friends and his neighbors, saying to them, 'Rejoice with me, for I have found my sheep which was lost.' ⁷ Even so, I tell you, there will be more joy in heaven over one sinner who repents than over ninety-nine righteous persons who need no repentance.

8 "Or what woman, having ten silver coins,ᶻ if she loses one coin, does not light a lamp and sweep the house and seek diligently until she finds it? ⁹ And when she has found it, she calls together her friends and neighbors, saying, 'Rejoice with me, for I have found the coin which I had lost.' ¹⁰ Even so, I tell you, there is joy before the angels of God over one sinner who repents."

11 And he said, "There was a man who had two sons; ¹² and the younger of them said to his father, 'Father, give me the share of property that falls to me.' And he divided his living between them. ¹³ Not many days later, the younger son gathered all he had and took his journey into a far country, and there he squandered his property in loose living. ¹⁴ And when he had spent everything, a great famine arose in that country, and he began to be in want. ¹⁵ So he went and joined himself to one of the citizens of that country, who sent him into his fields to feed swine. ¹⁶ And he would gladly have fed onᵃ the pods that the swine ate; and no one gave him anything. ¹⁷ But when he came to himself he said, 'How many of my father's hired servants have bread enough

---

ᶻ The drachma, rendered here by *silver coin*, was about sixteen cents.
ᵃ Many ancient authorities read *filled his belly with*.

15. 4–7: *Mt. 18. 10–14.   **15. 7:** Jas. 5. 20; Lk. 19. 10; 15. 10.   **15. 11:** Mt. 21. 28.
15. 12: Deut. 21. 15–17.

and to spare, but I perish here with hunger! [18] I will arise and go to my father, and I will say to him, Father, I have sinned against heaven and before you; [19] I am no longer worthy to be called your son; treat me as one of your hired servants.' [20] And he arose and came to his father. But while he was yet at a distance, his father saw him and had compassion, and ran and embraced him and kissed him. [21] And the son said to him, 'Father, I have sinned against heaven and before you; I am no longer worthy to be called your son.[b]' [22] But the father said to his servants, 'Bring quickly the best robe, and put it on him; and put a ring on his hand, and shoes on his feet; [23] and bring the fatted calf and kill it, and let us eat and make merry; [24] for this my son was dead, and is alive again; he was lost, and is found.' And they began to make merry.

25 "Now his elder son was in the field; and as he came and drew near to the house, he heard music and dancing. [26] And he called one of the servants and asked what this meant. [27] And he said to him, 'Your brother has come, and your father has killed the fatted calf, because he has received him safe and sound.' [28] But he was angry and refused to go in. His father came out and entreated him, [29] but he answered his father, 'Lo, these many years I have served you, and I never disobeyed your command; yet you never gave me a kid, that I might make merry with my friends. [30] But when this son of yours came, who has devoured your living with harlots, you killed for him the fatted calf!' [31] And he said to him, 'Son, you are always with me, and all that is mine is yours. [32] It was fitting to make merry and be glad, for this your brother was dead, and is alive; he was lost, and is found.'"

---

[b] Some ancient authorities add *treat me as one of your hired servants.*

15. 22: Gen. 41. 42; Zech. 3. 4.   **15. 24:** 1 Tim. 5. 6; Eph. 2. 1; Lk. 9. 60.

16 He also said to the disciples, "There was a rich man who had a steward, and charges were brought to him that this man was wasting his goods. [2] And he called him and said to him, 'What is this that I hear about you? Turn in the account of your stewardship, for you can no longer be steward.' [3] And the steward said to himself, 'What shall I do, since my master is taking the stewardship away from me? I am not strong enough to dig, and I am ashamed to beg. [4] I have decided what to do, so that people may receive me into their houses when I am put out of the stewardship.' [5] So, summoning his master's debtors one by one, he said to the first, 'How much do you owe my master?' [6] He said, 'A hundred measures of oil.' And he said to him, 'Take your bill, and sit down quickly and write fifty.' [7] Then he said to another, 'And how much do you owe?' He said, 'A hundred measures of wheat.' He said to him, 'Take your bill, and write eighty.' [8] The master commended the dishonest steward for his prudence; for the sons of this world[c] are wiser in their own generation than the sons of light. [9] And I tell you, make friends for yourselves by means of unrighteous mammon, so that when it fails they may receive you into the eternal habitations.

10 "He who is faithful in a very little is faithful also in much; and he who is dishonest in a very little is dishonest also in much. [11] If then you have not been faithful in the unrighteous mammon, who will entrust to you the true riches? [12] And if you have not been faithful in that which is another's, who will give you that which is your own? [13] No servant can serve two masters; for either he will hate the one and love the other, or he will be devoted to the one and despise the other. You cannot serve God and mammon."

[c] Greek *age*.

16. 8: 1 Thess. 5. 5; Eph. 5. 8; Lk. 20. 34; Jn. 12. 36.   **16. 9:** Lk. 12. 33; 18. 22.
16. 10: Mt. 25. 21; Lk. 19. 17.   **16. 13:** Mt. 6. 24.

14 The Pharisees, who were lovers of money, heard all this, and they scoffed at him. [15] But he said to them, "You are those who justify yourselves before men, but God knows your hearts; for what is exalted among men is an abomination in the sight of God.

16 "The law and the prophets were until John; since then the good news of the kingdom of God is preached, and every one enters it violently. [17] But it is easier for heaven and earth to pass away, than for one dot of the law to become void.

18 "Every one who divorces his wife and marries another commits adultery, and he who marries a woman divorced from her husband commits adultery.

19 "There was a rich man, who was clothed in purple and fine linen and who feasted sumptuously every day. [20] And at his gate lay a poor man named Laz'a-rus, full of sores, [21] who desired to be fed with what fell from the rich man's table; moreover the dogs came and licked his sores. [22] The poor man died and was carried by the angels to Abraham's bosom. The rich man also died and was buried; [23] and in Hades, being in torment, he lifted up his eyes, and saw Abraham far off and Laz'a-rus in his bosom. [24] And he called out, 'Father Abraham, have mercy upon me, and send Laz'a-rus to dip the end of his finger in water and cool my tongue; for I am in anguish in this flame.' [25] But Abraham said, 'Son, remember that you in your lifetime received your good things, and Laz'a-rus in like manner evil things; but now he is comforted here, and you are in anguish. [26] And besides all this, between us and you a great chasm has been fixed, in order that those who would pass from here to you may not be able, and none may cross from there to us.' [27] And he said, 'Then I beg you, father, to send him

16. 15: 1 Sam. 16. 7; Prov. 21. 2; Acts 1. 24; Lk. 10. 29.   **16. 16:** Mt. 11. 12–13.
16. 17: Mt. 5. 17–18; Lk. 21. 33.   **16. 18:** Mt. 5. 31–32; 19. 9; Mk. 10. 11–12;
1 Cor. 7. 10–11.   **16. 20:** Jn. 11. 1–44; 12. 1, 9.   **16. 22:** Jn. 13. 23.   **16. 25:** Lk. 6. 24.

to my father's house, [28] for I have five brothers, so that he may warn them, lest they also come into this place of torment.' [29] But Abraham said, 'They have Moses and the prophets; let them hear them.' [30] And he said, 'No, father Abraham; but if some one goes to them from the dead, they will repent.' [31] He said to him, 'If they do not hear Moses and the prophets, neither will they be convinced if some one should rise from the dead.'"

17 And he said to his disciples, "Temptations to sin[d] are sure to come; but woe to him by whom they come! [2] It would be better for him if a millstone were hung round his neck and he were cast into the sea, than that he should cause one of these little ones to sin.[e] [3] Take heed to yourselves; if your brother sins, rebuke him, and if he repents, forgive him; [4] and if he sins against you seven times in the day, and turns to you seven times, and says, 'I repent,' you must forgive him."

[5] The apostles said to the Lord, "Increase our faith!" [6] And the Lord said, "If you had faith as a grain of mustard seed, you could say to this sycamine tree, 'Be rooted up, and be planted in the sea,' and it would obey you.

[7] "Will any one of you, who has a servant plowing or keeping sheep, say to him when he has come in from the field, 'Come at once and sit down at table'? [8] Will he not rather say to him, 'Prepare supper for me, and gird yourself and serve me, till I eat and drink; and afterward you shall eat and drink'? [9] Does he thank the servant because he did what was commanded? [10] So you also, when you have done all that is commanded you, say, 'We are unworthy servants; we have only done what was our duty.'"

[d] Or *stumbling-blocks.*   [e] Or *stumble.*

16. 29: Jn. 5. 45–47; Acts 15. 21; Lk. 4. 17.   **16. 30:** Lk. 3. 8; 19. 9.
17. 1–2: Mt. 18. 6–7; Mk. 9. 42; 1 Cor. 8. 12.   **17. 3–4:** Mt. 18. 15, 21–22.   **17. 5–6:**
Mt. 17. 20; 21. 21; Mk. 11. 22–23.   **17. 5:** Lk, 7, 13.   **17. 8:** Lk. 12. 37; Jn. 13. 3–5.

11 On the way to Jerusalem he was passing along between Sa-ma'ri-a and Galilee. ¹² And as he entered a village, he was met by ten lepers, who stood at a distance ¹³ and lifted up their voices and said, "Jesus, Master, have mercy on us." ¹⁴ When he saw them he said to them, "Go and show yourselves to the priests." And as they went they were cleansed. ¹⁵ Then one of them, when he saw that he was healed, turned back, praising God with a loud voice; ¹⁶ and he fell on his face at Jesus' feet, giving him thanks. Now he was a Samaritan. ¹⁷ Then said Jesus, "Were not ten cleansed? Where are the nine? ¹⁸ Was no one found to return and give praise to God except this foreigner?" ¹⁹ And he said to him, "Rise and go your way; your faith has made you well."

20 Being asked by the Pharisees when the kingdom of God was coming, he answered them, "The kingdom of God is not coming with signs to be observed; ²¹ nor will they say, 'Lo, here it is!' or 'There!' for behold, the kingdom of God is in the midst of*ᶠ* you."

22 And he said to the disciples, "The days are coming when you will desire to see one of the days of the Son of man, and you will not see it. ²³ And they will say to you, 'Lo, there!' or 'Lo, here!' Do not go, do not follow them. ²⁴ For as the lightning flashes and lights up the sky from one side to the other, so will the Son of man be in his day.*ᵍ* ²⁵ But first he must suffer many things and be rejected by this generation. ²⁶ As it was in the days of Noah, so will it be in the days of the Son of man. ²⁷ They ate, they drank, they married, they were given in marriage, until the day when

---

ᶠ Or *within.*   *ᵍ* Some ancient authorities omit *in his day.*

17. 11: Lk. 9. 51; 13. 22; 19. 11.   **17. 12:** Lev. 13. 45–46.   **17. 13:** Lk. 5. 5; 8. 24, 45; 9. 33, 49.   **17. 14:** Lk. 5. 14; Mt. 8. 4; Mk. 1. 44; Lev. 14. 2–32.   **17. 19:** Mt. 9. 22; Mk. 5. 34; Lk. 8. 48; 18. 42.   **17. 20:** Lk. 19. 11; 21. 7; Acts 1. 6.   **17. 22:** Mt. 9. 15; Mk. 2. 20; Lk. 5. 35.   **17. 23:** Mt. 24. 23; Mk. 13. 21.   **17. 24:** Mt. 24. 27; Rev. 1. 7.   **17. 25:** Lk. 9. 22.   **17. 26–27:** Mt. 24. 37–39; Gen. 6. 5–8; 7. 6–24.

171

Noah entered the ark, and the flood came and destroyed them all. [28] Likewise as it was in the days of Lot — they ate, they drank, they bought, they sold, they planted, they built, [29] but on the day when Lot went out from Sodom fire and brimstone rained from heaven and destroyed them all — [30] so will it be on the day when the Son of man is revealed. [31] On that day, let him who is on the housetop, with his goods in the house, not come down to take them away; and likewise let him who is in the field not turn back. [32] Remember Lot's wife. [33] Whoever seeks to gain his life will lose it, but whoever loses his life will preserve it. [34] I tell you, in that night there will be two men in one bed; one will be taken and the other left. [35] There will be two women grinding together; one will be taken and the other left." [h] [37] And they said to him, "Where, Lord?" He said to them, "Where the body is, there the eagles [i] will be gathered together."

18 And he told them a parable, to the effect that they ought always to pray and not lose heart. [2] He said, "In a certain city there was a judge who neither feared God nor regarded man; [3] and there was a widow in that city who kept coming to him and saying, 'Vindicate me against my adversary.' [4] For a while he refused; but afterward he said to himself, 'Though I neither fear God nor regard man, [5] yet because this widow bothers me, I will vindicate her, or she will wear me out by her continual coming.'" [6] And the Lord said, "Hear what the unrighteous judge says. [7] And will not God vindicate his elect, who cry to him day and night? Will he delay long over them? [8] I tell you, he

---

[h] Some ancient authorities add verse 36, "*Two men will be in the field; one will be taken and the other left.*"   [i] Or *vultures.*

17. **28–30**: Gen. 18. 20–33; 19. 24–25.   17. **31**: Mt. 24. 17–18; Mk. 13. 15–16; Lk. 21. 21.
17. **32**: Gen. 19. 26.   17. **33**: Mt. 10. 39; 16. 25; Mk. 8. 35; Lk. 9. 24; Jn. 12. 25.
17. **34–35**: Mt. 24. 40–41.   17. **37**: Mt. 24. 28.
18. **1–8**: Lk. 11. 5–8.   18. **6**: Lk. 7. 13.   18. **7**: Rev. 6. 10; Mt. 24. 22; Rom. 8. 33;
Col. 3. 12; 2 Tim. 2. 10.

will vindicate them speedily. Nevertheless, when the Son of man comes, will he find faith on earth?"

9 He also told this parable to some who trusted in themselves that they were righteous and despised others: [10] "Two men went up into the temple to pray, one a Pharisee and the other a tax collector. [11] The Pharisee stood and prayed thus with himself, 'God, I thank thee that I am not like other men, extortioners, unjust, adulterers, or even like this tax collector. [12] I fast twice a week, I give tithes of all that I get.' [13] But the tax collector, standing far off, would not even lift up his eyes to heaven, but beat his breast, saying, 'God, be merciful to me a sinner!' [14] I tell you, this man went down to his house justified rather than the other; for every one who exalts himself will be humbled, but he who humbles himself will be exalted."

15 Now they were bringing even infants to him that he might touch them; and when the disciples saw it, they rebuked them. [16] But Jesus called them to him, saying, "Let the children come to me, and do not hinder them; for to such belongs the kingdom of God. [17] Truly, I say to you, whoever does not receive the kingdom of God like a child shall not enter it."

18 And a ruler asked him, "Good Teacher, what shall I do to inherit eternal life?" [19] And Jesus said to him, "Why do you call me good? No one is good but God alone. [20] You know the commandments: Do not commit adultery, Do not kill, Do not steal, Do not bear false witness, Honor your father and mother." [21] And he said, "All these I have kept from my youth." [22] And when Jesus heard it, he said to him, "One thing you still lack. Sell all that you have and distribute to the poor, and you will have treasure in heaven;

18. 11: Mt. 6. 5; Mk. 11. 25.   **18. 12:** Lk. 5. 33; 11. 42.   **18. 14:** Mt. 18. 4; 23. 12; Lk. 14. 11; 1 Pet. 5. 6.   **18. 15–17:** Mt. 19. 13–15; 18. 3; Mk. 10. 13–16.   **18. 18–23:** Mt. 19. 16–22; Mk. 10. 17–22.   **18. 18:** Lk. 10. 25.   **18. 20:** Ex. 20. 12–16; Deut. 5. 16–20; Rom. 13. 9; Jas. 2. 11.   **18. 22:** Lk. 12. 33; Acts 2. 45; 4. 32.

and come, follow me." ²³ But when he heard this he became sad, for he was very rich. ²⁴ Jesus looking at him said, "How hard it is for those who have riches to enter the kingdom of God! ²⁵ For it is easier for a camel to go through the eye of a needle than for a rich man to enter the kingdom of God." ²⁶ Those who heard it said, "Who then can be saved?" ²⁷ But he said, "What is impossible with men is possible with God." ²⁸ And Peter said, "Lo, we have left our homes and followed you." ²⁹ And he said to them, "Truly, I say to you, there is no man who has left house or wife or brothers or parents or children, for the sake of the kingdom of God, ³⁰ who will not receive manifold more in this time, and in the age to come eternal life."

31 And taking the twelve aside, he said to them, "Behold, we are going up to Jerusalem, and everything that is written of the Son of man by the prophets will be accomplished. ³² For he will be delivered to the Gentiles, and will be mocked and shamefully treated and spit upon; ³³ they will scourge him and kill him, and on the third day he will rise." ³⁴ But they understood none of these things; this saying was hid from them, and they did not grasp what was said.

35 As he drew near to Jericho, a blind man was sitting by the roadside begging; ³⁶ and hearing a multitude going by, he inquired what this meant. ³⁷ They told him, "Jesus of Nazareth is passing by." ³⁸ And he cried, "Jesus, Son of David, have mercy on me!" ³⁹ And those who were in front rebuked him, telling him to be silent; but he cried out all the more, "Son of David, have mercy on me!" ⁴⁰ And Jesus stopped, and commanded him to be brought to him; and when he came near, he asked him, ⁴¹ "What do you want me to do for you?" He said, "Lord, let me receive my

18. 24–27: Mt. 19. 23–26; Mk. 10. 23–27.   **18. 27**: Gen. 18. 14; Job 42. 2; Jer. 32. 17; Lk. 1. 37.   **18. 28–30**: Mt. 19. 27–30; Mk. 10. 28–31; Lk. 5. 1–11.   **18. 31–34**: Mt. 20. 17–19; Mk. 10. 32–34; Lk. 9. 22, 44–45; 17. 25,   **18. 35–43**: Mt. 20. 29–34; Mk. 10. 46–52; Mt. 9. 27–31; Mk. 8. 22; Jn. 9. 1–7.

sight." ⁴² And Jesus said to him, "Receive your sight; your faith has made you well." ⁴³ And immediately he received his sight and followed him, glorifying God; and all the people, when they saw it, gave praise to God.

19 He entered Jericho and was passing through. ² And there was a man named Zac-chae′us; he was a chief tax collector, and rich. ³ And he sought to see who Jesus was, but could not, on account of the crowd, because he was small of stature. ⁴ So he ran on ahead and climbed up into a sycamore tree to see him, for he was to pass that way. ⁵ And when Jesus came to the place, he looked up and said to him, "Zac-chae′us, make haste and come down; for I must stay at your house today." ⁶ So he made haste and came down, and received him joyfully. ⁷ And when they saw it they all murmured, "He has gone in to be the guest of a man who is a sinner." ⁸ And Zac-chae′us stood and said to the Lord, "Behold, Lord, the half of my goods I give to the poor; and if I have defrauded any one of anything, I restore it fourfold." ⁹ And Jesus said to him, "Today salvation has come to this house, since he also is a son of Abraham. ¹⁰ For the Son of man came to seek and to save that which was lost."

11 As they heard these things, he proceeded to tell a parable, because he was near to Jerusalem, and because they supposed that the kingdom of God was to appear immediately. ¹² He said therefore, "A nobleman went into a far country to receive kingly power[j] and then return. ¹³ Calling ten of his servants, he gave them ten pounds,[k] and said to them, 'Trade with these till I come.' ¹⁴ But

[j] Greek *a kingdom.*   [k] The mina, rendered here by *pound*, was equal to about twenty dollars.

18. 42: Mt. 9. 22; Mk. 5. 34; 10. 52; Lk. 7. 50; 8. 48; 17. 19.
19. 1: Mk. 10. 46.   **19. 7:** Lk. 5. 29–30; 15. 1–2.   **19. 8:** Lk. 7. 13; 3. 14; Ex. 22. 1; Lev. 6. 5; Num. 5. 6–7.   **19. 9:** Lk. 3. 8; 13. 16; Rom. 4. 16.   **19. 11:** Lk. 9. 51, 13. 22; 17. 11; 18. 31; 9. 27.   **19. 12–28:** Mt. 25. 14–30.   **19. 12:** Mk. 13. 34.

his citizens hated him and sent an embassy after him, saying, 'We do not want this man to reign over us.' [15] When he returned, having received the kingly power,[j] he commanded these servants, to whom he had given the money, to be called to him, that he might know what they had gained by trading. [16] The first came before him, saying, 'Lord, your pound has made ten pounds more.' [17] And he said to him, 'Well done, good servant! Because you have been faithful in a very little, you shall have authority over ten cities.' [18] And the second came, saying, 'Lord, your pound has made five pounds.' [19] And he said to him, 'And you are to be over five cities.' [20] Then another came, saying, 'Lord, here is your pound, which I kept laid away in a napkin; [21] for I was afraid of you, because you are a severe man; you take up what you did not lay down, and reap what you did not sow.' [22] He said to him, 'I will condemn you out of your own mouth, you wicked servant! You knew that I was a severe man, taking up what I did not lay down and reaping what I did not sow? [23] Why then did you not put my money into the bank, and at my coming I should have collected it with interest?' [24] And he said to those who stood by, 'Take the pound from him, and give it to him who has the ten pounds.' [25] (And they said to him, 'Lord, he has ten pounds!') [26] 'I tell you, that to every one who has will more be given; but from him who has not, even what he has will be taken away. [27] But as for these enemies of mine, who did not want me to reign over them, bring them here and slay them before me.'"

28 And when he had said this, he went on ahead, going up to Jerusalem. [29] When he drew near to Beth'pha-ge and Bethany, at the mount that is called Olivet, he sent two

[j] Greek *a kingdom*

19. 17: Lk. 16. 10.   **19. 26:** Mt. 13. 12; Mk. 4. 25; Lk. 8. 18.   **19. 28:** Mk. 10. 32.
19. 29–38: Mt. 21. 1–9; Mk. 11. 1–10; Jn. 12. 12–18.

of the disciples, ³⁰ saying, "Go into the village opposite,
where on entering you will find a colt tied, on which no one
has ever yet sat; untie it and bring it here. ³¹ If any one asks
you, 'Why are you untying it?' you shall say this, 'The
Lord has need of it.'" ³² So those who were sent went away
and found it as he had told them. ³³ And as they were untying the colt, its owners said to them, "Why are you untying the colt?" ³⁴ And they said, "The Lord has need of
it." ³⁵ And they brought it to Jesus, and throwing their
garments on the colt they set Jesus upon it. ³⁶ And as he
rode along, they spread their garments on the road. ³⁷ As
he was now drawing near, at the descent of the Mount of
Olives, the whole multitude of the disciples began to rejoice
and praise God with a loud voice for all the mighty works
that they had seen, ³⁸ saying,

"Blessed be the King who comes in the name of the Lord!
    Peace in heaven and glory in the highest!"

³⁹ And some of the Pharisees in the multitude said to him,
"Teacher, rebuke your disciples." ⁴⁰ He answered, "I tell
you, if these were silent, the very stones would cry out."

41 And when he drew near and saw the city he wept over
it, ⁴² saying, "Would that even today you knew the things
that make for peace! But now they are hid from your eyes.
⁴³ For the days shall come upon you, when your enemies
will cast up a bank about you and surround you, and hem
you in on every side, ⁴⁴ and dash you to the ground, you
and your children within you, and they will not leave one
stone upon another in you; because you did not know the
time of your visitation."

45 And he entered the temple and began to drive out
those who sold, ⁴⁶ saying to them, "It is written, 'My house

19. 32: Lk. 22. 13.   **19. 34:** Lk. 7. 13.   **19. 36:** 2 Kings 9. 13.   **19. 38:** Ps. 118. 26;
Lk. 13. 35; 2. 14.   **19. 39–40:** Mt. 21. 15–16; Hab. 2. 11.   **19. 41:** Lk. 13. 33–34.
19. 43: Lk. 21. 21–24; 21. 6; Is. 29. 3; Jer. 6. 6; Ezek. 4. 2.   **19. 44:** 1 Pet. 2. 12.
19. 45–46: Mt. 21. 12–13; Mk. 11. 15–17; Jn. 2. 13–17.

shall be a house of prayer'; but you have made it a den of robbers."

47 And he was teaching daily in the temple. The chief priests and the scribes and the principal men of the people sought to destroy him; ⁴⁸ but they did not find anything they could do, for all the people hung upon his words.

20 One day, as he was teaching the people in the temple and preaching the gospel, the chief priests and the scribes with the elders came up ² and said to him, "Tell us by what authority you do these things, or who it is that gave you this authority." ³ He answered them, "I also will ask you a question; now tell me, ⁴ Was the baptism of John from heaven or from men?" ⁵ And they discussed it with one another, saying, "If we say, 'From heaven,' he will say, 'Why did you not believe him?' ⁶ But if we say, 'From men,' all the people will stone us; for they are convinced that John was a prophet." ⁷ So they answered that they did not know whence it was. ⁸ And Jesus said to them, "Neither will I tell you by what authority I do these things."

9 And he began to tell the people this parable: "A man planted a vineyard, and let it out to tenants, and went into another country for a long while. ¹⁰ When the time came, he sent a servant to the tenants, that they should give him some of the fruit of the vineyard; but the tenants beat him, and sent him away empty-handed. ¹¹ And he sent another servant; him also they beat and treated shamefully, and sent him away empty-handed. ¹² And he sent yet a third; this one they wounded and cast out. ¹³ Then the owner of the vineyard said, 'What shall I do? I will send my beloved son; it may be they will respect him.' ¹⁴ But when the tenants

19. 47–48: Mk. 11. 18; Lk. 21. 37; 22. 53.
20. 1–8: Mt. 21. 23–27; Mk. 11. 27–33. **20. 2:** Jn. 2. 18. **20. 6:** Mt. 14. 5; Lk. 7. 29.
20. 9–19: Mt. 21. 33–46; Mk. 12. 1–12. **20. 9:** Is. 5. 1–7; Mt. 25. 14.

saw him, they said to themselves, 'This is the heir; let us kill him, that the inheritance may be ours.' ¹⁵ And they cast him out of the vineyard and killed him. What then will the owner of the vineyard do to them? ¹⁶ He will come and destroy those tenants, and give the vineyard to others." When they heard this, they said, "God forbid!" ¹⁷ But he looked at them and said, "What then is this that is written:

'The very stone which the builders rejected
has become the head of the corner'?

¹⁸ Every one who falls on that stone will be broken to pieces; but when it falls on any one it will crush him."

19 The scribes and the chief priests tried to lay hands on him at that very hour, but they feared the people; for they perceived that he had told this parable against them. ²⁰ So they watched him, and sent spies, who pretended to be sincere, that they might take hold of what he said, so as to deliver him up to the authority and jurisdiction of the governor. ²¹ They asked him, "Teacher, we know that you speak and teach rightly, and show no partiality, but truly teach the way of God. ²² Is it lawful for us to give tribute to Caesar, or not?" ²³ But he perceived their craftiness, and said to them, ²⁴ "Show me a coin.¹ Whose likeness and inscription has it?" They said, "Caesar's." ²⁵ He said to them, "Then render to Caesar the things that are Caesar's, and to God the things that are God's." ²⁶ And they were not able in the presence of the people to catch him by what he said; but marveling at his answer they were silent.

27 There came to him some Sad'du-cees, those who say that there is no resurrection, ²⁸ and they asked him a question, saying, "Teacher, Moses wrote for us that if a man's

¹ Greek *denarius*.

20. 16: Acts 13. 46; 18. 6; 28. 28.   **20. 17:** Ps. 118. 22–23; Acts 4. 11; 1 Pet. 2. 6–7.
20. 18: Is. 8. 14–15.   **20. 19:** Lk. 19. 47.   **20. 20–26:** Mt. 22. 15–22; Mk. 12. 13–17.
20. 21: Jn. 3. 2.   **20. 25:** Rom. 13. 7; Lk. 23. 2.   **20. 27–38:** Mt. 22. 23–33;
Mk. 12. 18–27.   **20. 27:** Acts 4. 1–2; 23. 6–10.   **20. 28:** Deut. 25. 5.

brother dies, having a wife but no children, the man[^m] must take the wife and raise up children for his brother. [^29] Now there were seven brothers; the first took a wife, and died without children; [^30] and the second [^31] and the third took her, and likewise all seven left no children and died. [^32] Afterward the woman also died. [^33] In the resurrection, therefore, whose wife will the woman be? For the seven had her as wife."

34 And Jesus said to them, "The sons of this age marry and are given in marriage; [^35] but those who are accounted worthy to attain to that age and to the resurrection from the dead neither marry nor are given in marriage, [^36] for they cannot die any more, because they are equal to angels and are sons of God, being sons of the resurrection. [^37] But that the dead are raised, even Moses showed, in the passage about the bush, where he calls the Lord the God of Abraham and the God of Isaac and the God of Jacob. [^38] Now he is not God of the dead, but of the living; for all live to him." [^39] And some of the scribes answered, "Teacher, you have spoken well." [^40] For they no longer dared to ask him anything.

41 But he said to them, "How can they say that the Christ is David's son? [^42] For David himself says in the Book of Psalms,

'The Lord said to my Lord,
  Sit thou at my right hand,
[^43] till I make thy enemies a stool for thy feet.'
[^44] David thus calls him Lord; so how is he his son?"

45 And in the hearing of all the people he said to his disciples, [^46] "Beware of the scribes, who like to go about

[^m]: Greek *his brother.*

20. 37: Ex. 3. 6.   **20. 39:** Mk. 12. 28.   **20. 40:** Mk. 12. 34; Mt. 22. 46.   **20. 41–44:** Mt. 22. 41–45; Mk. 12. 35–37; Ps. 110. 1.   **20. 45–47:** Mk. 12. 38–40; Mt. 23. 6–7; Lk. 11. 43; 14. 7–11.

in long robes, and love salutations in the market places and the best seats in the synagogues and the places of honor at feasts, ⁴⁷ who devour widows' houses and for a pretense make long prayers. They will receive the greater condemnation."

21 He looked up and saw the rich putting their gifts into the treasury; ² and he saw a poor widow put in two copper coins. ³ And he said, "Truly I tell you, this poor widow has put in more than all of them; ⁴ for they all contributed out of their abundance, but she out of her poverty put in all the living that she had."

5 And as some spoke of the temple, how it was adorned with noble stones and offerings, he said, ⁶ "As for these things which you see, the days will come when there shall not be left here one stone upon another that will not be thrown down." ⁷ And they asked him, "Teacher, when will this be, and what will be the sign when this is about to take place?" ⁸ And he said, "Take heed that you are not led astray; for many will come in my name, saying, 'I am he!' and, 'The time is at hand!' Do not go after them. ⁹ And when you hear of wars and tumults, do not be terrified; for this must first take place, but the end will not be at once."

10 Then he said to them, "Nation will rise against nation, and kingdom against kingdom; ¹¹ there will be great earthquakes, and in various places famines and pestilences; and there will be terrors and great signs from heaven. ¹² But before all this they will lay their hands on you and persecute you, delivering you up to the synagogues and prisons, and you will be brought before kings and governors for my name's sake. ¹³ This will be a time for you to bear testimony.

21. 1–4: Mk. 12. 41–44.   **21. 5–23:** Mt. 24. 1–19; Mk. 13. 1–17.   **21. 6:** Lk. 19. 43–44; Mk. 14. 58; 15. 29; Acts 6. 14.   **21. 7:** Lk. 17. 20; Acts 1. 6.   **21. 8:** Lk. 17. 23; Mk. 13. 21; 1 Jn. 2. 18.   **21. 10:** 2 Chr. 15. 6; Is. 19. 2.   **21. 12–17:** Mt. 10. 17–21. **21. 12:** Acts 25. 24; Jn. 16. 2.   **21. 13:** Phil. 1. 12.

[14] Settle it therefore in your minds, not to meditate beforehand how to answer; [15] for I will give you a mouth and wisdom, which none of your adversaries will be able to withstand or contradict. [16] You will be delivered up even by parents and brothers and kinsmen and friends, and some of you they will put to death; [17] you will be hated by all for my name's sake. [18] But not a hair of your head will perish. [19] By your endurance you will gain your lives.

20 "But when you see Jerusalem surrounded by armies, then know that its desolation has come near. [21] Then let those who are in Judea flee to the mountains, and let those who are inside the city depart, and let not those who are out in the country enter it; [22] for these are days of vengeance, to fulfill all that is written. [23] Alas for those who are with child and for those who give suck in those days! For great distress shall be upon the earth and wrath upon this people; [24] they will fall by the edge of the sword, and be led captive among all nations; and Jerusalem will be trodden down by the Gentiles, until the times of the Gentiles are fulfilled.

25 "And there will be signs in sun and moon and stars, and upon the earth distress of nations in perplexity at the roaring of the sea and the waves, [26] men fainting with fear and with foreboding of what is coming on the world; for the powers of the heavens will be shaken. [27] And then they will see the Son of man coming in a cloud with power and great glory. [28] Now when these things begin to take place, look up and raise your heads, because your redemption is drawing near."

29 And he told them a parable: "Look at the fig tree, and all the trees; [30] as soon as they come out in leaf, you

21. 14-15: Lk. 12. 11-12.   21. 16: Lk. 12. 52-53.   21. 17: Mt. 10. 22; Jn. 15. 18-25.
21. 18: Lk. 12. 7; Mt. 10. 30; Acts 27. 34; 1 Sam. 14. 45.   21. 19: Mt. 10. 22; Rev.
2. 7.   21. 20-22: Lk. 19. 41-44; 23. 28-31; 17. 31.   21. 23: Lk. 23. 29.   21. 24:
Rom. 11. 25; Is. 63. 18; Dan. 8. 13; Rev. 11. 2.   21. 25-27: Mt. 24. 29-30; Mk.
13. 24-26.   21. 25: Rev. 6. 12-13; Is. 13. 10; Joel 2. 10; Zeph. 1. 15.   21. 27: Lk. 9. 27;
Dan. 7. 13-14.   21. 28: Lk. 18. 7-8.   21. 29-33: Mt. 24. 32-35; Mk. 13. 28-31.

see for yourselves and know that the summer is already near. [31] So also, when you see these things taking place, you know that the kingdom of God is near. [32] Truly, I say to you, this generation will not pass away till all has taken place. [33] Heaven and earth will pass away, but my words will not pass away.

34 "But take heed to yourselves lest your hearts be weighed down with dissipation and drunkenness and cares of this life, and that day come upon you suddenly like a snare; [35] for it will come upon all who dwell upon the face of the whole earth. [36] But watch at all times, praying that you may have strength to escape all these things that will take place, and to stand before the Son of man."

37 And every day he was teaching in the temple, but at night he went out and lodged on the mount called Olivet. [38] And early in the morning all the people came to him in the temple to hear him.

22 Now the feast of Unleavened Bread drew near, which is called the Passover. [2] And the chief priests and the scribes were seeking how to put him to death; for they feared the people.

3 Then Satan entered into Judas called Iscariot, who was of the number of the twelve; [4] he went away and conferred with the chief priests and captains how he might betray him to them. [5] And they were glad, and engaged to give him money. [6] So he agreed, and sought an opportunity to betray him to them in the absence of the multitude.

7 Then came the day of Unleavened Bread, on which the passover lamb had to be sacrificed. [8] So Jesus[n] sent Peter and John, saying, "Go and prepare the passover for us, that

[n] Greek *he.*

21. 32: Lk. 9. 27.   **21. 33:** Lk. 16. 17.   **21. 34:** Lk. 12. 45; Mk. 4. 19; 1 Thess. 5. 6–7.   **21. 36:** Mk. 13. 33.   **21. 37:** Lk. 19. 47; Mk. 11. 19.   **22. 1–2:** Mt. 26. 2–5; Mk. 14. 1–2; Jn. 11. 47–53.   **22. 3–6:** Mt. 26. 14–16; Mk. 14. 10–11; Jn. 13. 2.   **22. 7–13:** Mt. 26. 17–19; Mk. 14. 12–16.   **22. 7:** Ex. 12. 18–20; Deut. 16. 5–8.   **22. 8:** Acts 3. 1; Lk. 19. 29.

we may eat it." ⁹ They said to him, "Where will you have us prepare it?" ¹⁰ He said to them, "Behold, when you have entered the city, a man carrying a jar of water will meet you; follow him into the house which he enters, ¹¹ and tell the householder, 'The Teacher says to you, Where is the guest room, where I am to eat the passover with my disciples?' ¹² And he will show you a large upper room furnished; there make ready." ¹³ And they went, and found it as he had told them; and they prepared the passover.

14 And when the hour came, he sat at table, and the apostles with him. ¹⁵ And he said to them, "I have earnestly desired to eat this passover with you before I suffer; ¹⁶ for I tell you I shall never eat it again*⁰* until it is fulfilled in the kingdom of God." ¹⁷ And he took a cup, and when he had given thanks he said, "Take this, and divide it among yourselves; ¹⁸ for I tell you that from now on I shall not drink of the fruit of the vine until the kingdom of God comes." ¹⁹ And he took bread, and when he had given thanks he broke it and gave it to them, saying, "This is my body.*ᵖ* ²¹ But behold the hand of him who betrays me is with me on the table. ²² For the Son of man goes as it has been determined; but woe to that man by whom he is betrayed!" ²³ And they began to question one another, which of them it was that would do this.

24 A dispute also arose among them, which of them was to be regarded as the greatest. ²⁵ And he said to them, "The kings of the Gentiles exercise lordship over them; and those in authority over them are called benefactors. ²⁶ But not so with you; rather let the greatest among you become as

ᵒ Some ancient authorities omit *again*.   *ᵖ* Many ancient authorities add *which is given for you. Do this in remembrance of me.*" ²⁰ *And likewise the cup after supper, saying, "This cup which is poured out for you is the new covenant in my blood.*

22. 14: Mt. 26. 20; Mk. 14. 17; Jn. 13. 17.   **22. 15:** Lk. 12. 49–50.   **22. 16:** Lk. 14. 15.
22. 17: Mt. 26. 27; Mk. 14. 23; 1 Cor. 10. 16.   **22. 18:** Mt. 26. 29; Mk. 14. 25.
22. 19: Mt. 26. 26; Mk. 14. 22; 1 Cor. 10. 16; 11. 23–26; Lk. 9. 16.   **22. 21–23:** Mt. 26. 21–24; Mk. 14. 18–21; Ps. 41. 9; Jn. 13. 21–30.   **22. 24:** Lk. 9. 46; Mk. 9. 34.
22. 25–27: Mt. 20. 25–28; Mk. 10. 42–45; Jn. 13. 3–16.   **22. 26:** Lk. 9. 48.

the youngest, and the leader as one who serves. ²⁷ For which is the greater, one who sits at table, or one who serves? Is it not the one who sits at table? But I am among you as one who serves.

28 "You are those who have continued with me in my trials; ²⁹ as my Father appointed a kingdom for me, so do I appoint for you ³⁰ that you may eat and drink at my table in my kingdom, and sit on thrones judging the twelve tribes of Israel.

31 "Simon, Simon, behold, Satan demanded to have you,*q* that he might sift you*q* like wheat, ³² but I have prayed for you that your faith may not fail; and when you have turned again, strengthen your brethren." ³³ And he said to him, "Lord, I am ready to go with you to prison and to death." ³⁴ He said, "I tell you, Peter, the cock will not crow this day, until you three times deny that you know me."

35 And he said to them, "When I sent you out with no purse or bag or sandals, did you lack anything?" They said, "Nothing." ³⁶ He said to them, "But now, let him who has a purse take it, and likewise a bag. And let him who has no sword sell his mantle and buy one. ³⁷ For I tell you that this scripture must be fulfilled in me, 'And he was reckoned with transgressors'; for what is written about me has its fulfillment." ³⁸ And they said, "Look, Lord, here are two swords." And he said to them, "It is enough."

39 And he came out, and went, as was his custom, to the Mount of Olives; and the disciples followed him. ⁴⁰ And when he came to the place he said to them, "Pray that you may not enter into temptation." ⁴¹ And he withdrew

---

q The Greek word for *you* here is plural; in verse 32 it is singular.

22. 28–30: Mt. 19. 28.   **22. 28:** Lk. 4. 13; Heb. 2. 18; 4. 15.   **22. 29:** Mk. 14. 24; Heb. 9. 20.   **22. 30:** Mk. 10. 37; Rev. 3. 21; 20. 4. **22. 31:** Job 1. 6–12; Amos 9. 9.
22. 32: Jn. 17. 15; 21. 15–17.   **22. 33–34:** Mt. 26. 33–35; Mk. 14. 29–31; Jn. 13. 37–38.
22. 35: Lk. 10. 4; Mt. 10. 9.   **22. 36:** Lk. 22. 49–50.   **22. 37:** Is. 53. 12.   **22. 39:** Mt. 26. 30; Mk. 14. 26; Jn. 18. 1.   **22. 40–46:** Mt. 26. 36–46; Mk. 14. 32–42; Heb. 5. 7–8.   **22. 40:** Lk. 11. 4.

from them about a stone's throw, and knelt down and prayed, [42] saying, "Father, if thou art willing, remove this cup from me; nevertheless not my will, but thine, be done." [43] And there appeared to him an angel from heaven, strengthening him. [44] And being in an agony he prayed more earnestly; and his sweat became like great drops of blood falling down upon the ground.[r] [45] And when he rose from prayer, he came to the disciples and found them sleeping for sorrow, [46] and he said to them, "Why do you sleep? Rise and pray that you may not enter into temptation."

47 While he was still speaking, there came a crowd, and the man called Judas, one of the twelve, was leading them. He drew near to Jesus to kiss him; [48] but Jesus said to him, "Judas, would you betray the Son of man with a kiss?" [49] And when those who were about him saw what would follow, they said, "Lord, shall we strike with the sword?" [50] And one of them struck the slave of the high priest and cut off his right ear. [51] But Jesus said, "No more of this!" And he touched his ear and healed him. [52] Then Jesus said to the chief priests and captains of the temple and elders, who had come out against him, "Have you come out as against a robber, with swords and clubs? [53] When I was with you day after day in the temple, you did not lay hands on me. But this is your hour, and the power of darkness."

54 Then they seized him and led him away, bringing him into the high priest's house. Peter followed at a distance; [55] and when they had kindled a fire in the middle of the courtyard and sat down together, Peter sat among them. [56] Then a maid, seeing him as he sat in the light and gazing at him, said, "This man also was with him."

[r] Many ancient authorities omit verses 43 and 44.

22. 42: Mk. 10. 38; Jn. 18. 11; 5. 30.   **22. 47–53:** Mt. 26. 47–56; Mk. 14. 43–49; Jn. 18. 3–11.   **22. 49:** Lk. 22. 38.   **22. 53:** Lk. 19. 47.   **22. 54–55:** Mt. 26. 57–58; Mk. 14. 53–54; Jn. 18. 12–16.   **22. 56–62:** Mt. 26. 69–75; Mk. 14. 66–72; Jn. 18. 16–18, 25–27.

[57] But he denied it, saying, "Woman, I do not know him." [58] And a little later some one else saw him and said, "You also are one of them." But Peter said, "Man, I am not." [59] And after an interval of about an hour still another insisted, saying, "Certainly this man also was with him; for he is a Galilean." [60] But Peter said, "Man, I do not know what you are saying." And immediately, while he was still speaking, the cock crowed. [61] And the Lord turned and looked at Peter. And Peter remembered the word of the Lord, how he had said to him, "Before the cock crows today, you will deny me three times." [62] And he went out, and wept bitterly.

63 Now the men who were holding Jesus mocked him and beat him; [64] they also blindfolded him and asked him, "Prophesy! Who is it that struck you?" [65] And they spoke many other words against him, reviling him.

66 When day came, the assembly of the elders of the people gathered together, both chief priests and scribes; and they led him away to their council, and they said, [67] "If you are the Christ, tell us." But he said to them, "If I tell you, you will not believe; [68] and if I ask you, you will not answer. [69] But from now on the Son of man shall be seated at the right hand of the power of God." [70] And they all said, "Are you the Son of God, then?" And he said to them, "You say that I am." [71] And they said, "What further testimony do we need? We have heard it ourselves from his own lips."

23 Then the whole company of them arose, and brought him before Pilate. [2] And they began to accuse him, saying, "We found this man perverting our nation, and forbidding us to give tribute to Caesar, and saying that he himself is Christ a king." [3] And Pilate asked him, "Are

22. 61: Lk. 7. 13; 22. 34.   **22. 63–65:** Mt. 26. 67–68; Mk. 14. 65; Jn. 18. 22–24.
22. 66: Mt. 26. 57; Mk. 14. 53; Lk. 22. 54.   **22. 67–71:** Mt. 26. 63–66; Mk. 14. 61–64;
Jn. 18. 19–21.   **22. 70:** Lk. 23. 3; Mt. 27. 11.
23. 1: Mt. 27. 1–2; Mk. 15. 1; Jn. 18. 28.   **23. 2:** Lk. 20. 25.   **23. 3:** Mt. 27. 11–12;
Mk. 15. 2–3; Jn. 18. 29–38; Lk. 22. 70.

you the King of the Jews?" And he answered him, "You
have said so." [4] And Pilate said to the chief priests and the
multitudes, "I find no crime in this man." [5] But they were
urgent, saying, "He stirs up the people, teaching throughout
all Judea, from Galilee even to this place."

6 When Pilate heard this, he asked whether the man
was a Galilean. [7] And when he learned that he belonged
to Herod's jurisdiction, he sent him over to Herod, who was
himself in Jerusalem at that time. [8] When Herod saw Jesus,
he was very glad, for he had long desired to see him, because
he had heard about him, and he was hoping to see some sign
done by him. [9] So he questioned him at some length; but he
made no answer. [10] The chief priests and the scribes stood
by, vehemently accusing him. [11] And Herod with his soldiers
treated him with contempt and mocked him; then, arraying
him in gorgeous apparel, he sent him back to Pilate. [12] And
Herod and Pilate became friends with each other that very
day, for before this they had been at enmity with each other.

13 Pilate then called together the chief priests and the
rulers and the people, [14] and said to them, "You brought
me this man as one who was perverting the people; and
after examining him before you, behold, I did not find this
man guilty of any of your charges against him; [15] neither
did Herod, for he sent him back to us. Behold, nothing
deserving death has been done by him; [16] I will therefore
chastise him and release him."[s]

18 But they all cried out together, "Away with this man,
and release to us Bar-ab′bas" — [19] a man who had been
thrown into prison for an insurrection started in the city,

---

[s] Here, or after verse 19, some ancient authorities add verse 17, *Now he was obliged to release one man to them at the festival.*

23. 4: Lk. 23. 14, 22, 41; Mt. 27. 24; Jn. 19. 4, 6; Acts 13. 28.　　　**23. 8:** Lk. 9. 9;
Acts 4. 27–28.　　**23. 9:** Mk. 15. 5.　　**23. 11:** Mk. 15. 17–19; Jn. 19. 2–3.　　**23. 14:**
Lk. 23. 4; 22, 41.　　**23. 16:** Lk. 23. 22; Jn. 19. 12–14.　　**23. 18–23:** Mt. 27. 20–23;
Mk. 15 11–14; Acts 3. 13–14; Jn. 18. 38–40; 19. 14–15.

and for murder. [20] Pilate addressed them once more, desiring to release Jesus; [21] but they shouted out, "Crucify, crucify him!" [22] A third time he said to them, "Why, what evil has he done? I have found in him no crime deserving death; I will therefore chastise him and release him." [23] But they were urgent, demanding with loud cries that he should be crucified. And their voices prevailed. [24] So Pilate gave sentence that their demand should be granted. [25] He released the man who had been thrown into prison for insurrection and murder, whom they asked for; but Jesus he delivered up to their will.

26 And as they led him away, they seized one Simon of Cy-re′ne, who was coming in from the country, and laid on him the cross, to carry it behind Jesus. [27] And there followed him a great multitude of the people, and of women who bewailed and lamented him. [28] But Jesus turning to them said, "Daughters of Jerusalem, do not weep for me, but weep for yourselves and for your children. [29] For behold, the days are coming when they will say, 'Blessed are the barren, and the wombs that never bore, and the breasts that never gave suck!' [30] Then they will begin to say to the mountains, 'Fall on us'; and to the hills, 'Cover us.' [31] For if they do this when the wood is green, what will happen when it is dry?"

32 Two others also, who were criminals, were led away to be put to death with him. [33] And when they came to the place which is called The Skull, there they crucified him, and the criminals, one on the right and one on the left. [34] And Jesus said, "Father, forgive them; for they know not what they do."[t] And they cast lots to divide his garments. [35] And the

---

[t] Some ancient authorities omit the sentence *And Jesus . . . . what they do.*

23. 23–25: Mt. 27. 26; Mk. 15. 15.   **23. 26:** Mt. 27. 32; Mk. 15. 21; Jn. 19. 17.
23. 28–31: Lk. 21. 23–24; 19. 41–44.   **23. 33–39:** Mt. 27. 33–44; Mk. 15. 22–32;
Jn. 19. 17–24.   **23. 34:** Acts 7. 60; Ps. 22. 18.   **23. 35:** Lk. 4. 23.

people stood by, watching; but the rulers scoffed at him, saying, "He saved others; let him save himself, if he is the Christ of God, his Chosen One!" [36] The soldiers also mocked him, coming up and offering him vinegar, [37] and saying, "If you are the King of the Jews, save yourself!" [38] There was also an inscription over him,[u] "This is the King of the Jews."

39 One of the criminals who were hanged railed at him, saying, "Are you not the Christ? Save yourself and us!" [40] But the other rebuked him, saying, "Do you not fear God, since you are under the same sentence of condemnation? [41] And we indeed justly; for we are receiving the due reward of our deeds; but this man has done nothing wrong." [42] And he said, "Jesus, remember me when you come in your kingly power."[v] [43] And he said to him, "Truly, I say to you, today you will be with me in Paradise."

44 It was now about the sixth hour, and there was darkness over the whole land[w] until the ninth hour, [45] while the sun's light failed;[x] and the curtain of the temple was torn in two. [46] Then Jesus, crying with a loud voice, said, "Father, into thy hands I commit my spirit!" And having said this he breathed his last. [47] Now when the centurion saw what had taken place, he praised God, and said, "Certainly this man was innocent!" [48] And all the multitudes who assembled to see the sight, when they saw what had taken place, returned home beating their breasts. [49] And all his acquaintances and the women who had followed him from Galilee stood at a distance and saw these things.

50 Now there was a man named Joseph from the Jewish town of Ar-i-ma-the'a. He was a member of the council, a

---

[u] Many ancient authorities add *in letters of Greek and Latin and Hebrew*.
[v] Greek *kingdom*. [w] Or *earth*. [x] Or *the sun was eclipsed*. Many ancient authorities read *the sun was darkened*.

23. 36: Mk. 15. 23; Ps. 69. 21.   **23. 41:** Lk. 23. 4, 14, 22.   **23. 43:** 2 Cor. 12. 4; Rev. 2. 7.   **23. 44–49:** Mt. 27. 45–56; Mk. 15. 33–41; Jn. 19. 25–30.   **23. 45:** Ex. 26. 31–35; Heb. 9. 8; 10. 19.   **23. 49:** Lk. 8. 1–3; 23. 55–56; 24. 10.   **23. 50–56:** Mt. 27. 57–61; Mk. 15. 42–47; Jn. 19. 38–42; Acts 13. 29.

good and righteous man, [51] who had not consented to their purpose and deed, and he was looking for the kingdom of God. [52] This man went to Pilate and asked for the body of Jesus. [53] Then he took it down and wrapped it in a linen shroud, and laid him in a rock-hewn tomb, where no one had ever yet been laid. [54] It was the day of Preparation, and the sabbath was beginning.[y] [55] The women who had come with him from Galilee followed, and saw the tomb, and how his body was laid; [56] then they returned, and prepared spices and ointments.

On the sabbath they rested according to the commandment.

24 But on the first day of the week, at early dawn, they went to the tomb, taking the spices which they had prepared. [2] And they found the stone rolled away from the tomb, [3] but when they went in they did not find the body.[z] [4] While they were perplexed about this, behold, two men stood by them in dazzling apparel; [5] and as they were frightened and bowed their faces to the ground, the men said to them, "Why do you seek the living among the dead?[a] [6] Remember how he told you, while he was still in Galilee, [7] that the Son of man must be delivered into the hands of sinful men, and be crucified, and on the third day rise." [8] And they remembered his words, [9] and returning from the tomb they told all this to the eleven and to all the rest. [10] Now it was Mary Mag'da-lene and Jo-an'na and Mary the mother of James and the other women with them who told this to the apostles; [11] but these words seemed to them an idle tale, and they did not believe them.[b]

[y] Greek *was dawning*.   [z] Some ancient authorities add *of the Lord Jesus*.
[a] Some ancient authorities add *He is not here, but has risen*.   [b] Some ancient authorities add verse 12, *But Peter rose and ran to the tomb; stooping and looking in, he saw the linen cloths by themselves; and he went home wondering at what had happened.*

23. 56: Mk. 16. 1; Ex. 12. 16; 20. 10.
24. 1–9: Mt. 28. 1–8; Mk. 16. 1–7; Jn. 20. 1, 11–13.   **24. 6:** Lk. 9. 22; 13. 32–33.
24. 10: Mk. 16. 1; Lk. 8. 1–3; Jn. 20. 2.

13 That very day two of them were going to a village named Em-ma'us, about seven miles[c] from Jerusalem, [14] and talking with each other about all these things that had happened. [15] While they were talking and discussing together, Jesus himself drew near and went with them. [16] But their eyes were kept from recognizing him. [17] And he said to them, "What is this conversation which you are holding with each other as you walk?" And they stood still, looking sad. [18] Then one of them, named Cle'o-pas, answered him, "Are you the only visitor to Jerusalem who does not know the things that have happened there in these days?" [19] And he said to them, "What things?" And they said to him, "Concerning Jesus of Nazareth, who was a prophet mighty in deed and word before God and all the people, [20] and how our chief priests and rulers delivered him up to be condemned to death and crucified him. [21] But we had hoped that he was the one to redeem Israel. Yes, and besides all this, it is now the third day since this happened. [22] Moreover, some women of our company amazed us. They were at the tomb early in the morning [23] and did not find his body; and they came back saying that they had even seen a vision of angels, who said that he was alive. [24] Some of those who were with us went to the tomb, and found it just as the women had said; but him they did not see." [25] And he said to them, "O foolish men, and slow of heart to believe all that the prophets have spoken! [26] Was it not necessary that the Christ should suffer these things and enter into his glory?" [27] And beginning with Moses and all the prophets, he interpreted to them in all the scriptures the things concerning himself.

28 So they drew near to the village to which they were

[c] Greek *sixty stadia.*

24. 16: Jn. 20. 14; 21. 4.   **24. 19:** Mt. 21. 11; Lk. 7. 16; 13. 33; Acts 3. 22.
24. 24: Jn. 20. 3–10.   **24. 27:** Lk. 24. 44–45; Acts 28. 23; 1 Pet. 1. 11.   **24. 28:** Mk. 6. 48.

going; and he made as though he would go further, ²⁹ but they constrained him, saying, "Stay with us, for it is toward evening and the day is now far spent." So he went in to stay with them. ³⁰ When he was at table with them, he took the bread and blessed, and broke it, and gave it to them. ³¹ And their eyes were opened and they recognized him; and he vanished out of their sight. ³² They said to each other, "Did not our hearts burn within us while he talked to us on the road, while he opened to us the scriptures?" ³³ And they rose that same hour and returned to Jerusalem; and they found the eleven gathered together and those who were with them, ³⁴ who said, "The Lord has risen indeed, and has appeared to Simon!" ³⁵ Then they told what had happened on the road, and how he was known to them in the breaking of the bread.

36 As they were saying this, Jesus himself stood among them.ᵈ ³⁷ But they were startled and frightened, and supposed that they saw a spirit. ³⁸ And he said to them, "Why are you troubled, and why do questionings rise in your hearts? ³⁹ See my hands and my feet, that it is I myself; handle me, and see; for a spirit has not flesh and bones as you see that I have.ᵉ ⁴¹ And while they still disbelieved for joy, and wondered, he said to them, "Have you anything here to eat?" ⁴² They gave him a piece of broiled fish, ⁴³ and he took it and ate before them.

44 Then he said to them, "These are my words which I spoke to you, while I was still with you, that everything written about me in the law of Moses and the prophets and the psalms must be fulfilled." ⁴⁵ Then he opened their minds to understand the scriptures, ⁴⁶ and said to them,

---

ᵈ Some ancient authorities add *and said to them, "Peace to you!"*   ᵉ Some ancient authorities add verse 40, *And when he had said this, he showed them his hands and his feet.*

24. 30: Lk. 9. 16; 22. 19.   **24. 34:** 1 Cor. 15. 5.   **24. 36–43:** Jn. 20. 19–20, 27; Jn. 21. 5, 9–13; 1 Cor. 15. 5; Acts 10. 40–41.   **24. 39:** 1 Jn. 1. 1.   **24. 44:** Lk. 24. 26–27; Acts 28. 23.   **24. 46:** Hos. 6. 2; 1 Cor. 15. 3–4.

"Thus it is written, that the Christ should suffer and on the third day rise from the dead, [47] and that repentance and forgiveness of sins should be preached in his name to all nations,[f] beginning from Jerusalem. [48] You are witnesses of these things. [49] And behold, I send the promise of my Father upon you; but stay in the city, until you are clothed with power from on high."

50 Then he led them out as far as Bethany, and lifting up his hands he blessed them. [51] While he blessed them, he parted from them.[g] [52] And they[h] returned to Jerusalem with great joy, [53] and were continually in the temple blessing God.

THE GOSPEL ACCORDING TO

JOHN

1 In the beginning was the Word, and the Word was with God, and the Word was God. [2] He was in the beginning with God; [3] all things were made through him, and without him was not anything made that was made. [4] In him was life,[a] and the life was the light of men. [5] The light shines in the darkness, and the darkness has not overcome it.

6 There was a man sent from God, whose name was John. [7] He came for testimony, to bear witness to the light, that all might believe through him. [8] He was not the light, but came to bear witness to the light.

9 The true light that enlightens every man was coming into the world; [10] he was in the world, and the world was

---

[f] Or *nations. Beginning from Jerusalem you are witnesses.*   [g] Many ancient authorities add *and was carried up into heaven.*   [h] Many ancient authorities add *worshiped him, and.*
[a] Or *was not anything made. That which has been made was life in him.*

24. 47: Acts 1. 4–8; Mt. 28. 19.   24. 49: Acts 2. 1–4; Jn. 14. 26; 20. 21–23.
24. 51: Acts 1. 9–11.   24. 52–53: Acts 1. 12–14.
1. 1: Gen. 1. 1; 1 Jn. 1. 1; Rev. 19. 13; Jn. 17. 5.   1. 3: Col. 1. 16; 1 Cor. 8. 6;
Heb. 1. 2.   1. 4: Jn. 5. 26; 11. 25; 14. 6.   1. 5: Jn. 9. 5; 12. 46.   1. 6: Mk. 1. 4;
Mt. 3. 1; Lk. 3. 3; Jn. 1. 19–23.   1. 9: 1 Jn. 2. 8.

made through him, yet the world knew him not; [11] he came to his own home, and his own people received him not. [12] But to all who received him, who believed in his name, he gave power to become children of God; [13] who were born, not of blood nor of the will of the flesh nor of the will of man, but of God.

14 And the Word became flesh and dwelt among us, full of grace and truth; we have beheld his glory, glory as of the only Son from the Father. ([15] John bore witness to him, and cried, "This was he of whom I said, 'He who comes after me ranks before me, for he was before me.'") [16] And from his fullness have we all received, grace upon grace. [17] For the law was given through Moses; grace and truth came through Jesus Christ. [18] No one has ever seen God; the only Son, who is in the bosom of the Father, he has made him known.

19 And this is the testimony of John, when the Jews sent priests and Levites from Jerusalem to ask him, "Who are you?" [20] He confessed, he did not deny, but confessed, "I am not the Christ." [21] And they asked him, "What then? Are you Elijah?" He said, "I am not." "Are you the prophet?" And he answered, "No." [22] They said to him then, "Who are you? Let us have an answer for those who sent us. What do you say about yourself?" [23] He said, "I am the voice of one crying in the wilderness, 'Make straight the way of the Lord,' as the prophet Isaiah said."

24 Now they had been sent from the Pharisees. [25] They asked him, "Then why are you baptizing, if you are neither the Christ, nor Elijah, nor the prophet?" [26] John answered them, "I baptize with water; but among you stands one whom you do not know, [27] even he who comes after me, the

1. 12: Gal. 3. 26; Jn. 3. 18; 1 Jn. 5. 13.   **1. 13:** Jn. 3. 5; 1 Pet. 1. 23; Jas. 1. 18;
1 Jn. 3. 9.   **1. 14:** Rom. 1. 3; Gal. 4. 4; Phil. 2. 7; 1 Tim. 3. 16; Heb. 2. 14; 1 Jn. 4. 2.
1. 15: Jn. 1. 30.   **1. 16:** Col. 1. 19; 2. 9; Eph. 1. 23; Rom. 5. 21.   **1. 17:** Jn. 7. 19.
1. 18: Ex. 33. 20; Jn. 6. 26; 1 Jn. 4. 12; Jn. 3. 11.   **1. 19:** Jn. 1. 6.   **1. 20:** Jn. 3. 28.
1. 21: Mt. 11. 14; 16. 14; Mk. 9. 13; Mt. 17. 13; Deut. 18. 15, 18.   **1. 23:** Is. 40. 3;
Mk. 1. 3; Mt. 3. 3; Lk. 3. 4.   **1. 26-27:** Mk. 1. 7-8; Mt. 3. 11; Lk. 3. 16.

thong of whose sandal I am not worthy to untie." ²⁸ This took place in Bethany beyond the Jordan, where John was baptizing.

29 The next day he saw Jesus coming toward him, and said, "Behold, the Lamb of God, who takes away the sin of the world! ³⁰ This is he of whom I said, 'After me comes a man who ranks before me, for he was before me.' ³¹ I myself did not know him; but for this I came baptizing with water, that he might be revealed to Israel." ³² And John bore witness, "I saw the Spirit descend as a dove from heaven, and it remained on him. ³³ I myself did not know him; but he who sent me to baptize with water said to me, 'He on whom you see the Spirit descend and remain, this is he who baptizes with the Holy Spirit.' ³⁴ And I have seen and have borne witness that this is the Son of God."

35 The next day again John was standing with two of his disciples; ³⁶ and he looked at Jesus as he walked, and said, "Behold, the Lamb of God!" ³⁷ The two disciples heard him say this, and they followed Jesus. ³⁸ Jesus turned, and saw them following, and said to them, "What do you seek?" And they said to him, "Rabbi (which means Teacher), where are you staying?" ³⁹ He said to them, "Come and see." They came and saw where he was staying; and they stayed with him that day, for it was about the tenth hour. ⁴⁰ One of the two who heard John speak, and followed him, was Andrew, Simon Peter's brother. ⁴¹ He first found his brother Simon, and said to him, "We have found the Messiah" (which means Christ). ⁴² He brought him to Jesus. Jesus looked at him, and said, "So you are Simon the son of John? You shall be called Ce′phas" (which means Rock*b*).

b Greek *Peter.*

1. 28: Jn. 3. 26; 10. 40.   **1. 29:** Jn. 1. 36; Is. 53. 7; Acts 8. 32; 1 Pet. 1. 19; Rev. 5. 6; 1 Jn. 3. 5.   **1. 30:** Jn. 1. 15.   **1. 32:** Mk. 1. 10; Mt. 3. 16; Lk. 3. 22.   **1. 35:** Lk. 7. 18.   **1. 40–42:** Mt. 4. 18–22; Mk. 1. 16–20; Lk. 5. 2–11.   **1. 41:** Dan. 9. 25; Jn. 4. 25.   **1. 42:** Jn. 21. 15–17; 1 Cor. 15. 5; Mt. 16. 18.

43 The next day Jesus decided to go to Galilee. And he found Philip and said to him, "Follow me." [44] Now Philip was from Beth-sa'i-da, the city of Andrew and Peter. [45] Philip found Na-than'a-el, and said to him, "We have found him of whom Moses in the law and also the prophets wrote, Jesus of Nazareth, the son of Joseph." [46] Na-than'a-el said to him, "Can anything good come out of Nazareth?" Philip said to him, "Come and see." [47] Jesus saw Na-than'a-el coming to him, and said of him, "Behold, an Israelite indeed, in whom is no guile!" [48] Na-than'a-el said to him, "How do you know me?" Jesus answered him, "Before Philip called you, when you were under the fig tree, I saw you." [49] Na-than'a-el answered him, "Rabbi, you are the Son of God! You are the King of Israel!" [50] Jesus answered him, "Because I said to you, I saw you under the fig tree, do you believe? You shall see greater things than these." [51] And he said to him, "Truly, truly, I say to you, you will see heaven opened, and the angels of God ascending and descending upon the Son of man."

2 On the third day there was a marriage at Cana in Galilee, and the mother of Jesus was there; [2] Jesus also was invited to the marriage, with his disciples. [3] When the wine failed, the mother of Jesus said to him, "They have no wine." [4] And Jesus said to her, "O woman, what have you to do with me? My hour has not yet come." [5] His mother said to the servants, "Do whatever he tells you." [6] Now six stone jars were standing there, for the Jewish rites of purification, each holding two or three measures.[c] [7] Jesus said to them, "Fill the jars with water." And they filled them up to the brim. [8] He said to them, "Now draw some

[c] That is, about twenty or thirty gallons.

1. 43: Mt. 10. 3; Jn. 6. 5; 12. 21; 14. 8.   **1. 45:** Lk. 24. 27.   **1. 46:** Jn. 7. 41; Mk. 6. 2.   **1. 49:** Ps. 2. 7; Mk. 15. 32; Jn. 12. 13.   **1. 51:** Lk. 3. 21; Gen. 28. 12. **2. 1:** Jn. 4. 46; 21. 2.   **2. 3:** Jn. 19. 26; Mk. 3. 31.   **2. 4:** Mk. 1. 24; 5. 7; Jn. 7. 6, 30; 8. 20.   **2. 6:** Mk. 7. 3; Jn. 3. 25.

out, and take it to the steward of the feast." So they took it.
⁹ When the steward of the feast tasted the water now become wine, and did not know where it came from (though
the servants who had drawn the water knew), the steward
of the feast called the bridegroom ¹⁰ and said to him, "Every
man serves the good wine first; and when men have drunk
freely, then the poor wine; but you have kept the good wine
until now." ¹¹ This, the first of his signs, Jesus did at Cana in
Galilee, and manifested his glory; and his disciples believed
in him.

12 After this he went down to Ca-per′na-um, with his
mother and his brothers and his disciples; and there they
stayed for a few days.

13 The Passover of the Jews was at hand, and Jesus went
up to Jerusalem. ¹⁴ In the temple he found those who were
selling oxen and sheep and pigeons, and the money-changers
at their business. ¹⁵ And making a whip of cords, he drove
them all, with the sheep and oxen, out of the temple; and
he poured out the coins of the money-changers and overturned their tables. ¹⁶ And he told those who sold the pigeons, "Take these things away; you shall not make my
Father's house a house of trade." ¹⁷ His disciples remembered
that it was written, "Zeal for thy house will consume me."
¹⁸ The Jews then said to him, "What sign have you to show
us for doing this?" ¹⁹ Jesus answered them, "Destroy this
temple, and in three days I will raise it up." ²⁰ The Jews then
said, "It has taken forty-six years to build this temple, and
will you raise it up in three days?" ²¹ But he spoke of the
temple of his body. ²² When therefore he was raised from
the dead, his disciples remembered that he had said this;

2. 11: Jn. 2. 23; 3. 2; 4. 54; 6. 2.   **2. 12:** Mt. 4. 13; Jn. 7. 3; Mk. 3. 31.
2. 13: Jn. 6. 4; 11. 55; Deut. 16. 1–6; Lk. 2. 41.   **2. 14–16:** Mt. 21. 12–13; Mk. 11.
15–17; Lk. 19. 45–46.   **2. 16:** Lk. 2. 49.   **2. 17:** Ps. 69. 9.   **2. 18:** Mk. 11. 28;
Mt. 21. 23; Lk. 20. 2.   **2. 19:** Mk. 14. 58; Acts 6. 14.   **2. 21:** 1 Cor. 6. 19; Jn. 8. 57.
2. 22: Jn. 12. 16; 14. 26.

and they believed the scripture and the word which Jesus had spoken.

23 Now when he was in Jerusalem at the Passover feast, many believed in his name when they saw his signs which he did; [24] but Jesus did not trust himself to them, [25] because he knew all men and needed no one to bear witness of man; for he himself knew what was in man.

3 Now there was a man of the Pharisees, named Nic-o-de'mus, a ruler of the Jews. [2] This man came to Jesus[d] by night and said to him, "Rabbi, we know that you are a teacher come from God; for no one can do these signs that you do, unless God is with him." [3] Jesus answered him, "Truly, truly, I say to you, unless one is born anew, he cannot see the kingdom of God." [4] Nic-o-de'mus said to him, "How can a man be born when he is old? Can he enter a second time into his mother's womb and be born?" [5] Jesus answered, "Truly, truly, I say to you, unless one is born of water and the Spirit, he cannot enter the kingdom of God. [6] That which is born of the flesh is flesh, and that which is born of the Spirit is spirit.[e] [7] Do not marvel that I said to you, 'You must be born anew.' [8] The wind[e] blows where it wills, and you hear the sound of it, but you do not know whence it comes or whither it goes; so it is with every one who is born of the Spirit." [9] Nic-o-de'mus said to him, "How can this be?" [10] Jesus answered him, "Are you a teacher of Israel, and yet you do not understand this? [11] Truly, truly, I say to you, we speak of what we know, and bear witness to what we have seen; but you do not receive our testimony. [12] If I have told you earthly things and you do not believe, how can you believe if I tell you heavenly things? [13] No one

[d] Greek *him.*   [e] The same Greek word means both *wind* and *spirit.*

2. 25: Jn. 1. 47; 6. 61; 13. 11; Mk. 2. 8.
3. 1: Jn. 7. 50; 19. 39; Lk. 23. 13; Jn. 7. 26.   **3. 2:** Jn. 2. 11; 7. 31; 9. 16; Acts 10. 38.
3. 3: Jn. 1. 13; 1 Pet. 1. 23; Jas. 1. 18; 1 Jn. 3. 9.   **3. 5:** Ezek. 36. 25–27;
Eph. 5. 26; Tit. 3. 5.   **3. 6:** 1 Cor. 15. 50.   **3. 8:** Ezek. 37. 9.   **3. 11:** Jn. 8. 26;
1. 18; 3. 32.   **3. 13:** Rom. 10. 6; Eph. 4. 9.

has ascended into heaven but he who descended from heaven, the Son of man.*ᶠ* ¹⁴ And as Moses lifted up the serpent in the wilderness, so must the Son of man be lifted up, ¹⁵ that whoever believes in him may have eternal life."

16 For God so loved the world that he gave his only Son, that whoever believes in him should not perish but have eternal life. ¹⁷ For God sent the Son into the world, not to condemn the world, but that the world might be saved through him. ¹⁸ He who believes in him is not condemned; he who does not believe is condemned already, because he has not believed in the name of the only Son of God. ¹⁹ And this is the judgment, that the light has come into the world, and men loved darkness rather than light, because their deeds were evil. ²⁰ For every one who does evil hates the light, and does not come to the light, lest his deeds should be exposed. ²¹ But he who does what is true comes to the light, that it may be clearly seen that his deeds have been wrought in God.

22 After this Jesus and his disciples went into the land of Judea; there he remained with them and baptized. ²³ John also was baptizing at Ae′non near Salim, because there was much water there; and people came and were baptized. ²⁴ For John had not yet been put in prison.

25 Now a discussion arose between John's disciples and a Jew over purifying. ²⁶ And they came to John, and said to him, "Rabbi, he who was with you beyond the Jordan, to whom you bore witness, here he is, baptizing, and all are going to him." ²⁷ John answered, "No one can receive anything except what is given him from heaven. ²⁸ You yourselves bear me witness, that I said, I am not the Christ, but I have been

---

ᶠ Some ancient authorities add *who is in heaven.*

3. 14: Num. 21. 9; Jn. 8. 28; 12. 34.   **3. 16:** Rom. 5. 8; 8. 32; Eph. 2. 4; 1 Jn. 4. 9–10.
3. 17: Jn. 8. 15; 12. 47; Lk. 19. 10; 1 Jn. 4. 14.   **3. 19:** Jn. 1. 4; 8. 12; Eph. 5. 11, 13.
3. 21: 1 Jn. 1. 6.   **3. 22:** Jn. 4. 2.   **3. 24:** Mk. 1. 14; 6. 17–18.   **3. 26:** Jn. 1. 7, 28.
3. 27: 1 Cor. 4. 7.   **3. 28:** Jn. 1. 20, 23.

sent before him. ²⁹ He who has the bride is the bridegroom; the friend of the bridegroom, who stands and hears him, rejoices greatly at the bridegroom's voice; therefore this joy of mine is now full. ³⁰ He must increase, but I must decrease."

31 He who comes from above is above all; he who is of the earth belongs to the earth, and of the earth he speaks; he who comes from heaven is above all. ³² He bears witness to what he has seen and heard, yet no one receives his testimony; ³³ he who receives his testimony sets his seal to this, that God is true. ³⁴ For he whom God has sent utters the words of God, for it is not by measure that he gives the Spirit; ³⁵ the Father loves the Son, and has given all things into his hand. ³⁶ He who believes in the Son has eternal life; he who does not obey the Son shall not see life, but the wrath of God rests upon him.

4 Now when the Lord knew that the Pharisees had heard that Jesus was making and baptizing more disciples than John ² (although Jesus himself did not baptize, but only his disciples), ³ he left Judea and departed again to Galilee. ⁴ He had to pass through Sa-ma′ri-a. ⁵ So he came to a city of Sa-ma′ri-a, called Sy′char, near the field that Jacob gave to his son Joseph. ⁶ Jacob's well was there, and so Jesus, wearied as he was with his journey, sat down beside the well. It was about the sixth hour.

7 There came a woman of Sa-ma′ri-a to draw water. Jesus said to her, "Give me a drink." ⁸ For his disciples had gone away into the city to buy food. ⁹ The Samaritan woman said to him, "How is it that you, a Jew, ask a drink of me, a woman of Sa-ma′ri-a?" For Jews have no dealings with Samaritans. ¹⁰ Jesus answered her, "If you knew the gift of

3. 29: Mk. 2. 19–20; Mt. 25. 1; Jn. 15. 11.   **3. 31:** Jn. 3. 13; 8. 23; 1 Jn. 4. 5.   **3. 32:** Jn. 3. 11.   **3. 36:** Jn. 3. 16; 5. 24.
4. 1: Jn. 3. 22.   **4. 4:** Lk. 9. 52; 17. 11.   **4. 5:** Gen. 33. 19; 48. 22; Josh. 24. 32.
4. 9: Mt. 10. 5; Jn. 8. 48; Ezr. 4. 3–6.   **4. 10:** Jn. 7. 37; Rev. 21. 6; 22. 17.

God, and who it is that is saying to you, 'Give me a drink,' you would have asked him, and he would have given you living water." [11] The woman said to him, "Sir, you have nothing to draw with, and the well is deep; where do you get that living water? [12] Are you greater than our father Jacob, who gave us the well, and drank from it himself, and his sons, and his cattle?" [13] Jesus said to her, "Every one who drinks of this water will thirst again, [14] but whoever drinks of the water that I shall give him will never thirst; the water that I shall give him will become in him a spring of water welling up to eternal life." [15] The woman said to him, "Sir, give me this water, that I may not thirst, nor come here to draw."

16 Jesus said to her, "Go, call your husband, and come here." [17] The woman answered him, "I have no husband." Jesus said to her, "You are right in saying, 'I have no husband'; [18] for you have had five husbands, and he whom you now have is not your husband; this you said truly." [19] The woman said to him, "Sir, I perceive that you are a prophet. [20] Our fathers worshiped on this mountain; and you say that in Jerusalem is the place where men ought to worship." [21] Jesus said to her, "Woman, believe me, the hour is coming when neither on this mountain nor in Jerusalem will you worship the Father. [22] You worship what you do not know; we worship what we know, for salvation is from the Jews. [23] But the hour is coming, and now is, when the true worshipers will worship the Father in spirit and truth, for such the Father seeks to worship him. [24] God is spirit, and those who worship him must worship in spirit and truth." [25] The woman said to him, "I know that Messiah is coming (he who is called Christ); when he comes, he will show us all things." [26] Jesus said to her, "I who speak to you am he."

4. 14: Jn. 6. 35; 7. 38.   **4. 15:** Jn. 6. 34.
4. 20: Deut. 11. 29; Josh. 8. 33; Lk. 9. 53.
4. 22: 2 Kings 17. 28–41; Is. 2. 3; Rom. 9. 4.
4. 18: 2 Kings 17. 24; Hos. 2. 7.
4. 21: Jn. 5. 25; 16. 2, 32; Mal. 1. 11.
4. 24: Phil. 3. 3.   **4. 26:** Jn. 8. 24.

27 Just then his disciples came. They marveled that he was talking with a woman, but none said, "What do you wish?" or, "Why are you talking with her?" [28] So the woman left her water jar, and went away into the city, and said to the people, [29] "Come, see a man who told me all that I ever did. Can this be the Christ?" [30] They went out of the city and were coming to him.

31 Meanwhile the disciples besought him, saying, "Rabbi, eat." [32] But he said to them, "I have food to eat of which you do not know." [33] So the disciples said to one another, "Has any one brought him food?" [34] Jesus said to them, "My food is to do the will of him who sent me, and to accomplish his work. [35] Do you not say, 'There are yet four months, then comes the harvest'? I tell you, lift up your eyes, and see how the fields are already white for harvest. [36] He who reaps receives wages, and gathers fruit for eternal life, so that sower and reaper may rejoice together. [37] For here the saying holds true, 'One sows and another reaps.' [38] I sent you to reap that for which you did not labor; others have labored, and you have entered into their labor."

39 Many Samaritans from that city believed in him because of the woman's testimony, "He told me all that I ever did." [40] So when the Samaritans came to him, they asked him to stay with them; and he stayed there two days. [41] And many more believed because of his word. [42] They said to the woman, "It is no longer because of your words that we believe, for we have heard for ourselves, and we know that this is indeed the Savior of the world."

43 After the two days he departed to Galilee. [44] For Jesus himself testified that a prophet has no honor in his own country. [45] So when he came to Galilee, the Galileans

4. 29: Jn. 7. 26; Mt. 12. 23.   **4. 32:** Mt. 4. 4.   **4. 34:** Jn. 5. 30; 6. 38; 17. 4.   **4. 35:** Lk. 10. 2; Mt. 9. 37.   **4. 37:** Job 31. 8; Mic. 6. 15.   **4. 42:** 1 John 4. 14; 2 Tim. 1. 10. **4. 44:** Mk. 6. 4; Mt. 13. 57.

welcomed him, having seen all that he had done in Jerusalem at the feast, for they too had gone to the feast.

46 So he came again to Cana in Galilee, where he had made the water wine. And at Ca-per′na-um there was an official whose son was ill. [47] When he heard that Jesus had come from Judea to Galilee, he went and begged him to come down and heal his son, for he was at the point of death. [48] Jesus therefore said to him, "Unless you see signs and wonders you will not believe." [49] The official said to him, "Sir, come down before my child dies." [50] Jesus said to him, "Go; your son will live." The man believed the word that Jesus spoke to him and went his way. [51] As he was going down, his servants met him and told him that his son was living. [52] So he asked them the hour when he began to mend, and they said to him, "Yesterday at the seventh hour the fever left him." [53] The father knew that was the hour when Jesus had said to him, "Your son will live"; and he himself believed, and all his household. [54] This was now the second sign that Jesus did when he had come from Judea to Galilee.

5 After this there was a feast of the Jews, and Jesus went up to Jerusalem.

2 Now there is in Jerusalem by the sheep gate a pool, in Hebrew called Beth-za′tha,[g] which has five porticoes. [3] In these lay a multitude of invalids, blind, lame, paralyzed. [5] One man was there, who had been ill for thirty-eight years. [6] When Jesus saw him and knew that he had been lying there a long time, he said to him, "Do you want to be healed?" [7] The sick man answered him, "Sir, I have no man to put me into the pool when the water is troubled, and while I am going another steps down before me." [8] Jesus said to

---

[g] Some ancient authorities read *Bethesda*, others *Bethsaida*.

4. 46: Jn. 2. 1–11; Mt. 8. 5–10; Lk. 7. 2–10.   **4. 48:** Dan. 4. 2; Mk. 13. 22; Acts 2. 19; 4. 30; Rom. 15. 19; Heb. 2. 4.   **4. 53:** Acts 11. 14.   **4. 54:** Jn. 2. 11. **5. 2:** Neh. 3. 1; 12. 39.   **5. 8:** Mk. 2. 11; Mt. 9. 6; Lk. 5. 24.

him, "Rise, take up your pallet, and walk." ⁹ And at once the man was healed, and he took up his pallet and walked.

Now that day was the sabbath. ¹⁰ So the Jews said to the man who was cured, "It is the sabbath, it is not lawful for you to carry your pallet." ¹¹ But he answered them, "The man who healed me said to me, 'Take up your pallet, and walk.'" ¹² They asked him, "Who is the man who said to you, 'Take up your pallet, and walk'?" ¹³ Now the man who had been healed did not know who it was, for Jesus had withdrawn, as there was a crowd in the place. ¹⁴ Afterward, Jesus found him in the temple, and said to him, "See, you are well! Sin no more, that nothing worse befall you." ¹⁵ The man went away and told the Jews that it was Jesus who had healed him. ¹⁶ And this was why the Jews persecuted Jesus, because he did this on the sabbath. ¹⁷ But Jesus answered them, "My Father is working still, and I am working." ¹⁸ This was why the Jews sought all the more to kill him, because he not only broke the sabbath but also called God his Father, making himself equal with God.

19 Jesus said to them, "Truly, truly, I say to you, the Son can do nothing of his own accord, but only what he sees the Father doing; for whatever he does, that the Son does likewise. ²⁰ For the Father loves the Son, and shows him all that he himself is doing; and greater works than these will he show him, that you may marvel. ²¹ For as the Father raises the dead and gives them life, so also the Son gives life to whom he will. ²² The Father judges no one, but has given all judgment to the Son, that all may honor the Son, ²³ even as they honor the Father. He who does not honor the Son does not honor the Father who sent him. ²⁴ Truly, truly, I say to you, he who hears my word and believes him who

5. 10: Neh. 13. 19; Jer. 17. 21; Jn. 7. 23; 9. 16; Mk. 2. 24.   **5. 14:** Mk. 2. 5.
5. 17: Gen. 2. 3.   **5. 18:** Jn. 7. 1; 10. 33.   **5. 19:** Jn. 5. 30; 8. 28; 14. 10.
5. 20: Jn. 14. 12.   **5. 21:** Rom. 4. 17; 8. 11; Jn. 11. 25.   **5. 23:** Lk. 10. 16; 1 Jn. 2. 23.
5. 24: Jn. 3. 18.

sent me, has eternal life; he does not come into judgment, but has passed from death to life.

25 "Truly, truly, I say to you, the hour is coming, and now is, when the dead will hear the voice of the Son of God, and those who hear will live. [26] For as the Father has life in himself, so he has granted the Son also to have life in himself, [27] and has given him authority to execute judgment, because he is the Son of man. [28] Do not marvel at this; for the hour is coming when all who are in the tombs will hear his voice [29] and come forth, those who have done good, to the resurrection of life, and those who have done evil, to the resurrection of judgment.

30 "I can do nothing on my own authority; as I hear, I judge; and my judgment is just, because I seek not my own will but the will of him who sent me. [31] If I bear witness to myself, my testimony is not true; [32] there is another who bears witness to me, and I know that the testimony which he bears to me is true. [33] You sent to John, and he has borne witness to the truth. [34] Not that the testimony which I receive is from man; but I say this that you may be saved. [35] He was a burning and shining lamp, and you were willing to rejoice for a while in his light. [36] But the testimony which I have is greater than that of John; for the works which the Father has granted me to accomplish, these very works which I am doing, bear me witness that the Father has sent me. [37] And the Father who sent me has himself borne witness to me. His voice you have never heard, his form you have never seen; [38] and you do not have his word abiding in you, for you do not believe him whom he has sent. [39] You search the scriptures, because you think that in them you have eternal life; and it is they that bear witness to me; [40] yet

5. 25: Jn. 4. 21; 16. 2, 32.   **5. 29**: Dan. 12. 2; Acts 24. 15; Jn. 11. 24; Mt. 25. 46; 1 Cor. 15. 52.   **5. 30**: Jn. 5. 19; 8. 16; 6. 38.   **5. 31–37**: Jn. 8. 14–18.   **5. 33**: Jn. 1. 7, 19.   **5. 34**: 1 Jn. 5. 9.   **5. 36**: Jn. 10. 25; 14. 11; 15. 24; Mt. 11. 4. **5. 39**: Lk. 24. 27; Acts 13. 27.

you refuse to come to me that you may have life. [41] I do not receive glory from men. [42] But I know that you have not the love of God within you. [43] I have come in my Father's name, and you do not receive me; if another comes in his own name, him you will receive. [44] How can you believe, who receive glory from one another and do not seek the glory that comes from the only God? [45] Do not think that I shall accuse you to the Father; it is Moses who accuses you, on whom you set your hope. [46] If you believed Moses, you would believe me, for he wrote of me. [47] But if you do not believe his writings, how will you believe my words?"

6 After this Jesus went to the other side of the sea of Galilee, which is the sea of Ti-be'ri-as. [2] And a multitude followed him, because they saw the signs which he did on those who were diseased. [3] Jesus went up into the hills, and there sat down with his disciples. [4] Now the Passover, the feast of the Jews, was at hand. [5] Lifting up his eyes, then, and seeing that a multitude was coming to him, Jesus said to Philip, "How are we to buy bread, so that these people may eat?" [6] This he said to test him, for he himself knew what he would do. [7] Philip answered him, "Two hundred denarii[h] would not buy enough bread for each of them to get a little." [8] One of his disciples, Andrew, Simon Peter's brother, said to him, [9] "There is a lad here who has five barley loaves and two fish; but what are they among so many?" [10] Jesus said, "Make the people sit down." Now there was much grass in the place; so the men sat down, in number about five thousand. [11] Jesus then took the loaves, and when he had given thanks, he distributed them to those who were seated; so also the fish, as much as they wanted. [12] And when they had eaten their fill, he told his disciples, "Gather

[h] See on Mt. 18. 28.

5. 43: Mt. 24. 5.   **5. 45:** Jn. 9. 28; Rom. 2. 17.   **5. 47:** Lk. 16. 29, 31.
6. 1–13: Mt. 14. 13–21; Mk. 6. 32–44; Lk. 9. 10–17.   **6. 5:** Jn. 1. 43; 12. 21.   **6. 8:** Jn. 1. 40; 12. 22.   **6. 9:** Jn. 21. 9–13.

up the fragments left over, that nothing may be lost." [13] So they gathered them up and filled twelve baskets with fragments from the five barley loaves, left by those who had eaten. [14] When the people saw the sign which he had done, they said, "This is indeed the prophet who is to come into the world!"

15 Perceiving then that they were about to come and take him by force to make him king, Jesus withdrew again to the hills by himself.

16 When evening came, his disciples went down to the sea, [17] got into a boat, and started across the sea to Ca-per′na-um. It was now dark, and Jesus had not yet come to them. [18] The sea rose because a strong wind was blowing. [19] When they had rowed about three or four miles,[i] they saw Jesus walking on the sea and drawing near to the boat. They were frightened, [20] but he said to them, "It is I; do not be afraid." [21] Then they were glad to take him into the boat, and immediately the boat was at the land to which they were going.

22 On the next day the people who remained on the other side of the sea saw that there had been only one boat there, and that Jesus had not entered the boat with his disciples, but that his disciples had gone away alone. [23] However, boats from Ti-be′ri-as came near the place where they ate the bread after the Lord had given thanks. [24] So when the people saw that Jesus was not there, nor his disciples, they themselves got into the boats and went to Ca-per′na-um, seeking Jesus.

25 When they found him on the other side of the sea, they said to him, "Rabbi, when did you come here?" [26] Jesus answered them, "Truly, truly, I say to you, you seek me, not because you saw signs, but because you ate your fill of the

[i] Greek *twenty-five or thirty stadia.*

6. 14: Mt. 21. 11.   **6. 15:** Jn. 6. 3; 18. 36.   **6. 16–21:** Mt. 14. 22–27; Mk. 6. 45–51.

loaves. [27] Do not labor for the food which perishes, but for the food which endures to eternal life, which the Son of man will give to you; for on him has God the Father set his seal." [28] Then they said to him, "What must we do, to be doing the work of God?" [29] Jesus answered them, "This is the work of God, that you believe in him whom he has sent." [30] So they said to him, "Then what sign do you do, that we may see, and believe you? What work do you perform? [31] Our fathers ate the manna in the wilderness; as it is written, 'He gave them bread from heaven to eat.'" [32] Jesus then said to them, "Truly, truly, I say to you, it was not Moses who gave you the bread from heaven; my Father gives you the true bread from heaven. [33] For the bread of God is that which comes down from heaven, and gives life to the world." [34] They said to him, "Lord, give us this bread always."

[35] Jesus said to them, "I am the bread of life; he who comes to me shall not hunger, and he who believes in me shall never thirst. [36] But I said to you that you have seen me and yet do not believe. [37] All that the Father gives me will come to me; and him who comes to me I will not cast out. [38] For I have come down from heaven, not to do my own will, but the will of him who sent me; [39] and this is the will of him who sent me, that I should lose nothing of all that he has given me, but raise it up at the last day. [40] For this is the will of my Father, that every one who sees the Son and believes in him should have eternal life; and I will raise him up at the last day."

[41] The Jews then murmured at him, because he said, "I am the bread which came down from heaven." [42] They said, "Is not this Jesus, the son of Joseph, whose father and mother we know? How does he now say, 'I have come down

6. 27: Is. 55. 2.   **6. 29:** 1 Thess. 1. 3; 1 Jn. 3. 23.   **6. 30:** Mt. 12. 38; Mk. 8. 11.
6. 31: Ex. 16. 4, 15; Num. 11. 8; Neh. 9. 15; Ps. 78. 24; 105. 40.   **6. 34:** Jn. 4. 15;
Mt. 6. 11.   **6. 35:** Jn. 6. 48–50; 4. 14.   **6. 37:** Jn. 17. 2.   **6. 38:** Jn. 4. 34; 5. 30.
6. 39: Jn. 17. 12; 18. 9.   **6. 40:** Jn. 5. 29; 11. 24; 6. 54.   **6. 42:** Lk. 4. 22; Jn. 7. 27.

from heaven'?" [43] Jesus answered them, "Do not murmur among yourselves. [44] No one can come to me unless the Father who sent me draws him; and I will raise him up at the last day. [45] It is written in the prophets, 'And they shall all be taught by God.' Every one who has heard and learned from the Father comes to me. [46] Not that any one has seen the Father except him who is from God; he has seen the Father. [47] Truly, truly, I say to you, he who believes has eternal life. [48] I am the bread of life. [49] Your fathers ate the manna in the wilderness, and they died. [50] This is the bread which comes down from heaven, that a man may eat of it and not die. [51] I am the living bread which came down from heaven; if any one eats of this bread, he will live for ever; and the bread which I shall give for the life of the world is my flesh."

52 The Jews then disputed among themselves, saying, "How can this man give us his flesh to eat?" [53] So Jesus said to them, "Truly, truly, I say to you, unless you eat the flesh of the Son of man and drink his blood, you have no life in you; [54] he who eats my flesh and drinks my blood has eternal life, and I will raise him up at the last day. [55] For my flesh is food indeed, and my blood is drink indeed. [56] He who eats my flesh and drinks my blood abides in me, and I in him. [57] As the living Father sent me, and I live because of the Father, so he who eats me will live because of me. [58] This is the bread which came down from heaven, not such as the fathers ate and died; he who eats this bread will live forever." [59] This he said in the synagogue, as he taught at Ca-per'na-um.

60 Many of his disciples, when they heard it, said, "This is a hard saying; who can listen to it?" [61] But Jesus, knowing in

6. 44: Jer. 31. 3; Hos. 11. 4; Jn. 12. 32; 6. 65.   **6. 45:** 1 Thess. 4. 9; 1 Jn. 2. 27;
Is. 54. 13.   **6. 46:** Jn. 1. 18.   **6. 52:** Jn. 3. 4; 4. 9.   **6. 56:** Jn. 15. 4; 1 Jn. 3. 24;
4. 15.   **6. 58:** Jn. 6. 41, 51.   **6. 59:** Jn. 6. 25.   **6. 61:** Mt. 11. 6.

himself that his disciples murmured at it, said to them, "Do you take offense at this? [62] Then what if you were to see the Son of man ascending where he was before? [63] It is the spirit that gives life, the flesh is of no avail; the words that I have spoken to you are spirit and life. [64] But there are some of you that do not believe." For Jesus knew from the first who those were that did not believe, and who it was that should betray him. [65] And he said, "This is why I told you that no one can come to me unless it is granted him by the Father."

66 After this many of his disciples drew back and no longer went about with him. [67] Jesus said to the twelve, "Will you also go away?" [68] Simon Peter answered him, "Lord, to whom shall we go? You have the words of eternal life; [69] and we have believed, and have come to know, that you are the Holy One of God." [70] Jesus answered them, "Did I not choose you, the twelve, and one of you is a devil?" [71] He spoke of Judas the son of Simon Iscariot, for he, one of the twelve, was to betray him.

7 After this Jesus went about in Galilee; he would not go about in Judea, because the Jews[j] sought to kill him. [2] Now the Jews' feast of Tabernacles was at hand. [3] So his brothers said to him, "Leave here and go to Judea, that your disciples may see the works you are doing. [4] For no man works in secret if he seeks to be known openly. If you do these things, show yourself to the world." [5] For even his brothers did not believe in him. [6] Jesus said to them, "My time has not yet come, but your time is always here. [7] The world cannot hate you, but it hates me because I testify of it that its works are evil. [8] Go to the feast your-

[j] Or *Judeans*.

6. 62: Jn. 3. 13; 17. 5.   6. 63: 2 Cor. 3. 6; Jn. 6. 68.   6. 64: Jn. 2. 25.   6. 65: Jn. 6. 44; 3. 27.   6. 68–69: Mk. 8. 27–30.   6. 70: Jn. 15. 16, 19.   6. 71: Jn. 13. 2, 27; 17. 12. 7. 2: Lev. 23. 34; Deut. 16. 16.   7. 3: Mk. 3. 21, 31; Mt. 12. 46.   7. 6: Mt. 26. 18; Jn. 2. 4; 7. 30.

selves; I am not[k] going up to the feast, for my time has not yet fully come." [9] So saying, he remained in Galilee.

10 But after his brothers had gone up to the feast, then he also went up, not publicly but in private. [11] The Jews were looking for him at the feast, and saying, "Where is he?" [12] And there was much muttering about him among the people. While some said, "He is a good man," others said, "No, he is leading the people astray." [13] Yet for fear of the Jews no one spoke openly of him.

14 About the middle of the feast Jesus went up into the temple and taught. [15] The Jews marveled at it, saying, "How is it that this man has learning,[l] when he has never studied?" [16] So Jesus answered them, "My teaching is not mine, but his who sent me; [17] if any man's will is to do his will, he shall know whether the teaching is from God or whether I am speaking on my own authority. [18] He who speaks on his own authority seeks his own glory; but he who seeks the glory of him who sent him is true, and in him there is no falsehood. [19] Did not Moses give you the law? Yet none of you keeps the law. Why do you seek to kill me?" [20] The people answered, "You have a demon! Who is seeking to kill you?" [21] Jesus answered them, "I did one deed, and you all marvel at it. [22] Moses gave you circumcision (not that it is from Moses, but from the fathers), and you circumcise a man upon the sabbath. [23] If on the sabbath a man receives circumcision, so that the law of Moses may not be broken, are you angry with me because on the sabbath I made a man's whole body well? [24] Do not judge by appearances, but judge with right judgment."

25 Some of the people of Jerusalem therefore said, "Is not

---

[k] Many ancient authorities add *yet*.   [l] Or *this man knows his letters*.

7. 7: Jn. 15. 18–21.   **7. 12:** Jn. 7. 40–43.   **7. 13:** Jn. 19. 38; 20. 19.   **7. 19:** Jn. 1. 17.   **7. 20:** Jn. 8. 48; 10. 20; Mt. 11. 18; Mk. 3. 22.   **7. 21:** Jn. 5. 2–9.   **7. 22:** Lev. 12. 3; Gen. 17. 10; 21. 4.   **7. 23:** Mk. 3. 5; Lk. 13. 12; 14. 4.   **7. 24:** Jn. 8. 15; Is. 11. 3; Zech. 7. 9.

this the man whom they seek to kill? [26] And here he is, speaking openly, and they say nothing to him! Can it be that the authorities really know that this is the Christ? [27] Yet we know where this man comes from; and when the Christ appears, no one will know where he comes from." [28] So Jesus proclaimed, as he taught in the temple, "You know me, and you know where I come from? But I have not come of my own accord; he who sent me is true, and him you do not know. [29] I know him, for I come from him, and he sent me." [30] So they sought to arrest him; but no one laid hands on him, because his hour had not yet come. [31] Yet many of the people believed in him; they said, "When the Christ appears, will he do more signs than this man has done?"

32 The Pharisees heard the crowd thus muttering about him, and the chief priests and Pharisees sent officers to arrest him. [33] Jesus then said, "I shall be with you a little longer, and then I go to him who sent me; [34] you will seek me and you will not find me; where I am you cannot come." [35] The Jews said to one another, "Where does this man intend to go that we shall not find him? Does he intend to go to the Dispersion among the Greeks and teach the Greeks? [36] What does he mean by saying, 'You will seek me and you will not find me,' and, 'Where I am you cannot come'?"

37 On the last day of the feast, the great day, Jesus stood up and proclaimed, "If any one thirst, let him come to me and drink. [38] He who believes in me, as[m] the scripture has said, 'Out of his heart shall flow rivers of living water.'" [39] Now this he said about the Spirit, which those who believed in him were to receive; for as yet the Spirit had not been given, because Jesus was not yet glorified.

[m] Or *let him come to me, and let him who believes in me drink. As.*

7. 27: Jn. 6. 42; 7. 41; 9. 29.   **7. 28:** Jn. 8. 42.   **7. 29:** Jn. 8. 55; 17. 25; Mt. 11. 27.
7. 30: Jn. 7. 44; 10. 39; Mk. 12. 12; Jn. 8. 20.   **7. 31:** Jn. 8. 30; 10. 42; 11. 45.
7. 33: Jn. 8. 21; 12. 35; 13. 33; 14. 19; 16. 16–19.   **7. 35:** Jas. 1. 1; 1 Pet. 1. 1; Jn. 12.
20; Acts 11. 20.   **7. 37:** Lev. 23. 36; Jn. 4. 10, 14.   **7. 38:** Is. 44. 3; 55. 1.
7. 39: Jn. 20. 22; 12. 23.

40 When they heard these words, some of the people said, "This is really the prophet." [41] Others said, "This is the Christ." But some said, "Is the Christ to come from Galilee? [42] Has not the scripture said that the Christ is descended from David, and comes from Bethlehem, the village where David was?" [43] So there was a division among the people over him. [44] Some of them wanted to arrest him, but no one laid hands on him.

45 The officers then went back to the chief priests and Pharisees, who said to them, "Why did you not bring him?" [46] The officers answered, "No man ever spoke like this man!" [47] The Pharisees answered them, "Are you led astray, you also? [48] Have any of the authorities or of the Pharisees believed in him? [49] But this crowd, who do not know the law, are accursed." [50] Nic-o-de'mus, who had gone to him before, and who was one of them, said to them, [51] "Does our law judge a man without first giving him a hearing and learning what he does?" [52] They replied, "Are you from Galilee too? Search and you will see that no prophet is to rise from Galilee."[n]

[n] Most of the ancient authorities either omit 7. 53–8. 11, or insert it, with variations of the text, here or at the end of this gospel or after Luke 21. 38.

8 [53] *They went each to his own house,* [1] *but Jesus went to the Mount of Olives.* [2] *Early in the morning he came again to the temple; all the people came to him, and he sat down and taught them.* [3] *The scribes and the Pharisees brought a woman who had been caught in adultery, and placing her in the midst* [4] *they said to him, "Teacher, this woman has been caught in the act of adultery.* [5] *Now in the law Moses commanded us to stone such. What do you say about her?"* [6] *This they said to test him, that they might have some charge to bring against him. Jesus bent down and wrote with his finger on the ground.* [7] *And as they continued to ask him, he stood up and said to them, "Let him who is without sin among you be the first to throw a stone at her."* [8] *And once more he bent down and wrote with his finger on the ground.* [9] *But when they heard it, they went away, one by one, beginning with the eldest, and Jesus was left alone with the woman standing before him.* [10] *Jesus looked up and said to her, "Woman, where are they? Has no one condemned you?"* [11] *She said, "No one, Lord." And Jesus said, "Neither do I condemn you; go, and do not sin again."*

7. 40: Jn. 1. 21; Mt. 21. 11.   7. 42: Mic. 5. 2; Mt. 1. 1; Lk. 2. 4.   7. 44: Jn. 7. 30; 10. 39.   7. 46: Mt. 7. 28.   7. 50: Jn. 3. 1; 19. 39.   7. 51: Deut. 17. 6; Ex. 23. 1. 7. 52: 2 Kings 14. 25.

8 [12] Again Jesus spoke to them, saying, "I am the light of the world; he who follows me will not walk in darkness, but will have the light of life." [13] The Pharisees then said to him, "You are bearing witness to yourself; your testimony is not true." [14] Jesus answered, "Even if I do bear witness to myself, my testimony is true, for I know whence I have come and whither I am going, but you do not know whence I come or whither I am going. [15] You judge according to the flesh, I judge no one. [16] Yet even if I do judge, my judgment is true, for it is not I alone that judge, but I and he[o] who sent me. [17] In your law it is written that the testimony of two men is true; [18] I bear witness to myself, and the Father who sent me bears witness to me." [19] They said to him therefore, "Where is your Father?" Jesus answered, "You know neither me nor my Father; if you knew me, you would know my Father also." [20] These words he spoke in the treasury, as he taught in the temple; but no one arrested him, because his hour had not yet come.

21 Again he said to them, "I go away, and you will seek me and die in your sin; where I am going, you cannot come." [22] Then said the Jews, "Will he kill himself, since he says, 'Where I am going, you cannot come'?" [23] He said to them, "You are from below, I am from above; you are of this world, I am not of this world. [24] I told you that you would die in your sins, for you will die in your sins unless you believe that I am he." [25] They said to him, "Who are you?" Jesus said to them, "Even what I have told you from the beginning.[b] [26] I have much to say about you and much to judge; but he who sent me is true, and I declare to the world what I have heard from him." [27] They did not understand that

[o] Many ancient authorities read *the Father*.   [p] Or *Why do I talk to you at all?*

8. 12: Jn. 9. 5; 12. 35; 1. 4.   **8. 13–18:** Jn. 5. 31–39.   **8. 15:** Jn. 7. 24; 3. 17.   **8. 16:** Jn. 5. 30.   **8. 17:** Deut. 19. 15; Mt. 18. 16.   **8. 19:** Jn. 14. 7.   **8. 20:** Mk. 12. 41; Jn. 7. 30.   **8. 21–22:** Jn. 7. 33–36.   **8. 23:** Jn. 3. 31; 17. 14; 1 Jn. 4. 5.   **8. 24:** Jn. 8. 28; 4. 26; 13. 19; Mk. 13. 6.

he spoke to them of the Father. [28] So Jesus said, "When you have lifted up the Son of man, then you will know that I am he, and that I do nothing on my own authority but speak thus as the Father taught me. [29] And he who sent me is with me; he has not left me alone, for I always do what is pleasing to him." [30] As he spoke thus, many believed in him.

31 Jesus then said to the Jews who had believed in him, "If you continue in my word, you are my disciples, [32] and you will know the truth, and the truth will make you free." [33] They answered him, "We are descendants of Abraham, and have never been in bondage to anyone. How is it that you say, 'You will be made free'?"

34 Jesus answered them, "Truly, truly, I say to you, every one who commits sin is a slave to sin. [35] The slave does not continue in the house forever; the son continues forever. [36] So if the Son makes you free, you will be free indeed. [37] I know that you are descendants of Abraham; yet you seek to kill me, because my word finds no place in you. [38] I speak of what I have seen with my Father, and you do what you have heard from your father."

39 They answered him, "Abraham is our father." Jesus said to them, "If you were Abraham's children, you would do what Abraham did, [40] but now you seek to kill me, a man who has told you the truth which I heard from God; this is not what Abraham did. [41] You do what your father did." They said to him, "We were not born of fornication; we have one Father, even God." [42] Jesus said to them, "If God were your Father, you would love me, for I proceeded and came forth from God; I came not of my own accord, but he sent me. [43] Why do you not understand what I say? It is because

8. 28: Jn. 3. 14; 12. 32.   8. 30: Jn. 7. 31; 10. 42; 11. 45.   8. 31: Jn. 15. 7; 2 Jn. 9.
8. 32: 2 Cor. 3. 17; Gal. 5. 1.   8. 33: Mt. 3. 9; Gal. 3. 7.   8. 34: Rom. 6. 16; 2 Pet.
2. 19.   8. 35: Gen. 21. 10; Gal. 4. 30.   8. 41: Deut. 32. 6; Is. 63. 16; 64. 8.
8. 42: Jn. 13. 3; 16. 28.

you cannot bear to hear my word. [44] You are of your father the devil, and your will is to do your father's desires. He was a murderer from the beginning, and has nothing to do with the truth, because there is no truth in him. When he lies, he speaks according to his own nature, for he is a liar and the father of lies. [45] But, because I tell the truth, you do not believe me. [46] Which of you convicts me of sin? If I tell the truth, why do you not believe me? [47] He who is of God hears the words of God; the reason why you do not hear them is that you are not of God."

48 The Jews answered him, "Are we not right in saying that you are a Samaritan and have a demon?" [49] Jesus answered, "I have not a demon; I honor my Father, and you dishonor me. [50] Yet I do not seek my own glory; there is One who seeks it and he will be the judge. [51] Truly, truly, I say to you, if any one keeps my word, he will never see death." [52] The Jews said to him, "Now we know that you have a demon. Abraham died, as did the prophets; and you say, 'If any one keeps my word, he will never taste death.' [53] Are you greater than our father Abraham, who died? And the prophets died! Whom do you make yourself to be?" [54] Jesus answered, "If I glorify myself, my glory is nothing; it is my Father who glorifies me, of whom you say that he is your God. [55] But you have not known him; I know him. If I said, I do not know him, I should be a liar like you; but I do know him and I keep his word. [56] Your father Abraham rejoiced that he was to see my day; he saw it and was glad." [57] The Jews then said to him, "You are not yet fifty years old, and have you seen Abraham?"[q] [58] Jesus said to them, "Truly, truly, I say to you, before Abraham was, I am."

---

[q] Some ancient authorities read *has Abraham seen you?*

8. 44: 1 Jn. 3. 8, 15; Gen. 3. 4; 1 Jn. 2. 4; Mt. 12. 34. **8. 46:** 1 Jn. 3. 5; Jn. 18. 37.
8. 48: Jn. 7. 20; 10. 20; 4. 9.   **8. 53:** Jn. 4. 12.   **8. 56:** Mt. 13. 17; Heb. 11. 13.
8. 57: Jn. 2. 20.   **8. 58:** Jn. 1. 1; 17. 5, 24.

⁵⁹ So they took up stones to throw at him; but Jesus hid himself, and went out of the temple.

9 As he passed by, he saw a man blind from his birth. ² And his disciples asked him, "Rabbi, who sinned, this man or his parents, that he was born blind?" ³ Jesus answered, "It was not that this man sinned, or his parents, but that the works of God might be made manifest in him. ⁴ We must work the works of him who sent me, while it is day; night comes, when no one can work. ⁵ As long as I am in the world, I am the light of the world." ⁶ As he said this, he spat on the ground and made clay of the spittle and anointed the man's eyes with the clay, ⁷ saying to him, "Go, wash in the pool of Si-lo′am" (which means Sent). So he went and washed and came back seeing. ⁸ The neighbors and those who had seen him before as a beggar, said, "Is not this the man who used to sit and beg?" ⁹ Some said, "It is he"; others said, "No, but he is like him." He said, "I am the man." ¹⁰ They said to him, "Then how were your eyes opened?" ¹¹ He answered, "The man called Jesus made clay and anointed my eyes and said to me, 'Go to Si-lo′am and wash'; so I went and washed and received my sight." ¹² They said to him, "Where is he?" He said, "I do not know."

13 They brought to the Pharisees the man who had formerly been blind. ¹⁴ Now it was a sabbath day when Jesus made the clay and opened his eyes. ¹⁵ The Pharisees again asked him how he had received his sight. And he said to them, "He put clay on my eyes, and I washed, and I see." ¹⁶ Some of the Pharisees said, "This man is not from God, for he does not keep the sabbath." But others said, "How can a man who is a sinner do such signs?" There was a

8. 59: Jn. 10. 31; 11. 8.
9. 2: Lk. 13. 2; Acts 28. 4; Ezek. 18. 20; Ex. 20. 5.   9. 3: Jn. 11. 4.   9. 4: Jn. 11. 9; 12. 35.   9. 5: Jn. 1. 4; 8. 12; 12. 46.   9. 6: Mk. 7. 33; 8. 23.   9. 7: Lk. 13. 4.
9. 16: Mt. 12. 2; Jn. 5. 9; 7. 43; 10. 19.

division among them. [17] So they again said to the blind man, "What do you say about him, since he has opened your eyes?" He said, "He is a prophet."

18 The Jews did not believe that he had been blind and had received his sight, until they called the parents of the man who had received his sight, [19] and asked them, "Is this your son, who you say was born blind? How then does he now see?" [20] His parents answered, "We know that this is our son, and that he was born blind; [21] but how he now sees we do not know, nor do we know who opened his eyes. Ask him; he is of age, he will speak for himself." [22] His parents said this because they feared the Jews, for the Jews had already agreed that if any one should confess him to be Christ, he was to be put out of the synagogue. [23] Therefore his parents said, "He is of age, ask him."

24 So for the second time they called the man who had been blind, and said to him, "Give God the praise; we know that this man is a sinner." [25] He answered, "Whether he is a sinner, I do not know; one thing I know, that though I was blind, now I see." [26] They said to him, "What did he do to you? How did he open your eyes?" [27] He answered them, "I have told you already, and you would not listen. Why do you want to hear it again? Do you too want to become his disciples?" [28] And they reviled him, saying, "You are his disciple, but we are disciples of Moses. [29] We know that God has spoken to Moses, but as for this man, we do not know where he comes from." [30] The man answered, "Why, this is a marvel! You do not know where he comes from, and yet he opened my eyes. [31] We know that God does not listen to sinners, but if any one is a worshiper of God and does his will, God listens to him. [32] Never since the world began has it been heard that any one opened the eyes of a man born blind.

9. 22: Jn. 7. 13; 12. 42; Lk. 6. 22.   **9. 28:** Jn. 5. 45.

³³ If this man were not from God, he could do nothing." ³⁴ They answered him, "You were born in utter sin, and would you teach us?" And they cast him out.

35 Jesus heard that they had cast him out, and having found him he said, "Do you believe in the Son of man?"ʳ ³⁶ He answered, "And who is he, sir, that I may believe in him?" ³⁷ Jesus said to him, "You have seen him, and it is he who speaks to you." ³⁸ He said, "Lord, I believe"; and he worshiped him. ³⁹ Jesus said, "For judgment I came into this world, that those who do not see may see, and that those who see may become blind." ⁴⁰ Some of the Pharisees near him heard this, and they said to him, "Are we also blind?" ⁴¹ Jesus said to them, "If you were blind, you would have no guilt; but now that you say, 'We see,' your guilt remains.

10 "Truly, truly, I say to you, he who does not enter the sheepfold by the door but climbs in by another way, that man is a thief and a robber; ² but he who enters by the door is the shepherd of the sheep. ³ To him the gatekeeper opens; the sheep hear his voice, and he calls his own sheep by name and leads them out. ⁴ When he has brought out all his own, he goes before them, and the sheep follow him, for they know his voice. ⁵ A stranger they will not follow, but they will flee from him, for they do not know the voice of strangers." ⁶ This figure Jesus used with them, but they did not understand what he was saying to them.

7 So Jesus again said to them, "Truly, truly, I say to you, I am the door of the sheep. ⁸ All who came before me are thieves and robbers; but the sheep did not heed them. ⁹ I am the door; if any one enters by me, he will be saved, and

---

ʳ Many ancient authorities read *the Son of God.*

9. 38: Mt. 28. 9.   **9. 39:** Jn. 5. 27; 3. 19; Mt. 15. 14.   **9. 41:** Jn. 15. 22.
10. 2: Mk. 6. 34.   **10. 6:** Jn. 16. 25.   **10. 8:** Jer. 23. 1; Ezek. 34. 2.   **10. 11:** Is. 40. 11;
Ezek. 34. 11–16; Heb. 13. 20; 1 Pet. 5. 4; Rev. 7. 17; 1 Jn. 3. 16; Jn. 15. 13.

will go in and out and find pasture. [10] The thief comes only to steal and kill and destroy; I came that they may have life, and have it abundantly. [11] I am the good shepherd. The good shepherd lays down his life for the sheep. [12] He who is a hireling and not a shepherd, whose own the sheep are not, sees the wolf coming and leaves the sheep and flees; and the wolf snatches them and scatters them. [13] He flees because he is a hireling and cares nothing for the sheep. [14] I am the good shepherd; I know my own and my own know me, [15] as the Father knows me and I know the Father; and I lay down my life for the sheep. [16] And I have other sheep, that are not of this fold; I must bring them also, and they will heed my voice. So there shall be one flock, one shepherd. [17] For this reason the Father loves me, because I lay down my life, that I may take it again. [18] No one takes it from me, but I lay it down of my own accord. I have power to lay it down, and I have power to take it again; this charge I have received from my Father."

19 There was again a division among the Jews because of these words. [20] Many of them said, "He has a demon, and he is mad; why listen to him?" [21] Others said, "These are not the sayings of one who has a demon. Can a demon open the eyes of the blind?"

22 It was the feast of the Dedication at Jerusalem; [23] it was winter, and Jesus was walking in the temple, in the portico of Solomon. [24] So the Jews gathered round him and said to him, "How long will you keep us in suspense? If you are the Christ, tell us plainly." [25] Jesus answered them, "I told you, and you do not believe. The works that I do in my Father's name, they bear witness to me; [26] but you do not believe, because you do not belong to my sheep. [27] My

10. 15: Mt. 11. 27.   **10. 16:** Is. 56. 8; Jn. 11. 52; 17. 20; Eph. 2. 13–18; 1 Pet. 2. 25.
10. 18: Jn. 14. 31; 15. 10; Phil. 2. 8; Heb. 5. 8.   **10. 19:** Jn. 7. 43; 9. 16.   **10. 20:** Jn. 7. 20; 8. 48; Mt. 11. 18.   **10. 21:** Jn. 9. 32; Ex. 4. 11.   **10. 23:** Acts 3. 11; 5. 12.
10. 25: Jn. 5. 36; 10. 38.   **10. 26:** Jn. 8. 47.

sheep hear my voice, and I know them, and they follow me; [28] and I give them eternal life, and they shall never perish, and no one shall snatch them out of my hand. [29] My Father, who has given them to me,[s] is greater than all, and no one is able to snatch them out of the Father's hand. [30] I and the Father are one."

31 The Jews took up stones again to stone him. [32] Jesus answered them, "I have shown you many good works from the Father; for which of these do you stone me?" [33] The Jews answered him, "We stone you for no good work but for blasphemy; because you, being a man, make yourself God." [34] Jesus answered them, "Is it not written in your law, 'I said, you are gods'? [35] If he called them gods to whom the word of God came (and scripture cannot be broken), [36] do you say of him whom the Father consecrated and sent into the world, 'You are blaspheming,' because I said, 'I am the Son of God'? [37] If I am not doing the works of my Father, then do not believe me; [38] but if I do them, even though you do not believe me, believe the works, that you may know and understand that the Father is in me and I am in the Father." [39] Again they tried to arrest him, but he escaped from their hands.

40 He went away again across the Jordan to the place where John at first baptized, and there he remained. [41] And many came to him; and they said, "John did no sign, but everything that John said about this man was true." [42] And many believed in him there.

11 Now a certain man was ill, Laz'a-rus of Bethany, the village of Mary and her sister Martha. [2] It was Mary who anointed the Lord with ointment and wiped his

[s] Some ancient authorities read *What my Father has given to me.*

10. 28: Jn. 17. 2; 1 Jn. 2. 25.   **10. 30:** Jn. 17. 21.   **10. 31:** Jn. 8. 59; 11. 8.
10. 33: Lev. 24. 16; Mk. 14. 64.   **10. 34:** Jn. 8. 17; Ps. 82. 6.   **10. 39:** Jn. 7. 30;
8. 59; Lk. 4. 30.   **10. 40:** Jn. 1. 28.   **10. 42:** Jn. 7. 31; 11. 45.
11. 1: Mk. 11. 1; Lk. 10. 38.   **11. 2:** Jn. 12. 3; Lk. 7. 38; Mk. 14. 3.

feet with her hair, whose brother Laz'a-rus was ill. [3] So the sisters sent to him, saying, "Lord, he whom you love is ill." [4] But when Jesus heard it he said, "This illness is not unto death; it is for the glory of God, so that the Son of God may be glorified by means of it."

5 Now Jesus loved Martha and her sister and Laz'a-rus. [6] So when he heard that he was ill, he stayed two days longer in the place where he was. [7] Then after this he said to the disciples, "Let us go into Judea again." [8] The disciples said to him, "Rabbi, the Jews were but now seeking to stone you, and are you going there again?" [9] Jesus answered, "Are there not twelve hours in the day? If any one walks in the day, he does not stumble, because he sees the light of this world. [10] But if any one walks in the night, he stumbles, because the light is not in him." [11] Thus he spoke, and then he said to them, "Our friend Laz'a-rus has fallen asleep, but I go to awake him out of sleep." [12] The disciples said to him, "Lord, if he has fallen asleep, he will recover." [13] Now Jesus had spoken of his death, but they thought that he meant taking rest in sleep. [14] Then Jesus told them plainly, "Laz'a-rus is dead; [15] and for your sake I am glad that I was not there, so that you may believe. But let us go to him." [16] Thomas, called the Twin, said to his fellow disciples, "Let us also go, that we may die with him."

17 Now when Jesus came, he found that Laz'a-rus*[t]* had already been in the tomb four days. [18] Bethany was near Jerusalem, about two miles*[u]* off, [19] and many of the Jews had come to Martha and Mary to console them concerning their brother. [20] When Martha heard that Jesus was coming, she went and met him, while Mary sat in the house. [21] Martha said to Jesus, "Lord, if you had been here, my

---

[t] Greek *he.*   *[u]* Greek *fifteen stadia.*
11. 4: Jn. 9. 3.   **11. 8:** Jn. 8. 59; 10. 31.   **11. 9:** Jn. 9. 4; 12. 35; Lk. 13. 33.
11. 11: Mk. 5. 39; Acts 7. 60.   **11. 16:** Mt. 10. 3; Jn. 20. 24–28.   **11. 19:** Job 2. 11.

brother would not have died. ²² And even now I know that whatever you ask from God, God will give you." ²³ Jesus said to her, "Your brother will rise again." ²⁴ Martha said to him, "I know that he will rise again in the resurrection at the last day." ²⁵ Jesus said to her, "I am the resurrection and the life;ᵛ he who believes in me, though he die, yet shall he live, ²⁶ and whoever lives and believes in me shall never die. Do you believe this?" ²⁷ She said to him, "Yes, Lord; I believe that you are the Christ, the Son of God, he who is coming into the world."

28 When she had said this, she went and called her sister Mary, saying quietly, "The Teacher is here and is calling for you." ²⁹ And when she heard it, she rose quickly and went to him. ³⁰ Now Jesus had not yet come to the village, but was still in the place where Martha had met him. ³¹ When the Jews who were with her in the house, consoling her, saw Mary rise quickly and go out, they followed her, supposing that she was going to the tomb to weep there. ³² Then Mary, when she came where Jesus was and saw him, fell at his feet, saying to him, "Lord, if you had been here, my brother would not have died." ³³ When Jesus saw her weeping, and the Jews who came with her also weeping, he was deeply moved in spirit and troubled; and ³⁴ he said, "Where have you laid him?" They said to him, "Lord, come and see." ³⁵ Jesus wept. ³⁶ So the Jews said, "See how he loved him!" ³⁷ But some of them said, "Could not he who opened the eyes of the blind man have kept this man from dying?"

38 Then Jesus, deeply moved again, came to the tomb; it was a cave, and a stone lay upon it. ³⁹ Jesus said, "Take away the stone." Martha, the sister of the dead man, said

---

ᵛ A few ancient authorities omit *and the life.*

11. 24: Dan. 12. 2; Jn. 5. 28; Acts 24. 15.   **11. 25:** Jn. 1. 4; 5. 26; Rev. 1. 18.
11. 26: Jn. 6. 47; 8. 51.   **11. 27:** Mt. 16. 16.   **11. 32:** Jn. 11. 22.   **11. 35:** Lk. 19. 41.
11. 37: Jn. 9. 7.   **11. 38:** Mt. 27. 60; Mk. 15. 46; Lk. 24. 2; Jn. 20. 1.

to him, "Lord, by this time there will be an odor, for he has been dead four days." [40] Jesus said to her, "Did I not tell you that if you would believe you would see the glory of God?" [41] So they took away the stone. And Jesus lifted up his eyes and said, "Father, I thank thee that thou hast heard me. [42] I knew that thou hearest me always, but I have said this on account of the people standing by, that they may believe that thou didst send me." [43] When he had said this, he cried with a loud voice, "Laz′a-rus, come out." [44] The dead man came out, his hands and feet bound with bandages, and his face wrapped with a cloth. Jesus said to them, "Unbind him, and let him go."

45 Many of the Jews therefore, who had come with Mary and had seen what he did, believed in him; [46] but some of them went to the Pharisees and told them what Jesus had done. [47] So the chief priests and the Pharisees gathered the council, and said, "What are we to do? For this man performs many signs. [48] If we let him go on thus, every one will believe in him, and the Romans will come and destroy both our holy place[w] and our nation." [49] But one of them, Ca′-ia-phas, who was high priest that year, said to them, "You know nothing at all; [50] you do not understand that it is expedient for you that one man should die for the people, and not that the whole nation should perish." [51] He did not say this of his own accord, but being high priest that year he prophesied that Jesus should die for the nation, [52] and not for the nation only, but to gather into one the children of God who are scattered abroad. [53] So from that day on they took counsel how to put him to death.

54 Jesus therefore no longer went about openly among the Jews, but went from there to the country near the wilder-

[w] Greek *our place.*

11. 41: Jn. 17. 1; Mt. 11. 25.   11. 42: Jn. 12. 30.   11. 44: Jn. 19. 40; 20. 7.
11. 49: Mt. 26. 3.   11. 52: Jn. 10. 16; 17. 21.

ness, to a town called E'phra-im; and there he stayed with the disciples.

55 Now the Passover of the Jews was at hand, and many went up from the country to Jerusalem before the Passover, to purify themselves. ⁵⁶ They were looking for Jesus and saying to one another as they stood in the temple, "What do you think? That he will not come to the feast?" ⁵⁷ Now the chief priests and the Pharisees had given orders that if any one knew where he was, he should let them know, so that they might arrest him.

12 Six days before the Passover, Jesus came to Bethany, where Laz'a-rus was, whom Jesus had raised from the dead. ² There they made him a supper; Martha served, but Laz'a-rus was one of those at table with him. ³ Mary took a pound^x of costly ointment of pure nard and anointed the feet of Jesus and wiped his feet with her hair; and the house was filled with the fragrance of the ointment. ⁴ But Judas Iscariot, one of his disciples (he who was to betray him), said, ⁵ "Why was this ointment not sold for three hundred denarii^y and given to the poor?" ⁶ This he said, not that he cared for the poor but because he was a thief, and as he had the money box he used to take what was put into it. ⁷ Jesus said, "Let her alone, let her keep it for the day of my burial. ⁸ The poor you always have with you, but you do not always have me."

9 When the great crowd of the Jews learned that he was there, they came, not only on account of Jesus but also to see Laz'a-rus, whom he had raised from the dead. ¹⁰ So the chief priests planned to put Laz'a-rus also to death, ¹¹ because on account of him many of the Jews were going away and believing in Jesus.

^{x} Greek *litra*. ^{y} See on Mt. 18. 28.
11. 55: Mt. 26. 1; Mk. 14. 1; Lk. 22. 1; Jn. 13. 1.   **11. 56:** Jn. 7. 11.
12. 1–8: Mt. 26. 6–13; Mk. 14. 3–9; Lk. 7. 37–38.   **12. 4:** Jn. 6. 71; 13. 26.
12. 6: Lk. 8. 3.   **12. 7:** Jn. 19. 40.   **12. 10:** Mk. 14. 1.

12 The next day a great crowd who had come to the feast heard that Jesus was coming to Jerusalem. [13] So they took branches of palm trees and went out to meet him, crying, "Hosanna! Blessed be he who comes in the name of the Lord, even the King of Israel!" [14] And Jesus found a young ass and sat upon it; as it is written,

[15] "Fear not, daughter of Zion;
    behold thy king is coming,
    sitting on an ass's colt!"

[16] His disciples did not understand this at first; but when Jesus was glorified, then they remembered that this had been written of him and had been done to him. [17] The crowd that had been with him when he called Laz'a-rus out of the tomb and raised him from the dead bore witness. [18] The reason why the crowd went to meet him was that they heard he had done this sign. [19] The Pharisees then said to one another, "You see that you can do nothing; look, the world has gone after him."

20 Now among those who went up to worship at the feast were some Greeks. [21] So these came to Philip, who was from Beth-sa'i-da in Galilee, and said to him, "Sir, we wish to see Jesus." [22] Philip went and told Andrew; Andrew went with Philip and they told Jesus. [23] And Jesus answered them, "The hour has come for the Son of man to be glorified. [24] Truly, truly, I say to you, unless a grain of wheat falls into the earth and dies, it remains alone; but if it dies, it bears much fruit. [25] He who loves his life loses it, and he who hates his life in this world will keep it for eternal life. [26] If any one serves me, he must follow me; and where I am, there shall my servant be also; if any one serves me, the Father will honor him.

12. 12–15: Mt. 21. 4–9; Mk. 11. 7–10; Lk. 19. 35–38.   12. 13: Ps. 118. 25; Jn. 1. 49.
12. 15: Zech. 9. 9.   12. 16: Mk. 9. 32; Jn. 2. 22.   12. 20: Jn. 7. 35; Acts 11. 20.
12. 21: Jn. 1. 44; 6. 5.   12. 23: Jn. 13. 1; 17. 1; Mk. 14. 35, 41.   12. 24: 1 Cor. 15. 36.
12. 25: Mt. 10. 39; Mk. 8. 35; Lk. 9. 24; 14. 26.

Jesus Facing Death

27 "Now is my soul troubled. And what shall I say? 'Father, save me from this hour'? No, for this purpose I have come to this hour. [28] Father, glorify thy name." Then a voice came from heaven, "I have glorified it, and I will glorify it again." [29] The crowd standing by heard it and said that it had thundered. Others said, "An angel has spoken to him." [30] Jesus answered, "This voice has come for your sake, not for mine. [31] Now is the judgment of this world, now shall the ruler of this world be cast out; [32] and I, when I am lifted up from the earth, will draw all men to myself." [33] He said this to show by what death he was to die. [34] The crowd answered him, "We have heard from the law that the Christ remains forever. How can you say that the Son of man must be lifted up? Who is this Son of man?" [35] Jesus said to them, "The light is with you for a little longer. Walk while you have the light, lest the darkness overtake you; he who walks in the darkness does not know where he goes. [36] While you have the light, believe in the light, that you may become sons of light."

When Jesus had said this, he departed and hid himself from them. [37] Though he had done so many signs before them, yet they did not believe in him; [38] it was that the word spoken by the prophet Isaiah might be fulfilled:

"Lord, who has believed our report,
    and to whom has the arm of the Lord been revealed?"
[39] Therefore they could not believe. For Isaiah again said,
    [40] "He has blinded their eyes and hardened their heart,
        lest they should see with their eyes and perceive with
            their heart,
        and turn for me to heal them."

12. 27: Jn. 11. 33; Mt. 26. 38; Mk. 14. 34. **12. 28:** Mk. 1. 11; 9. 7. **12. 31:** Jn. 16. 11; 2 Cor. 4. 4; Eph. 2. 2. **12. 32:** Jn. 3. 14; 8. 28. **12. 34:** Ps. 110. 4; Is. 9. 7; Ezek. 37. 25; Dan. 7. 14. **12. 35:** Jn. 7. 33; 9. 4; Eph. 5. 8; 1 Jn. 2. 11. **12. 36:** Lk. 16. 8; Jn. 8. 59. **12. 38:** Is. 53. 1; Rom. 10. 16. **12. 40:** Is. 6. 10; Mt. 13. 14.

[41] Isaiah said this because he saw his glory and spoke of him. [42] Nevertheless many even of the authorities believed in him, but for fear of the Pharisees they did not confess it, lest they should be put out of the synagogue; [43] for they loved the praise of men more than the praise of God.

44 And Jesus cried out and said, "He who believes in me, believes not in me but in him who sent me. [45] And he who sees me sees him who sent me. [46] I have come as light into the world, that whoever believes in me may not remain in darkness. [47] If any one hears my sayings and does not keep them, I do not judge him; for I did not come to judge the world but to save the world. [48] He who rejects me and does not receive my sayings has a judge; the word that I have spoken will be his judge on the last day. [49] For I have not spoken on my own authority; the Father who sent me has himself given me commandment what to say and what to speak. [50] And I know that his commandment is eternal life. What I say, therefore, I say as the Father has bidden me."

13 Now before the feast of the Passover, when Jesus knew that his hour had come to depart out of this world to the Father, having loved his own who were in the world, he loved them to the end. [2] And during supper, when the devil had already put it into the heart of Judas Iscariot, Simon's son, to betray him, [3] Jesus, knowing that the Father had given all things into his hands, and that he had come from God and was going to God, [4] rose from supper, laid aside his garments, and girded himself with a towel. [5] Then he poured water into a basin, and began to wash the disciples' feet, and to wipe them with the towel with which he was girded. [6] He came to Simon Peter; and Peter said to

---

12. 41: Is. 6. 1; Lk. 24. 27. Jn. 5. 24.   **12. 45:** Jn. 14. 9.   **12. 42:** Jn. 9. 22; Lk. 6. 22.   **12. 46:** Jn. 1. 4; 8. 12; 9. 5.   **12. 44:** Mt. 10. 40; **12. 47:** Jn. 3. 17.
12. 48: Mt. 10. 14–15. **13. 1:** Jn. 11. 55; 12. 23; 16. 28. 22. 27.   **13. 2:** Jn. 6. 71; Mk. 14. 10.   **13. 5:** Lk. 7. 44;

him, "Lord, do you wash my feet?" ⁷ Jesus answered him, "What I am doing you do not know now, but afterward you will understand." ⁸ Peter said to him, "You shall never wash my feet." Jesus answered him, "If I do not wash you, you have no part in me." ⁹ Simon Peter said to him, "Lord, not my feet only but also my hands and my head!" ¹⁰ Jesus said to him, "He who has bathed does not need to wash, except for his feet,ᶻ but he is clean all over; and you are clean, but not all of you." ¹¹ For he knew who was to betray him; that was why he said, "You are not all clean."

12 When he had washed their feet, and taken his garments, and resumed his place, he said to them, "Do you know what I have done to you? ¹³ You call me Teacher and Lord; and you are right, for so I am. ¹⁴ If I then, your Lord and Teacher, have washed your feet, you also ought to wash one another's feet. ¹⁵ For I have given you an example, that you also should do as I have done to you. ¹⁶ Truly, truly, I say to you, a servantᵃ is not greater than his master; nor is he who is sent greater than he who sent him. ¹⁷ If you know these things, blessed are you if you do them. ¹⁸ I am not speaking of you all; I know whom I have chosen; it is that the scripture may be fulfilled, 'He who ate my bread has lifted his heel against me.' ¹⁹ I tell you this now, before it takes place, that when it does take place you may believe that I am he. ²⁰ Truly, truly, I say to you, he who receives any one whom I send receives me; and he who receives me receives him who sent me."

21 When Jesus had thus spoken, he was troubled in spirit, and testified, "Truly, truly, I say to you, one of you will betray me." ²² The disciples looked at one another, uncertain

---

ᶻ Some ancient authorities omit *except for his feet.*   ᵃ Or *slave.*

13. 8: Deut. 12. 12; Jn. 3. 5; 9. 7.   **13. 11:** Jn. 13. 2.   **13. 15:** 1 Pet. 2. 21.
13. 16: Mt. 10. 24; Lk. 6. 40.   **13. 17:** Lk. 11. 28; Jas. 1. 25.   **13. 18:** Ps. 41. 9.
13. 19: Jn. 14. 29; 8. 28.   **13. 20:** Mt. 10. 40; Lk. 10. 16.   **13. 21-26:** Mt. 26. 21-25;
Mk. 14. 18-21; Lk. 22. 21-23.

of whom he spoke. ²³ One of his disciples, whom Jesus loved, was lying close to the breast of Jesus; ²⁴ so Simon Peter beckoned to him and said, "Tell us who it is of whom he speaks." ²⁵ So lying thus, close to the breast of Jesus, he said to him, "Lord, who is it?" ²⁶ Jesus answered, "It is he to whom I shall give this morsel when I have dipped it." So when he had dipped the morsel, he gave it to Judas, the son of Simon Iscariot. ²⁷ Then after the morsel, Satan entered into him. Jesus said to him, "What you are going to do, do quickly." ²⁸ Now no one at the table knew why he said this to him. ²⁹ Some thought that, because Judas had the money box, Jesus was telling him, "Buy what we need for the feast"; or, that he should give something to the poor. ³⁰ So, after receiving the morsel, he immediately went out; and it was night.

31 When he had gone out, Jesus said, "Now is the Son of man glorified, and in him God is glorified; ³² if God is glorified in him, God will also glorify him in himself, and glorify him at once. ³³ Little children, yet a little while I am with you. You will seek me; and as I said to the Jews so now I say to you, 'Where I am going you cannot come.' ³⁴ A new commandment I give to you, that you love one another; even as I have loved you, that you also love one another. ³⁵ By this all men will know that you are my disciples, if you have love for one another."

36 Simon Peter said to him, "Lord, where are you going?" Jesus answered, "Where I am going you cannot follow me now; but you shall follow afterward." ³⁷ Peter said to him, "Lord, why cannot I follow you now? I will lay down my life for you." ³⁸ Jesus answered, "Will you lay

---

13. 23: Jn. 19. 26; 20. 2; 21. 7, 20.   **13. 26:** Jn. 6. 71.   **13. 29:** Jn. 12. 6.
13. 30: Lk. 22. 53   **13. 31–32:** Jn. 17. 1.   **13. 33:** 1 Jn. 2. 1; Jn. 7. 33.
13. 34: Jn. 15. 12, 17; 1 Jn. 3. 23; 2 Jn. 5; Lev. 19. 18; 1 Thess. 4. 9; 1 Pet. 1. 22; Heb. 13. 1; Eph. 5. 2; 1 Jn. 4. 10.   **13. 36:** Jn. 21. 18; 2 Pet. 1. 14.   **13. 37–38:** Mt. 26. 33–35; Mk. 14. 29–31; Lk. 22. 33–34.

down your life for me? Truly, truly, I say to you, the cock will not crow, till you have denied me three times.

14 "Let not your hearts be troubled; believe in God, believe also in me. [2] In my Father's house are many rooms; if it were not so, would I have told you that I go to prepare a place for you? [3] And when I go and prepare a place for you, I will come again and will take you to myself, that where I am you may be also. [4] And you know the way where I am going."[b] [5] Thomas said to him, "Lord, we do not know where you are going; how can we know the way?" [6] Jesus said to him, "I am the way, and the truth, and the life; no one comes to the Father, but by me. [7] If you had known me, you would have known my Father also; henceforth you know him and have seen him."

[8] Philip said to him, "Lord, show us the Father, and we shall be satisfied." [9] Jesus said to him, "Have I been with you so long, and yet you do not know me, Philip? He who has seen me has seen the Father; how can you say, 'Show us the Father'? [10] Do you not believe that I am in the Father and the Father in me? The words that I say to you I do not speak on my own authority; but the Father who dwells in me does his works. [11] Believe me that I am in the Father and the Father in me; or else believe me for the sake of the works themselves.

[12] "Truly, truly, I say to you, he who believes in me will also do the works that I do; and greater works than these will he do, because I go to the Father. [13] Whatever you ask in my name, I will do it, that the Father may be glorified in the Son; [14] if you ask[c] anything in my name, I will do it.

[15] "If you love me, you will keep my commandments.

---

[b] Some ancient authorities read *where I am going you know, and the way you know.*
[c] Many ancient authorities add *me.*

14. 2: Jn. 13. 33.   **14. 5:** Jn. 11. 16.   **14. 6:** Jn. 10. 9; 1. 4, 14.   **14. 9:** Jn. 12. 45.
14. 11: Jn. 10. 38.   **14. 13:** Mt. 7. 7; Jn. 15. 7, 16; 16. 23; Jas. 1. 5.   **14. 15:** Jn. 15. 10;
1 Jn. 5. 3; 2 Jn. 6.

[16] And I will pray the Father, and he will give you another Counselor, to be with you forever, [17] even the Spirit of truth, whom the world cannot receive, because it neither sees him nor knows him; you know him, for he dwells with you, and will be in you.

18 "I will not leave you desolate; I will come to you. [19] Yet a little while, and the world will see me no more, but you will see me; because I live, you will live also. [20] In that day you will know that I am in my Father, and you in me, and I in you. [21] He who has my commandments and keeps them, he it is who loves me; and he who loves me will be loved by my Father, and I will love him and manifest myself to him." [22] Judas (not Iscariot) said to him, "Lord, how is it that you will manifest yourself to us, and not to the world?" [23] Jesus answered him, "If a man loves me, he will keep my word, and my Father will love him, and we will come to him and make our home with him. [24] He who does not love me does not keep my words; and the word which you hear is not mine but the Father's who sent me.

25 "These things I have spoken to you, while I am still with you. [26] But the Counselor, the Holy Spirit, whom the Father will send in my name, he will teach you all things, and bring to your remembrance all that I have said to you. [27] Peace I leave with you; my peace I give to you; not as the world gives do I give to you. Let not your hearts be troubled, neither let them be afraid. [28] You heard me say to you, 'I go away, and I will come to you.' If you loved me, you would have rejoiced, because I go to the Father; for the Father is greater than I. [29] And now I have told you before it takes place, so that when it does take place, you may believe. [30] I will no longer talk much with you, for the ruler

14. 16: Jn. 14. 26; 15. 26; 16. 7; 1 Jn. 2. 1. **14. 19:** Jn. 7. 33. **14. 22:** Acts 1. 13; 10. 40–41. **14. 23:** 1 Jn. 2. 24; Rev. 21. 3. **14. 27:** Jn. 16. 33; Phil. 4. 7; Col. 3. 15; Jn. 20. 19. **14. 29:** Jn. 13. 19. **14. 30:** Jn. 12. 31.

of this world is coming. He has no power over me; [31] but I do as the Father has commanded me, so that the world may know that I love the Father. Rise, let us go hence.

15 "I am the true vine, and my Father is the vine-dresser. [2] Every branch of mine that bears no fruit, he takes away, and every branch that does bear fruit he prunes, that it may bear more fruit. [3] You are already made clean by the word which I have spoken to you. [4] Abide in me, and I in you. As the branch cannot bear fruit by itself, unless it abides in the vine, neither can you, unless you abide in me. [5] I am the vine, you are the branches. He who abides in me, and I in him, he it is that bears much fruit, for apart from me you can do nothing. [6] If a man does not abide in me, he is cast forth as a branch and withers; and the branches are gathered, thrown into the fire and burned. [7] If you abide in me, and my words abide in you, ask whatever you will, and it shall be done for you. [8] By this my Father is glorified, that you bear much fruit, and so prove to be my disciples. [9] As the Father has loved me, so have I loved you; abide in my love. [10] If you keep my commandments, you will abide in my love, just as I have kept my Father's commandments and abide in his love. [11] These things I have spoken to you, that my joy may be in you, and that your joy may be full.

[12] "This is my commandment, that you love one another as I have loved you. [13] Greater love has no man than this, that a man lay down his life for his friends. [14] You are my friends if you do what I command you. [15] No longer do I call you servants,[d] for the servant[e] does not know what his master is doing; but I have called you friends, for all that

[d] Or *slaves.*   [e] Or *slave.*

14. 31: Mk. 14. 42; Jn. 18. 1.
15. 1: Is. 5. 1–7; Ezek. 19. 10; Mk. 12. 1–9; Mt. 15. 13; Rom. 11. 17.   **15. 3:** Jn. 13. 10.
15. 4: Jn. 6. 56; 1 Jn. 2. 6.   **15. 7:** Jn. 14. 13; 16. 23; Mt. 7. 7; Jas. 1. 5.   **15. 8:** Mt.
5. 16.   **15. 10:** Jn. 14. 15; 1 Jn. 5. 3.   **15. 12:** Jn. 13. 34.   **15. 13:** Rom.
5. 7; Jn. 10. 11.   **15. 14:** Lk. 12. 4.

I have heard from my Father I have made known to you. [16] You did not choose me, but I chose you and appointed you that you should go and bear fruit and that your fruit should abide; so that whatever you ask the Father in my name, he may give it to you. [17] This I command you, to love one another.

18 "If the world hates you, know that it has hated me before it hated you. [19] If you were of the world, the world would love its own; but because you are not of the world, but I chose you out of the world, therefore the world hates you. [20] Remember the word that I said to you, 'A servant^f is not greater than his master.' If they persecuted me, they will persecute you; if they kept my word, they will keep yours also. [21] But all this they will do to you on my account, because they do not know him who sent me. [22] If I had not come and spoken to them, they would not have sin; but now they have no excuse for their sin. [23] He who hates me hates my Father also. [24] If I had not done among them the works which no one else did, they would not have sin; but now they have seen and hated both me and my Father. [25] It is to fulfill the word that is written in their law, 'They hated me without a cause.' [26] But when the Counselor comes, whom I shall send to you from the Father, even the Spirit of truth, who proceeds from the Father, he will bear witness to me; [27] and you also are witnesses, because you have been with me from the beginning.

16 "I have said all this to you to keep you from falling away. [2] They will put you out of the synagogues; indeed, the hour is coming when whoever kills you

---

^f Or *slave.*

15. 16: Jn. 6. 70; 13. 18; 14. 13; 16. 23.   **15. 18:** Jn. 7. 7; 1 Jn. 3. 13; Mt. 10. 22; 24. 9.   **15. 20:** Jn. 13. 16; Mt. 10. 24; 1 Cor. 4. 12; Acts 4. 17; 1 Pet. 4. 14; Rev. 2. 3.
15. 22: Jn. 9. 41.   **15. 25:** Ps. 35. 19; 69. 4.   **15. 26:** Jn. 14. 16, 26; 16. 7; 1 Jn. 2. 1; 5. 7.   **15. 27:** Jn. 19. 35; 21. 24; 1 Jn. 4. 14.
16. 2: Jn. 9. 22; Acts 26. 9–11; Is. 66. 5.

will think he is offering service to God. [3] And they will do this because they have not known the Father, nor me. [4] But I have said these things to you, that when their hour comes you may remember that I told you of them.

"I did not say these things to you from the beginning, because I was with you. [5] But now I am going to him who sent me; yet none of you asks me, 'Where are you going?' [6] But because I have said these things to you, sorrow has filled your hearts. [7] Nevertheless I tell you the truth: it is to your advantage that I go away, for if I do not go away, the Counselor will not come to you; but if I go, I will send him to you. [8] And when he comes, he will convince the world of sin and of righteousness and of judgment: [9] of sin, because they do not believe in me; [10] of righteousness, because I go to the Father, and you will see me no more; [11] of judgment, because the ruler of this world is judged.

12 "I have yet many things to say to you, but you cannot bear them now. [13] When the Spirit of truth comes, he will guide you into all the truth; for he will not speak on his own authority, but whatever he hears he will speak, and he will declare to you the things that are to come. [14] He will glorify me, for he will take what is mine and declare it to you. [15] All that the Father has is mine; therefore I said that he will take what is mine and declare it to you.

16 "A little while, and you will see me no more; again a little while, and you will see me." [17] Some of his disciples said to one another, "What is this that he says to us, 'A little while, and you will not see me, and again a little while, and you will see me'; and, 'because I go to the Father?'" [18] They said, "What does he mean by 'a little while'? We do not know what he means." [19] Jesus knew that they

16. 5: Jn. 7. 33; 14. 5.   16. 7: Jn. 14. 16, 26; 15. 26.   16. 9: Jn. 15. 22.
16. 10: Acts 3. 14; 7. 52; 1 Pet. 3. 18.   16. 11: Jn. 12. 31.   16. 14: Jn. 7. 39.
16. 16–24: Jn. 14. 18–24.

wanted to ask him; so he said to them, "Is this what you are asking yourselves, what I meant by saying, 'A little while, and you will not see me, and again a little while, and you will see me'? [20] Truly, truly, I say to you, you will weep and lament, but the world will rejoice; you will be sorrowful, but your sorrow will turn into joy. [21] When a woman is in travail she has sorrow, because her hour has come; but when she is delivered of the child, she no longer remembers the anguish, for joy that a child[g] is born into the world. [22] So you have sorrow now, but I will see you again and your hearts will rejoice, and no one will take your joy from you. [23] On that day you will ask me no questions. Truly, truly, I say to you, if you ask anything of the Father, he will give it to you in my name. [24] Hitherto you have asked nothing in my name; ask, and you will receive, that your joy may be full.

[25] "I have said this to you in figures; the hour is coming when I shall no longer speak to you in figures but tell you plainly of the Father. [26] In that day you will ask in my name; and I do not say to you that I shall pray the Father for you; [27] for the Father himself loves you, because you have loved me and have believed that I came from the Father. [28] I came from the Father and have come into the world; again, I am leaving the world and going to the Father."

[29] His disciples said, "Ah, now you are speaking plainly, not in any figure! [30] Now we know that you know all things, and need none to question you; by this we believe that you came from God." [31] Jesus answered them, "Do you now believe? [32] The hour is coming, indeed it has come, when you will be scattered, every man to his home, and will leave me alone; yet I am not alone, for the Father is with me.

[g] Greek *a human being.*

16. 20: Jn. 20. 20.　　　　16. 21: Is. 13. 8; Hos. 13. 13; Mic. 4. 9; 1 Thess. 5. 3.
16. 24: Jn. 14. 14; 15. 11.　　16. 25: Jn. 10. 6; Mt. 13. 34.　　16. 32: Jn. 4. 23;
Mk. 14. 27; Zech. 13. 7.

[33] I have said this to you, that in me you may have peace. In the world you have tribulation; but be of good cheer, I have overcome the world."

17 When Jesus had spoken these words, he lifted up his eyes to heaven and said, "Father, the hour has come; glorify thy Son that the Son may glorify thee, [2] since thou hast given him power over all flesh, so that he might give eternal life to all whom thou hast given him. [3] And this is eternal life, that they know thee the only true God, and Jesus Christ whom thou hast sent. [4] I glorified thee on earth, having accomplished the work which thou gavest me to do; [5] and now, Father, glorify thou me in thy own presence with the glory which I had with thee before the world was made.

6 "I have manifested thy name to the men whom thou gavest me out of the world; thine they were, and thou gavest them to me, and they have kept thy word. [7] Now they know that everything that thou hast given me is from thee; [8] for I have given them the words which thou gavest me, and they have received them and know in truth that I came from thee; and they have believed that thou didst send me. [9] I am praying for them; I am not praying for the world but for those whom thou hast given me, for they are thine; [10] all mine are thine, and thine are mine, and I am glorified in them. [11] And now I am no more in the world, but they are in the world, and I am coming to thee. Holy Father, keep them in thy name which thou hast given me, that they may be one, even as we are one. [12] While I was with them, I kept them in thy name which thou hast given me; I have guarded them, and none of them is lost but the son of perdition, that the scripture might be fulfilled. [13] But now I am

16. 33: Jn. 14. 27; 15. 18; Rom. 8. 37; 2 Cor. 2. 14; Rev. 3. 21.
17. 1: Jn. 11. 41; 13. 31.   **17. 5:** Jn. 1. 1; 8. 58; Phil. 2. 6.   **17. 9:** Lk. 22. 32; Jn. 14. 16.   **17. 11:** Phil. 2. 9; Rev. 19. 12; Rom. 12. 5; Gal. 3. 28; Jn. 17. 21.
17. 12: Ps. 41. 9; Jn. 6. 70; 18. 9.

coming to thee; and these things I speak in the world, that they may have my joy fulfilled in themselves. [14] I have given them thy word; and the world has hated them because they are not of the world, even as I am not of the world. [15] I do not pray that thou shouldst take them out of the world, but that thou shouldst keep them from the evil one.[h] [16] They are not of the world, even as I am not of the world. [17] Consecrate them in the truth; thy word is truth. [18] As thou didst send me into the world, so I have sent them into the world. [19] And for their sake I consecrate myself, that they also may be consecrated in truth.

20 "I do not pray for these only, but also for those who are to believe in me through their word, [21] that they may all be one; even as thou, Father, art in me, and I in thee, that they also may be in us, so that the world may believe that thou hast sent me. [22] The glory which thou hast given me I have given to them, that they may be one even as we are one, [23] I in them and thou in me, that they may become perfectly one, so that the world may know that thou hast sent me and hast loved them even as thou hast loved me. [24] Father, I desire that they also, whom thou hast given me, may be with me where I am, to behold my glory which thou hast given me in thy love for me before the foundation of the world. [25] O righteous Father, the world has not known thee, but I have known thee; and these know that thou hast sent me. [26] I made known to them thy name, and I will make it known, that the love with which thou hast loved me may be in them, and I in them."

18 When Jesus had spoken these words, he went forth with his disciples across the Kidron valley, where there was a garden, which he and his disciples entered.

[h] Or *from evil.*

17. 14: Jn. 15. 19; 8. 23.   **17. 21:** Jn. 10. 38; 17. 11.   **17. 24:** Jn. 1. 14; 17. 5; Mt. 25. 34.
18. 1: Mt. 26. 30, 36; Mk. 14. 26, 32; Lk. 22. 39; 2 Sam. 15. 23.

² Now Judas, who betrayed him, also knew the place; for Jesus often met there with his disciples. ³ So Judas, procuring a band of soldiers and some officers from the chief priests and the Pharisees, went there with lanterns and torches and weapons. ⁴ Then Jesus, knowing all that was to befall him, came forward and said to them, "Whom do you seek?" ⁵ They answered him, "Jesus of Nazareth." Jesus said to them, "I am he." Judas, who betrayed him, was standing with them. ⁶ When he said to them, "I am he," they drew back and fell to the ground. ⁷ Again he asked them, "Whom do you seek?" And they said, "Jesus of Nazareth." ⁸ Jesus answered, "I told you that I am he; so, if you seek me, let these men go." ⁹ This was to fulfill the word which he had spoken, "Of those whom thou gavest me I lost not one." ¹⁰ Then Simon Peter, having a sword, drew it and struck the high priest's slave and cut off his right ear. The slave's name was Malchus. ¹¹ Jesus said to Peter, "Put your sword into its sheath; shall I not drink the cup which the Father has given me?"

12 So the band of soldiers and their captain and the officers of the Jews seized Jesus and bound him. ¹³ First they led him to Annas; for he was the father-in-law of Ca′ia-phas, who was high priest that year. ¹⁴ It was Ca′-ia-phas who had given counsel to the Jews that it was expedient that one man should die for the people.

15 Simon Peter followed Jesus, and so did another disciple. As this disciple was known to the high priest, he entered the court of the high priest along with Jesus, ¹⁶ while Peter stood outside at the door. So the other disciple, who was known to the high priest, went out and spoke to the maid who kept the door, and brought Peter in.

18. 3–11: Mt. 26. 47–56; Mk. 14. 43–50; Lk. 22. 47–53.   18. 4: Jn. 6. 64; 13. 1.   18. 9: Jn. 17. 12; 6.39.   18. 11: Mk. 10. 38; 14. 36.   18. 12–13: Mt. 26. 57; Mk. 14. 53; Lk. 22. 54; 3. 2.   18. 14: Jn. 11. 49–51.   18. 15–16: Mt. 26. 58; Mk. 14. 54; Lk. 22. 54.

[17] The maid who kept the door said to Peter, "Are not you also one of this man's disciples?" He said, "I am not." [18] Now the servants[i] and officers had made a charcoal fire, because it was cold, and they were standing and warming themselves; Peter also was with them, standing and warming himself.

19 The high priest then questioned Jesus about his disciples and his teaching. [20] Jesus answered him, "I have spoken openly to the world; I have always taught in synagogues and in the temple, where all Jews come together; I have said nothing secretly. [21] Why do you ask me? Ask those who have heard me, what I said to them; they know what I said." [22] When he had said this, one of the officers standing by struck Jesus with his hand, saying, "Is that how you answer the high priest?" [23] Jesus answered him, "If I have spoken wrongly, bear witness to the wrong; but if I have spoken rightly, why do you strike me?" [24] Annas then sent him bound to Ca′ia-phas the high priest.

25 Now Simon Peter was standing and warming himself. They said to him, "Are not you also one of his disciples?" He denied it and said, "I am not." [26] One of the servants[i] of the high priest, a kinsman of the man whose ear Peter had cut off, asked, "Did I not see you in the garden with him?" [27] Peter again denied it; and at once the cock crowed.

28 Then they led Jesus from the house of Ca′ia-phas to the praetorium. It was early. They themselves did not enter the praetorium, so that they might not be defiled, but might eat the passover. [29] So Pilate went out to them and said, "What accusation do you bring against this man?" [30] They answered him, "If this man were not an evil-doer, we would

[i] Or *slaves*.

18. 17-18: Mt. 26. 69-72; Mk. 14. 66-69; Lk. 22. 56-58.   18. 19-23: Mt. 26. 59-66; Mk. 14. 55-64; Lk. 22. 67-71.   18. 23: Mt. 5. 39; Acts 23. 2-5.   18. 24: Jn. 18. 13; Lk. 3. 2.   18. 25-27: Mt. 26. 73-75; Mk. 14. 70-72; Lk. 22. 59-62.   18. 28: Jn. 11 55; Mt. 27. 1-2; Mk. 15. 1; Lk. 23. 1.   18. 29-38: Mt. 27. 11-14; Mk. 15. 2-5; Lk. 23. 2-3.

not have handed him over." ³¹ Pilate said to them, "Take him yourselves and judge him by your own law." The Jews said to him, "It is not lawful for us to put any man to death." ³² This was to fulfill the word which Jesus had spoken to show by what death he was to die.

33 Pilate entered the praetorium again and called Jesus, and said to him, "Are you the King of the Jews?" ³⁴ Jesus answered, "Do you say this of your own accord, or did others say it to you about me?" ³⁵ Pilate answered, "Am I a Jew? Your own nation and the chief priests have handed you over to me; what have you done?" ³⁶ Jesus answered, "My kingship is not of this world; if my kingship were of this world, my servants would fight, that I might not be handed over to the Jews; but my kingship is not from the world." ³⁷ Pilate said to him, "So you are a king?" Jesus answered, "You say that I am a king. For this I was born, and for this I have come into the world, to bear witness to the truth. Every one who is of the truth hears my voice." ³⁸ Pilate said to him, "What is truth?"

After he had said this, he went out to the Jews again, and told them, "I find no crime in him. ³⁹ But you have a custom that I should release one man for you at the Passover; will you have me release for you the King of the Jews?" ⁴⁰ They cried out again, "Not this man, but Barab'bas!" Now Bar-ab'bas was a robber.

19 Then Pilate took Jesus and scourged him. ² And the soldiers plaited a crown of thorns, and put it on his head, and arrayed him in a purple robe; ³ they came up to him, saying, "Hail, King of the Jews!" and struck him with their hands. ⁴ Pilate went out again, and said to them, "Behold, I am bringing him out to you, that you may

18. 32: Jn. 3. 14; 12. 32.   **18. 36:** Jn. 6. 15; Mt. 26. 53.   **18. 37:** Jn. 3. 32; 8. 14, 47; 1 Jn. 4. 6.   **18. 38–40:** Mt. 27. 15–26; Mk. 15. 6–15; Lk. 23. 18–19; Acts 3. 14. **19. 2–3:** Mt. 27. 27–31; Mk. 15. 16–20; Lk. 22. 63–65; 23. 11.   **19. 4:** Jn. 18. 38; 19. 6; Lk. 23. 4.

know that I find no crime in him." ⁵ So Jesus came out, wearing the crown of thorns and the purple robe. Pilate said to them, "Here is the man!" ⁶ When the chief priests and the officers saw him, they cried out, "Crucify him, crucify him!" Pilate said to them, "Take him yourselves and crucify him, for I find no crime in him." ⁷ The Jews answered him, "We have a law, and by that law he ought to die, because he has made himself the Son of God." ⁸ When Pilate heard these words, he was the more afraid; ⁹ he entered the praetorium again and said to Jesus, "Where are you from?" But Jesus gave no answer. ¹⁰ Pilate therefore said to him, "You will not speak to me? Do you not know that I have power to release you, and power to crucify you?" ¹¹ Jesus answered him, "You would have no power over me unless it had been given you from above; therefore he who delivered me to you has the greater sin."

12 Upon this Pilate sought to release him, but the Jews cried out, "If you release this man, you are not Caesar's friend; every one who makes himself a king sets himself against Caesar." ¹³ When Pilate heard these words, he brought Jesus out and sat down on the judgment seat at a place called The Pavement, and in Hebrew, Gab′ba-tha. ¹⁴ Now it was the day of Preparation for the Passover; it was about the sixth hour. He said to the Jews, "Here is your King!" ¹⁵ They cried out, "Away with him, away with him, crucify him!" Pilate said to them, "Shall I crucify your King?" The chief priests answered, "We have no king but Caesar." ¹⁶ Then he handed him over to them to be crucified.

17 So they took Jesus, and he went out, bearing his own cross, to the place called the place of a skull, which is called

in Hebrew Gol'go-tha. [18] There they crucified him, and with him two others, one on either side, and Jesus between them. [19] Pilate also wrote a title and put it on the cross; it read, "Jesus of Nazareth, the King of the Jews." [20] Many of the Jews read this title, for the place where Jesus was crucified was near the city; and it was written in Hebrew, in Latin, and in Greek. [21] The chief priests of the Jews then said to Pilate, "Do not write, 'The King of the Jews,' but, 'This man said, I am King of the Jews.'" [22] Pilate answered, "What I have written I have written."

23 When the soldiers had crucified Jesus they took his garments and made four parts, one for each soldier. But his tunic was without seam, woven from top to bottom; [24] so they said to one another, "Let us not tear it, but cast lots for it to see whose it shall be." This was to fulfill the scripture,

"They parted my garments among them,
    and for my clothing they cast lots."

25 So the soldiers did this; but standing by the cross of Jesus were his mother, and his mother's sister, Mary the wife of Clo'pas, and Mary Mag'da-lene. [26] When Jesus saw his mother, and the disciple whom he loved standing near, he said to his mother, "Woman, behold your son!" [27] Then he said to the disciple, "Behold your mother!" And from that hour the disciple took her to his own home.

28 After this Jesus, knowing that all was now finished, said (to fulfill the scripture), "I thirst." [29] A bowl full of sour wine stood there; so they put a sponge full of the wine on hyssop and held it to his mouth. [30] When Jesus had received the wine, he said, "It is finished"; and he bowed his head and gave up his spirit.

19. 24: Ex. 28. 32; Ps. 22. 18.   **19. 25:** Mt. 27. 55–56; Mk. 15. 40–41; Lk. 23. 49; Jn. 2. 3; Mk. 3. 31; Lk. 24. 18; Jn. 20. 1, 18.   **19. 26:** Jn. 13. 23; 20. 2; 21. 20. **19. 28–30:** Ps. 69. 21; Mt. 27. 45–50; Mk. 15. 33–37; Lk. 23. 44–46; Jn. 17. 4.

31 Since it was the day of Preparation, in order to prevent the bodies from remaining on the cross on the sabbath (for that sabbath was a high day), the Jews asked Pilate that their legs might be broken, and that they might be taken away. ³² So the soldiers came and broke the legs of the first, and of the other who had been crucified with him; ³³ but when they came to Jesus and saw that he was already dead, they did not break his legs. ³⁴ But one of the soldiers pierced his side with a spear, and at once there came out blood and water. ³⁵ He who saw it has borne witness—his testimony is true, and he knows that he tells the truth—that you also may believe. ³⁶ For these things took place that the scripture might be fulfilled, "Not a bone of him shall be broken." ³⁷ And again another scripture says, "They shall look on him whom they have pierced."

38 After this Joseph of Ar-i-ma-the′a, who was a disciple of Jesus, but secretly, for fear of the Jews, asked Pilate that he might take away the body of Jesus; and Pilate gave him leave. So he came and took away his body. ³⁹ Nic-o-de′mus also, who had at first come to him by night, came bringing a mixture of myrrh and aloes, about a hundred pounds′ʲ weight. ⁴⁰ They took the body of Jesus, and bound it in linen cloths with the spices, as is the burial custom of the Jews. ⁴¹ Now in the place where he was crucified there was a garden, and in the garden a new tomb where no one had ever been laid. ⁴² So because of the Jewish day of Preparation, as the tomb was close at hand, they laid Jesus there.

20 Now on the first day of the week Mary Mag′dalene came to the tomb early, while it was still dark, and saw that the stone had been taken away from the tomb.

ʲ Greek *litras.*

19. 31: Deut. 21. 23; Ex. 12. 16.   19. 34: 1 Jn. 5. 6–8.   19. 35: Jn. 15. 27; 21. 24.
19. 36: Ex. 12. 46; Num. 9. 12; Ps. 34. 20.   19. 37: Zech. 12. 10.   19. 38–42:
Mt. 27. 57–61; Mk. 15. 42–47; Lk. 23. 50–56.   19. 39: Jn. 3. 1; 7. 50.   19. 40: Mk. 16. 1;
14. 8.   20. 1–10: Mt. 28. 1–8; Mk. 16. 1–8; Lk. 24. 1–10.

[2] So she ran, and went to Simon Peter and the other disciple, the one whom Jesus loved, and said to them, "They have taken the Lord out of the tomb, and we do not know where they have laid him." [3] Peter then came out with the other disciple, and they went toward the tomb. [4] They both ran, but the other disciple outran Peter and reached the tomb first; [5] and stooping to look in, he saw the linen cloths lying there, but he did not go in. [6] Then Simon Peter came, following him, and he went into the tomb; he saw the linen cloths lying, [7] and the napkin, which had been on his head, not lying with the linen cloths but rolled up in a place by itself. [8] Then the other disciple, who reached the tomb first, also went in, and he saw and believed; [9] for as yet they did not know the scripture, that he must rise from the dead. [10] Then the disciples went back to their homes.

11 But Mary stood weeping outside the tomb, and as she wept she stooped to look into the tomb; [12] and she saw two angels in white, sitting where the body of Jesus had lain, one at the head and one at the feet. [13] They said to her, "Woman, why are you weeping?" She said to them, "Because they have taken away my Lord, and I do not know where they have laid him." [14] Saying this, she turned round and saw Jesus standing, but she did not know that it was Jesus. [15] Jesus said to her, "Woman, why are you weeping? Whom do you seek?" Supposing him to be the gardener, she said to him, "Sir, if you have carried him away, tell me where you have laid him, and I will take him away." [16] Jesus said to her, "Mary." She turned and said to him in Hebrew, "Rab-bo'ni!" (which means Teacher). [17] Jesus said to her, "Do not hold me, for I have not yet ascended to the Father; but go to my brethren and say to them, 'I

20. 3–10: Lk. 24. 11–12. 20. 9: Lk. 24. 26, 46. 20. 12: Lk. 24. 4; Mt. 28. 5; Mk. 16. 5. 20. 13: Jn. 20. 2. 20. 14: Mt. 28. 9; Jn. 21. 4. 20. 17: Jn. 20. 27; Mt. 28. 10; Jn. 7. 33.

am ascending to my Father and your Father, to my God and your God.'" [18] Mary Mag′da-lene went and said to the disciples, "I have seen the Lord"; and she told them that he had said these things to her.

19 On the evening of that day, the first day of the week, the doors being shut where the disciples were, for fear of the Jews, Jesus came and stood among them and said to them, "Peace be with you." [20] When he had said this, he showed them his hands and his side. Then the disciples were glad when they saw the Lord. [21] Jesus said to them again, "Peace be with you. As the Father has sent me, even so I send you." [22] And when he had said this, he breathed on them, and said to them, "Receive the Holy Spirit. [23] If you forgive the sins of any, they are forgiven; if you retain the sins of any, they are retained."

24 Now Thomas, one of the twelve, called the Twin, was not with them when Jesus came. [25] So the other disciples told him, "We have seen the Lord." But he said to them, "Unless I see in his hands the print of the nails, and place my finger in the mark of the nails, and place my hand in his side, I will not believe."

26 Eight days later, his disciples were again in the house, and Thomas was with them. The doors were shut, but Jesus came and stood among them, and said, "Peace be with you." [27] Then he said to Thomas, "Put your finger here, and see my hands; and put out your hand, and place it in my side; do not be faithless, but believing." [28] Thomas answered him, "My Lord and my God!" [29] Jesus said to him, "Have you believed because you have seen me? Blessed are those who have not seen and yet believe."

30 Now Jesus did many other signs in the presence of the

20. 18: Lk. 24. 10, 23.   **20. 19–20:** Lk. 24. 36–39.   **20. 21:** Jn. 17. 18; Mt. 28. 19.
20. 22: Acts 2. 4, 33.   **20. 23:** Mt. 16. 19; 18. 18.   **20. 24:** Jn. 11. 16.
20. 27: Lk. 24. 40.   **20. 29:** 1 Pet. 1. 8.   **20. 30:** Jn. 21. 25.

disciples, which are not written in this book; [31] but these are written that you may believe that Jesus is the Christ, the Son of God, and that believing you may have life in his name.

21 After this Jesus revealed himself again to the disciples by the Sea of Ti-be′ri-as; and he revealed himself in this way. [2] Simon Peter, Thomas called the Twin, Na-than′a-el of Cana in Galilee, the sons of Zeb′e-dee, and two others of his disciples were together. [3] Simon Peter said to them, "I am going fishing." They said to him, "We will go with you." They went out and got into the boat; but that night they caught nothing.

4 Just as day was breaking, Jesus stood on the beach; yet the disciples did not know that it was Jesus. [5] Jesus said to them, "Children, have you any fish?" They answered him, "No." [6] He said to them, "Cast the net on the right side of the boat, and you will find some." So they cast it, and now they were not able to haul it in, for the quantity of fish. [7] That disciple whom Jesus loved said to Peter, "It is the Lord!" When Simon Peter heard that it was the Lord, he put on his clothes, for he was stripped for work, and sprang into the sea. [8] But the other disciples came in the boat, dragging the net full of fish, for they were not far from the land, but about a hundred yards[k] off.

9 When they got out on land, they saw a charcoal fire there, with fish lying on it, and bread. [10] Jesus said to them, "Bring some of the fish that you have just caught." [11] So Simon Peter went aboard and hauled the net ashore, full of large fish, a hundred and fifty-three of them; and although there were so many, the net was not torn. [12] Jesus said to

---

[k] Greek *two hundred cubits.*

20. 31: Jn. 3. 15.
21. 2: Jn. 11. 16; 1. 45; Lk. 5. 10.   **21. 3–6:** Lk. 5. 3–7.   **21. 4:** Jn. 20. 14;
Lk. 24. 16.   **21. 5:** Lk. 24. 41.   **21. 7:** Jn. 13. 23; 19. 26; 20. 2; 21. 20.

them, "Come and have breakfast." Now none of the disciples dared ask him, "Who are you?" They knew it was
the Lord. [13] Jesus came and took the bread and gave it to
them, and so with the fish. [14] This was now the third time
that Jesus was revealed to the disciples after he was raised
from the dead.

15 When they had finished breakfast, Jesus said to Simon
Peter, "Simon, son of John, do you love me more than
these?" He said to him, "Yes, Lord; you know that I love
you." [16] He said to him, "Feed my lambs." A second time
he said to him, "Simon, son of John, do you love me?"
He said to him, "Yes, Lord; you know that I love you."
He said to him, "Tend my sheep." [17] He said to him the
third time, "Simon, son of John, do you love me?" Peter
was grieved because he said to him the third time, "Do you
love me?" And he said to him, "Lord, you know everything;
you know that I love you." Jesus said to him, "Feed my
sheep. [18] Truly, truly, I say to you, when you were young,
you girded yourself and walked where you would; but when
you are old, you will stretch out your hands, and another
will gird you and carry you where you do not wish to go."
[19] (This he said to show by what death he was to glorify
God.) And after this, he said to him, "Follow me."

20 Peter turned and saw following them the disciple whom
Jesus loved, who had lain close to his breast at the supper
and had said, "Lord, who is it that is going to betray you?"
[21] When Peter saw him, he said to Jesus, "Lord, what about
this man?" [22] Jesus said to him, "If it is my will that he
remain until I come, what is that to you? Follow me!"
[23] The saying spread abroad among the brethren that the
disciple was not to die; yet Jesus did not say to him that he

21. 14: Jn. 20. 19, 26.   **21. 15:** Jn. 1. 42; 13. 37; Mk. 14. 29–31; Lk. 12. 32.
21. 16: Mt. 2. 6; Acts 20. 28; 1 Pet. 5. 2; Rev. 7. 17.   **21. 19:** 2 Pet. 1. 14; Mk. 1. 17.
21. 20: Jn. 13. 25.   **21. 22:** 1 Cor. 4. 5; Jas. 5. 7; Rev. 2. 25; Mt. 16. 28.

was not to die, but, "If it is my will that he remain until I come, what is that to you?"

24 This is the disciple who is bearing witness to these things, and who has written these things; and we know that his testimony is true.

25 But there are also many other things which Jesus did; were every one of them to be written, I suppose that the world itself could not contain the books that would be written.

THE

ACTS OF THE APOSTLES

1 In the first book, O The-oph'i-lus, I have dealt with all that Jesus began to do and teach, [2] until the day when he was taken up, after he had given commandment through the Holy Spirit to the apostles whom he had chosen. [3] To them he presented himself alive after his passion by many proofs, appearing to them during forty days, and speaking of the kingdom of God. [4] And while staying[a] with them he charged them not to depart from Jerusalem, but to wait for the promise of the Father, which, he said, "you heard from me, [5] for John baptized with water, but before many days you shall be baptized with the Holy Spirit."

6 So when they had come together, they asked him, "Lord, will you at this time restore the kingdom to Israel?" [7] He said to them, "It is not for you to know times or seasons which the Father has fixed by his own authority. [8] But you shall receive power when the Holy Spirit has come upon you; and you shall be my witnesses in Jerusalem and in all Judea and Sa-ma'ri-a and to the end of the earth." [9] And

[a] Or *eating*.

21. 24: Jn. 15. 27; 19. 35.   21. 25: Jn. 20. 30.
1. 1: Lk. 1. 1–4.   1. 4: Lk. 24. 49.   1. 8: Lk. 24. 48–49.   1. 9–12: Lk. 24 50–53.

when he had said this, as they were looking on, he was lifted up, and a cloud took him out of their sight. [10] And while they were gazing into heaven as he went, behold, two men stood by them in white robes, [11] and said, "Men of Galilee, why do you stand looking into heaven? This Jesus, who was taken up from you into heaven, will come in the same way as you saw him go into heaven."

12 Then they returned to Jerusalem from the mount called Olivet, which is near Jerusalem, a sabbath day's journey away; [13] and when they had entered, they went up to the upper room, where they were staying, Peter and John and James and Andrew, Philip and Thomas, Bartholomew and Matthew, James the son of Alphaeus and Simon the Zealot and Judas the son of James. [14] All these with one accord devoted themselves to prayer, together with the women and Mary the mother of Jesus, and with his brothers.

15 In those days Peter stood up among the brethren (the company of persons was in all about a hundred and twenty), and said, [16] "Brethren, the scripture had to be fulfilled, which the Holy Spirit spoke beforehand by the mouth of David, concerning Judas who was guide to those who arrested Jesus. [17] For he was numbered among us, and was allotted his share in this ministry. [18] (Now this man bought a field with the reward of his wickedness; and falling headlong he burst open in the middle and all his bowels gushed out. [19] And it became known to all the inhabitants of Jerusalem, so that the field was called in their language A-kel′da-ma, that is, Field of Blood.) [20] For it is written in the book of Psalms,

'Let his habitation become desolate,
    and let there be no one to live in it';
and
    'His office let another take.'

1. 13: Mt. 10. 2–4; Mk. 3. 16–19; Lk. 6. 14–16.   **1. 16–19:** Mt. 27. 3–10.
1. 20: Ps. 69. 25; 109. 8.

²¹ So one of the men who have accompanied us during all the time that the Lord Jesus went in and out among us, ²² beginning from the baptism of John until the day when he was taken up from us — one of these men must become with us a witness to his resurrection." ²³ And they put forward two, Joseph called Bar′sab-bas, who was surnamed Justus, and Mat-thi′as. ²⁴ And they prayed and said, "Lord, who knowest the hearts of all men, show which one of these two thou hast chosen ²⁵ to take the place in this ministry and apostleship from which Judas turned aside, to go to his own place." ²⁶ And they cast lots for them, and the lot fell on Mat-thi′as; and he was enrolled with the eleven apostles.

2 When the day of Pentecost had come, they were all together in one place. ² And suddenly a sound came from heaven like the rush of a mighty wind, and it filled all the house where they were sitting. ³ And there appeared to them tongues as of fire, distributed and resting on each one of them. ⁴ And they were all filled with the Holy Spirit and began to speak in other tongues, as the Spirit gave them utterance.

5 Now there were dwelling in Jerusalem Jews, devout men from every nation under heaven. ⁶ And at this sound the multitude came together, and they were bewildered, because each one heard them speaking in his own language. ⁷ And they were amazed and wondered, saying, "Are not all these who are speaking Galileans? ⁸ And how is it that we hear, each of us in his own native language? ⁹ Par′thians and Medes and E′lam-ites and residents of Mes-o-po-ta′mi-a, Judea and Cap-pa-do′ci-a, Pontus and Asia, ¹⁰ Phryg′i-a and Pam-phyl′i-a, Egypt and the parts of Libya belonging to Cy-re′ne, and visitors from Rome, both Jews and proselytes, ¹¹ Cre′tans and Arabians, we hear

them telling in our own tongues the mighty works of God."
[12] And all were amazed and perplexed, saying to one another, "What does this mean?" [13] But others mocking said, "They are filled with new wine."

14 But Peter, standing with the eleven, lifted up his voice and addressed them, "Men of Judea and all who dwell in Jerusalem, let this be known to you, and give ear to my words. [15] For these men are not drunk, as you suppose, since it is only the third hour of the day; [16] but this is what was spoken by the prophet Joel:

> [17] 'And in the last days it shall be, God declares,
>   that I will pour out my Spirit upon all flesh,
>   and your sons and your daughters shall prophesy,
>   and your young men shall see visions,
>   and your old men shall dream dreams;
> [18] yea, and on my menservants and my maidservants in
>   those days
>   I will pour out my Spirit, and they shall prophesy.
> [19] And I will show wonders in the heaven above
>   and signs on the earth beneath,
>   blood, and fire, and vapor of smoke;
> [20] the sun shall be turned into darkness
>   and the moon into blood,
>   before the day of the Lord comes,
>   the great and manifest day.
> [21] And it shall be that whoever calls on the name of the
>   Lord shall be saved.'

22 "Men of Israel, hear these words: Jesus of Nazareth, a man attested to you by God with mighty works and wonders and signs which God did through him in your midst, as you yourselves know — [23] this Jesus, delivered up according to the definite plan and foreknowledge of God, you

2. 17–21: Joel 2. 28–32.

crucified and killed by the hands of lawless men. [24] But God raised him up, having loosed the pangs of death, because it was not possible for him to be held by it. [25] For David says concerning him,

> 'I saw the Lord always before me,
>> for he is at my right hand that I may not be shaken;
> [26] therefore my heart was glad, and my tongue rejoiced;
>> moreover my flesh will dwell in hope.
> [27] For thou wilt not abandon my soul to Hades,
>> nor let thy Holy One see corruption.
> [28] Thou hast made known to me the ways of life;
>> thou wilt make me full of gladness with thy presence.'

29 "Brethren, I may say to you confidently of the patriarch David that he both died and was buried, and his tomb is with us to this day. [30] Being therefore a prophet, and knowing that God had sworn with an oath to him that he would set one of his descendants upon his throne, [31] he foresaw and spoke of the resurrection of the Christ, that he was not abandoned to Hades, nor did his flesh see corruption. [32] This Jesus God raised up, and of that we all are witnesses. [33] Being therefore exalted at the right hand of God, and having received from the Father the promise of the Holy Spirit, he has poured out this which you see and hear. [34] For David did not ascend into the heavens; but he himself says,

> 'The Lord said to my Lord, Sit at my right hand,
> [35] till I make thy enemies a stool for thy feet.'

[36] Let all the house of Israel therefore know assuredly that God has made him both Lord and Christ, this Jesus whom you crucified."

37 Now when they heard this they were cut to the heart, and said to Peter and the rest of the apostles, "Brethren, what shall we do?" [38] And Peter said to them, "Repent,

2. 25–28: Ps. 16. 8–11.   **2. 30:** Ps. 132. 11.   **2. 31:** Ps. 16. 10.   **2. 34–35:** Ps. 110. 1.

and be baptized every one of you in the name of Jesus Christ for the forgiveness of your sins; and you shall receive the gift of the Holy Spirit. ³⁹ For the promise is to you and to your children and to all that are far off, every one whom the Lord our God calls to him." ⁴⁰ And he testified with many other words and exhorted them, saying, "Save yourselves from this crooked generation." ⁴¹ So those who received his word were baptized, and there were added that day about three thousand souls. ⁴² And they devoted themselves to the apostles' teaching and fellowship, to the breaking of bread and the prayers.

43 And fear came upon every soul; and many wonders and signs were done through the apostles. ⁴⁴ And all who believed were together and had all things in common; ⁴⁵ and they sold their possessions and goods and distributed them to all, as any had need. ⁴⁶ And day by day, attending the temple together and breaking bread in their homes, they partook of food with glad and generous hearts, ⁴⁷ praising God and having favor with all the people. And the Lord added to their number day by day those who were being saved.

3 Now Peter and John were going up to the temple at the hour of prayer, the ninth hour. ² And a man lame from birth was being carried, whom they laid daily at that gate of the temple which is called Beautiful to ask alms of those who entered the temple. ³ Seeing Peter and John about to go into the temple, he asked for alms. ⁴ And Peter directed his gaze at him, with John, and said, "Look at us." ⁵ And he fixed his attention upon them, expecting to receive something from them. ⁶ But Peter said, "I have no silver and gold, but I give you what I have; in the name of Jesus Christ of Nazareth, walk." ⁷ And he took him by the

2. 39: Is. 57. 19; Joel 2. 32.   **2. 44–45:** Acts 4. 32–35.

255

right hand and raised him up; and immediately his feet and ankles were made strong. [8] And leaping up he stood and walked and entered the temple with them, walking and leaping and praising God. [9] And all the people saw him walking and praising God, [10] and recognized him as the one who sat for alms at the Beautiful Gate of the temple; and they were filled with wonder and amazement at what had happened to him.

11 While he clung to Peter and John, all the people ran together to them in the portico called Solomon's, astounded. [12] And when Peter saw it he addressed the people, "Men of Israel, why do you wonder at this, or why do you stare at us, as though by our own power or piety we had made him walk? [13] The God of Abraham and of Isaac and of Jacob, the God of our fathers, glorified his servant[b] Jesus, whom you delivered up and denied in the presence of Pilate, when he had decided to release him. [14] But you denied the Holy and Righteous One, and asked for a murderer to be granted to you, [15] and killed the Author of life, whom God raised from the dead. To this we are witnesses. [16] And his name, by faith in his name, has made this man strong whom you see and know; and the faith which is through Jesus[c] has given the man this perfect health in the presence of you all.

17 "And now, brethren, I know that you acted in ignorance, as did also your rulers. [18] But what God foretold by the mouth of all the prophets, that his Christ should suffer, he thus fulfilled. [19] Repent therefore, and turn again, that your sins may be blotted out, that times of refreshing may come from the presence of the Lord, [20] and that he may send the Christ appointed for you, Jesus, [21] whom heaven must receive until the time for establishing all that God spoke

[b] Or *child*.   [c] Greek *him*.

3. 13: Ex. 3. 6; Is. 52. 13.

by the mouth of his holy prophets from of old. [22] Moses said, 'The Lord God will raise up for you a prophet from your brethren as he raised me up. You shall listen to him in whatever he tells you. [23] And it shall be that every soul that does not listen to that prophet shall be destroyed from the people.' [24] And all the prophets who have spoken, from Samuel and those who came afterwards, also proclaimed these days. [25] You are the sons of the prophets and of the covenant which God gave to your fathers, saying to Abraham, 'And in your posterity shall all the families of the earth be blessed.' [26] God, having raised up his servant,[b] sent him to you first, to bless you in turning every one of you from your wickedness."

4 And as they were speaking to the people, the priests and the captain of the temple and the Sad'du-cees came upon them, [2] annoyed because they were teaching the people and proclaiming in Jesus the resurrection from the dead. [3] And they arrested them and put them in custody until the morrow, for it was already evening. [4] But many of those who heard the word believed; and the number of the men came to about five thousand.

5 On the morrow their rulers and elders and scribes were gathered together in Jerusalem, [6] with Annas the high priest and Ca'ia-phas and John and Alexander, and all who were of the high-priestly family. [7] And when they had set them in the midst, they inquired, "By what power or by what name did you do this?" [8] Then Peter, filled with the Holy Spirit, said to them, "Rulers of the people and elders, [9] if we are being examined today concerning a good deed done to a cripple, by what means this man has been healed, [10] be it known to you all, and to all the people of Israel, that by

[b] Or *child*.

3. 22: Deut. 18. 15–16.   3. 23: Deut. 18. 19; Lev. 23. 29.   3. 25: Gen. 22. 18.

the name of Jesus Christ of Nazareth, whom you crucified, whom God raised from the dead, by him this man is standing before you well. [11] This is the stone which was rejected by you builders, but which has become the head of the corner. [12] And there is salvation in no one else, for there is no other name under heaven given among men by which we must be saved."

13 Now when they saw the boldness of Peter and John, and perceived that they were uneducated, common men, they wondered; and they recognized that they had been with Jesus. [14] But seeing the man that had been healed standing beside them, they had nothing to say in opposition. [15] But when they had commanded them to go aside out of the council, they conferred with one another, [16] saying, "What shall we do with these men? For that a notable sign has been performed through them is manifest to all the inhabitants of Jerusalem, and we cannot deny it. [17] But in order that it may spread no further among the people, let us warn them to speak no more to any one in this name." [18] So they called them and charged them not to speak or teach at all in the name of Jesus. [19] But Peter and John answered them, "Whether it is right in the sight of God to listen to you rather than to God, you must judge; [20] for we cannot but speak of what we have seen and heard." [21] And when they had further threatened them, they let them go, finding no way to punish them, because of the people; for all men praised God for what had happened. [22] For the man on whom this sign of healing was performed was more than forty years old.

23 When they were released they went to their friends and reported what the chief priests and the elders had said to them. [24] And when they heard it, they lifted their voices

4. 11: Ps. 118. 22.   4. 24: Ex. 20. 11; Ps. 146. 6.

together to God and said, "Sovereign Lord, who didst make
the heaven and the earth and the sea and everything in
them, [25] who by the mouth of our father David, thy servant,[b]
didst say by the Holy Spirit,

'Why did the Gentiles rage,
and the peoples imagine vain things?
[26] The kings of the earth set themselves in array,
and the rulers were gathered together,
against the Lord and against his Anointed'[d]—

[27] for truly in this city there were gathered together against
thy holy servant[b] Jesus, whom thou didst anoint, both Herod
and Pontius Pilate, with the Gentiles and the peoples of
Israel, [28] to do whatever thy hand and thy plan had predestined to take place. [29] And now, Lord, look upon their
threats, and grant to thy servants[e] to speak thy word with
all boldness, [30] while thou stretchest out thy hand to heal,
and signs and wonders are performed through the name
of thy holy servant[b] Jesus." [31] And when they had prayed,
the place in which they were gathered together was shaken;
and they were all filled with the Holy Spirit and spoke the
word of God with boldness.

32 Now the company of those who believed were of one
heart and soul, and no one said that any of the things which
he possessed was his own, but they had everything in common. [33] And with great power the apostles gave their testimony to the resurrection of the Lord Jesus, and great
grace was upon them all. [34] There was not a needy person
among them, for as many as were possessors of lands or
houses sold them, and brought the proceeds of what was
sold [35] and laid it at the apostles' feet; and distribution
was made to each as any had need. [36] Thus Joseph who

[b] Or *child.*   [d] Or *Christ.*   [e] Or *slaves.*

4. 25–26: Ps. 2. 1–2.   **4. 27:** Ps. 2. 2; 2. 1.   **4. 32–35:** Acts 2. 44–45.

was surnamed by the apostles Barnabas (which means, Son of encouragement), a Levite, a native of Cyprus, ³⁷ sold a field which belonged to him, and brought the money and laid it at the apostles' feet.

5 But a man named An-a-ni'as with his wife Sap-phi'ra sold a piece of property, ² and with his wife's knowledge he kept back some of the proceeds, and brought only a part and laid it at the apostles' feet. ³ But Peter said, "An-a-ni'as, why has Satan filled your heart to lie to the Holy Spirit and to keep back part of the proceeds of the land? ⁴ While it remained unsold, did it not remain your own? And after it was sold, was it not at your disposal? How is it that you have contrived this deed in your heart? You have not lied to men but to God." ⁵ When An-a-ni'as heard these words, he fell down and died. And great fear came upon all who heard of it. ⁶ The young men rose and wrapped him up and carried him out and buried him.

7 After an interval of about three hours his wife came in, not knowing what had happened. ⁸ And Peter said to her, "Tell me whether you sold the land for so much." And she said, "Yes, for so much." ⁹ But Peter said to her, "How is it that you have agreed together to tempt the Spirit of the Lord? Hark, the feet of those that have buried your husband are at the door, and they will carry you out." ¹⁰ Immediately she fell down at his feet and died. When the young men came in they found her dead, and they carried her out and buried her beside her husband. ¹¹ And great fear came upon the whole church, and upon all who heard of these things.

12 Now many signs and wonders were done among the people by the hands of the apostles. And they were all together in Solomon's Portico. ¹³ None of the rest dared join them, but the people held them in high honor. ¹⁴ And more

than ever believers were added to the Lord, multitudes both of men and women, [15] so that they even carried out the sick into the streets, and laid them on beds and pallets, that as Peter came by at least his shadow might fall on some of them. [16] The people also gathered from the towns around Jerusalem, bringing the sick and those afflicted with unclean spirits, and they were all healed.

17 But the high priest rose up and all who were with him, that is, the party of the Sad'du-cees, and filled with jealousy [18] they arrested the apostles and put them in the common prison. [19] But at night an angel of the Lord opened the prison doors and brought them out and said, [20] "Go and stand in the temple and speak to the people all the words of this Life." [21] And when they heard this, they entered the temple at daybreak and taught.

Now the high priest came and those who were with him and called together the council and all the senate of Israel, and sent to the prison to have them brought. [22] But when the officers came, they did not find them in the prison, and they returned and reported, [23] "We found the prison securely locked and the sentries standing at the doors, but when we opened it we found no one inside." [24] Now when the captain of the temple and the chief priests heard these words, they were much perplexed about them, wondering what this would come to. [25] And some one came and told them, "The men whom you put in prison are standing in the temple and teaching the people." [26] Then the captain with the officers went and brought them, but without violence, for they were afraid of being stoned by the people.

27 And when they had brought them, they set them before the council. And the high priest questioned them, [28] saying, "We strictly charged you not to teach in this name, yet here you have filled Jerusalem with your teaching and you

intend to bring this man's blood upon us." ²⁹ But Peter and the apostles answered, "We must obey God rather than men. ³⁰ The God of our fathers raised Jesus whom you killed by hanging him on a tree. ³¹ God exalted him at his right hand as Leader and Savior, to give repentance to Israel and forgiveness of sins. ³² And we are witnesses to these things, and so is the Holy Spirit whom God has given to those who obey him."

33 When they heard this they were enraged and wanted to kill them. ³⁴ But a Pharisee in the council named Gama'li-el, a teacher of the law, held in honor by all the people, stood up and ordered the men to be put outside for a while. ³⁵ And he said to them, "Men of Israel, take care what you do with these men. ³⁶ For before these days Theu'das arose, giving himself out to be somebody, and a number of men, about four hundred, joined him; but he was slain and all who followed him were dispersed and came to nothing. ³⁷ After him Judas the Galilean arose in the days of the census and drew away some of the people after him; he also perished, and all who followed him were scattered. ³⁸ So in the present case I tell you, keep away from these men and let them alone; for if this plan or this undertaking is of men, it will fail; ³⁹ but if it is of God, you will not be able to overthrow them. You might even be found opposing God!"

40 So they took his advice, and when they had called in the apostles, they beat them and charged them not to speak in the name of Jesus, and let them go. ⁴¹ Then they left the presence of the council, rejoicing that they were counted worthy to suffer dishonor for the name. ⁴² And every day in the temple and at home they did not cease teaching and preaching Jesus as the Christ.

5. 30: Deut. 21. 22–23.

6 Now in these days when the disciples were increasing in number, the Hellenists murmured against the Hebrews because their widows were neglected in the daily distribution. [2] And the twelve summoned the body of the disciples and said, "It is not right that we should give up preaching the word of God to serve tables. [3] Therefore, brethren, pick out from among you seven men of good repute, full of the Spirit and of wisdom, whom we may appoint to this duty. [4] But we will devote ourselves to prayer and to the ministry of the word." [5] And what they said pleased the whole multitude, and they chose Stephen, a man full of faith and of the Holy Spirit, and Philip, and Proch'o-rus, and Ni-ca'nor, and Timon, and Par'me-nas, and Nic-o-la'us, a proselyte of Antioch. [6] These they set before the apostles, and they prayed and laid their hands upon them.

7 And the word of God increased; and the number of the disciples multiplied greatly in Jerusalem, and a great many of the priests were obedient to the faith.

8 And Stephen, full of grace and power, did great wonders and signs among the people. [9] Then some of those who belonged to the synagogue of the Freedmen (as it was called), and of the Cy-re'ni-ans, and of the Alexandrians, and of those from Ci-li'cia and Asia, arose and disputed with Stephen. [10] But they could not withstand the wisdom and the Spirit with which he spoke. [11] Then they secretly instigated men, who said, "We have heard him speak blasphemous words against Moses and God." [12] And they stirred up the people and the elders and the scribes, and they came upon him and seized him and brought him before the council, [13] and set up false witnesses who said, "This man never ceases to speak words against this holy place and the law; [14] for we have heard him say that this Jesus of Nazareth

will destroy this place, and will change the customs which Moses delivered to us." [15] And gazing at him, all who sat in the council saw that his face was like the face of an angel.

7 And the high priest said, "Is this so?" [2] And Stephen said:

"Brethren and fathers, hear me. The God of glory appeared to our father Abraham, when he was in Mes-o-po-ta'mi-a, before he lived in Haran, [3] and said to him, 'Depart from your land and from your kindred and go into the land which I will show you.' [4] Then he departed from the land of the Chal-de'ans, and lived in Haran. And after his father died, God removed him from there into this land in which you are now living; [5] yet he gave him no inheritance in it, not even a foot's length, but promised to give it to him in possession and to his posterity after him, though he had no child. [6] And God spoke to this effect, that his posterity would be aliens in a land belonging to others, who would enslave them and ill-treat them four hundred years. [7] 'But I will judge the nation which they serve,' said God, 'and after that they shall come out and worship me in this place.' [8] And he gave him the covenant of circumcision. And so Abraham became the father of Isaac, and circumcised him on the eighth day; and Isaac became the father of Jacob, and Jacob of the twelve patriarchs.

9 "And the patriarchs, jealous of Joseph, sold him into Egypt; but God was with him, [10] and rescued him out of all his afflictions, and gave him favor and wisdom before Pharaoh, king of Egypt, who made him governor over Egypt and over all his household. [11] Now there came a famine throughout all Egypt and Canaan, and great affliction,

7. 2: Ps. 29. 3; Gen. 11. 31; 15. 7.   **7. 3:** Gen. 12. 1.   **7. 4:** Gen. 11. 31; 15. 7; 12. 5.
7. 5: Deut. 2. 5; Gen. 12. 7; 17. 8.   **7. 6–7:** Gen. 15. 13–14.   **7. 7:** Ex. 3. 12.
7. 8: Gen. 17. 10–14; 21. 2–4; 25. 26; 29. 31–35; 30. 1–24; 35. 16–18; 35. 23–26.   **7. 9:** Gen. 37. 11, 28; 45. 4.   **7. 9–10:** Gen. 39. 2–3, 21.   **7. 10:** Gen. 41. 40–46; Ps. 105. 21.
7. 11: Gen. 41. 54–55; 42. 5.

and our fathers could find no food. [12] But when Jacob heard that there was grain in Egypt, he sent forth our fathers the first time. [13] And at the second visit Joseph made himself known to his brothers, and Joseph's family became known to Pharaoh. [14] And Joseph sent and called to him Jacob his father and all his kindred, seventy-five souls; [15] and Jacob went down into Egypt. And he died, himself and our fathers, [16] and they were carried back to She'chem and laid in the tomb that Abraham had bought for a sum of silver from the sons of Hamor in She'chem.

17 "But as the time of the promise drew near, which God had granted to Abraham, the people grew and multiplied in Egypt [18] till there arose over Egypt another king who had not known Joseph. [19] He dealt craftily with our race and forced our fathers to expose their infants, that they might not be kept alive. [20] At this time Moses was born, and was beautiful before God. And he was brought up for three months in his father's house; [21] and when he was exposed, Pharaoh's daughter adopted him and brought him up as her own son. [22] And Moses was instructed in all the wisdom of the Egyptians, and he was mighty in his words and deeds.

23 "When he was forty years old, it came into his heart to visit his brethren, the sons of Israel. [24] And seeing one of them being wronged, he defended the oppressed man and avenged him by striking the Egyptian. [25] He supposed that his brethren understood that God was giving them deliverance by his hand, but they did not understand. [26] And on the following day he appeared to them as they were quarreling and would have reconciled them, saying, 'Men, you are brethren, why do you wrong each other?' [27] But the man

7. 12: Gen. 42. 2. **7. 13:** Gen. 45. 1–4. **7. 14:** Gen. 45. 9–10. **7. 14–15:** Deut. 10. 22. **7. 16:** Josh. 24. 32; Gen. 50. 13. **7. 17–18:** Ex. 1. 7–8. **7. 19:** Ex. 1. 10–11; 1. 15–22. **7. 20:** Ex. 2. 2. **7. 21:** Ex. 2. 5–6, 10. **7. 23–29:** Ex. 2. 11–15.

who was wronging his neighbor thrust him aside, saying, 'Who made you a ruler and a judge over us? [28] Do you want to kill me as you killed the Egyptian yesterday?' [29] At this retort Moses fled, and became an exile in the land of Midian, where he became the father of two sons.

30 "Now when forty years had passed, an angel appeared to him in the wilderness of Mount Sinai, in a flame of fire in a thornbush. [31] When Moses saw it he wondered at the sight; and as he drew near to look, the voice of the Lord came, [32] 'I am the God of your fathers, the God of Abraham and of Isaac and of Jacob.' And Moses trembled and did not dare to look. [33] And the Lord said to him, 'Take off the shoes from your feet, for the place where you are standing is holy ground. [34] I have surely seen the ill-treatment of my people that are in Egypt and heard their groaning, and I have come down to deliver them. And now come, I will send you to Egypt.'

35 "This Moses whom they refused, saying, 'Who made you a ruler and a judge?' God sent as both ruler and deliverer by the hand of the angel that appeared to him in the thornbush. [36] He led them out, having performed wonders and signs in Egypt and at the Red Sea, and in the wilderness for forty years. [37] This is the Moses who said to the Israelites, 'God will raise up for you a prophet from your brethren as he raised me up.' [38] This is he who was in the congregation in the wilderness with the angel who spoke to him at Mount Sinai, and with our fathers; and he received living oracles to give to us. [39] Our fathers refused to obey him, but thrust him aside, and in their hearts they turned to Egypt, [40] saying to Aaron, 'Make for us gods to go before us; as for this Moses who led us out from the land of Egypt,

7. 29: Ex. 2. 22; 18. 3–4.   **7. 30–34:** Ex. 3. 1–10.   **7. 35:** Ex. 2. 14.   **7. 36:** Ex. 7. 3; 14. 21; Num. 14. 33.   **7. 37:** Deut. 18. 15, 18.   **7. 38:** Ex. 19.   **7. 39:** Num. 14. 3–4. **7. 40:** Ex. 32. 1, 23.

we do not know what has become of him.' ⁴¹ And they made a calf in those days, and offered a sacrifice to the idol and rejoiced in the works of their hands. ⁴² But God turned and gave them over to worship the host of heaven, as it is written in the book of the prophets:

> 'Did you offer to me slain beasts and sacrifices,
> forty years in the wilderness, O house of Israel?
> ⁴³ And you took up the tent of Moloch,
> and the star of the god Rephan,
> the figures which you made to worship;
> and I will remove you beyond Babylon.'

44 "Our fathers had the tent of witness in the wilderness, even as he who spoke to Moses directed him to make it, according to the pattern that he had seen. ⁴⁵ Our fathers in turn brought it in with Joshua when they dispossessed the nations which God thrust out before our fathers. So it was until the days of David, ⁴⁶ who found favor in the sight of God and asked leave to find a habitation for the God of Jacob. ⁴⁷ But it was Solomon who built a house for him. ⁴⁸ Yet the Most High does not dwell in houses made with hands; as the prophet says,

> ⁴⁹ 'Heaven is my throne,
> and earth my footstool.
> What house will you build for me, says the Lord,
> or what is the place of my rest?
> ⁵⁰ Did not my hand make all these things?'

51 "You stiff-necked people, uncircumcised in heart and ears, you always resist the Holy Spirit. As your fathers did, so do you. ⁵² Which of the prophets did not your fathers persecute? And they killed those who announced beforehand the coming of the Righteous One, whom you have now

7. 41: Ex. 32. 4, 6.   **7. 42:** Jer. 19. 13.   **7. 42–43:** Amos 5. 25–27.   **7. 44:** Ex. 25. 9, 40.   **7. 45:** Josh. 3. 14–17; Deut. 32. 49.   **7. 46:** 2 Sam. 7. 8–16; Ps. 132. 1–5. **7. 47:** 1 Kings 6.   **7. 49–50:** Is. 66. 1–2.   **7. 51:** Ex. 33. 3, 5; Jer. 9. 26; 6. 10; Num. 27. 14; Is. 63. 10.

betrayed and murdered, [53] you who received the law as delivered by angels and did not keep it."

54 Now when they heard these things they were enraged, and they ground their teeth against him. [55] But he, full of the Holy Spirit, gazed into heaven and saw the glory of God, and Jesus standing at the right hand of God; [56] and he said, "Behold, I see the heavens opened, and the Son of man standing at the right hand of God." [57] But they cried out with a loud voice and stopped their ears and rushed together upon him. [58] Then they cast him out of the city and stoned him; and the witnesses laid down their garments at the feet of a young man named Saul. [59] And as they were stoning Stephen, he prayed, "Lord Jesus, receive my spirit." [60] And he knelt down and cried with a loud voice, "Lord, do not hold this sin against them." And when he had said

8 this, he fell asleep. [1] And Saul was consenting to his death. And on that day a great persecution arose against the church in Jerusalem; and they were all scattered throughout the region of Judea and Sa-ma'ri-a, except the apostles. [2] Devout men buried Stephen, and made great lamentation over him. [3] But Saul laid waste the church, and entering house after house, he dragged off men and women and committed them to prison.

4 Now those who were scattered went about preaching the word. [5] Philip went down to a city of Sa-ma'ri-a, and proclaimed to them the Christ. [6] And the multitudes with one accord gave heed to what was said by Philip, when they heard him and saw the signs which he did. [7] For unclean spirits came out of many who were possessed, crying with a loud voice; and many who were paralyzed or lame were healed. [8] So there was much joy in that city.

9 But there was a man named Simon who had previously

8. 1: Acts 11. 19.

practiced magic in the city and amazed the nation of Sa-ma'ri-a, saying that he himself was somebody great. [10] They all gave heed to him, from the least to the greatest, saying, "This man is that power of God which is called Great." [11] And they gave heed to him, because for a long time he had amazed them with his magic. [12] But when they believed Philip as he preached good news about the kingdom of God and the name of Jesus Christ, they were baptized, both men and women. [13] Even Simon himself believed, and after being baptized he continued with Philip. And seeing signs and great miracles performed, he was amazed.

14 Now when the apostles at Jerusalem heard that Sa-ma'ri-a had received the word of God, they sent to them Peter and John, [15] who came down and prayed for them that they might receive the Holy Spirit; [16] for it had not yet fallen on any of them, but they had only been baptized in the name of the Lord Jesus. [17] Then they laid their hands on them and they received the Holy Spirit. [18] Now when Simon saw that the Spirit was given through the laying on of the apostles' hands, he offered them money, [19] saying, "Give me also this power, that any one on whom I lay my hands may receive the Holy Spirit." [20] But Peter said to him, "Your silver perish with you, because you thought you could obtain the gift of God with money! [21] You have neither part nor lot in this matter, for your heart is not right before God. [22] Repent therefore of this wickedness of yours, and pray to the Lord that, if possible, the intent of your heart may be forgiven you. [23] For I see that you are in the gall of bitterness and in the bond of iniquity." [24] And Simon answered, "Pray for me to the Lord, that nothing of what you have said may come upon me."

8. 21: Ps. 78. 37.   **8. 23**: Is. 58. 6.

25 Now when they had testified and spoken the word of the Lord, they returned to Jerusalem, preaching the gospel to many villages of the Samaritans.

26 But an angel of the Lord said to Philip, "Rise and go toward the south[f] to the road that goes down from Jerusalem to Gaza." This is a desert road. 27 And he rose and went. And behold, an Ethiopian, a eunuch, a minister of Can-da'ce the queen of the Ethiopians, in charge of all her treasure, had come to Jerusalem to worship 28 and was returning; seated in his chariot, he was reading the prophet Isaiah. 29 And the Spirit said to Philip, "Go up and join this chariot." 30 So Philip ran to him, and heard him reading Isaiah the prophet, and asked, "Do you understand what you are reading?" 31 And he said, "How can I, unless some one guides me?" And he invited Philip to come up and sit with him. 32 Now the passage of the scripture which he was reading was this:

"As a sheep led to the slaughter
   or a lamb before its shearer is dumb,
   so he opens not his mouth.
33 In his humiliation justice was denied him.
   Who can describe his generation?
   For his life is taken up from the earth."

34 And the eunuch said to Philip, "About whom, pray, does the prophet say this, about himself or about some one else?" 35 Then Philip opened his mouth, and beginning with this scripture he told him the good news of Jesus. 36 And as they went along the road they came to some water, and the eunuch said, "See, here is water! What is to prevent my being baptized?"[g] 38 And he commanded the chariot to stop, and

[f] Or *at noon.*
[g] Some ancient authorities add all or most of verse 37, *And Philip said, "If you believe with all your heart, you may." And he replied, "I believe that Jesus Christ is the Son of God."*
8. 32–33: Is. 53. 7–8.

they both went down into the water, Philip and the eunuch, and he baptized him. [39] And when they came up out of the water, the Spirit of the Lord caught up Philip; and the eunuch saw him no more, and went on his way rejoicing. [40] But Philip was found at A-zo'tus, and passing on he preached the gospel to all the towns till he came to Caes-a-re'a.

9 But Saul, still breathing threats and murder against the disciples of the Lord, went to the high priest [2] and asked him for letters to the synagogues at Damascus, so that if he found any belonging to the Way, men or women, he might bring them bound to Jerusalem. [3] Now as he journeyed he approached Damascus, and suddenly a light from heaven flashed about him. [4] And he fell to the ground and heard a voice saying to him, "Saul, Saul, why do you persecute me?" [5] And he said, "Who are you, Lord?" And he said, "I am Jesus, whom you are persecuting; [6] but rise and enter the city, and you will be told what you are to do." [7] The men who were traveling with him stood speechless, hearing the voice but seeing no one. [8] Saul arose from the ground; and when his eyes were opened, he could see nothing; so they led him by the hand and brought him into Damascus. [9] And for three days he was without sight, and neither ate nor drank.

10 Now there was a disciple at Damascus named An-a-ni'as. The Lord said to him in a vision, "An-a-ni'as." And he said, "Here I am, Lord." [11] And the Lord said to him, "Rise and go to the street called Straight, and inquire in the house of Judas for a man of Tarsus named Saul; for behold, he is praying, [12] and he has seen a man named An-a-ni'as come in and lay his hands on him so that he might regain his sight." [13] But An-a-ni'as answered, "Lord, I

9. 1–19: Acts 22. 4–16; 26. 9–18.

have heard from many about this man, how much evil he has done to thy saints at Jerusalem; [14] and here he has authority from the chief priests to bind all who call upon thy name." [15] But the Lord said to him, "Go, for he is a chosen instrument of mine to carry my name before the Gentiles and kings and the sons of Israel; [16] for I will show him how much he must suffer for the sake of my name." [17] So An-a-ni'as departed and entered the house. And laying his hands on him he said, "Brother Saul, the Lord Jesus who appeared to you on the road by which you came, has sent me that you may regain your sight and be filled with the Holy Spirit." [18] And immediately something like scales fell from his eyes and he regained his sight. Then he rose and was baptized, [19] and took food and was strengthened.

For several days he was with the disciples at Damascus. [20] And in the synagogues immediately he proclaimed Jesus, saying, "He is the Son of God." [21] And all who heard him were amazed, and said, "Is not this the man who made havoc in Jerusalem of those who called on this name? And he has come here for this purpose, to bring them bound before the chief priests." [22] But Saul increased all the more in strength, and confounded the Jews who lived in Damascus by proving that Jesus was the Christ.

23 When many days had passed, the Jews plotted to kill him, [24] but their plot became known to Saul. They were watching the gates day and night, to kill him; [25] but his disciples took him by night and let him down over the wall, lowering him in a basket.

26 And when he had come to Jerusalem he attempted to join the disciples; and they were all afraid of him, for they did not believe that he was a disciple. [27] But Barnabas took him, and brought him to the apostles, and declared

9. 24–25: 2 Cor. 11. 32–33.

to them how on the road he had seen the Lord, who spoke to him, and how at Damascus he had preached boldly in the name of Jesus. ²⁸ So he went in and out among them at Jerusalem, ²⁹ preaching boldly in the name of the Lord. And he spoke and disputed against the Hellenists; but they were seeking to kill him. ³⁰ And when the brethren knew it, they brought him down to Caes-a-re′a, and sent him off to Tarsus.

31 So the church throughout all Judea and Galilee and Sa-ma′ri-a had peace and was built up; and walking in the fear of the Lord and in the comfort of the Holy Spirit it was multiplied.

32 Now as Peter went here and there among them all, he came down also to the saints that lived at Lydda. ³³ There he found a man named Ae-ne′as, who had been bedridden for eight years and was paralyzed. ³⁴ And Peter said to him, "Ae-ne′as, Jesus Christ heals you; rise and make your bed." And immediately he rose. ³⁵ And all the residents of Lydda and Sharon saw him, and they turned to the Lord.

36 Now there was at Joppa a disciple named Tabitha, which means Dorcas or Gazelle. She was full of good works and acts of charity. ³⁷ In those days she fell sick and died; and when they had washed her, they laid her in an upper room. ³⁸ Since Lydda was near Joppa, the disciples, hearing that Peter was there, sent two men to him entreating him, "Please come to us without delay." ³⁹ So Peter rose and went with them. And when he had come, they took him to the upper room. All the widows stood beside him weeping, and showing coats and garments which Dorcas made while she was with them. ⁴⁰ But Peter put them all outside and knelt down and prayed; then turning to the body he said, "Tabitha, rise." And she opened her eyes, and when she saw Peter she sat up. ⁴¹ And he gave her his hand and lifted

her up. Then calling the saints and widows he presented her alive. ⁴² And it became known throughout all Joppa, and many believed in the Lord. ⁴³ And he stayed in Joppa for many days with one Simon, a tanner.

10 At Caes-a-re′a there was a man named Cornelius, a centurion of what was known as the Italian Cohort, ² a devout man who feared God with all his household, gave alms liberally to the people, and prayed constantly to God. ³ About the ninth hour of the day he saw clearly in a vision an angel of God coming in and saying to him, "Cornelius." ⁴ And he stared at him in terror, and said, "What is it, Lord?" And he said to him, "Your prayers and your alms have ascended as a memorial before God. ⁵ And now send men to Joppa, and bring one Simon who is called Peter; ⁶ he is lodging with Simon, a tanner, whose house is by the seaside." ⁷ When the angel who spoke to him had departed, he called two of his servants and a devout soldier from among those that waited on him, ⁸ and having related everything to them, he sent them to Joppa.

9 The next day, as they were on their journey and coming near the city, Peter went up on the housetop to pray, about the sixth hour. ¹⁰ And he became hungry and desired something to eat; but while they were preparing it, he fell into a trance ¹¹ and saw the heaven opened, and something descending, like a great sheet, let down by four corners upon the earth. ¹² In it were all kinds of animals and reptiles and wild birds. ¹³ And there came a voice to him, "Rise, Peter; kill and eat." ¹⁴ But Peter said, "No, Lord; for I have never eaten anything that is common or unclean." ¹⁵ And the voice came to him again a second time, "What God has cleansed, you must not call common." ¹⁶ This happened three times, and the thing was taken up at once to heaven.

10. 1–48: Acts 11. 4–17.

17 Now while Peter was inwardly perplexed as to what the vision which he had seen might mean, behold, the men that were sent by Cornelius, having made inquiry for Simon's house, stood before the gate [18] and called out to ask whether Simon who was called Peter was lodging there. [19] And while Peter was pondering the vision, the Spirit said to him, "Behold, three men are looking for you. [20] Rise and go down, and accompany them without hesitation; for I have sent them." [21] And Peter went down to the men and said, "I am the one you are looking for; what is the reason for your coming?" [22] And they said, "Cornelius, a centurion, an upright and God-fearing man, who is well spoken of by the whole Jewish nation, was directed by a holy angel to send for you to come to his house, and to hear what you have to say." [23] So he called them in to be his guests.

The next day he rose and went off with them, and some of the brethren from Joppa accompanied him. [24] And on the following day they entered Caes-a-re'a. Cornelius was expecting them and had called together his kinsmen and close friends. [25] When Peter entered, Cornelius met him and fell down at his feet and worshiped him. [26] But Peter lifted him up, saying, "Stand up; I too am a man." [27] And as he talked with him, he went in and found many persons gathered; [28] and he said to them, "You yourselves know how unlawful it is for a Jew to associate with or to visit any one of another nation; but God has shown me that I should not call any man common or unclean. [29] So when I was sent for, I came without objection. I ask then why you sent for me."

30 And Cornelius said, "Four days ago, about this hour, I was keeping the ninth hour of prayer in my house; and behold, a man stood before me in bright apparel, [31] saying, 'Cornelius, your prayer has been heard and your alms have

been remembered before God. [32] Send therefore to Joppa and ask for Simon who is called Peter; he is lodging in the house of Simon, a tanner, by the seaside.' [33] So I sent to you at once, and you have been kind enough to come. Now therefore we are all here present in the sight of God, to hear all that you have been commanded by the Lord."

34 And Peter opened his mouth and said: "Truly I perceive that God shows no partiality, [35] but in every nation any one who fears him and does what is right is acceptable to him. [36] You know the word which he sent to Israel, preaching good news of peace by Jesus Christ (he is Lord of all), [37] the word which was proclaimed throughout all Judea, beginning from Galilee after the baptism which John preached: [38] how God anointed Jesus of Nazareth with the Holy Spirit and with power; how he went about doing good and healing all that were oppressed by the devil, for God was with him. [39] And we are witnesses to all that he did both in the country of the Jews and in Jerusalem. They put him to death by hanging him on a tree; [40] but God raised him on the third day and made him manifest, [41] not to all the people but to us who were chosen by God as witnesses, who ate and drank with him after he rose from the dead. [42] And he commanded us to preach to the people, and to testify that he is the one ordained by God to be judge of the living and the dead. [43] To him all the prophets bear witness that every one who believes in him receives forgiveness of sins through his name."

44 While Peter was still saying this, the Holy Spirit fell on all who heard the word. [45] And the believers from among the circumcised who came with Peter were amazed, because the gift of the Holy Spirit had been poured out even on the Gentiles. [46] For they heard them speaking in tongues and extolling God. Then Peter declared, [47] "Can any one for-

bid water for baptizing these people who have received the Holy Spirit just as we have?" ⁴⁸ And he commanded them to be baptized in the name of Jesus Christ. Then they asked him to remain for some days.

11 Now the apostles and the brethren who were in Judea heard that the Gentiles also had received the word of God. ² So when Peter went up to Jerusalem, the circumcision party criticized him, ³ saying, "Why did you go to uncircumcised men and eat with them?" ⁴ But Peter began and explained to them in order: ⁵ "I was in the city of Joppa praying; and in a trance I saw a vision, something descending, like a great sheet, let down from heaven by four corners; and it came down to me. ⁶ Looking at it closely I observed animals and beasts of prey and reptiles and wild birds. ⁷ And I heard a voice saying to me, 'Rise, Peter; kill and eat.' ⁸ But I said, 'No, Lord: for nothing common or unclean has ever entered my mouth.' ⁹ But the voice answered a second time from heaven, 'What God has cleansed you must not call common.' ¹⁰ This happened three times, and all was drawn up again into heaven. ¹¹ At that very moment three men arrived at the house in which we were, sent to me from Caes-a-re′a. ¹² And the Spirit told me to go with them without hesitation. These six brethren also accompanied me, and we entered the man's house. ¹³ And he told us how he had seen the angel standing in his house and saying, 'Send to Joppa and bring Simon called Peter; ¹⁴ he will declare to you a message by which you will be saved, you and all your household.' ¹⁵ As I began to speak, the Holy Spirit fell on them just as on us at the beginning. ¹⁶ And I remembered the word of the Lord, how he said, 'John baptized with water, but you shall be baptized with the Holy Spirit.' ¹⁷ If then God gave the same gift to them as he gave to us

11. 4–17: Acts 10. 1–48.   **11. 16:** Acts 1. 5.

277

when we believed in the Lord Jesus Christ, who was I that I could withstand God?" [18] When they heard this they were silenced. And they glorified God, saying, "Then to the Gentiles also God has granted repentance unto life."

19 Now those who were scattered because of the persecution that arose over Stephen traveled as far as Phoe-ni'ci-a and Cyprus and Antioch, speaking the word to none except Jews. [20] But there were some of them, men of Cyprus and Cy-re'ne, who on coming to Antioch spoke to the Greeks[h] also, preaching the Lord Jesus. [21] And the hand of the Lord was with them, and a great number that believed turned to the Lord. [22] News of this came to the ears of the church in Jerusalem, and they sent Barnabas to Antioch. [23] When he came and saw the grace of God, he was glad; and he exhorted them all to remain faithful to the Lord with steadfast purpose; [24] for he was a good man, full of the Holy Spirit and of faith. And a large company was added to the Lord. [25] So Barnabas went to Tarsus to look for Saul; [26] and when he had found him, he brought him to Antioch. For a whole year they met with[i] the church, and taught a large company of people; and in Antioch the disciples were for the first time called Christians.

27 Now in these days prophets came down from Jerusalem to Antioch. [28] And one of them named Ag'a-bus stood up and foretold by the Spirit that there would be a great famine over all the world; and this took place in the days of Claudius. [29] And the disciples determined, every one according to his ability, to send relief to the brethren who lived in Judea; [30] and they did so, sending it to the elders by the hand of Barnabas and Saul.

12 About that time Herod the king laid violent hands upon some who belonged to the church. [2] He killed James the brother of John with the sword; [3] and when he

[h] Some ancient authorities read *Hellenists*.   [i] Or *were guests of*.
11. 19: Acts 8. 4.

saw that it pleased the Jews, he proceeded to arrest Peter also. This was during the days of Unleavened Bread. ⁴ And when he had seized him, he put him in prison, and delivered him to four squads of soldiers to guard him, intending after the Passover to bring him out to the people. ⁵ So Peter was kept in prison; but earnest prayer for him was made to God by the church.

6 The very night when Herod was about to bring him out, Peter was sleeping between two soldiers, bound with two chains, and sentries before the door were guarding the prison; ⁷ and behold, an angel of the Lord appeared, and a light shone in the cell; and he struck Peter on the side and woke him, saying, "Get up quickly." And the chains fell off his hands. ⁸ And the angel said to him, "Dress yourself and put on your sandals." And he did so. And he said to him, "Wrap your mantle around you and follow me." ⁹ And he went out and followed him; he did not know that what was done by the angel was real, but thought he was seeing a vision. ¹⁰ When they had passed the first and the second guard, they came to the iron gate leading into the city. It opened to them of its own accord, and they went out and passed on through one street; and immediately the angel left him. ¹¹ And Peter came to himself, and said, "Now I am sure that the Lord has sent his angel and rescued me from the hand of Herod and from all that the Jewish people were expecting."

12 When he realized this, he went to the house of Mary, the mother of John whose other name was Mark, where many were gathered together and were praying. ¹³ And when he knocked at the door of the gateway, a maid named Rhoda came to answer. ¹⁴ Recognizing Peter's voice, in her joy she did not open the gate but ran in and told that Peter was standing at the gate. ¹⁵ They said to her, "You are

mad." But she insisted that it was so. They said, "It is his angel!" [16] But Peter continued knocking; and when they opened, they saw him and were amazed. [17] But motioning to them with his hand to be silent, he described to them how the Lord had brought him out of the prison. And he said, "Tell this to James and to the brethren." Then he departed and went to another place.

18 Now when day came, there was no small stir among the soldiers over what had become of Peter. [19] And when Herod had sought for him and could not find him, he examined the sentries and ordered that they should be put to death. Then he went down from Judea to Caes-a-re′a, and remained there.

20 Now Herod was angry with the people of Tyre and Sidon; and they came to him in a body, and having persuaded Blastus, the king's chamberlain, they asked for peace, because their country depended on the king's country for food. [21] On an appointed day Herod put on his royal robes, took his seat upon the throne, and made an oration to them. [22] And the people shouted, "The voice of a god, and not of a a man!" [23] Immediately an angel of the Lord smote him, because he did not give God the glory; and he was eaten by worms and died.

24 But the word of God grew and multiplied.

25 And Barnabas and Saul returned from[j] Jerusalem when they had fulfilled their mission, bringing with them John whose other name was Mark.

13 Now in the church at Antioch there were prophets and teachers, Barnabas, Symeon who was called Niger, Lucius of Cy-re′ne, Man′a-en a member of the court of Herod the tetrarch, and Saul. [2] While they were worshiping the Lord and fasting, the Holy Spirit said, "Set apart

---

[j] Many ancient authorities read *to.*

280

for me Barnabas and Saul for the work to which I have called them." ³ Then after fasting and praying they laid their hands on them and sent them off.

4 So, being sent out by the Holy Spirit, they went down to Se-leu′ci-a; and from there they sailed to Cyprus. ⁵ When they arrived at Sal′a-mis, they proclaimed the word of God in the synagogues of the Jews. And they had John to assist them. ⁶ When they had gone through the whole island as far as Pa′phos, they came upon a certain magician,ᵏ a Jewish false prophet, named Bar-Jesus. ⁷ He was with the proconsul, Sergius Paulus, a man of intelligence, who summoned Barnabas and Saul and sought to hear the word of God. ⁸ But El′y-mas the magician (for that is the meaning of his name) withstood them, seeking to turn away the proconsul from the faith. ⁹ But Saul, who is also called Paul, filled with the Holy Spirit, looked intently at him ¹⁰ and said, "You son of the devil, you enemy of all righteousness, full of all deceit and villainy, will you not stop making crooked the straight paths of the Lord? ¹¹ And now, behold, the hand of the Lord is upon you, and you shall be blind and unable to see the sun for a time." Immediately mist and darkness fell upon him and he went about seeking people to lead him by the hand. ¹² Then the proconsul believed, when he saw what had occurred, for he was astonished at the teaching of the Lord.

13 Now Paul and his company set sail from Pa′phos, and came to Perga in Pam-phyl′i-a. And John left them and returned to Jerusalem; ¹⁴ but they passed on from Perga and came to Antioch of Pi-sid′i-a. And on the sabbath day they went into the synagogue and sat down. ¹⁵ After the reading of the law and the prophets, the rulers of the syna-

ᵏ Greek *magus* (as in Matthew 2. 1).
13. 10: Hos. 14. 9.

gogue sent to them, saying, "Brethren, if you have any word of exhortation for the people, say it." ¹⁶ So Paul stood up, and motioning with his hand said:

"Men of Israel, and you that fear God, listen. ¹⁷ The God of this people Israel chose our fathers and made the people great during their stay in the land of Egypt, and with uplifted arm he led them out of it. ¹⁸ And for about forty years he bore with¹ them in the wilderness. ¹⁹ And when he had destroyed seven nations in the land of Canaan, he gave them their land as an inheritance, for about four hundred and fifty years. ²⁰ And after that he gave them judges until Samuel the prophet. ²¹ Then they asked for a king; and God gave them Saul the son of Kish, a man of the tribe of Benjamin, for forty years. ²² And when he had removed him, he raised up David to be their king; of whom he testified and said, 'I have found in David the son of Jesse a man after my heart, who will do all my will.' ²³ Of this man's posterity God has brought to Israel a Savior, Jesus, as he promised. ²⁴ Before his coming John had preached a baptism of repentance to all the people of Israel. ²⁵ And as John was finishing his course, he said, 'What do you suppose that I am? I am not he. No, but after me one is coming, the sandals of whose feet I am not worthy to untie.'

26 "Brethren, sons of the family of Abraham, and those among you that fear God, to us has been sent the message of this salvation. ²⁷ For those who live in Jerusalem and their rulers, because they did not recognize him nor understand the utterances of the prophets which are read every sabbath, fulfilled these by condemning him. ²⁸ Though they could charge him with nothing deserving death, yet they

¹ Some ancient authorities read *cared for* (Deut. 1. 31).

13. 17: Ex. 6. 1, 6.   **13. 18:** Deut. 1. 31.   **13. 19:** Deut. 7. 1; Josh. 14. 1.
13. 22: Ps. 89. 20; 1 Sam. 13. 14; Is. 44. 28.   **13. 24:** Mk. 1. 1–4.   **13. 25:** Jn. 1. 20;
Mt. 3. 11; Mk. 1. 7; Lk. 3. 16.   **13. 26:** Ps. 107. 20.

asked Pilate to have him killed. [29] And when they had fulfilled all that was written of him, they took him down from
the tree, and laid him in a tomb. [30] But God raised him from
the dead; [31] and for many days he appeared to those who
came up with him from Galilee to Jerusalem, who are now
his witnesses to the people. [32] And we bring you the good
news that what God promised to the fathers, [33] this he has
fulfilled to us their children by raising Jesus; as also it is
written in the second psalm,

> 'Thou art my Son,
>   today I have begotten thee.'

[34] And as for the fact that he raised him from the dead, no
more to return to corruption, he spoke in this way,

> 'I will give you the holy and sure blessings of David.'

[35] Therefore he says also in another psalm,

> 'Thou wilt not let thy Holy One see corruption.'

[36] For David, after he had served the counsel of God in his
own generation, fell asleep, and was laid with his fathers,
and saw corruption; [37] but he whom God raised up saw no
corruption. [38] Let it be known to you therefore, brethren,
that through this man forgiveness of sins is proclaimed to
you, [39] and by him every one that believes is freed from
everything from which you could not be freed by the law
of Moses. [40] Beware, therefore, lest there come upon you
what is said in the prophets:

> [41] 'Behold, you scoffers, and wonder, and perish;
>   for I do a deed in your days,
>   a deed you will never believe, if one declares it to
>   you.'"

42 As they went out, the people begged that these things
might be told them the next sabbath. [43] And when the meet-
ing of the synagogue broke up, many Jews and devout con-

13. 33: Ps. 2. 7.   **13. 34:** Is. 55. 3.   **13. 35:** Ps. 16. 10.   **13. 41:** Hab. 1. 5.

verts to Judaism followed Paul and Barnabas, who spoke to them and urged them to continue in the grace of God.

44 The next sabbath almost the whole city gathered together to hear the word of God. ⁴⁵ But when the Jews saw the multitudes, they were filled with jealousy, and contradicted what was spoken by Paul, and reviled him. ⁴⁶ And Paul and Barnabas spoke out boldly, saying, "It was necessary that the word of God should be spoken first to you. Since you thrust it from you, and judge yourselves unworthy of eternal life, behold, we turn to the Gentiles. ⁴⁷ For so the Lord has commanded us, saying,

'I have set you to be a light for the Gentiles,
        that you may bring salvation to the uttermost parts
            of the earth.'"

48 And when the Gentiles heard this, they were glad and glorified the word of God; and as many as were ordained to eternal life believed. ⁴⁹ And the word of the Lord spread throughout all the region. ⁵⁰ But the Jews incited the devout women of high standing and the leading men of the city, and stirred up persecution against Paul and Barnabas, and drove them out of their district. ⁵¹ But they shook off the dust from their feet against them, and went to I-co'ni-um. ⁵² And the disciples were filled with joy and with the Holy Spirit.

14 Now at I-co'ni-um they entered together into the Jewish synagogue, and so spoke that a great company believed, both of Jews and of Greeks. ² But the unbelieving Jews stirred up the Gentiles and poisoned their minds against the brethren. ³ So they remained for a long time, speaking boldly for the Lord, who bore witness to the word of his grace, granting signs and wonders to be done by their hands. ⁴ But the people of the city were divided; some

13. 47: Is. 49. 6.

sided with the Jews, and some with the apostles. ⁵ When an attempt was made by both Gentiles and Jews, with their rulers, to molest them and to stone them, ⁶ they learned of it and fled to Lystra and Der'be, cities of Lyc-a-o'ni-a, and to the surrounding country; ⁷ and there they preached the gospel.

8 Now at Lystra there was a man sitting, who could not use his feet; he was a cripple from birth, who had never walked. ⁹ He listened to Paul speaking; and Paul, looking intently at him and seeing that he had faith to be made well, ¹⁰ said in a loud voice, "Stand upright on your feet." And he sprang up and walked. ¹¹ And when the crowds saw what Paul had done, they lifted up their voices, saying in Lyc-a-o'ni-an, "The gods have come down to us in the likeness of men!" ¹² Barnabas they called Zeus, and Paul, because he was the chief speaker, they called Her'mes. ¹³ And the priest of Zeus, whose temple was in front of the city, brought oxen and garlands to the gates and wanted to offer sacrifice with the people. ¹⁴ But when the apostles Barnabas and Paul heard of it, they tore their garments and rushed out among the multitude, crying, ¹⁵ "Men, why are you doing this? We also are men, of like nature with you, and bring you good news, that you should turn from these vain things to a living God who made the heaven and the earth and the sea and all that is in them. ¹⁶ In past generations he allowed all the nations to walk in their own ways; ¹⁷ yet he did not leave himself without witness, for he did good and gave you from heaven rains and fruitful seasons, satisfying your hearts with food and gladness." ¹⁸ With these words they scarcely restrained the people from offering sacrifice to them.

19 But Jews came there from Antioch and I-co'ni-um;

14. 15: Ex. 20. 11; Ps. 146. 6.   **14. 19:** 2 Cor. 11. 25.

and having persuaded the people, they stoned Paul and dragged him out of the city, supposing that he was dead. [20] But when the disciples gathered about him, he rose up and entered the city; and on the next day he went on with Barnabas to Der'be. [21] When they had preached the gospel to that city and had made many disciples, they returned to Lystra and to I-co'ni-um and to Antioch, [22] strengthening the souls of the disciples, exhorting them to continue in the faith, and saying that through many tribulations we must enter the kingdom of God. [23] And when they had appointed elders for them in every church, with prayer and fasting, they committed them to the Lord in whom they believed.

24 Then they passed through Pi-sid'i-a, and came to Pam-phyl'i-a. [25] And when they had spoken the word in Perga, they went down to At-ta-li'a; [26] and from there they sailed to Antioch, where they had been commended to the grace of God for the work which they had fulfilled. [27] And when they arrived, they gathered the church together and declared all that God had done with them, and how he had opened a door of faith to the Gentiles. [28] And they remained no little time with the disciples.

15 But some men came down from Judea and were teaching the brethren, "Unless you are circumcised according to the custom of Moses, you cannot be saved." [2] And when Paul and Barnabas had no small dissension and debate with them, Paul and Barnabas and some of the others were appointed to go up to Jerusalem to the apostles and the elders about this question. [3] So, being sent on their way by the church, they passed through both Phoe-ni'ci-a and Sa-ma'ri-a, reporting the conversion of the Gentiles, and they gave great joy to all the brethren. [4] When they came to Jerusalem, they were welcomed by the church and

15. 1–30: Gal. 2. 1–10.

the apostles and the elders, and they declared all that God had done with them. [5] But some believers who belonged to the party of the Pharisees rose up, and said, "It is necessary to circumcise them, and to charge them to keep the law of Moses."

6 The apostles and the elders were gathered together to consider this matter. [7] And after there had been much debate, Peter rose and said to them, "Brethren, you know that in the early days God made choice among you, that by my mouth the Gentiles should hear the word of the gospel and believe. [8] And God who knows the heart bore witness to them, giving them the Holy Spirit just as he did to us; [9] and he made no distinction between us and them, but cleansed their hearts by faith. [10] Now therefore why do you make trial of God by putting a yoke upon the neck of the disciples which neither our fathers nor we have been able to bear? [11] But we believe that we shall be saved through the grace of the Lord Jesus, just as they will."

12 And all the assembly kept silence; and they listened to Barnabas and Paul as they related what signs and wonders God had done through them among the Gentiles. [13] After they finished speaking, James replied, "Brethren, listen to me. [14] Symeon has related how God first visited the Gentiles, to take out of them a people for his name. [15] And with this the words of the prophets agree, as it is written,

[16] 'After this I will return,
        and I will rebuild the dwelling of David, which has
            fallen;
    I will rebuild its ruins,
        and I will set it up,
[17] that the rest of men may seek the Lord,
        and all the Gentiles who are called by my name,

15. 16–18: Amos 9. 11–12; Jer. 12. 15; Is. 45. 21.

[18] says the Lord, who has made these things known from of old.'

[19] Therefore my judgment is that we should not trouble those of the Gentiles who turn to God, [20] but should write to them to abstain from the pollutions of idols and from unchastity and from what is strangled[m] and from blood. [21] For from early generations Moses has had in every city those who preach him, for he is read every sabbath in the synagogues."

22 Then it seemed good to the apostles and the elders, with the whole church, to choose men from among them and send them to Antioch with Paul and Barnabas. They sent Judas called Bar′sab-bas, and Silas, leading men among the brethren, [23] with the following letter: "The brethren, both the apostles and the elders, to the brethren who are of the Gentiles in Antioch and Syria and Ci-li′cia, greeting. [24] Since we have heard that some persons from us have troubled you with words, unsettling your minds, although we gave them no instructions, [25] it has seemed good to us in assembly to choose men and send them to you with our beloved Barnabas and Paul, [26] men who have risked their lives for the sake of our Lord Jesus Christ. [27] We have therefore sent Judas and Silas, who themselves will tell you the same things by word of mouth. [28] For it has seemed good to the Holy Spirit and to us to lay upon you no greater burden than these necessary things: [29] that you abstain from what has been sacrificed to idols and from blood and from what is strangled[m] and from unchastity. If you keep yourselves from these, you will do well. Farewell."

30 So when they were sent off, they went down to Antioch; and having gathered the congregation together, they delivered the letter. [31] And when they read it, they rejoiced at the exhortation. [32] And Judas and Silas, who were them-

[m] A few early authorities omit *and from what is strangled*.

selves prophets, exhorted the brethren with many words and strengthened them. ³³ And after they had spent some time, they were sent off in peace by the brethren to those who had sent them." ³⁵ But Paul and Barnabas remained in Antioch, teaching and preaching the word of the Lord, with many others also.

36 And after some days Paul said to Barnabas, "Come, let us return and visit the brethren in every city where we proclaimed the word of the Lord, and see how they are." ³⁷ And Barnabas wanted to take with them John called Mark. ³⁸ But Paul thought best not to take with them one who had withdrawn from them in Pam-phyl′i-a, and had not gone with them to the work. ³⁹ And there arose a sharp contention, so that they separated from each other; Barnabas took Mark with him and sailed away to Cyprus, ⁴⁰ but Paul chose Silas and departed, being commended by the brethren to the grace of the Lord. ⁴¹ And he went through Syria and Ci-li′cia, strengthening the churches.

16 And he came also to Der′be and to Lystra. A disciple was there, named Timothy, the son of a Jewish woman who was a believer; but his father was a Greek. ² He was well spoken of by the brethren at Lystra and I-co′ni-um. ³ Paul wanted Timothy to accompany him; and he took him and circumcised him because of the Jews that were in those places, for they all knew that his father was a Greek. ⁴ As they went on their way through the cities, they delivered to them for observance the decisions which had been reached by the apostles and elders who were at Jerusalem. ⁵ So the churches were strengthened in the faith, and they increased in numbers daily.

6 And they went through the region of Phryg′i-a and Galatia, having been forbidden by the Holy Spirit to speak

---

ⁿ Some ancient authorities insert verse 34, *But it seemed good to Silas to remain there.*

the word in Asia. ⁷ And when they had come opposite My′si-a, they attempted to go into Bi-thyn′i-a, but the Spirit of Jesus did not allow them; ⁸ so, passing by My′si-a, they went down to Tro′as. ⁹ And a vision appeared to Paul in the night: a man of Mac-e-do′ni-a was standing beseeching him and saying, "Come over to Mac-e-do′ni-a and help us." ¹⁰ And when he had seen the vision, immediately we sought to go on into Mac-e-do′ni-a, concluding that God had called us to preach the gospel to them.

11 Setting sail therefore from Tro′as, we made a direct voyage to Sam′o-thrace, and the following day to Ne-ap′o-lis, ¹² and from there to Philippi, which is the leading city of the district of Mac-e-do′ni-a, and a Roman colony. We remained in this city some days; ¹³ and on the sabbath day we went outside the gate to the riverside, where we supposed there was a place of prayer; and we sat down and spoke to the women who had come together. ¹⁴ One who heard us was a woman named Lydia, from the city of Thy-a-ti′ra, a seller of purple goods, who was a worshiper of God. The Lord opened her heart to give heed to what was said by Paul. ¹⁵ And when she was baptized, with her household, she besought us, saying, "If you have judged me to be faithful to the Lord, come to my house and stay." And she prevailed upon us.

16 As we were going to the place of prayer, we were met by a slave girl who had a spirit of divination and brought her owners much gain by soothsaying. ¹⁷ She followed Paul and us, crying, "These men are servants of the Most High God, who proclaim to you the way of salvation." ¹⁸ And this she did for many days. But Paul was annoyed, and turned and said to the spirit, "I charge you in the name of Jesus Christ to come out of her." And it came out that very hour.

19 But when her owners saw that their hope of gain was gone, they seized Paul and Silas and dragged them into the market place before the rulers; [20] and when they had brought them to the magistrates they said, "These men are Jews and they are disturbing our city. [21] They advocate customs which it is not lawful for us Romans to accept or practice." [22] The crowd joined in attacking them; and the magistrates tore the garments off them and gave orders to beat them with rods. [23] And when they had inflicted many blows upon them, they threw them into prison, charging the jailer to keep them safely. [24] Having received this charge, he put them into the inner prison and fastened their feet in the stocks.

25 But about midnight Paul and Silas were praying and singing hymns to God, and the prisoners were listening to them, [26] and suddenly there was a great earthquake, so that the foundations of the prison were shaken; and immediately all the doors were opened and every one's fetters were unfastened. [27] When the jailer woke and saw that the prison doors were open, he drew his sword and was about to kill himself, supposing that the prisoners had escaped. [28] But Paul cried with a loud voice, "Do not harm yourself, for we are all here." [29] And he called for lights and rushed in, and trembling with fear he fell down before Paul and Silas, [30] and brought them out and said, "Men, what must I do to be saved?" [31] And they said, "Believe in the Lord Jesus, and you will be saved, you and your household." [32] And they spoke the word of the Lord to him and to all that were in his house. [33] And he took them the same hour of the night, and washed their wounds, and he was baptized at once, with all his family. [34] Then he brought them up into his house, and set food before them; and he rejoiced with all his household that he had believed in God.

16. 22–23: 2 Cor. 11. 25.

35 But when it was day, the magistrates sent the police, saying, "Let those men go." ³⁶ And the jailer reported the words to Paul, saying, "The magistrates have sent to let you go; now therefore come out and go in peace." ³⁷ But Paul said to them, "They have beaten us publicly, uncondemned, men who are Roman citizens, and have thrown us into prison; and do they now cast us out secretly? No! let them come themselves and take us out." ³⁸ The police reported these words to the magistrates, and they were afraid when they heard that they were Roman citizens; ³⁹ so they came and apologized to them. And they took them out and asked them to leave the city. ⁴⁰ So they went out of the prison, and visited Lydia; and when they had seen the brethren, they exhorted them and departed.

17 Now when they had passed through Am-phip′o-lis and Ap-ol-lo′ni-a, they came to Thes-sa-lo-ni′ca, where there was a synagogue of the Jews. ² And Paul went in, as was his custom, and for three weeks*ᵒ* he argued with them from the scriptures, ³ explaining and proving that it was necessary for the Christ to suffer and to rise from the dead, and saying, "This Jesus, whom I proclaim to you, is the Christ." ⁴ And some of them were persuaded, and joined Paul and Silas; as did a great many of the devout Greeks and not a few of the leading women. ⁵ But the Jews were jealous, and taking some wicked fellows of the rabble, they gathered a crowd, set the city in an uproar, and attacked the house of Jason, seeking to bring them out to the people. ⁶ And when they could not find them, they dragged Jason and some of the brethren before the city authorities, crying, "These men who have turned the world upside down have come here also, ⁷ and Jason has received them; and they are all acting against the decrees of Caesar, saying that there is

ᵒ Or *sabbaths.*

another king, Jesus." [8] And the people and the city authorities were disturbed when they heard this. [9] And when they had taken security from Jason and the rest, they let them go.

10 The brethren immediately sent Paul and Silas away by night to Be-roe′a; and when they arrived they went into the Jewish synagogue. [11] Now these Jews were more noble than those in Thes-sa-lo-ni′ca, for they received the word with all eagerness, examining the scriptures daily to see if these things were so. [12] Many of them therefore believed, with not a few Greek women of high standing as well as men. [13] But when the Jews of Thes-sa-lo-ni′ca learned that the word of God was proclaimed by Paul at Be-roe′a also, they came there too, stirring up and inciting the crowds. [14] Then the brethren immediately sent Paul off on his way to the sea, but Silas and Timothy remained there. [15] Those who conducted Paul brought him as far as Athens; and receiving a command for Silas and Timothy to come to him as soon as possible, they departed.

16 Now while Paul was waiting for them at Athens, his spirit was provoked within him as he saw that the city was full of idols. [17] So he argued in the synagogue with the Jews and the devout persons, and in the market place every day with those who chanced to be there. [18] Some also of the Epicurean and Stoic philosophers met him. And some said, "What would this babbler say?" Others said, "He seems to be a preacher of foreign divinities." — because he preached Jesus and the resurrection. [19] And they took hold of him and brought him to the Ar-e-op′a-gus, saying, "May we know what this new teaching is which you present? [20] For you bring some strange things to our ears; we wish to know therefore what these things mean." [21] Now all the Athenians and the foreigners who lived there spent their time in nothing except telling or hearing something new.

22 So Paul, standing in the middle of the Ar-e-op'a-gus, said: "Men of Athens, I perceive that in every way you are very religious. [23] For as I passed along, and observed the objects of your worship, I found also an altar with this inscription, 'To an unknown god.' What therefore you worship as unknown, this I proclaim to you. [24] The God who made the world and everything in it, being Lord of heaven and earth, does not live in shrines made by man, [25] nor is he served by human hands, as though he needed anything, since he himself gives to all men life and breath and everything. [26] And he made from one every nation of men to live on all the face of the earth, having determined allotted periods and the boundaries of their habitation, [27] that they should seek God, in the hope that they might feel after him and find him. Yet he is not far from each one of us, [28] for

'In him we live and move and are;'
as even some of your poets have said,
'For we are indeed his offspring.'

[29] Being then God's offspring, we ought not to think that the Deity is like gold, or silver, or stone, a representation by the art and imagination of man. [30] The times of ignorance God overlooked, but now he commands all men everywhere to repent, [31] because he has fixed a day on which he will judge the world in righteousness by a man whom he has appointed, and of this he has given assurance to all men by raising him from the dead."

32 Now when they heard of the resurrection of the dead, some mocked; but others said, "We will hear you again about this." [33] So Paul went out from among them. [34] But some men joined him and believed, among them Di-o-nys'-i-us the Ar-e-op'a-gite and a woman named Dam'a-ris and others with them.

17. 24–25: Is. 42. 5.   17. 28: Aratus, *Phaenomena*, 5.   17. 31: Ps. 9. 8; 96. 13; 98. 9.

18 After this he left Athens and went to Corinth.
² And he found a Jew named Aquila, a native of
Pontus, lately come from Italy with his wife Priscilla, because Claudius had commanded all the Jews to leave Rome.
And he went to see them; ³ and because he was of the same
trade he stayed with them, and they worked, for by trade
they were tentmakers. ⁴ And he argued in the synagogue
every sabbath, and persuaded Jews and Greeks.

5 When Silas and Timothy arrived from Mac-e-do′ni-a,
Paul was occupied with preaching, testifying to the Jews
that the Christ was Jesus. ⁶ And when they opposed and
reviled him, he shook out his garments and said to them,
"Your blood be upon your heads! I am innocent. From now
on I will go to the Gentiles." ⁷ And he left there and went
to the house of a man named Titius*ᵖ* Justus, a worshiper of
God; his house was next door to the synagogue. ⁸ Crispus,
the ruler of the synagogue, believed in the Lord, together
with all his household; and many of the Corinthians hearing
Paul believed and were baptized. ⁹ And the Lord said to
Paul one night in a vision, "Do not be afraid, but speak and
do not be silent; ¹⁰ for I am with you, and no man shall attack
you to harm you; for I have many people in this city." ¹¹ And
he stayed a year and six months, teaching the word of God
among them.

12 But when Gallio was proconsul of A-cha′ia, the Jews
made a united attack upon Paul and brought him before
the tribunal, ¹³ saying, "This man is persuading men to
worship God contrary to the law." ¹⁴ But when Paul was
about to open his mouth, Gallio said to the Jews, "If it
were a matter of wrongdoing or vicious crime, I should have
reason to bear with you, O Jews; ¹⁵ but since it is a matter
of questions about words and names and your own law, see

ᵖ Some early authorities read *Titus.*
18. 9–10: Is. 43. 5; Jer. 1. 8.

to it yourselves; I refuse to be a judge of these things."
[16] And he drove them from the tribunal. [17] And they all
seized Sos'the-nes, the ruler of the synagogue, and beat him
in front of the tribunal. But Gallio paid no attention to this.

18 After this Paul stayed many days longer, and then took
leave of the brethren and sailed for Syria, and with him Priscilla and Aquila. At Cen'chre-ae he cut his hair, for he had
a vow. [19] And they came to Ephesus, and he left them there;
but he himself went into the synagogue and argued with the
Jews. [20] When they asked him to stay for a longer period,
he declined; [21] but on taking leave of them he said, "I will
return to you if God wills," and he set sail from Ephesus.

22 When he had landed at Caes-a-re'a, he went up and
greeted the church, and then went down to Antioch. [23] After
spending some time there he departed and went from place
to place through the region of Galatia and Phryg'i-a,
strengthening all the disciples.

24 Now a Jew named A-pol'los, a native of Alexandria,
came to Ephesus. He was an eloquent man, well versed in
the scriptures. [25] He had been instructed in the way of the
Lord; and being fervent in spirit, he spoke and taught accurately the things concerning Jesus, though he knew only
the baptism of John. [26] He began to speak boldly in the
synagogue; but when Priscilla and Aquila heard him, they
took him and expounded to him the way of God more accurately. [27] And when he wished to cross to A-cha'ia, the
brethren encouraged him, and wrote to the disciples to receive
him. When he arrived, he greatly helped those who through
grace had believed, [28] for he powerfully confuted the Jews
in public, showing by the scriptures that the Christ was Jesus.

19 While A-pol'los was at Corinth, Paul passed through
the upper country and came to Ephesus. There he
found some disciples. [2] And he said to them, "Did you receive

the Holy Spirit when you believed?" And they said, "No, we have never even heard that there is a Holy Spirit." ³ And he said, "Into what then were you baptized?" They said, "Into John's baptism." ⁴ And Paul said, "John baptized with the baptism of repentance, telling the people to believe in the one who was to come after him, that is, Jesus." ⁵ On hearing this, they were baptized in the name of the Lord Jesus. ⁶ And when Paul had laid his hands upon them, the Holy Spirit came on them; and they spoke with tongues and prophesied. ⁷ There were about twelve of them in all.

8 And he entered the synagogue and for three months spoke boldly, arguing and pleading about the kingdom of God; ⁹ but when some were stubborn and disbelieved, speaking evil of the Way before the congregation, he withdrew from them, taking the disciples with him, and argued daily in the hall of Ty·ran′nus.*q* ¹⁰ This continued for two years, so that all the residents of Asia heard the word of the Lord, both Jews and Greeks.

11 And God did extraordinary miracles by the hands of Paul, ¹² so that handkerchiefs or aprons were carried away from his body to the sick, and diseases left them and the evil spirits came out of them. ¹³ Then some of the itinerant Jewish exorcists undertook to pronounce the name of the Lord Jesus over those who had evil spirits, saying, "I adjure you by the Jesus whom Paul preaches." ¹⁴ Seven sons of a Jewish high priest named Sce′va were doing this. ¹⁵ But the evil spirit answered them, "Jesus I know, and Paul I know; but who are you?" ¹⁶ And the man in whom the evil spirit was leaped on them, mastered all of them, and overpowered them, so that they fled out of that house naked and wounded. ¹⁷ And this became known to all residents of Ephesus, both Jews and Greeks; and fear fell upon them

---

q Some ancient authorities add, *from eleven o'clock to four.*

all; and the name of the Lord Jesus was extolled. [18] Many also of those who were now believers came, confessing and divulging their practices. [19] And a number of those who practiced magical arts brought their books together and burned them in the sight of all; and they counted the value of them and found it came to fifty thousand pieces of silver. [20] So the word of the Lord grew and prevailed mightily.

21 Now after these events Paul resolved in the Spirit to pass through Mac-e-do'ni-a and A-cha'ia and go to Jerusalem, saying, "After I have been there, I must also see Rome." [22] And having sent into Mac-e-do'ni-a two of his helpers, Timothy and E-ras'tus, he himself stayed in Asia for a while.

23 About that time there arose no little stir concerning the Way. [24] For a man named De-me'tri-us, a silversmith, who made silver shrines of Artemis, brought no little business to the craftsmen. [25] These he gathered together, with the workmen of like occupation, and said, "Men, you know that from this business we have our wealth. [26] And you see and hear that not only at Ephesus but almost throughout all Asia this Paul has persuaded and turned away a considerable company of people, saying that gods made with hands are not gods. [27] And there is danger not only that this trade of ours may come into disrepute but also that the temple of the great goddess Ar'te-mis may count for nothing, and that she may even be deposed from her magnificence, she whom all Asia and the world worship."

28 When they heard this they were enraged, and cried out, "Great is Ar'te-mis of the Ephesians!" [29] So the city was filled with the confusion; and they rushed together into the theater, dragging with them Ga'ius and Ar-is-tar'chus, Mac-e-do'ni-ans who were Paul's companions in travel. [30] Paul wished to go in among the crowd, but the disciples

would not let him; [31] some of the A'si-archs also, who were friends of his, sent to him and begged him not to venture into the theater. [32] Now some cried one thing, some another; for the assembly was in confusion, and most of them did not know why they had come together. [33] Some of the crowd prompted Alexander, whom the Jews had put forward. And Alexander motioned with his hand, wishing to make a defense to the people. [34] But when they recognized that he was a Jew, for about two hours they all with one voice cried out, "Great is Ar'te-mis of the Ephesians!" [35] And when the town clerk had quieted the crowd, he said, "Men of Ephesus, what man is there who does not know that the city of the Ephesians is temple keeper of the great Ar'te-mis, and of the sacred stone that fell from the sky?[r] [36] Seeing then that these things cannot be contradicted, you ought to be quiet and do nothing rash. [37] For you have brought these men here who are neither sacrilegious nor blasphemers of our goddess. [38] If therefore De-me'tri-us and the craftsmen with him have a complaint against any one, the courts are open, and there are proconsuls; let them bring charges against one another. [39] But if you seek anything further,[s] it shall be settled in the regular assembly. [40] For we are in danger of being charged with rioting today, there being no cause that we can give to justify this commotion." [41] And when he had said this, he dismissed the assembly.

20 After the uproar ceased, Paul sent for the disciples and having exhorted them took leave of them and departed for Mac-e-do'ni-a. [2] When he had gone through these parts and had given them much encouragement, he came to Greece. [3] There he spent three months, and when a plot was made against him by the Jews as he was about to set sail for Syria, he determined to return through Mac-e-

[r] The meaning of the Greek is uncertain.   [s] Many ancient authorities read *about other matters.*

do'ni-a. ⁴ Sop'a-ter of Be-roe'a, the son of Pyr'rhus, accompanied him; and of the Thes-sa-lo'ni-ans, Ar-is-tar'chus and Se-cun'dus; and Ga'ius of Der'be, and Timothy; and the Asians, Tych'i-cus and Troph'i-mus. ⁵ These went on and were waiting for us at Tro'as, ⁶ but we sailed away from Philippi after the days of Unleavened Bread, and in five days we came to them at Tro'as, where we stayed for seven days.

7 On the first day of the week, when we were gathered together to break bread, Paul talked with them, intending to depart on the morrow; and he prolonged his speech until midnight. ⁸ There were many lights in the upper chamber where we were gathered. ⁹ And a young man named Eu'ty-chus was sitting in the window. He sank into a deep sleep as Paul talked still longer; and being overcome by sleep, he fell down from the third story and was taken up dead. ¹⁰ But Paul went down and bent over him, and embracing him said, "Do not be alarmed, for his life is in him." ¹¹ And when Paul had gone up and had broken bread and eaten, he conversed with them a long while, until daybreak, and so departed. ¹² And they took the lad away alive, and were not a little comforted.

13 But going ahead to the ship, we set sail for As'sos, intending to take Paul aboard there; for so he had arranged, intending himself to go by land. ¹⁴ And when he met us at As'sos, we took him on board and came to Mit-y-le'ne. ¹⁵ And sailing from there we came the following day opposite Chi'os; the next day we touched at Sa'mos; and*t* the day after that we came to Mi-le'tus. ¹⁶ For Paul had decided to sail past Ephesus, so that he might not have to spend time in Asia; for he was hastening to be at Jerusalem, if possible, on the day of Pentecost.

17 And from Mi-le'tus he sent to Ephesus and called to

---

t Some ancient authorities add *after remaining at Trogyllium.*

him the elders of the church. [18] And when they came to him, he said to them:

"You yourselves know how I lived among you all the time from the first day that I set foot in Asia, [19] serving the Lord with all humility and with tears and with trials which befell me through the plots of the Jews; [20] how I did not shrink from declaring to you anything that was profitable, and teaching you in public and from house to house, [21] testifying both to Jews and to Greeks of repentance to God and of faith in our Lord Jesus Christ. [22] And now, behold, I am going to Jerusalem, bound in the Spirit, not knowing what shall befall me there; [23] except that the Holy Spirit testifies to me in every city that imprisonment and afflictions await me. [24] But I do not account my life of any value nor as precious to myself, if only I may accomplish my course and the ministry which I received from the Lord Jesus, to testify to the gospel of the grace of God. [25] And now, behold, I know that all you among whom I have gone about preaching the kingdom will see my face no more. [26] Therefore I testify to you this day that I am innocent of the blood of all of you, [27] for I did not shrink from declaring to you the whole counsel of God. [28] Take heed to yourselves and to all the flock, in which the Holy Spirit has made you guardians, to feed the church of the Lord[u] which he obtained for himself with his own blood.[v] [29] I know that after my departure fierce wolves will come in among you, not sparing the flock; [30] and from among your own selves will arise men speaking perverse things, to draw away the disciples after them. [31] Therefore be alert, remembering that for three years I did not cease night or day to admonish every one with tears. [32] And now I commend you to God and to the word of his grace, which is able to build you up and to give you the inheritance among all

---

[u] Many ancient authorities read *of God*.   [v] Or *with the blood of his Own*.

those who are consecrated. [33] I coveted no one's silver or gold or apparel. [34] You yourselves know that these hands ministered to my necessities, and to those who were with me. [35] In all things I have shown you that by so toiling one must help the weak, remembering the words of the Lord Jesus, how he said, 'It is more blessed to give than to receive.'"

36 And when he had spoken thus, he knelt down and prayed with them all. [37] And they all wept and embraced Paul and kissed him, [38] sorrowing most of all because of the word he had spoken, that they should see his face no more. And they brought him to the ship.

21 And when we had parted from them and set sail, we came by a straight course to Cos, and the next day to Rhodes, and from there to Pat'a-ra.[w] [2] And having found a ship crossing to Phoe-ni'ci-a, we went aboard, and set sail. [3] When we had come in sight of Cyprus, leaving it on the left we sailed to Syria, and landed at Tyre; for there the ship was to unload its cargo. [4] And having sought out the disciples, we stayed there for seven days. Through the Spirit they told Paul not to go on to Jerusalem. [5] And when our days there were ended, we departed and went on our journey; and they all, with wives and children, brought us on our way till we were outside the city; and kneeling down on the beach we prayed and bade one another farewell. [6] Then we went on board the ship, and they returned home.

7 When we had finished the voyage from Tyre, we arrived at Ptol-e-ma'is; and we greeted the brethren and stayed with them for one day. [8] On the morrow we departed and came to Caes-a-re'a; and we entered the house of Philip the evangelist, who was one of the seven, and stayed with him. [9] And he had four unmarried daughters, who prophesied.

[w] Some ancient authorities add *and Myra.*

[10] While we were staying for some days, a prophet named Ag′a-bus came down from Judea. [11] And coming to us he took Paul's girdle and bound his own feet and hands, and said, "Thus says the Holy Spirit, 'So shall the Jews at Jerusalem bind the man who owns this girdle and deliver him into the hands of the Gentiles.'" [12] When we heard this, we and the people there begged him not to go up to Jerusalem. [13] Then Paul answered, "What are you doing, weeping and breaking my heart? For I am ready not only to be imprisoned but even to die at Jerusalem for the name of the Lord Jesus." [14] And when he would not be persuaded, we ceased and said, "The will of the Lord be done."

15 After these days we made ready and went up to Jerusalem. [16] And some of the disciples from Caes-a-re′a went with us, bringing us to the house of Mna′son of Cyprus, an early disciple, with whom we should lodge.

17 When we had come to Jerusalem, the brethren received us gladly. [18] On the following day Paul went in with us to James; and all the elders were present. [19] After greeting them, he related one by one the things that God had done among the Gentiles through his ministry. [20] And when they heard it, they glorified God. And they said to him, "You see, brother, how many thousands there are among the Jews of those who have believed; they are all zealous for the law, [21] and they have been told about you that you teach all the Jews who are among the Gentiles to forsake Moses, telling them not to circumcise their children or observe the customs. [22] What then is to be done? They will certainly hear that you have come. [23] Do therefore what we tell you. We have four men who are under a vow; [24] take these men and purify yourself along with them and pay their expenses, so that they may shave their heads. Thus all will know that there is nothing in what they have been told about you, but

that you yourself live in observance of the law. [25] But as for the Gentiles who have believed, we have sent a letter with our judgment that they should abstain from what has been sacrificed to idols and from blood and from what is strangled and from unchastity." [26] Then Paul took the men, and the next day he purified himself with them and went into the temple, to give notice when the days of purification would be fulfilled and the offering presented for every one of them.

27 When the seven days were almost completed, the Jews from Asia, who had seen him in the temple, stirred up all the crowd, and laid hands on him, [28] crying out, "Men of Israel, help! This is the man who is teaching men everywhere against the people and the law and this place; moreover he also brought Greeks into the temple, and he has defiled this holy place." [29] For they had previously seen Troph'i-mus the Ephesian with him in the city, and they supposed that Paul had brought him into the temple. [30] Then all the city was aroused, and the people ran together; they seized Paul and dragged him out of the temple, and at once the gates were shut. [31] And as they were trying to kill him, word came to the tribune of the cohort that all Jerusalem was in confusion. [32] He at once took soldiers and centurions, and ran down to them; and when they saw the tribune and the soldiers, they stopped beating Paul. [33] Then the tribune came up and arrested him, and ordered him to be bound with two chains. He inquired who he was and what he had done. [34] Some in the crowd shouted one thing, some another; and as he could not learn the facts because of the uproar, he ordered him to be brought into the barracks. [35] And when he came to the steps, he was actually carried by the soldiers because of the violence of the crowd; [36] for the mob of the people followed, crying, "Away with him!"

37 As Paul was about to be brought into the barracks, he

said to the tribune, "May I say something to you?" And he said, "Do you know Greek? ³⁸ Are you not the Egyptian, then, who recently stirred up a revolt and led the four thousand men of the Assassins out into the wilderness?" ³⁹ Paul replied, "I am a Jew, from Tarsus in Ci-li′cia, a citizen of no mean city; I beg you, let me speak to the people." ⁴⁰ And when he had given him leave, Paul, standing on the steps, motioned with his hand to the people; and when there was a great hush, he spoke to them in the Hebrew language, saying:

22 "Brethren and fathers, hear the defense which I now make before you."

2 And when they heard that he addressed them in the Hebrew language, they were the more quiet. And he said:

3 "I am a Jew, born at Tarsus in Ci-li′cia, but brought up in this city at the feet of Ga-ma′li-el, educated according to the strict manner of the law of our fathers, being zealous for God as you all are this day. ⁴ I persecuted this Way to the death, binding and delivering to prison both men and women, ⁵ as the high priest and the whole council of elders bear me witness. From them I received letters to the brethren, and I journeyed to Damascus to take those also who were there and bring them in bonds to Jerusalem to be punished.

6 "As I made my journey and drew near to Damascus, about noon a great light from heaven suddenly shone about me. ⁷ And I fell to the ground and heard a voice saying to me, 'Saul, Saul, why do you persecute me?' ⁸ And I answered, 'Who are you, Lord?' And he said to me, 'I am Jesus of Nazareth whom you are persecuting.' ⁹ Now those who were with me saw the light but did not hear the voice of the one who was speaking to me. ¹⁰ And I said, 'What shall I do, Lord?' And the Lord said to me, 'Rise, and go

22. 4–16: Acts 9. 1–19; 26. 9–18; Gal. 1. 14.

into Damascus, and there you will be told all that is appointed for you to do.' [11] And when I could not see because of the brightness of that light, I was led by the hand by those who were with me, and came into Damascus.

12 "And one An-a-ni'as, a devout man according to the law, well spoken of by all the Jews who lived there, [13] came to me, and standing by me said to me, 'Brother Saul, receive your sight.' And in that very hour I received my sight and saw him. [14] And he said, 'The God of our fathers appointed you to know his will, to see the Just One and to hear a voice from his mouth; [15] for you will be a witness for him to all men of what you have seen and heard. [16] And now why do you wait? Rise and be baptized, and wash away your sins, calling on his name.'

17 "When I had returned to Jerusalem and was praying in the temple, I fell into a trance [18] and saw him saying to me, 'Make haste and get quickly out of Jerusalem, because they will not accept your testimony about me.' [19] And I said, 'Lord, they themselves know that in every synagogue I imprisoned and beat those who believed in thee. [20] And when the blood of Stephen thy witness was shed, I also was standing by and approving, and keeping the garments of those who killed him.' [21] And he said to me, 'Depart; for I will send you far away to the Gentiles.'"

22 Up to this word they listened to him; then they lifted up their voices and said, "Away with such a fellow from the earth! For he ought not to live." [23] And as they cried out and waved their garments and threw dust into the air, [24] the tribune commanded him to be brought into the barracks, and ordered him to be examined by scourging, to find out why they shouted thus against him. [25] But when they had tied him up with the thongs, Paul said to the centurion who was standing by, "Is it lawful for you to scourge a man

who is a Roman citizen, and uncondemned?" ²⁶ When the
centurion heard that, he went to the tribune and said to
him, "What are you about to do? For this man is a Roman
citizen." ²⁷ So the tribune came and said to him, "Tell me,
are you a Roman citizen?" And he said, "Yes." ²⁸ The
tribune answered, "I bought this citizenship for a large sum."
Paul said, "But I was born a citizen." ²⁹ So those who were
about to examine him withdrew from him instantly; and
the tribune also was afraid, for he realized that Paul was a
Roman citizen and that he had bound him.

30 But on the morrow, desiring to know the real reason
why the Jews accused him, he unbound him, and commanded
the chief priests and all the council to meet, and he brought
Paul down and set him before them.

23 And Paul, looking intently at the council, said,
"Brethren, I have lived before God in all good
conscience up to this day." ² And the high priest An-a-ni'as
commanded those who stood by him to strike him on the
mouth. ³ Then Paul said to him, "God shall strike you, you
whitewashed wall! Are you sitting to judge me according
to the law, and yet contrary to the law you order me to be
struck?" ⁴ Those who stood by said, "Would you revile God's
high priest?" ⁵ And Paul said, "I did not know, brethren,
that he was the high priest; for it is written, 'You shall not
speak evil of a ruler of your people.'"

6 But when Paul perceived that one part were Sad'du-
cees and the other Pharisees, he cried out in the council,
"Brethren, I am a Pharisee, a son of Pharisees; with respect
to the hope and the resurrection of the dead I am on trial."
⁷ And when he had said this, a dissension arose between the
Pharisees and the Sad'du-cees; and the assembly was divided. ⁸ For the Sad'du-cees say that there is no resurrec-

23. 5: Ex. 22. 28.

tion, nor angel, nor spirit; but the Pharisees acknowledge them all. 9 Then a great clamor arose; and some of the scribes of the Pharisees' party stood up and contended, "We find nothing wrong in this man. What if a spirit or an angel spoke to him?" 10 And when the dissension became violent, the tribune, afraid that Paul would be torn in pieces by them, commanded the soldiers to go down and take him by force from among them and bring him into the barracks.

11 The following night the Lord stood by him and said, "Take courage, for as you have testified about me at Jerusalem, so you must bear witness also at Rome."

12 When it was day, the Jews made a plot and bound themselves by an oath neither to eat nor drink till they had killed Paul. 13 There were more than forty who made this conspiracy. 14 And they went to the chief priests and elders, and said, "We have strictly bound ourselves by an oath to taste no food till we have killed Paul. 15 You therefore, along with the council, give notice now to the tribune to bring him down to you, as though you were going to determine his case more exactly. And we are ready to kill him before he comes near."

16 Now the son of Paul's sister heard of their ambush; so he went and entered the barracks and told Paul. 17 And Paul called one of the centurions and said, "Bring this young man to the tribune; for he has something to tell him." 18 So he took him and brought him to the tribune and said, "Paul the prisoner called me and asked me to bring this young man to you, as he has something to say to you." 19 The tribune took him by the hand, and going aside asked him privately, "What is it that you have to tell me?" 20 And he said, "The Jews have agreed to ask you to bring Paul down to the council tomorrow, as though they were going to inquire

somewhat more closely about him. [21] But do not yield to them; for more than forty of their men lie in ambush for him, having bound themselves by an oath neither to eat nor drink till they have killed him; and now they are ready, waiting for the promise from you." [22] So the tribune dismissed the young man, charging him, "Tell no one that you have informed me of this."

23 Then he called two of the centurions and said, "At the third hour of the night get ready two hundred soldiers with seventy horsemen and two hundred spearmen to go as far as Caes-a-re′a. [24] Also provide mounts for Paul to ride, and bring him safely to Felix the governor." [25] And he wrote a letter to this effect:

26 "Claudius Lys′i-as to his Excellency the governor Felix, greeting. [27] This man was seized by the Jews, and was about to be killed by them, when I came upon them with the soldiers and rescued him, having learned that he was a Roman citizen. [28] And desiring to know the charge on which they accused him, I brought him down to their council. [29] I found that he was accused about questions of their law, but charged with nothing deserving death or imprisonment. [30] And when it was disclosed to me that there would be a plot against the man, I sent him to you at once, ordering his accusers also to state before you what they have against him."

31 So the soldiers, according to their instructions, took Paul and brought him by night to An-tip′a-tris. [32] And on the morrow they returned to the barracks, leaving the horsemen to go on with him. [33] When they came to Caes-a-re′a and delivered the letter to the governor, they presented Paul also before him. [34] On reading the letter, he asked to what province he belonged. When he learned that he was from Ci-li′cia [35] he said, "I will hear you when your ac-

cusers arrive." And he commanded him to be guarded in Herod's praetorium.

24 And after five days the high priest An-a-ni′as came down with some elders and a spokesman, one Ter-tul′lus. They laid before the governor their case against Paul; ² and when he was called, Ter-tul′lus began to accuse him, saying:

"Since through you we enjoy much peace, and since by your provision, most excellent Felix, reforms are introduced on behalf of this nation, ³ in every way and everywhere we accept this with all gratitude. ⁴ But, to detain you no further, I beg you in your kindness to hear us briefly. ⁵ For we have found this man a pestilent fellow, an agitator among all the Jews throughout the world, and a ringleader of the sect of the Nazarenes. ⁶ He even tried to profane the temple, but we seized him.ˣ ⁸ By examining him yourself you will be able to learn from him about everything of which we accuse him."

9 The Jews also joined in the charge, affirming that all this was so.

10 And when the governor had motioned to him to speak, Paul replied:

"Realizing that for many years you have been judge over this nation, I cheerfully make my defense. ¹¹ As you may ascertain, it is not more than twelve days since I went up to worship at Jerusalem; ¹² and they did not find me disputing with any one or stirring up a crowd, either in the temple or in the synagogues, or in the city. ¹³ Neither can they prove to you what they now bring up against me. ¹⁴ But this I admit to you, that according to the Way, which they call a sect, I worship the God of our fathers, believing everything laid down by the law or written in the prophets,

---

ˣ Some ancient authorities add *and we would have judged him according to our law.* ⁷ *But the chief captain Lysias came and with great violence took him out of our hands,* ⁸ *commanding his accusers to come before you.*

[15] having a hope in God which these themselves accept, that there will be a resurrection of both the just and the unjust. [16] So I always take pains to have a clear conscience toward God and toward men. [17] Now after some years I came to bring to my nation alms and offerings. [18] As I was doing this, they found me purified in the temple, without any crowd or tumult. But some Jews from Asia — [19] they ought to be here before you and to make an accusation, if they have anything against me. [20] Or else let these men themselves say what wrongdoing they found when I stood before the council, [21] except this one thing which I cried out while standing among them, 'With respect to the resurrection of the dead I am on trial before you this day.'"

22 But Felix, having a rather accurate knowledge of the Way, put them off, saying, "When Lys'i-as the tribune comes down, I will decide your case." [23] Then he gave orders to the centurion that he should be kept in custody but should have some liberty, and that none of his friends should be prevented from attending to his needs.

24 After some days Felix came with his wife Dru-sil'la, who was a Jewess; and he sent for Paul and heard him speak upon faith in Christ Jesus. [25] And as he argued about justice and self-control and future judgment, Felix was alarmed and said, "Go away for the present; when I have an opportunity I will summon you." [26] At the same time he hoped that money would be given him by Paul. So he sent for him often and conversed with him. [27] But when two years had elapsed, Felix was succeeded by Por'cius Festus; and desiring to do the Jews a favor, Felix left Paul in prison.

25 Now when Festus had come into his province, after three days he went up to Jerusalem from Caes-a-re'a. [2] And the chief priests and the principal men of the Jews informed him against Paul; and they urged him,

³ asking as a favor to have the man sent to Jerusalem, planning an ambush to kill him on the way. ⁴ Festus replied that Paul was being kept at Caes-a-re′a, and that he himself intended to go there shortly. ⁵ "So," said he, "let the men of authority among you go down with me, and if there is anything wrong about the man, let them accuse him."

6 When he had stayed among them not more than eight or ten days, he went down to Caes-a-re′a; and the next day he took his seat on the tribunal and ordered Paul to be brought. ⁷ And when he had come, the Jews who had gone down from Jerusalem stood about him, bringing against him many serious charges which they could not prove. ⁸ Paul said in his defense, "Neither against the law of the Jews, nor against the temple, nor against Caesar have I offended at all." ⁹ But Festus, wishing to do the Jews a favor, said to Paul, "Do you wish to go up to Jerusalem, and there be tried on these charges before me?" ¹⁰ But Paul said, "I am standing before Caesar's tribunal, where I ought to be tried; to the Jews I have done no wrong, as you know very well. ¹¹ If then I am a wrongdoer, and have committed anything for which I deserve to die, I do not seek to escape death; but if there is nothing in their charges against me, no one can give me up to them. I appeal to Caesar." ¹² Then Festus, when he had conferred with his council, answered, "You have appealed to Caesar; to Caesar you shall go."

13 Now when some days had passed, Agrippa the king and Ber-ni′ce arrived at Caes-a-re′a to welcome Festus. ¹⁴ And as they stayed there many days, Festus laid Paul's case before the king, saying, "There is a man left prisoner by Felix; ¹⁵ and when I was at Jerusalem, the chief priests and the elders of the Jews gave information about him, asking for sentence against him. ¹⁶ I answered them that it

was not the custom of the Romans to give up any one before the accused met the accusers face to face, and had opportunity to make his defense concerning the charge laid against him. [17] When therefore they came together here, I made no delay, but on the next day took my seat on the tribunal and ordered the man to be brought in. [18] When the accusers stood up, they brought no charge in his case of such evils as I supposed; [19] but they had certain points of dispute with him about their own superstition and about one Jesus, who was dead, but whom Paul asserted to be alive. [20] Being at a loss how to investigate these questions, I asked whether he wished to go to Jerusalem and be tried there regarding them. [21] But when Paul had appealed to be kept in custody for the decision of the emperor, I commanded him to be held until I could send him to Caesar." [22] And Agrippa said to Festus, "I should like to hear the man myself." "Tomorrow," said he, "you shall hear him."

23 So on the morrow Agrippa and Ber-ni′ce came with great pomp, and they entered the audience hall with the military tribunes and the prominent men of the city. Then by command of Festus Paul was brought in. [24] And Festus said, "King Agrippa and all who are present with us, you see this man about whom the whole Jewish people petitioned me, both at Jerusalem and here, shouting that he ought not to live any longer. [25] But I found that he had done nothing deserving death; and as he himself appealed to the emperor, I decided to send him. [26] But I have nothing definite to write to my lord about him. Therefore I have brought him before you, and especially before you, King Agrippa, that, after we have examined him, I may have something to write. [27] For it seems to me unreasonable, in sending a prisoner, not to indicate the charges against him."

26 Agrippa said to Paul, "You have permission to speak for yourself." Then Paul stretched out his hand and made his defense:

2 "I think myself fortunate that it is before you, King Agrippa, I am to make my defense today against all the accusations of the Jews, ³ because you are especially familiar with all customs and controversies of the Jews; therefore I beg you to listen to me patiently.

4 "My manner of life from my youth, spent from the beginning among my own nation and at Jerusalem, is known by all the Jews. ⁵ They have known for a long time, if they are willing to testify, that according to the strictest party of our religion I have lived as a Pharisee. ⁶ And now I stand here on trial for hope in the promise made by God to our fathers, ⁷ to which our twelve tribes hope to attain, as they earnestly worship night and day. And for this hope I am accused by Jews, O king! ⁸ Why is it thought incredible by any of you that God raises the dead?

9 "I myself was convinced that I ought to do many things in opposing the name of Jesus of Nazareth. ¹⁰ And I did so in Jerusalem; I not only shut up many of the saints in prison, by authority from the chief priests, but when they were put to death I cast my vote against them. ¹¹ And I punished them often in all the synagogues and tried to make them blaspheme; and in raging fury against them, I persecuted them even to foreign cities.

12 "Thus I journeyed to Damascus with the authority and commission of the chief priests. ¹³ At midday, O king, I saw on the way a light from heaven, brighter than the sun, shining round me and those who journeyed with me. ¹⁴ And when we had all fallen to the ground, I heard a voice saying to me in the Hebrew language, 'Saul, Saul, why do you persecute me? It hurts you to kick against the goads.'

[15] And I said, 'Who are you, Lord?' And the Lord said, 'I am Jesus whom you are persecuting. [16] But rise and stand upon your feet; for I have appeared to you for this purpose, to appoint you to serve and bear witness to the things in which you have seen me and to those in which I will appear to you, [17] delivering you from the people and from the Gentiles — to whom I send you [18] to open their eyes, that they may turn from darkness to light and from the power of Satan to God, that they may receive forgiveness of sins and a place among those who are consecrated by faith in me.'

19 "Wherefore, O King Agrippa, I was not disobedient to the heavenly vision, [20] but declared first to those at Damascus, then at Jerusalem and throughout all the country of Judea, and also to the Gentiles, that they should repent and turn to God and perform deeds worthy of their repentance. [21] For this reason the Jews seized me in the temple and tried to kill me. [22] To this day I have had the help that comes from God, and so I stand here testifying both to small and great, saying nothing but what the prophets and Moses said would come to pass: [23] that the Christ must suffer, and that, by being the first to rise from the dead, he would proclaim light both to the people and to the Gentiles."

24 And as he thus made his defense, Festus said with a loud voice, "Paul, you are mad; your great learning is turning you mad." [25] But Paul said, "I am not mad, most excellent Festus, but I am speaking the sober truth. [26] For the king knows about these things, and to him I speak freely; for I am persuaded that none of these things has escaped his notice, for this was not done in a corner. [27] King Agrippa, do you believe the prophets? I know that you believe."

26. 9–18: Acts 9. 1–8; 22. 4–16.   **26. 16–17:** Ezek. 2. 1, 3.   **26. 18:** Is. 42. 7, 16.

²⁸ And Agrippa said to Paul, "In a short time you think to make me a Christian!" ²⁹ And Paul said, "Whether short or long, I would to God that not only you but also all who hear me this day might become such as I am — except for these chains."

30 Then the king rose, and the governor and Ber-ni′ce and those who were sitting with them; ³¹ and when they had withdrawn, they said to one another, "This man is doing nothing to deserve death or imprisonment." ³² And Agrippa said to Festus, "This man could have been set free if he had not appealed to Caesar."

27 And when it was decided that we should sail for Italy, they delivered Paul and some other prisoners to a centurion of the Augustan Cohort, named Julius. ² And embarking in a ship of Ad-ra-myt′ti-um, which was about to sail to the ports along the coast of Asia, we put to sea, accompanied by Ar-is-tar′chus, a Mac-e-do′ni-an from Thes-sa-lo-ni′ca. ³ The next day we put in at Sidon; and Julius treated Paul kindly, and gave him leave to go to his friends and be cared for. ⁴ And putting to sea from there we sailed under the lee of Cyprus, because the winds were against us. ⁵ And when we had sailed across the sea which is off Ci-li′cia and Pam-phyl′i-a, we came to Myra in Ly′ci-a. ⁶ There the centurion found a ship of Alexandria sailing for Italy, and put us on board. ⁷ We sailed slowly for a number of days, and arrived with difficulty off Cni′-dus, and as the wind did not allow us to go on, we sailed under the lee of Crete off Sal-mo′ne. ⁸ Coasting along it with difficulty, we came to a place called Fair Havens, near which was the city of La-se′a.

9 As much time had been lost, and the voyage was already dangerous because the fast had already gone by, Paul advised them, ¹⁰ saying, "Sirs, I perceive that the voyage

will be with injury and much loss, not only of the cargo and the ship, but also of our lives." ¹¹ But the centurion paid more attention to the captain and to the owner of the ship than to what Paul said. ¹² And because the harbor was not suitable to winter in, the majority advised to put to sea from there, on the chance that somehow they could reach Phoenix, a harbor of Crete, looking northeast and southeast,*ʸ* and winter there.

13 And when the south wind blew gently, supposing that they had obtained their purpose, they weighed anchor and sailed along Crete, close inshore. ¹⁴ But soon a tempestuous wind, called the northeaster, struck down from the land; ¹⁵ and when the ship was caught and could not face the wind, we gave way to it and were driven. ¹⁶ And running under the lee of a small island called Cau'da,*ᶻ* we managed with difficulty to secure the boat; ¹⁷ after hoisting it up, they took measures*ᵃ* to undergird the ship; then, fearing that they should run on the Syr'tis, they lowered the gear, and so were driven. ¹⁸ As we were violently storm-tossed, they began next day to throw the cargo overboard; ¹⁹ and the third day they cast out with their own hands the tackle of the ship. ²⁰ And when neither sun nor stars appeared for many a day, and no small tempest lay on us, all hope of our being saved was at last abandoned.

21 As they had been long without food, Paul then came forward among them and said, "Men, you should have listened to me, and should not have set sail from Crete and incurred this injury and loss. ²² I now bid you take heart; for there will be no loss of life among you, but only of the ship. ²³ For this very night there stood by me an angel of the God to whom I belong and whom I worship, ²⁴ and he said, 'Do not be afraid, Paul; you must stand before Caesar;

ʸ Or *southwest and northwest.*   *ᶻ* Many ancient authorities read *Clauda.*
ᵃ Greek *helps.*

and lo, God has granted you all those who sail with you.'
[25] So take heart, men, for I have faith in God that it will be
exactly as I have been told. [26] But we shall have to run on
some island."

27 When the fourteenth night had come, as we were drift-
ing across the sea of A'dri-a, about midnight the sailors
suspected that they were nearing land. [28] So they sounded
and found twenty fathoms; a little farther on they sounded
again and found fifteen fathoms. [29] And fearing that we
might run on the rocks, they let out four anchors from the
stern, and prayed for day to come. [30] And as the sailors
were seeking to escape from the ship, and had lowered the
boat into the sea, under pretense of laying out anchors from
the bow, [31] Paul said to the centurion and the soldiers, "Unless these men stay in the ship, you cannot be saved."
[32] Then the soldiers cut away the ropes of the boat, and let
it go.

33 As day was about to dawn, Paul urged them all to
take some food, saying, "Today is the fourteenth day that
you have continued in suspense and without food, having
taken nothing. [34] Therefore I urge you to take some food;
it will give you strength, since not a hair is to perish from
the head of any of you." [35] And when he had said this, he
took bread, and giving thanks to God in the presence of all
he broke it and began to eat. [36] Then they all were encouraged and ate some food themselves. [37] (We were in all
two hundred and seventy-six[b] persons in the ship.) [38] And
when they had eaten enough, they lightened the ship,
throwing out the wheat into the sea.

39 Now when it was day, they did not recognize the land,
but they noticed a bay with a beach, on which they planned
if possible to bring the ship ashore. [40] So they cast off the

[b] Some ancient authorities read *seventy-six* or *about seventy-six*.

anchors and left them in the sea, at the same time loosening
the ropes that tied the rudders; then hoisting the foresail
to the wind they made for the beach. ⁴¹ But striking a shoal^c
they ran the vessel aground; the bow stuck and remained
immovable, and the stern was broken up by the surf. ⁴² The
soldiers' plan was to kill the prisoners, lest any should swim
away and escape; ⁴³ but the centurion, wishing to save Paul,
kept them from carrying out their purpose. He ordered
those who could swim to throw themselves overboard first
and make for the land, ⁴⁴ and the rest on planks or on pieces
of the ship. And so it was that all escaped to land.

28 After we had escaped, we then learned that the
island was called Malta. ² And the natives showed
us unusual kindness, for they kindled a fire and welcomed
us all, because it had begun to rain and was cold. ³ Paul
had gathered a bundle of sticks and put them on the fire,
when a viper came out because of the heat and fastened on
his hand. ⁴ When the natives saw the creature hanging from
his hand, they said to one another, "No doubt this man is
a murderer. Though he has escaped from the sea, justice
has not allowed him to live." ⁵ He, however, shook off the
creature into the fire and suffered no harm. ⁶ They waited,
expecting him to swell up or suddenly fall down dead; but
when they had waited a long time and saw no misfortune
come to him, they changed their minds and said that he
was a god.

7 Now in the neighborhood of that place were lands belonging to the chief man of the island, named Publius, who
received us and entertained us hospitably for three days.
⁸ It happened that the father of Publius lay sick with fever
and dysentery; and Paul visited him and prayed, and putting his hands on him healed him. ⁹ And when this had

---

^c Greek *place of two seas.*

taken place, the rest of the people on the island who had diseases also came and were cured. [10] They presented many gifts to us;[d] and when we sailed, they put on board whatever we needed.

11 After three months we set sail in a ship which had wintered in the island, a ship of Alexandria, with the Twin Brothers as figurehead. [12] Putting in at Syracuse, we stayed there for three days. [13] And from there we made a circuit and arrived at Rhe′gi-um; and after one day a south wind sprang up, and on the second day we came to Pu-te′o-li. [14] There we found brethren, and were invited to stay with them for seven days. And so we came to Rome. [15] And the brethren there, when they heard of us, came as far as the Forum of Ap′pi-us and Three Taverns to meet us. On seeing them Paul thanked God and took courage. [16] And when we came into Rome, Paul was allowed to stay by himself, with the soldier that guarded him.

17 After three days he called together the local leaders of the Jews; and when they had gathered, he said to them, "Brethren, though I had done nothing against the people or the customs of our fathers, yet I was delivered prisoner from Jerusalem into the hands of the Romans. [18] When they had examined me, they wished to set me at liberty, because there was no reason for the death penalty in my case. [19] But when the Jews objected, I was compelled to appeal to Caesar — though I had no charge to bring against my nation. [20] For this reason therefore I have asked to see you and speak with you, since it is because of the hope of Israel that I am bound with this chain." [21] And they said to him, "We have received no letters from Judea about you, and none of the brethren coming here has reported or spoken any evil about you. [22] But we desire to hear from you what

[d] Or *honored us with many honors.*

your views are; for with regard to this sect we know that everywhere it is spoken against."

23 When they had appointed a day for him, they came to him at his lodging in great numbers. And he expounded the matter to them from morning till evening, testifying to the kingdom of God and trying to convince them about Jesus both from the law of Moses and from the prophets. [24] And some were convinced by what he said, while others disbelieved. [25] So, as they disagreed among themselves, they departed, after Paul had made one statement: "The Holy Spirit was right in saying to your fathers through Isaiah the prophet:

> [26] 'Go to this people, and say,
>> You shall indeed hear but never understand,
>> and you shall indeed see but never perceive.
> [27] For this people's heart has grown dull,
>> and their ears are heavy of hearing,
>> and their eyes they have closed;
>> lest they should perceive with their eyes,
>> and hear with their ears,
>> and understand with their heart,
>> and turn for me to heal them.'

[28] Let it be known to you then that this salvation of God has been sent to the Gentiles; they will listen."[e]

30 And he lived there two whole years at his own expense,[f] and welcomed all who came to him, [31] preaching the kingdom of God and teaching about the Lord Jesus Christ quite openly and unhindered.

[e] Some ancient authorities add verse 29, *And when he had said these words, the Jews departed, holding much dispute among themselves.*   [f] Or *in his own hired dwelling.*

28. 26–27: Is. 6. 9–10.   **28. 28**: Ps. 67. 2.

THE

LETTER OF PAUL TO THE ROMANS

1 Paul, a servant*a* of Jesus Christ, called to be an apostle, set apart for the gospel of God ²which he promised beforehand through his prophets in the holy scriptures, ³the gospel concerning his Son, who was descended from David according to the flesh ⁴and designated Son of God in power according to the Spirit of holiness by his resurrection from the dead, Jesus Christ our Lord, ⁵through whom we have received grace and apostleship to bring about obedience to the faith for the sake of his name among all the Gentiles, ⁶including yourselves who are called to belong to Jesus Christ;

7 To all God's beloved in Rome, who are called to be saints:

Grace to you and peace from God our Father and the Lord Jesus Christ.

8 First, I thank my God through Jesus Christ for all of you, because your faith is proclaimed in all the world. ⁹For God is my witness, whom I serve with my spirit in the gospel of his Son, that without ceasing I mention you always in my prayers, ¹⁰asking that somehow by God's will I may now at last succeed in coming to you. ¹¹For I long to see you, that I may impart to you some spiritual gift to strengthen you, ¹²that is, that we may be mutually encouraged by each other's faith, both yours and mine.

---

a Or *slave.*

1. 1: Acts 9. 15; 13. 2; 1 Cor. 1. 1; 2 Cor. 1. 1; Gal. 1. 15.   **1. 5:** Acts 26. 16–18; Rom. 15. 18; Gal. 2. 7, 9.   **1. 7:** 1 Cor. 1. 3; 2 Cor. 1. 2; Gal. 1. 3; Eph. 1. 2; Phil. 1. 2; Col. 1. 2; 1 Thess. 1. 2; 2 Thess. 1. 2; 1 Tim. 1. 2; 2 Tim. 1. 2; Tit. 1. 4; Philem. 3; 2 Jn. 3.   **1. 8:** Rom. 16. 19.   **1. 10:** Rom. 15. 23, 32; Acts 19. 21.

¹³ I want you to know, brethren, that I have often intended to come to you (but thus far have been prevented), in order that I may reap some harvest among you as well as among the rest of the Gentiles. ¹⁴ I am under obligation both to Greeks and to barbarians, both to the wise and to the foolish; ¹⁵ so I am eager to preach the gospel to you also who are in Rome.

16 For I am not ashamed of the gospel: it is the power of God for salvation to every one who has faith, to the Jew first and also to the Greek. ¹⁷ For in it the righteousness of God is revealed through faith for faith; as it is written, "He who through faith is righteous shall live." *b*

18 For the wrath of God is revealed from heaven against all ungodliness and wickedness of men who by their wickedness suppress the truth. ¹⁹ For what can be known about God is plain to them, because God has shown it to them. ²⁰ Ever since the creation of the world his invisible nature, namely, his eternal power and deity, has been clearly perceived in the things that have been made. So they are without excuse; ²¹ for although they knew God they did not honor him as God or give thanks to him, but they became futile in their thinking and their senseless minds were darkened. ²² Claiming to be wise, they became fools, ²³ and exchanged the glory of the immortal God for images resembling mortal man or birds or animals or reptiles.

24 Therefore God gave them up in the lusts of their hearts to impurity, to the dishonoring of their bodies among themselves, ²⁵ because they exchanged the truth about God for a lie and worshiped and served the creature rather than the Creator, who is blessed forever! Amen.

b Or *The righteous shall live by faith.*

1. 13: Rom. 15. 22.   **1. 14:** 1 Cor. 9. 16.   **1. 16:** 1 Cor. 1. 18, 24.   **1. 17:** Rom. 3. 21; Gal. 3. 11; Phil. 3. 9; Heb. 10. 38; Hab. 2. 4.   **1. 18:** Eph. 5. 6; Col. 3. 6.   **1. 20:** Ps. 19. 1–4.   **1. 21:** Eph. 4. 17–18.   **1. 23:** Acts 17. 29.

26 For this reason God gave them up to dishonorable passions. Their women exchanged natural relations for unnatural, [27] and the men likewise gave up natural relations with women and were consumed with passion for one another, men committing shameless acts with men and receiving in their own persons the due penalty for their error.

28 And since they did not see fit to acknowledge God, God gave them up to a base mind and to improper conduct. [29] They were filled with all manner of wickedness, evil, covetousness, malice. Full of envy, murder, strife, deceit, malignity, they are gossips, [30] slanderers, haters of God, insolent, haughty, boastful, inventors of evil, disobedient to parents, [31] foolish, faithless, heartless, ruthless. [32] Though they know God's decree that those who do such things deserve to die, they not only do them but approve those who practice them.

2 Therefore you have no excuse, O man, whoever you are, when you judge another; for in passing judgment upon him you condemn yourself, because you, the judge, are doing the very same things. [2] We know that the judgment of God rightly falls upon those who do such things. [3] Do you suppose, O man, that when you judge those who do such things and yet do them yourself, you will escape the judgment of God? [4] Or do you presume upon the riches of his kindness and forbearance and patience? Do you not know that God's kindness is meant to lead you to repentance? [5] But by your hard and impenitent heart you are storing up wrath for yourself on the day of wrath when God's righteous judgment will be revealed. [6] For he will render to every man according to his works: [7] to those who by patience in well-doing seek for glory and honor and

2. 1: Rom. 14. 22.　　**2. 4:** Eph. 1. 7; 2. 7; Phil. 4. 19; Col. 1. 27.　　**2. 6:** Mt. 16. 27; 1 Cor. 3. 8; 2 Cor. 5. 10; Rev. 22. 12.

immortality, he will give eternal life; [8] but for those who
are factious and do not obey the truth, but obey wickedness, there will be wrath and fury. [9] There will be tribulation and distress for every human being who does evil,
the Jew first and also the Greek, [10] but glory and honor
and peace for every one who does good, the Jew first and
also the Greek. [11] For God shows no partiality.

12 All who have sinned without the law will also perish
without the law, and all who have sinned under the law
will be judged by the law. [13] For it is not the hearers of the
law who are righteous before God, but the doers of the law
who will be justified. [14] When Gentiles who have not the
law do by nature what the law requires, they are a law to
themselves, even though they do not have the law. [15] They
show that what the law requires is written on their hearts,
while their conscience also bears witness and their conflicting
thoughts accuse or perhaps excuse them [16] on that day
when, according to my gospel, God judges the secrets of
men by Christ Jesus.

17 But if you call yourself a Jew and rely upon the law
and boast of your relation to God [18] and know his will and
approve what is excellent, because you are instructed in
the law, [19] and if you are sure that you are a guide to the
blind, a light to those who are in darkness, [20] a corrector
of the foolish, a teacher of children, having in the law the
embodiment of knowledge and truth — [21] you then who
teach others, will you not teach yourself? While you preach
against stealing, do you steal? [22] You who say that one
must not commit adultery, do you commit adultery? You
who abhor idols, do you rob temples? [23] You who boast
in the law, do you dishonor God by breaking the law?

2. 11: Deut. 10. 17; 2 Chr. 19. 7; Gal. 2. 6; Eph. 6. 9; Col. 3. 25; 1 Pet. 1. 17.   **2. 12:** Rom.
3. 19; 1 Cor. 9. 21.   **2. 13:** Jas. 1. 22–23, 25.   **2. 16:** Eccl. 12. 14; Rom. 16. 25;
1 Cor. 4. 5.   **2. 18:** Phil. 1. 10.   **2. 20:** Rom. 6. 17; 2 Tim. 1. 13.   **2. 21:** Mt. 23. 3–4.

²⁴ For, as it is written, "The name of God is blasphemed among the Gentiles because of you."

25 Circumcision indeed is of value if you obey the law; but if you break the law, your circumcision becomes uncircumcision. ²⁶ So, if a man who is uncircumcised keeps the precepts of the law, will not his uncircumcision be regarded as circumcision? ²⁷ Then those who are physically uncircumcised but keep the law will condemn you who have the written code and circumcision but break the law. ²⁸ For he is not a real Jew who is one outwardly, nor is true circumcision something external and physical. ²⁹ He is a Jew who is one inwardly, and real circumcision is a matter of the heart, spiritual and not literal. His praise is not from men but from God.

3 Then what advantage has the Jew? Or what is the value of circumcision? ² Much in every way. To begin with, the Jews were entrusted with the oracles of God. ³ What if some were unfaithful? Does their faithlessness nullify the faithfulness of God? ⁴ By no means! Let God be true though every man be false, as it is written,

"That thou mayest be justified in thy words,
    and prevail when thou art judged."

⁵ But if our wickedness serves to show the justice of God, what shall we say? That God is unjust to inflict wrath on us? (I speak in a human way.) ⁶ By no means! For then how could God judge the world? ⁷ But if through my falsehood God's truthfulness abounds to his glory, why am I still being condemned as a sinner? ⁸ And why not do evil that good may come?— as some people slanderously charge us with saying. Their condemnation is just.

2. 24: Is. 52. 5.   **2. 25:** Jer. 9. 25.   **2. 26:** 1 Cor. 7. 19; Acts 10. 35.
2. 27: Mt. 12. 41.   **2. 28:** Mt. 3. 9; Jn. 8. 39; Rom. 9. 6–7; Gal. 6. 15.
2. 29: 2 Cor. 3. 6; Phil. 3. 3; Col. 2. 11; 1 Pet. 3. 4.   **3. 2:** Ps. 147. 19; Rom. 9. 4.
3. 4: Ps. 51. 4.   **3. 5:** Rom. 5. 9; 6. 19; 1 Cor. 9. 8; Gal. 3. 15.
3. 8: Rom. 6. 1, 15.

9 What then? Are we Jews any better off?[c] No, not at all; for I[d] have already charged that all men, both Jews and Greeks, are under the power of sin, [10] as it is written:

> "None is righteous, no, not one;
>
> [11] no one understands, no one seeks for God.
>
> [12] All have turned aside, together they have gone wrong;
>
> no one does good, not even one."
>
> [13] "Their throat is an open grave,
>
> they use their tongues to deceive."
>
> "The venom of asps is under their lips."
>
> [14] "Their mouth is full of curses and bitterness."
>
> [15] "Their feet are swift to shed blood,
>
> [16] in their paths are ruin and misery,
>
> [17] and the way of peace they do not know."
>
> [18] "There is no fear of God before their eyes."

19 Now we know that whatever the law says it speaks to those who are under the law, so that every mouth may be stopped, and the whole world may be held accountable to God. [20] For no human being will be justified in his sight by works of the law since through the law comes knowledge of sin.

21 But now the righteousness of God has been manifested apart from law, although the law and the prophets bear witness to it, [22] the righteousness of God through faith in Jesus Christ for all who believe. For there is no distinction; [23] since all have sinned and fall short of the glory of God, [24] they are justified by his grace as a gift, through the redemption which is in Christ Jesus, [25] whom God put forward as an expiation by his blood, to be received by faith. This was to show God's righteousness, because in his divine

[c] Or *at any disadvantage?*   [d] Greek *we.*

3. 9: Rom. 1. 18–32; 2. 1–29; 11. 32; 3. 23.   **3. 10–12:** Ps. 14. 1–2; 53. 1–2.   **3. 13:** Ps. 5. 9; 140. 3.   **3. 14:** Ps. 10. 7.   **3. 15–17:** Is. 59. 7–8.   **3. 18:** Ps. 36. 1.   **3. 19:** Rom. 2. 12.   **3. 20:** Acts 13. 39; Gal. 2. 16; 3. 11; Rom. 7. 7.   **3. 21:** Rom. 1. 17; Phil. 3. 9; 2 Pet. 1. 1.   **3. 22:** Rom. 4. 5; 9. 30; 10. 12; Gal. 2. 16.   **3. 23:** Rom. 3. 9.   **3. 24:** Rom. 4. 16; 5. 9; Eph. 2. 8; Tit. 3. 7; Eph. 1. 7; Col. 1. 14; Heb. 9. 15.

forbearance he had passed over former sins; [26] it was to prove at the present time that he himself is righteous and that he justifies him who has faith in Jesus.

27 Then what becomes of our boasting? It is excluded. On what principle? On the principle of works? No, but on the principle of faith. [28] For we hold that a man is justified by faith apart from works of law. [29] Or is God the God of Jews only? Is he not the God of Gentiles also? Yes, of Gentiles also, [30] since God is one; and he will justify the circumcised on the ground of their faith and the uncircumcised because of their faith. [31] Do we then overthrow the law by this faith? By no means! On the contrary, we uphold the law.

4 What then shall we say about[e] Abraham, our forefather according to the flesh? [2] For if Abraham was justified by works, he has something to boast about, but not before God. [3] For what does the scripture say? "Abraham believed God, and it was reckoned to him as righteousness." [4] Now to one who works, his wages are not reckoned as a gift but as his due. [5] And to one who does not work but trusts him who justifies the ungodly, his faith is reckoned as righteousness. [6] So also David pronounces a blessing upon the man to whom God reckons righteousness apart from works:

[7] "Blessed are those whose iniquities are forgiven, and whose sins are covered;

[8] blessed is the man against whom the Lord will not reckon his sin."

9 Is this blessing pronounced only upon the circumcised, or also upon the uncircumcised? We say that faith was reckoned to Abraham as righteousness. [10] How then was

[e] Some ancient authorities read *was gained by.*

3. 26: 1 Jn. 2. 2; Col. 1. 20.   **3. 28:** Acts 13. 39; Rom. 5. 1; Eph. 2. 9.   **3. 29:** Rom. 9. 24; Acts 10. 34–35.   **3. 30:** Rom. 4. 11–12, 16.   **3. 31:** Rom. 8. 4; Mt. 5. 17. **4. 2:** 1 Cor. 1. 31.   **4. 3:** Gen. 15. 6; Rom. 4. 9, 22; Gal. 3. 6; Jas. 2. 23.   **4. 4:** Rom. 11. 6.   **4. 5:** Rom. 3. 22.   **4. 7:** Ps. 32. 1–2.

it reckoned to him? Was it before or after he had been circumcised? It was not after, but before he was circumcised. [11] He received circumcision as a sign or seal of the righteousness which he had by faith while he was still uncircumcised. The purpose was to make him the father of all who believe without being circumcised and who thus have righteousness reckoned to them, [12] and likewise the father of the circumcised who are not merely circumcised but also follow the example of the faith which our father Abraham had before he was circumcised.

13 The promise to Abraham and his descendants, that they should inherit the world, did not come through the law but through the righteousness of faith. [14] If it is the adherents of the law who are to be the heirs, faith is null and the promise is void. [15] For the law brings wrath, but where there is no law there is no transgression.

16 That is why it depends on faith, in order that the promise may rest on grace and be guaranteed to all his descendants — not only to the adherents of the law but also to those who share the faith of Abraham, for he is the father of us all, [17] as it is written, "I have made you the father of many nations" — in the presence of the God in whom he believed, who gives life to the dead and calls into existence the things that do not exist. [18] In hope he believed against hope, that he should become the father of many nations; as he had been told, "So shall your descendants be." [19] He did not weaken in faith when he considered his own body, which was as good as dead because he was about a hundred years old, or when he considered the barrenness of Sarah's womb. [20] No distrust made him waver concerning the promise of God, but he grew strong in his faith as he gave

4. 11: Gen. 17. 10; Rom. 3. 22, 30.   **4. 13:** Gen. 17. 4–6; 22. 17–18; Gal. 3. 29.
4. 14: Gal. 3. 18.   **4. 15:** Gal. 3. 10.   **4. 17:** Gen. 17. 5; Jn. 5. 21.   **4. 18:** Gen. 15. 5.
4. 19: Heb. 11. 12; Gen. 17. 17; 18. 11.

glory to God, [21] fully convinced that God was able to do what he had promised. [22] That is why his faith was "reckoned to him as righteousness." [23] But the words, "it was reckoned to him," were written not for his sake alone, [24] but for ours also. It will be reckoned to us who believe in him that raised from the dead Jesus our Lord, [25] who was put to death for our trespasses and raised for our justification.

5 Therefore, since we are justified by faith, we[f] have peace with God through our Lord Jesus Christ. [2] Through him we have obtained access[g] to this grace in which we stand, and we[h] rejoice in our hope of sharing the glory of God. [3] More than that, we[h] rejoice in our sufferings, knowing that suffering produces endurance, [4] and endurance produces character, and character produces hope, [5] and hope does not disappoint us, because God's love has been poured into our hearts through the Holy Spirit which has been given to us.

6 While we were yet helpless, at the right time Christ died for the ungodly. [7] Why, one will hardly die for a righteous man — though perhaps for a good man one will dare even to die. [8] But God shows his love for us in that while we were yet sinners Christ died for us. [9] Since, therefore, we are now justified by his blood, much more shall we be saved by him from the wrath of God. [10] For if while we were enemies we were reconciled to God by the death of his Son, much more, now that we are reconciled, shall we be saved by his life. [11] Not only so, but we also rejoice in God through our Lord Jesus Christ, through whom we have now received our reconciliation.

[f] Many ancient authorities read *let us.*   [g] Some ancient authorities add *by faith.*   [h] Or *let us.*

4. 22: Rom. 4. 3.   **4. 23–24:** Rom. 15. 4; 1 Cor. 9. 10; 10. 11.   **4. 25:** Rom. 8. 32.
5. 1: Rom. 3. 28.   **5. 2:** Eph. 2. 18; 3. 12; Heb. 10. 19–20.   **5. 3:** Rom. 5. 11;
2 Cor. 12. 10; Jas. 1. 3.   **5. 5:** Ps. 119. 116; Acts 2. 33; Phil. 1. 20.   **5. 8:** Jn. 15. 13;
Rom. 8. 32; 1 Pet. 3. 18; 1 Jn. 3. 16; 4. 10.   **5. 9:** Rom. 3. 5, 24–25; Eph. 1. 7;
1 Thess. 1. 10.   **5. 10:** Col. 1. 21.   **5. 11:** Rom. 5. 3.

12 Therefore as sin came into the world through one man and death through sin, and so death spread to all men because all men sinned — [13] sin indeed was in the world before the law was given, but sin is not counted where there is no law. [14] Yet death reigned from Adam to Moses, even over those whose sins were not like the transgression of Adam, who was a type of the one who was to come.

15 But the free gift is not like the trespass. For if many died through one man's trespass, much more have the grace of God and the free gift in the grace of that one man Jesus Christ abounded for many. [16] And the free gift is not like the effect of that one man's sin. For the judgment following one trespass brought condemnation, but the free gift following many trespasses brings justification. [17] If, because of one man's trespass, death reigned through that one man, much more will those who receive the abundance of grace and the free gift of righteousness reign in life through the one man Jesus Christ.

18 Then as one man's trespass led to condemnation for all men, so one man's act of righteousness leads to acquittal and life for all men. [19] For as by one man's disobedience many were made sinners, so by one man's obedience many will be made righteous. [20] Law came in, to increase the trespass; but where sin increased, grace abounded all the more, [21] so that, as sin reigned in death, grace also might reign through righteousness to eternal life through Jesus Christ our Lord.

6 What shall we say then? Are we to continue in sin that grace may abound? [2] By no means! How can we who died to sin still live in it? [3] Do you not know that all

---

5. 12: 1 Cor. 15. 21–22; Rom. 6. 23; Jas. 1. 15.   **5. 14:** 1 Cor. 15. 22, 45.   **5. 15:** Acts 15. 11.   **5. 16:** Rom. 8. 1.   **5. 19:** Phil. 2. 8.   **5. 20:** Rom. 7. 7–8; Gal. 3. 19; 1 Tim. 1. 14.   **5. 21:** Rom. 6. 23.   **6. 1:** Rom. 3. 8; 6. 15.   **6. 2:** Rom. 7. 4, 6; Gal. 2. 19; 1 Pet. 2. 24.   **6. 3:** Acts 2. 38; 8. 16; 19. 5.

of us who have been baptized into Christ Jesus were baptized into his death? [4] We were buried therefore with him by baptism into death, so that as Christ was raised from the dead by the glory of the Father, we too might walk in newness of life.

5 For if we have been united with him in a death like his, we shall certainly be united with him in a resurrection like his. [6] We know that our old self was crucified with him so that the sinful body might be destroyed, and we might no longer be enslaved to sin. [7] For he who has died is freed from sin. [8] But if we have died with Christ, we believe that we shall also live with him. [9] For we know that Christ being raised from the dead will never die again; death no longer has dominion over him. [10] The death he died he died to sin, once for all, but the life he lives he lives to God. [11] So you also must consider yourselves dead to sin and alive to God in Christ Jesus.

12 Let not sin therefore reign in your mortal bodies, to make you obey their passions. [13] Do not yield your members to sin as instruments of wickedness, but yield yourselves to God as men who have been brought from death to life, and your members to God as instruments of righteousness. [14] For sin will have no dominion over you, since you are not under law but under grace.

15 What then? Are we to sin because we are not under law but under grace? By no means! [16] Do you not know that if you yield yourselves to any one as obedient slaves, you are slaves of the one whom you obey, either of sin, which leads to death, or of obedience, which leads to righteousness? [17] But thanks be to God, that you who were once slaves of sin have become obedient from the heart to the

6. 4: Col. 2. 12.   **6. 5:** 2 Cor. 4. 10; Col. 2. 12.   **6. 6:** Rom. 7. 24; Col. 2. 13.
6. 7: 1 Pet. 4. 1.   **6. 8:** 2 Tim. 2. 11.   **6. 9:** Acts 2. 24; Rev. 1. 18.   **6. 11:** Rom.
7. 4, 6; Gal. 2. 19; 1 Pet. 2. 24.   **6. 13:** Rom. 6. 19; 7. 5; 12. 1.   **6. 14:** Rom. 8. 2.
6. 15: Rom. 3. 8; 6. 1.   **6. 16:** Mt. 6. 24; Jn. 8. 34; Rom. 12. 1.

standard of teaching to which you were committed, [18] and, having been set free from sin, have become slaves of righteousness. [19] I am speaking in human terms, because of your natural limitations. For just as you once yielded your members to impurity and to greater and greater iniquity, so now yield your members to righteousness for sanctification.

20 When you were slaves of sin, you were free in regard to righteousness. [21] But then what return did you get from the things of which you are now ashamed? The end of those things is death. [22] But now that you have been set free from sin and have become slaves of God, the return you get is sanctification and its end, eternal life. [23] For the wages of sin is death, but the free gift of God is eternal life in Christ Jesus our Lord.

7 Do you not know, brethren — for I am speaking to those who know the law — that the law is binding on a person only during his life? [2] Thus a married woman is bound by law to her husband as long as he lives; but if her husband dies she is discharged from the law concerning the husband. [3] Accordingly, she will be called an adulteress if she lives with another man while her husband is alive. But if her husband dies she is free from that law, and if she marries another man she is not an adulteress.

4 Likewise, my brethren, you have died to the law through the body of Christ, so that you may belong to another, to him who has been raised from the dead in order that we may bear fruit for God. [5] While we were living in the flesh, our sinful passions, aroused by the law, were at work in our members to bear fruit for death. [6] But now we are discharged from the law, dead to that which held us captive, so that

6. 18: Rom. 8. 2.   **6. 19:** Rom. 3. 5; 6. 13; 12. 1.   **6. 20:** Mt. 6. 24; Jn. 8. 34.
6. 21: Rom. 7. 5; 8. 6, 13, 21.   **6. 23:** Rom. 5. 12, 21; Gal. 6. 7, 8.
7. 2: 1 Cor. 7. 39.   **7. 4:** Rom. 6. 2, 11; Gal. 2. 19; Col. 1. 22.   **7. 5:** Rom. 6. 13, 21; 8. 8; Jas. 1. 15.

we serve not under the old written code but in the new life of the Spirit.

7 What then shall we say? That the law is sin? By no means! Yet, if it had not been for the law, I should not have known sin. I should not have known what it is to covet if the law had not said, "You shall not covet." [8] But sin, finding opportunity in the commandment, wrought in me all kinds of covetousness. Apart from the law sin lies dead. [9] I was once alive apart from the law, but when the commandment came, sin revived and I died; [10] the very commandment which promised life proved to be death to me. [11] For sin, finding opportunity in the commandment, deceived me and by it killed me. [12] So the law is holy, and the commandment is holy and just and good.

13 Did that which is good, then, bring death to me? By no means! It was sin, working death in me through what is good, in order that sin might be shown to be sin, and through the commandment might become sinful beyond measure. [14] We know that the law is spiritual; but I am carnal, sold under sin. [15] I do not understand my own actions. For I do not do what I want, but I do the very thing I hate. [16] Now if I do what I do not want, I agree that the law is good. [17] So then it is no longer I that do it, but sin which dwells within me. [18] For I know that nothing good dwells within me, that is, in my flesh. I can will what is right, but I cannot do it. [19] For I do not do the good I want, but the evil I do not want is what I do. [20] Now if I do what I do not want, it is no longer I that do it, but sin which dwells within me.

21 So I find it to be a law that when I want to do right, evil lies close at hand. [22] For I delight in the law of God,

7. 7: Rom. 3. 20; 5. 20; Ex. 20. 17; Deut. 5. 21.   **7. 8**: 1 Cor. 15. 56.   **7. 10**: Lev. 18. 5; Rom. 10. 5.   **7. 12**: 1 Tim. 1. 8.   **7. 14**: 1 Cor. 3. 1.   **7. 15**: Gal. 5. 17. **7. 22**: Ps. 1. 2.

in my inmost self, [23] but I see in my members another law at war with the law of my mind and making me captive to the law of sin which dwells in my members. [24] Wretched man that I am! Who will deliver me from this body of death? [25] Thanks be to God through Jesus Christ our Lord! So then, I of myself serve the law of God with my mind, but with my flesh I serve the law of sin.

8 There is therefore now no condemnation for those who are in Christ Jesus. [2] For the law of the Spirit of life in Christ Jesus has set me free from the law of sin and death. [3] For God has done what the law, weakened by the flesh, could not do: sending his own Son in the likeness of sinful flesh and for sin,[i] he condemned sin in the flesh, [4] in order that the just requirement of the law might be fulfilled in us, who walk not according to the flesh but according to the Spirit. [5] For those who live according to the flesh set their minds on the things of the flesh, but those who live according to the Spirit set their minds on the things of the Spirit. [6] To set the mind on the flesh is death, but to set the mind on the Spirit is life and peace. [7] For the mind that is set on the flesh is hostile to God; it does not submit to God's law, indeed it cannot; [8] and those who are in the flesh cannot please God.

9 But you are not in the flesh, you are in the Spirit, if the Spirit of God really dwells in you. Any one who does not have the Spirit of Christ does not belong to him. [10] But if Christ is in you, although your bodies are dead because of sin, your spirits are alive because of righteousness. [11] If the Spirit of him who raised Jesus from the dead dwells in you, he who raised Christ Jesus from the dead will give life

[i] Or *and as a sin-offering.*

7. 23: Gal. 5. 17.   **7. 24:** Rom. 6. 6; Col. 2. 11.
8. 1: Rom. 5. 16.   **8. 2:** 1 Cor. 15. 45; Rom. 6. 14, 18.   **8. 3:** Acts 13. 39; Heb. 7. 18; 10. 1–2; Phil. 2. 7; Heb. 2. 14.   **8. 4:** Rom. 3. 31; Gal. 5. 16, 25.   **8. 5:** Gal. 5. 19–25.
8. 6: Rom. 6. 21; 8. 13, 27; Gal. 6. 8.   **8. 8:** Rom. 7. 5.   **8. 9:** 1 Cor. 3. 16; 6. 19; 2 Cor. 6. 16; 2 Tim. 1. 14.   **8. 10:** Gal. 2. 20; Eph. 3. 17.   **8. 11:** Jn. 5. 21.

to your mortal bodies also through his Spirit which dwells in you.

12 So then, brethren, we are debtors, not to the flesh, to live according to the flesh — [13] for if you live according to the flesh you will die, but if by the Spirit you put to death the deeds of the body you will live. [14] For all who are led by the Spirit of God are sons of God. [15] For you did not receive the spirit of slavery to fall back into fear, but you have received the spirit of sonship. When we cry, "Abba! Father!" [16] it is the Spirit himself bearing witness with our spirit that we are children of God, [17] and if children, then heirs, heirs of God and fellow heirs with Christ, provided we suffer with him in order that we may also be glorified with him.

18 I consider that the sufferings of this present time are not worth comparing with the glory that is to be revealed to us. [19] For the creation waits with eager longing for the revealing of the sons of God; [20] for the creation was subjected to futility, not of its own will but by the will of him who subjected it in hope; [21] because the creation itself will be set free from its bondage to decay and obtain the glorious liberty of the children of God. [22] We know that the whole creation has been groaning in travail together until now; [23] and not only the creation, but we ourselves, who have the first fruits of the Spirit, groan inwardly as we wait for adoption as sons, the redemption of our bodies. [24] For in this hope we were saved. Now hope that is seen is not hope. For who hopes for what he sees? [25] But if we hope for what we do not see, we wait for it with patience.

26 Likewise the Spirit helps us in our weakness; for we

8. 13: Rom. 8. 6; Col. 3. 5.   **8. 14:** Gal. 5. 18.   **8. 15:** Rom. 9. 4; Gal. 4. 5–7; Mk. 14. 36.   **8. 16:** Acts 5. 32.   **8. 17:** Gal. 3. 29; 4. 7; 2 Cor. 1. 5, 7; 2 Tim. 2. 12; 1 Pet. 4. 13.   **8. 18:** 2 Cor. 4. 17; Col. 3. 4; 1 Pet. 5. 1.   **8. 19:** 1 Pet. 1. 7, 13; 1 Jn. 3. 2.   **8. 20:** Eccl. 1. 2.   **8. 21:** Acts 3. 21; Rom. 6. 21; 2 Pet. 3. 13; Rev. 21. 1. **8. 22:** Jer. 12. 4, 11.   **8. 23:** 2 Cor. 1. 22; 5. 2, 4; Gal. 5. 5.   **8. 24:** 2 Cor. 5. 7; Heb. 11. 1.

do not know how to pray as we ought, but the Spirit himself intercedes for us with sighs too deep for words. [27] And he who searches the hearts of men knows what is the mind of the Spirit, because[j] the Spirit intercedes for the saints according to the will of God.

28 We know that in everything God works for good[k] with those who love him,[l] who are called according to his purpose. [29] For those whom he foreknew he also predestined to be conformed to the image of his Son, in order that he might be the first-born among many brethren. [30] And those whom he predestined he also called; and those whom he called he also justified; and those whom he justified he also glorified.

31 What then shall we say to this? If God is for us, who is against us? [32] He who did not spare his own Son but gave him up for us all, will he not also give us all things with him? [33] Who shall bring any charge against God's elect? It is God who justifies; [34] who is to condemn? Is it Christ Jesus, who died, yes, who was raised from the dead, who is at the right hand of God, who indeed intercedes for us?[m] [35] Who shall separate us from the love of Christ? Shall tribulation, or distress, or persecution, or famine, or nakedness, or peril, or sword? [36] As it is written,

> "For thy sake we are being killed all the day long;
> we are regarded as sheep to be slaughtered."

[37] No, in all these things we are more than conquerors through him who loved us. [38] For I am sure that neither death, nor life, nor angels, nor principalities, nor things present, nor things to come, nor powers, [39] nor height, nor depth, nor anything else in all creation, will be able to separate us from the love of God in Christ Jesus our Lord.

[j] Or *that*.   [k] Some ancient authorities read *in everything he works for good*, or *everything works for good*.   [l] Greek *God*.   [m] Or *It is Christ Jesus . . . for us*.

8. 27: Ps. 139. 1–2; Lk. 16. 15; Rev. 2. 23; Rom. 8. 6, 34.   **8. 29:** Rom. 9. 23; 11. 2; 1 Pet. 1. 2, 20; Eph. 1. 5, 11.   **8. 31:** Ps. 118. 6.   **8. 32:** Jn. 3. 16; Rom. 4. 25; 5. 8.   **8. 33:** Lk. 18. 7; Is. 50. 8–9.   **8. 34:** Rom. 8. 27.   **8. 36:** Ps. 44. 22.   **8. 37:** 1 Cor. 15. 57.

9 I am speaking the truth in Christ, I am not lying; my conscience bears me witness in the Holy Spirit, [2] that I have great sorrow and unceasing anguish in my heart. [3] For I could wish that I myself were accursed and cut off from Christ for the sake of my brethren, my kinsmen by race. [4] They are Israelites, and to them belong the sonship, the glory, the covenants, the giving of the law, the worship, and the promises; [5] to them belong the patriarchs, and of their race, according to the flesh, is the Christ. God who is over all be blessed forever.[n] Amen.

6 But it is not as though the word of God had failed. For not all who are descended from Israel belong to Israel, [7] and not all are children of Abraham because they are his descendants; but, "Your descendants will be reckoned through Isaac." [8] This means that it is not the children of the flesh who are the children of God, but the children of the promise are reckoned as descendants. [9] For this is what the promise said, "About this time I will return and Sarah shall have a son." [10] And not only so, but also when Rebecca had conceived children by one man, our forefather Isaac, [11] though they were not yet born and had done nothing either good or bad, in order that God's purpose of election might continue, not because of works but because of his call, [12] she was told, "The elder will serve the younger." [13] As it is written, "Jacob I loved, but Esau I hated."

14 What shall we say then? Is there injustice on God's part? By no means! [15] For he says to Moses, "I will have mercy on whom I have mercy, and I will have compassion on whom I have compassion." [16] So it depends not upon man's will or exertion, but upon God's mercy. [17] For the

[n] Or *Christ, who is God over all, blessed forever.*

9. 3: Ex. 32. 32.   **9. 4:** Rom. 3. 2; 8. 15. Heb. 11. 18.   **9. 8:** Gal. 3. 29; 4. 28.   **9. 12:** Gen. 25. 23.   **9. 13:** Mal. 1. 2–3.   **9. 17:** Ex. 9. 16.   **9. 6:** Rom. 2. 28–29.   **9. 9:** Gen. 18. 10.   **9. 14:** 2 Chr. 19. 7.   **9. 7:** Gen. 21. 12;   **9. 10:** Gen. 25. 21.   **9. 15:** Ex. 33. 19.

scripture says to Pharaoh, "I have raised you up for the very purpose of showing my power in you, so that my name may be proclaimed in all the earth." [18] So then he has mercy upon whomever he wills, and he hardens the heart of whomever he wills.

19 You will say to me then, "Why does he still find fault? For who can resist his will?" [20] But, who are you, a man, to answer back to God? Will what is molded say to its molder, "Why have you made me thus?" [21] Has the potter no right over the clay, to make out of the same lump one vessel for beauty and another for menial use? [22] What if God, desiring to show his wrath and to make known his power, has endured with much patience the vessels of wrath made for destruction, [23] in order to make known the riches of his glory for the vessels of mercy, which he has prepared beforehand for glory, [24] even us whom he has called, not from the Jews only but also from the Gentiles? [25] As indeed he says in Ho-se′a,

> "Those who were not my people
> I will call 'my people,'
> and her who was not beloved
> I will call 'my beloved.'"

[26] "And in the very place where it was said to them, 'You are not my people,'
> they will be called 'sons of the living God.'"

27 And Isaiah cries out concerning Israel: "Though the number of the sons of Israel be as the sand of the sea, only a remnant of them will be saved; [28] for the Lord will execute his sentence upon the earth with rigor and dispatch." [29] And as Isaiah predicted,

9. 18: Rom. 11. 7.   **9. 20:** Is. 29. 16; 45. 9.   **9. 21:** 2 Tim. 2. 20.   **9. 22:** Prov. 16. 4.
9. 23: Rom. 8. 29.   **9. 24:** Rom. 3. 29.   **9. 25:** Hos. 2. 23; 1 Pet. 2. 10.
9. 26: Hos. 1. 10.   **9. 27:** Is. 10. 22–23; Gen. 22. 17; Hos. 1. 10; Rom. 11. 5; 2 Kings
19. 4; Is. 11. 11.   **9. 29:** Is. 1. 9.

"If the Lord of hosts had not left us children,
we would have fared like Sodom and been made
like Go-mor'rah."

30 What shall we say, then? That Gentiles who did not
pursue righteousness have attained it, that is, righteousness
through faith; [31] but that Israel who pursued the righteousness which is based on law did not succeed in fulfilling that
law. [32] Why? Because they did not pursue it through faith,
but as if it were based on works. They have stumbled over
the stumbling-stone, [33] as it is written,

"Behold I am laying in Zion a stone that will make
men stumble,
a rock that will make them fall;
and he who believes in him will not be put to shame."

10 Brethren, my heart's desire and prayer to God for
them is that they may be saved. [2] I bear them witness
that they have a zeal for God, but it is not enlightened.
[3] For, being ignorant of the righteousness that comes from
God, and seeking to establish their own, they did not submit to God's righteousness. [4] For Christ is the end of the
law, that every one who has faith may be justified.

5 Moses writes that the man who practices the righteousness which is based on the law shall live by it. [6] But the
righteousness based on faith says, "Do not say in your
heart, 'Who will ascend into heaven?' (that is, to bring
Christ down) [7] or 'Who will descend into the abyss?'"
(that is, to bring Christ up from the dead). [8] But what does
it say? "The word is near you, on your lips and in your
heart" (that is, the word of faith which we preach); [9] because, if you confess with your lips that Jesus is Lord and

9. 30: Rom. 3. 22; 10. 6, 20; Gal. 2. 16; 3. 24; Phil. 3. 9; Heb. 11. 7.   **9. 31:** Is. 51. 1;
Rom. 10. 2–3; 11. 7.   **9. 32:** 1 Pet. 2. 8.   **9. 33:** Is. 28. 16; Rom. 10. 11.
10. 2–4: Rom. 9. 31.   **10. 3:** Rom. 1. 17.   **10. 4:** Gal. 3. 24; Rom. 3. 22; 7. 1–4.
10. 5: Lev. 18. 5; Neh. 9. 29; Ezek. 20. 11, 13, 21; Rom. 7. 10.   **10. 6:** Deut. 30. 12–13;
Rom. 9. 30.   **10. 8:** Deut. 30. 14.   **10. 9:** Mt. 10. 32; Lk. 12. 8; Acts 16. 31.

believe in your heart that God raised him from the dead, you will be saved. [10] For man believes with his heart and so is justified, and he confesses with his lips and so is saved. [11] The scripture says, "No one who believes in him will be put to shame." [12] For there is no distinction between Jew and Greek; the same Lord is Lord of all and bestows his riches upon all who call upon him. [13] For, "every one who calls upon the name of the Lord will be saved."

14 But how are men to call upon him in whom they have not believed? And how are they to believe in him of whom they have never heard? And how are they to hear without a preacher? [15] And how can men preach unless they are sent? As it is written, "How beautiful are the feet of those who preach good news!" [16] But they have not all heeded the gospel; for Isaiah says, "Lord, who has believed what he has heard from us?" [17] So faith comes from what is heard, and what is heard comes by the preaching of Christ.

18 But I ask, have they not heard? Indeed they have; for
"Their voice has gone out to all the earth,
and their words to the ends of the world."

[19] Again I ask, did Israel not understand? First Moses says,
"I will make you jealous of those who are not a nation;
with a foolish nation I will make you angry."

[20] Then Isaiah is so bold as to say,
"I have been found by those who did not seek me;
I have shown myself to those who did not ask for
me."

[21] But of Israel he says, "All day long I have held out my hands to a disobedient and contrary people."

10. 11: Is. 28. 16; Rom. 9. 33.   **10. 12:** Rom. 3. 22, 29; Gal. 3. 28; Col. 3. 11;
Acts 10. 36.   **10. 13:** Joel 2. 32; Acts 2. 21.   **10. 15:** Is. 52. 7.   **10. 16:** Is. 53. 1.
Jn. 12. 38.   **10. 18:** Ps. 19. 4; Col. 1. 6, 23.   **10. 19:** Deut. 32. 21; Rom. 11. 11, 14;
10. 20: Is. 65. 1; Rom. 9. 30.   **10. 21:** Is. 65. 2.

11 I ask, then, has God rejected his people? By no means! I myself am an Israelite, a descendant of Abraham, a member of the tribe of Benjamin. [2] God has not rejected his people whom he foreknew. Do you not know what the scripture says of Elijah, how he pleads with God against Israel? [3] "Lord, they have killed thy prophets, they have demolished thy altars, and I alone am left, and they seek my life." [4] But what is God's reply to him? "I have kept for myself seven thousand men who have not bowed the knee to Ba'al." [5] So too at the present time there is a remnant, chosen by grace. [6] But if it is by grace, it is no longer on the basis of works; otherwise grace would no longer be grace.

7 What then? Israel failed to obtain what it sought. The elect obtained it, but the rest were hardened, [8] as it is written,

> "God gave them a spirit of stupor,
>> eyes that should not see and ears that should not hear,
> down to this very day."

[9] And David says,

> "Let their feast become a snare and a trap,
> a pitfall and a retribution for them;
>> [10] let their eyes be darkened so that they cannot see,
> and bend their backs forever."

11 So I ask, have they stumbled so as to fall? By no means! But through their transgression salvation has come to the Gentiles, so as to make Israel jealous. [12] Now if their transgression means riches for the world, and if their failure means riches for the Gentiles, how much more will their full inclusion mean!

11. 1: 1 Sam. 12. 22; Jer. 31. 37; 33. 24–26; 2 Cor. 11. 22; Phil. 3. 5. **11. 2:** Ps. 94. 14; 1 Kings 19. 10. **11. 4:** 1 Kings 19. 18. **11. 5:** 2 Kings 19. 4; Is. 11. 11; Rom. 9. 27. **11. 6:** Rom. 4. 4. **11. 7:** Rom. 9. 18, 31; 11. 25. **11. 8:** Is. 29. 10; Deut. 29. 4; Mt. 13. 13–14. **11. 9:** Ps. 69. 22–23. **11. 11:** Rom. 10. 19; 11. 14.

13 Now I am speaking to you Gentiles. Inasmuch then as I am an apostle to the Gentiles, I magnify my ministry [14] in order to make my fellow Jews jealous, and thus save some of them. [15] For if their rejection means the reconciliation of the world, what will their acceptance mean but life from the dead? [16] If the dough offered as first fruits is holy, so is the whole lump; and if the root is holy, so are the branches.

17 But if some of the branches were broken off, and you, a wild olive shoot, were grafted in their place to share the richness[o] of the olive tree, [18] do not boast over the branches. If you do boast, remember it is not you that support the root, but the root that supports you. [19] You will say, "Branches were broken off so that I might be grafted in." [20] That is true. They were broken off because of their unbelief, but you stand fast only through faith. So do not become proud, but stand in awe. [21] For if God did not spare the natural branches, neither will he spare you. [22] Note then the kindness and the severity of God: severity toward those who have fallen, but God's kindness to you, provided you continue in his kindness; otherwise you too will be cut off. [23] And even the others, if they do not persist in their unbelief, will be grafted in, for God has the power to graft them in again. [24] For if you have been cut from what is by nature a wild olive tree, and grafted, contrary to nature, into a cultivated olive tree, how much more will these natural branches be grafted back into their own olive tree.

25 Lest you be wise in your own conceits, I want you to understand this mystery, brethren: a hardening has come upon part of Israel, until the full number of the Gentiles come in, [26] and so all Israel will be saved; as it is written,

[o] Some ancient authorities read *rich root.*

11. 13: Acts 9. 15.   **11. 14:** Rom. 10. 19; 11. 11; 1 Cor. 9. 22.   **11. 15:** Lk. 15. 24, 32. **11. 20:** 2 Cor. 1. 24.   **11. 25:** 1 Cor. 2. 7–10; Eph. 3. 3–5, 9; Rom. 9. 18; 11. 7; Lk. 21. 24.   **11. 26:** Is. 59. 20–21.

"The Deliverer will come from Zion,
  he will banish ungodliness from Jacob";
²⁷ "and this will be my covenant with them
  when I take away their sins."
²⁸ As regards the gospel they are enemies of God, for your
sake; but as regards his election they are beloved for the
sake of their forefathers. ²⁹ For the gifts and the call of God
are irrevocable. ³⁰ Just as you were once disobedient to
God but now have received mercy because of their disobedience, ³¹ so they have now been disobedient in order that
by the mercy shown to you they also may[p] receive mercy.
³² For God has consigned all men to disobedience, that he
may have mercy upon all.

33 O the depth of the riches and wisdom and knowledge
of God! How unsearchable are his judgments and how
inscrutable his ways!
³⁴ "For who has known the mind of the Lord
  or who has been his counselor?"
³⁵ "Or who has given a gift to him
  that he might be repaid?"
³⁶ For from him and through him and to him are all things.
To him be glory forever. Amen.

12 I appeal to you therefore, brethren, by the mercies
of God, to present your bodies as a living sacrifice,
holy and acceptable to God, which is your spiritual worship.
² Do not be conformed to this world[q] but be transformed
by the renewal of your mind, that you may prove what is
the will of God, what is good and acceptable and perfect.[r]

3 For by the grace given to me I bid every one among

---

[p] Some ancient authorities add *now*.
[q] Greek *age*.   [r] Or *what is the good and acceptable and perfect will of God*.
11. 27: Jer. 31. 33; Is. 27. 9.   **11. 32:** Rom. 3. 9; Gal. 3. 22–31.   **11. 33:** Col. 2. 3.
11. 34: Is. 40. 13–14; 1 Cor. 2. 16.   **11. 35:** Job 35. 7; 41. 11.   **11. 36:** 1 Cor. 8. 6;
11. 12; Col. 1. 16; Heb. 2. 10.
12. 1: Rom. 6. 13, 16, 19; 1 Pet. 2. 5.   **12. 2:** 1 Jn. 2. 15; Eph. 4. 23; 5. 10.

you not to think of himself more highly than he ought to think, but to think with sober judgment, each according to the measure of faith which God has assigned him. [4] For as in one body we have many members, and all the members do not have the same function, [5] so we, though many, are one body in Christ, and individually members one of another. [6] Having gifts that differ according to the grace given to us, let us use them: if prophecy, in proportion to our faith; [7] if service, in our serving; he who teaches, in his teaching; [8] he who exhorts, in his exhortation; he who contributes, in liberality; he who gives aid, with zeal; he who does acts of mercy, with cheerfulness.

9 Let love be genuine; hate what is evil, hold fast to what is good; [10] love one another with brotherly affection; outdo one another in showing honor. [11] Never flag in zeal, be aglow with the Spirit, serve the Lord. [12] Rejoice in your hope, be patient in tribulation, be constant in prayer. [13] Contribute to the needs of the saints, practice hospitality.

14 Bless those who persecute you; bless and do not curse them. [15] Rejoice with those who rejoice, weep with those who weep. [16] Live in harmony with one another; do not be haughty, but associate with the lowly;[s] never be conceited. [17] Repay no one evil for evil, but take thought for what is noble in the sight of all. [18] If possible, so far as it depends upon you, live peaceably with all. [19] Beloved, never avenge yourselves, but leave it[t] to the wrath of God; for it is written, "Vengeance is mine, I will repay, says the Lord." [20] No, "if your enemy is hungry, feed him; if he is thirsty, give him drink; for by so doing you will heap burning coals upon

---

[s] Or *give yourselves to humble tasks.*   [t] Greek *give place.*

12. 4: 1 Cor. 12. 12–14; Eph. 4. 4, 16.   **12. 5:** 1 Cor. 10. 17; 12. 20, 27; Eph. 4. 25.
12. 6–8: 1 Cor. 7. 7; 12. 4–11; 1 Pet. 4. 10–11.   **12. 12:** Acts 1. 14; Rom. 5. 2;
1 Thess. 5. 17.   **12. 14:** Mt. 5. 44; Lk. 6. 28.   **12. 16:** Rom. 11. 25; 15. 5;
1 Cor. 1. 10; 2 Cor. 13. 11; Phil. 2. 2; 4. 2; Prov. 3. 7; 26. 12.   **12. 17:** Prov. 20. 22;
2 Cor. 8. 21; 1 Thess. 5. 15.   **12. 18:** Mk. 9. 50; Rom. 14. 19.   **12. 19:** Lev. 19. 18;
Deut. 32. 35; Heb. 10. 30.   **12. 20:** Prov. 25. 21–22; Mt. 5. 44; Lk. 6. 27.

his head." [21] Do not be overcome by evil, but overcome evil with good.

13 Let every person be subject to the governing authorities. For there is no authority except from God, and those that exist have been instituted by God. [2] Therefore he who resists the authorities resists what God has appointed, and those who resist will incur judgment. [3] For rulers are not a terror to good conduct, but to bad. Would you have no fear of him who is in authority? Then do what is good, and you will receive his approval, [4] for he is God's servant for your good. But if you do wrong, be afraid, for he does not bear the sword in vain; he is the servant of God to execute his wrath on the wrong-doer. [5] Therefore one must be subject, not only to avoid God's wrath but also for the sake of conscience. [6] For the same reason you also pay taxes, for the authorities are ministers of God, attending to this very thing. [7] Pay all of them their dues, taxes to whom taxes are due, revenue to whom revenue is due, respect to whom respect is due, honor to whom honor is due.

[8] Owe no one anything, except to love one another; for he who loves his neighbor has fulfilled the law. [9] The commandments, "You shall not commit adultery, You shall not kill, You shall not steal, You shall not covet," and any other commandment, are summed up in this sentence, "You shall love your neighbor as yourself." [10] Love does no wrong to a neighbor; therefore love is the fulfilling of the law.

[11] Besides this you know what hour it is, how it is full time now for you to wake from sleep. For salvation is nearer to us now than when we first believed; [12] the night is far gone, the day is at hand. Let us then cast off the works of

13. 1: Tit. 3. 1; 1 Pet. 2. 13–14; Prov. 8. 15; Jn. 19. 11.   **13. 3:** 1 Pet. 2. 14.
13. 4: 1 Thess. 4. 6.   **13. 7:** Mt. 22. 21; Mk. 12. 17; Lk. 20. 25.   **13. 8:** Mt. 22. 39–40;
Rom. 13. 10; Gal. 5. 14; Col. 3. 14; Jas. 2. 8.   **13. 9:** Ex. 20. 13–14; Deut. 5. 17–18;
Lev. 19. 18; Mt. 19. 19.   **13. 10:** Mt. 22. 39–40; Rom. 13. 8; Gal. 5. 14; Jas. 2. 8.
13. 11: Eph. 5. 14; 1 Thess. 5. 6.   **13. 12:** 1 Jn. 2. 8; Eph. 5. 11; 1 Thess. 5. 8.

darkness and put on the armor of light; [13] let us conduct ourselves becomingly as in the day, not in reveling and drunkenness, not in debauchery and licentiousness, not in quarreling and jealousy. [14] But put on the Lord Jesus Christ, and make no provision for the flesh, to gratify its desires.

14 As for the man who is weak in faith, welcome him, but not for disputes over opinions. [2] One believes he may eat anything, while the weak man eats only vegetables. [3] Let not him who eats despise him who abstains, and let not him who abstains pass judgment on him who eats; for God has welcomed him. [4] Who are you to pass judgment on the servant of another? It is before his own master that he stands or falls. And he will be upheld, for the Master is able to make him stand.

5 One man esteems one day as better than another, while another man esteems all days alike. Let every one be fully convinced in his own mind. [6] He who observes the day, observes it in honor of the Lord. He also who eats, eats in honor of the Lord, since he gives thanks to God; while he who abstains, abstains in honor of the Lord and gives thanks to God. [7] None of us lives to himself, and none of us dies to himself. [8] If we live, we live to the Lord, and if we die, we die to the Lord; so then, whether we live or whether we die, we are the Lord's. [9] For to this end Christ died and lived again, that he might be Lord both of the dead and of the living.

10 Why do you pass judgment on your brother? Or you, why do you despise your brother? For we shall all stand before the judgment seat of God; [11] for it is written,

> "As I live, says the Lord, every knee shall bow to me,
>   and every tongue shall give praise[u] to God."

[12] So each of us shall give account of himself to God.

[u] Or *confess.*

13. 13: 1 Thess. 4. 12; Gal. 5. 19–21.   **13. 14:** Gal. 3. 27; 5. 16.
14. 3: Col. 2. 16.   **14. 5:** Gal. 4. 10.   **14. 7:** Gal. 2. 20; 2 Cor. 5. 15.
14. 8: Phil. 1. 20.   **14. 10:** 2 Cor. 5. 10.   **14. 11:** Is. 45. 23; Phil. 2. 10–11.

13 Then let us no more pass judgment on one another, but rather decide never to put a stumbling-block or hindrance in the way of a brother. [14] I know and am persuaded in the Lord Jesus that nothing is unclean in itself; but it is unclean for any one who thinks it unclean. [15] If your brother is being injured by what you eat, you are no longer walking in love. Do not let what you eat cause the ruin of one for whom Christ died. [16] So do not let what is good to you be spoken of as evil. [17] For the kingdom of God does not mean food and drink but righteousness and peace and joy in the Holy Spirit; [18] he who thus serves Christ is acceptable to God and approved by men. [19] Let us then pursue what makes for peace and for mutual upbuilding. [20] Do not, for the sake of food, destroy the work of God. Everything is indeed clean, but it is wrong for any one to make others fall by what he eats; [21] it is right not to eat meat or drink wine or do anything that makes your brother stumble.*v* [22] The faith that you have, keep between yourself and God; happy is he who has no reason to judge himself for what he approves. [23] But he who has doubts is condemned, if he eats, because he does not act from faith; for whatever does not proceed from faith is sin.*w*

15 We who are strong ought to bear with the failings of the weak, and not to please ourselves; [2] let each of us please his neighbor for his good, to edify him. [3] For Christ did not please himself; but, as it is written, "The reproaches of those who reproached thee fell on me." [4] For whatever was written in former days was written for our instruction, that by steadfastness and by the encouragement of the scriptures we might have hope. [5] May the God of

v Many ancient authorities add *or be upset or be weakened.*
w Many authorities, some ancient, insert here ch. 16. 25–27.
14. 13: Mt. 7. 1; 1 Cor. 8. 13.   **14. 15:** Rom. 14. 20; 1 Cor. 8. 11.   **14. 16:** 1 Cor. 10. 30.
14. 19: Mk. 9. 50; Rom. 12. 18; 1 Thess. 5. 11.   **14. 20:** Rom. 14. 15; 1 Cor. 8. 9–12.
14. 21: 1 Cor. 8. 13.   **14. 22:** Rom. 2. 1.
15. 3: Ps. 69. 9.   **15. 4:** Rom. 4. 23–24; 1 Cor. 9. 10; 2 Tim. 3. 16.   **15. 5:** Rom. 12. 16;
1 Cor. 1. 10; 2 Cor. 13. 11; Phil. 2. 2; 4. 2.

steadfastness and encouragement grant you to live in such harmony with one another, in accord with Christ Jesus, [6] that together you may with one voice glorify the God and Father of our Lord Jesus Christ.

7 Welcome one another, therefore, as Christ has welcomed you, for the glory of God. [8] For I tell you that Christ became a servant to the circumcised to show God's truthfulness, in order to confirm the promises given to the patriarchs, [9] and in order that the Gentiles might glorify God for his mercy. As it is written,

> "Therefore I will praise thee among the Gentiles,
>   and sing to thy name";

[10] and again it is said,

> "Rejoice, O Gentiles, with his people";

[11] and again,

> "Praise the Lord, all Gentiles,
>   and let all the peoples praise him";

[12] and further Isaiah says,

> "The root of Jesse shall come,
>   he who rises to rule the Gentiles;
>   in him shall the Gentiles hope."

[13] May the God of hope fill you with all joy and peace in believing, so that by the power of the Holy Spirit you may abound in hope.

14 I myself am satisfied about you, my brethren, that you yourselves are full of goodness, filled with all knowledge, and able to instruct one another. [15] But on some points I have written to you very boldly by way of reminder, because of the grace given me by God [16] to be a minister of Christ Jesus to the Gentiles in the priestly service of the gospel of God, so that the offering of the Gentiles may be acceptable, consecrated by the Holy Spirit. [17] In Christ

15. 9: Ps. 18. 49; 2 Sam. 22. 50.   **15. 10:** Deut. 32. 43.   **15. 11:** Ps. 117. 1.
15. 12: Is. 11. 10; Mt. 12. 21.   **15. 16:** Acts 9. 15.

Jesus, then, I have reason to be proud of my work for God.
[18] For I will not venture to speak of anything except what
Christ has wrought through me to win obedience from the
Gentiles, by word and deed, [19] by the power of signs and
wonders, by the power of the Holy Spirit, so that from
Jerusalem and as far round as Il-lyr'i-cum I have fully
preached the gospel of Christ, [20] thus making it my ambition
to preach the gospel, not where Christ has already been
named, lest I build on another man's foundation, [21] but
as it is written,

> "They shall see who have never been told of him,
>> and they shall understand who have never heard of
>> him."

22 This is the reason why I have so often been hindered
from coming to you. [23] But now, since I no longer have
any room for work in these regions, and since I have
longed for many years to come to you, [24] I hope to see you
in passing as I go to Spain, and to be sped on my journey
there by you, once I have enjoyed your company for a little.
[25] At present, however, I am going to Jerusalem with aid
for the saints. [26] For Mac-e-do'ni-a and A-cha'ia have been
pleased to make some contribution for the poor among the
saints at Jerusalem; [27] they were pleased to do it, and indeed
they are in debt to them, for if the Gentiles have come to
share in their spiritual blessings, they ought also to be of
service to them in material blessings. [28] When therefore I
have completed this, and have delivered to them what has
been raised,[x] I shall go on by way of you to Spain; [29] and
I know that when I come to you I shall come in the fullness
of the blessing[y] of Christ.

[x] Greek *sealed to them this fruit.*   [y] Some ancient authorities insert *of the gospel.*

15. 18: Rom. 1. 5; Acts 15. 12; 21. 19.   **15. 19:** Acts 19. 11; 2 Cor. 12. 12.   **15. 20:** 2 Cor.
10. 15–16.   **15. 21:** Is. 52. 15.   **15. 22:** Rom. 1. 13.   **15. 23:** Acts 19. 21; Rom. 1. 10–11;
15. 32.   **15. 24:** Rom. 15. 28.   **15. 25:** Acts 19. 21; 24. 17; 15. 31.   **15. 26:** 2 Cor. 8. 1–5;
9. 2; 1 Thess. 1. 7f.   **15. 27:** 1 Cor. 9. 11.   **15. 28:** Rom. 15. 24.   **15. 29:** Acts 19. 21.

30 I appeal to you, brethren, by our Lord Jesus Christ and by the love of the Spirit, to strive together with me in your prayers to God on my behalf, [31] that I may be delivered from the unbelievers in Judea, and that my service for Jerusalem may be acceptable to the saints, [32] so that by God's will I may come to you with joy and be refreshed in your company. [33] The God of peace be with you all. Amen.

16 I commend to you our sister Phoebe, a deaconess of the church at Cen'chre-ae, [2] that you may receive her in the Lord as befits the saints, and help her in whatever she may require from you, for she has been a helper of many and of myself as well.

3 Greet Pris'ca and Aquila, my fellow workers in Christ Jesus, [4] who risked their necks for my life, to whom not only I but also all the churches of the Gentiles give thanks; [5] greet also the church in their house. Greet my beloved E-pae'ne-tus, who was the first convert in Asia for Christ. [6] Greet Mary, who has worked hard among you. [7] Greet An-dron'i-cus and Ju'ni-as, my kinsmen and my fellow prisoners; they are men of note among the apostles, and they were in Christ before me. [8] Greet Am-pli-a'tus, my beloved in the Lord. [9] Greet Ur-ba'nus, our fellow worker in Christ, and my beloved Sta'chys. [10] Greet A-pel'les, who is approved in Christ. Greet those who belong to the family of A-ris-tob'u-lus. [11] Greet my kinsman He-ro'di-on. Greet those in the Lord who belong to the family of Nar-cis'sus. [12] Greet those workers in the Lord, Try-phae'na and Try-pho'sa. Greet the beloved Persis, who has worked hard in the Lord. [13] Greet Rufus, eminent in the Lord, also his mother and mine. [14] Greet A-syn'cri-tus,

15. 31: 2 Thess. 3. 2; Rom. 15. 25–26; 2 Cor. 8. 4; 9. 1.   **15. 32:** Rom. 1. 10; Acts 19. 21.
15. 33: 2 Cor. 13. 11; Phil. 4. 9.
16. 3: Acts 18. 2.   **16. 5:** 1 Cor. 16. 19.

Phle'gon, Her'mes, Pat'ro-bas, Her'mas, and the brethren who are with them. [15] Greet Phi-lol'o-gus, Julia, Ne'reus and his sister, and O-lym'pas, and all the saints who are with them. [16] Greet one another with a holy kiss. All the churches of Christ greet you.

17 I appeal to you, brethren, to take note of those who create dissensions and difficulties, in opposition to the doctrine which you have been taught; avoid them. [18] For such persons do not serve our Lord Christ, but their own appetites,[z] and by fair and flattering words they deceive the hearts of the simple-minded. [19] For while your obedience is known to all, so that I rejoice over you, I would have you wise as to what is good and guileless as to what is evil; [20] then the God of peace will soon crush Satan under your feet. The grace of our Lord Jesus Christ be with you.[a]

21 Timothy, my fellow worker, greets you; so do Lucius and Jason and So-sip'a-ter, my kinsmen.

22 I Ter'tius, the writer of this letter, greet you in the Lord.

23 Ga'ius, who is host to me and to the whole church, greets you. E-ras'tus, the city treasurer, and our brother Quartus, greet you.[b]

25 Now to him who is able to strengthen you according to my gospel and the preaching of Jesus Christ, according to the revelation of the mystery which was kept secret for long ages [26] but is now disclosed and through the prophetic writings is made known to all nations, according to the command of the eternal God, to bring about obedience to the faith — [27] to the only wise God be glory for evermore through Jesus Christ! Amen.

[z] Greek *their own belly* (Phil. 3. 19).   [a] Many ancient authorities omit this sentence.
[b] Some ancient authorities insert verse 24, *The grace of our Lord Jesus Christ be with you all. Amen.*

16. 16: 2 Cor. 13. 12; 1 Thess. 5. 26; 1 Pet. 5. 14.   **16. 17:** Gal. 1. 8–9; 2 Thess. 3. 6, 14; 2 Jn. 10.   **16. 19:** Rom. 1. 8; 1 Cor. 14. 20.   **16. 20:** 1 Cor. 16. 23; 2 Cor. 13. 14; Gal. 6. 18; Phil. 4. 23; 1 Thess. 5. 28; 2 Thess. 3. 18; Rev. 22. 21.   **16. 21:** Acts 16. 1. **16. 23:** 1 Cor. 1. 14.

THE FIRST LETTER OF PAUL TO THE
CORINTHIANS

1 Paul, called by the will of God to be an apostle of Christ Jesus, and our brother Sos'the-nes,

2 To the church of God which is at Corinth, to those consecrated in Christ Jesus, called to be saints together with all those who in every place call on the name of our Lord Jesus Christ, both their Lord and ours:

3 Grace to you and peace from God our Father and the Lord Jesus Christ.

4 I give thanks to God[a] always for you because of the grace of God which was given you in Christ Jesus, [5] that in every way you were enriched in him with all speech and all knowledge — [6] even as the testimony to Christ was confirmed among you — [7] so that you are not lacking in any spiritual gift, as you wait for the revealing of our Lord Jesus Christ; [8] who will sustain you to the end, guiltless in the day of our Lord Jesus Christ. [9] God is faithful, by whom you were called into the fellowship of his Son, Jesus Christ our Lord.

10 I appeal to you, brethren, by the name of our Lord Jesus Christ, that all of you agree and that there be no dissensions among you, but that you be united in the same mind and the same judgment. [11] For it has been reported to me by Chlo'e's people that there is quarreling among you, my brethren. [12] What I mean is that each one of you says, "I belong to Paul," or "I belong to A-pol'los," or "I belong to Ce'phas," or "I belong to Christ." [13] Is Christ

---

[a] Many ancient authorities read *my God*.

1. 1: Rom. 1. 1; Acts 18. 17.   **1. 2:** Acts 18. 1.   **1. 3:** Rom. 1. 7.   **1. 4:** Rom. 1. 8.
1. 8: 1 Cor. 5. 5; 2 Cor. 1. 14.   **1. 9:** Rom. 8. 28; 1 Jn. 1. 3.   **1. 12:** 1 Cor. 3. 4;
Acts 18. 24; 1 Cor. 3. 22; Jn. 1. 42; 1 Cor. 9. 5; 15. 5.   **1. 13:** Mt. 28. 19; Acts 2. 38.

divided? Was Paul crucified for you? Or were you baptized in the name of Paul? [14] I am thankful[b] that I baptized none of you except Crispus and Ga′ius; [15] lest any one should say that you were baptized in my name. [16] (I did baptize also the household of Steph′a-nas. Beyond that, I do not know whether I baptized any one else.) [17] For Christ did not send me to baptize but to preach the gospel, and not with eloquent wisdom, lest the cross of Christ be emptied of its power.

18 For the word of the cross is folly to those who are perishing, but to us who are being saved it is the power of God. [19] For it is written,

"I will destroy the wisdom of the wise,
    and the cleverness of the clever I will thwart."

[20] Where is the wise man? Where is the scribe? Where is the debater of this age? Has not God made foolish the wisdom of the world? [21] For since, in the wisdom of God, the world did not know God through wisdom, it pleased God through the folly of what we preach to save those who believe. [22] For Jews demand signs and Greeks seek wisdom, [23] but we preach Christ crucified, a stumbling-block to Jews and folly to Gentiles, [24] but to those who are called, both Jews and Greeks, Christ the power of God and the wisdom of God. [25] For the foolishness of God is wiser than men, and the weakness of God is stronger than men.

26 For consider your call, brethren; not many of you were wise according to worldly standards, not many were powerful, not many were of noble birth; [27] but God chose what is foolish in the world to shame the wise, God chose what is weak in the world to shame the strong, [28] God chose what is low and despised in the world, even things that are not,

[b] A few ancient authorities read *I thank God.*

1. 14: Acts 18. 8; Rom. 16. 23.   1. 16: 1 Cor. 16. 15.   1. 17: Jn. 4. 2; Acts 10. 48; 1 Cor. 2. 1; 4, 13.   1. 19: Is. 29. 14.   1. 22: Mt. 12. 38.   1. 23: 1 Cor. 2. 2; Gal. 3. 1; 5. 11.   1. 27: Jas. 2. 5.   1. 28: Rom. 4. 17.

to bring to nothing things that are, [29] so that no human being might boast in the presence of God. [30] He is the source of your life in Christ Jesus, whom God made our wisdom, our righteousness and consecration and redemption; [31] therefore, as it is written, "Let him who boasts, boast of the Lord."

2 When I came to you, brethren, I did not come proclaiming to you the testimony[c] of God in lofty words or wisdom. [2] For I decided to know nothing among you except Jesus Christ and him crucified. [3] And I was with you in weakness and in much fear and trembling; [4] and my speech and my message were not in plausible words of wisdom, but in demonstration of the Spirit and power, [5] that your faith might not rest in the wisdom of men but in the power of God.

6 Yet among the mature we do impart wisdom, although it is not a wisdom of this age or of the rulers of this age, who are doomed to pass away. [7] But we impart a secret and hidden wisdom of God, which God decreed before the ages for our glorification. [8] None of the rulers of this age understood this; for if they had, they would not have crucified the Lord of glory. [9] But, as it is written,

"What no eye has seen, nor ear heard,

nor the heart of man conceived,

what God has prepared for those who love him,"

[10] God has revealed to us through the Spirit. For the Spirit searches everything, even the depths of God. [11] For what person knows a man's thoughts except the spirit of the man which is in him? So also no one comprehends the

---

[c] Many ancient authorities read *mystery* (or *secret*).

1. 29: Eph. 2. 9.   **1. 30:** 1 Cor. 4. 15; Rom. 8. 1; 2 Cor. 5. 21; 1 Cor. 6. 11; 1 Thess. 5. 23; Eph. 1. 7, 14; Col. 1. 14; Rom. 3. 24.   **1. 31:** Jer. 9. 24; 2 Cor. 10. 17.
2. 1: 1 Cor. 1. 17.   **2. 2:** Gal. 6. 14; 1 Cor. 1. 23.   **2. 3:** Acts 18. 1, 6, 12; 1 Cor. 4. 10; 2 Cor. 11. 30.   **2. 4:** Rom. 15. 19; 1 Cor. 4. 20.   **2. 5:** 2 Cor. 4. 7; 6. 7; 1 Cor. 12. 9.   **2. 6:** Eph. 4. 13.   **2. 7:** Rom. 8. 29–30.   **2. 8:** Acts 7. 2; Jas. 2. 1. **2. 9:** Is. 64. 4; 65. 17.   **2. 10:** Mt. 11. 25; 13. 11; 16. 17; Eph. 3. 3, 5.

thoughts of God except the Spirit of God. [12] Now we have received not the spirit of the world, but the Spirit which is from God, that we might understand the gifts bestowed on us by God. [13] And we impart this in words not taught by human wisdom but taught by the Spirit, interpreting spiritual truths to those who possess the Spirit.[d]

14 The unspiritual[e] man does not receive the gifts of the Spirit of God, for they are folly to him, and he is not able to understand them because they are spiritually discerned. [15] The spiritual man judges all things, but is himself to be judged by no one. [16] "For who has known the mind of the Lord so as to instruct him?" But we have the mind of Christ.

3 But I, brethren, could not address you as spiritual men, but as men of the flesh, as babes in Christ. [2] I fed you with milk, not solid food; for you were not ready for it; and even yet you are not ready, [3] for you are still of the flesh. For while there is jealousy and strife among you, are you not of the flesh, and behaving like ordinary men? [4] For when one says, "I belong to Paul," and another, "I belong to A-pol'los," are you not merely men?

5 What then is A-pol'los? What is Paul? Servants through whom you believed, as the Lord assigned to each. [6] I planted, A-pol'los watered, but God gave the growth. [7] So neither he who plants nor he who waters is anything, but only God who gives the growth. [8] He who plants and he who waters are equal, and each shall receive his wages according to his labor. [9] For we are fellow workmen for God; you are God's field, God's building.

10 According to the commission of God given to me, like

---

[d] Or *interpreting spiritual truths in spiritual language;* or *comparing spiritual things with spiritual.*   [e] Or *natural.*

2. 12: Rom. 8. 15.   **2. 13:** 1 Cor. 1. 17.   **2. 14:** 1 Cor. 1. 18; Jas. 3. 15.
2. 15: 1 Cor. 3. 1; 14. 37; Gal. 6. 1.   **2. 16:** Is. 40. 13; Rom. 11. 34.
3. 1: Rom. 7. 14; Heb. 5. 13.   **3. 2:** Heb. 5. 12–13; 1 Pet. 2. 2.   **3. 4:** 1 Cor. 1. 12.
3. 5: 2 Cor. 6. 4; Eph. 3. 7; Col. 1. 25.   **3. 6:** Acts 18. 4–11, 24–27; 1 Cor. 1. 12.
3. 9: Is. 61. 3; Eph. 2. 20–22; 1 Pet. 2. 5.   **3. 10:** Rom. 12. 3; 1 Cor. 15. 10.

a skilled master-builder I laid a foundation, and another man is building upon it. Let each man take care how he builds upon it. [11] For no other foundation can any one lay than that which is laid, which is Jesus Christ. [12] Now if any one builds on the foundation with gold, silver, precious stones, wood, hay, stubble — [13] each man's work will become manifest; for the Day will disclose it, because it will be revealed with fire, and the fire will test what sort of work each one has done. [14] If the work which any man has built on the foundation survives, he will receive a reward. [15] If any man's work is burned up, he will suffer loss, though he himself will be saved, but only as through fire.

16 Do you not know that you are God's temple and that God's Spirit dwells in you? [17] If any one destroys God's temple, God will destroy him. For God's temple is holy, and that temple you are.

18 Let no one deceive himself. If any one among you thinks that he is wise in this age, let him become a fool that he may become wise. [19] For the wisdom of this world is folly with God. For it is written, "He catches the wise in their craftiness," [20] and again, "The Lord knows that the thoughts of the wise are futile." [21] So let no one boast of men. For all things are yours, [22] whether Paul or A-pol′los or Ce′phas or the world or life or death or the present or the future, all are yours; [23] and you are Christ's; and Christ is God's.

4 This is how one should regard us, as servants of Christ and stewards of the mysteries of God. [2] Moreover it is required of stewards that they be found trustworthy. [3] But with me it is a very small thing that I should be judged by you or by any human court. I do not even judge myself.

3. 11: Eph. 2. 20.　　**3. 13:** 2 Thess. 1. 7–10.　　**3. 15:** Job 23. 10.　　**3. 16:** 1 Cor. 6. 19; 2 Cor. 6. 16.　　**3. 18:** Is. 5. 21; 1 Cor. 8. 2; Gal. 6. 3.　　**3. 19:** Job. 5. 13; 1 Cor. 1. 20. **3. 20:** Ps. 94. 11.　　**3. 21:** 1 Cor. 4. 6; Rom. 8. 32.　　**3. 22:** 1 Cor. 1. 12; Rom. 8. 38. **4. 1:** 1 Cor. 9. 17; Rom. 11. 25; 16. 25.

⁴ I am not aware of anything against myself, but I am not thereby acquitted. It is the Lord who judges me. ⁵ Therefore do not pronounce judgment before the time, before the Lord comes, who will bring to light the things now hidden in darkness and will disclose the purpose of men's hearts. Then every man will receive his commendation from God.

6 I have applied all this to myself and A-pol'los for your benefit, brethren, that you may learn by us to live according to scripture, that none of you may be puffed up in favor of one against another. ⁷ For who sees anything different in you? What have you that you did not receive? If then you received it, why do you boast as if it were not a gift?

8 Already you are filled! Already you have become rich! Without us you have become kings! And would that you did reign, so that we might share the rule with you! ⁹ For I think that God has exhibited us apostles as last of all, like men sentenced to death; because we have become a spectacle to the world, to angels and to men. ¹⁰ We are fools for Christ's sake, but you are wise in Christ. We are weak, but you are strong. You are held in honor, but we in disrepute. ¹¹ To the present hour we hunger and thirst, we are ill-clad and buffeted and homeless, ¹² and we labor, working with our own hands. When reviled, we bless; when persecuted, we endure; ¹³ when slandered, we try to conciliate; we have become, and are now, as the refuse of the world, the offscouring of all things.

14 I do not write this to make you ashamed, but to admonish you as my beloved children. ¹⁵ For though you have countless guides in Christ, you do not have many fathers. For I became your father in Christ Jesus through the gospel.

4. 4: 2 Cor. 1. 12.   4. 5: Rom. 2. 16; 1 Cor. 3. 13; 2 Cor. 10. 18; Rom. 2. 29.
4. 6: 1 Cor. 1. 19, 31; 3. 19–20; 1. 12; 3. 4.   4. 9: 1 Cor. 15. 31; 2 Cor. 11. 23; Rom.
8. 36; Heb. 10. 33.   4. 10: 1 Cor. 1. 18; 2 Cor. 11. 19; 1 Cor. 3. 18; 2 Cor. 13. 9;
1 Cor. 2. 3.   4. 11: Rom. 8. 35; 2 Cor. 11. 23–27.   4. 12: Acts 18. 3; 1 Pet. 3. 9.
4. 15: 1 Cor. 1. 30; Philem. 10.

¹⁶ I urge you, then, be imitators of me. ¹⁷ Therefore I sent to you Timothy, my beloved and faithful child in the Lord, to remind you of my ways in Christ, as I teach them everywhere in every church. ¹⁸ Some are arrogant, as though I were not coming to you. ¹⁹ But I will come to you soon, if the Lord wills, and I will find out not the talk of these arrogant people but their power. ²⁰ For the kingdom of God does not consist in talk but in power. ²¹ What do you wish? Shall I come to you with a rod, or with love in a spirit of gentleness?

5 It is actually reported that there is immorality among you, and of a kind that is not found even among pagans; for a man is living with his father's wife. ² And you are arrogant! Ought you not rather to mourn? Let him who has done this be removed from among you.

3 For though absent in body I am present in spirit, and as if present, I have already pronounced judgment ⁴ in the name of the Lord Jesus on the man who has done such a thing. When you are assembled, and my spirit is present, with the power of our Lord Jesus, ⁵ you are to deliver this man to Satan for the destruction of the flesh, that his spirit may be saved in the day of the Lord Jesus.ᶠ

6 Your boasting is not good. Do you not know that a little leaven ferments the whole lump of dough? ⁷ Cleanse out the old leaven that you may be fresh dough, as you really are unleavened. For Christ, our paschal lamb, has been sacrificed. ⁸ Let us, therefore, celebrate the festival, not with the old leaven, the leaven of malice and evil, but with the unleavened bread of sincerity and truth.

ᶠ Some ancient authorities omit *Jesus*.

4. 17: 1 Cor. 16. 10; Acts 16. 1; 1 Cor. 7. 17.   4. 21: 2 Cor. 1. 23.
5. 1: Deut. 22. 30; 27. 20.   5. 3: Col. 2. 5.   5. 4: 2 Thess. 3. 6.   5. 5: Mt. 4. 10;
1 Cor. 1. 8.   5. 6: Gal. 5. 9.   5. 8: Ex. 12. 19; 13. 7; Deut. 16. 3.

9 I wrote to you in my letter not to associate with immoral men; [10] not at all meaning the immoral of this world, or the greedy and robbers, or idolaters, since then you would need to go out of the world. [11] But rather I wrote to you not to associate with any one who bears the name of brother if he is guilty of immorality or greed, or is an idolater, reviler, drunkard, or robber — not even to eat with such a one. [12] For what have I to do with judging outsiders? Is it not those inside the church whom you are to judge? [13] God judges those outside. Drive out the wicked person from among you.

6 When one of you has a grievance against a brother, does he dare go to law before the unrighteous instead of the saints? [2] Do you not know that the saints will judge the world? And if the world is to be judged by you, are you incompetent to try trivial cases? [3] Do you not know that we are to judge angels? How much more, matters pertaining to this life! [4] If then you have such cases, why do you lay them before those who are least esteemed by the church? [5] I say this to your shame. Can it be that there is no man among you wise enough to decide between members of the brotherhood, [6] but brother goes to law against brother, and that before unbelievers?

7 To have lawsuits at all with one another is defeat for you. Why not rather suffer wrong? Why not rather be defrauded? [8] But you yourselves wrong and defraud, and that even your own brethren.

9 Do you not know that the unrighteous will not inherit the kingdom of God? Do not be deceived; neither the immoral, nor idolaters, nor adulterers, nor homosexuals,[g] [10] nor thieves, nor the greedy, nor drunkards, nor revilers, nor robbers will inherit the kingdom of God. [11] And such

[g] Two Greek words are rendered by this expression.

5. 9: 2 Cor. 6. 14.   **5. 10:** 1 Cor. 10. 27.   **5. 11:** 2 Thess. 3. 6; 1 Cor. 10. 7, 14, 20–21.
5. 12: Mk. 4. 11.   **5. 13:** 1 Cor. 5. 2.
6. 1: Mt. 18. 17.   **6. 7:** Mt. 5. 39–40.   **6. 9:** 1 Cor. 15. 50.   **6. 11:** Acts 22. 16; Rom. 8. 30.

were some of you. But you were washed, you were consecrated, you were justified in the name of the Lord Jesus
Christ and in the Spirit of our God.

12 "All things are lawful for me," but not all things are
helpful. "All things are lawful for me," but I will not be
enslaved by anything. [13] "Food is meant for the stomach
and the stomach for food" — and God will destroy both one
and the other. The body is not meant for immorality, but
for the Lord, and the Lord for the body. [14] And God raised
the Lord and will also raise us up by his power. [15] Do you
not know that your bodies are members of Christ? Shall I
therefore take the members of Christ and make them members of a prostitute? Never! [16] Do you not know that he who
joins himself to a prostitute becomes one body with her?
For, as it is written, "The two shall become one."
[17] But he who is united to the Lord becomes one Spirit with
him. [18] Shun immorality. Every other sin which a man
commits is outside the body; but the immoral man sins
against his own body. [19] Do you not know that your body is
a temple of the Holy Spirit within you, which you have
from God? You are not your own; [20] you were bought with
a price. So glorify God in your body.

7 Now concerning the matters about which you wrote.
It is well for a man not to touch a woman. [2] But because of the temptation to immorality, each man should
have his own wife and each woman her own husband. [3] The
husband should give to his wife her conjugal rights, and
likewise the wife to her husband. [4] For the wife does not
rule over her own body, but the husband does; likewise
the husband does not rule over his own body, but the wife

6. 12: 1 Cor. 10. 23.   **6. 15:** Rom. 12. 5; 1 Cor. 12. 27.   **6. 16:** Gen. 2. 24; Mt.
19. 5; Mk. 10. 8; Eph. 5. 31.   **6. 17:** Jn. 17. 21–23; Rom. 8. 9; Gal. 2. 20.
6. 19: Jn. 2. 21.   **6. 20:** 1 Cor. 7. 23; Acts 20. 28; Rom. 12. 1.

does. ⁵ Do not refuse one another except perhaps by agreement for a season, that you may devote yourselves to prayer; but then come together again, lest Satan tempt you through lack of self-control. ⁶ I say this by way of concession, not of command. ⁷ I wish that all were as I myself am. But each has his own special gift from God, one of one kind and one of another.

8 To the unmarried and the widows I say that it is well for them to remain single as I do. ⁹ But if they cannot exercise self-control, they should marry. For it is better to marry than to be aflame with passion.

10 To the married I give charge, not I but the Lord, that the wife should not separate from her husband ¹¹ (but if she does, let her remain single or else be reconciled to her husband) — and that the husband should not divorce his wife.

12 To the rest I say, not the Lord, that if any brother has a wife who is an unbeliever, and she consents to live with him, he should not divorce her. ¹³ If any woman has a husband who is an unbeliever, and he consents to live with her, she should not divorce him. ¹⁴ For the unbelieving husband is consecrated through his wife, and the unbelieving wife is consecrated through her husband. Otherwise, your children would be unclean, but as it is they are holy. ¹⁵ But if the unbelieving partner desires to separate, let it be so; in such a case the brother or sister is not bound. For God has called us*ʰ* to peace. ¹⁶ Wife, how do you know whether you will save your husband? Husband, how do you know whether you will save your wife?

17 Only, let every one lead the life which the Lord has assigned to him, and in which God has called him. This is my rule in all the churches. ¹⁸ Was any one at the time

---

ʰ Many ancient authorities read *you.*

7. 5: Ex. 19. 15.   **7. 7:** 1 Cor. 7. 8; 9. 5.   **7. 9:** 1 Tim. 5. 14.   **7. 12:** 2 Cor. 11. 17.
7. 16: 1 Pet. 3. 1.   **7. 17:** Rom. 12. 3; 1 Cor. 14. 33; 2 Cor. 8. 18; 11. 28.
7. 18: 1 Macc. 1. 15; Acts 15. 1f.

of his call already circumcised? Let him not seek to remove the marks of circumcision. Was any one at the time of his call uncircumcised? Let him not seek circumcision. ¹⁹ For neither circumcision counts for anything nor uncircumcision, but keeping the commandments of God. ²⁰ Every one should remain in the state in which he was called. ²¹ Were you a slave when called? Never mind. But if you can gain your freedom, avail yourself of the opportunity. ²² For he who was called in the Lord as a slave is a freedman of the Lord. Likewise he who was free when called is a slave of Christ. ²³ You were bought with a price; do not become slaves of men. ²⁴ So, brethren, in whatever state each was called, there let him remain with God.

25 Now concerning the unmarried, I have no command of the Lord, but I give my opinion as one who by the Lord's mercy is trustworthy. ²⁶ I think that in view of the impending*ⁱ* distress it is well for a person to remain as he is. ²⁷ Are you bound to a wife? Do not seek to be free. Are you free from a wife? Do not seek marriage. ²⁸ But if you marry, you do not sin, and if a girl marries she does not sin. Yet those who marry will have worldly troubles, and I would spare you that. ²⁹ I mean, brethren, the appointed time has grown very short; from now on, let those who have wives live as though they had none, ³⁰ and those who mourn as though they were not mourning, and those who rejoice as though they were not rejoicing, and those who buy as though they had no goods, ³¹ and those who deal with the world as though they had no dealings with it. For the form of this world is passing away.

32 I want you to be free from all anxieties. The unmarried man is anxious about the affairs of the Lord, how to please

---

ⁱ Or *present.*

7. 19: Gal. 5. 6; 6. 15; Rom. 2. 25.   **7. 22**: Jn. 8. 32, 36.   **7. 23**: 1 Cor. 6. 20.
7. 29: Rom. 13. 11–12; 1 Cor. 7. 31.   **7. 32**: 1 Tim. 5. 5.

the Lord; [33] but the married man is anxious about worldly affairs, how to please his wife, [34] and his interests are divided. And the unmarried woman or girl is anxious about the affairs of the Lord, how to be consecrated in body and spirit; but the married woman is anxious about worldly affairs, how to please her husband. [35] I say this for your own benefit, not to lay any restraint upon you, but to promote good order and to secure your undivided devotion to the Lord.

36 If any one thinks that he is not behaving properly toward his betrothed, if his passions are strong, and if it has to be, let him do what he will, he does not sin; let them marry. [37] But whoever is firmly established in his heart, being under no necessity but having his desire under control, and has determined this in his heart, to keep her as his betrothed, he will do well. [38] So that he who marries his betrothed does well; and he who refrains from marriage will do better.

39 A wife is bound to her husband as long as he lives. If the husband dies, she is free to be married to whom she wishes, only in the Lord. [40] But in my judgment she is happier if she remains as she is. And I think that I have the Spirit of God.

8 Now concerning food offered to idols: we know that "all of us possess knowledge." "Knowledge" puffs up, but love builds up. [2] If any one imagines that he knows something, he does not yet know as he ought to know. [3] But if one loves God, one is known by him.

4 Hence, as to the eating of food offered to idols, we know that "an idol has no real existence," and that "there is no God but one." [5] For although there may be so-called gods

7. 39: Rom. 7. 2.　　**7. 40:** 1 Cor. 7. 25.
8. 1: Rom. 15. 14.　　**8. 2:** 1 Cor. 3. 18; 13. 8, 9, 12.　　**8. 3:** Gal. 4. 9; Rom. 8. 29.
8. 4: 1 Cor. 10. 19; Deut. 6. 4.

in heaven or on earth — as indeed there are many "gods" and many "lords" — ⁶ yet for us there is one God, the Father, from whom are all things and for whom we exist, and one Lord, Jesus Christ, through whom are all things and through whom we exist.

7 However, not all possess this knowledge. But some, through being hitherto accustomed to idols, eat food as really offered to an idol; and their conscience, being weak, is defiled. ⁸ Food will not commend us to God. We are no worse off if we do not eat, and no better off if we do. ⁹ Only take care lest this liberty of yours somehow become a stumbling-block to the weak. ¹⁰ For if any one sees you, a man of knowledge, at table in an idol's temple, might he not be encouraged, if his conscience is weak, to eat food offered to idols? ¹¹ And so by your knowledge this weak man is destroyed, the brother for whom Christ died. ¹² Thus, sinning against your brethren and wounding their conscience when it is weak, you sin against Christ. ¹³ Therefore, if food is a cause of my brother's falling, I will never eat meat, lest I cause my brother to fall.

9 Am I not free? Am I not an apostle? Have I not seen Jesus our Lord? Are not you my workmanship in the Lord? ² If to others I am not an apostle, at least I am to you; for you are the seal of my apostleship in the Lord.

3 This is my defense to those who would examine me. ⁴ Do we not have the right to our food and drink? ⁵ Do we not have the right to be accompanied by a wife,ʲ as the other apostles and the brothers of the Lord and Ce′phas? ⁶ Or is it only Barnabas and I who have no right to refrain

---

ʲ Greek *a sister as wife.*
8. 6: Mal. 2. 10; Eph. 4. 6; Rom. 11. 36; 1 Cor. 1. 2; Eph. 4. 5; Jn. 1. 3; Col. 1. 16. 8. 7: 1 Cor. 8. 4–5.   8. 8: Rom. 14. 17.   8. 9: 1 Cor. 8. 10–11; Rom. 14. 1. 8. 11: Rom. 14. 15, 20.   8. 12: Mt. 18. 6; Rom. 14. 20.   8. 13: Rom. 14. 21. 9. 1: 1 Cor. 9. 19; 2 Cor. 12. 12; 1 Thess. 2. 6; Acts 9. 3, 17; 1 Cor. 15. 8.   9. 4: 1 Cor. 9. 14.   9. 5: 1 Cor. 7. 7–8; Mt. 12. 46; 8. 14; Jn. 1. 42.   9. 6: Acts 4. 36.

from working for a living? ⁷ Who serves as a soldier at his own expense? Who plants a vineyard without eating any of its fruit? Who tends a flock without getting some of the milk?

8 Do I say this on human authority? Does not the law say the same? ⁹ For it is written in the law of Moses, "You shall not muzzle an ox when it is treading out the grain." Is it for oxen that God is concerned? ¹⁰ Does he not speak entirely for our sake? It was written for our sake, because the plowman should plow in hope and the thresher thresh in hope of a share in the crop. ¹¹ If we have sown spiritual good among you, is it too much if we reap your material benefits? ¹² If others share this rightful claim upon you, do not we still more?

Nevertheless, we have not made use of this right, but we endure anything rather than put an obstacle in the way of the gospel of Christ. ¹³ Do you not know that those who are employed in the temple service get their food from the temple, and those who serve at the altar share in the sacrificial offerings? ¹⁴ In the same way, the Lord commanded that those who proclaim the gospel should get their living by the gospel.

15 But I have made no use of any of these rights, nor am I writing this to secure any such provision. For I would rather die than have any one deprive me of my ground for boasting. ¹⁶ For if I preach the gospel, that gives me no ground for boasting. For necessity is laid upon me. Woe to me if I do not preach the gospel! ¹⁷ For if I do this of my own will, I have a reward; but if not of my own will, I am entrusted with a commission. ¹⁸ What then is my reward? Just this: that in my preaching I may make the gospel free of charge, not making full use of my right in the gospel.

9. 9: Deut. 25. 4; 1 Tim. 5. 18. **9. 10:** 2 Tim. 2. 6. **9. 11:** Rom. 15. 27. **9. 12:** 2 Cor. 6. 3. **9. 13:** Deut. 18. 1. **9. 14:** Mt. 10. 10; Lk. 10. 7-8. **9. 15:** 2 Cor. 11. 10. **9. 17:** 1 Cor. 4. 1; Gal. 2. 7. **9. 18:** 2 Cor. 11. 7.

19 For though I am free from all men, I have made myself a slave to all, that I might win the more. ²⁰ To the Jews I became as a Jew, in order to win Jews; to those under the law I became as one under the law — though not being myself under the law — that I might win those under the law. ²¹ To those outside the law I became as one outside the law — not being without law toward God but under the law of Christ — that I might win those outside the law. ²² To the weak I became weak, that I might win the weak. I have become all things to all men, that I might by all means save some. ²³ I do it all for the sake of the gospel, that I may share in its blessings.

24 Do you not know that in a race all the runners compete, but only one receives the prize? So run that you may obtain it. ²⁵ Every athlete exercises self-control in all things. They do it to receive a perishable wreath, but we an imperishable. ²⁶ Well, I do not run aimlessly, I do not box as one beating the air; ²⁷ but I pommel my body and subdue it, lest after preaching to others I myself should be disqualified.

10 I want you to know, brethren, that our fathers were all under the cloud, and all passed through the sea, ² and all were baptized into Moses in the cloud and in the sea, ³ and all ate the same supernatural*ᵏ* food ⁴ and all drank the same supernatural*ᵏ* drink. For they drank from the supernatural*ᵏ* Rock which followed them, and the Rock was Christ. ⁵ Nevertheless with most of them God was not pleased; for they were overthrown in the wilderness.

6 Now these things are warnings for us, not to desire evil

ᵏ Greek *spiritual.*

9. 20: Rom. 11. 14.   **9. 21:** Rom. 2. 12, 14.   **9. 22:** 2 Cor. 11. 29; Rom. 15. 1; 1 Cor. 10. 33; Rom. 11. 14.   **9. 24:** Heb. 12. 1.   **9. 25:** 2 Tim. 2. 5; 4. 8; Jas. 1. 12; 1 Pet. 5. 4. **10. 1:** Rom. 1. 13; Ex. 13. 21; 14. 22, 29.   **10. 2:** Rom. 6. 3; Gal. 3. 27.   **10. 3:** Ex. 16. 4, 35. **10. 4:** Ex. 17. 6; Num. 20. 11. **10. 5:** Num. 14. 29–30. **10. 6:** Num. 11. 4, 34.

as they did. ⁷ Do not be idolaters as some of them were; as it is written, "The people sat down to eat and drink and rose up to dance." ⁸ We must not indulge in immorality as some of them did, and twenty-three thousand fell in a single day. ⁹ We must not put the Lord¹ to the test, as some of them did and were destroyed by serpents; ¹⁰ nor grumble, as some of them did and were destroyed by the Destroyer. ¹¹ Now these things happened to them as a warning, but they were written down for our instruction, upon whom the end of the ages has come. ¹² Therefore let any one who thinks that he stands take heed lest he fall. ¹³ No temptation has overtaken you that is not common to man. God is faithful, and he will not let you be tempted beyond your strength, but with the temptation will also provide the way of escape, that you may be able to endure it.

14 Therefore, my beloved, shun the worship of idols. ¹⁵ I speak as to sensible men; judge for yourselves what I say. ¹⁶ The cup of blessing which we bless, is it not a participation*ᵐ* in the blood of Christ? The bread which we break, is it not a participation*ᵐ* in the body of Christ? ¹⁷ Because there is one loaf, we who are many are one body, for we all partake of the same loaf. ¹⁸ Consider the practice of Israel; are not those who eat the sacrifices partners in the altar? ¹⁹ What do I imply then? That food offered to idols is anything, or that an idol is anything? ²⁰ No, I imply that what pagans sacrifice they offer to demons and not to God. I do not want you to be partners with demons. ²¹ You cannot drink the cup of the Lord and the cup of demons. You cannot partake of the table of the Lord and the table of demons. ²² Shall we provoke the Lord to jealousy? Are we stronger than he?

---

¹ Some ancient authorities read *Christ*.   *ᵐ* Or *communion*.

10. 7: Ex. 32. 4, 6.   **10. 8:** Num. 25. 1–21.   **10. 9:** Num. 21. 5–6.   **10. 10:** Num. 16. 41, 49.   **10. 13:** 1 Cor. 1. 9.   **10. 14:** 1 Jn. 5. 21.   **10. 16:** Mt. 26. 27–28; Acts 2. 42.   **10. 17:** Rom. 12. 5.   **10. 18:** Lev. 7. 6.   **10. 20:** Deut. 32. 17. **10. 21:** 2 Cor. 6. 16.   **10. 22:** Deut. 32. 21; Eccl. 6. 10; Is. 45. 9.

23 "All things are lawful," but not all things are helpful. "All things are lawful," but not all things build up. ²⁴ Let no one seek his own good, but the good of his neighbor. ²⁵ Eat whatever is sold in the meat market without raising any question on the ground of conscience. ²⁶ For "the earth is the Lord's, and everything in it." ²⁷ If one of the unbelievers invites you to dinner and you are disposed to go, eat whatever is set before you without raising any question on the ground of conscience. ²⁸ (But if some one says to you, "This has been offered in sacrifice," then out of consideration for the man who informed you, and for conscience' sake — ²⁹ I mean his conscience, not yours — do not eat it.) For why should my liberty be determined by another man's scruples? ³⁰ If I partake with thankfulness, why am I denounced because of that for which I give thanks?

31 So, whether you eat or drink, or whatever you do, do all to the glory of God. ³² Give no offense to Jews or to Greeks or to the church of God, ³³ just as I try to please all men in everything I do, not seeking my own advantage,

11 but that of many, that they may be saved. ¹ Be imitators of me, as I am of Christ.

2 I commend you because you remember me in everything and maintain the traditions even as I have delivered them to you. ³ But I want you to understand that the head of every man is Christ, the head of a woman is her husband, and the head of Christ is God. ⁴ Any man who prays or prophesies with his head covered dishonors his head, ⁵ but any woman who prays or prophesies with her head unveiled dishonors her head — it is the same as if her head were shaven. ⁶ For if a woman will not veil herself,

10. 23: 1 Cor. 6. 12; Phil. 2. 21.   **10. 26:** Ps. 24. 1; 50. 12.   **10. 28:** 1 Cor. 8. 7, 10–12.
10. 32: 1 Cor. 8. 13.   **10. 33:** 1 Cor. 9. 22; Rom. 15. 2; 1 Cor. 13. 5.
11. 1: 1 Cor. 4. 16.   **11. 2:** 2 Thess. 2. 15.   **11. 3:** Eph. 1. 22; 4. 15; 5. 23; Col. 1. 8; 2. 19.   **11. 5:** Lk. 2. 36; Acts 21. 9; 1 Cor. 14. 34.

then she should cut off her hair; but if it is disgraceful for a woman to be shorn or shaven, let her wear a veil. [7] For a man ought not to cover his head, since he is the image and glory of God; but woman is the glory of man. [8] (For man was not made from woman, but woman from man. [9] Neither was man created for woman, but woman for man.) [10] That is why a woman ought to have a veil[n] on her head, because of the angels. [11] (Nevertheless, in the Lord woman is not independent of man nor man of woman; [12] for as woman was made from man, so man is now born of woman. And all things are from God.) [13] Judge for yourselves; is it proper for a woman to pray to God with her head uncovered? [14] Does not nature itself teach you that for a man to wear long hair is degrading to him, [15] but if a woman has long hair, it is her pride? For her hair is given to her for a covering. [16] If any one is disposed to be contentious, we recognize no other practice, nor do the churches of God.

17 But in the following instructions I do not commend you, because when you come together it is not for the better but for the worse. [18] For, in the first place, when you assemble as a church, I hear that there are divisions among you; and I partly believe it, [19] for there must be factions among you in order that those who are genuine among you may be recognized. [20] When you meet together, it is not the Lord's supper that you eat. [21] For in eating, each one goes ahead with his own meal, and one is hungry and another is drunk. [22] What! Do you not have houses to eat and drink in? Or do you despise the church of God and humiliate those who have nothing? What shall I say to you? Shall I commend you in this? No, I will not.

23 For I received from the Lord what I also delivered

[n] Greek *authority* (the veil being a symbol of this).

11. 7: Gen. 1. 26.   **11. 8:** Gen. 2. 21–23.   **11. 9:** Gen. 2. 18.   **11. 12:** 2 Cor. 5. 18; Rom. 11. 36.   **11. 16:** 1 Cor. 7. 17.   **11. 18:** 1 Cor. 1. 10.   **11. 23:** 1 Cor. 15. 3.   **11. 23–25:** Mt. 26. 26–28; Mk. 14. 22–24; Lk. 22. 17–19; 1 Cor. 10. 16.

to you, that the Lord Jesus on the night when he was betrayed took bread, [24] and when he had given thanks, he broke it, and said, "This is my body which is broken[o] for you. Do this in remembrance of me." [25] In the same way also the cup, after supper, saying, "This cup is the new covenant in my blood. Do this, as often as you drink it, in remembrance of me." [26] For as often as you eat this bread and drink the cup, you proclaim the Lord's death until he comes.

27 Whoever, therefore, eats the bread or drinks the cup of the Lord in an unworthy manner will be guilty of profaning the body and blood of the Lord. [28] Let a man examine himself, and so eat of the bread and drink of the cup. [29] For any one who eats and drinks without discerning the body eats and drinks judgment upon himself. [30] That is why many of you are weak and ill, and some have died.[p] [31] But if we judged ourselves truly, we should not be judged. [32] But when we are judged by the Lord, we are chastened[q] so that we may not be condemned along with the world.

33 So then, my brethren, when you come together to eat, wait for one another — [34] if any one is hungry, let him eat at home — lest you come together to be condemned. About the other things I will give directions when I come.

12 Now concerning spiritual gifts, brethren, I do not want you to be uninformed. [2] You know that when you were heathen, you were led astray to dumb idols, however you may have been moved. [3] Therefore I want you to understand that no one speaking by the Spirit of God ever says "Jesus be cursed!" and no one can say "Jesus is Lord" except by the Holy Spirit.

[o] Many ancient authorities omit *broken;* a few read *given.*
[p] Greek *have fallen asleep* (as in 15. 6, 20).
[q] Or *when we are judged we are being chastened by the Lord.*

11. 25: 2 Cor. 3. 6; Lk. 22. 20.	**11. 26:** 1 Cor. 4. 5.	**11. 32:** 1 Cor. 1. 20.
11. 34: 1 Cor. 4. 19.		
12. 2: Eph. 2. 11–12.	**12. 3:** Rom. 10. 9.	

4 Now there are varieties of gifts, but the same Spirit;
⁵ and there are varieties of service, but the same Lord; ⁶ and
there are varieties of working, but it is the same God who
inspires them all in every one. ⁷ To each is given the mani-
festation of the Spirit for the common good. ⁸ To one is given
through the Spirit the utterance of wisdom, and to another
the utterance of knowledge according to the same Spirit,
⁹ to another faith by the same Spirit, to another gifts of
healing by the one Spirit, ¹⁰ to another the working of miracles, to another prophecy, to another the ability to distinguish between spirits, to another various kinds of tongues,
to another the interpretation of tongues. ¹¹ All these are
inspired by one and the same Spirit, who apportions to each
one individually as he wills.

12 For just as the body is one and has many members,
and all the members of the body, though many, are one body,
so it is with Christ. ¹³ For by one Spirit we were all baptized
into one body — Jews or Greeks, slaves or free — and all
were made to drink of one Spirit.

14 For the body does not consist of one member but of
many. ¹⁵ If the foot should say, "Because I am not a hand,
I do not belong to the body," that would not make it any
less a part of the body. ¹⁶ And if the ear should say, "Because
I am not an eye, I do not belong to the body," that would
not make it any less a part of the body. ¹⁷ If the whole body
were an eye, where would be the hearing? If the whole body
were an ear, where would be the sense of smell? ¹⁸ But as
it is, God arranged the organs in the body, each one of them,
as he chose. ¹⁹ If all were a single organ, where would the
body be? ²⁰ As it is, there are many parts, yet one body.
²¹ The eye cannot say to the hand, "I have no need of you,"

12. 10: 1 Cor. 14. 26. **12. 12:** Rom. 12. 4. **12. 13:** Gal. 3. 28; Col. 3. 11; Eph. 2.
13–18; Jn. 7. 37–39.

nor again the head to the feet, "I have no need of you." ²² On the contrary, the parts of the body which seem to be weaker are indispensable, ²³ and those parts of the body which we think less honorable we invest with the greater honor, and our unpresentable parts are treated with greater modesty, ²⁴ which our more presentable parts do not require. But God has so adjusted the body, giving the greater honor to the inferior part, ²⁵ that there may be no discord in the body, but that the members may have the same care for one another. ²⁶ If one member suffers, all suffer together; if one member is honored, all rejoice together.

27 Now you are the body of Christ and individually members of it. ²⁸ And God has appointed in the church first apostles, second prophets, third teachers, then workers of miracles, then healers, helpers, administrators, speakers in various kinds of tongues. ²⁹ Are all apostles? Are all prophets? Are all teachers? Do all work miracles? ³⁰ Do all possess gifts of healing? Do all speak with tongues? Do all interpret? ³¹ But earnestly desire the higher gifts.

And I will show you a still more excellent way.

13 If I speak in the tongues of men and of angels, but have not love, I am a noisy gong or a clanging cymbal. ² And if I have prophetic powers, and understand all mysteries and all knowledge, and if I have all faith, so as to remove mountains, but have not love, I am nothing. ³ If I give away all I have, and if I deliver my body to be burned,ʳ but have not love, I gain nothing.

4 Love is patient and kind; love is not jealous or boastful; ⁵ it is not arrogant or rude. Love does not insist on its own way; it is not irritable or resentful; ⁶ it does not rejoice at

---

ʳ Some ancient authorities read *body that I may glory.*

12. 27: Eph. 1. 23; 4. 12; Col. 1. 18, 24; Eph. 5. 30; Rom. 12. 5.   **12. 28:** Eph. 4. 11; 2. 20; 3. 5.
13. 1: Ps. 150. 5.   **13. 2:** 1 Cor. 14. 2; Mt. 17. 20; 21. 21.   **13. 5:** 1 Cor. 10. 24.

wrong, but rejoices in the right. [7] Love bears all things, believes all things, hopes all things, endures all things.

8 Love never ends; as for prophecy, it will pass away; as for tongues, they will cease; as for knowledge, it will pass away. [9] For our knowledge is imperfect and our prophecy is imperfect; [10] but when the perfect comes, the imperfect will pass away. [11] When I was a child, I spoke like a child, I thought like a child, I reasoned like a child; when I became a man, I gave up childish ways. [12] For now we see in a mirror dimly, but then face to face. Now I know in part; then I shall understand fully, even as I have been fully understood. [13] So faith, hope, love abide, these three; but the greatest of these is love.

14 Make love your aim, and earnestly desire the spiritual gifts, especially that you may prophesy. [2] For one who speaks in a tongue speaks not to men but to God; for no one understands him, but he utters mysteries in the Spirit. [3] On the other hand, he who prophesies speaks to men for their upbuilding and encouragement and consolation. [4] He who speaks in a tongue edifies himself, but he who prophesies edifies the church. [5] Now I want you all to speak in tongues, but even more to prophesy. He who prophesies is greater than he who speaks in tongues, unless someone interprets, so that the church may be edified.

6 Now, brethren, if I come to you speaking in tongues, how shall I benefit you unless I bring you some revelation or knowledge or prophecy or teaching? [7] If even lifeless instruments, such as the flute or the harp, do not give distinct notes, how will anyone know what is played? [8] And if the bugle gives an indistinct sound, who will get ready for battle? [9] So with yourselves; if you in a tongue utter speech that is not intelligible, how will anyone know what

13. 7: 1 Cor. 9. 12.

is said? For you will be speaking into the air. [10] There are doubtless many different languages in the world, and none is without meaning; [11] but if I do not know the meaning of the language, I shall be a foreigner to the speaker and the speaker a foreigner to me. [12] So with yourselves; since you are eager for manifestations of the Spirit, strive to excel in building up the church.

13 Therefore, he who speaks in a tongue should pray for the power to interpret. [14] For if I pray in a tongue, my spirit prays but my mind is unfruitful. [15] What am I to do? I will pray with the spirit and I will pray with the mind also; I will sing with the spirit and I will sing with the mind also. [16] Otherwise, if you bless[s] with the spirit, how can any one in the position of an outsider[t] say the "Amen" to your thanksgiving when he does not know what you are saying? [17] For you may give thanks well enough, but the other man is not edified. [18] I thank God that I speak in tongues more than you all; [19] nevertheless, in church I would rather speak five words with my mind, in order to instruct others, than ten thousand words in a tongue.

20 Brethren, do not be children in your thinking; be babes in evil, but in thinking be mature. [21] In the law it is written, "By men of strange tongues and by the lips of foreigners will I speak to this people, and even then they will not listen to me, says the Lord." [22] Thus, tongues are a sign not for believers but for unbelievers, while prophecy is not for unbelievers but for believers. [23] If, therefore, the whole church assembles and all speak in tongues, and outsiders or unbelievers enter, will they not say that you are mad? [24] But if all prophesy, and an unbeliever or outsider enters, he is convicted by all, he is called to account by all, [25] the secrets

---

[s] That is, *give thanks to God.*   [t] Or *him that is without gifts.*

14. 15: Eph. 5. 19; Col. 3. 16.   **14. 16:** 1 Chr. 16. 36; Ps. 106. 48; Mt. 15. 36.
14. 20: Eph. 4. 14.   **14. 21:** Is. 28. 11–12.

of his heart are disclosed; and so, falling on his face, he will worship God and declare that God is really among you.

26 What then, brethren? When you come together, each one has a hymn, a lesson, a revelation, a tongue, or an interpretation. Let all things be done for edification. [27] If any speak in a tongue, let there be only two or at most three, and each in turn; and let one interpret. [28] But if there is no one to interpret, let each of them keep silence in church and speak to himself and to God. [29] Let two or three prophets speak, and let the others weigh what is said. [30] If a revelation is made to another sitting by, let the first be silent. [31] For you can all prophesy one by one, so that all may learn and all be encouraged; [32] and the spirits of prophets are subject to prophets. [33] For God is not a God of confusion but of peace.

As in all the churches of the saints, [34] the women should keep silence in the churches. For they are not permitted to speak, but should be subordinate, as even the law says. [35] If there is anything they desire to know, let them ask their husbands at home. For it is shameful for a woman to speak in church. [36] What! Did the word of God originate with you, or are you the only ones it has reached?

37 If any one thinks that he is a prophet, or spiritual, he should acknowledge that what I am writing to you is a command of the Lord. [38] If any one does not recognize this, he is not recognized. [39] So, my brethren, earnestly desire to prophesy, and do not forbid speaking in tongues; [40] but all things should be done decently and in order.

15 Now I would remind you, brethren, in what terms I preached to you the gospel, which you received, in which you stand, [2] by which you are saved, if you hold it fast — unless you believed in vain.

14. 26: Eph. 5. 19. 14. 34: 1 Tim. 2. 11–12; 1 Pet. 3. 1.

3 For I delivered to you as of first importance what I also received, that Christ died for our sins in accordance with the scriptures, ⁴ that he was buried, that he was raised on the third day in accordance with the scriptures, ⁵ and that he appeared to Ce′phas, then to the twelve. ⁶ Then he appeared to more than five hundred brethren at one time, most of whom are still alive, though some have fallen asleep. ⁷ Then he appeared to James, then to all the apostles. ⁸ Last of all, as to one untimely born, he appeared also to me. ⁹ For I am the least of the apostles, unfit to be called an apostle, because I persecuted the church of God. ¹⁰ But by the grace of God I am what I am, and his grace toward me was not in vain. On the contrary, I worked harder than any of them, though it was not I, but the grace of God which is with me. ¹¹ Whether then it was I or they, so we preach and so you believed.

12 Now if Christ is preached as raised from the dead, how can some of you say that there is no resurrection of the dead? ¹³ But if there is no resurrection of the dead, then Christ has not been raised; ¹⁴ if Christ has not been raised, then our preaching is in vain and your faith is in vain. ¹⁵ We are even found to be misrepresenting God, because we testified of God that he raised Christ, whom he did not raise if it is true that the dead are not raised. ¹⁶ For if the dead are not raised, then Christ has not been raised. ¹⁷ If Christ has not been raised, your faith is futile and you are still in your sins. ¹⁸ Then those also who have died in Christ have perished. ¹⁹ If in this life we who are in Christ have only hope,ᵘ we are of all men most to be pitied.

20 But in fact Christ has been raised from the dead, the first fruits of those who have fallen asleep. ²¹ For as by a

ᵘ Or *If in this life only we have hoped in Christ.*
15. 3: 1 Cor. 11. 23; 1 Pet. 2. 24; Is. 53. 5–12.   **15. 4:** Mt. 16. 21; Ps. 16. 8–9.
15. 5: Lk. 24. 34; Mt. 28. 17.   **15. 8:** 1 Cor. 9. 1; Gal. 1. 16; Acts 9. 3–6.   **15. 9:**
Acts 8. 3.   **15. 14:** 1 Thess. 4. 14.   **15. 18:** 1 Thess. 4. 16.   **15. 21:** Rom. 5. 12.

man came death, by a man has come also the resurrection of the dead. ²² For as in Adam all die, so also in Christ shall all be made alive. ²³ But each in his own order: Christ the first fruits, then at his coming those who belong to Christ. ²⁴ Then comes the end, when he delivers the kingdom to God the Father after destroying every rule and every authority and power. ²⁵ For he must reign until he has put all his enemies under his feet. ²⁶ The last enemy to be destroyed is death. ²⁷ "For God" has put all things in subjection under his feet." But when it says, "All things are put in subjection under him," it is plain that he is excepted who put all things under him. ²⁸ When all things are subjected to him, then the Son himself will also be subjected to him who put all things under him, that God may be everything to every one.

29 Otherwise, what do people mean by being baptized on behalf of the dead? If the dead are not raised at all, why are people baptized on their behalf? ³⁰ Why am I in peril every hour? ³¹ I protest, brethren, by my pride in you which I have in Christ Jesus our Lord, I die every day! ³² What do I gain if, humanly speaking, I fought with beasts at Ephesus? If the dead are not raised, "Let us eat and drink, for tomorrow we die." ³³ Do not be deceived: "Bad company ruins good morals." ³⁴ Come to your right mind, and sin no more. For some have no knowledge of God. I say this to your shame.

35 But some one will ask, "How are the dead raised? With what kind of body do they come?" ³⁶ You foolish man! What you sow does not come to life unless it dies. ³⁷ And what you sow is not the body which is to be, but a bare kernel, perhaps of wheat or of some other grain. ³⁸ But God

---

ᵛ Greek *he.*

15. 22: Rom. 5. 14–18.   **15. 23:** 1 Thess. 2. 19.   **15. 25:** Ps. 110. 1.   **15. 27:** Ps. 8. 6; Eph. 1. 22.   **15. 28:** Phil. 3. 21.   **15. 30:** 2 Esdr. 7. 89.   **15. 31:** Rom. 8. 36. **15. 32:** 2 Cor. 1. 8, 9; Is. 22. 13.   **15. 34:** Rom. 13. 11.   **15. 36:** Jn. 12. 24. **15. 38:** Gen. 1. 11.

gives it a body as he has chosen, and to each kind of seed its own body. [39] For not all flesh is alike, but there is one kind for men, another for animals, another for birds, and another for fish. [40] There are celestial bodies and there are terrestrial bodies; but the glory of the celestial is one, and the glory of the terrestrial is another. [41] There is one glory of the sun, and another glory of the moon, and another glory of the stars; for star differs from star in glory.

42 So is it with the resurrection of the dead. What is sown is perishable, what is raised is imperishable. [43] It is sown in dishonor, it is raised in glory. It is sown in weakness, it is raised in power. [44] It is sown a physical body, it is raised a spiritual body. If there is a physical body, there is also a spiritual body. [45] Thus it is written, "The first man Adam became a living being"; the last Adam became a life-giving spirit. [46] But it is not the spiritual which is first but the physical, and then the spiritual. [47] The first man was from the earth, a man of dust; the second man is from heaven. [48] As was the man of dust, so are those who are of the dust; and as is the man of heaven, so are those who are of heaven. [49] Just as we have borne the image of the man of dust, we shall[w] also bear the image of the man of heaven. [50] I tell you this, brethren: flesh and blood cannot inherit the kingdom of God, nor does the perishable inherit the imperishable.

51 Lo! I tell you a mystery. We shall not all sleep, but we shall all be changed, [52] in a moment, in the twinkling of an eye, at the last trumpet. For the trumpet will sound, and the dead will be raised imperishable, and we shall be changed. [53] For this perishable nature must put on the imperishable, and this mortal nature must put on immortality.

[w] Many ancient authorities read *let us.*

15. 42: Dan. 12. 3.   **15. 47:** Gen. 2. 7.   **15. 51–52:** 1 Thess. 4. 15–17.

[54] When the perishable puts on the imperishable, and the mortal puts on immortality, then shall come to pass the saying that is written:

"Death is swallowed up in victory."
[55] "O death, where is thy victory?
O death, where is thy sting?"

[56] The sting of death is sin, and the power of sin is the law. [57] But thanks be to God, who gives us the victory through our Lord Jesus Christ.

58 Therefore, my beloved brethren, be steadfast, immovable, always abounding in the work of the Lord, knowing that in the Lord your labor is not in vain.

16 Now concerning the contribution for the saints: as I directed the churches of Galatia, so you also are to do. [2] On the first day of every week, each of you is to put something aside and save, as he may prosper, so that contributions need not be made when I come. [3] And when I arrive, I will send those whom you accredit by letter to carry your gift to Jerusalem. [4] If it seems advisable that I should go also, they will accompany me.

5 I will visit you after passing through Mac-e-do′ni-a, for I intend to pass through Mac-e-do′ni-a, [6] and perhaps I will stay with you or even spend the winter, so that you may speed me on my journey, wherever I go. [7] For I do not want to see you now just in passing; I hope to spend some time with you, if the Lord permits. [8] But I will stay in Ephesus until Pentecost, [9] for a wide door for effective work has opened to me, and there are many adversaries.

10 When Timothy comes, see that you put him at ease among you, for he is doing the work of the Lord, as I am.

15. 54: Is. 25. 8.   **15. 55:** Hos. 13. 15.   **16. 1:** Acts 24. 17.   **16. 2:** Acts 20. 7; 2 Cor. 9. 4–5.   **16. 3:** 2 Cor. 8. 18–19.   **16. 5:** Rom. 15. 26; Acts 19. 21. **16. 7:** Acts 18. 21.   **16. 8:** Acts 18. 19.   **16. 9:** Acts 19. 9.   **16. 10:** Acts 16. 1.

¹¹ So let no one despise him. Speed him on his way in peace, that he may return to me; for I am expecting him with the brethren.

12 As for our brother A-pol′los, I strongly urged him to visit you with the other brethren, but it was not at all God's will for him to go^x now. He will come when he has opportunity.

13 Be watchful, stand firm in your faith, be courageous, be strong. ¹⁴ Let all that you do be done in love.

15 Now, brethren, you know that the household of Steph′a-nas were the first converts in A-cha′ia, and they have devoted themselves to the service of the saints; ¹⁶ I urge you to be subject to such men and to every fellow worker and laborer. ¹⁷ I rejoice at the coming of Steph′a-nas and For-tu-na′tus and A-cha′i-cus, because they have made up for your absence; ¹⁸ for they refreshed my spirit as well as yours. Give recognition to such men.

19 The churches of Asia send greetings. Aquila and Pris′ca, together with the church that meets in their house, send you hearty greetings in the Lord. ²⁰ All the brethren send greetings. Greet one another with a holy kiss.

21 I, Paul, write this greeting with my own hand. ²² If any one has no love for the Lord, let him be accursed. Our Lord, come!^{y} ²³ The grace of the Lord Jesus be with you. ²⁴ My love be with you all in Christ Jesus. Amen.

^{x} Or *his will to go*. ^{y} Greek *Maranatha*.

16. 12: Acts 18. 24.   **16. 13:** Ps. 31. 24; Eph. 6. 10.   **16. 19:** Acts 18. 2;
Rom. 16. 5.   **16. 20:** Rom. 16. 16.   **16. 21:** Col. 4. 18; Gal. 6. 11; 2 Thess. 3. 17.
16. 22: Rom. 9. 3.   **16. 23:** Rom. 16. 20.

THE SECOND LETTER OF PAUL TO THE
CORINTHIANS

1 Paul, an apostle of Christ Jesus by the will of God,
and Timothy our brother,

To the church of God which is at Corinth, with all the
saints who are in the whole of A-cha′ia:

2 Grace to you and peace from God our Father and the
Lord Jesus Christ.

3 Blessed be the God and Father of our Lord Jesus Christ,
the Father of mercies and God of all comfort, ⁴ who comforts us in all our affliction, so that we may be able to comfort those who are in any affliction, with the comfort with
which we ourselves are comforted by God. ⁵ For as we share
abundantly in Christ's sufferings, so through Christ we
share abundantly in comfort too.ᵃ ⁶ If we are afflicted, it
is for your comfort and salvation; and if we are comforted,
it is for your comfort, which you experience when you
patiently endure the same sufferings that we suffer. ⁷ Our
hope for you is unshaken; for we know that as you share
in our sufferings, you will also share in our comfort.

8 For we do not want you to be ignorant, brethren, of
the affliction we experienced in Asia; for we were so utterly,
unbearably crushed that we despaired of life itself. ⁹ Why,
we felt that we had received the sentence of death; but that
was to make us rely not on ourselves but on God who raises
the dead; ¹⁰ he delivered us from such a deadly peril, and he
will deliver us; on him we have set our hope that he will
deliver us again. ¹¹ You also must help us by prayer, so that

---

ᵃ Or, *For as. the sufferings of Christ abound for us, so also our comfort abounds through
Christ.*

1. 1: Eph. 1. 1; Col. 1. 1; 2 Cor. 1. 19; Acts 16. 1; 18. 1. **1. 2:** Rom. 1. 7. **1. 3:** Eph.
1. 3; 1 Pet. 1. 3; Rom. 15. 5. **1. 4:** 2 Cor. 7. 6, 7, 13.

many will give thanks on our behalf for the blessing granted us in answer to many prayers.

12 For our boast is this, the testimony of our conscience that we have behaved in the world, and still more toward you, with holiness and godly sincerity, not by earthly wisdom but by the grace of God. [13] For we write you nothing but what you can read and understand; I hope you will understand fully, [14] as you have understood in part, that you can be proud of us as we can be of you, on the day of the Lord Jesus.

15 Because I was sure of this, I wanted to come to you first, so that you might have a double pleasure;[b] [16] I wanted to visit you on my way to Mac-e-do'ni-a, and to come back to you from Mac-e-do'ni-a and have you send me on my way to Judea. [17] Was I vacillating when I wanted to do this? Do I make my plans like a worldly man, ready to say Yes and No at once? [18] As surely as God is faithful, our word to you has not been Yes and No. [19] For the Son of God, Jesus Christ, whom we preached among you, Silva'nus and Timothy and I, was not Yes and No; but in him it is always Yes. [20] For all the promises of God find their Yes in him. That is why we utter the Amen through him, to the glory of God. [21] But it is God who establishes us with you in Christ, and has commissioned us; [22] he has put his seal upon us and given us his Spirit in our hearts as a guarantee.

23 But I call God to witness against me — it was to spare you that I refrained from coming to Corinth. [24] Not that we lord it over your faith; we work with you for your joy, for you stand firm in your faith. [1] For I made up my mind not to make you another painful visit. [2] For if I

[b] Some ancient authorities read *favor.*

1. 16: Acts 19. 21.   **1. 19:** 1 Thess. 1. 1; Acts 15. 22.   **1. 20:** 1 Cor. 14. 16; Rev. 3. 14.

cause you pain, who is there to make me glad but the one whom I have pained? ³ And I wrote as I did, so that when I came I might not be pained by those who should have made me rejoice, for I felt sure of all of you, that my joy would be the joy of you all. ⁴ For I wrote you out of much affliction and anguish of heart and with many tears, not to cause you pain but to let you know the abundant love that I have for you.

5 But if any one has caused pain, he has caused it not to me, but in some measure — not to put it too severely — to you all. ⁶ For such a one this punishment by the majority is enough; ⁷ so you should rather turn to forgive and comfort him, or he may be overwhelmed by excessive sorrow. ⁸ So I beg you to reaffirm your love for him. ⁹ For this is why I wrote, that I might test you and know whether you are obedient in everything. ¹⁰ Any one whom you forgive, I also forgive. What I have forgiven, if I have forgiven anything, has been for your sake in the presence of Christ, ¹¹ to keep Satan from gaining the advantage over us; for we are not ignorant of his designs.

12 When I came to Tro′as to preach the gospel of Christ, a door was opened for me in the Lord; ¹³ but my mind could not rest because I did not find my brother Titus there. So I took leave of them and went on to Mac-e-do′ni-a.

14 But thanks be to God, who in Christ always leads us in triumph, and through us spreads the fragrance of the knowledge of him everywhere. ¹⁵ For we are the aroma of Christ to God among those who are being saved and among those who are perishing, ¹⁶ to one a fragrance from death to death, to the other a fragrance from life to life. Who is sufficient for these things? ¹⁷ For we are not, like so many, peddlers of God's word; but as men of sincerity,

2. 12: Acts 16. 8.

as commissioned by God, in the sight of God we speak in Christ.

3 Are we beginning to commend ourselves again? Or do we need, as some do, letters of recommendation to you, or from you? [2] You yourselves are our letter of recommendation, written on your[c] hearts, to be known and read by all men; [3] and you show that you are a letter from Christ delivered by us, written not with ink but with the Spirit of the living God, not on tablets of stone but on tablets of human hearts.

4 Such is the confidence that we have through Christ toward God. [5] Not that we are sufficient of ourselves to claim anything as coming from us; our sufficiency is from God, [6] who has qualified us to be ministers of a new covenant, not in a written code but in the Spirit; for the written code kills, but the Spirit gives life.

7 Now if the dispensation of death, carved in letters on stone, came with such splendor that the Israelites could not look at Moses' face because of its brightness, fading as this was, [8] why should not the dispensation of the Spirit be attended with greater splendor? [9] For if there was splendor in the dispensation of condemnation, the dispensation of righteousness must far exceed it in splendor. [10] Indeed, in this case, what once had splendor has come to have no splendor at all, because of the splendor that surpasses it. [11] For if what faded away came with splendor, what is permanent must have much more splendor.

12 Since we have such a hope, we are very bold, [13] not like Moses, who put a veil over his face so that the Israelites might not see the end of the fading splendor. [14] But their minds were hardened; for to this day, when they read the

[c] Many ancient authorities read *our.*

3. 1: Acts 18. 27; Rom. 16. 1; 1 Cor. 16. 3.   **3. 3:** Ex. 24. 12; 31. 18; 32. 15–16; Jer. 31. 33.   **3. 6:** Jer. 31. 31.   **3. 7:** Ex. 34. 29–35.

old covenant, that same veil remains unlifted, because only through Christ is it taken away. [15] Yes, to this day whenever Moses is read a veil lies over their minds; [16] but when a man turns to the Lord the veil is removed. [17] Now the Lord is the Spirit, and where the Spirit of the Lord is, there is freedom. [18] And we all, with unveiled face, beholding[d] the glory of the Lord, are being changed into his likeness from one degree of glory to another; for this comes from the Lord who is the Spirit.

4 Therefore, being engaged in this service by the mercy of God,[e] we do not lose heart. [2] We have renounced disgraceful, underhanded ways; we refuse to practice cunning or to tamper with God's word, but by the open statement of the truth we would commend ourselves to every man's conscience in the sight of God. [3] And even if our gospel is veiled, it is veiled only to those who are perishing. [4] In their case the god of this world has blinded the minds of the unbelievers, to keep them from seeing the light of the gospel of the glory of Christ, who is the likeness of God. [5] For what we preach is not ourselves, but Jesus Christ as Lord, with ourselves as your servants[f] for Jesus' sake. [6] For it is the God who said, "Let light shine out of darkness," who has shone in our hearts to give the light of the knowledge of the glory of God in the face of Christ.

7 But we have this treasure in earthen vessels, to show that the transcendent power belongs to God and not to us. [8] We are afflicted in every way, but not crushed; perplexed, but not driven to despair; [9] persecuted, but not forsaken; struck down, but not destroyed; [10] always carrying in the body the death of Jesus, so that the life of Jesus may also be manifested in our bodies. [11] For while we live we are

---

[d] Or *reflecting.*   [e] Greek *as we have received mercy.*   [f] Or *slaves.*
3. 17: Is. 61. 1–2.
4. 4: Jn. 12. 31; Col. 1. 15.   **4. 6:** Gen. 1. 3.

always being given up to death for Jesus' sake, so that the life of Jesus may be manifested in our mortal flesh. [12] So death is at work in us, but life in you.

13 Since we have the same spirit of faith as he had who wrote, "I believed, and so I spoke," we too believe, and so we speak, [14] knowing that he who raised the Lord Jesus will raise us also with Jesus and bring us with you into his presence. [15] For it is all for your sake, so that as grace extends to more and more people it may increase thanksgiving, to the glory of God.

16 So we do not lose heart. Though our outer nature is wasting away, our inner nature is being renewed every day. [17] For this slight momentary affliction is preparing for us an eternal weight of glory beyond all comparison, [18] because we look not to the things that are seen but to the things that are unseen; for the things that are seen are transient, but the things that are unseen are eternal.

5 For we know that if the earthly tent we live in is destroyed, we have a building from God, a house not made with hands, eternal in the heavens. [2] Here indeed we groan, and long to put on our heavenly dwelling, [3] so that by putting it on we may not be found naked. [4] For while we are still in this tent, we sigh with anxiety; not that we would be unclothed, but that we would be further clothed, so that what is mortal may be swallowed up by life. [5] He who has prepared us for this very thing is God, who has given us the Spirit as a guarantee.

6 So we are always of good courage; we know that while we are at home in the body we are away from the Lord, [7] for we walk by faith, not by sight. [8] We are of good courage, and we would rather be away from the body and at home with the Lord. [9] So whether we are at home or away, we

4. 13: Ps. 116. 10.   **4. 14:** 1 Thess. 4. 14.

make it our aim to please him. [10] For we must all appear before the judgment seat of Christ, so that each one may receive good or evil, according to what he has done in the body.

11 Therefore, knowing the fear of the Lord, we persuade men; but what we are is known to God, and I hope it is known also to your conscience. [12] We are not commending ourselves to you again but giving you cause to be proud of us, so that you may be able to answer those who pride themselves on a man's position and not on his heart. [13] For if we are beside ourselves, it is for God; if we are in our right mind, it is for you. [14] For the love of Christ controls us, because we are convinced that one has died for all; therefore all have died. [15] And he died for all, that those who live might live no longer for themselves but for him who for their sake died and was raised.

16 From now on, therefore, we regard no one from a human point of view; even though we once regarded Christ from a human point of view, we regard him thus no longer. [17] Therefore, if any one is in Christ, he is a new creation;[g] the old has passed away, behold, the new has come. [18] All this is from God, who through Christ reconciled us to himself and gave us the ministry of reconciliation; [19] that is, God was in Christ reconciling[h] the world to himself, not counting their trespasses against them, and entrusting to us the message of reconciliation. [20] So we are ambassadors for Christ, God making his appeal through us. We beseech you on behalf of Christ, be reconciled to God. [21] For our sake he made him to be sin who knew no sin, so that in him we might become the righteousness of God.

[g] Or *creature*.
[h] Or *in Christ God was reconciling*.

5. 10: Mt. 16. 27.   **5. 12:** 2 Cor. 3. 1.   **5. 14:** Rom. 5. 15; 6. 6–7.   **5. 17:** Rom. 16. 7;
Gal. 6. 15.   **5. 18:** 1 Cor. 11. 12; Col. 1. 20; Rom. 5. 10.   **5. 20:** Eph. 6. 20.
5. 21: Heb. 4. 15; 7. 25; 1 Pet. 2. 22; 1 Jn. 3. 5; Acts 3. 14.

6 Working together with him, then, we entreat you not to accept the grace of God in vain. ² For he says,
"At the acceptable time I have listened to you,
and helped you on the day of salvation."
Behold, now is the acceptable time; behold, now is the day of salvation. ³ We put no obstacle in any one's way, so that no fault may be found with our ministry, ⁴ but as servants of God we commend ourselves in every way: through great endurance, in afflictions, hardships, calamities, ⁵ beatings, imprisonments, tumults, labors, watching, hunger; ⁶ by purity, knowledge, forbearance, kindness, the Holy Spirit, genuine love, ⁷ truthful speech, and the power of God; with the weapons of righteousness for the right hand and for the left; ⁸ in honor and dishonor, in ill repute and good repute. We are treated as impostors, and yet are true; ⁹ as unknown, and yet well known; as dying, and behold we live; as punished, and yet not killed; ¹⁰ as sorrowful, yet always rejoicing; as poor, yet making many rich; as having nothing, and yet possessing everything.

11 Our mouth is open to you, Corinthians; our heart is wide. ¹² You are not restricted by us, but you are restricted in your own affections. ¹³ In return — I speak as to children — widen your hearts also.

14 Do not be mismated with unbelievers. For what partnership have righteousness and iniquity? Or what fellowship has light with darkness? ¹⁵ What accord has Christ with Be'li-al?ⁱ Or what has a believer in common with an unbeliever? ¹⁶ What agreement has the temple of God with idols? For we are the temple of the living God; as God said,

ⁱ Greek *Beliar.*

6. 2: Is. 49. 8.   **6. 4:** 2 Cor. 4. 8–11; 11. 23–27.   **6. 5:** Acts 16. 23.   **6. 7:** 2 Cor. 10. 4; Rom. 13. 12; Eph. 6. 11–12.   **6. 9:** Rom. 8. 36.   **6. 10:** Rom. 8. 32; 1 Cor. 3. 21. **6. 11:** Ezek. 33. 22; Is. 60. 5.   **6. 16:** 1 Cor. 10. 21; 3. 16; Ex. 25. 8; 29. 45; Lev. 26. 12; Ezek. 37. 27; Jer. 31. 1.

"I will live in them and move among them,
and I will be their God,
and they shall be my people.
¹⁷ Therefore come out from them,
and be separate from them, says the Lord,
and touch nothing unclean;
then I will welcome you,
¹⁸ and I will be a father to you,
and you shall be my sons and daughters,
says the Lord Almighty."

7 Since we have these promises, beloved, let us cleanse
ourselves from every defilement of body and spirit,
and make holiness perfect in the fear of God.

2 Open your hearts to us; we have wronged no one, we
have corrupted no one, we have taken advantage of no
one. ³ I do not say this to condemn you, for I said before
that you are in our hearts, to die together and to live together. ⁴ I have great confidence in you; I have great pride
in you; I am filled with comfort. With all our affliction, I
am overjoyed.

5 For even when we came into Mac-e-do'ni-a, our bodies
had no rest but we were afflicted at every turn — fighting
without and fear within. ⁶ But God, who comforts the down-
cast, comforted us by the coming of Titus, ⁷ and not only
by his coming but also by the comfort with which he was
comforted in you, as he told us of your longing, your mourning, your zeal for me, so that I rejoiced still more. ⁸ For
even if I made you sorry with my letter, I do not regret it
(though I did regret it), for I see that that letter grieved
you, though only for a while. ⁹ As it is, I rejoice, not because

6. 17: Is. 52. 11.   6. 18: Hos. 1. 10; Is. 43. 6.
7. 2: 2 Cor. 6. 12–13.   7. 3: 2 Cor. 6. 11–12.   7. 5: 2 Cor. 2. 13; 4. 8.   7. 6: 2 Cor.
2. 13; 7. 13–14.   7. 8: 2 Cor. 2. 2.

you were grieved, but because you were grieved into repenting; for you felt a godly grief, so that you suffered no loss through us. [10] For godly grief produces a repentance that leads to salvation and brings no regret, but worldly grief produces death. [11] For see what earnestness this godly grief has produced in you, what eagerness to clear yourselves, what indignation, what alarm, what longing, what zeal, what punishment! At every point you have proved yourselves guiltless in the matter. [12] So although I wrote to you, it was not on account of the one who did the wrong, nor on account of the one who suffered the wrong, but in order that your zeal for us might be revealed to you in the sight of God. [13] Therefore we are comforted.

And besides our own comfort we rejoiced still more at the joy of Titus, because his mind has been set at rest by you all. [14] For if I have expressed to him some pride in you, I was not put to shame; but just as everything we said to you was true, so our boasting before Titus has proved true. [15] And his heart goes out all the more to you, as he remembers the obedience of you all, and the fear and trembling with which you received him. [16] I rejoice, because I have perfect confidence in you.

8 We want you to know, brethren, about the grace of God which has been shown in the churches of Mac-e-do'ni-a, [2] for in a severe test of affliction, their abundance of joy and their extreme poverty have overflowed in a wealth of liberality on their part. [3] For they gave according to their means, as I can testify, and beyond their means, of their own free will, [4] begging us earnestly for the favor of taking part in the relief of the saints — [5] and this, not as we expected, but first they gave themselves to the Lord

7. **12**: 2 Cor. 7. 8; 2. 3, 9.
8. **3**: 1 Cor. 16. 2.　　**8. 4**: Acts 24. 17; Rom. 15. 31.

and to us by the will of God. ⁶ Accordingly we have urged Titus that as he had already made a beginning, he should also complete among you this gracious work. ⁷ Now as you excel in everything — in faith, in utterance, in knowledge, in all earnestness, and in your love for us — see that you excel in this gracious work also.

8 I say this not as a command, but to prove by the earnestness of others that your love also is genuine. ⁹ For you know the grace of our Lord Jesus Christ, that though he was rich, yet for your sake he became poor, so that by his poverty you might become rich. ¹⁰ And in this matter I give my advice: it is best for you now to complete what a year ago you began not only to do but to desire, ¹¹ so that your readiness in desiring it may be matched by your completing it out of what you have. ¹² For if the readiness is there, it is acceptable according to what a man has, not according to what he has not. ¹³ I do not mean that others should be eased and you burdened, ¹⁴ but that as a matter of equality your abundance at the present time should supply their want, so that their abundance may supply your want, that there may be equality. ¹⁵ As it is written, "He who gathered much had nothing over, and he who gathered little had no lack."

16 But thanks be to God who puts the same earnest care for you into the heart of Titus. ¹⁷ For he not only accepted our appeal, but being himself very earnest he is going to you of his own accord. ¹⁸ With him we are sending the brother who is famous among all the churches for his preaching of the gospel; ¹⁹ and not only that, but he has been appointed by the churches to travel with us in this gracious work which we are carrying on, for the glory of the Lord and to show our good will. ²⁰ We intend that no one should blame

8. 6: 2 Cor. 8. 16, 23; 2. 13.   **8. 9:** 2 Cor. 6. 10.   **8. 10:** 2 Cor. 9. 2; 1 Cor. 16. 2–3.
8. 15: Ex. 16. 18.   **8. 18:** 2 Cor. 12. 18.   **8. 19:** 1 Cor. 16. 3–4.

us about this liberal gift which we are administering, [21] for we aim at what is honorable not only in the Lord's sight but also in the sight of men. [22] And with them we are sending our brother whom we have often tested and found earnest in many matters, but who is now more earnest than ever because of his great confidence in you. [23] As for Titus, he is my partner and fellow worker in your service; and as for our brethren, they are messengers[j] of the churches, the glory of Christ. [24] So give proof, before the churches, of your love and of our boasting about you to these men.

9 Now it is superfluous for me to write to you about the offering for the saints,[2] for I know your readiness, of which I boast about you to the people of Mac-e-do'ni-a, saying that A-cha'ia has been ready since last year; and your zeal has stirred up most of them. [3] But I am sending the brethren so that our boasting about you may not prove vain in this case, so that you may be ready, as I said you would be; [4] lest if some Mac-e-do'ni-ans come with me and find that you are not ready, we be humiliated — to say nothing of you — for being so confident. [5] So I thought it necessary to urge the brethren to go on to you before me, and arrange in advance for this gift you have promised, so that it may be ready not as an exaction but as a willing gift.

[6] The point is this: he who sows sparingly will also reap sparingly, and he who sows bountifully will also reap bountifully. [7] Each one must do as he has made up his mind, not reluctantly or under compulsion, for God loves a cheerful giver. [8] And God is able to provide you with every blessing in abundance, so that you may always have enough of everything and may provide in abundance for every good work. [9] As it is written,

[j] Greek *apostles.*

9. 1: 2 Cor. 8. 4.   **9. 2:** Rom. 15. 26; 2 Cor. 8. 10.   **9. 3:** 1 Cor. 16. 2.   **9. 7:** Prov. 22. 8 (Sept.).   **9. 8:** Eph. 3. 20.   **9. 9:** Ps. 112. 9.

"He scatters abroad, he gives to the poor;
    his righteousness[k] endures forever."

[10] He who supplies seed to the sower and bread for food will supply and multiply your resources[l] and increase the harvest of your righteousness.[k] [11] You will be enriched in every way for great generosity, which through us will produce thanksgiving to God; [12] for the rendering of this service not only supplies the wants of the saints but also overflows in many thanksgivings to God. [13] Under the test of this service, you[m] will glorify God by your obedience in acknowledging the gospel of Christ, and by the generosity of your contribution for them and for all others; [14] while they long for you and pray for you, because of the surpassing grace of God in you. [15] Thanks be to God for his inexpressible gift!

10

I, Paul, myself entreat you, by the meekness and gentleness of Christ — I who am humble when face to face with you, but bold to you when I am away! — [2] I beg of you that when I am present I may not have to show boldness with such confidence as I count on showing against some who suspect us of acting in worldly fashion. [3] For though we live in the world we are not carrying on a worldly war, [4] for the weapons of our warfare are not worldly but have divine power to destroy strongholds. [5] We destroy arguments and every proud obstacle to the knowledge of God, and take every thought captive to obey Christ, [6] being ready to punish every disobedience, when your obedience is complete.

[7] Look at what is before your eyes. If any one is confident that he is Christ's, let him remind himself that as he is

k Or *benevolence.*   l Greek *sowing.*   m Or *they.*

9. 10: Is. 55. 10; Hos. 10. 12.   **9. 13:** 2 Cor. 8. 4; Rom. 15. 31.   **9. 15:** Rom. 5. 15–16.
10. 1: 2 Cor. 10. 10.   **10. 2:** 2 Cor. 13. 2, 10; 1 Cor. 4. 21.   **10. 6:** 2 Cor. 2. 9.
10. 7: 1 Cor. 1. 12.

Christ's, so are we. ⁸ For even if I boast a little too much of our authority, which the Lord gave for building you up and not for destroying you, I shall not be put to shame. ⁹ I would not seem to be frightening you with letters. ¹⁰ For they say, "His letters are weighty and strong, but his bodily presence is weak, and his speech of no account." ¹¹ Let such people understand that what we say by letter when absent, we do when present. ¹² Not that we venture to class or compare ourselves with some of those who commend themselves. But when they measure themselves by one another, and compare themselves with one another, they are without understanding.

13 But we will not boast beyond limit, but will keep to the limits God has apportioned us, to reach even to you. ¹⁴ For we are not overextending ourselves, as though we did not reach you; we were the first to come all the way to you with the gospel of Christ. ¹⁵ We do not boast beyond limit, in other men's labors; but our hope is that as your faith increases, our field among you may be greatly enlarged, ¹⁶ so that we may preach the gospel in lands beyond you, without boasting of work already done in another's field. ¹⁷ "Let him who boasts, boast of the Lord." ¹⁸ For it is not the man who commends himself that is accepted, but the man whom the Lord commends.

11 I wish you would bear with me in a little foolishness. Do bear with me! ² I feel a divine jealousy for you, for I betrothed you to Christ to present you as a pure bride to her one husband. ³ But I am afraid that as the serpent deceived Eve by his cunning, your thoughts will be led astray from a sincere and pure devotion to Christ. ⁴ For if some one comes and preaches another Jesus than

10. 10: 1 Cor. 2. 3.   **10. 15:** Rom. 15. 20.   **10. 17:** Jer. 9. 24.
11. 1: 2 Cor. 11. 21.   **11. 2:** Hos. 2. 19–20; Eph. 5. 26–27.   **11. 3:** Gen. 3. 4.
11. 4: Gal. 1. 6.

the one we preached, or if you receive a different spirit from the one you received, or if you accept a different gospel from the one you accepted, you submit to it readily enough. [5] I think that I am not in the least inferior to these superlative apostles. [6] Even if I am unskilled in speaking, I am not in knowledge; in every way we have made this plain to you in all things.

7 Did I commit a sin in abasing myself so that you might be exalted, because I preached God's gospel without cost to you? [8] I robbed other churches by accepting support from them in order to serve you. [9] And when I was with you and was in want, I did not burden any one, for my needs were supplied by the brethren who came from Mac-e-do'-ni-a. So I refrained and will refrain from burdening you in any way. [10] As the truth of Christ is in me, this boast of mine shall not be silenced in the regions of A-cha'ia. [11] And why? Because I do not love you? God knows I do!

12 And what I do I will continue to do, in order to undermine the claim of those who would like to claim that in their boasted mission they work on the same terms as we do. [13] For such men are false apostles, deceitful workmen, disguising themselves as apostles of Christ. [14] And no wonder, for even Satan disguises himself as an angel of light. [15] So it is not strange if his servants also disguise themselves as servants of righteousness. Their end will correspond to their deeds.

16 I repeat, let no one think me foolish; but even if you do, accept me as a fool, so that I too may boast a little. [17] (What I am saying I say not with the Lord's authority but as a fool, in this boastful confidence; [18] since many boast of worldly things, I too will boast.) [19] For you gladly bear

11. 5: 2 Cor. 12. 11; Gal. 2. 6.   **11. 6:** 1 Cor. 1. 17.   **11. 7:** 2 Cor. 12. 13; 1 Cor. 9. 18.
11. 8: Phil. 4. 15, 18.   **11. 10:** 1 Cor. 9. 15.   **11. 11:** 2 Cor. 12. 15.   **11. 12:** 1 Cor.
9. 12.   **11. 17:** 1 Cor. 7. 12, 25.   **11. 19:** 1 Cor. 4. 10.

with fools, being wise yourselves! [20] For you bear it if a man makes slaves of you, or preys upon you, or takes advantage of you, or puts on airs, or strikes you in the face. [21] To my shame, I must say, we were too weak for that!

But whatever any one dares to boast of — I am speaking as a fool — I also dare to boast of that. [22] Are they Hebrews? So am I. Are they Israelites? So am I. Are they descendants of Abraham? So am I. [23] Are they servants of Christ? I am a better one — I am talking like a madman — with far greater labors, far more imprisonments, with countless beatings, and often near death. [24] Five times I have received at the hands of the Jews the forty lashes less one. [25] Three times I have been beaten with rods; once I was stoned. Three times I have been shipwrecked; a night and a day I have been adrift at sea; [26] on frequent journeys, in danger from rivers, danger from robbers, danger from my own people, danger from Gentiles, danger in the city, danger in the wilderness, danger at sea, danger from false brethren; [27] in toil and hardship, through many a sleepless night, in hunger and thirst, often without food, in cold and exposure. [28] And, apart from other things, there is the daily pressure upon me of my anxiety for all the churches. [29] Who is weak, and I am not weak? Who is made to fall, and I am not indignant?

30 If I must boast, I will boast of the things that show my weakness. [31] The God and Father of the Lord Jesus, he who is blessed forever, knows that I do not lie. [32] At Damascus, the governor under King Ar′e-tas guarded the city of Damascus in order to seize me, [33] but I was let down in a basket through a window in the wall, and escaped his hands.

11. 23: Acts 16. 23; 2 Cor. 6. 5. 14. 19.   **11. 26:** Acts 9. 23; 14. 5.   **11. 32–33:** Acts 9. 24–25.   **11. 24:** Deut. 25. 3.   **11. 27:** 1 Cor. 4. 11.   **11. 25:** Acts 16. 22; **11. 29:** 1 Cor. 9. 22.

12 I must boast; there is nothing to be gained by it, but I will go on to visions and revelations of the Lord. [2] I know a man in Christ who fourteen years ago was caught up to the third heaven — whether in the body or out of the body I do not know, God knows. [3] And I know that this man was caught up into Paradise — whether in the body or out of the body I do not know, God knows — [4] and he heard things that cannot be told, which man may not utter. [5] On behalf of this man I will boast, but on my own behalf I will not boast, except of my weaknesses. [6] Though if I wish to boast, I shall not be a fool, for I shall be speaking the truth. But I refrain from it, so that no one may think more of me than he sees in me or hears from me. [7] And to keep me from being too elated by the abundance of revelations, a thorn was given me in the flesh, a messenger of Satan, to harass me, to keep me from being too elated. [8] Three times I besought the Lord about this, that it should leave me; [9] but he said to me, "My grace is sufficient for you, for my power is made perfect in weakness." I will all the more gladly boast of my weaknesses, that the power of Christ may rest upon me. [10] For the sake of Christ, then, I am content with weaknesses, insults, hardships, persecutions, and calamities; for when I am weak, then I am strong.

11 I have been a fool! You forced me to it, for I ought to have been commended by you. For I am not at all inferior to these superlative apostles, even though I am nothing. [12] The signs of a true apostle were performed among you in all patience, with signs and wonders and mighty works. [13] For in what were you less favored than the rest of the churches, except that I myself did not burden you? Forgive me this wrong!

---

12. 4: Lk. 23. 43.   **12. 7:** Job 2. 6.   **12. 10:** Rom. 5. 3; 2 Cor. 6. 4–5.
12. 11: 2 Cor. 11. 5.   **12. 13:** 2 Cor. 11. 7.

14 Here for the third time I am ready to come to you. And I will not be a burden, for I seek not what is yours but you; for children ought not to lay up for their parents, but parents for their children. ¹⁵ I will most gladly spend and be spent for your souls. If I love you the more, am I to be loved the less? ¹⁶ But granting that I myself did not burden you, I was crafty, you say, and got the better of you by guile. ¹⁷ Did I take advantage of you through any of those whom I sent to you? ¹⁸ I urged Titus to go, and sent the brother with him. Did Titus take advantage of you? Did we not act in the same spirit? Did we not take the same steps?

19 Have you been thinking all along that we have been defending ourselves before you? It is in the sight of God that we have been speaking in Christ, and all for your up-building, beloved. ²⁰ For I fear that perhaps I may come and find you not what I wish, and that you may find me not what you wish; that perhaps there may be quarreling, jealousy, anger, selfishness, slander, gossip, conceit, and disorder. ²¹ I fear that when I come again my God may humble me before you, and I may have to mourn over many of those who sinned before and have not repented of the impurity, immorality, and licentiousness which they have practiced.

13 This is the third time I am coming to you. Any charge must be sustained by the evidence of two or three witnesses. ² I warned those who sinned before and all the others, and I warn them now while absent, as I did when present on my second visit, that if I come again I will not spare them — ³ since you desire proof that Christ is speaking in me. He is not weak in dealing with you, but is powerful

12. 16: 2 Cor. 11. 9.   12. 18: 2 Cor. 2. 13; 8. 18.   12. 20: 2 Cor. 2. 1-4; 1 Cor. 1. 11; 3. 3.
13. 1: 2 Cor. 12. 14; Deut. 19. 15.

in you. [4] For he was crucified in weakness, but lives by the power of God. For we are weak in him, but in dealing with you we shall live with him by the power of God.

5 Examine yourselves, to see whether you are holding to your faith. Test yourselves. Do you not realize that Jesus Christ is in you? — unless indeed you fail to meet the test! [6] I hope you will find out that we have not failed. [7] But we pray God that you may not do wrong — not that we may appear to have met the test, but that you may do what is right, though we may seem to have failed. [8] For we cannot do anything against the truth, but only for the truth. [9] For we are glad when we are weak and you are strong. What we pray for is your improvement. [10] I write this while I am away from you, in order that when I come I may not have to be severe in my use of the authority which the Lord has given me for building up and not for tearing down.

11 Finally, brethren, farewell. Mend your ways, heed my appeal, agree with one another, live in peace, and the God of love and peace will be with you. [12] Greet one another with a holy kiss. [13] All the saints greet you.

14 The grace of the Lord Jesus Christ and the love of God and the fellowship of[n] the Holy Spirit be with you all.

[n] Or *and participation in.*

13. 4: Phil. 2. 7–8; Rom. 6. 8. **13. 10:** 2 Cor. 2. 3. **13. 12:** Rom. 16. 16.
13. 13: Phil. 4. 22. **13. 14:** Rom. 16. 20.

THE LETTER OF PAUL TO THE
GALATIANS

1 Paul an apostle — not from men nor through man, but through Jesus Christ and God the Father, who raised him from the dead — ² and all the brethren who are with me,

To the churches of Galatia:

3 Grace to you and peace from God the Father and our Lord Jesus Christ, ⁴ who gave himself for our sins to deliver us from the present evil age, according to the will of our God and Father; ⁵ to whom be the glory for ever and ever. Amen.

6 I am astonished that you are so quickly deserting him who called you in the grace of Christ and turning to a different gospel — ⁷ not that there is another gospel, but there are some who trouble you and want to pervert the gospel of Christ. ⁸ But even if we, or an angel from heaven, should preach to you a gospel contrary to that which we preached to you, let him be accursed. ⁹ As we have said before, so now I say again, If any one is preaching to you a gospel contrary to that which you received, let him be accursed.

10 Am I now seeking the favor of men, or of God? Or am I trying to please men? If I were still pleasing men, I should not be a servant^a of Christ.

11 For I would have you know, brethren, that the gospel which was preached by me is not man's^b gospel. ¹² For I did not receive it from man, nor was I taught it, but it came through a revelation of Jesus Christ. ¹³ For you have heard of my former life in Judaism, how I persecuted the church

---

^{a} Or *slave.* ^{b} Greek *according to* (or *after*) *man.*

1. 3: Rom. 1. 7.   **1. 4:** Gal. 2. 20; 1 Tim. 2. 6.   **1. 5:** Rom. 16. 27.   **1. 8:** 2 Cor. 11. 4.
1. 10: 1 Thess. 2. 4.   **1. 11:** Rom. 1. 16–17.   **1. 13:** Acts 8. 3.

of God violently and tried to destroy it; [14] and I advanced in Judaism beyond many of my own age among my people, so extremely zealous was I for the traditions of my fathers. [15] But when he who had set me apart before I was born, and had called me through his grace, [16] was pleased to reveal his Son to[c] me, in order that I might preach him among the Gentiles, I did not confer with flesh and blood, [17] nor did I go up to Jerusalem to those who were apostles before me, but I went away into Arabia; and again I returned to Damascus.

[18] Then after three years I went up to Jerusalem to visit Ce'phas, and remained with him fifteen days. [19] But I saw none of the other apostles except James the Lord's brother. [20] (In what I am writing to you, before God, I do not lie!) [21] Then I went into the regions of Syria and Ci-li'cia. [22] And I was still not known by sight to the churches of Christ in Judea; [23] they only heard it said, "He who once persecuted us is now preaching the faith he once tried to destroy." [24] And they glorified God because of me.

2 Then after fourteen years I went up again to Jerusalem with Barnabas, taking Titus along with me. [2] I went up by revelation; and I laid before them (but privately before those who were of repute) the gospel which I preach among the Gentiles, lest somehow I should be running or had run in vain. [3] But even Titus, who was with me, was not compelled to be circumcised, though he was a Greek. [4] But because of false brethren secretly brought in, who slipped in to spy out our freedom which we have in Christ Jesus, that they might bring us into bondage — [5] to them we did not yield submission even for a moment, that the truth of the gospel might be preserved for you. [6] And

---

[c] Greek *in*.

1. 14: Acts 22. 3.   **1. 15:** Acts 9. 1–19; Is. 49. 1; Jer. 1. 5.   **1. 18:** Acts 9. 26–30; 11. 30.   **2. 1:** Acts 15. 2.   **2. 5:** Acts 15. 23–29.   **2. 6:** Deut. 10. 17.

from those who were reputed to be something (what they were makes no difference to me; God shows no partiality) — those, I say, who were of repute added nothing to me; [7] but on the contrary, when they saw that I had been entrusted with the gospel to the uncircumcised, just as Peter had been entrusted with the gospel to the circumcised [8] (for he who worked through Peter for the mission to the circumcised worked through me also for the Gentiles), [9] and when they perceived the grace that was given to me, James and Ce′phas and John, who were reputed to be pillars, gave to me and Barnabas the right hand of fellowship, that we should go to the Gentiles and they to the circumcised; [10] only they would have us remember the poor, which very thing I was eager to do.

11 But when Ce′phas came to Antioch I opposed him to his face, because he stood condemned. [12] For before certain men came from James, he ate with the Gentiles; but when they came he drew back and separated himself, fearing the circumcision party. [13] And with him the rest of the Jews acted insincerely, so that even Barnabas was carried away by their insincerity. [14] But when I saw that they were not straightforward about the truth of the gospel, I said to Ce′phas before them all, "If you, though a Jew, live like a Gentile and not like a Jew, how can you compel the Gentiles to live like Jews?" [15] We ourselves, who are Jews by birth and not Gentile sinners, [16] yet who know that a man is not justified[d] by works of the law but through faith in Jesus Christ, even we have believed in Christ Jesus, in order to be justified by faith in Christ, and not by works of the law, because by works of the law shall no one be justified. [17] But if, in our endeavor to be justified in Christ, we our-

---

[d] Or *reckoned righteous;* and so elsewhere.

2. 11: Acts 11. 19–26.   **2. 16:** Ps. 143. 2; Rom. 3. 20.

selves also were found to be sinners, is Christ then an agent of sin? Certainly not! [18] But if I build up again those things which I tore down, then I prove myself a transgressor. [19] For I through the law died to the law, that I might live to God. [20] I have been crucified with Christ; it is no longer I who live, but Christ who lives in me; and the life I now live in the flesh I live by faith in the Son of God, who loved me and gave himself for me. [21] I do not nullify the grace of God; for if justification[e] were through the law, then Christ died to no purpose.

3 O foolish Galatians! Who has bewitched you, before whose eyes Jesus Christ was publicly portrayed as crucified? [2] Let me ask you only this: Did you receive the Spirit by works of the law, or by hearing with faith? [3] Are you so foolish? Having begun with the Spirit, are you now ending with the flesh? [4] Did you suffer so many things in vain? — if it really is in vain. [5] Does he who supplies the Spirit to you and works miracles among you do so by works of the law, or by hearing with faith?

6 Thus Abraham "believed God, and it was reckoned to him as righteousness." [7] So you see that it is men of faith who are the sons of Abraham. [8] And the scripture, foreseeing that God would justify the Gentiles by faith, preached the gospel beforehand to Abraham, saying, "In thee shall all the nations be blessed." [9] So then, those who are men of faith are blessed with Abraham who had faith.

10 For all who rely on works of the law are under a curse; for it is written, "Cursed be every one who does not abide by all things written in the book of the law, and do them." [11] Now it is evident that no man is justified before God by

[e] Or *righteousness*.
2. 20: Gal. 1. 4.
3. 6: Gen. 15. 6; Rom. 4. 3.   **3. 8:** Gen. 12. 3; 18. 18; Acts 3. 25.   **3. 9:** Rom. 4. 16.
3. 10: Deut. 27. 26.   **3. 11:** Hab. 2. 4; Rom. 1. 17; Heb. 10. 38.

the law; for "He who through faith is righteous shall live";[f]
[12] but the law does not rest on faith, for "He who does them
shall live by them." [13] Christ redeemed us from the curse
of the law, having become a curse for us — for it is written,
"Cursed be every one who hangs on a tree" — [14] that in
Christ Jesus the blessing of Abraham might come upon the
Gentiles, that we might receive the promise of the Spirit
through faith.

15 To give a human example, brethren: no one annuls
even a man's will,[g] or adds to it, once it has been ratified.
[16] Now the promises were made to Abraham and to his offspring. It does not say, "And to offsprings," referring to
many; but, referring to one, "And to your offspring," which
is Christ. [17] This is what I mean: the law, which came four
hundred and thirty years afterward, does not annul a covenant previously ratified by God, so as to make the promise
void. [18] For if the inheritance is by the law, it is no longer
by promise; but God gave it to Abraham by a promise.

19 Why then the law? It was added because of transgressions, till the offspring should come to whom the promise
had been made; and it was ordained by angels through an
intermediary. [20] Now an intermediary implies more than
one; but God is one.

21 Is the law then against the promises of God? Certainly
not; for if a law had been given which could make alive, then
righteousness would indeed be by the law. [22] But the scripture consigned all things to sin, that what was promised
to faith in Jesus Christ might be given to those who believe.

23 Now before faith came, we were confined under the
law, kept under restraint until faith should be revealed.
[24] So that the law was our custodian until Christ came, that

[f] Or *the righteous shall live by faith.*   [g] Or *covenant* (as in verse 17).

3. 12: Lev. 18. 5; Rom. 10. 5.   **3. 13:** Deut. 21. 23.   **3. 16:** Gen. 12. 7.   **3. 17:** Ex.
12. 40.   **3. 18:** Rom. 11. 6.   **3. 19:** Rom. 5. 20.   **3. 21:** Rom. 8. 2–4.   **3. 22:** Rom.
3. 9–19; 11. 32.

405

we might be justified by faith. [25] But now that faith has come, we are no longer under a custodian; [26] for in Christ Jesus you are all sons of God, through faith. [27] For as many of you as were baptized into Christ have put on Christ. [28] There is neither Jew nor Greek, there is neither slave nor free, there is neither male nor female; for you are all one in Christ Jesus. [29] And if you are Christ's, then you are Abraham's offspring, heirs according to promise.

4 I mean that the heir, as long as he is a child, is no better than a slave, though he is the owner of all the estate; [2] but he is under guardians and trustees until the date set by the father. [3] So with us; when we were children, we were slaves to the elemental spirits of the universe. [4] But when the time had fully come, God sent forth his Son, born of woman, born under the law, to redeem those who were under the law, [5] so that we might receive adoption as sons. [6] And because you are sons, God has sent the Spirit of his Son into our hearts, crying, "Abba! Father!" [7] So through God you are no longer a slave but a son, and if a son then an heir.

8 Formerly, when you did not know God, you were in bondage to beings that by nature are no gods; [9] but now that you have come to know God, or rather to be known by God, how can you turn back again to the weak and beggarly elemental spirits, whose slaves you want to be once more? [10] You observe days, and months, and seasons, and years! [11] I am afraid I have labored over you in vain.

12 Brethren, I beseech you, become as I am, for I also have become as you are. You did me no wrong; [13] you know it was because of a bodily ailment that I preached the gospel to you at first; [14] and though my condition was a trial to you, you did not scorn or despise me, but received me as

3. 28: Rom. 10. 12.
4. 3: Col. 2. 20.   **4. 6:** Rom. 8. 15.   **4. 13:** Acts 16. 6.

an angel of God, as Christ Jesus. [15] What has become of the satisfaction you felt? For I bear you witness that, if possible, you would have plucked out your eyes and given them to me. [16] Have I then become your enemy by telling you the truth?[h] [17] They make much of you, but for no good purpose; they want to shut you out, that you may make much of them. [18] For a good purpose it is always good to be made much of, and not only when I am present with you. [19] My little children, with whom I am again in travail until Christ be formed in you! [20] I could wish to be present with you now and to change my tone, for I am perplexed about you.

21 Tell me, you who desire to be under law, do you not hear the law? [22] For it is written that Abraham had two sons, one by a slave and one by a free woman. [23] But the son of the slave was born according to the flesh, the son of the free woman through promise. [24] Now this is an allegory: these women are two covenants. One is from Mount Si′nai, bearing children for slavery; she is Hagar. [25] Now Hagar is Mount Si′nai in Arabia;[i] she corresponds to the present Jerusalem, for she is in slavery with her children. [26] But the Jerusalem above is free, and she is our mother. [27] For it is written,

> "Rejoice, O barren one that dost not bear;
> break forth and shout, thou who art not in travail;
> for the desolate hath more children
> than she who hath a husband."

[28] Now we,[j] brethren, like Isaac, are children of promise. [29] But as at that time he who was born according to the flesh persecuted him who was born according to the Spirit, so it is now. [30] But what does the scripture say? "Cast out

[h] Or *by dealing truly with you.*
[i] Many ancient authorities read *For Sinai is a mountain in Arabia.*　　[j] Many ancient authorities read *you.*

4. 19: 1 Cor. 4. 15.　　**4. 22:** Gen. 16. 15; 21. 2, 9.　　**4. 23:** Rom. 9. 7–9.　　**4. 27:** Is. 54. 1.
4. 29: Gen. 21. 9.　　**4. 30:** Gen. 21. 10–12.

the slave and her son; for the son of the slave shall not inherit with the son of the free woman." [31] So, brethren, we are not children of the slave but of the free woman.

5 For freedom Christ has set us free; stand fast therefore, and do not submit again to a yoke of slavery. 2 Now I, Paul, say to you that if you receive circumcision, Christ will be of no advantage to you. [3] I testify again to every man who receives circumcision that he is bound to keep the whole law. [4] You are severed from Christ, you who would be justified by the law; you have fallen away from grace. [5] For through the Spirit, by faith, we wait for the hope of righteousness. [6] For in Christ Jesus neither circumcision nor uncircumcision is of any avail, but faith working through love. [7] You were running well; who hindered you from obeying the truth? [8] This persuasion is not from him who called you. [9] A little yeast leavens the whole lump. [10] I have confidence in the Lord that you will take no other view than mine; and he who is troubling you will bear his judgment, whoever he is. [11] But if I, brethren, still preach circumcision, why am I still persecuted? In that case the stumbling-block of the cross has been removed. [12] I wish those who unsettle you would mutilate themselves!

13 For you were called to freedom, brethren; only do not use your freedom as an opportunity for the flesh, but through love be servants of one another. [14] For the whole law is fulfilled in one word, "You shall love your neighbor as yourself." [15] But if you bite and devour one another take heed that you are not consumed by one another.

16 But I say, walk by the Spirit, and do not gratify the desires of the flesh. [17] For the desires of the flesh are against

5. 6: 1 Cor. 7. 19; Gal. 6. 15.   **5. 9:** 1 Cor. 5. 6.   **5. 14:** Lev. 19. 18; Rom. 13. 8–10.
5. 17: Rom. 7. 15–23.

the Spirit, and the desires of the Spirit are against the flesh; for these are opposed to each other, to prevent you from doing what you would. [18] But if you are led by the Spirit you are not under the law. [19] Now the works of the flesh are plain: immorality, impurity, licentiousness, [20] idolatry, sorcery, enmity, strife, jealousy, anger, selfishness, dissension, party spirit, [21] envy,[k] drunkenness, carousing, and the like. I warn you, as I warned you before, that those who do such things shall not inherit the kingdom of God. [22] But the fruit of the Spirit is love, joy, peace, patience, kindness, goodness, faithfulness, [23] gentleness, self-control; against such there is no law. [24] And those who belong to Christ Jesus have crucified the flesh with its passions and desires.

25 If we live by the Spirit, let us also walk by the Spirit. [26] Let us have no self-conceit, no provoking of one another, no envy of one another.

6 Brethren, if a man is overtaken in any trespass, you who are spiritual should restore him in a spirit of gentleness. Look to yourself, lest you too be tempted. [2] Bear one another's burdens, and so fulfill the law of Christ. [3] For if any one thinks he is something, when he is nothing, he deceives himself. [4] But let each one test his own work, and then his reason to boast will be in himself alone and not in his neighbor. [5] For each man will have to bear his own load.

6 Let him who is taught the word share all good things with him who teaches.

7 Do not be deceived; God is not mocked, for whatever a man sows, that he will also reap. [8] For he who sows to his own flesh will from the flesh reap corruption; but he who sows to the Spirit will from the Spirit reap eternal life. [9] And let us not grow weary in well-doing, for in due season we shall reap, if we do not lose heart. [10] So then, as we have

[k] Many ancient authorities add *murder*.
5. 19: Rom. 1. 28.

opportunity, let us do good to all men, and especially to those who are of the household of faith.

11 See with what large letters I am writing to you with my own hand. [12] It is those who want to make a good showing in the flesh that would compel you to be circumcised, and only in order that they may not be persecuted for the cross of Christ. [13] For even those who receive circumcision do not themselves keep the law, but they desire to have you circumcised that they may glory in your flesh. [14] But far be it from me to glory except in the cross of our Lord Jesus Christ, by which[l] the world has been crucified to me, and I to the world. [15] For neither is circumcision anything, nor uncircumcision, but a new creation. [16] Peace and mercy be upon all who walk by this rule, upon the Israel of God.

17 Henceforth let no man trouble me; for I bear on my body the marks of Jesus.

18 The grace of our Lord Jesus Christ be with your spirit, brethren. Amen.

THE LETTER OF PAUL TO THE
EPHESIANS

1 Paul, an apostle of Christ Jesus by the will of God,
To the saints who are also faithful[a] in Christ Jesus:

2 Grace to you and peace from God our Father and the Lord Jesus Christ.

3 Blessed be the God and Father of our Lord Jesus Christ, who has blessed us in Christ with every spiritual blessing in the heavenly places, [4] even as he chose us in him before

[l] Or *through whom.*
[a] Some ancient authorities read *who are at Ephesus and faithful.*
6. 11: 1 Cor. 16. 21.   **6. 16:** Ps. 125. 5.
1. 3: 2 Cor. 1. 3.

the foundation of the world, that we should be holy and blameless before him. [5] He destined us in love[b] to be his sons through Jesus Christ, according to the purpose of his will, [6] to the praise of his glorious grace which he freely bestowed on us in the Beloved. [7] In him we have redemption through his blood, the forgiveness of our trespasses, according to the riches of his grace [8] which he lavished upon us. [9] For he has made known to us in all wisdom and insight the mystery of his will, according to his purpose which he set forth in Christ [10] as a plan for the fullness of time, to unite all things in him, things in heaven and things on earth.

11 In him, according to the purpose of him who accomplishes all things according to the counsel of his will, [12] we who first hoped in Christ have been destined and appointed to live for the praise of his glory. [13] In him you also, who have heard the word of truth, the gospel of your salvation, and have believed in him, were sealed with the promised Holy Spirit, [14] which is the guarantee of our inheritance until we acquire possession of it, to the praise of his glory.

15 For this reason, because I have heard of your faith in the Lord Jesus and your love[c] toward all the saints, [16] I do not cease to give thanks for you, remembering you in my prayers, [17] that the God of our Lord Jesus Christ, the Father of glory, may give you a spirit of wisdom and of revelation in the knowledge of him, [18] having the eyes of your hearts enlightened, that you may know what is the hope to which he has called you, what are the riches of his glorious inheritance in the saints, [19] and what is the immeasurable greatness of his power in us who believe, according to the working of his great might [20] which he accomplished in Christ when he raised him from the dead and made him sit at his right

[b] Or *before him in love, having destined us.*
[c] Many ancient authorities omit *and your love.*
1. 6: Col. 1. 13.   **1. 7:** Col. 1. 14.   **1. 10:** Gal. 4. 4   **1. 14:** 2 Cor. 1. 22.
1. 15: Col. 1. 9.   **1. 16:** Col. 1. 3.   **1. 18:** Deut. 33. 3.   **1. 20:** Ps. 110. 1.

hand in the heavenly places, [21] far above all rule and authority and power and dominion, and above every name that is named, not only in this age but also in that which is to come; [22] and he has put all things under his feet and has made him the head over all things for the church, [23] which is his body, the fullness of him who fills all in all.

2 And you he made alive, when you were dead through the trespasses and sins [2] in which you once walked, following the course of this world, following the prince of the power of the air, the spirit that is now at work in the sons of disobedience. [3] Among these we all once lived in the passions of our flesh, following the desires of body and mind, and so we were by nature children of wrath, like the rest of mankind. [4] But God, who is rich in mercy, out of the great love with which he loved us, [5] even when we were dead through our trespasses, made us alive together with Christ (by grace you have been saved), [6] and raised us up with him, and made us sit with him in the heavenly places in Christ Jesus, [7] that in the coming ages he might show the immeasurable riches of his grace in kindness toward us in Christ Jesus. [8] For by grace you have been saved through faith; and this is not your own doing, it is the gift of God — [9] not because of works, lest any man should boast. [10] For we are his workmanship, created in Christ Jesus for good works, which God prepared beforehand, that we should walk in them.

11 Therefore remember that at one time you Gentiles in the flesh, called the uncircumcision by what is called the circumcision, which is made in the flesh by hands — [12] remember that you were at that time separated from Christ, alienated from the commonwealth of Israel, and strangers to the covenants of promise, having no hope and without

1. 21: Col. 1. 6; 2. 10, 15.   **1. 22:** Ps. 8. 6; Col. 1. 19.   **1. 23:** Rom. 12. 5; Col. 2. 17.
2. 2: Col. 1. 13.   **2. 8:** Gal. 2. 16.   **2. 12:** Is. 57. 19.

God in the world. [13] But now in Christ Jesus you who once were far off have been brought near in the blood of Christ. [14] For he is our peace, who has made us both one, and has broken down the dividing wall of hostility, [15] by abolishing in his flesh the law of commandments and ordinances, that he might create in himself one new man in place of the two, so making peace, [16] and might reconcile us both to God in one body through the cross, thereby bringing the hostility to an end. [17] And he came and preached peace to you who were far off and peace to those who were near; [18] for through him we both have access in one Spirit to the Father. [19] So then you are no longer strangers and sojourners, but you are fellow citizens with the saints and members of the household of God, [20] built upon the foundation of the apostles and prophets, Christ Jesus himself being the chief cornerstone, [21] in whom the whole structure is joined together and grows into a holy temple in the Lord; [22] in whom you also are built into it for a dwelling place of God in the Spirit.

3 For this reason I Paul, a prisoner for Christ Jesus on behalf of you Gentiles — [2] assuming that you have heard of the stewardship of God's grace that was given to me for you, [3] how the mystery was made known to me by revelation, as I have written briefly. [4] When you read this you can perceive my insight into the mystery of Christ, [5] which was not made known to the sons of men in other generations as it has now been revealed to his holy apostles and prophets by the Spirit; [6] that is, how the Gentiles are fellow heirs, members of the same body, and partakers of the promise in Christ Jesus through the gospel.

7 Of this gospel I was made a minister according to the gift of God's grace which was given me by the working of his power. [8] To me, though I am the very least of all the

2. 17: Is. 57. 19.   **3. 2:** Col. 1. 25.   **3. 6:** Col. 1. 27.

saints, this grace was given, to preach to the Gentiles the unsearchable riches of Christ, [9] and to make all men see what is the plan of the mystery hidden for ages in[d] God who created all things; [10] that through the church the manifold wisdom of God might now be made known to the principalities and powers in the heavenly places. [11] This was according to the eternal purpose which he has realized in Christ Jesus our Lord, [12] in whom we have boldness and confidence of access through our faith in him. [13] So I ask you not to[e] lose heart over what I am suffering for you, which is your glory.

14 For this reason I bow my knees before the Father, [15] from whom every family in heaven and on earth is named, [16] that according to the riches of his glory he may grant you to be strengthened with might through his Spirit in the inner man, [17] and that Christ may dwell in your hearts through faith; that you, being rooted and grounded in love, [18] may have power to comprehend with all the saints what is the breadth and length and height and depth, [19] and to know the love of Christ which surpasses knowledge, that you may be filled with all the fullness of God.

20 Now to him who by the power at work within us is able to do far more abundantly than all that we ask or think, [21] to him be glory in the church and in Christ Jesus to all generations, for ever and ever. Amen.

4 I therefore, a prisoner for the Lord, beg you to lead a life worthy of the calling to which you have been called, [2] with all lowliness and meekness, with patience, forbearing one another in love, [3] eager to maintain the unity of the Spirit in the bond of peace. [4] There is one body and

[d] Or *by.*   [e] Or *I ask that I may not.*
3. 9: Col. 1. 26.
4. 2: Col. 3. 12–13.

one Spirit, just as you were called to the one hope that belongs to your call, [5] one Lord, one faith, one baptism, [6] one God and Father of us all, who is above all and through all and in all. [7] But grace was given to each of us according to the measure of Christ's gift. [8] Therefore it is said,

> "When he ascended on high he led a host of captives,
> and he gave gifts to men."

[9] (In saying, "He ascended," what does it mean but that he had also descended into the lower parts of the earth? [10] He who descended is he who also ascended far above all the heavens, that he might fill all things.) [11] And his gifts were that some should be apostles, some prophets, some evangelists, some pastors and teachers, [12] for the equipment of the saints, for the work of ministry, for building up the body of Christ, [13] until we all attain to the unity of the faith and of the knowledge of the Son of God, to mature manhood, to the measure of the stature of the fullness of Christ; [14] so that we may no longer be children, tossed to and fro and carried about with every wind of doctrine, by the cunning of men, by their craftiness in deceitful wiles. [15] Rather, speaking the truth in love, we are to grow up in every way into him who is the head, into Christ, [16] from whom the whole body, joined and knit together by every joint with which it is supplied, when each part is working properly, makes bodily growth and upbuilds itself in love.

17 Now this I affirm and testify in the Lord, that you must no longer live as the Gentiles do, in the futility of their minds; [18] they are darkened in their understanding, alienated from the life of God because of the ignorance that is in them, due to their hardness of heart; [19] they have become callous and have given themselves up to licentiousness, greedy to practice every kind of uncleanness. [20] You

4. 8: Ps. 68. 19.   **4. 15:** Col. 1. 18.   **4. 16:** Col. 2. 19.

did not so learn Christ! — ²¹ assuming that you have heard about him and were taught in him, as the truth is in Jesus. ²² Put off your old nature which belongs to your former manner of life and is corrupt through deceitful lusts, ²³ and be renewed in the spirit of your minds, ²⁴ and put on the new nature, created after the likeness of God in true righteousness and holiness.

25 Therefore, putting away falsehood, let every one speak the truth with his neighbor, for we are members one of another. ²⁶ Be angry but do not sin; do not let the sun go down on your anger, ²⁷ and give no opportunity to the devil. ²⁸ Let the thief no longer steal, but rather let him labor, doing honest work with his hands, so that he may be able to give to those in need. ²⁹ Let no evil talk come out of your mouths, but only such as is good for edifying, as fits the occasion, that it may impart grace to those who hear. ³⁰ And do not grieve the Holy Spirit of God, in whom you were sealed for the day of redemption. ³¹ Let all bitterness and wrath and anger and clamor and slander be put away from you, with all malice, ³² and be kind to one another, tenderhearted, forgiving one another, as God in Christ forgave you.

5 Therefore be imitators of God, as beloved children. ² And walk in love, as Christ loved us and gave himself up for us, a fragrant offering and sacrifice to God.

3 But immorality and all impurity or covetousness must not even be named among you, as is fitting among saints. ⁴ Let there be no filthiness, nor silly talk, nor levity, which are not fitting; but instead let there be thanksgiving. ⁵ Be sure of this, that no immoral or impure man, or one who is covetous (that is, an idolater), has any inheritance in the kingdom of Christ and of God. ⁶ Let no one deceive you with

4. 25: Zech. 8. 16; Rom. 12. 5.
5. 2: Ex. 29. 18; Ezek. 20. 41.

empty words, for it is because of these things that the wrath of God comes upon the sons of disobedience. [7] Therefore do not associate with them, [8] for once you were darkness, but now you are light in the Lord; walk as children of light [9] (for the fruit of light is found in all that is good and right and true), [10] and try to learn what is pleasing to the Lord. [11] Take no part in the unfruitful works of darkness, but instead expose them. [12] For it is a shame even to speak of the things that they do in secret; [13] but when anything is exposed by the light it becomes visible, for anything that becomes visible is light. [14] Therefore it is said,

> "Awake, O sleeper, and arise from the dead,
> and Christ shall give you light."

[15] Look carefully then how you walk, not as unwise men but as wise, [16] making the most of the time, because the days are evil. [17] Therefore do not be foolish, but understand what the will of the Lord is. [18] And do not get drunk with wine, for that is debauchery; but be filled with the Spirit, [19] addressing one another in psalms and hymns and spiritual songs, singing and making melody to the Lord with all your heart, [20] always and for everything giving thanks in the name of our Lord Jesus Christ to God the Father.

[21] Be subject to one another out of reverence for Christ. [22] Wives, be subject to your husbands, as to the Lord. [23] For the husband is the head of the wife as Christ is the head of the church, his body, and is himself its Savior. [24] As the church is subject to Christ, so let wives also be subject in everything to their husbands. [25] Husbands, love your wives, as Christ loved the church and gave himself up for her, [26] that he might consecrate her, having cleansed her by the washing of water with the word, [27] that the church might be presented before him in splendor, without spot

5. 16: Col. 4. 5.   **5. 19:** Col. 3. 16–17.   **5. 22–6. 9:** Col. 3. 18–4. 1.

or wrinkle or any such thing, that she might be holy and without blemish. ²⁸ Even so husbands should love their wives as their own bodies. He who loves his wife loves himself. ²⁹ For no man ever hates his own flesh, but nourishes and cherishes it, as Christ does the church, ³⁰ because we are members of his body. ³¹ "For this reason a man shall leave his father and mother and be joined to his wife, and the two shall become one." ³² This is a great mystery, and I take it to mean Christ and the church; ³³ however, let each one of you love his wife as himself, and let the wife see that she respects her husband.

6 Children, obey your parents in the Lord, for this is right. ² "Honor your father and mother" (this is the first commandment with a promise), ³ "that it may be well with you and that you may live long on the earth." ⁴ Fathers, do not provoke your children to anger, but bring them up in the discipline and instruction of the Lord.

5 Slaves, be obedient to those who are your earthly masters, with fear and trembling, in singleness of heart, as to Christ; ⁶ not in the way of eyeservice, as men-pleasers, but as servants*ᶠ* of Christ, doing the will of God from the heart, ⁷ rendering service with a good will as to the Lord and not to men, ⁸ knowing that whatever good any one does, he will receive the same again from the Lord, whether he is a slave or free. ⁹ Masters, do the same to them, and forbear threatening, knowing that he who is both their Master and yours is in heaven, and that there is no partiality with him.

10 Finally, be strong in the Lord and in the strength of his might. ¹¹ Put on the whole armor of God, that you may be able to stand against the wiles of the devil. ¹² For we are not contending against flesh and blood, but against

---

ᶠ Or *slaves*.

5. 31: Gen. 2. 24.
6. 2: Ex. 20. 12.   **6. 3:** Deut. 5. 16.

the principalities, against the powers, against the world rulers of this present darkness, against the spiritual hosts of wickedness in the heavenly places. [13] Therefore take the whole armor of God, that you may be able to withstand in the evil day, and having done all, to stand. [14] Stand therefore, having girded your loins with truth, and having put on the breastplate of righteousness, [15] and having shod your feet with the equipment of the gospel of peace; [16] above all taking the shield of faith, with which you can quench all the flaming darts of the evil one. [17] And take the helmet of salvation, and the sword of the Spirit, which is the word of God. [18] Pray at all times in the Spirit, with all prayer and supplication. To that end keep alert with all perseverance, making supplication for all the saints, [19] and also for me, that utterance may be given me in opening my mouth boldly to proclaim the mystery of the gospel, [20] for which I am an ambassador in chains; that I may declare it boldly, as I ought to speak.

21 Now that you also may know how I am and what I am doing, Tych'i-cus the beloved brother and faithful minister in the Lord will tell you everything. [22] I have sent him to you for this very purpose, that you may know how we are, and that he may encourage your hearts.

23 Peace be to the brethren, and love with faith, from God the Father and the Lord Jesus Christ. [24] Grace be with all who love our Lord Jesus Christ with love undying.

6. 14: Is. 11. 5; 59. 17; 1 Thess. 5. 8.   **6. 15:** Is. 52. 7.   **6. 21–22:** Col. 4. 7–8.

THE LETTER OF PAUL TO THE
PHILIPPIANS

1 Paul and Timothy, servants[a] of Christ Jesus,
  To all the saints in Christ Jesus who are at Philippi,
with the bishops and deacons:
  2 Grace to you and peace from God our Father and the
Lord Jesus Christ.

3 I thank my God in all my remembrance of you, [4] always
in every prayer of mine for you all making my prayer with
joy, [5] thankful for your partnership in the gospel from the
first day until now. [6] And I am sure that he who began a
good work in you will bring it to completion at the day of
Jesus Christ. [7] It is right for me to feel thus about you all,
because I hold you all in my heart as partakers with me
of grace, both in my imprisonment and in the defense and
confirmation of the gospel. [8] For God is my witness, how
I yearn for you all with the affection of Christ Jesus. [9] And
it is my prayer that your love may abound more and more,
with knowledge and all discernment, [10] so that you may approve what is excellent, and may be pure and blameless
for the day of Christ, [11] filled with the fruits of righteousness
which come through Jesus Christ, to the glory and praise of
God.

12 I want you to know, brethren, that what has happened to me has really served to advance the gospel, [13] so
that it has become known throughout the whole praetorian
guard[b] and to all the rest that my imprisonment is for Christ;
[14] and most of the brethren have been made confident in

---

[a] Or *slaves*.   [b] Greek *in the whole praetorium*.

1. 1: Acts 16. 1, 12–40; Rom. 1. 1; 2 Cor. 1. 1; Gal. 1. 10; Col. 1. 1; 1 Thess. 1. 1;
2 Thess. 1. 1; Philem. 1.   **1. 2:** Rom. 1. 7.   **1. 6, 10:** 1 Cor. 1. 8.   **1. 7:** Acts 21. 33;
2 Cor. 7. 3; Eph. 6. 20.   **1. 12:** Lk. 21. 13.   **1. 13:** Acts 28. 30; 2 Tim. 2. 9.

the Lord because of my imprisonment, and are much more bold to speak the word of God without fear.

15 Some indeed preach Christ from envy and rivalry, but others from good will. [16] The latter do it out of love, knowing that I am put here for the defense of the gospel; [17] the former proclaim Christ out of partisanship, not sincerely but thinking to afflict me in my imprisonment. [18] What then? Only that in every way, whether in pretense or in truth, Christ is proclaimed; and in that I rejoice.

19 Yes, and I shall rejoice. For I know that through your prayers and the help of the Spirit of Jesus Christ this will turn out for my deliverance, [20] as it is my eager expectation and hope that I shall not be at all ashamed, but that with full courage now as always Christ will be honored in my body, whether by life or by death. [21] For to me to live is Christ, and to die is gain. [22] If it is to be life in the flesh, that means fruitful labor for me. Yet which I shall choose I cannot tell. [23] I am hard pressed between the two. My desire is to depart and be with Christ, for that is far better. [24] But to remain in the flesh is more necessary on your account. [25] Convinced of this, I know that I shall remain and continue with you all, for your progress and joy in the faith, [26] so that in me you may have ample cause to glory in Christ Jesus, because of my coming to you again.

[27] Only let your manner of life be worthy of the gospel of Christ, so that whether I come and see you or am absent, I may hear of you that you stand firm in one spirit, with one mind striving side by side for the faith of the gospel, [28] and not frightened in anything by your opponents. This is a clear omen to them of their destruction, but of your salvation, and that from God. [29] For it has been granted to you that for the sake of Christ you should not only believe

1. 19: Acts 16. 7; 2 Cor. 1. 11.   1. 20: Rom. 14. 8.   1. 21: Gal. 2. 20.
1. 28: 2 Thess. 1. 5.

in him but also suffer for his sake, [30] engaged in the same conflict which you saw and now hear to be mine.

2 So if there is any encouragement in Christ, any incentive of love, any participation in the Spirit, any affection and sympathy, [2] complete my joy by being of the same mind, having the same love, being in full accord and of one mind. [3] Do nothing from selfishness or conceit, but in humility count others better than yourselves. [4] Let each of you look not only to his own interests, but also to the interests of others. [5] Have this mind among yourselves, which you have in Christ Jesus, [6] who, though he was in the form of God, did not count equality with God a thing to be grasped, [7] but emptied himself, taking the form of a servant,[c] being born in the likeness of men. [8] And being found in human form he humbled himself and became obedient unto death, even death on a cross. [9] Therefore God has highly exalted him and bestowed on him the name which is above every name, [10] that at the name of Jesus every knee should bow, in heaven and on earth and under the earth, [11] and every tongue confess that Jesus Christ is Lord, to the glory of God the Father.

12 Therefore, my beloved, as you have always obeyed, so now, not only as in my presence but much more in my absence, work out your own salvation with fear and trembling; [13] for God is at work in you, both to will and to work for his good pleasure.

14 Do all things without grumbling or questioning, [15] that you may be blameless and innocent, children of God without blemish in the midst of a crooked and perverse generation, among whom you shine as lights in the world, [16] holding fast the word of life, so that in the day of Christ I may be

---

[c] Or *slave*.

1. 30: Acts 16. 19–40; 1 Thess. 2. 2.
2. 1: 2 Cor. 13. 14.   **2. 3–4:** Rom. 12. 10; 15. 1–2.   **2. 5–8:** Mt. 11. 29; 20. 28; Jn. 1. 1; 2 Cor. 8. 9; Heb. 5. 8.   **2. 9–11:** Rom. 10. 9; 14. 9; Eph. 1. 20–21.
2. 13: 1 Cor. 15. 10.   **2. 15:** Mt. 5. 45, 48.

proud that I did not run in vain or labor in vain. [17] Even if I am to be poured as a libation upon the sacrificial offering of your faith, I am glad and rejoice with you all. [18] Likewise you also should be glad and rejoice with me.

19 I hope in the Lord Jesus to send Timothy to you soon, so that I may be cheered by news of you. [20] I have no one like him, who will be genuinely anxious for your welfare. [21] They all look after their own interests, not those of Jesus Christ. [22] But Timothy's worth you know, how as a son with a father he has served with me in the gospel. [23] I hope therefore to send him just as soon as I see how it will go with me; [24] and I trust in the Lord that shortly I myself shall come also.

25 I have thought it necessary to send to you E-paph-ro-di'tus my brother and fellow worker and fellow soldier, and your messenger and minister to my need, [26] for he has been longing for you all, and has been distressed because you heard that he was ill. [27] Indeed he was ill, near to death. But God had mercy on him, and not only on him but on me also, lest I should have sorrow upon sorrow. [28] I am the more eager to send him, therefore, that you may rejoice at seeing him again, and that I may be less anxious. [29] So receive him in the Lord with all joy; and honor such men, [30] for he nearly died for the work of Christ, risking his life to complete your service to me.

3 Finally, my brethren, rejoice in the Lord. To write the same things to you is not irksome to me, and is safe for you.

2 Look out for the dogs, look out for the evil-workers, look out for those who mutilate the flesh. [3] For we are the true circumcision, who worship God in spirit,[d] and glory

[d] Some ancient authorities read *worship by the Spirit of God.*
3. 3: Rom. 2. 28–29; Gal. 6. 14–15.

in Christ Jesus, and put no confidence in the flesh. [4] Though I myself have reason for confidence in the flesh also. If any other man thinks he has reason for confidence in the flesh, I have more: [5] circumcised on the eighth day, of the people of Israel, of the tribe of Benjamin, a Hebrew born of Hebrews; as to the law a Pharisee, [6] as to zeal a persecutor of the church, as to righteousness under the law blameless. [7] But whatever gain I had, I counted as loss for the sake of Christ. [8] Indeed I count everything as loss because of the surpassing worth of knowing Christ Jesus my Lord. For his sake I have suffered the loss of all things, and count them as refuse, in order that I may gain Christ [9] and be found in him, not having a righteousness of my own, based on law, but that which is through faith in Christ, the righteousness from God that depends on faith; [10] that I may know him and the power of his resurrection, and may share his sufferings, becoming like him in his death, [11] that if possible I may attain the resurrection from the dead.

12 Not that I have already obtained this or am already perfect; but I press on to make it my own, because Christ Jesus has made me his own. [13] Brethren, I do not consider that I have made it my own; but one thing I do, forgetting what lies behind and straining forward to what lies ahead, [14] I press on toward the goal for the prize of the upward call of God in Christ Jesus. [15] Let those of us who are mature be thus minded; and if in anything you are otherwise minded, God will reveal that also to you. [16] Only let us hold true to what we have attained.

17 Brethren, join in imitating me, and mark those who live as you have an example in us. [18] For many, of whom I have often told you and now tell you even with tears, live as enemies of the cross of Christ. [19] Their end is destruction,

3. 4–7: Acts 8. 3; 22. 3–21; 23. 6; 26. 4–23; Rom. 11. 1; 2 Cor. 11. 18–31.   **3. 17**: 1 Cor. 4. 15–17.

their god is the belly, and they glory in their shame, with minds set on earthly things. [20] But our commonwealth is in heaven, and from it we await a Savior, the Lord Jesus Christ, [21] who will change our lowly body to be like his glorious body, by the power which enables him even to subject all things to himself.

4 Therefore, my brethren, whom I love and long for, my joy and crown, stand firm thus in the Lord, my beloved.

2 I entreat Eu-o′di-a and I entreat Syn′ty-che to agree in the Lord. [3] And I ask you also, true yokefellow, help these women, for they have labored side by side with me in the gospel together with Clement and the rest of my fellow workers, whose names are in the book of life.

4 Rejoice in the Lord always; again I will say, Rejoice. [5] Let all men know your forbearance. The Lord is at hand. [6] Have no anxiety about anything, but in everything by prayer and supplication with thanksgiving let your requests be made known to God. [7] And the peace of God, which passes all understanding, will keep your hearts and your minds in Christ Jesus.

8 Finally, brethren, whatever is true, whatever is honorable, whatever is just, whatever is pure, whatever is lovely, whatever is gracious, if there is any excellence, if there is anything worthy of praise, think about these things. [9] What you have learned and received and heard and seen in me, do; and the God of peace will be with you.

10 I rejoice in the Lord greatly that now at length you have revived your concern for me; you were indeed concerned for me, but you had no opportunity. [11] Not that I complain of want; for I have learned, in whatever state I

3. 21: 1 Cor. 15. 35–58; Col. 3. 4.
4. 3: Lk. 10. 20.   4. 6: Mt. 6. 25–34.   4. 9: Rom. 15. 33.   4. 10: 2 Cor. 11. 9.

am, to be content. [12] I know how to be abased, and I know how to abound; in any and all circumstances I have learned the secret of facing plenty and hunger, abundance and want. [13] I can do all things in him who strengthens me.

14 Yet it was kind of you to share my trouble. [15] And you Philippians yourselves know that in the beginning of the gospel, when I left Mac-e-do′ni-a, no church entered into partnership with me in giving and receiving except you only; [16] for even in Thes-sa-lo-ni′ca you sent me help[e] once and again. [17] Not that I seek the gift; but I seek the fruit which increases to your credit. [18] I have received full payment, and more; I am filled, having received from E-paph-ro-di′tus the gifts you sent, a fragrant offering, a sacrifice acceptable and pleasing to God. [19] And my God will supply every need of yours according to his riches in glory in Christ Jesus. [20] To our God and Father be glory for ever and ever. Amen.

21 Greet every saint in Christ Jesus. The brethren who are with me greet you. [22] All the saints greet you, especially those of Caesar's household.

23 The grace of the Lord Jesus Christ be with your spirit.

THE LETTER OF PAUL TO THE
COLOSSIANS

1   Paul, an apostle of Christ Jesus by the will of God, and Timothy our brother,

2 To the saints and faithful brethren in Christ at Co-los′sae:

Grace to you and peace from God our Father.

---

[e] Many ancient authorities read *money for my needs*.
4. 13: 2 Cor. 12. 9.   **4. 16:** Acts 17. 1–9; 1 Thess. 2. 9.   **4. 23:** Gal. 6. 18; Philem. 25.
1. 2: Rom. 1. 7.

3 We always thank God, the Father of our Lord Jesus Christ, when we pray for you, ⁴ because we have heard of your faith in Christ Jesus and of the love which you have for all the saints, ⁵ because of the hope laid up for you in heaven. Of this you have heard before in the word of the truth, the gospel ⁶ which has come to you, as indeed in the whole world it is bearing fruit and growing — so among yourselves, from the day you heard and understood the grace of God in truth, ⁷ as you learned it from Ep′a-phras our beloved fellow servant. He is a faithful minister of Christ on our*ᵃ* behalf ⁸ and has made known to us your love in the Spirit.

9 And so, from the day we heard of it, we have not ceased to pray for you, asking that you may be filled with the knowledge of his will in all spiritual wisdom and understanding, ¹⁰ to lead a life worthy of the Lord, fully pleasing to him, bearing fruit in every good work and increasing in the knowledge of God. ¹¹ May you be strengthened with all power, according to his glorious might, for all endurance and patience with joy, ¹² giving thanks to the Father, who has qualified us*ᵇ* to share in the inheritance of the saints in light. ¹³ He has delivered us from the dominion of darkness and transferred us to the kingdom of his beloved Son, ¹⁴ in whom we have redemption, the forgiveness of sins.

15 He is the image of the invisible God, the first-born of all creation; ¹⁶ for in him all things were created, in heaven and on earth, visible and invisible, whether thrones or dominions or principalities or authorities — all things were created through him and for him. ¹⁷ He is before all things, and in him all things hold together. ¹⁸ He is the head of the body, the church; he is the beginning, the first-born from the dead,

---

ᵃ Many ancient authorities read *your*.   *ᵇ* Some ancient authorities read *you*.
1. 3: Eph. 1. 16.   **1. 7:** Col. 4. 12; Philem. 23.   **1. 9:** Eph. 1. 15–17.   **1. 13:** Eph. 1. 21; 2. 2.   **1. 15:** 2 Cor. 4. 4.   **1. 17:** Prov. 8. 22–31.   **1. 18:** Eph. 4. 15.

that in everything he might be preëminent. [19] For in him all the fullness of God was pleased to dwell, [20] and through him to reconcile to himself all things, whether on earth or in heaven, making peace by the blood of his cross.

21 And you, who once were estranged and hostile in mind, doing evil deeds, [22] he has now reconciled in his body of flesh by his death, in order to present you holy and blameless and irreproachable before him, [23] provided that you continue in the faith, stable and steadfast, not shifting from the hope of the gospel which you heard, which has been preached to every creature under heaven, and of which I Paul became a minister.

24 Now I rejoice in my sufferings for your sake, and in my flesh I complete what remains of Christ's afflictions for the sake of his body, that is, the church, [25] of which I became a minister according to the divine office which was given to me for you, to make the word of God fully known, [26] the mystery hidden for ages and generations[c] but now made manifest to his saints. [27] To them God chose to make known how great among the Gentiles are the riches of the glory of this mystery, which is Christ in you, the hope of glory. [28] Him we proclaim, warning every man and teaching every man in all wisdom, that we may present every man mature in Christ. [29] For this I toil, striving with all the energy which he mightily inspires within me.

2 For I want you to know how greatly I strive for you, and for those at La-od-i-ce'a, and for all who have not seen my face, [2] that their hearts may be encouraged as they are knit together in love, to have all the riches of assured understanding and the knowledge of God's mystery, of Christ, [3] in whom are hid all the treasures of wisdom and

[c] Or *from angels and men.*
1. 25: Eph. 3. 2.   **1. 26:** Eph. 3. 9.
2. 3: Is. 45. 3.

knowledge. [4] I say this in order that no one may delude you with beguiling speech. [5] For though I am absent in body, yet I am with you in spirit, rejoicing to see your good order and the firmness of your faith in Christ.

6 As therefore you received Christ Jesus the Lord, so live in him, [7] rooted and built up in him and established in the faith, just as you were taught, abounding in thanksgiving.

8 See to it that no one makes a prey of you by philosophy and empty deceit, according to human tradition, according to the elemental spirits of the universe, and not according to Christ. [9] For in him dwells the whole fullness of deity bodily, [10] and you have come to fullness of life in him, who is the head of all rule and authority. [11] In him also you were circumcised with a circumcision made without hands, by putting off the body of flesh in the circumcision of Christ; [12] and you were buried with him in baptism, in which you were also raised with him through faith in the working of God, who raised him from the dead. [13] And you, who were dead in trespasses and the uncircumcision of your flesh, God made alive together with him, having forgiven us all our trespasses, [14] having canceled the bond which stood against us with its legal demands; this he set aside, nailing it to the cross. [15] He disarmed the principalities and powers and made a public example of them, triumphing over them in him.[d]

16 Therefore let no one pass judgment on you in questions of food and drink or with regard to a festival or a new moon or a sabbath. [17] These are only a shadow of what is to come; but the substance belongs to Christ. [18] Let no one disqualify you, insisting on self-abasement and worship of angels,

[d] Or *in it* (that is, the cross).

2. 10: Eph. 1. 21–22.   **2. 15:** Eph. 1. 21.   **2. 16:** Rom. 14. 1–12.   **2. 17:** Eph. 1. 23.

taking his stand on visions, puffed up without reason by his sensuous mind, [19] and not holding fast to the Head, from whom the whole body, nourished and knit together through its joints and ligaments, grows with a growth that is from God.

20 If with Christ you died to the elemental spirits of the universe, why do you live as if you still belonged to the world? Why do you submit to regulations, [21] "Do not handle, Do not taste, Do not touch" [22] (referring to things which all perish as they are used), according to human precepts and doctrines? [23] These have indeed an appearance of wisdom in promoting rigor of devotion and self-abasement and severity to the body, but they are of no value in checking the indulgence of the flesh.[e]

3 If then you have been raised with Christ, seek the things that are above, where Christ is, seated at the right hand of God. [2] Set your minds on things that are above, not on things that are on earth. [3] For you have died, and your life is hid with Christ in God. [4] When Christ who is our life appears, then you also will appear with him in glory.

5 Put to death therefore what is earthly in you: immorality, impurity, passion, evil desire, and covetousness, which is idolatry. [6] On account of these the wrath of God is coming upon the sons of disobedience,[f] [7] among whom you also once walked, when you lived in these things. [8] But now put away also all these: anger, wrath, malice, slander, and foul talk from your mouth. [9] Do not lie to one another, seeing that you have put off the old nature with its practices [10] and have put on the new nature, which is being renewed in knowledge after the image of its creator. [11] Here there cannot be Greek and Jew, circumcised and uncircumcised,

[e] Or *are of no value, serving only to indulge the flesh.*
[f] Some ancient authorities omit *upon the sons of disobedience,* and read *in which.*
2. 19: Eph. 1. 22; 4. 16.   **2. 20:** Gal. 4. 3.   **2. 22:** Is. 29. 13; Mk. 7. 7.
3. 1: Ps. 110. 1.   **3. 10:** Gen. 1. 26.

barbarian, Scyth'i-an, slave, free man, but Christ is all, and in all.

12 Put on then, as God's chosen ones, holy and beloved, compassion, kindness, lowliness, meekness, and patience, [13] forbearing one another and, if one has a complaint against another, forgiving each other; as the Lord has forgiven you, so you also must forgive. [14] And above all these put on love, which binds everything together in perfect harmony. [15] And let the peace of Christ rule in your hearts, to which indeed you were called in the one body. And be thankful. [16] Let the word of Christ dwell in you richly, as you teach and admonish one another in all wisdom, and as you sing psalms and hymns and spiritual songs with thankfulness in your hearts to God. [17] And whatever you do, in word or deed, do everything in the name of the Lord Jesus, giving thanks to God the Father through him.

18 Wives, be subject to your husbands, as is fitting in the Lord. [19] Husbands, love your wives, and do not be harsh with them. [20] Children, obey your parents in everything, for this pleases the Lord. [21] Fathers, do not provoke your children, lest they become discouraged. [22] Slaves, obey in everything those who are your earthly masters, not with eyeservice, as men-pleasers, but in singleness of heart, fearing the Lord. [23] Whatever your task, work heartily, as serving the Lord and not men, [24] knowing that from the Lord you will receive the inheritance as your reward; you are serving the Lord Christ. [25] For the wrongdoer will be paid back for the wrong he has done, and there is no partiality.

4 [1] Masters, treat your slaves justly and fairly, knowing that you also have a Master in heaven.

2 Continue steadfastly in prayer, being watchful in it

3. 12–13: Eph. 4. 2.   **3. 16–17:** Eph. 5. 19.   **3. 18–4. 1:** Eph. 5. 22–6. 9.   **3. 23:** Rom. 12. 11.
4. 1: Lev. 25. 43, 53   **4. 2:** Rom. 12. 12.

with thanksgiving; [3] and pray for us also, that God may open to us a door for the word, to declare the mystery of Christ, on account of which I am in prison, [4] that I may make it clear, as I ought to speak.

5 Conduct yourselves wisely toward outsiders, making the most of the time. [6] Let your speech always be gracious, seasoned with salt, so that you may know how you ought to answer every one.

7 Tych'i-cus will tell you all about my affairs; he is a beloved brother and faithful minister and fellow servant in the Lord. [8] I have sent him to you for this very purpose, that you may know how we are and that he may encourage your hearts, [9] and with him O-nes'i-mus, the faithful and beloved brother, who is one of yourselves. They will tell you of everything that has taken place here.

10 Ar-is-tar'chus my fellow prisoner greets you, and Mark the cousin of Barnabas (concerning whom you have received instructions — if he comes to you, receive him), [11] and Jesus who is called Justus. These are the only men of the circumcision among my fellow workers for the kingdom of God, and they have been a comfort to me. [12] Ep'a-phras, who is one of yourselves, a servant[g] of Christ Jesus, greets you, always remembering you earnestly in his prayers, that you may stand mature and fully assured in all the will of God. [13] For I bear him witness that he has worked hard for you and for those in La-od-i-ce'a and in Hi-e-rap'o-lis. [14] Luke the beloved physician and Demas greet you. [15] Give my greetings to the brethren at La-od-i-ce'a, and to Nym'pha and the church in her house. [16] And when this letter has been read among you, have it read also in the church of

[g] Or *slave*.

4. 5: Eph. 5. 16.   4. 7–8: Eph. 6. 21–22.   4. 9: Philem. 10.   4. 10–11: Acts 19. 29; 27. 2; Philem. 24.   4. 12: Col. 1. 7; Philem. 23.   4. 14: 2 Tim. 4. 10–11; Philem. 24.

the La-od-i-ce′ans; and see that you read also the letter
from La-od-i-ce′a. [17] And say to Ar-chip′pus, "See that
you fulfill the ministry which you have received in the Lord."

18 I, Paul, write this greeting with my own hand. Remember my fetters. Grace be with you.

THE FIRST LETTER OF PAUL TO THE
THESSALONIANS

1 Paul, Sil-va′nus, and Timothy,
To the church of the Thes-sa-lo′ni-ans in God the
Father and the Lord Jesus Christ:
Grace to you and peace.

2 We give thanks to God always for you all, constantly
mentioning you in our prayers, [3] remembering before our
God and Father your work of faith and labor of love and
steadfastness of hope in our Lord Jesus Christ. [4] For we
know, brethren beloved by God, that he has chosen you;
[5] for our gospel came to you not only in word, but also in
power and in the Holy Spirit and with full conviction. You
know what kind of men we proved to be among you for
your sake. [6] And you became imitators of us and of the Lord,
for you received the word in much affliction, with joy inspired by the Holy Spirit; [7] so that you became an example
to all the believers in Mac-e-do′ni-a and in A-cha′ia. [8] For
not only has the word of the Lord sounded forth from you
in Mac-e-do′ni-a and A-cha′ia, but your faith in God has

4. 18: 1 Cor. 16. 21.   **1. 1:** 2 Thess. 1. 1; 2 Cor. 1. 19; Acts 16. 1; Acts 17. 1; Rom. 1. 7.
1. 2: 2 Thess. 1. 3; 2. 13; Rom. 1. 9.   **1. 3:** 2 Thess. 1. 11; 1. 3; Rom. 8. 25; 15. 4;
Gal. 1. 4.   **1. 4:** 2 Thess. 2. 13; Rom. 1. 7; 2 Pet. 1. 10.   **1. 5:** 2 Thess. 2. 14; Rom.
15. 19.   **1. 6:** Col. 2. 2; 1 Thess. 2. 10; 1 Cor. 4. 16; 1 Cor. 11. 1; Acts 17. 5–10;
13. 52.   **1. 7:** Rom. 15. 26; Acts 18. 1   **1. 8:** 2 Thess. 3. 1; Rom. 1. 8.

gone forth everywhere, so that we need not say anything.
⁹ For they themselves report concerning us what a welcome
we had among you, and how you turned to God from idols,
to serve a living and true God, ¹⁰ and to wait for his Son
from heaven, whom he raised from the dead, Jesus who delivers us from the wrath to come.

2 For you yourselves know, brethren, that our visit
to you was not in vain; ² but though we had already
suffered and been shamefully treated at Philippi, as you
know, we had courage in our God to declare to you the gospel
of God in the face of great opposition. ³ For our appeal does
not spring from error or uncleanness, nor is it made with
guile; ⁴ but just as we have been approved by God to be
entrusted with the gospel, so we speak, not to please men,
but to please God who tests our hearts. ⁵ For we never used
either words of flattery, as you know, or a cloak for greed,
as God is witness; ⁶ nor did we seek glory from men, whether
from you or from others, though we might have made demands as apostles of Christ. ⁷ But we were gentle*a* among
you, like a nurse taking care of her children. ⁸ So, being
affectionately desirous of you, we were ready to share with
you not only the gospel of God but also our own selves,
because you had become very dear to us.

9 For you remember our labor and toil, brethren; we
worked night and day, that we might not burden any of
you, while we preached to you the gospel of God. ¹⁰ You
are witnesses, and God also, how holy and righteous and
blameless was our behavior to you believers; ¹¹ for you
know how, like a father with his children, we exhorted each
one of you and encouraged you and charged you ¹² to lead

---

a Many ancient authorities read *babes.*

1. 10: Mt. 3. 7.
2. 2: Acts 16. 19–24; 17. 1–9; Rom. 1. 1.   **2. 5:** Acts 20. 33.   **2. 6:** 1 Cor. 9. 1.
2. 7: 1 Thess. 2. 11; Gal. 4. 19.   **2. 8:** 2 Cor. 12. 15; 1 Jn. 3. 16.   **2. 11:** 1 Cor. 4. 14.
2. 12: 1 Pet. 5. 10.

a life worthy of God, who calls you into his own kingdom and glory.

13 And we also thank God constantly for this, that when you received the word of God which you heard from us, you accepted it not as the word of men but as what it really is, the word of God, which is at work in you believers. [14] For you, brethren, became imitators of the churches of God in Christ Jesus which are in Judea; for you suffered the same things from your own countrymen as they did from the Jews, [15] who killed both the Lord Jesus and the prophets, and drove us out, and displease God and oppose all men [16] by hindering us from speaking to the Gentiles that they may be saved — so as always to fill up the measure of their sins. But God's wrath has come upon them at last![b]

17 But since we were bereft of you, brethren, for a short time, in person not in heart, we endeavored the more eagerly and with great desire to see you face to face; [18] because we wanted to come to you — I, Paul, again and again — but Satan hindered us. [19] For what is our hope or joy or crown of boasting before our Lord Jesus at his coming? Is it not you? [20] For you are our glory and joy.

3 Therefore when we could bear it no longer, we were willing to be left behind at Athens alone, [2] and we sent Timothy, our brother and God's servant in the gospel of Christ, to establish you in your faith and to exhort you, [3] that no one be moved by these afflictions. You yourselves know that this is to be our lot. [4] For when we were with you, we told you beforehand that we were to suffer affliction; just as it has come to pass, and as you know. [5] For this

[b] Or *completely*, or *for ever*.

2. 13: 1 Thess. 1. 2.   2. 14: 1 Thess. 1. 6; 1 Cor. 7. 17; Gal. 1. 22; Acts 17. 5;
2 Thess. 1. 4.   2. 15: Lk. 24. 20; Acts 2. 23; 7. 52.   2. 16: Acts 9. 23;
13. 45, 50; 14. 2, 5, 19; 17. 5, 13; 18. 12; 21. 21, 27; 25. 2, 7; 1 Cor. 10. 33; Gen. 15. 16;
1 Thess. 1. 10.   2. 17: 1 Cor. 5. 3.   2. 19: Phil. 4. 1; 1 Thess. 3. 13; 4. 15; 5. 23;
Mt. 16. 27; Mk. 8. 38.   2. 20: 2 Cor. 1. 14.
3. 1: Phil. 2. 19; Acts 17. 15.   3. 2: 2 Cor. 1. 1; Col. 1. 1.   3. 3: Acts 14. 22.
3. 4: 1 Thess. 2. 14.   3. 5: Mt. 4. 3; Phil. 2. 16.

reason, when I could bear it no longer, I sent that I might know your faith, for fear that somehow the tempter had tempted you and that our labor would be in vain.

6 But now that Timothy has come to us from you, and has brought us the good news of your faith and love and reported that you always remember us kindly and long to see us, as we long to see you — ⁷ for this reason, brethren, in all our distress and affliction we have been comforted about you through your faith; ⁸ for now we live, if you stand fast in the Lord. ⁹ For what thanksgiving can we render to God for you, for all the joy which we feel for your sake before our God, ¹⁰ praying earnestly night and day that we may see you face to face and supply what is lacking in your faith?

11 Now may our God and Father himself, and our Lord Jesus, direct our way to you; ¹² and may the Lord make you increase and abound in love to one another and to all men, as we do to you, ¹³ so that he may establish your hearts unblamable in holiness before our God and Father, at the coming of our Lord Jesus with all his saints.

4 Finally, brethren, we beseech and exhort you in the Lord Jesus, that as you learned from us how you ought to live and to please God, just as you are doing, you do so more and more. ² For you know what instructions we gave you through the Lord Jesus. ³ For this is the will of God, your consecration: that you abstain from immorality; ⁴ that each one of you know how to take a wife for himself in consecration and honor, ⁵ not in the passion of lust like heathen who do not know God; ⁶ that no man transgress, and wrong his brother in this matter,ᶜ because the Lord is an avenger in all these things, as we solemnly forewarned

---

ᶜ Or *defraud his brother in business.*

3. 6: Acts 18. 5.   **3. 13:** 1 Cor. 1. 8; 1 Thess. 2. 19; 4. 17.
4. 3: 1 Cor. 6. 18.   **4. 4:** 1 Cor. 7. 2; 1 Pet. 3. 7.

you. [7] For God has not called us for uncleanness, but in consecration. [8] Therefore whoever disregards this, disregards not man but God, who gives his Holy Spirit to you.

9 But concerning love of the brethren you have no need to have any one write to you, for you yourselves have been taught by God to love one another; [10] and indeed you do love all the brethren throughout Mac-e-do'ni-a. But we exhort you, brethren, to do so more and more, [11] to aspire to live quietly, to mind your own affairs, and to work with your hands, as we charged you; [12] so that you may command the respect of outsiders, and be dependent on nobody.

13 But we would not have you ignorant, brethren, concerning those who are asleep, that you may not grieve as others do who have no hope. [14] For since we believe that Jesus died and rose again, even so, through Jesus, God will bring with him those who have fallen asleep. [15] For this we declare to you by the word of the Lord, that we who are alive, who are left until the coming of the Lord, shall not precede those who have fallen asleep. [16] For the Lord himself will descend from heaven with a cry of command, with the archangel's call, and with the sound of the trumpet of God. And the dead in Christ will rise first; [17] then we who are alive, who are left, shall be caught up together with them in the clouds to meet the Lord in the air; and so we shall always be with the Lord. [18] Therefore comfort one another with these words.

5 But as to the times and the seasons, brethren, you have no need to have anything written to you. [2] For you yourselves know well that the day of the Lord will come like a thief in the night. [3] When people say, "There is peace and security," then sudden destruction will come upon

4. 11: 2 Thess. 3. 12; Eph. 4. 28; 2 Thess. 3. 10–12. **4. 13:** Eph. 2. 12. **4. 14:** 2 Cor. 4. 14. **4. 16:** Mt. 24. 31; 1 Cor. 15. 23; 2 Thess. 2. 1. **5. 1:** Acts 1. 7. **5. 2:** 1 Cor. 1. 8. **5. 3:** 2 Thess. 1. 9.

them as travail comes upon a woman with child, and there will be no escape. ⁴ But you are not in darkness, brethren, for that day to surprise you like a thief. ⁵ For you are all sons of light and sons of the day; we are not of the night or of darkness. ⁶ So then let us not sleep, as others do, but let us keep awake and be sober. ⁷ For those who sleep sleep at night, and those who get drunk are drunk at night. ⁸ But, since we belong to the day, let us be sober, and put on the breastplate of faith and love, and for a helmet the hope of salvation. ⁹ For God has not destined us for wrath, but to obtain salvation through our Lord Jesus Christ, ¹⁰ who died for us so that whether we wake or sleep we might live with him. ¹¹ Therefore encourage one another and build one another up, just as you are doing.

12 But we beseech you, brethren, to respect those who labor among you and are over you in the Lord and admonish you, ¹³ and to esteem them very highly in love because of their work. Be at peace among yourselves. ¹⁴ And we exhort you, brethren, admonish the idle, encourage the faint-hearted, help the weak, be patient with them all. ¹⁵ See that none of you repays evil for evil, but always seek to do good to one another and to all. ¹⁶ Rejoice always, ¹⁷ pray constantly, ¹⁸ give thanks in all circumstances; for this is the will of God in Christ Jesus for you. ¹⁹ Do not quench the Spirit, ²⁰ do not despise prophesying, ²¹ but test everything; hold fast what is good, ²² abstain from every form of evil.

23 May the God of peace himself sanctify you wholly; and may your spirit and soul and body be kept sound and

5. 4: 1 Jn. 2. 8; Acts 26. 18.   5. 5: Lk. 16. 8.   5. 6: Rom. 13. 11; 1 Pet. 1. 13. 5. 7: Acts 2. 15; 2 Pet. 2. 13.   5. 8: Eph. 6. 14, 23, 17; Rom. 8. 24.   5. 9: 1 Thess. 1. 10; 2 Thess. 2. 13; Rom. 14. 9.   5. 12: 1 Cor. 16. 18; 1 Tim. 5. 17; 1 Cor. 16. 16; Rom. 16. 6, 12; 1 Cor. 15. 10; Heb. 13. 17.   5. 13: Mk. 9. 50.   5. 14: Is. 35. 4; Rom. 14. 1; 1 Cor. 8. 7; 2 Thess. 3. 6, 7, 11.   5. 15: Rom. 12. 17; 1 Pet. 3. 9. 5. 16: Phil. 4. 4.   5. 17: Eph. 6. 18.   5. 18: Eph. 5. 20.   5. 19: Eph. 4. 30. 5. 20: 1 Cor. 14. 31.   5. 21: 1 Cor. 14. 29; 1 Jn. 4. 1.   5. 23: Rom. 15. 33.

blameless at the coming of our Lord Jesus Christ. [24] He who calls you is faithful, and he will do it.

25 Brethren, pray for us.

26 Greet all the brethren with a holy kiss.

27 I adjure you by the Lord that this letter be read to all the brethren.

28 The grace of our Lord Jesus Christ be with you.

THE SECOND LETTER OF PAUL TO THE THESSALONIANS

1 Paul, Sil-va'nus, and Timothy,
To the church of the Thes-sa-lo'ni-ans in God our Father and the Lord Jesus Christ:

2 Grace to you and peace from God the Father and the Lord Jesus Christ.

3 We are bound to give thanks to God always for you, brethren, as is fitting, because your faith is growing abundantly, and the love of every one of you for one another is increasing. [4] Therefore we ourselves boast of you in the churches of God for your steadfastness and faith in all your persecutions and in the afflictions which you are enduring.

5 This is evidence of the righteous judgment of God, that you may be made worthy of the kingdom of God, for which you are suffering — [6] since indeed God deems it just to repay with affliction those who afflict you, [7] and to grant rest with us to you who are afflicted, when the Lord Jesus is revealed from heaven with his mighty angels in flaming fire, [8] inflicting vengeance upon those who do not know God and upon those who do not obey the gospel of our Lord

5. 26: Rom. 16. 16.   **5. 27:** Col. 4. 16.   **5. 28:** Rom. 16. 20; 2 Thess. 3. 18.
1. 1: 1 Thess. 1. 1; 2 Cor. 1. 19; Acts 16. 1.   **1. 2:** Rom. 1. 7.   **1. 3:** 1 Thess. 1. 2.
1. 8: Gal. 4. 8.

Jesus. ⁹ They shall suffer the punishment of eternal destruction and exclusion from the presence of the Lord and from the glory of his might, ¹⁰ when he comes on that day to be glorified in his saints, and to be marveled at in all who have believed, because our testimony to you was believed. ¹¹ To this end we always pray for you, that our God may make you worthy of his call, and may fulfill every good resolve and work of faith by his power, ¹² so that the name of our Lord Jesus may be glorified in you, and you in him, according to the grace of our God and the Lord Jesus Christ.

2 Now concerning the coming of our Lord Jesus Christ and our assembling to meet him, we beg you, brethren, ² not to be quickly shaken in mind or excited, either by spirit or by word, or by letter purporting to be from us, to the effect that the day of the Lord has come. ³ Let no one deceive you in any way; for that day will not come, unless the rebellion comes first, and the man of lawlessness[a] is revealed, the son of perdition, ⁴ who opposes and exalts himself against every so-called god or object of worship, so that he takes his seat in the temple of God, proclaiming himself to be God. ⁵ Do you not remember that when I was still with you I told you this? ⁶ And you know what is restraining him now so that he may be revealed in his time. ⁷ For the mystery of lawlessness is already at work; only he who now restrains it will do so until he is out of the way. ⁸ And then the lawless one will be revealed, and the Lord Jesus will slay him with the breath of his mouth and destroy him by his appearing and his coming. ⁹ The coming of the lawless one by the activity of Satan will be with all power

[a] Some ancient authorities read *sin*.

1. 11: 1 Thess. 1. 3.
2. 1: 1 Thess. 4. 15–17.   **2. 2:** 2 Thess. 3. 17.   **2. 3:** Eph. 5. 6–8; Dan. 7. 25; 8. 25; 11. 36; Rev. 13. 5; Jn. 17. 12.   **2. 4:** Ezek. 28. 2.   **2. 5:** 1 Thess. 3. 4.   **2. 8:** Is. 11. 4.
2. 9: Mt. 24. 24; Jn. 4. 48.

and with pretended signs and wonders, [10] and with all wicked deception for those who are to perish, because they refused to love the truth and so be saved. [11] Therefore God sends upon them a strong delusion, to make them believe what is false, [12] so that all may be condemned who did not believe the truth but had pleasure in unrighteousness.

13 But we are bound to give thanks to God always for you, brethren beloved by the Lord, because God chose you from the beginning[b] to be saved, through consecration by the Spirit[c] and belief in the truth. [14] To this he called you through our gospel, so that you may obtain the glory of our Lord Jesus Christ. [15] So then, brethren, stand firm and hold to the traditions which you were taught by us, either by word of mouth or by letter.

16 Now may our Lord Jesus Christ himself, and God our Father, who loved us and gave us eternal comfort and good hope through grace, [17] comfort your hearts and establish them in every good work and word.

3 Finally, brethren, pray for us, that the word of the Lord may speed on and triumph, as it did among you, [2] and that we may be delivered from wicked and evil men; for not all have faith. [3] But the Lord is faithful; he will strengthen you and guard you from evil.[d] [4] And we have confidence in the Lord about you, that you are doing and will do the things which we command. [5] May the Lord direct your hearts to the love of God and to the steadfastness of Christ.

6 Now we command you, brethren, in the name of our Lord Jesus Christ, that you keep away from any brother

[b] Many ancient authorities read *as the first converts.*   [c] Or *of spirit.*   [d] Or *the evil one.*
2. 11: Rom. 1. 28.   **2. 13:** 2 Thess. 1. 3; Eph. 1. 4; 1 Pet. 1. 2.   **2. 15:** 1 Cor. 16. 13; 11. 2.   **2. 16:** 1 Thess. 3. 11; 1 Pet. 1. 3.
3. 1: 1 Thess. 5. 25; 1. 8.   **3. 2:** Rom. 15. 31.   **3. 3:** 1 Cor. 1. 9; 1 Thess. 5. 24.
3. 6: 1 Cor. 5. 4, 5, 11; 1 Thess. 5. 14.

who is living in idleness and not in accord with the tradition that you received from us. [7] For you yourselves know how you ought to imitate us; we were not idle when we were with you, [8] we did not eat anyone's bread without paying, but with toil and labor we worked night and day, that we might not burden any of you. [9] It was not because we have not that right, but to give you in our conduct an example to imitate. [10] For even when we were with you, we gave you this command: If any one will not work, let him not eat. [11] For we hear that some of you are living in idleness, mere busybodies, not doing any work. [12] Now such persons we command and exhort in the Lord Jesus Christ to do their work in quietness and to earn their own living. [13] Brethren, do not be weary in well-doing.

14 If any one refuses to obey what we say in this letter, note that man, and have nothing to do with him, that he may be ashamed. [15] Do not look on him as an enemy, but warn him as a brother.

16 Now may the Lord of peace himself give you peace at all times in all ways. The Lord be with you all.

17 I, Paul, write this greeting with my own hand. This is the mark in every letter of mine; it is the way I write. [18] The grace of our Lord Jesus Christ be with you all.

3. 7: 1 Thess. 1. 6, 9.   **3. 8:** 1 Thess. 2. 9; Acts 18. 3; Eph. 4. 28.   **3. 9:** 2 Thess. 3. 7.
3. 10: 1 Thess. 4. 11.   **3. 11:** 2 Thess. 3. 6.   **3. 12:** 1 Thess. 4. 1, 11.   **3. 13:** Gal. 6. 9.
3. 16: Ruth 2. 4.   **3. 17:** 1 Cor. 16. 21.   **3. 18:** Rom. 16. 20; 1 Thess. 5. 28.

THE FIRST LETTER OF PAUL TO
TIMOTHY

1 Paul, an apostle of Christ Jesus by command of God our Savior and of Christ Jesus our hope,

2 To Timothy, my true child in the faith:

Grace, mercy, and peace from God the Father and Christ Jesus our Lord.

3 As I urged you when I was going to Mac-e-do'ni-a, remain at Ephesus that you may charge certain persons not to teach any different doctrine, [4] nor to occupy themselves with myths and endless genealogies which promote speculations rather than the divine training[a] that is in faith; [5] whereas the aim of our charge is love that issues from a pure heart and a good conscience and sincere faith. [6] Certain persons by swerving from these have wandered away into vain discussion, [7] desiring to be teachers of the law, without understanding either what they are saying or the things about which they make assertions.

8 Now we know that the law is good, if any one uses it lawfully, [9] understanding this, that the law is not laid down for the just but for the lawless and disobedient, for the ungodly and sinners, for the unholy and profane, for murderers of fathers and murderers of mothers, for manslayers, [10] immoral persons, sodomites, kidnapers, liars, perjurers, and whatever else is contrary to sound doctrine, [11] in accordance with the glorious gospel of the blessed God with which I have been entrusted.

12 I thank him who has given me strength for this, Christ Jesus our Lord, because he judged me faithful by appointing me to his service, [13] though I formerly blasphemed and

[a] Or stewardship, or order.

persecuted and insulted him; but I received mercy because I had acted ignorantly in unbelief, [14] and the grace of our Lord overflowed for me with the faith and love that are in Christ Jesus. [15] The saying is sure and worthy of full acceptance, that Christ Jesus came into the world to save sinners. And I am the foremost of sinners; [16] but I received mercy for this reason, that in me, as the foremost, Jesus Christ might display his perfect patience for an example to those who were to believe in him for eternal life. [17] To the King of ages, immortal, invisible, the only God, be honor and glory for ever and ever.[b] Amen.

18 This charge I commit to you, Timothy, my son, in accordance with the prophetic utterances which pointed to you, that inspired by them you may wage the good warfare, [19] holding faith and a good conscience. By rejecting conscience, certain persons have made shipwreck of their faith, [20] among them Hy-me-nae'us and Alexander, whom I have delivered to Satan that they may learn not to blaspheme.

2 First of all, then, I urge that supplications, prayers, intercessions, and thanksgivings be made for all men, [2] for kings and all who are in high positions, that we may lead a quiet and peaceable life, godly and respectful in every way. [3] This is good, and it is acceptable in the sight of God our Savior, [4] who desires all men to be saved and to come to the knowledge of the truth. [5] For there is one God, and there is one mediator between God and men, the man Christ Jesus, [6] who gave himself as a ransom for all, the testimony to which was borne at the proper time. [7] For this I was appointed a preacher and apostle (I am telling the truth, I am not lying), a teacher of the Gentiles in faith and truth.

[b] Greek *to the ages of ages.*

8 I desire then that in every place the men should pray, lifting holy hands without anger or quarreling; ⁹ also that women should adorn themselves modestly and sensibly in seemly apparel, not with braided hair or gold or pearls or costly attire ¹⁰ but by good deeds, as befits women who profess religion. ¹¹ Let a woman learn in silence with all submissiveness. ¹² I permit no woman to teach or to have authority over men; she is to keep silent. ¹³ For Adam was formed first, then Eve; ¹⁴ and Adam was not deceived, but the woman was deceived and became a transgressor. ¹⁵ Yet woman will be saved through bearing children,ᶜ if she con-tinuesᵈ in faith and love and holiness, with modesty.

3 The saying is sure: If anyone aspires to the office of bishop, he desires a noble task. ² Now a bishop must be above reproach, married only once, temperate, sensible, dignified, hospitable, an apt teacher, ³ no drunkard, not violent but gentle, not quarrelsome, and no lover of money. ⁴ He must manage his own household well, keeping his children submissive and respectful in every way; ⁵ for if a man does not know how to manage his own household, how can he care for God's church? ⁶ He must not be a recent convert, or he may be puffed up with conceit and fall into the condemnation of the devil;ᵉ ⁷ moreover he must be well thought of by outsiders, or he may fall into reproach and the snare of the devil.ᵉ

8 Deacons likewise must be serious, not double-tongued, not addicted to much wine, not greedy for gain; ⁹ they must hold the mystery of the faith with a clear conscience. ¹⁰ And let them also be tested first; then if they prove themselves blameless let them serve as deacons. ¹¹ The women likewise must be serious, no slanderers, but temperate, faithful in all things. ¹² Let deacons be married only once, and let them

ᶜ Or *by the birth of the child.*   ᵈ Greek *they continue.*   ᵉ Or *slanderer.*
3. 13: Gen. 2. 7, 21–22.   **2. 14:** Gen. 3. 1–6.

manage their children and their households well; [13] for those who serve well as deacons gain a good standing for themselves and also great confidence in the faith which is in Christ Jesus.

14 I hope to come to you soon, but I am writing these instructions to you so that, [15] if I am delayed, you may know how one ought to behave in the household of God, which is the church of the living God, the pillar and bulwark of the truth. [16] Great indeed, we confess, is the mystery of our religion:

> He[f] was manifested in the flesh,
> vindicated[g] in the Spirit,
>   seen by angels,
> preached among the nations,
> believed on in the world,
>   taken up in glory.

4 Now the Spirit expressly says that in later times some will depart from the faith by giving heed to deceitful spirits and doctrines of demons, [2] through the pretensions of liars whose consciences are seared, [3] who forbid marriage and enjoin abstinence from foods which God created to be received with thanksgiving by those who believe and know the truth. [4] For everything created by God is good, and nothing is to be rejected if it is received with thanksgiving; [5] for then it is consecrated by the word of God and prayer.

6 If you put these instructions before the brethren, you will be a good minister of Christ Jesus, nourished on the words of the faith and of the good doctrine which you have followed. [7] Have nothing to do with godless and silly myths. Train yourself in godliness; [8] for while bodily training is of some value, godliness is of value in every way, as it holds promise for the present life and also for the life to come.

---

[f] Greek *Who;* some ancient authorities read *God;* others, *Which.*   [g] Or *justified.*

⁹ The saying is sure and worthy of full acceptance. ¹⁰ For to this end we toil and strive,ʰ because we have our hope set on the living God, who is the Savior of all men, especially of those who believe.

11 Command and teach these things. ¹² Let no one despise your youth, but set the believers an example in speech and conduct, in love, in faith, in purity. ¹³ Till I come, attend to the public reading of scripture, to preaching, to teaching. ¹⁴ Do not neglect the gift you have, which was given you by prophetic utterance when the elders laid their hands upon you. ¹⁵ Practice these duties, devote yourself to them, so that all may see your progress. ¹⁶ Take heed to yourself and to your teaching; hold to that, for by so doing you will save both yourself and your hearers.

5 Do not rebuke an older man but exhort him as you would a father; treat younger men like brothers, ² older women like mothers, younger women like sisters, in all purity.

3 Honor widows who are real widows. ⁴ If a widow has children or grandchildren, let them first learn their religious duty to their own family and make some return to their parents; for this is acceptable in the sight of God. ⁵ She who is a real widow, and is left all alone, has set her hope on God and continues in supplications and prayers night and day; ⁶ whereas she who is self-indulgent is dead even while she lives. ⁷ Command this, so that they may be without reproach. ⁸ If any one does not provide for his relatives, and especially for his own family, he has disowned the faith and is worse than an unbeliever.

9 Let no one be enrolled as a widow who is under sixty years of age, or who has been married more than once; ¹⁰ and she must be well attested for her good deeds, as one who has brought up children, shown hospitality, washed

ʰ Some ancient authorities read *suffer reproach.*

the feet of the saints, relieved the afflicted, and devoted herself to doing good in every way. [11] But refuse to enroll younger widows; for when they grow wanton against Christ they desire to marry, [12] and so they incur condemnation for having violated their first pledge. [13] Besides that, they learn to be idlers, gadding about from house to house, and not only idlers but gossips and busybodies, saying what they should not. [14] So I would have younger widows marry, bear children, rule their households, and give the enemy no occasion to revile us. [15] For some have already strayed after Satan. [16] If any believing woman[i] has relatives who are widows, let her assist them; let the church not be burdened, so that it may assist those who are real widows.

17 Let the elders who rule well be considered worthy of double honor, especially those who labor in preaching and teaching; [18] for the scripture says, "You shall not muzzle an ox when it is treading out the grain," and, "The laborer deserves his wages." [19] Never admit any charge against an elder except on the evidence of two or three witnesses. [20] As for those who persist in sin, rebuke them in the presence of all, so that the rest may stand in fear. [21] In the presence of God and of Christ Jesus and of the elect angels I charge you to keep these rules without favor, doing nothing from partiality. [22] Do not be hasty in the laying on of hands, nor participate in another man's sins; keep yourself pure.

23 No longer drink only water, but use a little wine for the sake of your stomach and your frequent ailments.

24 The sins of some men are conspicuous, pointing to judgment, but the sins of others appear later. [25] So also good deeds are conspicuous; and even when they are not, they cannot remain hidden.

---

[i] Some ancient authorities read *man or woman;* others, simply *man.*

5. 18: Deut. 25. 4; 1 Cor. 9. 9; Mt. 10. 10; Lk. 10. 7; 1 Cor. 9. 14.   **5. 19:** Deut. 19. 15.

6 Let all who are under the yoke of slavery regard their masters as worthy of all honor, so that the name of God and the teaching may not be defamed. [2] Those who have believing masters must not be disrespectful on the ground that they are brethren; rather they must serve all the better since those who benefit by their service are believers and beloved.

Teach and urge these duties. [3] If any one teaches otherwise and does not agree with the sound words of our Lord Jesus Christ and the teaching which accords with godliness, [4] he is puffed up with conceit, he knows nothing; he has a morbid craving for controversy and for disputes about words, which produce envy, dissension, slander, base suspicions, [5] and wrangling among men who are depraved in mind and bereft of the truth, imagining that godliness is a means of gain. [6] There is great gain in godliness with contentment; [7] for we brought nothing into the world, and[j] we cannot take anything out of the world; [8] but if we have food and clothing, with these we shall be content. [9] But those who desire to be rich fall into temptation, into a snare, into many senseless and hurtful desires that plunge men into ruin and destruction. [10] For the love of money is the root of all evils; it is through this craving that some have wandered away from the faith and pierced their hearts with many pangs.

11 But as for you, man of God, shun all this; aim at righteousness, godliness, faith, love, steadfastness, gentleness. [12] Fight the good fight of the faith; take hold of the eternal life to which you were called when you made the good confession in the presence of many witnesses. [13] In the presence of God who gives life to all things, and of Christ Jesus who in his testimony before Pontius Pilate made the good con-

---

[j] Some ancient authorities insert *it is certain that.*
6. 13: Jn. 18. 37.

fession, [14] I charge you to keep the commandment unstained and free from reproach until the appearing of our Lord Jesus Christ; [15] and this will be made manifest at the proper time by the blessed and only Sovereign, the King of kings and Lord of lords, [16] who alone has immortality and dwells in unapproachable light, whom no man has ever seen or can see. To him be honor and eternal dominion. Amen.

17 As for the rich in this world, charge them not to be haughty, nor to set their hopes on uncertain riches but on God who richly furnishes us with everything to enjoy. [18] They are to do good, to be rich in good deeds, liberal and generous, [19] thus laying up for themselves a good foundation for the future, so that they may take hold of the life which is life indeed.

20 O Timothy, guard what has been entrusted to you. Avoid the godless chatter and contradictions of what is falsely called knowledge, [21] for by professing it some have missed the mark as regards the faith.

Grace be with you.

THE SECOND LETTER OF PAUL TO
TIMOTHY

1 Paul, an apostle of Christ Jesus by the will of God according to the promise of the life which is in Christ Jesus,

2 To Timothy, my beloved child:

Grace, mercy, and peace from God the Father and Christ Jesus our Lord.

3 I thank God whom I serve with a clear conscience, as did my fathers, when I remember you constantly in my

prayers. [4] As I remember your tears, I long night and day to see you, that I may be filled with joy. [5] I am reminded of your sincere faith, a faith that dwelt first in your grandmother Lo'is and your mother Eunice and now, I am sure, dwells in you. [6] Hence I remind you to rekindle the gift of God that is within you through the laying on of my hands; [7] for God did not give us a spirit of timidity but a spirit of power and love and self-control.

8 Do not be ashamed then of testifying to our Lord, nor of me his prisoner, but take your share of suffering for the gospel in the power of God, [9] who saved us and called us with a holy calling, not in virtue of our works but in virtue of his own purpose and the grace which he gave us in Christ Jesus ages ago, [10] and now has manifested through the appearing of our Savior Christ Jesus, who abolished death and brought life and immortality to light through the gospel. [11] For this gospel I was appointed a preacher and apostle and teacher, [12] and therefore I suffer as I do. But I am not ashamed, for I know whom I have believed and I am sure that he is able to guard until that Day what has been entrusted to me.[a] [13] Follow the pattern of the sound words which you have heard from me, in the faith and love which are in Christ Jesus; [14] guard the truth that has been entrusted to you, by the Holy Spirit who dwells within us.

15 You are aware that all who are in Asia turned away from me, and among them Phy-gel'us and Her-mog'e-nes. [16] May the Lord grant mercy to the household of On-e-siph'-o-rus, for he often refreshed me; he was not ashamed of my chains, [17] but when he arrived in Rome he searched for me eagerly and found me — [18] may the Lord grant him to find mercy from the Lord on that Day — and you well know all the service he rendered at Ephesus.

[a] Or *what I have entrusted to him.*
1. 5: Acts 16. 1.

2 You then, my son, be strong in the grace that is in Christ Jesus, [2] and what you have heard from me before many witnesses entrust to faithful men who will be able to teach others also. [3] Take your share of suffering as a good soldier of Christ Jesus. [4] No soldier on service gets entangled in civilian pursuits, since his aim is to satisfy the one who enlisted him. [5] An athlete is not crowned unless he competes according to the rules. [6] It is the hard-working farmer who ought to have the first share of the crops. [7] Think over what I say, for the Lord will grant you understanding in everything.

8 Remember Jesus Christ, risen from the dead, descended from David, as preached in my gospel, [9] the gospel for which I am suffering and wearing fetters, like a criminal. But the word of God is not fettered. [10] Therefore I endure everything for the sake of the elect, that they also may obtain the salvation which in Christ Jesus goes with eternal glory. [11] The saying is sure:

> If we have died with him, we shall also live with him;
> [12] if we endure, we shall also reign with him;
> if we deny him, he also will deny us;
> [13] if we are faithless, he remains faithful —

for he cannot deny himself.

14 Remind them of this, and charge them before the Lord[b] to avoid disputing about words, which does no good, but only ruins the hearers. [15] Do your best to present yourself to God as one approved, a workman who has no need to be ashamed, rightly handling the word of truth. [16] Avoid such godless chatter, for it will lead people into more and more ungodliness, [17] and their talk will eat its way like gangrene. Among them are Hy-me-nae'us and Phi-le'tus, [18] who have swerved from the truth by holding that the resurrection is

[b] Many ancient authorities read *God*.

452

past already. They are upsetting the faith of some. [19] But God's firm foundation stands, bearing this seal: "The Lord knows those who are his," and, "Let every one who names the name of the Lord depart from iniquity."

20 In a great house there are not only vessels of gold and silver but also of wood and earthenware, and some for noble use, some for ignoble. [21] If any one purifies himself from what is ignoble, then he will be a vessel for noble use, consecrated and useful to the master of the house, ready for any good work. [22] So shun youthful passions and aim at righteousness, faith, love, and peace, along with those who call upon the Lord from a pure heart. [23] Have nothing to do with stupid, senseless controversies; you know that they breed quarrels. [24] And the Lord's servant must not be quarrelsome but kindly to everyone, an apt teacher, forbearing, [25] correcting his opponents with gentleness. God may perhaps grant that they will repent and come to know the truth, [26] and they may escape from the snare of the devil, after being captured by him to do his will.[c]

3 But understand this, that in the last days there will come times of stress. [2] For men will be lovers of self, lovers of money, proud, arrogant, abusive, disobedient to their parents, ungrateful, unholy, [3] inhuman, implacable, slanderers, profligates, fierce, haters of good, [4] treacherous, reckless, swollen with conceit, lovers of pleasure rather than lovers of God, [5] holding the form of religion but denying the power of it. Avoid such people. [6] For among them are those who make their way into households and capture weak women, burdened with sins and swayed by various impulses, [7] who will listen to anybody and can never arrive at a knowledge of the truth. [8] As Jan′nes and Jam′bres

[c] Or *by him, to do his* (that is, God's) *will.*
2. 19: Num. 16. 5; Is. 26. 13.
3. 8: Ex. 7. 11.

opposed Moses, so these men also oppose the truth, men of corrupt minds and rejected as regards the faith; [9] but they will not get very far, for their folly will be plain to all, as was that of those two men.

10 Now you have observed my teaching, my conduct, my aim in life, my faith, my patience, my love, my steadfastness, [11] my persecutions, my sufferings, what befell me at Antioch, at I-co′ni-um, and at Lystra, what persecutions I endured; yet from them all the Lord rescued me. [12] Indeed all who desire to live a godly life in Christ Jesus will be persecuted, [13] while evil men and impostors will go on from bad to worse, deceivers and deceived. [14] But as for you, continue in what you have learned and have firmly believed, knowing from whom you learned it [15] and how from childhood you have been acquainted with the sacred writings which are able to instruct you for salvation through faith in Christ Jesus. [16] All scripture is inspired by God and[d] profitable for teaching, for reproof, for correction, and for training in righteousness, [17] that the man of God may be complete, equipped for every good work.

4 I charge you in the presence of God and of Christ Jesus who is to judge the living and the dead, and by his appearing and his kingdom: [2] preach the word, be urgent in season and out of season, convince, rebuke, and exhort, be unfailing in patience and in teaching. [3] For the time is coming when people will not endure sound teaching, but having itching ears they will accumulate for themselves teachers to suit their own likings, [4] and will turn away from listening to the truth and wander into myths. [5] As for you, always be steady, endure suffering, do the work of an evangelist, fulfill your ministry.

[d] Or *Every scripture inspired by God is also.*
3. 11: Acts 13. 14–52; 14. 1–20; 16. 1–5.

6 For I am already on the point of being sacrificed; the time of my departure has come. ⁷ I have fought the good fight, I have finished the race, I have kept the faith. ⁸ Henceforth there is laid up for me the crown of righteousness, which the Lord, the righteous judge, will award to me on that Day, and not only to me but also to all who have loved his appearing.

9 Do your best to come to me soon. ¹⁰ For Demas, in love with this present world, has deserted me and gone to Thes-sa-lo-ni′ca; Crescens has gone to Galatia,ᵉ Titus to Dalmatia. ¹¹ Luke alone is with me. Get Mark and bring him with you; for he is very useful in serving me. ¹² Tych′i-cus I have sent to Ephesus. ¹³ When you come, bring the cloak that I left with Carpus at Tro′as, also the books, and above all the parchments. ¹⁴ Alexander the coppersmith did me great harm; the Lord will requite him for his deeds. ¹⁵ Beware of him yourself, for he strongly opposed our message. ¹⁶ At my first defense no one took my part; all deserted me. May it not be charged against them! ¹⁷ But the Lord stood by me and gave me strength to proclaim the word fully, that all the Gentiles might hear it. So I was rescued from the lion's mouth. ¹⁸ The Lord will rescue me from every evil and save me for his heavenly kingdom. To him be the glory for ever and ever. Amen.

19 Greet Pris′ca and Aquila, and the household of On-e-siph′o-rus. ²⁰ E-ras′tus remained at Corinth; Troph′i-mus I left ill at Mi-le′tus. ²¹ Do your best to come before winter. Eu-bu′lus sends greetings to you, as do Pu′dens and Li′nus and Claudia and all the brethren.

22 The Lord be with your spirit. Grace be with you.

ᵉ Some ancient authorities read *Gaul*.

THE LETTER OF PAUL TO
TITUS

1 Paul, a servant[a] of God and an apostle of Jesus Christ, to further the faith of God's elect and their knowledge of the truth which accords with godliness, [2] in hope of eternal life which God, who never lies, promised ages ago [3] and at the proper time manifested in his word through the preaching with which I have been entrusted by command of God our Savior;

4 To Titus, my true child in a common faith:

Grace and peace from God the Father and Christ Jesus our Savior.

5 This is why I left you in Crete, that you might amend what was defective, and appoint elders in every town as I directed you, [6] men who are blameless, married only once, whose children are believers and not open to the charge of being profligate or insubordinate. [7] For a bishop, as God's steward, must be blameless; he must not be arrogant or quick-tempered or a drunkard or violent or greedy for gain, [8] but hospitable, a lover of goodness, master of himself, upright, holy, and self-controlled; [9] he must hold firm to the sure word as taught, so that he may be able to give instruction in sound doctrine and also to confute those who contradict it. [10] For there are many insubordinate men, empty talkers and deceivers, especially the circumcision party; [11] they must be silenced, since they are upsetting whole families by teaching for base gain what they have no right to teach. [12] One of themselves, a prophet of their own, said, "Cre'tans are always liars, evil beasts, lazy glut-

[a] Or slave.
1. 12: Epimenides.

456

tons." [13] This testimony is true. Therefore rebuke them sharply, that they may be sound in the faith, [14] instead of giving heed to Jewish myths or to commands of men who reject the truth. [15] To the pure all things are pure, but to the corrupt and unbelieving nothing is pure; their very minds and consciences are corrupted. [16] They profess to know God, but they deny him by their deeds; they are detestable, disobedient, unfit for any good deed.

2 But as for you, teach what befits sound doctrine. [2] Bid the older men be temperate, serious, sensible, sound in faith, in love, and in steadfastness. [3] Bid the older women likewise to be reverent in behavior, not to be slanderers or slaves to drink; they are to teach what is good, [4] and so train the young women to love their husbands and children, [5] to be sensible, chaste, domestic, kind, and submissive to their husbands, that the word of God may not be discredited. [6] Likewise urge the younger men to control themselves. [7] Show yourself in all respects a model of good deeds, and in your teaching show integrity, gravity, [8] and sound speech that cannot be censured, so that an opponent may be put to shame, having nothing evil to say of us. [9] Bid slaves to be submissive to their masters and to give satisfaction in every respect; they are not to be refractory, [10] nor to pilfer, but to show entire and true fidelity, so that in everything they may adorn the doctrine of God our Savior.

11 For the grace of God has appeared for the salvation of all men, [12] training us to renounce irreligion and worldly passions, and to live sober, upright, and godly lives in this world, [13] awaiting our blessed hope, the appearing of the glory of our great God and Savior[b] Jesus Christ, [14] who gave himself for us to redeem us from all iniquity and to

[b] Or *of the great God and our Savior.*
2. 14: Ps. 130. 8; Ezek. 37. 23; Deut. 14. 2.

purify for himself a people of his own who are zealous for good deeds.

15 Declare these things; exhort and reprove with all authority. Let no one disregard you.

3 Remind them to be submissive to rulers and authorities, to be obedient, to be ready for any honest work, [2] to speak evil of no one, to avoid quarreling, to be gentle, and to show perfect courtesy toward all men. [3] For we ourselves were once foolish, disobedient, led astray, slaves to various passions and pleasures, passing our days in malice and envy, hated by men and hating one another; [4] but when the goodness and loving kindness of God our Savior appeared, [5] he saved us, not because of deeds done by us in righteousness, but in virtue of his own mercy, by the washing of regeneration and renewal in the Holy Spirit, [6] which he poured out upon us richly through Jesus Christ our Savior, [7] so that we might be justified by his grace and become heirs in hope of eternal life. [8] The saying is sure.

I desire you to insist on these things, so that those who have believed in God may be careful to apply themselves to good deeds;[c] these are excellent and profitable to men. [9] But avoid stupid controversies, genealogies, dissensions, and quarrels over the law, for they are unprofitable and futile. [10] As for a man who is factious, after admonishing him once or twice, have nothing more to do with him, [11] knowing that such a person is perverted and sinful; he is self-condemned.

12 When I send Artemas or Tych'i-cus to you, do your best to come to me at Ni-cop'o-lis, for I have decided to spend the winter there. [13] Do your best to speed Zenas the lawyer and A-pol'los on their way; see that they lack noth-

[c] Or *enter honorable occupations.*

ing. [14] And let our people learn to apply themselves to good deeds,[d] so as to help cases of urgent need, and not to be unfruitful.

15 All who are with me send greetings to you. Greet those who love us in the faith.

Grace be with you all.

THE LETTER OF PAUL TO
PHILEMON

1 Paul, a prisoner for Christ Jesus, and Timothy our brother,

To Phi-le′mon our beloved fellow worker [2] and Ap′phi-a our sister and Ar-chip′pus our fellow soldier, and the church in your house:

3 Grace to you and peace from God our Father and the Lord Jesus Christ.

4 I thank my God always when I remember you in my prayers, [5] because I hear of your love and of the faith which you have toward the Lord Jesus and all the saints, [6] and I pray that the sharing of your faith may promote the knowledge of all the good that is ours in Christ. [7] For I have derived much joy and comfort from your love, my brother, because the hearts of the saints have been refreshed through you.

8 Accordingly, though I am bold enough in Christ to command you to do what is required, [9] yet for love's sake I prefer to appeal to you — I, Paul, an ambassador[a] and now a prisoner also for Christ Jesus — [10] I appeal to you for my child, O-nes′i-mus, whose father I have become in my

---

[d] Or *enter honorable occupations.*   [a] Or *an old man.*

3: Rom. 1. 7.   **4:** Rom. 1. 8.   **10:** Col. 4. 9.

imprisonment. ¹¹ (Formerly he was useless to you, but now he is indeed useful[b] to you and to me.) ¹² I am sending him back to you, sending my very heart. ¹³ I would have been glad to keep him with me, in order that he might serve me on your behalf during my imprisonment for the gospel; ¹⁴ but I preferred to do nothing without your consent in order that your goodness might not be by compulsion but of your own free will.

15 Perhaps this is why he was parted from you for a while, that you might have him back forever, ¹⁶ no longer as a slave but more than a slave, as a beloved brother, especially to me but how much more to you, both in the flesh and in the Lord. ¹⁷ So if you consider me your partner, receive him as you would receive me. ¹⁸ If he has wronged you at all, or owes you anything, charge that to my account. ¹⁹ I, Paul, write this with my own hand, I will repay it — to say nothing of your owing me even your own self. ²⁰ Yes, brother, I want some benefit from you in the Lord. Refresh my heart in Christ.

21 Confident of your obedience, I write to you, knowing that you will do even more than I say. ²² At the same time, prepare a guest room for me, for I am hoping through your prayers to be granted to you.

23 Epaphras, my fellow prisoner in Christ Jesus, sends greetings to you, ²⁴ and so do Mark, Ar-is-tar'chus, Demas, and Luke, my fellow workers.

25 The grace of the Lord Jesus Christ be with your spirit.

---

b The name Onesimus means *useful* or (verse 20) *beneficial*.
23: Col. 1. 7; 4. 12.   **24:** Col. 4. 10, 14.

THE LETTER TO THE
HEBREWS

1 In many and various ways God spoke of old to our fathers by the prophets; [2] but in these last days he has spoken to us by a Son, whom he appointed the heir of all things, through whom also he created the world. [3] He reflects the glory of God and bears the very stamp of his nature, upholding the universe by his word of power. When he had made purification for sins, he sat down at the right hand of the Majesty on high, [4] having become as much superior to angels as the name he has obtained is more excellent than theirs.

5 For to what angel did God ever say,

> "Thou art my Son,
>   today I have begotten thee"?

Or again,

> "I will be to him a father,
>   and he shall be to me a son"?

[6] And again, when he brings the first-born into the world, he says,

> "Let all God's angels worship him."

[7] Of the angels he says,

> "Who makes his angels winds,
>   and his servants flames of fire."

[8] But of the Son he says,

> "Thy throne, O God,[a] is for ever and ever,
>   the righteous scepter is the scepter of thy[b] kingdom.
> [9] Thou hast loved righteousness and hated lawlessness;

---

[a] Or *God is thy throne.*   [b] Some ancient authorities read *his.*

1. 5: Ps. 2. 7; 2 Sam. 7. 14.   **1. 6:** Deut. 32. 43 Sept.; Ps. 97. 7.   **1. 7:** Ps. 104. 4.
1. 8–9: Ps. 45. 6–7.

therefore God, thy God, has anointed thee
with the oil of gladness beyond thy comrades."
[10] And,

"Thou, Lord, didst found the earth in the beginning,
and the heavens are the work of thy hands;
[11] they will perish, but thou remainest;
they will all grow old like a garment,
[12] like a mantle thou wilt roll them up,
and they will be changed.[c]
But thou art the same,
and thy years will never end."
[13] But to what angel has he ever said,
"Sit at my right hand,
till I make thy enemies
a stool for thy feet"?
[14] Are they not all ministering spirits sent forth to serve, for the sake of those who are to obtain salvation?

2 Therefore we must pay the closer attention to what we have heard, lest we drift away from it. [2] For if the message declared by angels was valid and every transgression or disobedience received a just retribution, [3] how shall we escape if we neglect such a great salvation? It was declared at first by the Lord, and it was attested to us by those who heard him, [4] while God also bore witness by signs and wonders and various miracles and by gifts of the Holy Spirit distributed according to his own will.

5 For it was not to angels that God subjected the world to come, of which we are speaking. [6] It has been testified somewhere,

"What is man that thou art mindful of him,
or the son of man, that thou carest for him?

[c] Many ancient authorities add *like a garment*.
1. 10–12: Ps. 102. 25–27.   **1. 13**: Ps. 110. 1.
2. 6–9: Ps. 8. 4–6.

⁷ Thou didst make him for a little while lower than
      the angels,

   thou hast crowned him with glory and honor,*ᵈ*
⁸ putting everything in subjection under his feet."
Now in putting everything in subjection to man, he left
nothing outside his control. As it is, we do not yet see everything in subjection to him. ⁹ But we see Jesus, who for a
little while was made lower than the angels, crowned with
glory and honor because of the suffering of death, so that
by the grace of God he might taste death for every one.

10 For it was fitting that he, for whom and by whom
all things exist, in bringing many sons to glory, should
make the pioneer of their salvation perfect through suffering.
¹¹ For he who sanctifies and those who are sanctified have
all one origin. That is why he is not ashamed to call them
brethren, ¹² saying,

   "I will proclaim thy name to my brethren,

      in the midst of the congregation I will praise thee."
¹³ And again,

   "I will put my trust in him."
And again,

   "Here am I, and the children God has given me."
14 Since therefore the children share in flesh and blood,
he himself likewise partook of the same nature, that through
death he might destroy him who has the power of death,
that is, the devil, ¹⁵ and deliver all those who through fear
of death were subject to lifelong bondage. ¹⁶ For surely it is
not with angels that he is concerned but with the descendants
of Abraham. ¹⁷ Therefore he had to be made like his brethren
in every respect, so that he might become a merciful and
faithful high priest in the service of God, to make expiation

---

ᵈ Many ancient authorities insert *and didst set him over the works of thy hands.*
2. 12: Ps. 22. 22.   **2. 13:** Is. 8. 17–18.   **2. 16:** Is. 41. 8–9.

for the sins of the people. [18] For because he himself has suffered and been tempted, he is able to help those who are tempted.

3 Therefore, holy brethren, who share in a heavenly call, consider Jesus, the apostle and high priest of our confession. [2] He was faithful to him who appointed him, just as Moses also was faithful in[e] God's house. [3] Yet Jesus has been counted worthy of as much more glory than Moses as the builder of a house has more honor than the house. [4] (For every house is built by some one, but the builder of all things is God.) [5] Now Moses was faithful in all God's house as a servant, to testify to the things that were to be spoken later, [6] but Christ was faithful over God's[f] house as a son. And we are his house if we hold fast[g] our confidence and pride in our hope.

7 Therefore, as the Holy Spirit says,

"Today, when you hear his voice,
[8] do not harden your hearts as in the rebellion,
on the day of testing in the wilderness,
[9] where your fathers put me to the test
and saw my works for forty years.
[10] Therefore I was provoked with that generation,
and said, 'They always go astray in their hearts;
they have not known my ways.'
[11] As I swore in my wrath,
'They shall never enter my rest.'"

[12] Take care, brethren, lest there be in any of you an evil, unbelieving heart, leading you to fall away from the living God. [13] But exhort one another every day, as long as it is called "today," that none of you may be hardened by the

---

[e] Some ancient authorities insert *all*.   [f] Greek *his*.   [g] Some ancient authorities insert *firm to the end*.

3. 2: Num. 12. 7.   **3. 5:** Num. 12. 7.   **3. 7–11:** Ps. 95. 7–11.

deceitfulness of sin. [14] For we share in Christ, if only we hold our first confidence firm to the end. [15] While it is still "today," when you hear his voice, do not harden your hearts as in the rebellion. [16] Who were they that heard and yet were rebellious? Was it not all those who left Egypt under the leadership of Moses? [17] And with whom was he provoked forty years? Was it not with those who sinned, whose bodies fell in the wilderness? [18] And to whom did he swear that they should never enter his rest, but to those who were disobedient? [19] So we see that they were unable to enter because of unbelief.

4 Therefore, while the promise of entering his rest remains, let us fear lest any of you be judged to have failed to reach it. [2] For good news came to us just as to them; but the message which they heard did not benefit them, because it did not meet with faith in the hearers.[h] [3] For we who have believed enter that rest, as he has said,

"As I swore in my wrath,

'They shall never enter my rest,'"

although his works were finished from the foundation of the world. [4] For he has somewhere spoken of the seventh day in this way, "And God rested on the seventh day from all his works." [5] And again in this place he said,

"They shall never enter my rest."

[6] Since therefore it remains for some to enter it, and those who formerly received the good news failed to enter because of disobedience, [7] again he sets a certain day, "Today," saying through David so long afterward, in the words already quoted,

"Today, when you hear his voice,
do not harden your hearts."

[h] Many manuscripts read *they were not united in faith with those who heard.*
3. 15: Ps. 95. 7–8.   **3. 16–19**: Num. 14. 1–35.   **3. 17**: Num. 14. 29.
4. 3: Ps. 95. 11.   **4. 4**: Gen. 2. 2.   **4. 5**: Ps. 95. 11.   **4. 7**: Ps. 95. 7–8.

[8] For if Joshua had given them rest, God[i] would not speak later of another day. [9] So then, there remains a sabbath rest for the people of God; [10] for whoever enters God's rest also ceases from his labors as God did from his.

11 Let us therefore strive to enter that rest, that no one fall by the same sort of disobedience. [12] For the word of God is living and active, sharper than any two-edged sword, piercing to the division of soul and spirit, of joints and marrow, and discerning the thoughts and intentions of the heart. [13] And before him no creature is hidden, but all are open and laid bare to the eyes of him with whom we have to do.

14 Since then we have a great high priest who has passed through the heavens, Jesus, the Son of God, let us hold fast our confession. [15] For we have not a high priest who is unable to sympathize with our weaknesses, but one who in every respect has been tempted as we are, yet without sinning. [16] Let us then with confidence draw near to the throne of grace, that we may receive mercy and find grace to help in time of need.

5 For every high priest chosen from among men is appointed to act on behalf of men in relation to God, to offer gifts and sacrifices for sins. [2] He can deal gently with the ignorant and wayward, since he himself is beset with weakness. [3] Because of this he is bound to offer sacrifice for his own sins as well as for those of the people. [4] And one does not take the honor upon himself, but he is called by God, just as Aaron was.

5 So also Christ did not exalt himself to be made a high priest, but was appointed by him who said to him,

---

[i] Greek *he.*
4. 10: Gen. 2. 2.
5. 5: Ps. 2. 7.

"Thou art my Son,
today I have begotten thee";

⁶ as he says also in another place,

"Thou art a priest forever,
after the order of Mel-chiz'e-dek."

7 In the days of his flesh, Jesus*ʲ* offered up prayers and supplications, with loud cries and tears, to him who was able to save him from death, and he was heard for his godly fear. ⁸ Although he was a Son, he learned obedience through what he suffered; ⁹ and being made perfect he became the source of eternal salvation to all who obey him, ¹⁰ being designated by God a high priest after the order of Mel-chiz'e-dek.

11 About this we have much to say which is hard to explain, since you have become dull of hearing. ¹² For though by this time you ought to be teachers, you need some one to teach you again the first principles of God's word. You need milk, not solid food; ¹³ for every one who lives on milk is unskilled in the word of righteousness, for he is a child. ¹⁴ But solid food is for the mature, for those who have their faculties trained by practice to distinguish good from evil.

6 Therefore let us leave the elementary doctrines of Christ and go on to maturity, not laying again a foundation of repentance from dead works and of faith toward God, ² with instruction*ᵏ* about ablutions, the laying on of hands, the resurrection of the dead, and eternal judgment. ³ And this we will do if God permits.*ˡ* ⁴ For it is impossible to restore again to repentance those who have once been enlightened, who have tasted the heavenly gift, and have

ʲ Greek *he.*   *ᵏ* Many ancient manuscripts read *of instruction.*
ˡ Some ancient manuscripts read *let us do this if God permits.*

5. 6: Ps. 110. 4.   **5. 7:** Mt. 26. 36–46; Mk. 14. 32–42; Lk. 22. 40–46.   **5. 9:** Is. 45. 17.
5. 10: Ps. 110. 4.

become partakers of the Holy Spirit, [5] and have tasted the goodness of the word of God and the powers of the age to come, [6] if they then commit apostasy, since they crucify the Son of God on their own account and hold him up to contempt. [7] For land which has drunk the rain that often falls upon it, and brings forth vegetation useful to those for whose sake it is cultivated, receives a blessing from God. [8] But if it bears thorns and thistles, it is worthless and near to being cursed; its end is to be burned.

9 Though we speak thus, yet in your case, beloved, we feel sure of better things that belong to salvation. [10] For God is not so unjust as to overlook your work and the love which you showed for his sake in serving the saints, as you still do. [11] And we desire each one of you to show the same earnestness in realizing the full assurance of hope until the end, [12] so that you may not be sluggish, but imitators of those who through faith and patience inherit the promises.

13 For when God made a promise to Abraham, since he had no one greater by whom to swear, he swore by himself, [14] saying, "Surely I will bless you and multiply you." [15] And thus Abraham,[m] having patiently endured, obtained the promise. [16] Men indeed swear by a greater than themselves, and in all their disputes an oath is final for confirmation. [17] So when God desired to show more convincingly to the heirs of the promise the unchangeable character of his purpose, he interposed with an oath, [18] so that through two unchangeable things, in which it is impossible that God should prove false, we who have fled for refuge might have strong encouragement to seize the hope set before us. [19] We have this as a sure and steadfast anchor of the soul, a hope that enters into the inner shrine behind the

[m] Greek *he.*

6. 8: Gen. 3. 17–18.   **6. 13–14:** Gen. 22. 16–17.   **6. 19:** Lev. 16. 2.

curtain, [20] where Jesus has gone as a forerunner on our behalf, having become a high priest forever after the order of Mel-chiz′e-dek.

7 For this Mel-chiz′e-dek, king of Salem, priest of the most high God, met Abraham returning from the slaughter of the kings and blessed him; [2] and to him Abraham apportioned a tenth part of everything. He is first, by translation of his name, king of righteousness, and then he is also king of Salem, that is, king of peace. [3] He is without father or mother or genealogy, and has neither beginning of days nor end of life, but resembling the Son of God he continues a priest forever.

4 See how great he is! Abraham the patriarch gave him a tithe of the spoils. [5] And those descendants of Levi who receive the priestly office have a commandment in the law to take tithes from the people, that is, from their brethren, though these also are descended from Abraham. [6] But this man who has not their genealogy received tithes from Abraham and blessed him who had the promises. [7] It is beyond dispute that the inferior is blessed by the superior. [8] Here tithes are received by mortal men; there, by one of whom it is testified that he lives. [9] One might even say that Levi himself, who receives tithes, paid tithes through Abraham, [10] for he was still in the loins of his ancestor when Mel-chiz′e-dek met him.

11 Now if perfection had been attainable through the Le-vit′ic-al priesthood (for under it the people received the law), what further need would there have been for another priest to arise after the order of Mel-chiz′e-dek, rather than one named after the order of Aaron? [12] For when there is a change in the priesthood, there is necessarily a change in the law as well. [13] For the one of whom these things are

6. 20: Ps. 110. 4.   7. 1–10: Gen. 14. 17–20.   7. 11, 15, 17, 21, 28: Ps. 110. 4.

spoken belonged to another tribe, from which no one has ever served at the altar. [14] For it is evident that our Lord was decended from Judah, and in connection with that tribe Moses said nothing about priests.

15 This becomes even more evident when another priest arises in the likeness of Mel-chiz'e-dek, [16] who has become a priest, not according to a legal requirement concerning bodily descent but by the power of an indestructible life. [17] For it is witnessed of him,

"Thou art a priest forever,

after the order of Mel-chiz'e-dek."

[18] On the one hand, a former commandment is set aside because of its weakness and uselessness [19] (for the law made nothing perfect); on the other hand, a better hope is introduced, through which we draw near to God.

20 And it was not without an oath. [21] Those who formerly became priests took their office without an oath, but this one was addressed with an oath,

"The Lord has sworn

and will not change his mind,

'Thou art a priest forever.'"

[22] This makes Jesus the surety of a better covenant.

23 The former priests were many in number, because they were prevented by death from continuing in office; [24] but he holds his priesthood permanently, because he continues forever. [25] Consequently he is able for all time to save those who draw near to God through him, since he always lives to make intercession for them.

26 For it was fitting that we should have such a high priest, holy, blameless, unstained, separated from sinners, exalted above the heavens. [27] He has no need, like those high priests, to offer sacrifices daily, first for his own sins and then for those of the people; he did this once for all

when he offered up himself. [28] Indeed, the law appoints men
in their weakness as high priests, but the word of the oath,
which came later than the law, appoints a Son who has been
made perfect forever.

8 Now the point in what we are saying is this: we have
such a high priest, one who is seated at the right hand
of the throne of the Majesty in heaven, [2] a minister in the
sanctuary and the true tent[n] which is set up not by man
but by the Lord. [3] For every high priest is appointed to
offer gifts and sacrifices; hence it is necessary for this priest
also to have something to offer. [4] Now if he were on earth,
he would not be a priest at all, since there are priests who
offer gifts according to the law. [5] They serve a copy and
shadow of the heavenly sanctuary; for when Moses was
about to erect the tent,[n] he was instructed by God, saying,
"See that you make everything according to the pattern
which was shown you on the mountain." [6] But as it is, Christ[o]
has obtained a ministry which is as much more excellent
than the old as the covenant he mediates is better, since it
is enacted on better promises. [7] For if that first covenant
had been faultless, there would have been no occasion for a
second.

8 For he finds fault with them when he says:
   "The days will come, says the Lord,
       when I will establish a new covenant with the house
          of Israel
       and with the house of Judah;
   [9] not like the covenant that I made with their fathers
       on the day when I took them by the hand
       to lead them out of the land of Egypt;

[n] Or *tabernacle.*   [o] Greek *he.*
8. 1: Ps. 110. 1.   **8. 5:** Ex. 25. 40.   **8. 8–12:** Jer. 31. 31–34.

for they did not continue in my covenant,
and so I paid no heed to them, says the Lord.
¹⁰ This is the covenant that I will make with the house
     of Israel
after those days, says the Lord:
I will put my laws into their minds,
and write them on their hearts,
and I will be their God,
and they shall be my people.
¹¹ And they shall not teach every one his fellow
or every one his brother, saying, 'Know the Lord,'
for all shall know me,
from the least of them to the greatest.
¹² For I will be merciful toward their iniquities,
and I will remember their sins no more."
¹³ In speaking of a new covenant he treats the first as obsolete. And what is becoming obsolete and growing old is ready to vanish away.

9 Now even the first covenant had regulations for worship and an earthly sanctuary. ² For a tent*ᵖ* was prepared, the outer one, in which were the lampstand and the table and the bread of the Presence;*�q* it is called the Holy Place. ³ Behind the second curtain stood a tent*ᵖ* called the Holy of Holies, ⁴ having the golden altar of incense and the ark of the covenant covered on all sides with gold, which contained a golden urn holding the manna, and Aaron's rod that budded, and the tablets of the covenant; ⁵ above it were the cherubim of glory overshadowing the mercy seat. Of these things we cannot now speak in detail.

6 These preparations having thus been made, the priests go continually into the outer tent,*ᵖ* performing their ritual

ᵖ Or *tabernacle.*   *�q* Greek *the presentation of the loaves.*
9. 1–10: Ex. 25. 10–40.   **9. 2:** Lev. 24. 5.   **9. 3:** Ex. 26. 31–33.   **9. 4:** Ex. 30. 1–5; 16. 32–33; Num. 17. 8–10.

duties; [7] but into the second only the high priest goes, and he but once a year, and not without taking blood which he offers for himself and for the errors of the people. [8] By this the Holy Spirit indicates that the way into the sanctuary is not yet opened as long as the outer tent[s] is still standing [9] (which is symbolic for the present age). According to this arrangement, gifts and sacrifices are offered which cannot perfect the conscience of the worshiper, [10] but deal only with food and drink and various ablutions, regulations for the body imposed until the time of reformation.

11 But when Christ appeared as a high priest of the good things that have come,[r] then through the greater and more perfect tent[s] (not made with hands, that is, not of this creation) [12] he entered once for all into the Holy Place, taking[t] not the blood of goats and calves but his own blood, thus securing an eternal redemption. [13] For if sprinkling defiled persons with the blood of goats and bulls and with the ashes of a heifer sanctifies for the purification of the flesh, [14] how much more shall the blood of Christ, who through the eternal Spirit offered himself without blemish to God, purify your[u] conscience from dead works to serve the living God.

15 Therefore he is the mediator of a new covenant, so that those who are called may receive the promised eternal inheritance, since a death has occurred which redeems them from the transgressions under the first covenant.[v] [16] For where a will[v] is involved, the death of the one who made it must be established. [17] For a will[v] takes effect only at death, since it is not in force as long as the one who made it is alive. [18] Hence even the first covenant was not ratified without blood. [19] For when every commandment of the

[r] Some manuscripts read *good things to come*.   [s] Or *tabernacle*.   [t] Greek *through*.
[u] Many manuscripts read *our*.   [v] The Greek word here used means both *covenant* and *will*.
9. 7: Lev. 16.   **9. 13:** Lev. 16. 6, 16; Num. 19. 9, 17–18.   **9. 19–20:** Ex. 24. 6–8

law had been declared by Moses to all the people, he took the blood of calves and goats, with water and scarlet wool and hyssop, and sprinkled both the book itself and all the people, [20] saying, "This is the blood of the covenant which God commanded you." [21] And in the same way he sprinkled with the blood both the tent[w] and all the vessels used in worship. [22] Indeed, under the law almost everything is purified with blood, and without the shedding of blood there is no forgiveness of sins.

23 Thus it was necessary for the copies of the heavenly things to be purified with these rites, but the heavenly things themselves with better sacrifices than these. [24] For Christ has entered, not into a sanctuary made with hands, a copy of the true one, but into heaven itself, now to appear in the presence of God on our behalf. [25] Nor was it to offer himself repeatedly, as the high priest enters the Holy Place yearly with blood not his own; [26] for then he would have had to suffer repeatedly since the foundation of the world. But as it is, he has appeared once for all at the end of the age to put away sin by the sacrifice of himself. [27] And just as it is appointed for men to die once, and after that comes judgment, [28] so Christ, having been offered once to bear the sins of many, will appear a second time, not to deal with sin but to save those who are eagerly waiting for him.

10 For since the law has but a shadow of the good things to come instead of the true form of these realities, it can never, by the same sacrifices which are continually offered year after year, make perfect those who draw near. [2] Otherwise, would they not have ceased to be offered? If the worshipers had once been cleansed, they would no longer have any consciousness of sin. [3] But in these sacrifices there is a reminder of sin year after year. [4] For

[w] Or *tabernacle*.

it is impossible that the blood of bulls and goats should take away sins.

5 Consequently, when Christ[x] came into the world, he said,

> "Sacrifices and offerings thou hast not desired,
>   but a body hast thou prepared for me;
> [6] in burnt offerings and sin-offerings thou hast taken
>   no pleasure.
> [7] Then I said, 'Lo, I have come to do thy will, O God,'
>   as it is written of me in the roll of the book."

[8] When he said above, "Thou hast neither desired nor taken pleasure in sacrifices and offerings and burnt offerings and sin-offerings" (these are offered according to the law), [9] then he added, "Lo, I have come to do thy will." He abolishes the first in order to establish the second. [10] And by that will we have been consecrated through the offering of the body of Jesus Christ once for all.

11 And every priest stands daily at his service, offering repeatedly the same sacrifices, which can never take away sins. [12] But when Christ[y] had offered for all time a single sacrifice for sins, he sat down at the right hand of God, [13] then to wait until his enemies should be made a stool for his feet. [14] For by a single offering he has perfected for all time those who are consecrated. [15] And the Holy Spirit also bears witness to us; for after saying,

> [16] "This is the covenant that I will make with them
>   after those days, says the Lord:
>   I will put my laws on their hearts,
>   and write them on their minds,"
> [17] then he adds,
> "I will remember their sins and their misdeeds no more."

[x] Greek *he.*   [y] Greek *this one.*

10. 5–9: Ps. 40. 6–8.   **10. 12–13:** Ps. 110. 1.   **10. 16–17:** Jer. 31. 33–34.

¹⁸ Where there is forgiveness of these, there is no longer any offering for sin.

19 Therefore, brethren, since we have confidence to enter the sanctuary by the blood of Jesus, ²⁰ by the new and living way which he opened for us through the curtain, that is, through his flesh, ²¹ and since we have a great priest over the house of God, ²² let us draw near with a true heart in full assurance of faith, with our hearts sprinkled clean from an evil conscience and our bodies washed with pure water. ²³ Let us hold fast the confession of our hope without wavering, for he who promised is faithful; ²⁴ and let us consider how to stir up one another to love and good works, ²⁵ not neglecting to meet together, as is the habit of some, but encouraging one another, and all the more as you see the Day drawing near.

26 For if we sin deliberately after receiving the knowledge of the truth, there no longer remains a sacrifice for sins, ²⁷ but a fearful prospect of judgment, and a fury of fire which will consume the adversaries. ²⁸ A man who has violated the law of Moses dies without mercy at the testimony of two or three witnesses. ²⁹ How much worse punishment do you think will be deserved by the man who has spurned the Son of God, and profaned the blood of the covenant by which he was consecrated, and outraged the Spirit of grace? ³⁰ For we know him who said, "Vengeance is mine, I will repay." And again, "The Lord will judge his people." ³¹ It is a fearful thing to fall into the hands of the living God.

32 But recall the former days when, after you were enlightened, you endured a hard struggle with sufferings, ³³ sometimes being publicly exposed to abuse and affliction, and sometimes being partners with those so treated. ³⁴ For you had compassion on the prisoners, and you joyfully

10. 27: Is. 26. 11.   **10. 28:** Deut. 17. 2–6.   **10. 29:** Ex. 24. 8.   **10. 30:** Deut. 32. 35–36.

accepted the plundering of your property, since you knew that you yourselves had a better possession and an abiding one. [35] Therefore do not throw away your confidence, which has a great reward. [36] For you have need of endurance, so that you may do the will of God and receive what is promised.

> [37] "For yet a little while,
> and the coming one shall come and shall not tarry;
> [38] but my righteous one shall live by faith,
> and if he shrinks back,
> my soul has no pleasure in him."

[39] But we are not of those who shrink back and are destroyed, but of those who have faith and keep their souls.

11 Now faith is the assurance of things hoped for, the conviction of things not seen. [2] For by it the men of old received divine approval. [3] By faith we understand that the world was created by the word of God, so that what is seen was made out of things which do not appear.

4 By faith Abel offered[z] a more acceptable sacrifice than Cain, through which he received approval as righteous, God bearing witness by accepting his gifts; he died, but through his faith he is still speaking. [5] By faith Enoch was taken up so that he should not see death; and he was not found, because God had taken him. Now before he was taken he was attested as having pleased God. [6] And without faith it is impossible to please him. For whoever would draw near to God must believe that he exists and that he rewards those who seek him. [7] By faith Noah, being warned by God concerning events as yet unseen, took heed and constructed an ark for the saving of his household; by this he condemned

---

[z] Many ancient authorities add *to God.*

10. 37: Is. 26. 20 Sept.   **10. 37–38:** Hab. 2. 3–4.
11. 4: Gen. 4. 3–10.   **11. 5:** Gen. 5. 21–24.   **11. 7:** Gen. 6. 13–22.

the world and became an heir of the righteousness which comes by faith.

8 By faith Abraham obeyed when he was called to go out to a place which he was to receive as an inheritance; and he went out, not knowing where he was to go. ⁹ By faith he sojourned in the land of promise, as in a foreign land, living in tents with Isaac and Jacob, heirs with him of the same promise. ¹⁰ For he looked forward to the city which has foundations, whose builder and maker is God. ¹¹ By faith Sarah herself received power to conceive, even when she was past the age, since she considered him faithful who had promised. ¹² Therefore from one man, and him as good as dead, were born descendants as many as the stars of heaven and as the innumerable grains of sand by the seashore.

13 These all died in faith, not having received what was promised, but having seen it and greeted it from afar, and having acknowledged that they were strangers and exiles on the earth. ¹⁴ For people who speak thus make it clear that they are seeking a homeland. ¹⁵ If they had been thinking of that land from which they had gone out, they would have had opportunity to return. ¹⁶ But as it is, they desire a better country, that is, a heavenly one. Therefore God is not ashamed to be called their God, for he has prepared for them a city.

17 By faith Abraham, when he was tested, offered up Isaac, and he who had received the promises was ready to offer up his only son, ¹⁸ of whom it was said, "Through Isaac shall your posterity be named." ¹⁹ He considered that God was able to raise men even from the dead; hence, figuratively speaking, he did receive him back. ²⁰ By faith Isaac

11. 8–9: Gen. 12. 1–8.   11. 11: Gen. 17. 19; 18. 11–14; 21. 2.   11. 12: Gen. 15. 5–6; 22. 17; 32. 12.   11. 13: Ps. 39. 12; Gen. 23. 4.   11. 16: Ex. 3. 6, 15; 4. 5. 11. 17: Gen. 22. 1–10.   11. 18: Gen. 21. 12.   11. 20: Gen. 27. 27–29, 39–40.

invoked future blessings on Jacob and Esau. ²¹ By faith Jacob, when dying, blessed each of the sons of Joseph, bowing in worship over the head of his staff. ²² By faith Joseph, at the end of his life, made mention of the exodus of the Israelites and gave directions concerning his burial.*ᵃ*

23 By faith Moses, when he was born, was hid for three months by his parents, because they saw that the child was beautiful; and they were not afraid of the king's edict. ²⁴ By faith Moses, when he was grown up, refused to be called the son of Pharaoh's daughter, ²⁵ choosing rather to share ill-treatment with the people of God than to enjoy the fleeting pleasures of sin. ²⁶ He considered abuse suffered for the Christ greater wealth than the treasures of Egypt, for he looked to the reward. ²⁷ By faith he left Egypt, not being afraid of the anger of the king; for he endured as seeing him who is invisible. ²⁸ By faith he kept the Passover and sprinkled the blood, so that the Destroyer of the first-born might not touch them.

29 By faith the people crossed the Red Sea as if on dry land; but the Egyptians, when they attempted to do the same, were drowned. ³⁰ By faith the walls of Jericho fell down after they had been encircled for seven days. ³¹ By faith Rahab the harlot did not perish with those who were disobedient, because she had given friendly welcome to the spies.

32 And what more shall I say? For time would fail me to tell of Gideon, Barak, Samson, Jeph'thah, of David and Samuel and the prophets — ³³ who through faith conquered kingdoms, enforced justice, received promises, stopped the mouths of lions, ³⁴ quenched raging fire, escaped the

---

ᵃ Greek *bones*.

11. 21: Gen. 48; 47. 31 Sept. **11. 22:** Gen. 50. 24–25; Ex. 13. 19. **11. 23:** Ex. 2. 2; 1. 22. **11. 24:** Ex. 2. 10, 11–15. **11. 27:** Ex. 2. 15. **11. 28:** Ex. 12. 21–28, 29–30. **11. 29:** Ex. 14. 21–31. **11. 30:** Josh. 6. 12–21. **11. 31:** Josh. 2. 1–21; 6. 22–25. **11. 32:** Judg. 6–8; 4–5; 13–16; 11–12; 1 Sam. 16–30; 2 Sam. 1–24; 1 Kings 1–2. 11; 1 Sam. 1–12; 15; 16. 1–13. **11. 33:** Dan. 6.

edge of the sword, won strength out of weakness, became mighty in war, put foreign armies to flight. [35] Women received their dead by resurrection. Some were tortured, refusing to accept release, that they might rise again to a better life. [36] Others suffered mocking and scourging, and even chains and imprisonment. [37] They were stoned, they were sawn in two,[b] they were killed with the sword; they went about in skins of sheep and goats, destitute, afflicted, ill-treated — [38] of whom the world was not worthy — wandering over deserts and mountains, and in dens and caves of the earth.

39 And all these, though well attested by their faith, did not receive what was promised, [40] since God had foreseen something better for us, that apart from us they should not be made perfect.

12 Therefore, since we are surrounded by so great a cloud of witnesses, let us also lay aside every weight, and sin which clings so closely, and let us run with perseverance the race that is set before us, [2] looking to Jesus the pioneer and perfecter of our faith, who for the joy that was set before him endured the cross, despising the shame, and is seated at the right hand of the throne of God.

3 Consider him who endured from sinners such hostility against himself, so that you may not grow weary or faint-hearted. [4] In your struggle against sin you have not yet resisted to the point of shedding your blood. [5] And have you forgotten the exhortation which addresses you as sons? —

"My son, do not regard lightly the discipline of the Lord, nor lose courage when you are punished by him.

[6] For the Lord disciplines him whom he loves, and chastises every son whom he receives."

[b] Many manuscripts add *they were tempted*.

11. 34: Dan. 3.   **11. 35:** 1 Kings 17. 17–24; 2 Kings 4. 25–37.
12. 2: Ps. 110. 1.   **12. 5–8:** Prov. 3. 11–12.

⁷ It is for discipline that you have to endure. God is treating you as sons; for what son is there whom his father does not discipline? ⁸ If you are left without discipline, in which all have participated, then you are illegitimate children and not sons. ⁹ Besides this, we have had earthly fathers to discipline us and we respected them. Shall we not much more be subject to the Father of spirits and live? ¹⁰ For they disciplined us for a short time at their pleasure, but he disciplines us for our good, that we may share his holiness. ¹¹ For the moment all discipline seems painful rather than pleasant; later it yields the peaceful fruit of righteousness to those who have been trained by it.

12 Therefore lift your drooping hands and strengthen your weak knees, ¹³ and make straight paths for your feet, so that what is lame may not be put out of joint but rather be healed. ¹⁴ Strive for peace with all men, and for the consecration without which no one will see the Lord. ¹⁵ See to it that no one fail to obtain the grace of God; that no "root of bitterness" spring up and cause trouble, and by it the many become defiled; ¹⁶ that no one be immoral or irreligious like Esau, who sold his birthright for a single meal. ¹⁷ For you know that afterward, when he desired to inherit the blessing, he was rejected, for he found no chance to repent, though he sought it with tears.

18 For you have not come to what may be touched, a blazing fire, and darkness, and gloom, and a tempest, ¹⁹ and the sound of a trumpet, and a voice whose words made the hearers entreat that no further message be spoken to them. ²⁰ For they could not endure the order that was given, "If even a beast touches the mountain, it shall be stoned." ²¹ Indeed, so terrifying was the sight that Moses said, "I

12. 12: Is. 35. 3.   **12. 13:** Prov. 4. 26 Sept.   **12. 15:** Deut. 29. 18 Sept.   **12. 16:** Gen. 25. 29–34.   **12. 17:** Gen. 27. 30–40.   **12. 18–19:** Ex. 19. 12–22; 20. 18–21; Deut. 4. 11–12; 5. 22–27.   **12. 20:** Ex. 19. 12–13.   **12. 21:** Deut. 9. 19.

tremble with fear." ²² But you have come to Mount Zion and to the city of the living God, the heavenly Jerusalem, and to innumerable angels in festal gathering, ²³ and to the assembly^c of the first-born who are enrolled in heaven, and to a judge who is God of all, and to the spirits of just men made perfect, ²⁴ and to Jesus, the mediator of a new covenant, and to the sprinkled blood that speaks more graciously than the blood of Abel.

25 See that you do not refuse him who is speaking. For if they did not escape when they refused him who warned them on earth, much less shall we escape if we reject him who warns from heaven. ²⁶ His voice then shook the earth; but now he has promised, "Yet once more I will shake not only the earth but also the heaven." ²⁷ This phrase, "Yet once more," indicates the removal of what is shaken, as of what has been made, in order that what cannot be shaken may remain. ²⁸ Therefore let us be grateful for receiving a kingdom that cannot be shaken, and thus let us offer to God acceptable worship, with reverence and awe; ²⁹ for our God is a consuming fire.

13 Let brotherly love continue. ² Do not neglect to show hospitality to strangers, for thereby some have entertained angels unawares. ³ Remember those who are in prison, as though in prison with them; and those who are ill-treated, since you also are in the body. ⁴ Let marriage be held in honor among all, and let the marriage bed be undefiled; for God will judge the immoral and adulterous. ⁵ Keep your life free from love of money, and be content with what you have; for he has said, "I will never fail you nor forsake you." ⁶ Hence we can confidently say,

^c Or *angels, and to the festal gathering and assembly.*
12. 24: Gen. 4. 10.   **12. 25:** Ex. 20. 19.   **12. 26:** Hag. 2. 6.   **12. 29:** Deut. 4. 24.
13. 2: Gen. 18. 1–8; 19. 1–3.   **13. 5:** Deut. 31. 6, 8; Josh. 1. 5.   **13. 6:** Ps. 118. 6.

"The Lord is my helper,
I will not be afraid;
what can man do to me?"

7 Remember your leaders, those who spoke to you the word of God; consider the outcome of their life, and imitate their faith. [8] Jesus Christ is the same yesterday and today and forever. [9] Do not be led away by diverse and strange teachings; for it is well that the heart be strengthened by grace, not by foods, which have not benefited their adherents. [10] We have an altar from which those who serve the tent[d] have no right to eat. [11] For the bodies of those animals whose blood is brought into the sanctuary by the high priest as a sacrifice for sin are burned outside the camp. [12] So Jesus also suffered outside the gate in order to consecrate the people through his own blood. [13] Therefore let us go forth to him outside the camp, bearing abuse for him. [14] For here we have no lasting city, but we seek the city which is to come. [15] Through him then let us continually offer up a sacrifice of praise to God, that is, the fruit of lips that acknowledge his name. [16] Do not neglect to do good and to share what you have, for such sacrifices are pleasing to God.

17 Obey your leaders and submit to them; for they are keeping watch over your souls, as men who will have to give account. Let them do this joyfully, and not sadly, for that would be of no advantage to you.

18 Pray for us, for we are sure that we have a clear conscience, desiring to act honorably in all things. [19] I urge you the more earnestly to do this in order that I may be restored to you the sooner.

20 Now may the God of peace who brought again from the dead our Lord Jesus, the great shepherd of the sheep,

[d] Or *tabernacle*.
13. 11, 13: Lev. 16. 27.   **13. 15:** Lev. 7. 12; Is. 57. 19; Hos. 14. 2.   **13. 20:** Is. 63. 11; Zech. 9. 11; Is. 55. 3; Ezek. 37. 26.

by the blood of the eternal covenant, [21] equip you with everything good that you may do his will, working in you[e] that which is pleasing in his sight, through Jesus Christ; to whom be glory for ever and ever. Amen.

22 I appeal to you, brethren, bear with my word of exhortation, for I have written to you briefly. [23] You should understand that our brother Timothy has been released, with whom I shall see you if he comes soon. [24] Greet all your leaders and all the saints. Those who come from Italy send you greetings. [25] Grace be with all of you. Amen.

THE LETTER OF

JAMES

1 James, a servant of God and of the Lord Jesus Christ,
To the twelve tribes in the dispersion:
Greeting.

2 Count it all joy, my brethren, when you meet various trials, [3] for you know that the testing of your faith produces steadfastness. [4] And let steadfastness have its full effect, that you may be perfect and complete, lacking in nothing.

5 If any of you lacks wisdom, let him ask God who gives to all men generously and without reproaching, and it will be given him. [6] But let him ask in faith, with no doubting, for he who doubts is like a wave of the sea that is driven and tossed by the wind. [7, 8] For that person must not suppose that a double-minded man, unstable in all his ways, will receive anything from the Lord.

[e] Many ancient authorities read *us*.

9 Let the lowly brother boast in his exaltation, [10] and the rich in his humiliation, because like the flower of the grass he will pass away. [11] For the sun rises with its scorching heat and withers the grass; its flower falls, and its beauty perishes. So will the rich man fade away in the midst of his pursuits.

12 Blessed is the man who endures trial, for when he has stood the test he will receive the crown of life which God has promised to those who love him. [13] Let no one say when he is tempted, "I am tempted by God"; for God cannot be tempted with evil and he himself tempts no one; [14] but each person is tempted when he is lured and enticed by his own desire. [15] Then desire when it has conceived gives birth to sin; and sin when it is full-grown brings forth death.

16 Do not be deceived, my beloved brethren. [17] Every good endowment and every perfect gift is from above, coming down from the Father of lights with whom there is no variation or shadow due to change.[a] [18] Of his own will he brought us forth by the word of truth that we should be a kind of first fruits of his creatures.

19 Know this, my beloved brethren. Let every man be quick to hear, slow to speak, slow to anger, [20] for the anger of man does not work the righteousness of God. [21] Therefore put away all filthiness and rank growth of wickedness and receive with meekness the implanted word, which is able to save your souls.

22 But be doers of the word, and not hearers only, deceiving yourselves. [23] For if any one is a hearer of the word and not a doer, he is like a man who observes his natural face in a mirror; [24] for he observes himself and goes away and at once forgets what he was like. [25] But he who looks

[a] Some ancient authorities read *variation due to a shadow of turning.*
1. 10–11: Is. 40. 6–7.

into the perfect law, the law of liberty, and perseveres, being no hearer that forgets but a doer that acts, he shall be blessed in his doing.

26 If any one thinks he is religious, and does not bridle his tongue but deceives his heart, this man's religion is vain. [27] Religion that is pure and undefiled before God and the Father is this: to visit orphans and widows in their affliction, and to keep oneself unstained from the world.

2 My brethren, show no partiality as you hold the faith of our Lord Jesus Christ, the Lord of glory. [2] For if a man with gold rings and in fine clothing comes into your assembly, and a poor man in shabby clothing also comes in, [3] and you pay attention to the one who wears the fine clothing and say, "Have a seat here, please," while you say to the poor man, "Stand there," or, "Sit at my feet," [4] have you not made distinctions among yourselves, and become judges with evil thoughts? [5] Listen, my beloved brethren. Has not God chosen those who are poor in the world to be rich in faith and heirs of the kingdom which he has promised to those who love him? [6] But you have dishonored the poor man. Is it not the rich who oppress you, is it not they who drag you into court? [7] Is it not they who blaspheme that honorable name by which you are called?

8 If you really fulfill the royal law, according to the scripture, "You shall love your neighbor as yourself," you do well. [9] But if you show partiality, you commit sin, and are convicted by the law as transgressors. [10] For whoever keeps the whole law but fails in one point has become guilty of all of it. [11] For he who said, "Do not commit adultery," said also, "Do not kill." If you do not commit adultery but do kill, you have become a transgressor of the law. [12] So speak

2. 8: Lev. 19. 18.   **2. 11:** Ex. 20. 13–14; Deut. 5. 17–18.

and so act as those who are to be judged under the law of liberty. [13] For judgment is without mercy to one who has shown no mercy; mercy triumphs over judgment.

14 What does it profit, my brethren, if a man says he has faith but has not works? Can his faith save him? [15] If a brother or sister is ill-clad and in lack of daily food, [16] and one of you says to them, "Go in peace, be warmed and filled," without giving them the things needed for the body, what does it profit? [17] So faith by itself, if it has no works, is dead.

18 But some one will say, "You have faith and I have works." Show me your faith apart from your works, and I by my works will show you my faith. [19] You believe that God is one; you do well. Even the demons believe — and shudder. [20] Do you want to be shown, you foolish fellow, that faith apart from works is barren? [21] Was not Abraham our father justified by works, when he offered his son Isaac upon the altar? [22] You see that faith was active along with his works, and faith was completed by works, [23] and the scripture was fulfilled which says, "Abraham believed God, and it was reckoned to him as righteousness"; and he was called the friend of God. [24] You see that a man is justified by works and not by faith alone. [25] And in the same way was not also Rahab the harlot justified by works when she received the messengers and sent them out another way? [26] For as the body apart from the spirit is dead, so faith apart from works is dead.

3 Let not many of you become teachers, my brethren, for you know that we who teach shall be judged with greater strictness. [2] For we all make many mistakes, and if any one makes no mistakes in what he says he is a perfect

2. 21: Gen. 22. 1–14.   **2. 23**: Gen. 15. 6; Is. 41. 8; 2 Chr. 20. 7.   **2. 25**: Josh. 2. 1–21.

man, able to bridle the whole body also. ³ If we put bits into the mouths of horses that they may obey us, we guide their whole bodies. ⁴ Look at the ships also; though they are so great and are driven by strong winds, they are guided by a very small rudder wherever the will of the pilot directs. ⁵ So the tongue is a little member and boasts of great things. How great a forest is set ablaze by a small fire!

6 And the tongue is a fire. The tongue is an unrighteous world among our members, staining the whole body, setting on fire the cycle of nature,*b* and set on fire by hell.*c* ⁷ For every kind of beast and bird, of reptile and sea creature, can be tamed and has been tamed by humankind, ⁸ but no human being can tame the tongue — a restless evil, full of deadly poison. ⁹ With it we bless the Lord and Father, and with it we curse men, who are made in the likeness of God. ¹⁰ From the same mouth come blessing and cursing. My brethren, this ought not to be so. ¹¹ Does a spring pour forth from the same opening fresh water and brackish? ¹² Can a fig tree, my brethren, yield olives, or a grapevine figs? No more can salt water yield fresh.

13 Who is wise and understanding among you? By his good life let him show his works in the meekness of wisdom. ¹⁴ But if you have bitter jealousy and selfish ambition in your hearts, do not boast and be false to the truth. ¹⁵ This wisdom is not such as comes down from above, but is earthly, unspiritual, devilish. ¹⁶ For where jealousy and selfish ambition exist, there will be disorder and every vile practice. ¹⁷ But the wisdom from above is first pure, then peaceable, gentle, open to reason, full of mercy and good fruits, without uncertainty or insincerity. ¹⁸ And the harvest of righteousness is sown in peace by those who make peace.

b Or *wheel of birth.*   *c* Greek *Gehenna.*

4 What causes wars, and what causes fightings among you? Is it not your passions that are at war in your members? [2] You desire and do not have; so you kill. And you covet[d] and cannot obtain; so you fight and wage war. You do not have, because you do not ask. [3] You ask and do not receive, because you ask wrongly, to spend it on your passions. [4] Unfaithful creatures! Do you not know that friendship with the world is enmity with God? Therefore whoever wishes to be a friend of the world makes himself an enemy of God. [5] Or do you suppose it is in vain that the scripture says, "He yearns jealously over the spirit which he has made to dwell in us?" [6] But he gives more grace; therefore it says, "God opposes the proud, but gives grace to the humble." [7] Submit yourselves therefore to God. Resist the devil and he will flee from you. [8] Draw near to God and he will draw near to you. Cleanse your hands, you sinners, and purify your hearts, you men of double mind. [9] Be wretched and mourn and weep. Let your laughter be turned to mourning and your joy to dejection. [10] Humble yourselves before the Lord and he will exalt you.

11 Do not speak evil against one another, brethren. He that speaks evil against a brother or judges his brother, speaks evil against the law and judges the law. But if you judge the law, you are not a doer of the law but a judge. [12] There is one lawgiver and judge, he who is able to save and to destroy. But who are you that you judge your neighbor?

13 Come now, you who say, "Today or tomorrow we will go into such and such a town and spend a year there and trade and get gain"; [14] whereas you do not know about tomorrow. What is your life? For you are a mist that appears

---

[d] Or *you kill and you covet.*

4. 6: Prov. 3. 34.

for a little time and then vanishes. [15] Instead you ought to say, "If the Lord wills, we shall live and we shall do this or that." [16] As it is, you boast in your arrogance. All such boasting is evil. [17] Whoever knows what is right to do and fails to do it, for him it is sin.

5 Come now, you rich, weep and howl for the miseries that are coming upon you. [2] Your riches have rotted and your garments are moth-eaten. [3] Your gold and silver have rusted, and their rust will be evidence against you and will eat your flesh like fire. You have laid up treasure[e] for the last days. [4] Behold, the wages of the laborers who mowed your fields, which you kept back by fraud, cry out; and the cries of the harvesters have reached the ears of the Lord of hosts. [5] You have lived on the earth in luxury and in pleasure; you have fattened your hearts in a day of slaughter. [6] You have condemned, you have killed the righteous man; he does not resist you.

7 Be patient, therefore, brethren, until the coming of the Lord. Behold, the farmer waits for the precious fruit of the earth, being patient over it until it receives the early and the late rain. [8] You also be patient. Establish your hearts, for the coming of the Lord is at hand. [9] Do not grumble, brethren, against one another, that you may not be judged; behold, the Judge is standing at the doors. [10] As an example of suffering and patience, brethren, take the prophets who spoke in the name of the Lord. [11] Behold, we call those happy who were steadfast. You have heard of the steadfastness of Job, and you have seen the purpose of the Lord, how the Lord is compassionate and merciful.

12 But above all, my brethren, do not swear, either by heaven or by earth or with any other oath, but let your yes

---

[e] Or *will eat your flesh, since you have stored up fire.*

5. 11: Job 1. 21–22; 2. 10; Ps. 108. 8; 111. 4.   **5. 12:** Mt. 5. 37.

be yes and your no be no, that you may not fall under condemnation.

13 Is any one among you suffering? Let him pray. Is any cheerful? Let him sing praise. [14] Is any among you sick? Let him call for the elders of the church, and let them pray over him, anointing him with oil in the name of the Lord; [15] and the prayer of faith will save the sick man, and the Lord will raise him up; and if he has committed sins, he will be forgiven. [16] Therefore confess your sins to one another, and pray for one another, that you may be healed. The prayer of a righteous man has great power in its effects. [17] Elijah was a man of like nature with ourselves and he prayed fervently that it might not rain, and for three years and six months it did not rain on the earth. [18] Then he prayed again and the heaven gave rain, and the earth brought forth its fruit.

19 My brethren, if any one among you wanders from the truth and some one brings him back, [20] let him know that whoever brings back a sinner from the error of his way will save his soul from death and will cover a multitude of sins.

THE FIRST LETTER OF
PETER

1 Peter, an apostle of Jesus Christ,
To the exiles of the dispersion in Pontus, Galatia, Cap-pa-do′ci-a, Asia, and Bi-thyn′i-a, [2] chosen and destined by God the Father and sanctified by the Spirit for obedience to Jesus Christ and for sprinkling with his blood:

May grace and peace be multiplied to you.

5. 17: 1 Kings 17. 1; 18. 1; Luke 4. 25.   **5. 18:** 1 Kings 18. 42.

3 Blessed be the God and Father of our Lord Jesus Christ! By his great mercy we have been born anew to a living hope through the resurrection of Jesus Christ from the dead, [4] and to an inheritance which is imperishable, undefiled, and unfading, kept in heaven for you, [5] who by God's power are guarded through faith for a salvation ready to be revealed in the last time. [6] In this you rejoice,[a] though now for a little while you may have to suffer various trials, [7] so that the genuineness of your faith, more precious than gold which though perishable is tested by fire, may redound to praise and glory and honor at the revelation of Jesus Christ. [8] Without having seen[b] him you[c] love him; though you do not now see him you[c] believe in him and rejoice with unutterable and exalted joy. [9] As the outcome of your faith you obtain the salvation of your souls.

10 The prophets who prophesied of the grace that was to be yours searched and inquired about this salvation; [11] they inquired what person or time was indicated by the Spirit of Christ within them when predicting the sufferings of Christ and the subsequent glory. [12] It was revealed to them that they were serving not themselves but you, in the things which have now been announced to you by those who preached the good news to you through the Holy Spirit sent from heaven, things into which angels long to look.

13 Therefore gird up your minds, be sober, set your hope fully upon the grace that is coming to you at the revelation of Jesus Christ. [14] As obedient children, do not be conformed to the passions of your former ignorance, [15] but as he who called you is holy, be holy yourselves in all your conduct; [16] since it is written, "You shall be holy, for I am

[a] Or *Rejoice in this.*   [b] Some ancient authorities read *known.*   [c] Or omit *you.*
1. 16: Lev. 11. 44–45.

holy." [17] And if you invoke as Father him who judges each one impartially according to his deeds, conduct yourselves with fear throughout the time of your exile. [18] You know that you were ransomed from the futile ways inherited from your fathers, not with perishable things such as silver or gold, [19] but with the precious blood of Christ, like that of a lamb without blemish or spot. [20] He was destined before the foundation of the world but was made manifest at the end of the times for your sake. [21] Through him you have confidence in God, who raised him from the dead and gave him glory, so that your faith and hope are in God.[d]

22 Having purified your souls by your obedience to the truth for a sincere love of the brethren, love one another earnestly from the heart. [23] You have been born anew, not of perishable seed but of imperishable, through the living and abiding word of God; [24] for

"All flesh is like grass
and all its glory like the flower of grass.
The grass withers, and the flower falls,
[25] but the word of the Lord abides forever."

That word is the good news which was preached to you.

2 So put away all malice and all guile and insincerity and envy and all slander. [2] Like newborn babes, long for the pure spiritual milk, that by it you may grow up to salvation; [3] for you have tasted the kindness of the Lord.

4 Come to him, to that living stone, rejected by men but in God's sight chosen and precious; [5] and like living stones be yourselves built into a spiritual house, to be a holy priesthood, to offer spiritual sacrifices acceptable to God through Jesus Christ. [6] For it stands in scripture:

[d] Or *so that your faith is hope in God.*
1. 24–25: Is. 40. 6–9.
2. 3: Ps. 34. 8.   **2. 4:** Ps. 118. 22; Is. 28. 16.   **2. 6:** Is. 28. 16.

"Behold, I am laying in Zion a stone, a cornerstone
chosen and precious,
and he who believes in him will not be put to shame."
[7] To you therefore who believe, he is precious, but for those
who do not believe,

"The very stone which the builders rejected
has become the head of the corner,"
[8] and

"A stone that will make men stumble,
a rock that will make them fall";
for they stumble because they disobey the word, as they
were destined to do.

[9] But you are a chosen race, a royal priesthood, a holy
nation, God's own[e] people, that you may declare the wonderful deeds of him who called you out of darkness into his
marvelous light. [10] Once you were no people but now you
are God's people; once you had not received mercy but now
you have received mercy.

[11] Beloved, I beseech you as aliens and exiles to abstain
from the passions of the flesh that wage war against your
soul. [12] Maintain good conduct among the Gentiles, so that
in case they speak against you as wrongdoers, they may see
your good deeds and glorify God on the day of visitation.

[13] Be subject for the Lord's sake to every human institution,[f] whether it be to the emperor as supreme, [14] or to
governors as sent by him to punish those who do wrong and
to praise those who do right. [15] For it is God's will that
by doing right you should put to silence the ignorance of
foolish men. [16] Live as free men, yet without using your
freedom as a pretext for evil; but live as servants of God.

---

[e] Greek *a special.*   [f] Or *every institution ordained for men.*

2. 7: Ps. 118. 22.   **2. 8:** Is. 8. 14–15.   **2. 9:** Ex. 23. 22.   **2. 10:** Hos. 2. 23.

[17] Honor all men. Love the brotherhood. Fear God. Honor the emperor.

18 Servants, be submissive to your masters with all respect, not only to the kind and gentle but also to the overbearing. [19] For one is approved if, mindful of God, he endures pain while suffering unjustly. [20] For what credit is it, if when you do wrong and are beaten for it you take it patiently? But if when you do right and suffer for it you take it patiently, you have God's approval. [21] For to this you have been called, because Christ also suffered for you, leaving you an example, that you should follow in his steps. [22] He committed no sin; no guile was found on his lips. [23] When he was reviled, he did not revile in return; when he suffered, he did not threaten; but he trusted to him who judges justly. [24] He himself bore our sins in his body on the tree,[g] that we might die to sin and live to righteousness. By his wounds you have been healed. [25] For you were straying like sheep, but have now returned to the Shepherd and Guardian of your souls.

3 Likewise you wives, be submissive to your husbands, so that some, though they do not obey the word, may be won without a word by the behavior of their wives, [2] when they see your reverent and chaste behavior. [3] Let not yours be the outward adorning with braiding of hair, decoration of gold, and wearing of robes, [4] but let it be the hidden person of the heart with the imperishable jewel of a gentle and quiet spirit, which in God's sight is very precious. [5] So once the holy women who hoped in God used to adorn themselves and were submissive to their husbands, [6] as Sarah obeyed Abraham, calling him lord. And you are now her children if you do right and let nothing terrify you.

[g] Or *carried up . . . to the tree.*

2. 22: Is. 53. 9.   **2. 24:** Is. 53. 12. Sept.   **2. 24-25:** Is. 53. 5-6.
3. 6: Gen. 18. 12.

7 Likewise you husbands, live considerately with your wives, bestowing honor on the woman as the weaker sex, since you are joint heirs of the grace of life, in order that your prayers may not be hindered.

8 Finally, all of you, have unity of spirit, sympathy, love of the brethren, a tender heart and a humble mind. ⁹ Do not return evil for evil or reviling for reviling; but on the contrary bless, for to this you have been called, that you may obtain a blessing. ¹⁰ For

> "He that would love life
>   and see good days,
>   let him keep his tongue from evil
>   and his lips from speaking guile;
> ¹¹ let him turn away from evil and do right;
>   let him seek peace and pursue it.
> ¹² For the eyes of the Lord are upon the righteous,
>   and his ears are open to their prayer.
>   But the face of the Lord is against those that do evil."

13 Now who is there to harm you if you are zealous for what is right? ¹⁴ But even if you do suffer for righteousness' sake, you will be blessed. Have no fear of them, nor be troubled, ¹⁵ but in your hearts reverence Christ as Lord. Always be prepared to make a defense to any one who calls you to account for the hope that is in you, yet do it with gentleness and reverence; ¹⁶ and keep your conscience clear, so that, when you are abused, those who revile your good behavior in Christ may be put to shame. ¹⁷ For it is better to suffer for doing right, if that should be God's will, than for doing wrong. ¹⁸ For Christ also died[h] for sins once for all, the righteous for the unrighteous, that he might bring us to God, being put to death in the flesh but made alive in

[h] Some ancient authorities read *suffered*.

3. 10–12: Ps. 24. 12–16.   **3. 14–15:** Is. 8. 12–13.

the spirit; [19] in which he went and preached to the spirits in prison, [20] who formerly did not obey, when God's patience waited in the days of Noah, during the building of the ark, in which a few, that is, eight persons, were saved through water. [21] Baptism, which corresponds to this, now saves you, not as a removal of dirt from the body but as an appeal to God for a clear conscience, through the resurrection of Jesus Christ, [22] who has gone into heaven and is at the right hand of God, with angels, authorities, and powers subject to him.

4 Since therefore Christ suffered in the flesh,[i] arm yourselves with the same thought, for whoever has suffered in the flesh has ceased from sin, [2] so as to live for the rest of the time in the flesh no longer by human passions but by the will of God. [3] Let the time that is past suffice for doing what the Gentiles like to do, living in licentiousness, passions, drunkenness, revels, carousing, and lawless idolatry. [4] They are surprised that you do not now join them in the same wild profligacy, and they abuse you; [5] but they will give account to him who is ready to judge the living and the dead. [6] For this is why the gospel was preached even to the dead, that though judged in the flesh like men, they might live in the spirit like God.

7 The end of all things is at hand; keep sane and sober for your prayers. [8] Above all hold unfailing your love for one another, since love covers a multitude of sins. [9] Practice hospitality ungrudgingly to one another. [10] As each has received a gift, employ it for one another, as good stewards of God's varied grace: [11] whoever speaks, as one who utters oracles of God; whoever renders service, as one who renders it by the strength which God supplies; in order that in every-

---

[i] Some ancient authorities add *for us;* some *for you.*

3. 20: Gen. 6–8.

thing God may be glorified through Jesus Christ. To him belong glory and dominion for ever and ever. Amen.

12 Beloved, do not be surprised at the fiery ordeal which comes upon you to prove you, as though something strange were happening to you. [13] But rejoice in so far as you share Christ's sufferings, that you may also rejoice and be glad when his glory is revealed. [14] If you are reproached for the name of Christ, you are blessed, because the spirit of glory[j] and of God rests upon you. [15] But let none of you suffer as a murderer, or a thief, or a wrongdoer, or a mischief-maker; [16] yet if one suffers as a Christian, let him not be ashamed, but under that name let him glorify God. [17] For the time has come for judgment to begin with the household of God; and if it begins with us, what will be the end of those who do not obey the gospel of God? [18] And

"If the righteous man is scarcely saved,

where will the impious and sinner appear?"

[19] Therefore let those who suffer according to God's will do right and entrust their souls to a faithful creator.

5 So I exhort the elders among you, as a fellow elder and a witness of the sufferings of Christ as well as a partaker in the glory that is to be revealed. [2] Tend the flock of God that is your charge,[k] not by constraint but willingly,[l] not for shameful gain but eagerly, [3] not as domineering over those in your charge but being examples to the flock. [4] And when the chief Shepherd is manifested you will obtain the unfading crown of glory. [5] Likewise you that are younger be subject to the elders. Clothe yourselves, all of you, with humility toward one another, for "God opposes the proud, but gives grace to the humble."

[j] Some ancient authorities insert *and of power.*
[k] Some ancient authorities add *exercising the oversight.*   [l] Some ancient authorities add *as God would have you.*
4. 14: Is. 11. 2.   **4. 18:** Prov. 11. 31, Septuagint.   **5. 5:** Prov. 3. 34.

6 Humble yourselves therefore under the mighty hand of God, that in due time he may exalt you. ⁷ Cast all your anxieties on him, for he cares about you. ⁸ Be sober, be watchful. Your adversary the devil prowls around like a roaring lion, seeking someone to devour. ⁹ Resist him, firm in your faith, knowing that the same experience of suffering is required of your brotherhood throughout the world. ¹⁰ And after you have suffered a little while, the God of all grace, who has called you to his eternal glory in Christ, will himself restore, establish, and strengthen*ᵐ* you. ¹¹ To him be the dominion for ever and ever. Amen.

12 By Sil-va′nus, a faithful brother as I regard him, I have written briefly to you, exhorting and declaring that this is the true grace of God; stand fast in it. ¹³ She who is at Babylon, who is likewise chosen, sends you greetings; and so does my son Mark. ¹⁴ Greet one another with the kiss of love.

Peace to all of you that are in Christ.

THE SECOND LETTER OF
PETER

1 Simon Peter, a servant and apostle of Jesus Christ,
 To those who have obtained a faith of equal standing with ours in the righteousness of our God and Savior Jesus Christ:*ᵃ*

2 May grace and peace be multiplied to you in the knowledge of God and of Jesus our Lord.

3 His divine power has granted to us all things that pertain to life and godliness, through the knowledge of him who

---

ᵐ Many ancient authorities read *restore, establish, strengthen and settle.*
ᵃ Or *of our God and the Savior Jesus Christ.*
5. 7: Ps. 55. 22.

called us to[b] his own glory and excellence, [4] by which he has
granted to us his precious and very great promises, that
through these you may escape from the corruption that is
in the world because of passion, and become partakers of
the divine nature. [5] For this very reason make every effort
to supplement your faith with virtue, and virtue with
knowledge, [6] and knowledge with self-control, and self-
control with steadfastness, and steadfastness with godliness,
[7] and godliness with brotherly affection, and brotherly affection with love. [8] For if these things are yours and abound,
they keep you from being ineffective or unfruitful in the
knowledge of our Lord Jesus Christ. [9] For whoever lacks
these things is blind and shortsighted and has forgotten
that he was cleansed from his old sins. [10] Therefore, brethren, be the more zealous to confirm your call and election,
for if you do this you will never fall; [11] so there will be
richly provided for you an entrance into the eternal kingdom
of our Lord and Savior Jesus Christ.

12 Therefore I intend always to remind you of these
things, though you know them and are established in the
truth that you have. [13] I think it right, as long as I am in
this body,[c] to arouse you by way of reminder, [14] since I
know that the putting off of my body[c] will be soon, as our
Lord Jesus Christ showed me. [15] And I will see to it that
after my departure you may be able at any time to recall
these things.

16 For we did not follow cleverly devised myths when we
made known to you the power and coming of our Lord Jesus
Christ, but we were eyewitnesses of his majesty. [17] For
when he received honor and glory from God the Father and
the voice was borne to him by the Majestic Glory, "This is

[b] Or *by*.   [c] Greek *tent*.
1. 17–18: Mt. 17. 1–8; Mk. 9. 2–8; Lk. 9. 28–36.

my beloved Son,^d with whom I am well pleased," we heard this voice borne from heaven, for we were with him on the holy mountain. ¹⁹ And we have the prophetic word made more sure. You will do well to pay attention to this as to a lamp shining in a dark place, until the day dawns and the morning star rises in your hearts. ²⁰ First of all you must understand this, that no prophecy of scripture is a matter of one's own interpretation, ²¹ because no prophecy ever came by the impulse of man, but men moved by the Holy Spirit spoke from God.^e

2 But false prophets also arose among the people, just as there will be false teachers among you, who will secretly bring in destructive heresies, even denying the Master who bought them, bringing upon themselves swift destruction. ² And many will follow their licentiousness, and because of them the way of truth will be reviled. ³ And in their greed they will exploit you with false words; from of old their condemnation has not been idle, and their destruction has not been asleep.

4 For if God did not spare the angels when they sinned, but cast them into hell^f and committed them to pits of nether gloom to be kept until the judgment; ⁵ if he did not spare the ancient world, but preserved Noah, a herald of righteousness, with seven other persons, when he brought a flood upon the world of the ungodly; ⁶ if by turning the cities of Sodom and Go-mor'rah to ashes he condemned them to extinction and made them an example to those who were to be ungodly; ⁷ and if he rescued righteous Lot, greatly distressed by the licentiousness of the wicked ⁸ (for by what that righteous man saw and heard as he lived among them, he was vexed in his righteous soul day after day with

---

^d Or *my Son, my* (or *the*) *Beloved.*
^e Many authorities read *moved by the Holy Spirit holy men of God spoke.*   ^f Greek *Tartarus.*
2. 1–18: Jude 4–16.   **2. 5:** Gen. 8. 18, 6–8.   **2. 6:** Gen. 19. 24.   **2. 7:** Gen. 19. 16, 29.

their lawless deeds), ⁹ then the Lord knows how to rescue the godly from trial, and to keep the unrighteous under punishment until the day of judgment, ¹⁰ and especially those who indulge in the lust of defiling passion and despise authority.

Bold and wilful, they are not afraid to revile the glorious ones, ¹¹ whereas angels, though greater in might and power, do not pronounce a reviling judgment upon them before the Lord. ¹² But these, like irrational animals, creatures of instinct, born to be caught and killed, reviling in matters of which they are ignorant, will be destroyed in the same destruction with them, ¹³ suffering wrong for their wrongdoing. They count it pleasure to revel in the daytime. They are blots and blemishes, reveling in their dissipation,ᵍ carousing with you. ¹⁴ They have eyes full of adultery, insatiable for sin. They entice unsteady souls. They have hearts trained in greed. Accursed children! ¹⁵ Forsaking the right way they have gone astray; they have followed the way of Ba'laam, the son of Be'or, who loved gain from wrongdoing, ¹⁶ but was rebuked for his own transgression; a dumb ass spoke with human voice and restrained the prophet's madness.

17 These are waterless springs and mists driven by a storm; for them the nether gloom of darkness has been reserved. ¹⁸ For, uttering loud boasts of folly, they entice with licentious passions of the flesh men who have barely escaped from those who live in error. ¹⁹ They promise them freedom, but they themselves are slaves of corruption; for whatever overcomes a man, to that he is enslaved. ²⁰ For if, after they have escaped the defilements of the world through the knowledge of our Lord and Savior Jesus Christ, they are again entangled in them and overpowered, the last state has

ᵍ Some ancient authorities read *love feasts.*

2. 15: Num. 22. 5, 7.   **2. 16:** Num. 22. 21, 23, 28, 30–31.

become worse for them than the first. ²¹ For it would have been better for them never to have known the way of righteousness than after knowing it to turn back from the holy commandment delivered to them. ²² It has happened to them according to the true proverb, The dog turns back to his own vomit, and the sow is washed only to wallow in the mire.

3 This is now the second letter that I have written to you, beloved, and in both of them I have aroused your sincere mind by way of reminder; ² that you should remember the predictions of the holy prophets and the commandment of the Lord and Savior through your apostles. ³ First of all you must understand this, that scoffers will come in the last days with scoffing, following their own passions ⁴ and saying, "Where is the promise of his coming? For ever since the fathers fell asleep, all things have continued as they were from the beginning of creation." ⁵ They deliberately ignore this fact, that by the word of God heavens existed long ago, and an earth formed out of water and by means of water, ⁶ through which the world that then existed was deluged with water and perished. ⁷ But by the same word the heavens and earth that now exist have been stored up for fire, being kept until the day of judgment and destruction of ungodly men.

8 But do not ignore this one fact, beloved, that with the Lord one day is as a thousand years, and a thousand years as one day. ⁹ The Lord is not slow about his promise as some count slowness, but is forbearing toward you,^h not wishing that any should perish, but that all should reach repentance. ¹⁰ But the day of the Lord will come like a

---

^h Some ancient authorities read *on your account.*

2. 22: Prov. 26. 11.　　**3. 5–6:** Gen. 1. 6–8; 7. 11.　　**3. 8:** Ps. 90. 4.

thief, and then the heavens will pass away with a loud noise, and the elements will be dissolved with fire, and the earth and the works that are upon it will be burned up.

11 Since all these things are thus to be dissolved, what sort of persons ought you to be in lives of holiness and godliness, [12] waiting for and hastening[i] the coming of the day of God, because of which the heavens will be kindled and dissolved, and the elements will melt with fire. [13] But according to his promise we wait for new heavens and a new earth in which righteousness dwells.

14 Therefore, beloved, since you wait for these, be zealous to be found by him without spot or blemish, and at peace. [15] And count the forbearance of our Lord as salvation. So also our beloved brother Paul wrote to you according to the wisdom given him, [16] speaking of this as he does in all his letters. There are some things in them hard to understand, which the ignorant and unstable twist to their own destruction, as they do the other scriptures. [17] You therefore, beloved, knowing this beforehand, beware lest you be carried away with the error of lawless men and lose your own stability. [18] But grow in the grace and knowledge of our Lord and Savior Jesus Christ. To him be the glory both now and to the day of eternity. Amen.

THE FIRST LETTER OF
JOHN

1 That which was from the beginning, which we have heard, which we have seen with our eyes, which we have looked upon and touched with our hands, concerning the word of life — [2] the life was made manifest, and we saw it,

[i] Or *earnestly desiring.*

3. 12: Is. 34. 4.   **3. 13:** Is. 65. 17; 66. 22.   **1. 1–2:** Lk. 24. 39; Jn. 1. 1; 4, 14; 15. 27; 20. 20, 25; Acts 4. 20; 1 Jn. 2. 13.

and testify to it, and proclaim to you the eternal life which was with the Father and was made manifest to us — [3] that which we have seen and heard we proclaim also to you, so that you may have fellowship with us; and our fellowship is with the Father and with his Son Jesus Christ. [4] And we are writing this that our[a] joy may be complete.

[5] This is the message we have heard from him and proclaim to you, that God is light and in him is no darkness at all. [6] If we say we have fellowship with him while we walk in darkness, we lie and do not live according to the truth; [7] but if we walk in the light, as he is in the light, we have fellowship with one another, and the blood of Jesus his Son cleanses us from all sin. [8] If we say we have no sin, we deceive ourselves, and the truth is not in us. [9] If we confess our sins, he is faithful and just, and will forgive our sins and cleanse us from all unrighteousness. [10] If we say we have not sinned, we make him a liar, and his word is not in us.

[2] My little children, I am writing this to you so that you may not sin; but if any one does sin, we have an advocate with the Father, Jesus Christ the righteous; [2] and he is the expiation for our sins, and not for ours only but also for the sins of the whole world. [3] And by this we may be sure that we know him, if we keep his commandments. [4] He who says "I know him" but disobeys his commandments is a liar, and the truth is not in him; [5] but whoever keeps his word, in him truly love for God is perfected. By this we may be sure that we are in him: [6] he who says he abides in him ought to walk in the same way in which he walked.

---

[a] Some ancient authorities read *your*.

1. 4: Jn. 15. 11; 2 Jn. 12.   **1. 5:** 1 Jn. 3. 11.   **1. 6–8:** Jn. 3. 21; 1 Jn. 2. 4, 11.
1. 7: Rev. 1. 5.   **1. 10:** 1 Jn. 5. 10.
2. 1: Jn. 14. 16.   **2. 2:** Jn. 1. 29; 3. 14–16; 11. 51–52; 1 Jn. 4. 10.   **2. 3:** Jn. 15. 10.
2. 4: 1 Jn. 1. 6–8; 4. 20.   **2. 5:** Jn. 14. 21, 23; 1 Jn. 5. 3.   **2. 6:** Jn. 13. 15.

7 Beloved, I am writing you no new commandment, but an old commandment which you had from the beginning; the old commandment is the word which you have heard. ⁸ Yet I am writing you a new commandment, which is true in him and in you, because*ᵇ* the darkness is passing away and the true light is already shining. ⁹ He who says he is in the light and hates his brother is in the darkness still. ¹⁰ He who loves his brother abides in the light, and in it*ᶜ* there is no cause for stumbling. ¹¹ But he who hates his brother is in the darkness and walks in the darkness, and does not know where he is going, because the darkness has blinded his eyes.

12 I am writing to you, little children, because your sins are forgiven for his sake. ¹³ I am writing to you, fathers, because you know him who is from the beginning. I am writing to you, young men, because you have overcome the evil one. I write to you, children, because you know the Father. ¹⁴ I write to you, fathers, because you know him who is from the beginning. I write to you, young men, because you are strong, and the word of God abides in you, and you have overcome the evil one.

15 Do not love the world or the things in the world. If any one loves the world, love for the Father is not in him. ¹⁶ For all that is in the world, the lust of the flesh and the lust of the eyes and the pride of life, is not of the Father but is of the world. ¹⁷ And the world passes away, and the lust of it; but he who does the will of God abides forever.

18 Children, it is the last hour; and as you have heard that antichrist is coming, so now many antichrists have come; therefore we know that it is the last hour. ¹⁹ They

ᵇ Or *that.*　　*ᶜ* Or *him.*

2. 7: Jn. 13. 34.　　**2. 8:** Jn. 8. 12.　　**2. 10–11:** Jn. 11. 9–10; 1 Jn. 1. 6.　　**2. 13:** Jn. 1. 1; 1 Jn. 1. 1.　　**2. 18:** 1 Jn. 4. 3.

went out from us, but they were not of us; for if they had been of us, they would have continued with us; but they went out, that it might be plain that they all are not of us. ²⁰ But you have been anointed by the Holy One, and you all know.^d ²¹ I write to you, not because you do not know the truth, but because you know it, and know that no lie is of the truth. ²² Who is the liar but he who denies that Jesus is the Christ? This is the antichrist, he who denies the Father and the Son. ²³ No one who denies the Son has the Father. He who confesses the Son has the Father also. ²⁴ Let what you heard from the beginning abide in you. If what you heard from the beginning abides in you, then you will abide in the Son and in the Father. ²⁵ And this is what he has promised us,^e eternal life.

26 I write this to you about those who would deceive you; ²⁷ but the anointing which you received from him abides in you, and you have no need that any one should teach you; as his anointing teaches you about everything, and is true, and is no lie, just as it has taught you, abide in him.

28 And now, little children, abide in him, so that when he appears we may have confidence and not shrink from him in shame at his coming. ²⁹ If you know that he is righteous, you may be sure that every one who does right is born of him.

3 See what love the Father has given us, that we should be called children of God; and so we are. The reason why the world does not know us is that it did not know him. ² Beloved, we are God's children now; it does not yet appear what we shall be, but we know that when he appears we

---

^d Some ancient authorities read *you know everything.*   ^e Some ancient authorities read *you.*

2. 22: 2 Jn. 7.   **2. 23:** 1 Jn. 4. 15; 2 Jn. 9.   **2. 27:** Jn. 14. 26.   **2. 28:** 1 Jn. 4. 17.
2. 29: 1 Jn. 3. 7–10; 4. 7.
3. 1: Jn. 1. 12; 16. 3.

shall be like him, for we shall see him as he is. ³ And every one who thus hopes in him purifies himself as he is pure.

4 Every one who commits sin is guilty of lawlessness; sin is lawlessness. ⁵ You know that he appeared to take away sins, and in him there is no sin. ⁶ No one who abides in him sins; no one who sins has either seen him or known him. ⁷ Little children, let no one deceive you. He who does right is righteous, as he is righteous. ⁸ He who commits sin is of the devil; for the devil has sinned from the beginning. The reason the Son of God appeared was to destroy the works of the devil. ⁹ No one born of God commits sin; for God's*ᶠ* nature abides in him, and he cannot sin because he is*ᵍ* born of God. ¹⁰ By this it may be seen who are the children of God, and who are the children of the devil: no one who does not do right is of God, nor any one who does not love his brother.

11 For this is the message which you have heard from the beginning, that we should love one another, ¹² and not be like Cain who was of the evil one and murdered his brother. And why did he murder him? Because his own deeds were evil and his brother's righteous. ¹³ Do not wonder, brethren, that the world hates you. ¹⁴ We know that we have passed out of death into life, because we love the brethren. He who does not love remains in death. ¹⁵ Any one who hates his brother is a murderer, and you know that no murderer has eternal life abiding in him. ¹⁶ By this we know love, that he laid down his life for us; and we ought to lay down our lives for the brethren. ¹⁷ But if any one has the world's goods and sees his brother in need, yet closes his heart against him, how does God's love abide in him? ¹⁸ Little children, let us not love in word or speech but in deed and in truth.

ᶠ Greek *his.*   ᵍ Or *for the offspring of God abide in him, and they cannot sin because they are.*

3. 5: Jn. 1. 29.   **3. 8:** Jn. 8. 34, 44.   **3. 9:** 1 Jn. 5. 18.   **3. 11:** 1 Jn. 1. 5.
3. 13: Jn. 15. 18–19.   **3. 14:** Jn. 5. 24.   **3. 15:** Jn. 8. 44.   **3. 16:** Jn. 13. 1; 15. 13.
3. 18: Jas. 1. 22.

19 By this we shall know that we are of the truth, and reassure our hearts before him [20] whenever our hearts condemn us; for God is greater than our hearts, and he knows everything. [21] Beloved, if our hearts do not condemn us, we have confidence before God; [22] and we receive from him whatever we ask, because we keep his commandments and do what pleases him. [23] And this is his commandment, that we should believe in the name of his Son Jesus Christ and love one another, just as he has commanded us. [24] All who keep his commandments abide in him, and he in them. And by this we know that he abides in us, by the Spirit which he has given us.

4 Beloved, do not believe every spirit, but test the spirits to see whether they are of God; for many false prophets have gone out into the world. [2] By this you know the Spirit of God: every spirit which confesses that Jesus Christ has come in the flesh is of God, [3] and every spirit which does not confess Jesus is not of God. This is the spirit of antichrist, of which you heard that it was coming, and now it is in the world already. [4] Little children, you are of God, and have overcome them; for he who is in you is greater than he who is in the world. [5] They are of the world, therefore what they say is of the world, and the world listens to them. [6] We are of God. Whoever knows God listens to us, and he who is not of God does not listen to us. By this we know the spirit of truth and the spirit of error.

7 Beloved, let us love one another; for love is of God, and he who loves is born of God and knows God. [8] He who does not love does not know God; for God is love. [9] In this the love of God was made manifest among us, that God sent

3. 21: 1 Jn. 5. 14.   3. 23: Jn. 6. 29; 13. 34; 15. 17.   3. 24: 1 Jn. 4. 13.
4. 3: 1 Jn. 2. 18.   4. 5: Jn. 15. 19.   4. 6: Jn. 8. 47.   4. 7: 1 Jn. 2. 29.
4. 9: Jn. 3. 16.

his only Son into the world, so that we might live through him. [10] In this is love, not that we loved God but that he loved us and sent his Son to be the expiation for our sins. [11] Beloved, if God so loved us, we also ought to love one another. [12] No man has ever seen God; if we love one another, God abides in us and his love is perfected in us.

13 By this we know that we abide in him and he in us, because he has given us of his own Spirit. [14] And we have seen and testify that the Father has sent his Son as the Savior of the world. [15] Whoever confesses that Jesus is the Son of God, God abides in him, and he in God. [16] So we know and believe the love God has for us. God is love, and he who abides in love abides in God, and God abides in him. [17] In this is love perfected with us, that we may have confidence for the day of judgment, because as he is so are we in this world. [18] There is no fear in love, but perfect love casts out fear. For fear has to do with punishment, and he who fears is not perfected in love. [19] We love, because he first loved us. [20] If any one says, "I love God," and hates his brother, he is a liar; for he who does not love his brother whom he has seen, cannot[h] love God whom he has not seen. [21] And this commandment we have from him, that he who loves God should love his brother also.

5 Every one who believes that Jesus is the Christ is a child of God, and every one who loves the parent loves the child. [2] By this we know that we love the children of God, when we love God and obey his commandments. [3] For this is the love of God, that we keep his commandments. And his commandments are not burdensome. [4] For whatever is born of God overcomes the world; and this is the vic-

---

[h] Some ancient authorities read *how can he.*

4. 10: Jn. 15. 12; 1 Jn. 4. 19; 2. 2.   **4. 12:** Jn. 1. 18.   **4. 13:** 1 Jn. 3. 24.
4. 14: Jn. 4. 42; 3. 17.   **4. 17:** 1 Jn. 2. 28.   **4. 19:** 1 Jn. 4. 10.   **4. 20:** 1 Jn. 2. 4.
5. 1: Jn. 8. 42.   **5. 3:** Jn. 14. 15; 1 Jn. 2. 5; 2 Jn. 6.   **5. 4:** Jn. 16. 33.

tory that overcomes the world, our faith. ⁵ Who is it that overcomes the world but he who believes that Jesus is the Son of God?

6 This is he who came by water and blood, Jesus Christ, not with the water only but with the water and the blood. ⁷ And the Spirit is the witness, because the Spirit is the truth. ⁸ There are three witnesses, the Spirit, the water, and the blood; and these three agree. ⁹ If we receive the testimony of men, the testimony of God is greater; for this is the testimony of God that he has borne witness to his Son. ¹⁰ He who believes in the Son of God has the testimony in himself. He who does not believe God, has made him a liar, because he has not believed in the testimony that God has borne to his Son. ¹¹ And this is the testimony, that God gave us eternal life, and this life is in his Son. ¹² He who has the Son has life; he who has not the Son has not life.

13 I write this to you who believe in the name of the Son of God, that you may know that you have eternal life. ¹⁴ And this is the confidence which we have in him, that if we ask anything according to his will he hears us. ¹⁵ And if we know that he hears us in whatever we ask, we know that we have obtained the requests made of him. ¹⁶ If any one sees his brother committing what is not a mortal sin, he will ask, and God*ⁱ* will give him life for those whose sin is not mortal. There is sin which is mortal; I do not say that one is to pray for that. ¹⁷ All wrongdoing is sin, but there is sin which is not mortal.

18 We know that any one born of God does not sin, but He who was born of God keeps him, and the evil one does not touch him.

ⁱ Or *he.*

5. 6–8: Jn. 19. 34; 4. 23; 15. 26.   **5. 9:** Jn. 5. 32, 36; 8. 18.   **5. 10:** 1 Jn. 1. 10.
5. 12: Jn. 3. 36.   **5. 13:** Jn. 20. 31.   **5. 14:** Mt. 7. 7; 1 Jn. 3. 21.   **5. 18:** Jn. 17. 15;
1 Jn. 3. 9.

19 We know that we are of God, and the whole world is in the power of the evil one.

20 And we know that the Son of God has come and has given us understanding, to know him who is true; and we are in him who is true, in his Son Jesus Christ. This is the true God and eternal life. [21] Little children, keep yourselves from idols.

THE SECOND LETTER OF
JOHN

1 The elder to the elect lady and her children, whom I love in the truth, and not only I but also all who know the truth, [2] because of the truth which abides in us and will be with us forever:

3 Grace, mercy, and peace will be with us, from God the Father and from Jesus Christ the Father's Son, in truth and love.

4 I rejoiced greatly to find some of your children following the truth, just as we have been commanded by the Father. [5] And now I beg you, lady, not as though I were writing you a new commandment, but the one we have had from the beginning, that we love one another. [6] And this is love, that we follow his commandments; this is the commandment, as you have heard from the beginning, that you follow love. [7] For many deceivers have gone out into the world, men who will not acknowledge the coming of Jesus Christ in the flesh; such a one is the deceiver and the antichrist. [8] Look to yourselves, that you may not lose what you[a] have worked for, but may win a full reward. [9] Any one who goes

[a] Some ancient authorities read *we*.
5. 20–21: Jn. 17. 3; Rev. 3. 7.
1: 3 Jn. 1.   **5:** Jn. 13. 34.   **6:** 1 Jn. 5. 3.   **7:** 1 Jn. 2. 22.

ahead and does not abide in the doctrine of Christ does not have God; he who abides in the doctrine of Christ has both the Father and the Son. [10] If any one comes to you and does not bring this doctrine, do not receive him into the house or give him any greeting; [11] for he who greets him shares his wicked work.

12 Though I have much to write to you, I would rather not use paper and ink, but I hope to come to see you and talk with you face to face, so that our joy may be complete.

13 The children of your elect sister greet you.

THE THIRD LETTER OF

JOHN

1 The elder to the beloved Ga'ius, whom I love in the truth.

2 Beloved, I pray that all may go well with you and that you may keep well, as I know it is well with your soul. [3] For I greatly rejoiced when some of the brethren arrived and testified to the truth of your life, as indeed you do follow the truth. [4] No greater joy can I have than this, to hear that my children follow the truth.

5 Beloved, it is a loyal thing you do when you render any service to the brethren, especially to strangers, [6] who have testified to your love before the church. You will do well to send them on their journey as befits God's service. [7] For they have set out for his sake and have accepted nothing from the heathen. [8] So we ought to support such men, that we may be fellow workers in the truth.

9 I have written something to the church; but Di-ot're-phes, who likes to put himself first, does not acknowledge

12: 1 Jn. 1. 4; 3 Jn. 13.
1: Acts 19. 29; 2 Jn. 1.

my authority. ¹⁰ So if I come, I will bring up what he is doing, prating against me with evil words. And not content with that, he refuses himself to welcome the brethren, and also stops those who want to welcome them and puts them out of the church.

11 Beloved, do not imitate evil but imitate good. He who does good is of God; he who does evil has not seen God. ¹² De-me′tri-us has testimony from every one, and from the truth itself; I testify to him too, and you know my testimony is true.

13 I had much to write to you, but I would rather not write with pen and ink; ¹⁴ I hope to see you soon, and we will talk together face to face.

15 Peace be to you. The friends greet you. Greet the friends, every one of them.

THE LETTER OF
JUDE

1 Jude, a servant of Jesus Christ and brother of James,
To those who are called, beloved in God the Father and kept for Jesus Christ:

2 May mercy, peace, and love be multiplied to you.

3 Beloved, being very eager to write to you of our common salvation, I found it necessary to write appealing to you to contend for the faith which was once for all delivered to the saints. ⁴ For admission has been secretly gained by some who long ago were designated for this condemnation, ungodly persons who pervert the grace of our God into

12: Jn. 21. 24.   13: 2 Jn. 12.
4–16: 2 Pet. 2. 1–18.

514

licentiousness and deny our only Master and Lord, Jesus Christ.[a]

5 Now I desire to remind you, though you were once for all fully informed, that he[b] who saved a people out of the land of Egypt, afterward destroyed those who did not believe. [6] And the angels that did not keep their own position but left their proper dwelling have been kept by him in eternal chains in the nether gloom until the judgment of the great day; [7] just as Sodom and Go-mor′rah and the surrounding cities, which likewise acted immorally and indulged in unnatural lust, serve as an example by undergoing a punishment of eternal fire.

8 Yet in like manner these men in their dreamings defile the flesh, reject authority, and revile the glorious ones.[c] [9] But when the archangel Michael, contending with the devil, disputed about the body of Moses, he did not presume to pronounce a reviling judgment upon him, but said, "The Lord rebuke you." [10] But these men revile whatever they do not understand, and by those things that they know by instinct as irrational animals do, they are destroyed. [11] Woe to them! For they walk in the way of Cain, and abandon themselves for the sake of gain to Ba′laam's error, and perish in Korah's rebellion. [12] These are blemishes[d] on your love feasts, as they boldly carouse together, looking after themselves; waterless clouds, carried along by winds; fruitless trees in late autumn, twice dead, uprooted; [13] wild waves of the sea, casting up the foam of their own shame; wandering stars for whom the nether gloom of darkness has been reserved forever.

14 It was of these also that Enoch in the seventh generation from Adam prophesied, saying, "Behold, the Lord came

---

[a] Or *the only Master and our Lord Jesus Christ.* [b] Some ancient authorities read *Jesus* or *the Lord* or *God.* [c] Greek *glories.* [d] Or *reefs.*

7: Gen. 19. **9:** Zech. 3. 2. **11:** Gen. 4. 3–8; Num. 22–24; 16. **14–15:** Enoch 1. 9.

515

with his holy myriads, [15] to execute judgment on all, and to convict all the ungodly of all their deeds of ungodliness which they have committed in such an ungodly way, and of all the harsh things which ungodly sinners have spoken against him." [16] These are grumblers, malcontents, following their own passions, loud-mouthed boasters, flattering people to gain advantage.

[17] But you must remember, beloved, the predictions of the apostles of our Lord Jesus Christ; [18] they said to you, "In the last time there will be scoffers, following their own ungodly passions." [19] It is these who set up divisions, worldly people, devoid of the Spirit. [20] But you, beloved, build yourselves up on your most holy faith; pray in the Holy Spirit; [21] keep yourselves in the love of God; wait for the mercy of our Lord Jesus Christ unto eternal life. [22] And convince some, who doubt; [23] save some, by snatching them out of the fire; on some have mercy with fear, hating even the garment spotted by the flesh.[e]

[24] Now to him who is able to keep you from falling and to present you without blemish before the presence of his glory with rejoicing, [25] to the only God, our Savior through Jesus Christ our Lord, be glory, majesty, dominion, and authority, before all time and now and forever. Amen.

[e] The Greek text in this sentence is uncertain at several points.
23: Zech. 3. 3–4.

THE REVELATION TO
JOHN

1 The revelation of Jesus Christ, which God gave him to show to his servants what must soon take place; and he made it known by sending his angel to his servant John, [2] who bore witness to the word of God and to the testimony of Jesus Christ, even to all that he saw. [3] Blessed is he who reads aloud the words of the prophecy, and blessed are those who hear, and who keep what is written therein; for the time is near.

4 John to the seven churches that are in Asia:

Grace to you and peace from him who is and who was and who is to come, and from the seven spirits who are before his throne, [5] and from Jesus Christ the faithful witness, the first-born of the dead, and the ruler of kings on earth.

To him who loves us and has freed us from our sins by his blood [6] and made us a kingdom, priests to his God and Father, to him be glory and dominion for ever and ever. Amen. [7] Behold, he is coming with the clouds, and every eye will see him, every one who pierced him; and all tribes of the earth will wail on account of him. Even so. Amen.

8 "I am the Alpha and the Omega," says the Lord God, who is and who was and who is to come, the Almighty.

9 I John, your brother, who share with you in Jesus the tribulation and the kingdom and the patient endurance, was on the island called Patmos on account of the word of God and the testimony of Jesus. [10] I was in the Spirit on the Lord's day, and I heard behind me a loud voice like a trumpet [11] saying, "Write what you see in a book and send it to the seven churches, to Ephesus and to Smyrna and to Per'ga-

1. 4: Ex. 3. 14.   1. 5: Ps. 89. 27.   1. 6: Ex. 19. 6; Is. 61. 6.   1. 7: Dan. 7. 13;
Mk. 14. 62; Zech. 12. 10.   1. 8: Ex. 3. 14.

mum and to Thy-a-ti′ra and to Sardis and to Philadelphia and to La-od-i-ce′a."

12 Then I turned to see the voice that was speaking to me, and on turning I saw seven golden lampstands, [13] and in the midst of the lampstands one like a son of man, clothed with a long robe and a golden girdle round his breast; [14] his head and his hair were white as white wool, white as snow; his eyes were like a flame of fire, [15] his feet were like burnished bronze, refined as in a furnace, and his voice was like the sound of many waters; [16] in his right hand he held seven stars, from his mouth issued a sharp two-edged sword, and his face was like the sun shining in full strength.

17 When I saw him, I fell at his feet as though dead. But he laid his right hand upon me, saying, "Fear not, I am the first and the last, [18] and the living one; I died, and behold I am alive for evermore, and I have the keys of Death and Hades. [19] Now write what you see, what is and what is to take place hereafter. [20] As for the mystery of the seven stars which you saw in my right hand, and the seven golden lampstands, the seven stars are the angels of the seven churches and the seven lampstands are the seven churches.

2 "To the angel of the church in Ephesus write: 'The words of him who holds the seven stars in his right hand, who walks among the seven golden lampstands.

2 "'I know your works, your toil and your patient endurance, and how you cannot bear evil men but have tested those who call themselves apostles but are not, and found them to be false; [3] I know you are enduring patiently and bearing up for my name's sake, and you have not grown weary. [4] But I have this against you, that you have abandoned the love you had at first. [5] Remember then from what you have fallen, repent and do the works you did at

1. 13: Dan. 7. 13; 10. 5.   **1. 15:** Ezek. 1. 24.   **1. 16:** Ex. 34. 29.   **1. 17:** Is. 44. 2, 6.

first. If not, I will come to you and remove your lampstand from its place, unless you repent. ⁶ Yet this you have, you hate the works of the Nic-o-la'i-tans, which I also hate. ⁷ He who has an ear, let him hear what the Spirit says to the churches. To him who conquers I will grant to eat of the tree of life, which is in the paradise of God.'

8 "And to the angel of the church in Smyrna write: 'The words of the first and the last, who died and came to life.

9 "'I know your tribulation and your poverty (but you are rich) and the slander of those who say that they are Jews and are not, but are a synagogue of Satan. ¹⁰ Do not fear what you are about to suffer. Behold, the devil is about to throw some of you into prison, that you may be tested, and for ten days you will have tribulation. Be faithful unto death, and I will give you the crown of life. ¹¹ He who has an ear, let him hear what the Spirit says to the churches. He who conquers shall not be hurt by the second death.'

12 "And to the angel of the church in Per'ga-mum write: 'The words of him who has the sharp two-edged sword.

13 "'I know where you dwell, where Satan's throne is; you hold fast my name and you did not deny my faith even in the days of An'ti-pas my witness, my faithful one, who was killed among you, where Satan dwells. ¹⁴ But I have a few things against you: you have some there who hold the teaching of Ba'laam, who taught Balak to put a stumbling-block before the sons of Israel, that they might eat food sacrificed to idols and practice immorality. ¹⁵ So you also have some who hold the teaching of the Nic-o-la'i-tans. ¹⁶ Repent then. If not, I will come to you soon and war against them with the sword of my mouth. ¹⁷ He who has an ear, let him hear what the Spirit says to the churches. To him who conquers I will give some of the hidden manna,

2. 7: Gen. 2. 9.   **2. 8:** Is. 44. 6.   **2. 10:** Dan. 1. 12.   **2. 14:** Num. 31. 16; 25. 1–2.
2. 17: Ps. 78. 24; Is. 62. 2.

and I will give him a white stone, with a new name written on the stone which no one knows except him who receives it.'

18 "And to the angel of the church in Thy-a-ti'ra write: 'The words of the Son of God, who has eyes like a flame of fire, and whose feet are like burnished bronze.

19 "'I know your works, your love and faith and service and patient endurance, and that your latter works exceed the first. ²⁰ But I have this against you, that you tolerate the woman Jez'e-bel, who calls herself a prophetess and is teaching and beguiling my servants to practice immorality and to eat food sacrificed to idols. ²¹ I gave her time to repent, but she refuses to repent of her immorality. ²² Behold, I will throw her on a sickbed, and those who commit adultery with her I will throw into great tribulation, unless they repent of her doings; ²³ and I will strike her children dead. And all the churches shall know that I am he who searches mind and heart, and I will give to each of you as your works deserve. ²⁴ But to the rest of you in Thy-a-ti'ra, who do not hold this teaching, who have not learned what some call the deep things of Satan, to you I say, I do not lay upon you any other burden; ²⁵ only hold fast what you have, until I come. ²⁶ He who conquers and who keeps my works until the end, I will give him power over the nations, ²⁷ and he shall rule them with a rod of iron, as when earthen pots are broken in pieces, even as I myself have received power from my Father; ²⁸ and I will give him the morning star. ²⁹ He who has an ear, let him hear what the Spirit says to the churches.'

3 "And to the angel of the church in Sardis write: 'The words of him who has the seven spirits of God and the seven stars.

"'I know your works; you have the name of being alive,

2. 18: Dan. 10. 6.   **2. 20:** 1 Kings 16. 31; 2 Kings 9. 22, 30; Num. 25. 1.   **2. 23:** Jer. 17. 10; Ps. 62. 12.   **2. 26:** Ps. 2. 8–9.

and you are dead. ² Awake, and strengthen what remains and is on the point of death, for I have not found your works perfect in the sight of my God. ³ Remember then what you received and heard; keep that, and repent. If you will not awake, I will come like a thief, and you will not know at what hour I will come upon you. ⁴ Yet you have still a few names in Sardis, people who have not soiled their garments; and they shall walk with me in white, for they are worthy. ⁵ He who conquers shall be clad thus in white garments, and I will not blot his name out of the book of life; I will confess his name before my Father and before his angels. ⁶ He who has an ear, let him hear what the Spirit says to the churches.'

7 "And to the angel of the church in Philadelphia write: 'The words of the holy one, the true one, who has the key of David, who opens and no one shall shut, who shuts and no one opens.

8 "'I know your works. Behold, I have set before you an open door, which no one is able to shut; I know that you have but little power, and yet you have kept my word and have not denied my name. ⁹ Behold, I will make those of the synagogue of Satan who say that they are Jews and are not, but lie — behold, I will make them come and bow down before your feet, and learn that I have loved you. ¹⁰ Because you have kept my word of patient endurance, I will keep you from the hour of trial which is coming on the whole world, to try those who dwell upon the earth. ¹¹ I am coming soon; hold fast what you have, so that no one may seize your crown. ¹² He who conquers, I will make him a pillar in the temple of my God; never shall he go out of it, and I will write on him the name of my God, and the name of the city of my God, the new Jerusalem which comes

3. 5: Ex. 32. 32; Ps. 69. 28; Dan. 12. 1; Mt. 10. 32.   **3. 7:** Is. 22. 22.   **3. 9:** Is. 60. 14; 49. 23; 43. 4.   **3. 12:** Is. 62. 2; Ezek. 48. 35; Rev. 21. 2.

down from my God out of heaven, and my own new name. [13] He who has an ear, let him hear what the Spirit says to the churches.'

14 "And to the angel of the church in La-od-i-ce'a write: 'The words of the Amen, the faithful and true witness, the beginning of God's creation.

15 "'I know your works; you are neither cold nor hot. Would that you were cold or hot! [16] So, because you are lukewarm, and neither cold nor hot, I will spew you out of my mouth. [17] For you say, I am rich, I have prospered, and I need nothing; not knowing that you are wretched, pitiable, poor, blind and naked. [18] Therefore I counsel you to buy from me gold refined by fire, that you may be rich, and white garments to clothe you and to keep the shame of your nakedness from being seen, and salve to anoint your eyes, that you may see. [19] Those whom I love, I reprove and chasten; so be zealous and repent. [20] Behold, I stand at the door and knock; if any one hears my voice and opens the door, I will come in to him and eat with him, and he with me. [21] He who conquers, I will grant him to sit with me on my throne, as I myself conquered and sat down with my Father on his throne. [22] He who has an ear, let him hear what the Spirit says to the churches.'"

4 After this I looked, and lo, in heaven an open door! And the first voice, which I had heard speaking to me like a trumpet, said, "Come up hither, and I will show you what must take place after this." [2] At once I was in the Spirit, and lo, a throne stood in heaven, with one seated on the throne! [3] And he who sat there appeared like jasper and carnelian, and round the throne was a rainbow that looked like an emerald. [4] Round the throne were twenty-

3. 14: Ps. 89. 38; Prov. 8. 22; Jn. 1. 1–3.   3. 17: Hos. 12. 8.   3. 19: Prov. 3. 12.
4. 1: Ex. 19. 16, 24.   4. 2: Ezek. 1. 26–28.

four thrones, and seated on the thrones were twenty-four elders, clad in white garments, with golden crowns upon their heads. [5] From the throne issue flashes of lightning, and voices and peals of thunder, and before the throne burn seven torches of fire, which are the seven spirits of God; [6] and before the throne there is as it were a sea of glass, like crystal.

And round the throne, on each side of the throne, are four living creatures, full of eyes in front and behind: [7] the first living creature like a lion, the second living creature like an ox, the third living creature with the face of a man, and the fourth living creature like a flying eagle. [8] And the four living creatures, each of them with six wings, are full of eyes all round and within, and day and night they never cease to sing,

"Holy, holy, holy, is the Lord God Almighty,
who was and is and is to come!"
[9] And whenever the living creatures give glory and honor and thanks to him who is seated on the throne, who lives for ever and ever, [10] the twenty-four elders fall down before him who is seated on the throne and worship him who lives for ever and ever; they cast their crowns before the throne, singing,

[11] "Worthy art thou, our Lord and God,
to receive glory and honor and power,
for thou didst create all things,
and by thy will they existed and were created."

5 And I saw in the right hand of him who was seated on the throne a scroll written within and on the back, sealed with seven seals; [2] and I saw a strong angel proclaiming with a loud voice, "Who is worthy to open the

4. 5: Ex. 19. 16; Zech. 4. 2.   **4. 6:** Ezek. 1. 5, 18.   **4. 7:** Ezek. 1. 10.   **4. 8:** Is. 6. 2–3.
4. 9: Ps. 47. 8.
5. 1: Ezek. 2. 9; Is. 29. 11.

scroll and break its seals?" ³ And no one in heaven or on earth or under the earth was able to open the scroll or to look into it, ⁴ and I wept much that no one was found worthy to open the scroll or to look into it. ⁵ Then one of the elders said to me, "Weep not; lo, the Lion of the tribe of Judah, the Root of David, has conquered, so that he can open the scroll and its seven seals."

6 And between the throne and the four living creatures and among the elders, I saw a Lamb standing, as though it had been slain, with seven horns and with seven eyes, which are the seven spirits of God sent out into all the earth; ⁷ and he went and took the scroll from the right hand of him who was seated on the throne. ⁸ And when he had taken the scroll, the four living creatures and the twenty-four elders fell down before the Lamb, each holding a harp, and with golden bowls full of incense, which are the prayers of the saints; ⁹ and they sang a new song, saying,

"Worthy art thou to take the scroll and to open its seals,
for thou wast slain and by thy blood didst ransom men for God
from every tribe and tongue and people and nation,
¹⁰ and hast made them a kingdom and priests to our God, and they shall reign on earth."

¹¹ Then I looked, and I heard around the throne and the living creatures and the elders the voice of many angels, numbering myriads of myriads and thousands of thousands, ¹² saying with a loud voice, "Worthy is the Lamb who was slain, to receive power and wealth and wisdom and might and honor and glory and blessing!" ¹³ And I heard every creature in heaven and on earth and under the earth and in the sea, and all therein, saying, "To him who sits upon the throne and to the Lamb be blessing and honor and glory

5. 5: Gen. 49. 9.   **5. 6:** Is. 53. 7; Zech. 4. 10.   **5. 8:** Ps. 141. 2.   **5. 9:** Ps. 33. 3.
5. 10: Ex. 19. 6; Is. 61. 6.   **5. 11:** Dan. 7. 10.

and might for ever and ever!" [14] And the four living creatures said, "Amen!" and the elders fell down and worshiped.

6 Now I saw when the Lamb opened one of the seven
seals, and I heard one of the four living creatures say,
as with a voice of thunder, "Come!" [2] And I saw, and behold,
a white horse, and its rider had a bow; and a crown was
given to him, and he went out conquering and to conquer.

[3] When he opened the second seal, I heard the second
living creature say, "Come!" [4] And out came another horse,
bright red; its rider was permitted to take peace from the
earth, so that men should slay one another; and he was given
a great sword.

[5] When he opened the third seal, I heard the third living
creature say, "Come!" And I saw, and behold, a black
horse, and its rider had a balance in his hand; [6] and I heard
what seemed to be a voice in the midst of the four living
creatures saying, "A quart of wheat for a denarius,[a] and
three quarts of barley for a denarius;[a] but do not harm oil
and wine!"

[7] When he opened the fourth seal, I heard the voice of
the fourth living creature say, "Come!" [8] And I saw, and
behold, a pale horse, and its rider's name was Death, and
Hades followed him; and they were given power over a
fourth of the earth, to kill with sword and with famine and
with pestilence and by wild beasts of the earth.

[9] When he opened the fifth seal, I saw under the altar
the souls of those who had been slain for the word of God
and for the witness they had borne; [10] they cried out with
a loud voice, "O Sovereign Lord, holy and true, how long
before thou wilt judge and avenge our blood on those who

[a] See note on Mt. 18. 28.
6. 2: Zech. 1. 8; 6. 1–3.   **6. 6:** 2 Kings 6. 25.   **6. 8:** Hos. 13. 14; Ezek. 5. 12.
6. 10: Zech. 1. 12; Ps. 79. 5; Gen. 4. 10.

dwell upon the earth?" [11] Then they were each given a white robe and told to rest a little longer, until the number of their fellow servants and their brethren should be complete, who were to be killed as they themselves had been.

12 When he opened the sixth seal, I looked, and behold, there was a great earthquake; and the sun became black as sackcloth, the full moon became like blood, [13] and the stars of the sky fell to the earth as the fig tree sheds its winter fruit when shaken by a gale; [14] the sky vanished like a scroll that is rolled up, and every mountain and island was removed from its place. [15] Then the kings of the earth and the great men and the generals and the rich and the strong, and every one, slave and free, hid in the caves and among the rocks of the mountains, [16] calling to the mountains and rocks, "Fall on us and hide us from the face of him who is seated on the throne, and from the wrath of the Lamb; [17] for the great day of their wrath has come, and who can stand before it?"

7 After this I saw four angels standing at the four corners of the earth, holding back the four winds of the earth, that no wind might blow on earth or sea or against any tree. [2] Then I saw another angel ascend from the rising of the sun, with the seal of the living God, and he called with a loud voice to the four angels who had been given power to harm earth and sea, [3] saying, "Do not harm the earth or the sea or the trees, till we have sealed the servants of our God upon their foreheads." [4] And I heard the number of the sealed, a hundred and forty-four thousand sealed, out of every tribe of the sons of Israel, [5] twelve thousand sealed out of the tribe of Judah, twelve thousand of the tribe of Reuben, twelve thousand of the tribe of Gad, [6] twelve

6. 12: Joel 2. 31; Acts 2. 20.   **6. 13:** Is. 34. 4.   **6. 15:** Is. 2. 10.   **6. 16:** Hos. 10. 8.
6. 17: Joel 2. 11; Mal. 3. 2.
7. 1: Zech. 6. 5.   **7. 3:** Ezek. 9. 4.

thousand of the tribe of Asher, twelve thousand of the tribe of Naph′ta-li, twelve thousand of the tribe of Ma-nas′seh, [7] twelve thousand of the tribe of Simeon, twelve thousand of the tribe of Levi, twelve thousand of the tribe of Is′sachar, [8] twelve thousand of the tribe of Zeb′u-lun, twelve thousand of the tribe of Joseph, twelve thousand sealed out of the tribe of Benjamin.

9 After this I looked, and behold, a great multitude which no man could number, from every nation, from all tribes and peoples and tongues, standing before the throne and before the Lamb, clothed in white robes, with palm branches in their hands, [10] and crying out with a loud voice, "Salvation belongs to our God who sits upon the throne, and to the Lamb!" [11] And all the angels stood round the throne and round the elders and the four living creatures, and they fell on their faces before the throne and worshiped God, [12] saying, "Amen! Blessing and glory and wisdom and thanksgiving and honor and power and might be to our God for ever and ever! Amen."

13 Then one of the elders addressed me, saying, "Who are these, clothed in white robes, and whence have they come?" [14] I said to him, "Sir, you know." And he said to me, "These are they who have come out of the great tribulation; they have washed their robes and made them white in the blood of the Lamb.

[15] Therefore are they before the throne of God,
　　　and serve him day and night within his temple;
　　　and he who sits upon the throne will shelter them
　　　　　with his presence.
[16] They shall hunger no more, neither thirst any more;
　　　the sun shall not strike them, nor any scorching
　　　　　heat.

7. 14: Dan. 12. 1; Gen. 49. 11.　　**7. 16:** Is. 49. 10; Ps. 121. 6.

¹⁷ For the Lamb in the midst of the throne will be
their shepherd,
and he will guide them to springs of living water;
and God will wipe away every tear from their eyes."

8 When the Lamb opened the seventh seal, there was silence in heaven for about half an hour. ² Then I saw the seven angels who stand before God, and seven trumpets were given to them. ³ And another angel came and stood at the altar with a golden censer; and he was given much incense to mingle with the prayers of all the saints upon the golden altar before the throne; ⁴ and the smoke of the incense rose with the prayers of the saints from the hand of the angel before God. ⁵ Then the angel took the censer and filled it with fire from the altar and threw it on the earth; and there were peals of thunder, loud noises, flashes of lightning, and an earthquake.

6 Now the seven angels who had the seven trumpets made ready to blow them.

7 The first angel blew his trumpet, and there followed hail and fire, mixed with blood, which fell on the earth; and a third of the earth was burnt up, and a third of the trees were burnt up, and all green grass was burnt up.

8 The second angel blew his trumpet, and something like a great mountain, burning with fire, was thrown into the sea; ⁹ and a third of the sea became blood, a third of the living creatures in the sea died, and a third of the ships were destroyed.

10 The third angel blew his trumpet, and a great star fell from heaven, blazing like a torch, and it fell on a third of the rivers and on the fountains of water. ¹¹ The name of the star is Wormwood. A third of the waters became

7. 17: Ezek. 34. 23; Ps. 23. 2; Is. 25. 8.
8. 3: Amos 9. 1; Ps. 141. 2. **8. 5:** Lev. 16. 12; Ezek. 10. 2. **8. 7:** Ex. 9. 23–25.
8. 8: Jer. 51. 25. **8. 10:** Is. 14. 12.

wormwood, and many men died of the water, because it was made bitter.

12 The fourth angel blew his trumpet, and a third of the sun was struck, and a third of the moon, and a third of the stars, so that a third of their light was darkened; a third of the day was kept from shining, and likewise a third of the night.

13 Then I looked, and I heard an eagle crying with a loud voice, as it flew in midheaven, "Woe, woe, woe to those who dwell on the earth, at the blasts of the other trumpets which the three angels are about to blow!"

9 And the fifth angel blew his trumpet, and I saw a star fallen from heaven to earth, and he was given the key of the shaft of the bottomless pit; ² he opened the shaft of the bottomless pit, and from the shaft rose smoke like the smoke of a great furnace, and the sun and the air were darkened with the smoke from the shaft. ³ Then from the smoke came locusts on the earth, and they were given power like the power of scorpions of the earth; ⁴ they were told not to harm the grass of the earth or any green growth or any tree, but only those of mankind who have not the seal of God upon their foreheads; ⁵ they were allowed to torture them for five months, but not to kill them, and their torture was like the torture of a scorpion, when it stings a man. ⁶ And in those days men will seek death and will not find it; they will long to die, and death flies from them.

7 In appearance the locusts were like horses arrayed for battle; on their heads were what looked like crowns of gold; their faces were like human faces, ⁸ their hair like women's hair, and their teeth like lions' teeth; ⁹ they had scales like iron breastplates, and the noise of their wings was like the

9. 2: Gen. 19. 28; Ex. 19. 18; Joel 2. 10.   **9. 3:** Ex. 10. 12–15.   **9. 4:** Ezek. 9. 4.
9. 6: Job 3. 21.   **9. 7:** Joel 2. 4.   **9. 8:** Joel 1. 6.   **9. 9:** Joel 2. 5.

noise of many chariots with horses rushing into battle, [10] they have tails like scorpions, and stings, and their power of hurting men for five months lies in their tails. [11] They have as king over them the angel of the bottomless pit; his name in Hebrew is A-bad'don, and in Greek he is called A-pol'-lyon.[b]

12 The first woe has passed; behold, two woes are still to come.

13 Then the sixth angel blew his trumpet, and I heard a voice from the four horns of the golden altar before God, [14] saying to the sixth angel who had the trumpet, "Release the four angels who are bound at the great river Eu-phra'tes." [15] So the four angels were released, who had been held ready for the hour, the day, the month, and the year, to kill a third of mankind. [16] The number of the troops of cavalry was twice ten thousand times ten thousand; I heard their number. [17] And this was how I saw the horses in my vision: the riders wore breastplates the color of fire and of sapphire[c] and of sulphur, and the heads of the horses were like lions' heads, and fire and smoke and sulphur issued from their mouths. [18] By these three plagues a third of mankind was killed, by the fire and smoke and sulphur issuing from their mouths. [19] For the power of the horses is in their mouths and in their tails; their tails are like serpents, with heads, and by means of them they wound.

20 The rest of mankind, who were not killed by these plagues, did not repent of the works of their hands nor give up worshiping demons and idols of gold and silver and bronze and stone and wood, which cannot either see or hear or walk; [21] nor did they repent of their murders or their sorceries or their immorality or their thefts.

[b] Or *Destroyer*.   [c] Greek *hyacinth*.

9. 13: Ex. 30. 1–3.   **9. 20:** Is. 17. 8; Ps. 115. 4–7; 135. 15–17.

10 Then I saw another mighty angel coming down from heaven, wrapped in a cloud, with a rainbow over his head, and his face was like the sun, and his legs like pillars of fire. ² He had a little scroll open in his hand. And he set his right foot on the sea, and his left foot on the land, ³ and called out with a loud voice, like a lion roaring; when he called out, the seven thunders sounded. ⁴ And when the seven thunders had sounded, I was about to write, but I heard a voice from heaven saying, "Seal up what the seven thunders have said, and do not write it down." ⁵ And the angel whom I saw standing on sea and land lifted up his right hand to heaven ⁶ and swore by him who lives for ever and ever, who created heaven and what is in it, the earth and what is in it, and the sea and what is in it, that there should be no more delay, ⁷ but that in the days of the trumpet call to be sounded by the seventh angel, the mystery of God, as he announced to his servants the prophets, should be fulfilled.

8 Then the voice which I had heard from heaven spoke to me again, saying, "Go, take the scroll which is open in the hand of the angel who is standing on the sea and on the land." ⁹ So I went to the angel and told him to give me the little scroll; and he said to me, "Take it and eat; it will be bitter to your stomach, but sweet as honey in your mouth." ¹⁰ And I took the little scroll from the hand of the angel and ate it; it was sweet as honey in my mouth, but when I had eaten it my stomach was made bitter. ¹¹ And I was told, "You must again prophesy about many peoples and nations and tongues and kings."

11 Then I was given a measuring rod like a staff, and I was told: "Rise and measure the temple of God

10. 5: Deut. 32. 40; Dan. 12. 7.   **10. 9:** Ezek. 2. 8; 3. 1–3.   **10. 11:** Jer. 1. 10.
11. 1: Ezek. 40. 3.

and the altar and those who worship there, ² but do not measure the court outside the temple; leave that out, for it is given over to the nations, and they will trample over the holy city for forty-two months. ³ And I will grant my two witnesses power to prophesy for one thousand two hundred and sixty days, clothed in sackcloth."

4 These are the two olive trees and the two lampstands which stand before the Lord of the earth. ⁵ And if any one would harm them, fire pours from their mouth and consumes their foes; if any one would harm them, thus he is doomed to die. ⁶ They have power to shut the sky, that no rain may fall during the days of their prophesying, and they have power over the waters to turn them into blood, and to smite the earth with every plague, as often as they desire. ⁷ And when they have finished their testimony, the beast that ascends from the bottomless pit will make war upon them and conquer them and kill them, ⁸ and their dead bodies will lie in the street of the great city which is allegorically*ᵈ* called Sodom and Egypt, where their Lord was crucified. ⁹ For three days and a half men from the peoples and tribes and tongues and nations gaze at their dead bodies and refuse to let them be placed in a tomb, ¹⁰ and those who dwell on the earth will rejoice over them and make merry and exchange presents, because these two prophets had been a torment to those who dwell on the earth. ¹¹ But after the three and a half days a breath of life from God entered them, and they stood up on their feet, and great fear fell on those who saw them. ¹² Then they heard a loud voice from heaven saying to them, "Come up hither!" And in the sight of their foes they went up to heaven in

ᵈ Greek *spiritually*.

11. 2: Zech. 12. 3; Is. 63. 18; Lk. 21. 24. **11. 4:** Zech. 4. 3, 11–14. **11. 5:** 2 Kings 1. 10; Jer. 5. 14. **11. 6:** 1 Kings 17. 1; Ex. 7. 17, 19. **11. 7:** Dan. 7. 3, 7, 21. **11. 8:** Is. 1. 9. **11. 11:** Ezek. 37. 5, 10. **11. 12:** 2 Kings 2. 11.

a cloud. ¹³ And at that hour there was a great earthquake, and a tenth of the city fell; seven thousand people were killed in the earthquake, and the rest were terrified and gave glory to the God of heaven.

14 The second woe has passed; behold, the third woe is soon to come.

15 Then the seventh angel blew his trumpet, and there were loud voices in heaven, saying, "The kingdom of the world has become the kingdom of our Lord and of his Christ, and he shall reign for ever and ever." ¹⁶ And the twenty-four elders who sit on their thrones before God fell on their faces and worshiped God, ¹⁷ saying,

"We give thanks to thee, Lord God almighty, who
    art and who wast,
    that thou hast taken thy great power and begun
      to reign.
¹⁸ The nations raged, but thy wrath came,
    and the time for the dead to be judged,
    for rewarding thy servants, the prophets and saints,
    and those who fear thy name, both small and great,
    and for destroying the destroyers of the earth."

19 Then God's temple in heaven was opened, and the ark of his covenant was seen within his temple; and there were flashes of lightning, loud noises, peals of thunder, an earthquake, and heavy hail.

12 And a great portent appeared in heaven, a woman clothed with the sun, with the moon under her feet, and on her head a crown of twelve stars; ² she was with child and she cried out in her pangs of birth, in anguish for delivery. ³ And another portent appeared in heaven; behold

11. 15: Ps. 22. 28; Dan. 7. 14, 27.   **11. 18:** Ps. 2. 1.   **11. 19:** 1 Kings 8. 1–6;
2 Macc. 2. 4–8.
12. 3: Mic. 4. 10; Dan. 7. 7.

a great red dragon, with seven heads and ten horns, and seven diadems upon his heads. ⁴ His tail swept down a third of the stars of heaven, and cast them to the earth. And the dragon stood before the woman who was about to bear a child, that he might devour her child when she brought it forth; ⁵ she brought forth a male child, one who is to rule all the nations with a rod of iron, but her child was caught up to God and to his throne, ⁶ and the woman fled into the wilderness, where she has a place prepared by God, in which to be nourished for one thousand two hundred and sixty days.

7 Now war arose in heaven, Michael and his angels fighting against the dragon; and the dragon and his angels fought, ⁸ but they were defeated and there was no longer any place for them in heaven. ⁹ And the great dragon was thrown down, that ancient serpent, who is called the Devil and Satan, the deceiver of the whole world— he was thrown down to the earth, and his angels were thrown down with him. ¹⁰ And I heard a loud voice in heaven, saying, "Now the salvation and the power and the kingdom of our God and the authority of his Christ have come, for the accuser of our brethren has been thrown down, who accuses them day and night before our God. ¹¹ And they have conquered him by the blood of the Lamb and by the word of their testimony, for they loved not their lives even unto death. ¹² Rejoice then, O heaven and you that dwell therein! But woe to you, O earth and sea, for the devil has come down to you in great wrath, because he knows that his time is short!"

13 And when the dragon saw that he had been thrown down to the earth, he pursued the woman who had borne the male child. ¹⁴ But the woman was given the two wings

12. 4: Dan. 8. 10.   **12. 5:** Is. 66. 7; Ps. 2. 9.   **12. 7:** Dan. 10. 13.   **12. 9:** Gen. 3. 1, 14–15; Zech. 3. 1.   **12. 10:** Job 1. 9–11.   **12. 12:** Is. 44. 23; 49. 13.   **12. 14:** Dan. 7. 25; 12. 7.

of the great eagle that she might fly from the serpent into the wilderness, to the place where she is to be nourished for a time, and times, and half a time. [15] The serpent poured water like a river out of his mouth after the woman, to sweep her away with the flood. [16] But the earth came to the help of the woman, and the earth opened its mouth and swallowed the river which the dragon had poured from his mouth. [17] Then the dragon was angry with the woman, and went off to make war on the rest of her offspring, on those who keep the commandments of God and bear testimony to Jesus. And he stood[e] on the sand of the sea.

13 And I saw a beast rising out of the sea, with ten horns and seven heads, with ten diadems upon its horns and a blasphemous name upon its heads. [2] And the beast that I saw was like a leopard, its feet were like a bear's, and its mouth was like a lion's mouth. And to it the dragon gave his power and his throne and great authority. [3] One of its heads seemed to have a mortal wound, but its mortal wound was healed, and the whole earth followed the beast with wonder. [4] Men worshiped the dragon, for he had given his authority to the beast, and they worshiped the beast, saying, "Who is like the beast, and who can fight against it?"

5 And the beast was given a mouth uttering haughty and blasphemous words, and it was allowed to exercise authority for forty-two months; [6] it opened its mouth to utter blasphemies against God, blaspheming his name and his dwelling, that is, those who dwell in heaven. [7] Also it was allowed to make war on the saints and to conquer them.[f] And authority was given it over every tribe and people and tongue and nation, [8] and all who dwell on earth will worship it, every one whose name has not been written

[e] Some ancient authorities read *And I stood*, connecting the sentence with 13. 1.
[f] Some ancient authorities omit this sentence.
13. 1: Dan. 7. 1–6.   **13. 5:** Dan. 7. 8.   **13. 7:** Dan. 7. 21.

before the foundation of the world in the book of life of the Lamb that was slain. [9] If any one has an ear, let him hear:

[10] If any one is to be taken captive,
to captivity he goes;
if any one slays with the sword,
with the sword must he be slain.

Here is a call for the endurance and faith of the saints.

11 Then I saw another beast which rose out of the earth; it had two horns like a lamb and it spoke like a dragon. [12] It exercises all the authority of the first beast in its presence, and makes the earth and its inhabitants worship the first beast, whose mortal wound was healed. [13] It works great signs, even making fire come down from heaven to earth in the sight of men; [14] and by the signs which it is allowed to work in the presence of the beast, it deceives those who dwell on earth, bidding them make an image for the beast which was wounded by the sword and yet lived; [15] and it was allowed to give breath to the image of the beast so that the image of the beast should even speak, and to cause those who will not worship the image of the beast to be slain. [16] Also it causes all, both small and great, both rich and poor, both free and slave, to be marked on the right hand or the forehead, [17] so that no one can buy or sell unless he has the mark, that is, the name of the beast or the number of its name. [18] This calls for wisdom: let him who has understanding reckon the number of the beast, for it is a human number, its number is six hundred and sixty-six.[g]

14 Then I looked, and lo, on Mount Zion stood the Lamb, and with him a hundred and forty-four thousand who had his name and his Father's name written on their foreheads. [2] And I heard a voice from heaven like the

[g] A few ancient authorities read *six hundred and sixteen.*

13. 9: Mk. 4. 23.   **13. 10:** Jer. 15. 2.   **13. 14:** Deut. 13. 1–5.   **13. 15:** Dan. 3. 5.
14. 1: Ezek. 9. 4.

sound of many waters and like the sound of loud thunder; the voice I heard was like the sound of harpers playing on their harps, [3] and they sing a new song before the throne and before the four living creatures and before the elders. No one could learn that song except the hundred and forty-four thousand who had been redeemed from the earth. [4] It is these who have not defiled themselves with women, for they are chaste;[h] it is these who follow the Lamb wherever he goes; these have been redeemed from mankind as first fruits for God and the Lamb, [5] and in their mouth no lie was found, for they are spotless.

6 Then I saw another angel flying in midheaven, with an eternal gospel to proclaim to those who dwell on earth, to every nation and tribe and tongue and people; [7] and he said with a loud voice, "Fear God and give him glory, for the hour of his judgment has come; and worship him who made heaven and earth, the sea and the fountains of water."

8 Another angel, a second, followed, saying, "Fallen, fallen is Babylon the great, she who made all nations drink the wine of her impure passion."

9 And another angel, a third, followed, saying with a loud voice, "If any one worships the beast and its image, and receives a mark on his forehead or on his hand, [10] he also shall drink the wine of God's wrath, poured unmixed into the cup of his anger, and he shall be tormented with fire and brimstone in the presence of the holy angels and in the presence of the Lamb. [11] And the smoke of their torment goes up for ever and ever; and they have no rest, day or night, these worshipers of the beast and its image, and whoever receives the mark of its name."

12 Here is a call for the endurance of the saints, those who keep the commandments of God and the faith of Jesus.

[h] Greek *virgins.*

14. 8: Is. 21. 9.   **14. 10:** Jer. 51. 7; Gen. 19. 24.   **14. 11:** Is. 34. 10.

13 And I heard a voice from heaven saying, "Write this: Blessed are the dead who die in the Lord henceforth." "Blessed indeed," says the Spirit, "that they may rest from their labors, for their deeds follow them!"

14 Then I looked, and lo, a white cloud, and seated on the cloud one like a son of man, with a golden crown on his head, and a sharp sickle in his hand. [15] And another angel came out of the temple, calling with a loud voice to him who sat upon the cloud, "Put in your sickle, and reap, for the hour to reap has come, for the harvest of the earth is fully ripe." [16] So he who sat upon the cloud swung his sickle on the earth, and the earth was reaped.

17 And another angel came out of the temple in heaven, and he too had a sharp sickle. [18] Then another angel came out from the altar, the angel who has power over fire, and he called with a loud voice to him who had the sharp sickle, "Put in your sickle, and gather the clusters of the vine of the earth, for its grapes are ripe." [19] So the angel swung his sickle on the earth and gathered the vintage of the earth, and threw it into the great wine press of the wrath of God; [20] and the wine press was trodden outside the city, and blood flowed from the wine press, as high as a horse's bridle, for one thousand six hundred stadia.[i]

15 Then I saw another portent in heaven, great and wonderful, seven angels with seven plagues, which are the last, for with them the wrath of God is ended.

2 And I saw what appeared to be a sea of glass mingled with fire, and those who had conquered the beast and its image and the number of its name, standing beside the sea of glass with harps of God in their hands. [3] And they sing

[i] About two hundred miles.

14. 14: Dan. 7. 13.   **14. 15:** Joel 3. 13; Mt. 13. 30.   **14. 20:** Joel 3. 13.
15. 1: Lev. 26. 21.   **15. 3:** Ex. 15. 1; Ps. 145. 17.

the song of Moses, the servant of God, and the song of the
Lamb, saying,

"Great and wonderful are thy deeds,
        O Lord God the Almighty!
    Just and true are thy ways,
        O King of the ages!*[j]*
    [4] Who shall not fear and glorify thy name, O Lord?
        For thou alone art holy.
    All nations shall come and worship thee,
        for thy judgments have been revealed."

5 After this I looked, and the temple of the tent of witness
in heaven was opened, [6] and out of the temple came the
seven angels with the seven plagues, robed in pure bright
linen, and their breasts girded with golden girdles. [7] And
one of the four living creatures gave the seven angels seven
golden bowls full of the wrath of God who lives for ever
and ever; [8] and the temple was filled with smoke from the
glory of God and from his power, and no one could enter
the temple until the seven plagues of the seven angels were
ended.

16 Then I heard a loud voice from the temple telling
the seven angels, "Go and pour out on the earth
the seven bowls of the wrath of God."

2 So the first angel went and poured his bowl on the
earth, and foul and evil sores came upon the men who bore
the mark of the beast and worshiped its image.

3 The second angel poured his bowl into the sea, and it
became like the blood of a dead man, and every living thing
died that was in the sea.

4 The third angel poured his bowl into the rivers and

---

[j] Some ancient authorities read *the nations.*

15. 4: Jer. 10. 7; Ps. 86. 9–10.   **15. 5:** Ex. 40. 34.   **15. 8:** 1 Kings 8. 10; Is. 6. 4;
Ezek. 44. 4.
16. 1: Is. 66. 6; Ps. 69. 24.   **16. 2:** Ex. 9. 10–11; Deut. 28. 35.   **16. 3–4:** Ex. 7. 17–21.

the fountains of water, and they became blood. [5] And I heard the angel of water say,

> "Just art thou in these thy judgments,
> thou who art and wast, O Holy One.
> [6] For men have shed the blood of saints and prophets,
> and thou hast given them blood to drink.
> It is their due!"

[7] And I heard the altar cry,

> "Yea, Lord God the Almighty,
> true and just are thy judgments!"

8 The fourth angel poured his bowl on the sun, and it was allowed to scorch men with fire; [9] men were scorched by the fierce heat, and they cursed the name of God who had power over these plagues, and they did not repent and give him glory.

10 The fifth angel poured his bowl on the throne of the beast, and its kingdom was in darkness; men gnawed their tongues in anguish [11] and cursed the God of heaven for their pain and sores, and did not repent of their deeds.

12 The sixth angel poured his bowl on the great river Eu-phra′tes, and its water was dried up, to prepare the way for the kings from the east. [13] And I saw, issuing from the mouth of the dragon and from the mouth of the beast and from the mouth of the false prophet, three foul spirits like frogs; [14] for they are devil spirits, performing signs, who go abroad to the kings of the whole world, to assemble them for battle on the great day of God the Almighty. [15] ("Lo, I am coming like a thief! Blessed is he who is awake, keeping his garments that he may not go naked and be seen exposed!") [16] And they assembled them at the place which is called in Hebrew Ar-ma-ged′don.

---

16. 6: Ps. 79. 3.   **16. 7:** Ps. 119. 137.   **16. 10:** Ex. 10. 21.   **16. 12:** Is. 11. 15–16.
16. 13: 1 Kings 22. 21–23; Ex. 8. 3.   **16. 15:** 1 Thess. 5. 2.   **16. 16:** 2 Kings 9. 27.

17 The seventh angel poured his bowl into the air, and a great voice came out of the temple, from the throne, saying, "It is done!" [18] And there were flashes of lightning, loud noises, peals of thunder, and a great earthquake such as had never been since men were on the earth, so great was that earthquake. [19] The great city was split into three parts, and the cities of the nations fell, and God remembered great Babylon, to make her drain the cup of the fury of his wrath. [20] And every island fled away, and no mountains were to be found; [21] and great hailstones, heavy as a hundredweight, dropped on men from heaven, till men cursed God for the plague of the hail, so fearful was that plague.

17 Then one of the seven angels who had the seven bowls came and said to me, "Come, I will show you the judgment of the great harlot who is seated upon many waters, [2] with whom the kings of the earth have committed fornication, and with the wine of whose fornication the dwellers on earth have become drunk." [3] And he carried me away in the Spirit into a wilderness, and I saw a woman sitting on a scarlet beast which was full of blasphemous names, and it had seven heads and ten horns. [4] The woman was arrayed in purple and scarlet, and bedecked with gold and jewels and pearls, holding in her hand a golden cup full of abominations and the impurities of her fornication; [5] and on her forehead was written a name of mystery: "Babylon the great, mother of harlots and of earth's abominations." [6] And I saw the woman, drunk with the blood of the saints and the blood of the martyrs of Jesus.

When I saw her I marveled greatly. [7] But the angel said to me, "Why marvel? I will tell you the mystery of the woman, and of the beast with seven heads and ten horns that carries her. [8] The beast that you saw was, and is not, and is to ascend from the bottomless pit and go to perdition; and the dwellers on earth whose names have not been written in the book of life from the foundation of the world, will marvel to behold the beast, because it was and is not and is to come. [9] This calls for a mind with wisdom: the seven heads are seven hills on which the woman is seated; [10] they are also seven kings, five of whom have fallen, one is, the other has not yet come, and when he comes he must remain only a little while. [11] As for the beast that was and is not, it is an eighth but it belongs to the seven, and it goes to perdition. [12] And the ten horns that you saw are ten kings who have not yet received royal power, but they are to receive authority as kings for one hour, together with the beast. [13] These are of one mind and give over their power and authority to the beast; [14] they will make war on the Lamb, and the Lamb will conquer them, for he is Lord of lords and King of kings, and those with him are called and chosen and faithful."

15 And he said to me, "The waters that you saw, where the harlot is seated, are peoples and multitudes and nations and tongues. [16] And the ten horns that you saw, they and the beast will hate the harlot; they will make her desolate and naked, and devour her flesh and burn her up with fire, [17] for God has put it into their hearts to carry out his purpose by being of one mind and giving over their royal power to the beast, until the words of God shall be fulfilled. [18] And the woman that you saw is the great city which has dominion over the kings of the earth."

18 After this I saw another angel coming down from heaven, having great authority; and the earth was

17. 8: Dan. 7. 3; Rev. 3. 5.   **17. 12:** Dan. 7. 20–24.   **17. 14:** Dan. 2. 47.

made bright with his splendor. ² And he called out with a mighty voice,

"Fallen, fallen is Babylon the great!
It has become a dwelling place of demons,
a haunt of every foul spirit,
a haunt of every foul and hateful bird;
³ for all nations have drunk[k] the wine of her impure passion,
and the kings of the earth have committed fornication with her,
and the merchants of the earth have grown rich with the wealth of her wantonness."

⁴ Then I heard another voice from heaven saying,

"Come out of her, my people,
lest you take part in her sins,
lest you share in her plagues;
⁵ for her sins are heaped high as heaven,
and God has remembered her iniquities.
⁶ Render to her as she herself has rendered,
and repay her double for her deeds;
mix a double draught for her in the cup she mixed.
⁷ As she glorified herself and played the wanton,
so give her a like measure of torment and mourning.
Since in her heart she says, 'A queen I sit,
I am no widow, mourning I shall never see,'
⁸ so shall her plagues come in a single day,
pestilence and mourning and famine,
and she shall be burned with fire;
for mighty is the Lord God who judges her."

9 And the kings of the earth, who committed fornication and were wanton with her, will weep and wail over her

[k] Some ancient authorities read *fallen by.*

18. 2: Is. 21. 9; Jer. 50. 39.   **18. 3:** Jer. 25. 15, 27.   **18. 4:** Is. 48. 20; Jer. 50. 8.
18. 5: Jer. 51. 9.   **18. 6:** Ps. 137. 8.   **18. 7:** Is. 47. 8-9.   **18. 9:** Ezek. 26. 16-17.

when they see the smoke of her burning; [10] they will stand far off, in fear of her torment, and say,

> "Alas! alas! thou great city,
>> thou mighty city, Babylon!
>> In one hour has thy judgment come."

11 And the merchants of the earth weep and mourn for her, since no one buys their cargo any more, [12] cargo of gold, silver, jewels and pearls, fine linen, purple, silk and scarlet, all kinds of scented wood, all articles of ivory, all articles of costly wood, bronze, iron and marble, [13] cinnamon, spice, incense, myrrh, frankincense, wine, oil, fine flour and wheat, cattle and sheep, horses and chariots, and slaves, that is, human souls.

> [14] "The fruit for which thy soul longed has gone from thee,
>> and all thy dainties and thy splendor are lost to thee, never to be found again!"

[15] The merchants of these wares, who gained wealth from her, will stand far off, in fear of her torment, weeping and mourning aloud,

> [16] "Alas, alas, for the great city
>> that was clothed in fine linen, in purple and scarlet,
>> bedecked with gold, with jewels, and with pearls!
>> [17] In one hour all this wealth has been laid waste."

And all shipmasters and seafaring men, sailors and all whose trade is on the sea, stood far off [18] and cried out as they saw the smoke of her burning,

> "What city was like the great city?"

[19] And they threw dust on their heads, as they wept and mourned, crying out,

> "Alas, alas, for the great city

18. 11: Ezek. 27. 36.   **18. 12:** Ezek. 27. 12–13, 22.   **18. 15:** Ezek. 27. 36, 31.
18. 17: Is. 23. 14; Ezek. 27. 26–30.   **18. 19:** Ezek. 27. 30–34.

where all who had ships at sea grew rich by her
    wealth!
In one hour she has been laid waste.
[20] Rejoice over her, O heaven,
    O saints and apostles and prophets,
    for God has given judgment for you against her!"
21 Then a mighty angel took up a stone like a great millstone and threw it into the sea, saying,
    "So shall Babylon the great city be thrown down with
        violence,
    and shall be found no more;
[22] and the sound of harpers and minstrels, of flute
        players and trumpeters,
    shall be heard in thee no more;
    and a craftsman of any craft
    shall be found in thee no more;
    and the sound of the millstone
    shall be heard in thee no more;
[23] and the light of a lamp
    shall shine in thee no more;
    and the voice of bridegroom and bride
    shall be heard in thee no more;
    for thy merchants were the great men of the earth,
    and all nations were deceived by thy sorcery.
[24] And in her was found the blood of prophets and of
        saints,
    and of all who have been slain on earth."

19 After this I heard what seemed to be the mighty
    voice of a great multitude in heaven, crying,
    "Hallelujah! Salvation and glory and power belong to
        our God,

18. 20: Is. 44. 23; Jer. 51. 48.   **18. 21:** Jer. 51. 63; Ezek. 26. 21.   **18. 22:** Is. 24. 8;
Ezek. 26. 13.   **18. 23:** Jer. 25. 10.   **18. 24:** Jer. 51. 49.

² for his judgments are true and just;

 he has judged the great harlot who corrupted the
   earth with her fornication,

 and he has avenged on her the blood of his servants."

³ Once more they cried,

 "Hallelujah! The smoke of her goes up for ever and
   ever."

⁴ And the twenty-four elders and the four living creatures
fell down and worshiped God who is seated on the throne,
saying, "Amen. Hallelujah!" ⁵ And from the throne came a
voice crying,

 "Praise our God, all you his servants,

 you who fear him, small and great."

⁶ Then I heard what seemed to be the voice of a great multitude, like the sound of many waters and like the sound of
mighty thunderpeals, crying,

 "Hallelujah! For the Lord our God the Almighty
   reigns.

⁷ Let us rejoice and exult and give him the glory,

 for the marriage of the Lamb has come,

 and his Bride has made herself ready;

⁸ it was granted her to be clothed with fine linen,
   bright and pure" —

for the fine linen is the righteous deeds of the saints.

 9 And the angel said[1] to me, "Write this: Blessed are
those who are invited to the marriage supper of the Lamb."
And he said to me, "These are true words of God." ¹⁰ Then
I fell down at his feet to worship him, but he said to me,
"You must not do that! I am a fellow servant with you and
your brethren who hold the testimony of Jesus. Worship
God." For the testimony of Jesus is the spirit of prophecy.

[1] Greek *he said.*

19. 2: Deut. 32. 43.   **19. 3:** Is. 34. 10.   **19. 5:** Ps. 115. 13.   **19. 7:** Ps. 118. 24.

11 Then I saw heaven opened, and behold, a white horse! He who sat upon it is called Faithful and True, and in righteousness he judges and makes war. ¹² His eyes are like a flame of fire, and on his head are many diadems; and he has a name inscribed which no one knows but himself. ¹³ He is clad in a robe dipped in*ᵐ* blood, and the name by which he is called is The Word of God. ¹⁴ And the armies of heaven, arrayed in fine linen, white and pure, followed him on white horses. ¹⁵ From his mouth issues a sharp sword with which to smite the nations, and he will rule them with a rod of iron; he will tread the wine press of the fury of the wrath of God the Almighty. ¹⁶ On his robe and on his thigh he has a name inscribed, King of kings and Lord of lords.

17 Then I saw an angel standing in the sun, and with a loud voice he called to all the birds that fly in midheaven, "Come, gather for the great supper of God, ¹⁸ to eat the flesh of kings, the flesh of captains, the flesh of mighty men, the flesh of horses and their riders, and the flesh of all men, both free and slave, both small and great." ¹⁹ And I saw the beast and the kings of the earth with their armies gathered to make war against him who sits upon the horse and against his army. ²⁰ And the beast was captured, and with it the false prophet who in its presence had worked the signs by which he deceived those who had received the mark of the beast and those who worshiped its image. These two were thrown alive into the lake of fire that burns with brimstone. ²¹ And the rest were slain by the sword of him who sits upon the horse, the sword that issues from his mouth; and all the birds were gorged with their flesh.

20 Then I saw an angel coming down from heaven, holding in his hand the key of the bottomless pit and

ᵐ Some ancient authorities read *sprinkled with.*

19. 11: Ezek. 1. 1. **19. 12:** Dan. 10. 6. **19. 15:** Ps. 2. 9. **19. 16:** Deut. 10. 17; Dan. 2. 47. **19. 17:** Ezek. 39. 4, 17–20.

a great chain. [2] And he seized the dragon, that ancient serpent, who is the Devil and Satan, and bound him for a thousand years, [3] and threw him into the pit, and shut it and sealed it over him, that he should deceive the nations no more, till the thousand years were ended. After that he must be loosed for a little while.

4 Then I saw thrones, and seated on them were those to whom judgment was committed. Also I saw the souls of those who had been beheaded for their testimony to Jesus and for the word of God, and who had not worshiped the beast or its image and had not received its mark on their foreheads or their hands. They came to life again, and reigned with Christ a thousand years. [5] The rest of the dead did not come to life again until the thousand years were ended. This is the first resurrection. [6] Blessed and holy is he who shares in the first resurrection! Over such the second death has no power, but they shall be priests of God and of Christ, and they shall reign with him a thousand years.

7 And when the thousand years are ended, Satan will be loosed from his prison [8] and will come out to deceive the nations which are at the four corners of the earth, that is, Gog and Ma'gog, to gather them for battle; their number is like the sand of the sea. [9] And they marched up over the broad earth and surrounded the camp of the saints and the beloved city; but fire came down from heaven[n] and consumed them, [10] and the devil who had deceived them was thrown into the lake of fire and brimstone where the beast and the false prophet were, and they will be tormented day and night for ever and ever.

11 Then I saw a great white throne and him who sat upon it; from his presence earth and sky fled away, and

[n] Some ancient authorities read *from God, out of heaven*, or *out of heaven from God*.
20. 4: Dan. 7. 9, 22, 27.   **20. 8:** Ezek. 38. 2, 9, 15.   **20. 9:** 2 Kings 1. 10–12.
20. 11–12: Dan. 7. 9–10.

no place was found for them. ¹² And I saw the dead, great
and small, standing before the throne, and books were
opened. Also another book was opened, which is the book
of life. And the dead were judged by what was written
in the books, by what they had done. ¹³ And the sea gave
up the dead in it, Death and Hades gave up the dead in
them, and all were judged by what they had done. ¹⁴ Then
Death and Hades were thrown into the lake of fire. This is
the second death, the lake of fire; ¹⁵ and if anyone's name was
not found written in the book of life, he was thrown into
the lake of fire.

21 Then I saw a new heaven and a new earth; for the
first heaven and the first earth had passed away,
and the sea was no more. ² And I saw the holy city, new
Jerusalem, coming down out of heaven from God, prepared
as a bride adorned for her husband; ³ and I heard a great
voice from the throne saying, "Behold, the dwelling of God
is with men. He will dwell with them, and they shall be his
people,ᵒ and God himself will be with them;ᵖ ⁴ he will wipe
away every tear from their eyes, and death shall be no more,
neither shall there be mourning nor crying nor pain any
more, for the former things have passed away."

5 And he who sat upon the throne said, "Behold, I make
all things new." Also he said, "Write this, for these words
are trustworthy and true." ⁶ And he said to me, "It is done!
I am the Alpha and the Omega, the beginning and the end.
To the thirsty I will give water without price from the
fountain of the water of life. ⁷ He who conquers shall have
this heritage, and I will be his God and he shall be my son.

ᵒ Some ancient authorities read *peoples*.   ᵖ Some ancient authorities add *and be their God*.

20. 15: Rev. 3. 5.
21. 1: Is. 66. 22.   21. 2: Rev. 3. 12.
21. 3: Ezek. 37. 27.   21. 4: Is. 25. 8; 35. 10.
21. 5: Is. 43. 19.   21. 6: Is. 55. 1.   21. 7: Ps. 89. 27–28.

[8] But as for the cowardly, the faithless, the polluted, as for murderers, fornicators, sorcerers, idolaters, and all liars, their lot shall be in the lake that burns with fire and brimstone, which is the second death."

9 Then came one of the seven angels who had the seven bowls full of the seven last plagues, and spoke to me, saying, "Come, I will show you the Bride, the wife of the Lamb." [10] And in the Spirit he carried me away to a great, high mountain, and showed me the holy city Jerusalem coming down out of heaven from God, [11] having the glory of God, its radiance like a most rare jewel, like a jasper, clear as crystal. [12] It had a great, high wall, with twelve gates, and at the gates twelve angels, and on the gates the names of the twelve tribes of the sons of Israel were inscribed; [13] on the east three gates, on the north three gates, on the south three gates, and on the west three gates. [14] And the wall of the city had twelve foundations, and on them the twelve names of the twelve apostles of the Lamb.

15 And he who talked to me had a measuring rod of gold to measure the city and its gates and walls. [16] The city lies foursquare, its length the same as its breadth; and he measured the city with his rod, twelve thousand stadia;[q] its length and breadth and height are equal. [17] He also measured its wall, a hundred and forty-four cubits by a man's measure, that is, an angel's. [18] The wall was built of jasper, while the city was pure gold, clear as glass. [19] The foundations of the wall of the city were adorned with every jewel; the first was jasper, the second sapphire, the third agate, the fourth emerald, [20] the fifth onyx, the sixth carnelian, the seventh chrysolite, the eighth beryl, the ninth topaz, the tenth chrysoprase, the eleventh jacinth,

[q] About fifteen hundred miles.

21. 8: Is. 30. 33   **21. 10:** Ezek. 40. 2.   **21. 12:** Ezek. 48. 30–35; Ex. 28. 21.
21. 15: Ezek. 40. 5   **21. 19:** Is. 54. 11–12.

the twelfth amethyst. [21] And the twelve gates were twelve pearls, each of the gates made of a single pearl, and the street of the city was pure gold, transparent as glass.

22 And I saw no temple in the city, for its temple is the Lord God the Almighty and the Lamb. [23] And the city has no need of sun or moon to shine upon it, for the glory of God is its light, and its lamp is the Lamb. [24] By its light shall the nations walk; and the kings of the earth shall bring their glory into it, [25] and its gates shall never be shut by day — and there shall be no night there; [26] they shall bring into it the glory and the honor of the nations. [27] But nothing unclean shall enter it, nor any one who practices abomination or falsehood, but only those who are written in the Lamb's book of life.

22 Then he showed me the river of the water of life, bright as crystal, flowing from the throne of God and of the Lamb [2] through the middle of the street of the city;[r] also, on either side of the river, the tree of life with its twelve kinds of fruit, yielding its fruit each month; and the leaves of the tree were for the healing of the nations. [3] There shall no more be anything accursed, but the throne of God and of the Lamb shall be in it, and his servants shall worship him; [4] they shall see his face, and his name shall be on their foreheads. [5] And night shall be no more; they need no light of lamp or sun, for the Lord God will be their light, and they shall reign for ever and ever.

6 And he said to me, "These words are trustworthy and true. And the Lord, the God of the spirits of the prophets, has sent his angel to show his servants what must soon take place. [7] And behold, I am coming soon."

[r] Or *the Lamb. In the midst of the street of the city, and on either side of the river, was the tree of life,* etc.

21. 23: Is. 24. 23; 60. 1, 19.   **21. 25:** Is. 60. 11.   **21. 27:** Is. 52. 1; Rev. 3. 5.
22. 2: Gen. 2. 9.   **22. 3:** Zech. 14. 11.   **22. 4:** Ps. 17. 15.

Blessed is he who keeps the words of the prophecy of this book.

8 I John am he who heard and saw these things. And when I heard and saw them, I fell down to worship at the feet of the angel who showed them to me; ⁹ but he said to me, "You must not do that! I am a fellow servant with you and your brethren the prophets, and with those who keep the words of this book. Worship God."

10 And he said to me, "Do not seal up the words of the prophecy of this book, for the time is near. ¹¹ Let the evil-doer still do evil, and the filthy still be filthy, and the righteous still do right, and the holy still be holy."

12 "Behold, I am coming soon, bringing my recompense, to repay every one for what he has done. ¹³ I am the Alpha and the Omega, the first and the last, the beginning and the end."

14 Blessed are those who wash their robes,ˢ that they may have the right to the tree of life and that they may enter the city by the gates. ¹⁵ Outside are the dogs and sorcerers and fornicators and murderers and idolaters, and every one who loves and practices falsehood.

16 "I Jesus have sent my angel to you with this testimony for the churches. I am the root and the offspring of David, the bright morning star."

17 The Spirit and the Bride say, "Come." And let him who hears say, "Come." And let him who is thirsty come, let him who desires take the water of life without price.

18 I warn every one who hears the words of the prophecy of this book: if any one adds to them, God will add to him the plagues described in this book, ¹⁹ and if any one takes away from the words of the book of this prophecy, God

ˢ Some ancient authorities read *do his commandments.*

22. 11: Dan. 12. 10.　　**22. 12:** Is. 40. 10; Jer. 17. 10.　　**22. 13:** Is. 44. 6; 48. 12.
22. 14: Gen. 2. 9; 3. 22.　　**22. 16:** Is. 11. 1, 10.　　**22. 17:** Is. 55. 1.

will take away his share in the tree of life and in the holy city, which are described in this book.

20 He who testifies to these things says, "Surely I am coming soon." Amen. Come, Lord Jesus!

21 The grace of the Lord Jesus be with all the saints[t]. Amen.

[t] Some ancient authorities omit *all;* others omit *the saints.*
22. 21: 2 Thess. 3. 18.

PRINTED IN THE UNITED STATES OF AMERICA

146

5328 Delmar